FOUNDATIONS OF HOMELAND SECURITY

WILEY SERIES ON HOMELAND DEFENSE AND SECURITY

Series Editor

TED LEWIS   Professor, Naval Postgraduate School

Foundations of Homeland Security: Law and Policy / Martin J. Alperen, Esq.

FOUNDATIONS OF HOMELAND SECURITY

Law and Policy

MARTIN J. ALPEREN, Esq.

WILEY

A JOHN WILEY & SONS, INC., PUBLICATION

Published by John Wiley & Sons, Inc., Hoboken, New Jersey
Published simultaneously in Canada

For general information on our other products and services or for technical support, please contact our Customer Care Department within the United States at 877-762-2974, outside the United States at 317-572-3993 or fax 317- 572-4002.

Wiley also publishes its books in a variety of electronic formats. Some content that appears in print may not be available in electronic formats. For more information about Wiley products, visit our web site at www.wiley.com.

Library of Congress Cataloging-in-Publication Data:

Alperen, Martin J.
      Foundations of homeland security : homeland security law and policy / Martin J. Alperen.
          p. cm.
      Includes index.
      ISBN 978-0-470-59698-2 (cloth)
  1. National security–Law and legislation–United States.   2. Emergency management–Law and legislation–United States.   3. Terrorism–United States–Prevention.   4. National security–United States.   I. Title.
      KF4850 .A947
      344.7305′32–dc22
                                                                                                          2010025377

Printed in the United States

eBook ISBN: 978-0-470-92579-9
oBook ISBN: 978-0-470-92580-5
ePub ISBN: 978-0-470-93460-9

10 9 8 7 6 5 4 3

This book is dedicated to the memory of Alva A. Swan, Attorney General of the United States Virgin Islands. Attorney Swan cared deeply about the People and Territory of the VI. He supported the development of the VI's preparedness as well as homeland security education. He was liked and respected by all who had the privilege to have worked with him.

CONTENTS

1

INTRODUCTION

Until this text, homeland security educators did not have a collection of homeland security law and policy documents in one place. This text is a collection of those documents, edited and organized by topic. This chapter begins with a very short mention of 9/11 and references to the 9/11 Commission Report and other factual reporting about the attack. Next is a discussion of "what is homeland security?" followed by sections on what homeland security looks like from the outside and from the inside. It discusses "what is a homeland security curriculum?" "what is homeland security law?" and the development of homeland security law since 9/11. Finally are definitions of terrorism, learning objectives, and a little about this text.

9/11

A textbook on homeland security law and policy would be remiss without some mention of 9/11. Understanding what happened and how that day affected America and the world is an important foundation for understanding homeland security law and policy but is beyond the scope of this book. I recommend that readers familiarize themselves with September 11th's factual history and background. For a poignant video, see footnote.[1] The 9/11 Commission Report,[2] the result of an intensive government-sponsored investigation, is the official version of the events leading up to and including the attack and the U.S. government's and military's confusion in the moments after. The 9/11 Public Discourse Project[3] has subsequent documents related to the report. Columbia University's The World Trade Center Attack: The Official Documents[4] and

City University of New York/George Mason University's the September 11th Digital Archives[5] both have a wealth of information.

WHAT IS HOMELAND SECURITY?

Vision of Homeland Security

According to the Homeland Security Council, "the United States, through a concerted national effort that galvanizes the strengths and capabilities of Federal, State, local, and Tribal governments; the private and non-profit sectors; and regions, communities, and individual citizens – along with our partners in the international community – will work to achieve a secure Homeland that sustains our way of life as a free, prosperous, and welcoming America."[6]

Definition of Homeland Security

Homeland Security is "a concerted national effort to prevent terrorist attacks within the United States, reduce America's vulnerability to terrorism, and minimize the damage and recover from attacks that do occur."[7]

Despite this vision and definition, there is no agreement among practitioners as to what the term Homeland Security actually means. On the one hand, the two extremes of opinion are represented by those who feel homeland security is only about terrorism. They believe that focusing on anything additional dilutes, distracts, and weakens the homeland security mission. On the other hand, there are those for whom homeland security is about everything—that it implicates almost every sector of our lives and there is very little that does not relate to it in some way.

Foundations of Homeland Security: Law and Policy, First Edition. Martin J. Alperen.
© 2011 John Wiley & Sons, Inc. Published 2011 by John Wiley & Sons, Inc.

Christopher Bellavita, professor and Director of Academic Programs at the Naval Postgraduate School's Center for Homeland Defense and Security, points out that different groups view homeland security differently.[8] To some, it is just about terrorism. Others say that its focus is terrorism and natural disasters. Still others claim that homeland security is about "all hazards" (terrorism, man-made disasters, and natural disasters). One group views homeland security as focused on "jurisdictional hazards" (i.e., homeland security means different things to different jurisdictions depending upon that jurisdiction's particular hazards, risks, and level of preparedness).

Bellavita uses the term Meta Hazards for what Patrick Massey calls Generational Hazards. These are hazards created by the present generation that "take many decades to metastasize before finally reaching a disastrous end-state that impacts future generations."[9] Many people believe that the focus of homeland security is or should be national security. For those who think that homeland security includes everything already mentioned, plus global problems like global warming, universal health care, and social justice, homeland security is synonymous with "World Security."[10]

Massey[11] discusses how the focus of what we now call homeland security and the words we have used to describe it have changed over the years. During the Cold War, we called it civil defense. When the Cold War ended, the focus was on natural hazards. After 9/11, we called it homeland security focusing on terrorism. This was followed by the current all hazards approach (terrorism + natural disasters + man-made disasters). Lastly are Massey's generational hazards. Within this list of terms, "public safety" should also be included.

Further insight into what is homeland security can be gained by examining different models of emergency management. Michael D. Selves[12] describes two philosophically different views of emergency management: the emergency services model versus the public administration model. The "emergency services [model is] primarily concerned with the coordination of emergency services." Among other things, Selves points out that under the emergency services model,

> Organizational interactions tend to be primarily with emergency services agencies. Managers operating under the E-S model may be reluctant to interact with non-emergency services agencies and especially with senior, elected officials. Often emergency management functions are embedded within an emergency service agency. This has the effect of isolating them further from the policy making functions of the jurisdiction. Access to local executives and elected officials is often indirect and limited by the organizational structure. Interaction with policy level officials is also often characterized by an attitude that the "politicians" are a nuisance during response operations and should be "kept somewhere so they don't get in the way".

The "public administration" model is much broader:

> The P-A model is based on a philosophy which views emergency management as an element of the overall administration of government. It sees emergency management as that aspect of public administration which deals with the operation of government during crisis. Because of this, there is an interest in the political, social, and psychological factors that are involved in crisis management. The concern is focused on not just the emergency services response, but on the impact of the disaster/emergency in terms of larger jurisdictional issues. . .
>
> Practitioners operating under the P-A model tend to approach emergency management as a discipline, subject to academic research and debate with the results . . . being used as tools in implementing a local program. . .

Furthering the broad view of homeland security, President Obama stated that there is no distinction between homeland security and national security.[13] He "described the nation's energy challenges as both a matter of national security and environmental protection."[14] The U.S. Commission on National Security wrote, "We have taken a broad view of national security. In the new era, sharp distinctions between 'foreign' and 'domestic' no longer apply."[15] The Director of National Intelligence set forth the dire national security implications of growing worldwide energy demand, global warming, food and water shortages, and increasing population.[16] The Department of Defense National Defense Strategy reflects this same sentiment.[17] "The capacity of America's educational system to create a 21st century workforce second to none in the world is a national security issue of the first order."[18] "[B]ased on my career and professional experience, I can think of no more pressing threat, no greater vulnerability, than America's heavy dependence on a global petroleum market that is unpredictable, to say the least."[19]

Former president Jimmy Carter said in May 2009, "In closing, let me emphasize that our inseparable energy and environmental decisions will determine how well we can maintain a vibrant society, protect our strategic interests, regain worldwide political and economic leadership, meet relatively new competitive challenges, and deal with less fortunate nations. Collectively, nothing could be more important."[20]

WHAT DOES HOMELAND SECURITY LOOK LIKE FROM THE OUTSIDE?

Using an Office of Emergency Services (OES)[21] as an example, homeland security looks like or reflects the breadth-of-homeland-security view of its leaders. For those with an "emergency services" orientation we would expect to see major involvement by emergency services providers only (police, fire, EMS, Haz. Mat., etc.). This system might have the best equipment and respond with military precision, yet if these are the only participants, then OES has completed its task as soon as the scene is safe.

An OES with a "public administration" focus would have a vastly broader area of responsibility. This OES would involve not just a city's first responders but also all subsequent responders, those represented in part by the city agencies. Every city agency would be involved with the OES. After surviving a disaster, when the first responders are done, these subsequent responders will make a city resilient.

At the very least, a broad-minded OES will have all of its agencies working as soon after a disaster as possible. Ideally, all of the agencies have practiced working together in alternative locations and with limited communications capabilities. All agencies should have their own ways to obtain essential equipment, supplies, and other vital resources even without a fully functional city government. (For example, the public health department procures latex gloves from the local pharmacy when the traditional supplier is unavailable.) In addition, all of this should be practiced and coordinated with federal, state, and tribal governments, the private and non-profit sectors, and regions, communities, and individual citizens.

WHAT DOES HOMELAND SECURITY LOOK LIKE FROM THE INSIDE?

On every level, homeland security requires cooperation, joint operations, and collaboration. It is integrated, interrelated, and interagency. Emergency services agencies all over the country have a grand history of cooperating with each other. Thus, there is horizontal integration. Almost every statute and policy document related to homeland security requires that a certain plan or action be coordinated with federal, state, county, city, town, tribal, and regional governments, and with the private sector. Thus, there is at least in theory vertical integration.

Homeland security has many components and they are all critical. For example, no matter what type of incident, whether it is a storm, earthquake, flood, tornado, man-made disaster such as a train wreck with deadly chemicals aboard, or terrorism, without *communications*, intelligence cannot reach decision-makers and direction cannot be conveyed to the people in the position to take action. Without good *intelligence*, those in charge will not know the best actions to take, regardless of whether they can communicate with them. Without *trained, prepared,* and *properly equipped responders* to take action, communication and intelligence are meaningless.

WHAT IS A HOMELAND SECURITY CURRICULUM?

Homeland security is multi-disciplinary; it involves contributions from almost unlimited areas of expertise and academic backgrounds.[22] A survey of homeland security related curriculums[23] included approximately forty-five different areas of study.[24]

The U.S. has a "gross imbalance between powerful departments and agencies, yet weak interagency mechanisms."[25] Thus, homeland security practitioners also need to study human dynamics and interagency and civil interactions.[26]

On an individual level, homeland security demands a broad knowledge base that includes social sciences and humanities along with science, creative thinking, critical thinking, open mindedness, personal initiative, adaptability, flexibility, and leadership skills.

Homeland security education is still young but no longer in its infancy. Homeland security educators are moving to identify a core curriculum and accreditation standards. The Homeland Security and Defense Education Consortium Association is working toward this goal.[27] The Center for Homeland Defense and Security (CHDS) at the Naval Postgraduate School in Monterey, California, offered the first university-level courses about homeland defense and security.[28] CHDS offers several educational opportunities including a Masters Degree in "Security Studies (Homeland Security and Defense)." FEMA offers many higher education opportunities as well.[29]

WHAT IS HOMELAND SECURITY LAW?

One definition of homeland security is that it is "a concerted national effort to prevent terrorist attacks within the United States, reduce America's vulnerability to terrorism, and minimize the damage and recover from attacks that do occur."[30] Adding the Department of Homeland Security's all hazards approach, it follows logically, then, that Homeland Security Laws are those statutes enacted to prevent, mitigate, respond to, and recover from man-made or natural disasters, catastrophic accidents, or terrorist attacks.[31]

Homeland Security and Homeland Security Law had its official beginning on September 11, 2001. Prior to then, our nation "lacked a unifying vision, a cohesive strategic approach, and the necessary institutions within government to secure the Homeland against terrorism." "[That day] transformed our thinking."[32]

Six weeks later, October 26, 2001, Congress passed the USA Patriot Act.[33] On November 25, 2002, Congress passed the Homeland Security Act[34] establishing the Department of Homeland Security (DHS).

DHS's "overriding and urgent mission

> . . . is to lead the unified national effort to secure the country and preserve our freedoms. While the Department was created to secure our country against those who seek to disrupt the American way of life, our charter also includes preparation for and response to all hazards and disasters. . ."[35]

Documents called National Strategies enunciate the Nation's overriding homeland security strategies. For example, there is the National Strategy for Homeland Security, The

National Strategy to Combat Terrorism, the National Strategy to Secure Cyberspace, the National Strategy for the Protection of Critical Infrastructures and Key Assets, and others.

Homeland Security Presidential Directives[36] (HSPDs), issued by the President, are much shorter than the national strategies. Each one is directed toward a specific subject area. For example, HSPD 7 relates to Critical Infrastructure Identification, Prioritization, and Protection, HSPD 8 deals with National Preparedness, and number 9 is entitled Defense of United States Agriculture and Food. There are currently 24 HSPDs. Some are classified.

The Disaster Relief Act of 1974 established the procedures for presidential disaster declarations. The Federal Emergency Management Agency (FEMA), created during the administration of President Jimmy Carter in 1979, consolidated under one agency the disaster management functions that previously were scattered among several independent agencies. The Robert T. Stafford Disaster Relief and Emergency Assistance Act[37] (1988) amended and incorporated the provisions of the 1974 Disaster Relief Act. The Stafford Act, as it is called, sets forth the procedures for declaring a disaster and requesting federal assistance, and then guides the subsequent emergency response through ultimate recovery.

FEMA's mission is

> ... to reduce the loss of life and property and protect the Nation from all hazards, including natural disasters, acts of terrorism, and other man-made disasters, by leading and supporting the Nation in a risk-based, comprehensive emergency management system of preparedness, protection, response, recovery, and mitigation.[38]

After a clearly inadequate response to hurricane Katrina, the Post-Katrina Emergency Management Reform Act[39] (PKEMRA) made significant changes to FEMA and DHS, and helped to clarify the State and Federal Government's roles, as well as FEMA's and DHS's roles for responding to large-scale events.

The strategies, HSPDs, the Patriot Act, the Homeland Security Act, the Stafford Act, PKEMRA, and others, Executive Orders, plus portions of related statutes, comprise homeland security law and policy and are the homeland security framework. The Department of Homeland Security itself and all homeland security actions exist only in compliance with these foundational documents.

THE DEVELOPMENT OF HOMELAND SECURITY LAW

It is impossible to understand the complexity, scope, and depth of the Patriot Act without reading the statute; thus, significant portions have been reproduced here. The Patriot Act was extremely controversial and invoked public protests. One of its most controversial provisions involved increasing the availability of surveillance without the need for a judicially approved warrant. Supporters of the Patriot Act claim that it was accurately focused to achieve its goal as it moved decisively to correct some of the country's security weaknesses.[40]

Regardless of whether one approved of the Patriot Act or not, it was an intellectual accomplishment representing a tremendous effort in a very short time period. It involved understanding many complex and interrelated statutes covering many areas of existing law, and it created new law.

Although the Homeland Security Act was not written in the same short time period as the Patriot Act, and not under the immediate shock of 9/11, it too was a remarkable document. Even though many disagree with some of its provisions, organizational structure, or the inclusion of FEMA as an agency within DHS, in creating DHS the Act accomplished the largest reorganization of government in more than 50 years.

The Homeland Security Act created DHS, brought FEMA under DHS control, and "transferred more than two-dozen federal entities – some in their entirety, some only in part – and 180,000 employees to the new department."[41] DHS has a vast area of responsibility; it is an agency that influences many areas of our lives, on land, air, and sea.

From its inception, homeland security included an important focus on science and technology. Homeland security relies on technology for many purposes, including situational awareness, early detection and monitoring of weapons of mass destruction, and communication. DHS promotes the expedited development, acquisition, and introduction of new technology.

The Homeland Security Act mandated:

> ... that [DHS] agencies' databases be compatible with one another and with other federal agencies.
>
> It "established within the Department of Justice an Office of Science and Technology ... to serve as the national focal point for work on law enforcement technology; and ... to carry out programs that, through the provision of equipment, training, and technical assistance, improve the safety and effectiveness of law enforcement technology and improve access to such technology by Federal, State, and local law enforcement agencies."[42]

The homeland security framework was designed and implemented at an extraordinarily rapid pace. For example, in addition to the Patriot Act coming only six weeks after 9/11, a particular HSPD would have deadlines for each subsequent step, such as the design or implementation of the related national strategy. For example, for the National Incident Management System (NIMS), first mentioned in HSPD 5, dated February 28, 2003, the Secretary of DHS was directed to have guidelines, standards, and protocols to implement NIMS by June 1, 2003. Each Federal Department was to have a plan to adopt and fully implement NIMS by August 1, 2003.

A FEW DEFINITIONS OF TERRORISM

There is no agreement as to the definition of terrorism.[43]

DHS

(15) The term "terrorism" means any activity that—

    (A) involves an act that—

        (i) is dangerous to human life or potentially destructive of critical infrastructure or key resources; and

        (ii) is a violation of the criminal laws of the United States or of any State or other subdivision of the United States; and

    (B) appears to be intended—

        (i) to intimidate or coerce a civilian population;

        (ii) to influence the policy of a government by intimidation or coercion; or

        (ii) to affect the conduct of a government by mass destruction, assassination, or kidnapping.[44]

FBI

[Terrorism is] the unlawful use of force or violence against persons or property to intimidate or coerce a Government, the civilian population, or any segment thereof, in furtherance of political or social objectives.[45]

STATE DEPARTMENT

[T]errorism means premeditated, politically motivated violence perpetrated against noncombatant targets by subnational groups or clandestine agents, usually intended to influence an audience. . .

The term "international terrorism" means terrorism involving citizens or the territory of more than one country. The US Government has employed this definition of terrorism for statistical and analytical purposes since 1983.[46]

U.S. CRIMINAL CODE (18 USC 2331 (1))

"international terrorism" means activities that involve violent acts or acts dangerous to human life that are a violation of the criminal laws of the United States or of any State, or that would be a criminal violation if committed within the jurisdiction of the United States or of any State; appear to be intended to intimidate or coerce a civilian population; to influence the policy of a government by intimidation or coercion; or to affect the conduct of a government by mass destruction, assassination, or kidnapping; and occur primarily outside the territorial jurisdiction of the United States, or transcend national boundaries in terms of the means by which they are accomplished, the persons they appear intended to intimidate or coerce, or the locale in which their perpetrators operate or seek asylum. . .[47]

U.S. CRIMINAL CODE (18 USC 2331 (5))

"domestic terrorism" means activities that involve acts dangerous to human life that are a violation of the criminal laws of the United States or of any State; appear to be intended to intimidate or coerce a civilian population; to influence the policy of a government by intimidation or coercion; or to affect the conduct of a government by mass destruction, assassination, or kidnapping; and occur primarily within the territorial jurisdiction of the United States.[48]

LEARNING OBJECTIVES

The purpose of this text is to familiarize students and professionals with the extensive and complex legal codes that come under the heading of Homeland Security:

1. Know the threat terrorism presents.[49] The Strategic Environment Chapter describes the current and near future threats to the United States as well as some possible future strategic environments. See questions in Teaching Suggestions, as to whether other matters, such as global warming and population, should be included in an analysis of our strategic environment.

2. Put terrorism in perspective. We face Bird Flu, Swine Flu, global warming, migrating fire ants, killer bees, hurricanes, earthquakes, floods, tornadoes, and the full spectrum of man-made accidents. Terrorism is a real threat, but one of these other catastrophes is more likely to happen.

3. Develop a conceptual understanding of homeland security law and policy—the foundation and framework of homeland security.

4. Appreciate the complexity of this framework. For example, the Critical Infrastructure Protection Chapter has approximately twenty-five contributing documents. There are 100 legal authorities "that guide the structure, development, and implementation of the National Response Framework."[50]

5. Evaluate homeland security law and policy and its application. Does what we have established work? Why are we doing it? How can we improve it? Is that new idea being considered a good idea?

6. Engage in meaningful discussion about America's homeland security.

7. Recognize that the government, whether it is state, local, tribal, or federal, cannot protect us from every

hazard all the time. Whether it is a natural disaster, man-made disaster, or terrorism, it may take three or more days for rescue to arrive. Thus, we must be able to take care of our families, our neighbors, and ourselves without electricity, running water, or communications. The cry, "where's my FEMA water,"[51] may simply not be heard. Every community and everyone in that community must participate in preparedness.

8. Recognize that resiliency, our ability to return to normal after a disaster, catastrophic accident, or terrorist attack, depends both on us as individuals and on our infrastructure.

9. Recognize that a significant portion of our Nation's infrastructure is in need of repair. Recognize that there are several predictable, foreseeable, and preventable "cascading infrastructure failures"—disasters ready to happen.[52] Recognize that we must take action now to rebuild and repair our infrastructure, to achieve resiliency.

ABOUT THIS TEXT

The material included here is not exhaustive. There is an overwhelming volume of information available and including all of it would be unwieldy. Most of the statutes and other documents included here are edited. We have included those sections sufficient to present the essence of the document. Also, repetitive directions have been eliminated. For example, almost every directive contains instructions that the Secretary of the Department of Homeland Security or the Administrator of the Federal Emergency Management Agency is to cooperate with or consult with, followed by a long list of names. To save space and repetition, these have been omitted. In addition, almost every program came with a requirement for a mandatory report to Congress on the program's progress, and for the establishment of a method of measuring the program's performance, to monitor implementation. These paragraphs have been eliminated too.

Many of the acts, like the Patriot Act and the Homeland Security Act, have had changes or amendments made to them. The acts in this text are in their original form; these amendments have not been included. Because of the edits and omissions, this text should not be used as a substitute for up-to-the-minute authorities themselves.

Lastly, unless otherwise noted, references to the *United States Code* are reprinted with permission from Westlaw.

ENDNOTES

1. Video of the burning towers, the people, scene, etc., set to music by Enya. http://www.patriotwatch.com/911.htm.

2. 9/11 Commission Report. http://www.9-11commission .gov/report/911Report.pdf. http://govinfo.library.unt .edu/911/report/index.htm.

3. Public Discourse Project. www.9-11pdp.org.

4. Columbia University. http://www.columbia.edu/cu/ lweb/indiv/usgd/wtc.html.

5. The September 11 Digital Archives. http:// 911digitalarchive.org/.

6. National Strategy for Homeland Security, Homeland Security Council, October 5, 2007, p. 13. http://www .dhs.gov/xlibrary/assets/nat_strat_homelandsecurity_2007 .pdf.

7. National Strategy for Homeland Security, Homeland Security Council, October 5, 2007, p. 3. http://www.dhs .gov/xlibrary/assets/nat_strat_homelandsecurity_2007 .pdf.

8. Christopher Bellavita, "Changing Homeland Security: What is Homeland Security?" Homeland Security Affairs, Vol. IV, No. 2, June 2008. http://www .hsaj.org/?article=4.2.1.

9. Bellavita at page 10 quoting Patrick J. Massey, "Generational Hazards."

   Massey's "Generational" hazards are: 1. The Soaring Federal Fiscal and Current-Account Debts; 2. Global Warming; 3. Failing Math, Science, and Engineering Education; and 4. Decaying Physical Infrastructure. Patrick Massey, Generational Hazards, Homeland Security Affairs III, no. 3, September 2007, pp. 3–6. http://www .hsaj.org/?article=3.3.3.

10. The author's term.

11. Patrick Massey, Generational Hazards, Homeland Security Affairs III, no. 3, September 2007, pp. 3–6. http://www.hsaj.org/?article=3.3.3.

12. Local Emergency Management: A Tale of Two Models, by Michael D. Selves, July 27, 2004. http:// training.fema.gov/EMIweb/downloads/LOCAL% 20EMERGENCY%20MANAGEMENT.doc.

    See also "Understanding and Advancing Cross-Sector Collaboration in Homeland Security and Emergency Management," Forthcoming in the Journal of Emergency Management, 2009/2010, by David J. Kaufman and Jonathan Dake, Center for Naval Analysis, July 21, 2009. http://www.cna.org/documents/ Cross%20Sector%20Collaboration%20in%20HS.pdf.

13. President Obama, Presidential Study Directive 1, February 23, 2009, pp. 1–2. http://www.fas.org/irp/offdocs/ psd/psd-1.pdf.

14. "Obama defends climate bill's cap-and-trade plan," Richard S. Dunham, Hearst Washington Bureau

    Thursday, the San Francisco Chronicle, June 25, 2009.

    http://www.sfgate.com/cgi-bin/article.cgi?f=/c/a/ 2009/06/24/MNF518DBGI.DTL.

15. Road Map for National Security: Imperative for Change, The Phase III Report of the U.S. Commission on National Security/21st Century, *The United States Commission on National Security/21st Century*, February 15, 2001. http://www.au.af.mil/au/awc/awcgate/nssg/phaseIIIfr .pdf.

16. Dennis C. Blair, Director of National Intelligence, February 12, 2009, Annual Threat Assessment of the Intelligence Community for the Senate Select Committee on Intelligence, pp. 41–43. http://www.dni.gov/ testimonies/20090212_testimony.pdf.

    "Global Trends 2025: The National Intelligence Council's 2025 Project." http://www.dni.gov/nic/ NIC_2025_project.html.

    "Climate Change and Global Security: Challenges, Threats and Diplomatic Opportunities," Committee On Foreign Relations United States Senate, July 21, 2009.

    http://foreign.senate.gov/hearings/2009/hrg090721p .html.

    "Global Climate Change Impacts in the United States," June 16, 2009, United States Global Change Research Program.

    http://www.globalchange.gov/publications/reports/ scientific-assessments/us-impacts.

    "Emerging Global Trends and Potential Implications for National Security," by David J. Kay, Association of the United States Army, Institute of Land Warfare, National Security Watch, NSW 09-1, May 29, 2009. http://www3.ausa.org/marketing/NSW_Trends_May09 .pdf.

    "Wildlife crisis worse than economic crisis – IUCN." For Press Release, July 2, 2009.

    http://www.iucn.org/about/work/programmes/species/ ?3460/Wildlife-crisis-worse-than-economic-crisis– IUCN. For actual report see http://data.iucn.org/ dbtw-wpd/edocs/RL-2009-001.pdf.

    "Rising Temperatures, Rising Tensions, Climate Change and The Risk of Violent Conflict in The Middle East," by Oli Brown and Alec Crawford, International Institute for Sustainable Development, 2009. http:// www.iisd.org/pdf/2009/rising_temps_middle_east.pdf.

    "Potential Impacts of Climate Change in the United States, Congressional Budget Office," May 2009.

    http://www.cbo.gov/ftpdocs/101xx/doc10107/05-04-ClimateChange_forWeb.pdf.

17. National Defense Strategy, June 2008, p. 5. http:// www.defenselink.mil/news/2008%20national% 20defense%20strategy.pdf.

18. "Road Map for National Security: Imperative for Change," The Phase III Report of the U.S. Commission on National Security/21st Century, February 15, 2001, p. 38, Gary Hart and Warren B. Rudman, Co-Chairs. http://www.au.af.mil/au/awc/awcgate/nssg/phaseIIIfr .pdf.

19. Testimony of General Charles F. Wald, United States Air Force (Ret.), Member, Energy Security Leadership Council, Before the U.S. Senate Committee on Foreign Relations, May 12, 2009. http://foreign.senate.gov/ testimony/2009/WaldTestimony090512p.pdf.

20. The Honorable Jimmy Carter, Former President of the United States, Hearing Before The Committee on Foreign Relations United States, May 12, 2009. http:// foreign.senate.gov/hearings/2009/hrg090512p.html.

21. I consider the terms Office/Department/Agency of Emergency Services/Emergency Management/Homeland Security as synonyms.

22. In the call for papers for its March 2010 "Homeland Security—Global and Domestic Perspectives, A Multidisciplinary Academic Conference," the University of Central Missouri expects "representation … from a wide-variety of disciplines—agriculture, communication, journalism & media studies, computer information systems, criminal justice, disaster management, geography, history, health sciences, homeland security education, international studies, legal/justice studies, natural sciences, philosophy, political science, psychology, safety sciences, sociology." http://www.ucmo.edu/cjinst/ PDF%20Call.pdf.

23. Homeland Security and Defense Education Summit, Washington, DC, March 12–13, 2009. http:// www.hsdl.org/hslog/?q=node/4696.

24. Intelligence; law and policy; emergency management; terrorism; environmental science; risk analysis; critical infrastructure analysis and protection; Constitutional presidential power, separation of powers, enemy combatants, and war powers; the Geneva Conventions; civil liberties; federalism; the Patriot Act; Foreign Intelligence Surveillance Act (FISA); chemical and biological weapons; computer forensics; information security; encryption science and technology; environmental terrorism; national intelligence production and policy; law enforcement; criminal justice; aviation security; maritime security; transportation security; border control; transnational crime; international studies; emergency management; funding and grant evaluation; epistemology; critical thinking skills; philosophy of science; philosophy of social science; the study of how states organize science and technology to produce physical power; qualitative analysis; quantitative analysis; evaluation research; policy analysis; economics; biology; engineering; history; psychology; sociology; economics; ethics; and human rights.

25. The Honorable James R. Lochner, III, Project for National Security Reform, Keynote address, 2009 Unrestricted Warfare Symposium, Johns Hopkins Applied Physics Lab and Paul H. Nitze School of Advanced International Studies, Baltimore, MD, March 24, 2009. http://www.jhuapl.edu/urw_symposium/.

Also see, James Jay Carafano, Ph.D., Missing Pieces in Homeland Security: Interagency Education, Assignments, and Professional Accreditation, The Heritage Foundation, October 16, 2006. http://www.heritage.org/Research/HomelandSecurity/em1013.cfm.

"Our current national security system, and the manner in which it is governed and funded, does not permit the timely and effective integration of the diverse departmental expertise and capabilities required to protect the United States in an increasingly complex ... world. This gives the President a narrow range of options for dealing with national security affairs and causes an over-reliance on the military instrument of national power. Using a blunt and outmoded set of tools, the United States has jeopardized its national security ... This system was devised over sixty years ago for a different era ... Today, national security involves a much wider array of issues that can only be addressed with a broader set of highly synchronized and carefully calibrated capabilities ..." "The Project on National Security Reform was established to assist the nation as it seeks to better equip itself to operate in this 21st century security environment..."

http://www.pnsr.org/web/page/578/sectionid/578/pagelevel/1/interior.asp.

Also, "Today's inter-agency coordination efforts, although growing, are still discrete, purpose-driven and episodic... Today our nation employs millions of dedicated professionals, both directly and indirectly, engaged daily in delivering national security. Executing the mission is however encumbered and made more difficult by an ever-growing excrescence of constraints, policies, conflicting corporate cultures and bureaucratic constructs that overburden the efficiency and efficacy of the efforts. Much time, energy, money and scarce management bandwidth are spent on non-value added, agility-weakening 'industrial age' activities which result in a costly and cumbersome sub-optimal national security outcome incapable of the necessary agility to adapt to the dynamics of an ever-changing environment." Prepared Statement, Henry N. Dreifus, Committee on Armed Services, United States House of Representatives, April 2, 2009, "Becoming comfortable about being uncomfortable." http://armedservices.house.gov/pdfs/TUTC040209/Dreifus_Testimony040209.pdf.

26. Report of the Defense Science Board Task Force on Understanding Human Dynamics March 2009, Office of the Under Secretary of Defense for Acquisition, Technology, and Logistics, pp. vii–viii.

http://www.acq.osd.mil/dsb/reports/2009-03-Human_Dynamics.pdf.

Also see "Developing Critical Thinking Skills in Homeland Security and Emergency Management Courses," By Linda Kiltz, Journal of Homeland Security and Emergency Management, Manuscript 1558, Berkeley Electronic Press, 2009. http://www.bepress.com/jhsem/vol6/iss1/36/.

27. See www.hsdeca.org.

28. The author graduated from the CHDS Masters Program in March 2006. www.chds.us. "...Since 2002, CHDS has conducted a wide range of programs focused on assisting current and future leaders in Homeland Defense and Security to develop the policies, strategies, programs and organizational elements needed to defeat terrorism in the United States. The programs are developed in partnership with and are sponsored by the National Preparedness Directorate, FEMA..."

29. "The principal goal of FEMA's Emergency Management Higher Education Project is to enhance the professionalism and abilities of the next generation of hazards and emergency managers through solid college-based emergency management education programs."

http://www.fema.gov/institution/university.shtm#0.

30. National Strategy for Homeland Security, Homeland Security Council, October 5, 2007, p. 3. http://www.dhs.gov/xlibrary/assets/nat_strat_homelandsecurity_2007.pdf.

31. This is the author's definition. There is not yet an agreed upon definition.

32. National Strategy for Homeland Security, Homeland Security Council, October 5, 2007, p. 3. http://www.dhs.gov/xlibrary/assets/nat_strat_homelandsecurity_2007.pdf.

33. The USA Patriot Act: http://thomas.loc.gov/cgi-bin/bdquery/z?d107:hr03162:%5D.

34. The Homeland Security Act: http://www.dhs.gov/xabout/laws/law_regulation_rule_0011.shtm.

35. http://www.dhs.gov/xabout/strategicplan/index.shtm.

36. A complete list of HSPDs is available from DHS. http://www.dhs.gov/xabout/laws/editorial_0607.shtm.

37. The Stafford Act: http://www.fema.gov/about/stafact.shtm.

38. http://www.fema.gov/about/. These same words are in PKEMRA, s. 503(b)(1).

39. PKEMRA. http://frwebgate.access.gpo.gov/cgi-bin/getdoc.cgi?dbname=109_cong_public_laws&docid=f:publ295.109.pdf.

40. "... after the first National Security Council meeting, the President turned to the Attorney General and said very simply, "John you make sure this does not happen again." The Attorney General then turned to the men and women of the justice [sic] and asked for a very carefully vetted set of proposals that would serve to prosecute the war against terrorism on the short term and to win that war in the long term..."

"The USA Patriot Act served a very, very central purpose. That is to update the law to the technology so that the terrorists and other criminals ... can not evade investigations simply by switching cell phone [sic] or changing from phone to internet. And likewise and much more significantly, Congress allowed for the criminal investigators to communicate with our intelligence investigators and vice versa. So when all hands are on deck, in order to fight the common fight against terrorism the right hand knows what the left hand is doing so that we can coordinate action . . . contrary to the law of separation that existed prior to the USA Patriot Act. . ." Viet Dinh, principal author of the Patriot Act, interview by Bryant Gumbel, "Sacrifices of Security" with Bryant Gumbel and Gwen Ifil, July 15, 2003. http://www.pbs.org/flashpointsusa/20030715/infocus/ topic_03/trans_pat_act.html.

41. David Heyman and James Jay Carafano, Ph.D., "Homeland Security 3.0, Building a National Enterprise to Keep America Safe, Free, and Prosperous," The Heritage Foundation Special Report, Center for Strategic and International Studies, SR-23, September 18, 2008, p. 3. http://www.heritage.org/Research/HomelandDefense/ upload/sr_23.pdf.

42. Homeland Security Act, sec. 231(a). http://www .dhs.gov/xabout/laws/law_regulation_rule_0011.shtm.

43. For detailed historical discussions of terrorism. See "Terrorism: A Very Short Introduction" by Charles Townshend, Oxford University Press 2002; and "Inside Terrorism" by Bruce Hoffman, Columbia University Press, 2006.

44. Homeland Security Act of 2002, section 2(15). http://www.dhs.gov/xlibrary/assets/hr_5005_enr.pdf.

45. FBI. http://denver.fbi.gov/nfip.htm.

46. The State Department has chosen the definition of terrorism contained in Title 22 of the United States Code, Section 2656f(d). http://www.state.gov/ s/ct/rls/crt/2000/2419.htm.

47. United States Criminal Code. 18 USC 2331(1).

48. United States Criminal Code. 18 USC 2331(5).

49. "We lack insight into specific details, timing, and intended targets of potential, current US Homeland plots, although we assess al-Qa'ida continues to pursue plans for Homeland attacks and is likely focusing on prominent political, economic, and infrastructure targets designed to produce mass casualties, visually dramatic destruction, significant economic aftershocks, and/or fear among the population." Dennis C. Blair Director of National Intelligence, February 12, 2009, Annual Threat Assessment of the Intelligence Community for the Senate Select Committee on Intelligence, p. 6. http://www.dni.gov/testimonies/20090212_testimony .pdf.

50. http://www.fema.gov/pdf/emergency/nrf/nrf-authorities .pdf.

51. Lieutenant General Russell L. Honore, USA (ret). March 13, 2008, Third Annual Homeland Defense and Security Education Summit. George Washington University, March 13, 2009.

52. See "The Edge of Disaster," by Stephen Flynn, 2007, for several well described existing and predictable infrastructure failures.

2

THE STRATEGIC ENVIRONMENT

We must evaluate homeland security in the context of the current and future strategic reality. Although there are differing viewpoints on one or another aspect of our strategic reality, the one that matters most in the context of this book is the one that the United States Government propounds. Presented chronologically are the strategic environment or threat assessment portions of several strategies, intelligence reports, and some outside materials. The first one, New World Coming from 1999, provides a chronological reference point.

SOURCES

- New World Coming: American Security in the 21st Century, September 15, 1999[1]
- Road Map for National Security: Imperative for Change, February 15, 2001[2]
- National Strategy to Combat Weapons Of Mass Destruction, December 2002[3]
- National Strategy for Combating Terrorism, September 2006[4]
- Generational Hazards, Patrick J. Massey, September 2007[5]
- National Strategy for Homeland Security, October 2007[6]
- National Defense Strategy, June 2008[7]
- U.S. Department of Homeland Security Strategic Plan. Fiscal Years 2008–2013[8]
- DOD, Defense Science Board, "Defense Imperatives for the New Administration." August 2008[9]

- Commission on Prevention of WMD, House Armed Svc. Comm., January 22, 2009[10]
- Director of National Intelligence, Annual Threat Assessment of the Intelligence Community for the Senate Select Committee on Intelligence, February 12, 2009[11]
- FBI. Rightwing Extremism: Current Economic And Political Climate Fueling Resurgence In Radicalization And Recruitment, April 7, 2009[12]
- 2009 Annual Report to Congress. Department of Defense Chemical and Biological Defense Program[13]
- National Strategy for Countering Biological Threats, November 2009[14]
- Strategic Environment in 2025
  - The Horizon Project[15]
  - The National Intelligence Council[16]
- The National Intelligence Strategy, August 2009[17]

New World Coming: American Security In The 21st Century, Major Themes And Implications, The Phase I Report On The Emerging Global Security Environment For The First Quarter Of The 21st Century, The United States Commission On National Security/21st Century, September 15, 1999

...Conclusions

On the basis of the foregoing beliefs, and our understanding of the broad context of the international security environment that will emerge over the next quarter century, we conclude that:

(1) America will become increasingly vulnerable to hostile attack on our homeland, and our military superiority will not entirely protect us.

Foundations of Homeland Security: Law and Policy, First Edition. Martin J. Alperen.
© 2011 John Wiley & Sons, Inc. Published 2011 by John Wiley & Sons, Inc.

The United States will be both absolutely and relatively stronger than any other state or combination of states. Although a global competitor to the United States is unlikely to arise over the next 25 years, emerging powers—either singly or in coalition—will increasingly constrain U.S. options regionally and limit its strategic influence. As a result, we will remain limited in our ability to impose our will, and we will be vulnerable to an increasing range of threats against American forces and citizens overseas as well as at home. American influence will increasingly be both embraced and resented abroad, as U.S. cultural, economic, and political power persists and perhaps spreads. States, terrorists, and other disaffected groups will acquire weapons of mass destruction and mass disruption, and some will use them. Americans will likely die on American soil, possibly in large numbers.

(2) Rapid advances in information and biotechnologies will create new vulnerabilities for U.S. security...

(3) New technologies will divide the world as well as draw it together...

(4) The national security of all advanced states will be increasingly affected by the vulnerabilities of the evolving global economic infrastructure...

(5) Energy will continue to have major strategic significance.

(6) All borders will be more porous; some will bend and some will break...

(7) The sovereignty of states will come under pressure, but will endure...

(8) Fragmentation or failure of states will occur, with destabilizing effects on neighboring states.

(9) Foreign crises will be replete with atrocities and the deliberate terrorizing of civilian populations.

(10) Space will become a critical and competitive military environment.

(11) The essence of war will not change.

Despite the proliferation of highly sophisticated and remote means of attack, the essence of war will remain the same. There will be casualties, carnage, and death; it will not be like a video game. What will change will be the kinds of actors and the weapons available to them...

(12) U.S. intelligence will face more challenging adversaries, and even excellent intelligence will not prevent all surprises...

(13) The United States will be called upon frequently to intervene militarily in a time of uncertain alliances and with the prospect of fewer forward-deployed forces.

(14) The emerging security environment in the next quarter century will require different military and other national capabilities.

[See portions of Phase II of the above Report, "Seeking a National Strategy," in Chapter 9, "National Strategy for Homeland Security."]

Road Map For National Security: Imperative For Change, February 15, 2001

The combination of unconventional weapons proliferation with the persistence of international terrorism will end the relative invulnerability of the U.S. homeland to catastrophic attack. A direct attack against American citizens *on American soil* is likely over the next quarter century...

In this Commission's view, the inadequacies of our systems of research and education pose a greater threat to U.S. national security over the next quarter century than any potential conventional war that we might imagine. American national leadership must understand these deficiencies as threats to national security...

National Strategy To Combat Weapons Of Mass Destruction, December, 2002

"The possession and increased likelihood of use of WMD by hostile states and terrorists are realities of the contemporary security environment."

This is the primary reference to the strategic environment in the National Strategy to Combat WMD. Much more of this National Strategy is in Chapter 15, "Weapons of Mass Destruction."

National Strategy for Combating Terrorism, September 2006

"America is at war with a transnational terrorist movement fueled by a radical ideology of hatred, oppression, and murder..."

"The United States and our partners continue to pursue a significantly degraded but still dangerous al-Qaida network. Yet the enemy we face today in the War on Terror is not the same enemy we faced on September 11... Today, the principal terrorist enemy confronting the United States is a transnational movement of extremist organizations, networks, and individuals – and their state and non-state supporters – which have in common that they exploit Islam and use terrorism for ideological ends.

This transnational movement is not monolithic. Although al-Qaida functions as the movement's vanguard and remains, along with its affiliate groups and those inspired by them, the most dangerous present manifestation of the enemy, the movement is not controlled by any single individual, group, or state. What unites the movement is a common vision, a common set of ideas about the nature and destiny of the world, and a common goal of ushering in totalitarian rule. What unites the movement is the ideology of oppression, violence, and hate.[18,19]

Our terrorist enemies exploit Islam to serve a violent political vision. Fueled by a radical ideology and a false belief that the United States is the cause of most problems affecting Muslims today, our enemies seek to expel Western power and influence from the Muslim world and establish regimes that rule according to a violent and intolerant distortion of Islam. As illustrated by Taliban-ruled Afghanistan, such regimes would deny all political and religious freedoms and serve as sanctuaries for extremists to launch additional attacks against not only the United States, its allies and partners, but the Muslim world itself.

Some among the enemy, particularly al-Qaida, harbor even greater territorial and geopolitical ambitions and aim to establish a single, pan-Islamic, totalitarian regime that stretches from Spain to Southeast Asia...

For our terrorist enemies, violence is not only justified, it is necessary and even glorified – judged the only means to achieve a world vision darkened by hate, fear, and oppression... We cannot permit the world's most dangerous terrorists and their regime sponsors to threaten us with the world's most destructive weapons.

For the enemy, there is no peaceful coexistence with those who do not subscribe to their distorted and violent view of the world. They accept no dissent and tolerate no alternative points of view. Ultimately, the terrorist enemy we face threatens global peace, international security and prosperity, the rising tide of democracy, and the right of all people to live without fear of indiscriminate violence."

Generational Hazards, Patrick J. Massey, September 2007

Patrick J. Massey argues that the following are what he calls "Generational" or long-term security issues:

(1) The soaring Federal fiscal and current-account debts
(2) Global warming
(3) Failing math, science, and engineering education
(4) Decaying physical infrastructure

National Strategy For Homeland Security, October 2007

Today's Threat Environment Our Nation faces complex and dynamic threats from terrorism. In addition, other threats from catastrophic events...

Terrorism Despite concerted worldwide efforts in the aftermath of September 11 that have disrupted terrorist plots and constrained al-Qaida's ability to strike the Homeland, the United States faces a persistent and evolving terrorist threat, primarily from violent Islamic terrorist groups and cells.

Al-Qaida likely will ... intensify its efforts to place operatives here in the Homeland. We also must never lose sight of al-Qaida's persistent desire for weapons of mass destruction...

In addition to al-Qaida, [there are] a host of other groups... These include Lebanese Hizballah, ... [and] Iran, its principal sponsor.

The United States also is not immune to the emergence of homegrown radicalization and violent Islamic extremism within its borders...[20]

The terrorist threat...[includes]...white supremacist groups, animal rights extremists, and eco-terrorist groups...

Catastrophic Natural Disasters ... the American people also are at risk from natural catastrophes..... Naturally occurring infectious diseases... Increasing human contact with domesticated and wild animals (from which many human diseases emerge), the growing speed and volume of global travel and commerce, and a decline in the development of new infectious disease therapeutics complicate this challenge.

Natural disasters also encompass a variety of meteorological and geological hazards ... hurricanes ... earthquakes... floods ... tornadoes ... wildfires ...

Catastrophic Accidents and Other Hazards We also remain vulnerable to catastrophic domestic accidents involving industrial hazards and infrastructure failures...[21]

National Defense Strategy, June 2008[22]

The Strategic Environment For the foreseeable future, this environment will be defined by a global struggle against a violent extremist ideology that seeks to overturn the international state system. Beyond this transnational struggle, we face other threats, including a variety of irregular challenges, the quest by rogue states for nuclear weapons, and the rising military power of other states. These are long-term challenges. Success in dealing with them will require the orchestration of national and international power over years or decades to come.

Violent extremist movements such as al-Qaeda and its associates comprise a complex and urgent challenge...

The inability of many states to police themselves effectively or to work with their neighbors to ensure regional security represents a challenge to the international system...

Rogue states such as Iran and North Korea similarly threaten international order. The Iranian regime sponsors terrorism and is attempting to disrupt the fledgling democracies in Iraq and Afghanistan. Iran's pursuit of nuclear technology and enrichment capabilities poses a serious challenge to security in an already volatile region. The North Korean regime also poses a serious nuclear and missile proliferation concern for the U.S. and other responsible international stakeholders...

China is one ascendant state with the potential for competing with the United States...[23]

"Russia's retreat from openness and democracy could have significant security implications for the United States, our European allies, and our partners in other regions...

U.S. dominance in conventional warfare has given prospective adversaries, particularly non-state actors and their state sponsors, strong motivation to adopt asymmetric methods to counter our advantages. For this reason, we must display a mastery of irregular warfare comparable to that which we possess in conventional combat. Our adversaries also seek to develop or acquire catastrophic capabilities: chemical, biological, and especially nuclear weapons. In addition, they may develop disruptive technologies in an attempt to offset U.S. advantages. For example, the development and proliferation of anti-access technology[24] and weaponry is worrisome as it can restrict our future freedom of action. These challenges could come not only in the obvious forms we see today but also in less traditional forms of influence such as manipulating global opinion using mass communications venues and exploiting international commitments and legal avenues. Meeting these challenges require better and more diverse capabilities in both hard and soft power, and greater flexibility and skill in employing them.

We must develop better intelligence capabilities to detect, recognize, and analyze new forms of warfare as well as explore joint approaches and strategies to counter them. ....

These risks will require managing the divergent needs of massively increasing energy demand to maintain economic development and the need to tackle climate change...

The Strategic Framework ... The security of the United States is tightly bound up with the security of the broader international system. As a result, our strategy seeks to build the capacity of fragile or vulnerable partners to withstand internal threats and external aggression...

Win the Long War ... We face a global struggle. Like communism and fascism before it, extremist ideology has transnational pretensions, and like its secular antecedents, it draws adherents from around the world. The vision it offers is in opposition to globalization and the expansion of freedom it brings. Paradoxically, violent extremist movements use the very instruments of globalization – the unfettered flow of information and ideas, goods and services, capital, people, and technology – that they claim to reject to further their goals. ...

Promote Security ...The prospect that instability and collapse in a strategic state could provide extremists access to weapons of mass destruction or result in control of strategic resources is a particular concern.[25]

The United States welcomes the rise of a peaceful and prosperous China, and it encourages China to participate as a responsible stakeholder by taking on a greater share of burden for the stability, resilience, and growth of the international system...

...In addition, Russia's retreat from democracy and its increasing economic and political intimidation of its neighbors give cause for concern. We do not expect Russia to revert to outright global military confrontation, but the risk of miscalculation or conflict arising out of economic coercion has increased.

Deter Conflict ... In the contemporary strategic environment, the challenge is one of deterring or dissuading a range of potential adversaries from taking a variety of actions against the U.S. and our allies and interests...

Prevent Adversaries from Acquiring or Using Weapons of Mass Destruction (WMD)

There are few greater challenges than those posed by chemical, biological, and particularly nuclear weapons...

A number of hostile or potentially hostile states are actively seeking or have acquired WMD.

Technological and information advances of the last fifty years have led to the wide dissemination of WMD knowledge and lowered barriers to entry. Relatively sophisticated chemical agents, and even crude biological agents, are within the reach of many non-state actors with a modicum of scientific knowledge. Non-state actors may acquire WMD, either through clandestine production, state-sponsorship, or theft. Also of concern is the potential for severe instability in WMD states and resulting loss of control of these weapons.

Secure U.S. Strategic Access and Retain Freedom of Action The United States requires freedom of action in the global commons and strategic access to important regions of the world to meet our national security needs. The well-being of the global economy is contingent on ready access to energy resources...

Integrate and Unify Our Efforts: A New "Jointness" ...We also need capabilities to meet the challenges of the 21st century. Strategic communications within the Department and across government is a good example. Although the United States invented modern public relations, we are unable to communicate to the world effectively who we are and what we stand for as a society and culture, about freedom and democracy, and about our goals and aspirations...

DoD Capabilities and Means Strategic communications will play an increasingly important role in a unified approach to national security...DoD, in partnership with the

Department of State, has begun to make strides in this area, and will continue to do so. However, we should recognize that this is a weakness across the U.S. Government, and that a coordinated effort must be made to improve the joint planning and implementation of strategic communications.

Future Challenges Risk China is developing technologies to disrupt our traditional advantages. Examples include development of anti-satellite capabilities and cyber warfare.

One Team, One Mission, Securing Our Homeland U.S. Department Of Homeland Security Strategic Plan Fiscal Years 2008–2013

The bulk of this Strategic Plan is in Chapter 5, "Department of Homeland Security." Appendix A says, "There is the possibility that our adversaries will be able to surprise us particularly with rapid advances in biotechnology and threats to cyberspace that would inhibit our ability to protect the Nation" (p. 28).

Appendix B: Strategic Context and Stakeholder Outreach

Strategic Context
The DHS *2008 Strategic Plan* considers a multitude of internal and external forces likely to shape current and future challenges to our Nation's people, society, and economy. The *Plan* also considers how these forces may affect the United States' role in the world... For an independent assessment of how DHS might operate in the coming years, the Office of Strategic Plans commissioned a detailed report by the Homeland Security Institute (HSI), the Department's federally-funded research and development center...

The assessment identifies the two principal sources of risk our Nation faces – dangers posed by human architects or by nature. It also identifies a number of factors that could influence the environment in which the Department operates. First, the report considers it likely that nation-states will continue as the dominant players on the world stage. It also envisages, however, that governments will have less control over information, technology, disease, and migrants, and that the global community will continue to exist in a profound sense of uncertainty. The report indicates that non-state actors will likely play a larger role, to both positive and negative ends, in influencing the global framework. The report also concludes that greater inter-connectivity and networks will provide opportunities for transnational criminals.

The HSI assessment develops nine themes that will affect future homeland security decision-making... These themes are:

Increasing global interdependence of economies, enterprises, and governments;

Threats from domestic and transnational terrorists;

Challenges to U.S. homeland security emanating from nation-states;

Impact of transnational criminal networks;

Outbreak and rapid spread of virulent diseases;

Effect of large-scale natural disasters;

Proliferation and acquisition of weapons of mass destruction;

Advances in scientific knowledge and applications and resultant challenges and opportunities; and

Physical and cyber critical infrastructure in the United States.

DOD, Defense Science Board, "Defense Imperatives For The New Administration"[26]

"Weapons of mass destruction challenge the safety of our homeland and our military forces. A major factor in addressing the threat from weapons of mass destruction (WMD) is a fundamental lack of information needed for interdiction and deterrence, calling for a major increase in focus on the full range of WMD by our intelligence community. Furthermore, one of the easiest ways for terrorists to create weapons such as bio-weapons is from materials and equipment purchased or stolen in the United States, which places a particular premium on domestic intelligence."

Statement Of Senator Bob Graham, Chairman, Senator Jim Talent, Vice-Chairman, And Dr. Graham Allison Of The Commission On The Prevention Of Weapons Of Mass Destruction Proliferation And Terrorism Before A Hearing Of The House Armed Services Committee, January 22, 2009[27]

"... The Congress asked our Commission to assess the U.S. government's current activities, initiatives, and programs aimed at preventing WMD proliferation and terrorism, and to lay out a clear, comprehensive strategy for the President and Congress—including a set of practical, implementable recommendations...

Early on, the Commission decided to focus its inquiry and recommendations on nuclear and biological weapons because these two categories of WMD have the greatest potential to cause massive casualties... Indeed, we believe that unless urgent preventive action is taken, a terrorist attack involving a weapon of mass destruction—nuclear, biological, chemical, or radiological—is more likely than not to occur somewhere in the world in the next five years.

Our report concludes that although an incident of nuclear terrorism would be catastrophic, a biological attack that inflicts mass casualties is more likely in the near term because of the greater availability of the relevant dual-use materials, equipment, and know-how, which are spreading rapidly throughout the world...

Pakistan is a major focus of our report because of its terrorist networks, history of instability, and nuclear arsenal of several dozen warheads. Indeed, were one to map terrorism and WMD today, all roads would intersect in Pakistan. . .

Pakistan is a U.S. ally, but many government officials and outside experts believe that the next terrorist attack against the United States—possibly with weapons of mass destruction—is likely to originate from within the FATA in Pakistan. The Commission agrees. . .

At present, given the difficulty of weaponizing and disseminating significant quantities of a biological agent as an aerosol cloud, government officials and outside experts believe that no terrorist group has the operational capability to carry out a mass-casualty attack. . . Accordingly, the Commission concluded that the United States should be less concerned that terrorists will become biologists and far more concerned that biologists will become terrorists.

In addition to the current threat of bioweapons proliferation and terrorism, a set of over-the-horizon risks is emerging, associated with recent advances in the life sciences and biotechnology and the world-wide diffusion of these capabilities. One area of intense activity, based on the availability of automated machines that can synthesize long strands of DNA, is known as "synthetic genomics." By piecing together large fragments of genetic material, scientists have been able to assemble infectious viruses. . .

With respect to the threat of nuclear terrorism, al Qaeda is judged to be the sole terrorist group currently intent on conducting a nuclear attack against the United States. . .

Director Of National Intelligence, Annual Threat Assessment Of The Intelligence Community For The Senate Select Committee On Intelligence, February 12, 2009

"Continued escalation of energy demand will hasten the impacts of climate change. On the other hand, forcibly cutting back on fossil fuel use before substitutes are widely available could threaten continued economic development, particularly for countries like China, whose industries have not yet achieved high levels of energy efficiency.

Food and water also are intertwined with climate change, energy, and demography. . . Climatically, rainfall anomalies and constricted seasonal flows of snow and glacial melts are aggravating water scarcities, harming agriculture in many parts of the globe. Energy and climate dynamics also combine to amplify a number of other ills such as health problems, agricultural losses to pests, and storm damage. The greatest danger may arise from the convergence and interaction of many stresses simultaneously. . .

According to the United Nations Intergovernmental Panel on Climate Change (IPCC), a failure to act to reduce greenhouse gas emissions risks severe damage to the planet by the end of this century and even greater risk in coming centuries. . .

The Intelligence Community recently completed a National Intelligence Assessment on the national security impacts of global climate change to 2030. The IC judges global climate change will have important and extensive implications for US national security interests over the next 20 years.

FBI. Rightwing Extremism: Current Economic And Political Climate Fueling Resurgence In Radicalization And Recruitment, April 7, 2009

Prepared by the Extremism and Radicalization Branch, Homeland Environment Threat Analysis Division. Coordinated with the FBI.

Key Findings The DHS/Office of Intelligence and Analysis (I&A) has no specific information that domestic rightwing[28] terrorists are currently planning acts of violence, but rightwing extremists may be gaining new recruits by playing on their fears about several emergent issues. The economic downturn and the election of the first African American president present unique drivers for rightwing radicalization and recruitment.

The current economic and political climate has some similarities to the 1990s when rightwing extremism experienced a resurgence fueled largely by an economic recession, criticism about the outsourcing of jobs, and the perceived threat to U.S. power and sovereignty by other foreign powers. . .

The possible passage of new restrictions on firearms and the return of military veterans facing significant challenges reintegrating into their communities could lead to the potential emergence of terrorist groups or lone wolf extremists capable of carrying out violent attacks.

Proposed imposition of firearms restrictions and weapons bans likely would attract new members into the ranks of rightwing extremist groups, as well as potentially spur some of them to begin planning and training for violence against the government. The high volume of purchases and stockpiling of weapons and ammunition by rightwing extremists in anticipation of restrictions and bans in some parts of the country continue to be a primary concern to law enforcement.

Returning veterans possess combat skills and experience that are attractive to rightwing extremists.

Exploiting Economic Downturn Rightwing extremist chatter on the Internet continues to focus on the economy, the perceived loss of U.S. jobs in the manufacturing and construction sectors, and home foreclosures. Anti-Semitic extremists attribute these losses to a deliberate conspiracy conducted by a cabal of Jewish "financial elites."

Historical Presidential Election Rightwing extremists are harnessing this historical election as a recruitment tool. . .

Economic Hardship and Extremism Historically, domestic rightwing extremists have feared, predicted, and anticipated a cataclysmic economic collapse in the United States. . .

Illegal Immigration Rightwing extremists were concerned during the 1990s with the perception that illegal immigrants were taking away American jobs through their willingness to work at significantly lower wages...

DHS/I&A notes that prominent civil rights organizations have observed an increase in anti-Hispanic crimes over the past five years.

2009 Annual Report To Congress. Department Of Defense Chemical And Biological Defense Program

"The overall number of countries capable of producing chemical agents has grown and will continue to increase due to the availability of chemical production equipment and the globalization of the chemical industry. As technology dissemination progresses and dual-use equipment becomes increasingly available, the threat from CWs [chemical weapons] could become more diverse and more technically sophisticated...

Toxic industrial chemicals (TIC) and toxic industrial materials (TIM) also pose a serious risk to U.S. Armed Forces and civilians because of their potential lethality...

Between October 2006 and June 2007, Iraqi insurgents conducted multiple vehicle-borne improvised explosive device attacks employing industrial chlorine gas cylinders as improvised CWs. While these attacks showed little technical sophistication, they were initially successful in causing fear amongst the general populace and served as a clear sign that CW alternatives were being pursued by U.S. adversaries."

National Strategy for Countering Biological Threats, November 2009

The effective dissemination of a lethal biological agent within an unprotected population could place at risk the lives of hundreds of thousands of people. The unmitigated consequences of such an event could overwhelm our public health capabilities, potentially causing an untold number of deaths. The economic cost could exceed one trillion dollars for each such incident. In addition, there could be significant societal and political consequences that would derive from the incident's direct impact on our way of life and the public's trust in government...

Strategic Environment in 2025

Below are eight possible scenarios of what the world might be like in 2025: five from the Horizon Project and three from the National Intelligence Council. Although the state of the world and the United States 15 years from now is impossible to predict with certainty, scenarios are useful for planning.

The Horizon Project "brought together U.S. Government senior executives from global affairs agencies and the National Security Council staff to explore ways to improve U.S. Government interagency coordination in global affairs." They created a "set of five plausible alternative future operating environments or scenarios." They caution that the scenarios "are not intended to be forecasts of the future, and are 'valid' only as a set" and only for planning.

The Horizon Project

Asian Way Summary: In this version of 2025, the world economy is increasingly dominated by Asian megacorporations that are expanding at the expense of the formerly dominant American and European military/economic powers. The "Asian Way" of conducting business and national affairs in more discreet, shielded ways, through subtle personal networks, rather than in the Western mode of at least apparent insistence on transparency, disclosure, and – in politics – democratization, has yielded clear advantages both in the marketplace and in national affairs over the Western-style capitalism of the post-World War II era. America is trying to dig itself out of the fiscal and economic hole caused by its simultaneous attempts to insulate itself from terrorism (mainly successfully), fund the retirement of its elderly, maintain military supremacy, and keep its tax rates low.

The U.S. public feels secure from any imminent threat, but feels uneasy about what appears to be the end of the era of American dominance. While Asian governments are increasingly transferring power to influential, opaque corporate interests, Washington has found itself in gridlock and losing influence to state and local governments and corporations, all of which are cutting deals with the new Asian megacorporations. The U.S. economy is not in a depression, yet it has largely lost the technology edge that it possessed at the turn of the century. The youth of America are more and more drawn to the "Wild East" to find excitement, fortune, and opportunity. Asia is where the action is – in terms of business, culture, and even political power.

Be Careful What You Wish For Summary: Not without its problems to manage, this version of 2025 is a world of excitement, opportunity, freedom, and technological wonders. Democratic governments with some level of engaged and informed citizenry have emerged and prospered in all regions of the globe. The global economy is growing and wealth is being distributed more evenly than ever before, although significant areas of poverty, and even desperation, remain. Nation-states still command the global political landscape, but conflicts are low level and are usually resolved through peaceful means.

The world economy is different than forecasters in 2006 might have envisioned it. Social turmoil in China added to nearly six years of on-again, off-again geological instability in the Pacific Ring of Fire (from the Solomon Islands to Japan and the Aleutians and down the Americas' West Coast to Chile) has brought about the near disappearance of fragile just-in-time supply chains. In place of these systems, the investment portfolios of large organizations now emphasize resiliency, risk management, and geographic dispersion. The result, to a greater degree than ever before, has been manufacturing sites and transportation systems spread across the globe and new fast-growing middle classes in Asia, Africa, and Latin America.

The world faces a globally acknowledged environmental crisis created by a combination of human and natural causes. There is a U.S.-initiated worldwide movement to "Heal the Earth" that exerts a strong influence on government, social, and technological agendas. The U.S. is well off and well regarded, but, as the policeman and global first responder, is stretched very thin. The U.S. is finding that participating and leading in a world made up of activist fellow democracies is more chaotic and challenging than might ever have been foreseen in 2006.

Congagement Summary: This version of 2025 is a world in which political and economic power increasingly are organized regionally, rather than globally. This is a dynamic, tense, and highly competitive world with multiple points of friction. The emerging regional blocs revolve around three major power centers – the U.S., the EU, and China. Each of these is increasingly sharing power with regional authorities. The power blocs are not monolithic, however. The other major players – Brazil, Russia, and India – shift among them opportunistically to varying extents. The remaining nations in Africa, the Middle East and Central Asia with resources and/or major markets are the objects of energetic competition, while those nations with few resources or markets are neglected.

Among the U.S. population, there is a new focus on the Americas. Remaining U.S. troops in South Korea are increasingly unwelcome even as Venezuela has invited Chinese troops into their country. The Middle East remains unsettled. Energy access is so important that all parties tacitly agree to allow unimpeded shipments, even as global investment patterns have shifted to reflect a distinct regionalization of major trade flows. Oil rigs are appearing everywhere, even in the Polar Regions. The global commons are in jeopardy as there are few effective mechanisms for managing global issues. Trade, commerce, and capital flows still benefit from a legacy global architecture, but new investments follow the strong new intra-regional economic and political relationships. These dynamics create a continually shifting mixture of both tension and trade, both confrontation and engagement, or 'Congagement.'

Lockdown Summary: This version of 2025 is a multi-threat world marked by persistent terrorism, nuclear proliferation, and the most challenging economics the U.S. – and the world – have faced in more than 50 years. The U.S. has been the primary target of WMD attacks launched by a new, radical Islamic terror network. The assaults have exposed critical vulnerabilities in supply chain and transportation systems. In response, the U.S. has turned heavily defensive, protectionist, and isolationist. This has had a profoundly negative impact on nearly every aspect of economic life in the U.S., with harsh and bewildering effects across much of the global economy.

While Europe, too, has experienced terrorist violence (including a dirty bomb attack in its most important port), the frequency and human cost have been considerably less. Less isolated from the world, Europe is meeting its economic challenges relatively well. Meanwhile, nuclear proliferation continues unabated. An uneasy balance of terror hangs over the Middle East. Many developing countries are collapsing, without export markets or foreign aid. The heady era of globalization and multilateral interdependence is over. China is the principal victim of the U.S. lockdown, and its economic and political desperation is now taking an ominous turn.

Profits and Principles Summary: In this version of 2025, across much of the world, a new culture of global capitalism is fueling rapid economic growth, increasingly integrated markets, and dynamic technological innovation. The effects of this corporate-driven capitalism are pervasive. Foreign policy is strongly influenced by business leaders who are pulling the strings of increasingly powerful international bodies. The U.S. economy is thriving, but social safety nets have disappeared as the global business drive for profits ruthlessly discards those who cannot (or do not) contribute.

Poverty in many developing nations is exploding. An emerging moderate Pan-Islamic movement with a message that Islam cares (while global capitalism does not) is attempting to fill the void, and has gathered partners among other religious and social movements. Leaders of the new movement are benefiting from the significant income derived from hydrocarbon energy resources and are using some of this wealth to provide for those left behind. Although the top tier of Americans have benefited tremendously from hyper-capitalism, many others have not and the global clash between profits and principles is causing leaders from all sectors a high degree of anxiety. Optimists see these diverging paths as complementary and useful. Pessimists worry that they could end up on a collision course, with profound consequences for the U.S. and the world.

The National Intelligence Council

The National Intelligence Council is the "intelligence community's center for mid-term and long-term strategic thinking." "Global Scenarios to 2025" presents three of its own scenarios. Like the Horizon Project, this report also cautions that these are not forecasts.

Borrowed Time represents how the future might play out if the world follows the "business as usual" modus operandi. The notion that we can afford to wait much longer for technology's silver bullet without facing serious consequences is somewhat unrealistic. The implications of this scenario are that (1) unless serious changes are made now in terms of how decision makers at all levels (e.g., international institutions, states, business leaders, and citizens) prioritize issues and (2) there is a conscious awareness of the true interconnectedness of a globalized world, then we could soon pass the point of no return (particularly with regards to climate change issues). In addition, leaders and citizens alike must be cognizant of the fact that the repercussions of their actions (or inactions) could last several lifetimes and beyond, and that in many cases the long-term impact is potentially irreversible.

Fragmented World is a more selfish world, a future which can be reflected in the expression "every man for himself." Actors try to save themselves without much concern for the others. Economic growth is constrained and there is not a great deal of multilateral solidarity. There is more insecurity and less trust. This is a world that cannot keep pace with the problems, is overwhelmed, and is starting to come apart at the seams.

Constant Renewal describes a world in which nations realize that the international community must work collaboratively on a sustained basis to affect real change at the global level. This is not borne out of any sense of a desire to create a global "Kumbaya" community, but out of necessity—we are shocked into action—and a change in the way key players think about the issues. Leaders also develop a heightened sense of the scale and urgency of the problems facing the world. The journey to this future is full of pitfalls (and policies are fine-tuned as needed), but the main point is that there is a global momentum towards a sustainable future supported by lasting partnerships, cooperative agreements, and a clear change in ways of thinking about global problems.

The National Intelligence Strategy August 2009

THE STRATEGIC ENVIRONMENT The United States faces a complex and rapidly changing national security environment in which nation-states, highly capable non-state actors, and other transnational forces will continue to compete with and challenge U.S. national interests. Adversaries are likely to use asymmetric means and technology (either new or applied in a novel way) to counter U.S. interests at home and abroad.

A number of **nation-states** have the ability to challenge U.S. interests in traditional (e.g., military force and espionage) and emerging (e.g., cyber operations) ways.

Non-state and sub-state actors increasingly impact our national security.

- *Violent extremist groups* are planning to use terrorism—including the possible use of nuclear weapons or devices if they can acquire them—to attack the United States.

- *Insurgents* are attempting to destabilize vulnerable states in regions of strategic interest to the United States.

- Transnational criminal organizations, including those that traffic drugs, pose a threat to U.S. interests.

- The global economic crisis could accelerate and weaken U.S. security by fueling political turbulence...

- Failed states and ungoverned spaces offer terrorist and criminal organizations safe haven and possible access to weapons of mass destruction (WMD)...

- *Climate change and energy competition* may produce second-order effects for national security as states anticipate the effects of global warming (e.g., by contesting water resources in regions with limited potable sources) and seek to secure new energy sources, transport routes, and territorial claims.

- Rapid *technological change* and dissemination of information continue to alter social, economic, and political forces...

- As the 2009 H1N1 influenza outbreak vividly illustrates, the risk of *pandemic disease* presents a persistent challenge to global health, commerce, and economic well-being.

ENDNOTES

1. "New World Coming: American Security in The 21st Century, Major Themes and Implications," The Phase I Report on the Emerging Global Security Environment for the First Quarter of the 21st Century, The United States Commission on National Security/21st Century, September 15, 1999, pp. 4–7. Gary Hart and Warren B. Rudman, Co-Chairs. http://www.au.af.mil/au/awc/awcgate/nssg/nwc.pdf.

2. "Road Map for National Security: Imperative for Change," The Phase III Report of the U.S. Commission on National Security/21st Century, February 15, 2001, pp. viii–ix, Gary Hart and Warren B. Rudman, Co-Chairs. http://www.au.af.mil/au/awc/awcgate/nssg/phaseIIIfr.pdf.

3. National Strategy to Combat Weapons of Mass Destruction, December 2002, p. 2. http://merln.ndu.edu/archivepdf/nss/strategies/WMDStrategy.pdf.

4. National Strategy for Combating Terrorism, September 2006, pp. 1, 5–6. http://merln.ndu.edu/archivepdf/terrorism/WH/nsct2006.pdf.

5. Patrick J. Massey, "Generational Hazards," Homeland Security Affairs III, no. 3, September 2007, pp. 3–6, 20. http://www.hsaj.org/?article=3.3.3.

6. National Strategy for Homeland Security, October 2007, pp. 9–11. http://www.dhs.gov/xlibrary/assets/nat_strat_homelandsecurity_2007.pdf.

7. National Defense Strategy, June 2008, pp. i–22. http://www.defenselink.mil/pubs/2008NationalDefenseStrategy.pdf.

8. One Team, One Mission, Securing Our Homeland. U.S. Department of Homeland Security Strategic Plan. Fiscal Years 2008–2013, Appendix A, Appendix B. http://www.dhs.gov/xlibrary/assets/DHS_StratPlan_FINAL_spread.pdf.

9. Defense Science Board. http://www.acq.osd.mil/dsb/reports/2008-11-Defense_Imperatives.pdf.

10. Commission on Prevention of WMD, House Armed Svc. Comm., January 22, 2009. http://armedservices.house.gov/pdfs/FC012209/WMDCommission_Testimony012209.pdf.

11. Dennis C. Blair, Director of National Intelligence, Annual Threat Assessment of the Intelligence Community for the Senate Select Committee on Intelligence, February 12, 2009, pp. 41–43. http://www.dni.gov/testimonies/20090212_testimony.pdf.

12. DHS. Rightwing Extremism. . . . http://www.fas.org/irp/eprint/rightwing.pdf.

13. 2009 Annual Report to Congress. Department of Defense Chemical and Biological Defense Program, April 2009, pp. 2–3. https://www.hsdl.org/homesec/docs/dod/nps37-042109-03.pdf&code=02a7f04e2ca1160b97e7d1cd6104e6c3.

14. National Strategy for Countering Biological Threats, National Security Council, November 2009. http://www.whitehouse.gov/sites/default/files/National_Strategy_for_Countering_BioThreats.pdf.

15. Project Horizon Progress Report, Summer 2006, pp. 1, 12–16. Reprinted with permission. http://www.osif.us/images/Project_Horizon_Progress_Report.pdf.

16. The National Intelligence Council, "Global Scenarios to 2025," February 2008, pp. 59–60. http://www.dni.gov/nic/PDF_2025/2025_Global_Scenarios_to_2025.pdf.

17. The National Intelligence Strategy, August 2009. http://www.dni.gov/reports/2009_NIS.pdf.

18. . . . "Today in the Kingdom [of Saudi Arabia] . . . young people are systematically infused with hostility for "infidels." . . . "America . . . is the "Abode of the Infidel," the Christian and the Jew." (pp. 8, 11.) Center for Religious Freedom, "Saudi Publications On Hate Ideology Invade American Mosques," 2006. http://www.hudson.org/files/publications/SaudiPropoganda.pdf.

19. [Our] "opponents [are] suffused with a vision of a vengeful god whom they serve as executioners, men who regard death as a promotion. . .Ralph Peters, "Our Brilliant, Bloody Future," *Military Officer*, January 2006, p. 69.

20. "A Minneapolis mosque is again denying allegations it's responsible for a dozen or more young Somali men leaving the U.S. to join a terrorist group in East Africa. Abubakar al-Saddique mosque was one of two mosques named at a U.S. Senate committee hearing yesterday investigating Islamic extremist recruitment in America." By Sasha Aslanian, Minnesota Public Radio, March 11, 2009. http://minnesota.publicradio.org/display/web/2009/03/11/somalihearing_folo/?refid=0.

21. The American Society of Civil Engineers in its report, "America's Infrastructure, 2009 Report Card," March 25, 2009, assess our nation's infrastructure is in very bad condition. http://s3.amazonaws.com/ascereportcard/sites/default/files/RC2009_full_report.pdf [large file].

Stephen Flynn argues persuasively that our critical infrastructure is in dire need of reconstruction, repair, or rebuilding, thus exacerbating the cascading effect. The "Edge of Disaster, Rebuilding a Resilient Nation." Random House, 2007.

See Also, "Unconquerable Nation, Knowing Our Enemy Strengthening Ourselves," by Brian Michael Jenkins. Rand, 2006.

For other excellent examples see "Attack Here," a well-crafted scenario about terrorism in the Houston Ship Channel, November 2004. http://www.texasmonthly.com/2004-11-01/feature5.php.

"Considering The Effects of a Catastrophic Terrorist Attack," Charles Meade, Roger C. Molander, The RAND Center for Terrorism Risk Management Policy, 2006. http://www.rand.org/pubs/technical_reports/2006/RAND_TR391.pdf.

See the concept of resiliency in the Resiliency and a Culture of Preparedness Chapter of this text.

22. National Defense Strategy, June 2008. http://www.defenselink.mil/news/2008%20national%20defense%20strategy.pdf

23. "A vast electronic spying operation has infiltrated computers and has stolen documents from hundreds of government and private offices around the world, including those of the Dalai Lama, Canadian researchers have concluded. . . . researchers said that the system was being controlled from computers based almost exclusively in China, but that they could not say conclusively that the Chinese government was involved. . .]" John Markoff, "Vast Spy System Loots Computers in 103 Countries," New York Times, March 28, 2009. http://www.nytimes.com/2009/03/29/technology/29spy.html?_r=1&ref=todayspaper. For the complete report, see "Tracking Ghostnet: Investigating a Cyber Espionage Network," Information Warfare Monitor, March 29, 2009. www.infowar-monitor.net/ghostnet

24. "Since the end of the Cold War, U.S. strategists have become increasingly concerned with the possibility that, in the event of a conflict with the United States, an adversary might adopt and attempt to execute an "antiaccess" strategy intended to interfere with the U.S. military's ability to deploy to or operate within overseas theaters of operation.

This concern stems from two features of the post–Cold War world. First is that, with the disintegration of the Soviet Union, no country fields military forces comparable in both quantity and quality to those of the United States, and thus there is little likelihood that the U.S. military will be defeated in a conventional force-on-force engagement on the battlefield. The principal threat to defeat U.S. military forces, therefore, is through the use of an asymmetric approach, such as an antiaccess strategy.

The chances of success of an antiaccess strategy are increased by the second feature of the post–Cold War world: The absence of a single dominant adversary makes it impossible to predict where U.S. military forces will next be needed and, thus, makes it likely that the United States will have relatively few forward-deployed forces in the vicinity of a conflict about to erupt.

For potential opponents of the United States, the motives for adopting an antiaccess strategy are compelling. These countries must plan to face an adversary that enjoys tremendous military and technological superiority, and they undoubtedly recognize that, as long as the U.S. military can arrive in force and on time, it will almost certainly prevail. Thus, they may seek to impede the deployment of U.S. forces and restrict or disrupt the U.S. military's ability to operate within a theater far from U.S. territory. They may also calculate that, by mounting a credible threat to do so, they will be able to deter the United States from intervening in the first place, or at least limit the scale and scope of that intervention.

This monograph describes the types of antiaccess measures one particular country—China—might employ...

For purposes of this discussion, an *antiaccess* measure is considered to be any action by an opponent that has the effect of slowing the deployment of friendly forces into a theater, preventing them from operating from certain locations within that theater, or causing them to operate from distances farther from the locus of conflict than they would normally prefer... "Entering the Dragon's Lair, Chinese Antiaccess Strategies and Their Implications for the United States." Roger Cliff, Mark Burles, Michael S. Chase, Derek Eaton, Kevin L. Pollpeter. Prepared for the United States Air Force, Approved for public release; distribution unlimited. RAND Corporation, 2007. http://www.rand.org/pubs/monographs/2007/RAND_MG524.sum.pdf.

Also, "If anti-access (A2) strategies aim to prevent US forces entry into a theater of operations, then area-denial (AD) operations aim to prevent their freedom of action in the more narrow confines of the area under an enemy's direct control. AD operations thus include actions by an adversary in the air, on land, and on and under the sea to contest and prevent US joint operations within their defended battlespace." "Meeting the Anti-Access

and Area-Denial Challenge" by Andrew Krepinevich, Barry Watts, Robert Work. Center for Strategic and Budgetary Assessments, 2003. http://www.csbaonline.org/4Publications/Archive/R.20030520.Meeting_the_Anti-A/R.20030520.Meeting_the_Anti-A.pdf.

25. As this book is written, areas of concern include Pakistan, Iran, and North Korea.

26. DOD, Defense Science Board, "Defense Imperatives for the New Administration." August 2008, p. 2. http://www.acq.osd.mil/dsb/reports/2008-11-Defense_Imperatives.pdf.

27. Statement of Senator Bob Graham, Chairman, Senator Jim Talent, Vice-Chairman, and Dr. Graham Allison of the Commission on the Prevention of Weapons of Mass Destruction Proliferation and Terrorism Before a Hearing of the House Armed Services Committee, January 22, 2009. http://armedservices.house.gov/pdfs/FC012209/WMDCommission_Testimony012209.pdf.

28. Rightwing extremism in the United States can be broadly divided into those groups, movements, and adherents that are primarily hate-oriented (based on hatred of particular religious, racial or ethnic groups), and those that are mainly antigovernment, rejecting federal authority in favor of state or local authority, or rejecting government authority entirely. It may include groups and individuals that are dedicated to a single issue, such as opposition to abortion or immigration.

ADDITIONAL RESOURCES

"Global Risks 2010: A Global Risk Network Report, World Economic Forum, January 2010. http://opim.wharton.upenn.edu/risk/downloads/WEF_Global-Risks_2010.pdf.

"Transnational Threats Update," September 2009, Vol. 7, no. 7. http://csis.org/files/publication/ttu_0707.pdf.

"Global Strategic Assessment 2009, America's Security Role in a Changing World," Edited by Patrick M. Cronin, By National Defense University Press 2009. http://www.ndu.edu/inss/index.cfm?secID=8&pageID=126&type=section.

"Taking Up the Security Challenge of Climate Change," by Rymn J. Parsons, Strategic Studies Institute, United States Army War College. http://www.strategicstudiesinstitute.army.mil/pubs/display.cfm?pubID=932.

A Guide to Terrorism Events and Landmark Cases: Terrorism in the West 2008, by Daveed Gartenstein-Ross, Joshua D. Goodman, and Laura Grossman, FDD's Center for Terrorism Research. http://defenddemocracy.org/images/stories/Terrorism%20in%20the%20West%20Final%20Report.pdf.

"Confronting the New Faces of Hate: Hate Crimes in America, 2009," is an initiative of the Leadership Conference on Civil Rights Education Fund (LCCREF). http://www.civilrights.org/publications/hatecrimes/lccref_hate_crimes_report.pdf.

State And Nonstate Associated Gangs: Credible "Midwives Of New Social Orders," by Max G. Manwaring, May 2009,

Strategic Studies Institute. http://www.strategicstudiesinstitute. army.mil/pdffiles/PUB876.pdf.

"Emerging Threats and Security Planning: How Should We Decide What Hypothetical Threats to Worry About?" Brian A. Jackson, David R. Frelinger, Rand, 2009. http://www.rand.org/pubs/occasional_papers/2009/RAND_OP256.pdf.

Preventing Nuclear Terrorism: A Global Intelligence Imperative, by Rolf Mowatt-Larssen, April 30, 2009, The Washington Institute for Near East Policy. http://www.washingtoninstitute.org/templateC05.php?CID=3048.

Homegrown Terrorists in the U.S. and U.K.: An Empirical Examination of The Radicalization Process, Daveed Gartenstein-Ross and Laura Grossman, 04/27/2009, Center for Terrorism Research, Foundation for Defense of Democracies. http://www.defenddemocracy.org/index.php?option=com_content&task=view&id=11785395&Itemid=102.

"Nuclear Terrorism: Assessing the Threat, Developing a Response," Evan Montgomery, Center for Strategic and Budgetary Assessments, 04/22/2009. http://www.csbaonline.org/4Publications/PubLibrary/R.20090422.Nuclear_Terrorism/R.20090422.Nuclear_Terrorism.pdf.

"Missed by the Boom, Hurt by the Bust: Making Markets Work for Young People in the Middle East, An Agenda for Policy Reform and Greater Regional Cooperation." Middle East Youth Initiative, A Joint Project of The Dubai School of Government & The Wolfensohn Center for Development at Brookings. http://www.brookings.edu/~/media/Files/rc/reports/2009/05_middle_east_youth_dhillon/05_middle_east_youth_dhillon_final.pdf.

"Political Violence Against Americans 2008," United States Department of State, Bureau of Diplomatic Security. http://www.state.gov/documents/organization/125224.pdf.

3

HOMELAND SECURITY COUNCIL

The Homeland Security Council was established in 2001 to advise the President on homeland security issues, just as the National Security Council (NSC) advises the President about national security issues. It is relatively unknown. There is now discussion of eliminating it or merging it with the NSC.

SOURCES

- National Security Act Of 1947[1]
- Executive Order 13228 of October 8, 2001, Establishing the Office of Homeland Security and the Homeland Security Council[2]
- HSPD 1. Homeland Security Council, October 29, 2001[3]
- Executive Order 13260 of March 19, 2002, Establishing the President's Homeland Security Advisory Council and Senior Advisory Committees for Homeland Security[4]
- Homeland Security Act, November 25, 2002[5]
- Presidential Policy Directive 1 – Organization of the National Security Council System, February 13, 2009[6]

National Security Act Of 1947

SEC. 101.

(a) There is hereby established a council to be known as the National Security Council (thereinafter in this section referred to as the "Council"). The President of the United States shall preside over meetings of the Council: . . .The function of the Council shall be to advise the President with respect to the integration of domestic, foreign, and military policies relating to the national security so as to enable the military services and the other departments and agencies of the Government to cooperate more effectively in matters involving the national security.

Sec. 101.

The Council shall be composed of 1—

(1) the President;
(2) the Vice President;
(3) the Secretary of State;
(4) the Secretary of Defense;
(5) the Director for Mutual Security;
(6) the Chairman of the National Security Resources Board; and
(7) The Secretaries and Under Secretaries of other executive departments and the military departments, the Chairman of the Munitions Board, and the Chairman of the Research and Development Board, when appointed by the President by and with the advice and consent of the Senate, to serve at his pleasure.

(b). . . it shall, subject to the direction of the President, be the duty of the Council—

(1) to assess and appraise the objectives, commitments, and risks of the United States in relation to our actual and potential military power, in the interest of national security, for the purpose of making recommendations to the President in connection therewith; and

Foundations of Homeland Security: Law and Policy, First Edition. Martin J. Alperen.
© 2011 John Wiley & Sons, Inc. Published 2011 by John Wiley & Sons, Inc.

(2) to consider policies on matters of common interest to the departments and agencies of the Government concerned with the national security, and to make recommendations to the President in connection therewith.

Executive Order 13228 Of October 8, 2001, Establishing The Office Of Homeland Security And The Homeland Security Council

Sec. 1. Establishment.

I hereby establish within the Executive Office of the President an Office of Homeland Security (the "Office") to be headed by the Assistant to the President for Homeland Security.

Sec. 2. Mission.

The mission of the Office shall be to develop and coordinate the implementation of a comprehensive national strategy to secure the United States from terrorist threats or attacks.

Sec. 3. Functions.

The functions of the Office shall be to coordinate the executive branch's efforts to detect, prepare for, prevent, protect against, respond to, and recover from terrorist attacks within the United States.

(a) *National Strategy.* The Office shall work with executive departments and agencies, State and local governments, and private entities to ensure the adequacy of the national strategy for detecting, preparing for, preventing, protecting against, responding to, and recovering from terrorist threats or attacks within the United States and shall periodically review and coordinate revisions to that strategy as necessary.

(b) *Detection.* The Office shall identify priorities and coordinate efforts for collection and analysis of information. . . .

(i) In performing these functions, the Office shall work with Federal, State, and local agencies, as appropriate, to:

  (A) facilitate collection from State and local governments and private entities of information pertaining to terrorist threats or activities within the United States;

  (B) coordinate and prioritize the requirements for foreign intelligence relating to terrorism within the United States of executive departments and agencies responsible for homeland security and provide these requirements and priorities to the Director of Central Intelligence and other agencies responsible for collection of foreign intelligence;

  (C) coordinate efforts to ensure that all executive departments and agencies that have intelligence collection responsibilities have sufficient technological capabilities and resources. . .

  (D) coordinate development of monitoring protocols and equipment for use in detecting the release of biological, chemical, and radiological hazards; and

  (E) ensure that, to the extent permitted by law, all appropriate and necessary intelligence and law enforcement information relating to homeland security is disseminated to and exchanged among appropriate executive departments and agencies responsible for homeland security and, where appropriate for reasons of homeland security, promote exchange of such information with and among State and local governments and private entities.

(c) *Preparedness.* The Office of Homeland Security shall coordinate national efforts to prepare for and mitigate the consequences of terrorist threats or attacks within the United States. . .

(i) review and assess the adequacy of the portions of all Federal emergency response plans that pertain to terrorist threats or attacks within the United States;

(ii) coordinate domestic exercises and simulations designed to assess and practice systems that would be called upon to respond to a errorist threat or attack within the United States and coordinate programs and activities for training Federal, State, and local employees who would be called upon to respond to such a threat or attack;

(iii) coordinate national efforts to ensure public health preparedness for a terrorist attack, including reviewing vaccination policies and reviewing the adequacy of and, if necessary, increasing vaccine and pharmaceutical stockpiles and hospital capacity;

(iv) coordinate Federal assistance to State and local authorities and nongovernmental organizations to prepare for and respond to terrorist threats or attacks within the United States;

(v) ensure that national preparedness programs and activities for terrorist threats or attacks are developed and are regularly evaluated under appropriate standards and that resources are allocated to improving and sustaining preparedness based on such evaluations; and

(vi) ensure the readiness and coordinated deployment of Federal response teams to respond to terrorist threats or attacks, working with the Assistant to the President for National Security Affairs, when appropriate.

(d) *Prevention.* The Office shall coordinate efforts to. . .

(i) facilitate the exchange of information among such agencies relating to immigration and visa matters and shipments of cargo; and. . . ensure coordination among such agencies to prevent the entry of terrorists and terrorist materials and supplies into the United States and facilitate removal of such terrorists from the United States, when appropriate;

(ii) coordinate efforts to investigate terrorist threats and attacks within the United States; and

(iii) coordinate efforts to improve the security of United States borders, territorial waters, and airspace..

(e) *Protection.* The Office shall coordinate efforts to protect the United States and its critical infrastructure from the consequences of terrorist attacks.

(i) strengthen measures for protecting energy production, transmission, and distribution services and critical facilities; other utilities; telecommunications; facilities that produce, use, store, or dispose of nuclear material; and other critical infrastructure services and critical facilities within the United States from terrorist attack;

(ii) coordinate efforts to protect critical public and privately owned information systems. . .

(iii) develop criteria for reviewing whether appropriate security measures are in place at major public and privately owned facilities. . .

(iv) coordinate domestic efforts to ensure that special events determined by appropriate senior officials to have national significance are protected. . .

(v) coordinate efforts to protect transportation systems within the United States, including railways, highways, shipping, ports and waterways, and airports and civilian aircraft, from terrorist attack;

(vi) coordinate efforts to protect United States livestock, agriculture, and systems for the provision of water and food for human use and consumption from terrorist attack; and

(vii) coordinate efforts to prevent unauthorized access to, development of, and unlawful importation into the United States of, chemical, biological, radiological, nuclear, explosive, or other related materials that have the potential to be used in terrorist attacks.

(f) *Response and Recovery.* The Office shall coordinate efforts to respond to and promote recovery from terrorist threats or attacks within the United States. In performing this function, the Office shall work with Federal, State, and local agencies, and private entities, as appropriate, to:

(i) coordinate efforts to ensure rapid restoration of transportation systems, energy production, transmission, and distribution systems; telecommunications; other utilities; and other critical infrastructure facilities after disruption by a terrorist threat or attack;

(ii) coordinate efforts to ensure rapid restoration of public and private critical information systems after disruption by a terrorist threat or attack;

(iii) work with the National Economic Council to coordinate efforts to stabilize United States financial markets after a terrorist threat or attack and manage the immediate economic and financial consequences of the incident;

(iv) coordinate Federal plans and programs to provide medical, financial, and other assistance to victims of terrorist attacks and their families; and

(v) coordinate containment and removal of biological, chemical, radiological, explosive, or other hazardous materials in the event of a terrorist threat or attack involving such hazards and coordinate efforts to mitigate the effects of such an attack.

(g) *Incident Management.* The Assistant to the President for Homeland Security shall be the individual primarily responsible for coordinating the domestic response efforts of all departments and agencies in the event of an imminent terrorist threat and during and in the immediate aftermath of a terrorist attack within the United States and shall be the principal point of contact for and to the President with respect to coordination of such efforts. The Assistant to the President for Homeland Security shall coordinate with the Assistant to the President for National Security Affairs, as appropriate.

(h) *Continuity of Government.* The Assistant to the President for Homeland Security, in coordination with the Assistant to the President for National Security Affairs, shall review plans and preparations for ensuring the continuity of the Federal Government in the event of a terrorist attack that threatens the safety and security of the United States Government or its leadership.

(i) *Public Affairs.* The Office, subject to the direction of the White House Office of Communications, shall coordinate the strategy of the executive branch for communicating with the public in the event of a terrorist threat or attack within the United States. The Office also shall coordinate the development of programs for educating the public about the nature of terrorist threats and appropriate precautions and responses.

(j) *Cooperation with State and Local Governments and Private Entities.* The Office shall encourage and invite the participation of State and local governments and private entities, as appropriate, in carrying out the Office's functions.

Sec. 5. Establishment of Homeland Security Council.

(a) I hereby establish a Homeland Security Council (the "Council"), which shall be responsible for advising and assisting the President with respect to all aspects of homeland security. The Council shall serve as the mechanism for ensuring coordination of homeland security-related activities of executive departments and agencies and effective development and implementation of homeland security policies.

HSPD 1. Homeland Security Council, October 29, 2001

Subject: Organization and Operation of the Homeland Security Council

(A) Homeland Security Council
  Securing Americans from terrorist threats or attacks is a critical national security function. It requires extensive coordination across a broad spectrum of Federal, State, and local agencies... The Homeland Security Council (HSC) shall ensure coordination of all homeland security-related activities...

Executive Order 13260 Of March 19, 2002, Establishing The President's Homeland Security Advisory Council And Senior Advisory Committees For Homeland Security

Sec. 1. President's Homeland Security Advisory Council.

(a) *Establishment and Membership.* I hereby establish the President's Homeland Security Advisory Council (PHSAC). The PHSAC shall be composed of not more than 21 members appointed by the President...

(c) *Senior Advisory Committees.* (i) Establishment and Membership. The following four Senior Advisory Committees for Homeland Security (SACs) are hereby established to advise the PHSAC: (1) State and Local Officials; (2) Academia and Policy Research; (3) Private Sector; and (4) Emergency Services, Law Enforcement, and Public Health and Hospitals. Each SAC shall generally be composed of not more than 17 members selected by the Assistant to the President for Homeland Security (Assistant).

Sec. 2. Functions.

The PHSAC shall meet periodically at the Assistant's request to:

(a) provide advice to the President through the Assistant on developing and coordinating the implementation of a comprehensive national strategy to secure the United States from terrorist threats or attacks;

(b) recommend to the President through the Assistant ways to improve coordination, cooperation, and communication among Federal, State, and local officials and private and other entities, and provide a means to collect scholarly research, technological advice, and information concerning processes and organizational management practices both inside and outside of the Federal Government;

(c) provide advice to the President through the Assistant regarding the feasibility of implementing specific measures to detect, prepare for, prevent, protect against, respond to, and recover from terrorist threats or attacks within the United States;

(d) examine, and advise the President through the Assistant on, the effectiveness of the implementation of specific strategies to detect, prepare for, prevent, protect against, respond to, and recover from terrorist threats or attacks within the United States; and

Homeland Security Act, November 25, 2002

Sec. 901. National Homeland Security Council.

There is established within the Executive Office of the President a council to be known as the "Homeland Security Council" (in this title referred to as the "Council").

Sec. 902. Function.

The function of the Council shall be to advise the President on homeland security matters.

Sec. 904. Other Functions and Activities.

For the purpose of more effectively coordinating the policies and functions of the United States Government relating to homeland security, the Council shall—

(1) assess the objectives, commitments, and risks of the United States in the interest of homeland security and to make resulting recommendations to the President;

(2) oversee and review homeland security policies of the Federal Government and to make resulting recommendations to the President...

Sec. 906. Relation to the National Security Council.

The President may convene joint meetings of the Homeland Security Council and the National Security Council with participation by members of either Council or as the President may otherwise direct.

**Presidential Policy Directive 1 – Organization Of The
National Security Council System, February 13, 2009**

THE WHITE HOUSE

WASHINGTON

February 13, 2009

PRESIDENTIAL POLICY DIRECTIVE - 1

MEMORANDUM FOR THE VICE PRESIDENT
                THE SECRETARY OF STATE
                THE SECRETARY OF THE TREASURY
                THE SECRETARY OF DEFENSE
                THE ATTORNEY GENERAL
                THE SECRETARY OF COMMERCE
                THE SECRETARY OF ENERGY
                THE SECRETARY OF HOMELAND SECURITY
                THE ASSISTANT TO THE PRESIDENT AND CHIEF OF STAFF
                THE DIRECTOR OF THE OFFICE OF MANAGEMENT AND
                    BUDGET
                THE REPRESENTATIVE OF THE UNITED STATES
                    OF AMERICA TO THE UNITED NATIONS
                THE UNITED STATES TRADE REPRESENTATIVE
                THE CHAIR OF THE COUNCIL OF ECONOMIC ADVISERS
                THE ASSISTANT TO THE PRESIDENT FOR NATIONAL
                    SECURITY AFFAIRS
                THE DIRECTOR OF NATIONAL INTELLIGENCE
                THE ASSISTANT TO THE PRESIDENT FOR ECONOMIC
                    POLICY
                THE COUNSEL TO THE PRESIDENT
                THE DIRECTOR OF THE OFFICE OF SCIENCE AND
                    TECHNOLOGY POLICY
                THE CHAIRMAN OF THE JOINT CHIEFS OF STAFF

    SUBJECT: Organization of the National Security Council
                    System

To assist me in carrying out my responsibilities in the area of
national security, I hereby direct that the National Security
Council system be organized as follows.

A. The National Security Council

The National Security Council (NSC) shall be the principal forum
for consideration of national security policy issues requiring
Presidential determination. The functions, membership, and
responsibilities of the NSC shall be as set forth in the

National Security Act of 1947, as amended, and this Presidential
Policy Directive. The NSC shall advise and assist me in
integrating all aspects of national security policy as it affect
the United States -- domestic, foreign, military, intelligence,
and economic (in conjunction with the National Economic Council)
Along with its subordinate committees, the NSC shall be my
principal means for coordinating executive departments and
agencies in the development and implementation of national
security policy.

The NSC shall have as its members the President, Vice President,
Secretary of State, Secretary of Defense, and Secretary of
Energy, as prescribed by statute. In addition, the membership o
the NSC shall include the Secretary of the Treasury, the Attorne
General, the Secretary of Homeland Security, the Representative
of the United States of America to the United Nations, the
Assistant to the President and Chief of Staff (Chief of Staff to
the President), and the Assistant to the President for National
Security Affairs (National Security Advisor). The Director of
National Intelligence and the Chairman of the Joint Chiefs of
Staff, as statutory advisers to the NSC, shall attend NSC
meetings. The Counsel to the President shall be invited to
attend every NSC meeting, and the Assistant to the President
and Deputy National Security Advisor shall attend every meeting,
and serve as Secretary. When international economic issues
are on the agenda of the NSC, the NSC's regular attendees will
include the Secretary of Commerce, the United States Trade
Representative, the Assistant to the President for Economic
Policy, and the Chair of the Council of Economic Advisers. When
homeland security or counter-terrorism related issues are on the
agenda, the NSC's regular attendees will include the Assistant t
the President for Homeland Security and Counter-Terrorism. When
science and technology related issues are on the agenda, the
NSC's regular attendees will include the Director of the Office
of Science and Technology Policy. The heads of other executive
departments and agencies, and other senior officials, shall be
invited to attend meetings of the NSC as appropriate.

The NSC shall meet regularly and as required. The National
Security Advisor, at my direction and in consultation with
other members of the NSC, shall be responsible for determining
the agenda, ensuring that necessary papers are prepared, and
recording NSC actions and Presidential decisions in a timely
manner.

B.   The NSC Principals Committee

The NSC Principals Committee (NSC/PC) will continue to be the
senior interagency forum for consideration of policy issues

affecting national security, as it has been since 1989. The
National Security Advisor shall serve as Chair, and its regular
members will be the Secretary of State, the Secretary of the
Treasury, the Secretary of Defense, the Attorney General,
the Secretary of Energy, the Secretary of Homeland Security,
the Director of the Office of Management and Budget, the
Representative of the United States of America to the
United Nations, the Chief of Staff to the President, the Director
of National Intelligence, and the Chairman of the Joint Chiefs of
Staff. The Assistant to the President and Deputy National
Security Advisor, the Deputy Secretary of State, the Counsel
to the President, and the Assistant to the Vice President for
National Security Affairs shall be invited to attend every
meeting of the NSC/PC. When international economic issues are
on the agenda, the NSC/PC's regular attendees will include the
Secretary of Commerce, the United States Trade Representative,
the Chair of the Council of Economic Advisers, and the Assistant
to the President for Economic Policy, who, at the discretion of
the National Security Advisor, may serve as chair. When homeland
security or counter-terrorism related issues are on the agenda,
the NSC/PC's regular attendees will include the Assistant to the
President for Homeland Security and Counter-Terrorism, who, at
the discretion of the National Security Advisor, may serve as
chair. When science and technology related issues are on the
agenda, the NSC's regular attendees will include the Director of
the Office of Science and Technology Policy. The heads of other
executive departments and agencies, along with additional senior
officials, shall be invited as appropriate.

The NSC/PC shall meet at the call of the National Security
Advisor, in consultation with the members of the NSC/PC.
The National Security Advisor shall determine the agenda in
consultation with the other committee members, and shall
ensure that necessary papers are prepared and that conclusions
and decisions are communicated in a timely manner.

C.   The NSC Deputies Committee

The NSC Deputies Committee (NSC/DC) shall review and monitor
the work of the NSC interagency process (including Interagency
Policy Committees established pursuant to section D below).
The NSC/DC shall also help ensure that issues being brought
before the NSC/PC or the NSC have been properly analyzed and
prepared for decision. The NSC/DC shall focus significant
attention on policy implementation. Periodic reviews of the
Administration''s major foreign policy initiatives shall be
scheduled to ensure that they are being implemented in a timely
and effective manner. Such reviews should periodically consider
whether existing policy directives should be revamped or

rescinded. Finally, the NSC/DC shall be responsible for day-tc
day crisis management, reporting to the National Security
Council. Any NSC principal or deputy, as well as the National
Security Advisor, may request a meeting of the Deputies Committ
in its crisis management capacity.

The Assistant to the President and Deputy National Security
Advisor shall chair the NSC/DC. Its members are the Deputy
Secretary of State, the Deputy Secretary of the Treasury, the
Deputy Secretary of Defense, the Deputy Attorney General, the
Deputy Secretary of Energy, the Deputy Secretary of Homeland
Security, the Deputy Director of the Office of Management and
Budget, the Deputy to the United States Representative to the
United Nations, the Deputy Director of National Intelligence, t
Vice Chairman of the Joint Chiefs of Staff, and the Assistant t
the Vice President for National Security Affairs. When homelan
security or counter-terrorism related issues are on the agenda,
a regular attendee of meetings of the NSC/DC will include the
Assistant to the President for Homeland Security and Counter-
Terrorism and Deputy National Security Advisor, who, at the
discretion of the Assistant to the President and Deputy Nationa
Security Advisor, may serve as chair. When international
economic issues are on the agenda, a regular meeting of the
NSC/DC will include the Deputy Assistant to the President and
Deputy National Security Advisor for International Economics,
who, at the discretion of the Assistant to the President and
Deputy National Security Advisor, may serve as chair. When
science and technology related issues are on the agenda, a
regular meeting of the NSC/DC will include an Associate Directo
of the Office of Science and Technology Policy. The chair
may invite representatives of other executive departments and
agencies, and other senior officials, to attend meetings of the
NSC/DC as appropriate.

The Assistant to the President and Deputy National Security
Advisor shall be responsible -- in consultation with the member
of the NSC/DC -- for calling meetings of the NSC/DC, for
determining the agenda, for ensuring that the necessary papers
are prepared, and for preparing and circulating conclusions and
decisions in a timely manner. The NSC/DC shall ensure that all
papers to be discussed by the NSC or the NSC/PC fully analyze
the issues, fairly and adequately set out the facts, consider a
full range of views and options, and satisfactorily assess the
prospects, risks, and implications of each.

D.   Interagency Policy Committees

Management of the development and implementation of national
security policies by multiple agencies of the United States
Government shall be accomplished by the NSC Interagency Policy

Committees (NSC/IPCs). The NSC/IPCs shall be the main day-to-day fora for interagency coordination of national security policy. They shall provide policy analysis for consideration by the more senior committees of the NSC system and ensure timely responses to decisions made by the President. The NSC/IPCs shall be established at the direction of the Deputies Committee, and be chaired by the NSC (or NEC, as appropriate); at its discretion, the NSC/DC may add co-chairs to any NSC/IPC if desirable. The NSC/IPCs shall convene on a regular basis to review and coordinate the implementation of Presidential decisions in their policy areas. Strict guidelines shall be established governing the operation of the Interagency Policy Committees, including participants, decisionmaking path, and time frame.

An early meeting of the NSC/DC will be devoted to setting up the NSC/IPCs and providing their mandates for reviewing policies and developing options in their respective areas for early consideration by the interagency committees established by this directive. The NSC/IPCs will replace the existing system of Policy Coordination Committees.

The Vice President and I may attend any and all meetings of any entity established by or under this directive.

This document is the first in a series of Presidential Policy Directives that, along with Presidential Study Directives, shall replace National Security Presidential Directives as instruments for communicating presidential decisions about national security policies of the United States. This Directive shall supersede all other existing presidential guidance on the organization of the National Security Council system. With regard to its application to economic matters, this document shall be interpreted in concert with any Executive Order governing the National Economic Council and with Presidential documents signed hereafter that implement either this directive or that Executive Order.

ENDNOTES

1. National Security Act of 1947, (Chapter 343; 61 Stat. 496; approved July 26, 1947) [As Amended Through P.L. 110–53, Enacted August 3, 2007], Unofficial Version. http://intelligence.senate.gov/nsaact1947.pdf.
2. Executive Order 13228 of October 8, 2001, Establishing the Office of Homeland Security and the Homeland Security Council, Federal Register/Vol. 66, No. 196. http://frwebgate.access.gpo.gov/cgi-bin/getdoc.cgi?dbname=2001_register&docid=fr10oc01-144.pdf.
3. HSPD 1. http://www.dhs.gov/xabout/laws/gc_1213648320189.shtm#1.
4. Executive Order 13260 of March 19, 2002, Establishing the President's Homeland Security Advisory Council and Senior Advisory Committees for Homeland Security, Federal Register/Vol. 67, No. 55, (Revoked by: EO 13286, February 28, 2003 eff. March 31, 2003). http://frwebgate.access.gpo.gov/cgi-bin/getdoc.cgi?dbname=2002_register& docid=fr21mr02-104. pdf.
5. Homeland Security Act of 2002. http://www.dhs.gov/xabout/laws/law_regulation_rule_0011.shtm.
6. Presidential Policy Directive 1 – Organization of The National Security Council System, February 13, 2009. http://www.Fas.Org/Irp/Offdocs/Ppd/Ppd-1.Pdf.

ADDITIONAL RESOURCES

Homeland Security Advisory Council Home Page. http://www.dhs.gov/xinfoshare/committees/editorial_0331.shtm.

For a very short bio of the HSAC members see: "U.S. Department of Homeland Security Secretary Janet Napolitano swore in 16 members of the Homeland Security Advisory Council today during her first meeting with HSAC in Albuquerque, N.M." June 5, 2009. http://www.dhs.gov/ynews/releases/pr_1244227862914.shtm.

"Reforming the Culture of National Security: Vision, Clarity, and Accountability," Final Report of a Working Group of the Markle Foundation and the Center on Law and Security at the NYU School of Law,Markle Foundation, April 2009. http://www.markle.org/downloadable_assets/20090403_reforming_culture_natsec.pdf.

The Homeland Security Council: Considerations for the Future. Homeland Security Policy Institute Task Force Report, April 2009. http://www.gwumc.edu/hspi/pubs/TFReport_HSC_040109.pdf.

"Homeland Security Policymaking: HSC at a Crossroads and Presidential Study Directive 1" Full Committee, Thursday, April 02, 2009. United Sates House of Representatives, Committee on Homeland Security, Hearing. http://www.homeland.house.gov/hearings/index.asp?id=187.

"The National Intelligence Council: Issues and Options for Congress," by Richard A. Best, Jr., Congressional Research Service, September 2, 2009, R40505. http://opencrs.com/document/R40505/2009-09-02/?23891.

"The National Security Council: An Organizational Assessment," Richard A. Best, Jr., Congressional Research Service, March 31, 2009, RL3840. http://www.dtic.mil/cgi-bin/GetTRDoc?AD=ADA494866&Location=U2&doc=GetTRDoc.pdf.

"The National Security Council: An Organizational Assessment," Richard A. Best, Jr., February 6, 2009, CRS RL30840. http://fas.org/sgp/crs/natsec/RL30840.pdf.

"The most critical issue in merging the Homeland Security Council (HSC) and the National Security Council (NSC) is one that has received the least attention. Merger advocates emphasize that combining the councils will better integrate domestic and international policymaking. Paul Stockton agrees with the importance of that goal. He argues, however, that the most destructive gaps in policy integration lie between federal, state, and local governments. The HSC was originally supposed to include state and local representatives in its policymaking process. That never happened. The failure to give states and localities a sustained, institutionalized role in shaping the initiatives they implement has produced repeated policy and programmatic failures. Stockton argues that now, regardless of whether the administration merges the HSC and NSC, the time has come to include state and local representatives in their work. In this essay he proposes how to do so and also examines the special challenges that a merged council would face in terms of its span of control and other issues." "Beyond the HSC/NSC Merger: Integrating States and Localities into Homeland Security" Policymaking Journal Article, Author Paul Stockton - Senior Research Scholar at CISAC, Published by Homeland Security Affairs, Vol. V, no. 1, January 2009. http://cisac. stanford.edu/publications/beyond_the_hscnsc_merger_integrating_states_and_localities_into_homeland_security_ policymaking/.

"A growing number of scholars argue that the new administration should overturn a key decision by President George W. Bush administration's decision in 2002 to create a Homeland Security Council (HSC). Until the September 11 attacks, the National Security Council (NSC) coordinated the handful of institutions, (including the Department of Defense) that protected the United States from its adversaries. Bush responded to al Qaeda's attacks by organizing a sprawling parallel system of institutions to protect the United States from terrorism. The Department of Homeland Security (DHS) is only part of that system. The Bush administration also assigned terrorism prevention functions to the Departments of Agriculture (USDA), Health and Human Services, Interior, and other federal institutions which had never before played such significant roles in securing the United States from attack. Bush capped this parallel security system with the HSC to help guide and coordinate its activities.

A spate of recent studies argue that creating the HSC was a mistake and that the new administration should subsume the Council within the NSC. Such a merger, however, would impede the reforms that are most vital for securing the United States against future terrorist attacks and hurricanes or other natural hazards." "Reform, Don't Merge, the Homeland Security Council," Journal Article Author Paul Stockton - Stanford University Published by The Washington Quarterly, Vol. 32, no. 1, page(s) 107–114, January 2009. http://cisac.stanford.edu/publications/reform_dont_merge_ the_homeland_security_council/.

Project on National Security Reform, "The National Security Council: A Legal History of the President's Most Powerful Advisers," (2008). http://www.pnsr.org/data/images/the%20national%20security%20council.pdf.

"The Commission on the Intelligence Capabilities of the United States Regarding Weapons of Mass Destruction, Report to the President of the United States," March 31, 2005. http://www.gpoaccess.gov/wmd/index.html.

4

INTELLIGENCE GATHERING

This chapter presents the most important material in the area of intelligence gathering. For proper background and depth, it begins with the Fourth, Fifth, Sixth, and Fourteenth Constitutional Amendments, and portions of the National Security Act of 1947. Following is Title III of the Omnibus Crime Control and Safe Streets Act of 1968 regarding wiretapping and electronic surveillance. From 1978, there is the Foreign Intelligence Surveillance Act (FISA) and Executive Order 12333, in 1981. There are ten other documents presented including the Patriot Act of 2001 and the National Intelligence Strategy, 2009.

SOURCES

- U.S. Constitution, Amendments IV, V, VI, XIV[1]
- National Security Act of 1947, (as amended through August 6, 2007)[2]
- Title III of the Omnibus Crime Control and Safe Streets Act of 1968, Wiretapping and
- Electronic Surveillance, June 19, 1968[3]
- Foreign Intelligence Surveillance Act, October 25, 1978
- Executive Order 12139–Foreign intelligence electronic surveillance of May 23, 1979[4]
- Executive Order 12333, United States intelligence activities, December 4, 1981[5]
- Electronic Communications Privacy Act of 1986, October 21, 1986[6]
- Computer Matching and Privacy Act of 1988, 5 U.S.C. § 552a

- Patriot Act, October 26, 2001[7]
- E-Government Act of 2002, December 17, 2002[8]
- Intelligence Reform and Terrorism Prevention Act of 2004[9]
- Implementing Recommendations of the 9/11 Commission Act of 2007, August 3, 2007[10]
- Protect America Act of 2007, August 5, 2007[11]
- Executive Order 13462 of February 29, 2008, President's Intelligence Advisory Board and Intelligence Oversight Board[12]
- FISA Amendments Act of 2008, July 10, 2008[13]
- Executive Order 13475 of October 7, 2008, Further Amendments to Executive Orders 12139 And 12949 In Light of the Foreign Intelligence Surveillance Act of 1978, Amendments Act of 2008[14]
- The National Intelligence Strategy, August 2009[15]

U.S. Constitution, Amendments IV, V, VI, XIV[16]

Amendment IV, 1791 The right of the people to be secure in their persons, houses, papers, and effects, against unreasonable searches and seizures, shall not be violated, and no warrants shall issue, but upon probable cause, supported by oath or affirmation, and particularly describing the place to be searched, and the persons or things to be seized.

Amendment V, 1791 No person shall be held to answer for a capital, or otherwise infamous crime, unless on a presentment or indictment of a grand jury, except in cases arising in the land or naval forces, or in the militia, when in actual service in time of war or public danger; nor shall any person be subject for the same offense to be twice put in jeopardy of life or limb; nor shall be compelled in any criminal case to

Foundations of Homeland Security: Law and Policy, First Edition. Martin J. Alperen.
© 2011 John Wiley & Sons, Inc. Published 2011 by John Wiley & Sons, Inc.

be a witness against himself, nor be deprived of life, liberty, or property, without due process of law; nor shall private property be taken for public use, without just compensation.

Amendment VI, 1791 In all criminal prosecutions, the accused shall enjoy the right to a speedy and public trial, by an impartial jury of the state and district wherein the crime shall have been committed, which district shall have been previously ascertained by law, and to be informed of the nature and cause of the accusation; to be confronted with the witnesses against him; to have compulsory process for obtaining witnesses in his favor, and to have the assistance of counsel for his defense.

Amendment XIV, 1868

SEC. 1.

All persons born or naturalized in the United States, and subject to the jurisdiction thereof, are citizens of the United States and of the state wherein they reside. No state shall make or enforce any law which shall abridge the privileges or immunities of citizens of the United States; nor shall any state deprive any person of life, liberty, or property, without due process of law; nor deny to any person within its jurisdiction the equal protection of the laws.

SEC. 5.

The Congress shall have power to enforce, by appropriate legislation, the provisions of this article.

National Security Act Of 1947

An act to promote the national security by providing for a Secretary of Defense; for a National Military Establishment; for a Department of the Army, a Department of the Navy, and a Department of the Air Force; and for the coordination of the activities of the National Military Establishment with other departments and agencies of the Government concerned with the national security.

SHORT TITLE. That this Act may be cited as the "National Security Act of 1947".

DEFINITIONS As used in this Act:

(1) The term "intelligence" includes foreign intelligence and counterintelligence.

(2) The term "foreign intelligence" means information relating to the capabilities, intentions, or activities of foreign governments or elements thereof, foreign organizations, or foreign persons, or international terrorist activities.

(3) The term "counterintelligence" means information gathered, and activities conducted, to protect against

espionage, other intelligence activities, sabotage, or assassinations conducted by or on behalf of foreign governments or elements thereof, foreign organizations, or foreign persons, or international terrorist activities.

(4) The term "intelligence community" includes the following:

(A) The Office of the Director of National Intelligence.

(B) The Central Intelligence Agency.

(C) The National Security Agency.

(D) The Defense Intelligence Agency.

(E) The National Geospatial-Intelligence Agency.

(F) The National Reconnaissance Office.

(G) Other offices within the Department of Defense for the collection of specialized national intelligence through reconnaissance programs.

(H) The intelligence elements of the Army, the Navy, the Air Force, the Marine Corps, the Federal Bureau of Investigation, and the Department of Energy.

(I) The Bureau of Intelligence and Research of the Department of State.

(J) The Office of Intelligence and Analysis of the Department of the Treasury.

(K) The elements of the Department of Homeland Security concerned with the analysis of intelligence information, including the Office of Intelligence of the Coast Guard.

(L) Such other elements of any other department or agency as may be designated by the President, or designated jointly by the Director of National Intelligence and the head of the department or agency concerned, as an element of the intelligence community.

(5) The terms "national intelligence" and "intelligence related to national security" refer to all intelligence, regardless of the source from which derived and including information gathered within or outside the United States, that—

(A) pertains, as determined consistent with any guidance issued by the President, to more than one United States Government agency; and

(B) that involves—

(i) threats to the United States, its people, property, or interests;

(ii) the development, proliferation, or use of weapons of mass destruction; or

(iii) any other matter bearing on United States national or homeland security.

(6) The term "National Intelligence Program" refers to all programs, projects, and activities of the intelligence community, as well as any other programs of the intelligence community designated jointly by the Director of Central Intelligence and the head of a United States department or agency or by the President. Such term does not include programs, projects, or activities of the military departments to acquire intelligence solely for the planning and conduct of tactical military operations by United States Armed Forces.

(7) The term "congressional intelligence committees" means—

(A) the Select Committee on Intelligence of the Senate; and

(B) the Permanent Select Committee on Intelligence of the House of Representatives

Title III of the Omnibus Crime Control and Safe Streets Act, Wiretapping and Electronic Surveillance, June 19, 1968[17]

FINDINGS

SEC. 801.

On the basis of its own investigations and of published studies, the Congress makes the following findings:

(a) Wire communications are normally conducted through the use of facilities which form part of an interstate network. The same facilities are used for interstate and intrastate communications. There has been extensive wiretapping carried on without legal sanctions, and without the consent of any of the parties to the conversation. Electronic, mechanical, and other intercepting devices are being used to overhear oral conversations made in private, without the consent of any of the parties to such communications. The contents of these communications and evidence derived therefrom are being used by public and private parties as evidence in court and administrative proceedings, and by persons whose activities affect interstate commerce. The possession, manufacture, distribution, advertising, and use of these devices are facilitated by interstate commerce.

(b) . . . it is necessary for Congress to define on a uniform basis the circumstances and conditions under which the interception of wire and oral communications may be authorized, to prohibit any unauthorized interception of such communications, and the use of the contents thereof in evidence in courts and administrative proceedings.

(c) Organized criminals make extensive use of wire and oral communications in their criminal activities. . .

(d) To safeguard the privacy of innocent persons, the interception of wire or oral communications where none of the parties to the communication has consented to the interception should be allowed only when authorized by a court of competent jurisdiction and should remain under the control and supervision of the authorizing court. Interception of wire and oral communications should further be limited to certain major types of offenses and specific categories of crime with assurances that the interception is justified and that the information obtained thereby will not be misused.

SEC. 802.

Part I of title 18, United States Code, is amended by adding at the end of the following new chapter:

"CHAPTER 119. WIRE INTERCEPTION AND INTERCEPTION OF ORAL COMMUNICATIONS

§ 2511. Interception and Disclosure of Wire or Oral Communications Prohibited

"(1) Except as otherwise specifically provided in this chapter any person who-

"(a) willfully intercepts, endeavors to intercept, or procures any other person to intercept or endeavor to intercept, any wire or oral communication;

"(b) willfully uses, endeavors to use, or procures any other person to use or endeavor to use any electronic, mechanical, or other device to intercept any oral communication when-

"(i) such device is affixed to, or otherwise transmits a signal through, a wire, cable, or other like connection used in wire communication; or

"(ii) such device transmits communications by radio, or interferes with the transmission of such communication; or

"(iii) such person knows, or has reason to know, that such device or any component thereof has been sent through the mail or transported in interstate or foreign commerce; or

"(iv) such use or endeavor to use (A) takes place on the premises of any business or other commercial establishment. . .

or (B) obtains or is for the purpose of obtaining information relating to the operations of any business or other commercial establishment. . .; or "(v) such person acts in the District of Columbia, the Commonwealth of Puerto Rico, or any territory or possession of the United States;"

"(c) willfully discloses, or endeavors to disclose, to any other person the contents of any wire or oral communication, knowing or having reason to know that the information was obtained through the interception of a wire or oral communication in violation of this subsection; or

"(d) willfully uses, or endeavors to use, the contents of any wire or oral communication, knowing or having reason to know that the information was obtained through the interception of a wire or oral communication in violation of this subsection; shall be fined not more than $10,000 or imprisoned not more than five years, or both.

§ 2515. Prohibition of Use As Evidence of Intercepted Wire or Oral Communications

"Whenever any wire or oral communication has been intercepted, no part of the contents of such communication and no evidence derived therefrom may be received in evidence in any trial, hearing, or other proceeding in or before any court, grand jury, department, officer, agency, regulatory body, legislative committee, or other authority of the United States, a State, or a political subdivision thereof if the disclosure of that information would be in violation of this chapter.

§ 2516. Authorization for Interception of Wire or Oral Communications

"(1) The Attorney General, or any Assistant Attorney General specially designated by the Attorney General, may authorize an application to a Federal judge of competent jurisdiction for, and such judge may grant inconformity with section 2518 of this chapter an order authorizing or approving the interception of wire or oral communications by the Federal Bureau of Investigation, or a Federal agency having responsibility for the investigation of the offense as to which the application is made, when such interception may provide or has provided evidence of-

"(a) any offense punishable by death or by imprisonment for more than one year under sections 2274 through 2277 of title 42 of the United States Code (relating to the enforcement of the Atomic Energy Act of 1954), or under the following chapters of this title: chapter 37 (relating to espionage), chapter 105 (relating to sabotage), chapter 115 (relating to treason), or chapter 102 (relating to riots);

"(b) a violation of section 186 or section 501(c) of title 29, United States Code (dealing with restrictions on payments and loans to labor organizations), or

any offense which involves murder, kidnapping, robbery, or extortion, and which is punishable under this title;

"(c) any offense which is punishable under the following sections of this title...

"(2) The principal prosecuting attorney of any State, or the principal prosecuting attorney of any political subdivision thereof, if such attorney is authorized by a statute of that State to make application to a State court judge of competent jurisdiction for an order authorizing or approving the interception of wire or oral communications, may apply to such judge for, and such judge may grant in conformity with section 2518 of this chapter and with the applicable State statute an order authorizing, or approving the interception of wire or oral communications by investigative or law enforcement officers having responsibility for the investigation of the offense as to which the application is made, when such interception may provide or has provided evidence of the commission of the offense of murder, kidnapping, gambling, robbery, bribery, extortion, or dealing in narcotic drugs, marihuana or other dangerous drugs, or other crime dangerous to life, limb, or property, and punishable by imprisonment for more than one year, designated in any applicable State statute authorizing such interception, or any conspiracy to commit any of the foregoing offenses.

§ 2517. Authorization for Disclosure and Use of Intercepted Wire or Oral Communications

"(1) Any investigative or law enforcement officer who, by any means authorized by this chapter, has obtained knowledge of the contents of any wire or oral communication, or evidence derived therefrom, may disclose such contents to another investigative or law enforcement officer to the extent that such disclosure is appropriate to the proper performance of the official duties of the officer making or receiving the disclosure.

"(2) Any investigative or law enforcement officer who, by any means authorized by this chapter, has obtained knowledge of the contents of any wire or oral communication or evidence derived therefrom may use such contents to the extent such use is appropriate to the proper performance of his official duties.

"(3) Any person who has received, by any means authorized by this chapter, any information concerning a wire or oral communication, or evidence derived therefrom intercepted in accordance with the provisions of this chapter may disclose the contents of that communication or such derivative evidence while giving testimony under oath or affirmation in any criminal proceeding in any court of the United States or of any State or in any Federal or State grand jury proceeding.

"(4) No otherwise privileged wire or oral communication intercepted in accordance with, or in violation of, the provisions of this chapter shall lose its privileged character.

"(5) When an investigative or law enforcement officer, while engaged in intercepting wire or oral communications in the manner authorized herein, intercepts wire or oral communications relating to offenses other than those specified in the order of authorization or approval, the contents thereof, and evidence derived therefrom, may be disclosed... Such contents and any evidence derived therefrom may be used under subsection (3) of this section when authorized or approved by a judge of competent jurisdiction where such judge finds on subsequent application that the contents were otherwise intercepted in accordance with the provisions of this chapter. Such application shall be made as soon as practicable.

§ 2518. Procedure for Interception of Wire or Oral Communications

"(1) Each application for an order authorizing or approving the interception of a wire or oral communication shall be made in writing upon oath or affirmation to a judge of competent jurisdiction and shall state the applicant's authority to make such application. Each application shall include the following information:

"(a) the identity of the investigative or law enforcement officer making the application, and the officer authorizing the application;

"(b) a full and complete statement of the facts and circumstances relied upon by the applicant, to justify his belief that an order should be issued, including (i) details as to the particular offense that has been, is being, or is about to be committed, (ii) a particular description of the nature and location of the facilities from which or the place where the communication is to be intercepted, (iii) a particular description of the type of communications sought to be intercepted, (iv) the identity of the person, if known, committing the offense and whose communications are to be intercepted;

"(c) a full and complete statement as to whether or not other investigative procedures have been tried and failed or why they reasonably appear to be unlikely to succeed if tried or to be too dangerous;

"(d) a statement of the period of time for which the interception is required to be maintained. If the nature of the investigation is such that the authorization for interception should not automatically terminate when the described type of communication has been first obtained, a particular description of facts establishing probable cause to believe that additional communications of the same type will occur thereafter;

"(e) a full and complete statement of the facts concerning all previous applications known to the individual authorizing and making the application, made to any judge for authorization to intercept, or for approval of interceptions of, wire or oral communications involving any of the same persons, facilities or places specified in the application, and the action taken by the judge on each such application; and

"(f) where the application is for the extension of an order, a statement setting forth the results thus far obtained from the interception, or a reasonable explanation of the failure to obtain such results.

"(3) Upon such application the judge may enter an ex parte order, as requested or as modified, authorizing or approving interception of wire or oral communications within the territorial jurisdiction of the court in which the judge is sitting, if the judge determines on the basis of the facts submitted by the applicant that—

"(a) there is probable cause for belief that an individual is committing, has committed, or is about to commit a particular offense enumerated in section 2516 of this chapter;

"(b) there is probable cause for belief that particular communications concerning that offense will be obtained through such interception;

"(c) normal investigative procedures have been tried and have failed or reasonably appear to be unlikely to succeed if tried or to be too dangerous;

"(d) there is probable cause for belief that the facilities from which, or the place where, the wire or oral communications are to be intercepted are being used, or are about to be used, in connection with the commission of such offense, or are leased to, listed in the name of, or commonly used by such person.

"(4) Each order authorizing or approving the interception of any wire or oral communication shall specify—

"(a) the identity of the person, if known, whose communications are to be intercepted;

"(b) the nature and location of the communications facilities as to which, or the place where, authority to intercept is granted;

"(c) a particular description of the type of communication sought to be intercepted, and a statement of the particular offense to which it relates;

"(d) the identity of the agency authorized to intercept the communications, and of the person authorizing the application; and

"(e) the period of time during which such interception is authorized, including a statement as to whether or not the interception shall automatically terminate when the described communication has been first obtained.

"(5) No order entered under this section may authorize or approve the interception of any wire or oral communication for any period longer than is necessary to achieve the objective of the authorization, nor in any event longer than thirty days. Extensions of an order may be granted, but only upon application for an extension made in accordance with subsection (1) of this section and the court making the findings required by subsection (3) of this section.

"(7) Notwithstanding any other provision of this chapter, any investigative or law enforcement officer, specially designated by the Attorney General or by the principal prosecuting attorney of any State or subdivision thereof acting pursuant to a statute of that State, who reasonably determines that-

"(a) an emergency situation exists with respect to conspiratorial activities threatening the national security interest or to conspiratorial activities characteristic of organized crime that requires a wire or oral communication to be intercepted before an order authorizing such interception can with due diligence be obtained, and

"(b) there are grounds upon which an order could be entered under this chapter to authorize such interception, may intercept such wire or oral communication if an application for an order approving the interception is made in accordance with this section within forty-eight hours after the interception has occurred, or begins to occur. In the absence of an order, such interception shall immediately terminate when the communication sought is obtained or when the application for the order is denied, whichever is earlier. In the event such application for approval is denied, or in any other case where the interception is terminated without an order having been issued, the contents of any wire or oral communication intercepted shall be treated as having been obtained in violation of this chapter, and an inventory shall be served as provided for in subsection (d) of this section on the person named in the application.

"(8) (a) The contents of any wire or oral communication intercepted by any means authorized by this chapter shall, if possible, be recorded on tape or wire or other comparable device. The recording of the contents of any wire or oral communication under this subsection shall be done in such way as will protect the recording from editing or other alterations. Immediately upon the expiration of the period of the order, or extensions thereof, such recordings shall be made available to the judge issuing such order and sealed under his directions. Custody of the recordings shall be wherever the judge orders. They shall not be destroyed except upon an order of the issuing or denying judge and in any event shall be kept for ten years.

"(b) Applications made and orders granted under this chapter shall be sealed by the judge.

"(c) Any violation of the provisions of this subsection may be punished as contempt of the issuing or denying judge.

"(d) Within a reasonable time but not later than ninety days after the filing of an application for an order of approval under section 2518(7) (b) which is denied or the termination of the period of an order or extensions thereof, the issuing or denying judge shall cause to be served, on the persons named in the order or the application, and such other parties to intercepted communications as the judge may determine in his discretion that is in the interest of justice, an inventory which shall include notice of-

"(1) the fact of the entry of the order or the application;

"(2) the date of the entry and the period of authorized, approved or disapproved interception, or the denial of the application; and

"(3) the fact that during the period wire or oral communications were or were not intercepted. The judge, upon the filing of a motion, may in his discretion make available to such person or his counsel for inspection such portions of the intercepted communications, applications and orders as the judge determines to be in the interest of justice. On an ex parte showing of good cause to a judge of competent jurisdiction the serving of the inventory required by this subsection may be postponed.

"(9) The contents of any intercepted wire or oral communication or evidence derived therefrom shall not be received in evidence, or otherwise disclosed in any trial, hearing, or other proceeding in a Federal or-State court unless each party, not less than ten days before the trial, hearing, or proceeding, has been furnished with a copy of the court order, and accompanying application, under which the interception was authorized or approved.

"(10) (a) Any aggrieved person in any trial, hearing, or proceeding in or before any court, department, officer, agency, regulatory body, or other authority of the United States, a State, or a political subdivision thereof, may move to suppress the contents of any intercepted wire or oral communication, or evidence derived therefrom, on the grounds that-

   "(i) the communication was unlawfully intercepted;

   "(ii) the order of authorization or approval under which it was intercepted is insufficient on its face; or

   "(iii) the interception was not made in conformity with the order of authorization or approval. Such motion shall be made before the trial, hearing, or proceeding unless there was no opportunity to make such motion or the person was not aware of the grounds of the motion. If the motion is granted, the contents of the intercepted wire or oral communication, or evidence derived therefrom, shall be treated as having been obtained in violation of this chapter.

§ 2520. Recovery of Civil Damages Authorized

"Any person whose wire or oral communication is intercepted, disclosed, or used in violation of this chapter shall (1) have a civil cause of action against any person who intercepts, discloses, or uses, or procures any other person to intercept, disclose, or use such communications. . .

SEC. 803.

Section 605 of the Communications Act of 1934 (48 Stat. 1103; 47 U.S.C. 605) 25 is amended to read as follows:

"UNAUTHORIZED PUBLICATION OF COMMUNICATIONS

SEC. 605.

"Except as authorized by Chapter 119, title 18, United States Code, no person receiving, assisting in receiving, transmitting, or assisting in transmitting, any interstate or foreign communication by wire or radio shall divulge or publish the existence, contents, substance, purport, effect, or meaning thereof, except through authorized channels of transmission or reception, (1) to any person other than the addressee, his

agent, or attorney, (2) to a person employed or authorized to forward such communication to its destination, (3) to proper accounting or distributing officers of the various communicating centers over which the communication may be passed, (4) to the master of a ship under whom he is serving, (5) in response to a subpoena issued by a court of competent jurisdiction, or (6) on demand of other lawful authority. No person not being authorized by the sender shall intercept any radio communication and divulge or publish the existence, contents, substance, purport, effect, or meaning of such intercepted communication to any person. . .

Foreign Intelligence Surveillance Act October 25, 1978

The Foreign Intelligence Surveillance Act (FISA) was enacted in 1978 as Public Law 95–511, 92 *Stat.* 1783, October 25, 1978. There are no editable electronic versions of this statute that could be edited to fit within this text; however, complete uneditable versions can be found at http://intelligence.senate.gov/laws/pl95-511.pdf and also at ftp://cnss.org/PL%2095-511.pdf. Below is the statute as it exists today from the *United States Code*, 50 USC 1801 *et seq.*

§ 1801. Definitions

As used in this subchapter:

(a) "Foreign power" means–

   (1) a foreign government or any component thereof, whether or not recognized by the United States;

   (2) a faction of a foreign nation or nations, not substantially composed of United States persons;

   (3) an entity that is openly acknowledged by a foreign government or governments to be directed and controlled by such foreign government or governments;

   (4) a group engaged in international terrorism or activities in preparation therefor;

   (5) a foreign-based political organization, not substantially composed of United States persons;

   (6) an entity that is directed and controlled by a foreign government or governments; or

   (7) an entity not substantially composed of United States persons that is engaged in the international proliferation of weapons of mass destruction.

(b) "Agent of a foreign power" means–

   (1) any person other than a United States person, who–

      (A) acts in the United States as an officer or employee of a foreign power, or as a member of a foreign power as defined in subsection (a)(4) of this section;

(B) acts for or on behalf of a foreign power which engages in clandestine intelligence activities in the United States contrary to the interests of the United States, when the circumstances of such person's presence in the United States indicate that such person may engage in such activities in the United States, or when such person knowingly aids or abets any person in the conduct of such activities or knowingly conspires with any person to engage in such activities;

(C) engages in international terrorism or activities in preparation therefore;

(D) engages in the international proliferation of weapons of mass destruction, or activities in preparation therefor; or

(E) engages in the international proliferation of weapons of mass destruction, or activities in preparation therefor for or on behalf of a foreign power; or

(2) any person who—

(A) knowingly engages in clandestine intelligence gathering activities for or on behalf of a foreign power, which activities involve or may involve a violation of the criminal statutes of the United States;

(B) pursuant to the direction of an intelligence service or network of a foreign power, knowingly engages in any other clandestine intelligence activities for or on behalf of such foreign power, which activities involve or are about to involve a violation of the criminal statutes of the United States;

(C) knowingly engages in sabotage or international terrorism, or activities that are in preparation therefor, for or on behalf of a foreign power;

(D) knowingly enters the United States under a false or fraudulent identity for or on behalf of a foreign power or, while in the United States, knowingly assumes a false or fraudulent identity for or on behalf of a foreign power; or

(E) knowingly aids or abets any person in the conduct of activities described in subparagraph (A), (B), or (C) or knowingly conspires with any person to engage in activities described in subparagraph (A), (B), or (C).

(d) "Sabotage" means activities that involve a violation of Chapter 105 of Title 18, or that would involve such a violation if committed against the United States.

(e) "Foreign intelligence information" means–

(1) information that relates to, and if concerning a United States person is necessary to, the ability of the United States to protect against–

(A) actual or potential attack or other grave hostile acts of a foreign power or an agent of a foreign power;

(B) sabotage, international terrorism, or the international proliferation of weapons of mass destruction by a foreign power or an agent of a foreign power; or

(C) clandestine intelligence activities by an intelligence service or network of a foreign power or by an agent of a foreign power; or

(2) information with respect to a foreign power or foreign territory that relates to, and if concerning a United States person is necessary to–

(A) the national defense or the security of the United States; or

(B) the conduct of the foreign affairs of the United States.

(f) "Electronic surveillance" means–

(1) the acquisition by an electronic, mechanical, or other surveillance device of the contents of any wire or radio communication sent by or intended to be received by a particular, known United States person who is in the United States, if the contents are acquired by intentionally targeting that United States person, under circumstances in which a person has a reasonable expectation of privacy and a warrant would be required for law enforcement purposes;

(2) the acquisition by an electronic, mechanical, or other surveillance device of the contents of any wire communication to or from a person in the United States, without the consent of any party thereto, if such acquisition occurs in the United States, but does not include the acquisition of those communications of computer trespassers that would be permissible under section 2511(2)(i) of Title 18;

(3) the intentional acquisition by an electronic, mechanical, or other surveillance device of the contents of any radio communication, under circumstances in which a person has a reasonable expectation of privacy and a warrant would be required for law enforcement purposes, and if both the sender and all intended recipients are located within the United States; or

(4) the installation or use of an electronic, mechanical, or other surveillance device in the United States for monitoring to acquire information, other than from a wire or radio communication,

under circumstances in which a person has a reasonable expectation of privacy and a warrant would be required for law enforcement purposes.

(h) "Minimization procedures", with respect to electronic surveillance, means–

(1) specific procedures, which shall be adopted by the Attorney General, that are reasonably designed in light of the purpose and technique of the particular surveillance, to minimize the acquisition and retention, and prohibit the dissemination, of nonpublicly available information concerning unconsenting United States persons consistent with the need of the United States to obtain, produce, and disseminate foreign intelligence information;

(2) procedures that require that nonpublicly available information, which is not foreign intelligence information, as defined in subsection (e)(1) of this section, shall not be disseminated in a manner that identifies any United States person, without such person's consent, unless such person's identity is necessary to understand foreign intelligence information or assess its importance;

(3) notwithstanding paragraphs (1) and (2), procedures that allow for the retention and dissemination of information that is evidence of a crime which has been, is being, or is about to be committed and that is to be retained or disseminated for law enforcement purposes; and

(4) notwithstanding paragraphs (1), (2), and (3), with respect to any electronic surveillance approved pursuant to section 1802(a) of this title, procedures that require that no contents of any communication to which a United States person is a party shall be disclosed, disseminated, or used for any purpose or retained for longer than 72 hours unless a court order under section 1805 of this title is obtained or unless the Attorney General determines that the information indicates a threat of death or serious bodily harm to any person.

(i) "United States person" means a citizen of the United States, an alien lawfully admitted for permanent residence (as defined in section 1101(a)(20) of Title 8), an unincorporated association a substantial number of members of which are citizens of the United States or aliens lawfully admitted for permanent residence, or a corporation which is incorporated in the United States, but does not include a corporation or an association which is a foreign power, as defined in subsection (a)(1), (2), or (3) of this section.

(j) "United States", when used in a geographic sense, means all areas under the territorial sovereignty of the United States and the Trust Territory of the Pacific Islands.

(k) "Aggrieved person" means a person who is the target of an electronic surveillance or any other person whose communications or activities were subject to electronic surveillance.

(l) "Wire communication" means any communication while it is being carried by a wire, cable, or other like connection furnished or operated by any person engaged as a common carrier in providing or operating such facilities for the transmission of interstate or foreign communications.

(n) "Contents", when used with respect to a communication, includes any information concerning the identity of the parties to such communication or the existence, substance, purport, or meaning of that communication.

(o) "State" means any State of the United States, the District of Columbia, the Commonwealth of Puerto Rico, the Trust Territory of the Pacific Islands, and any territory or possession of the United States.

§ 1802. Electronic Surveillance Authorization Without Court Order; Certification by Attorney General; Reports to Congressional Committees; Transmittal Under Seal; Duties and Compensation of Communication Common Carrier; Applications; Jurisdiction of Court

(a) (1) Notwithstanding any other law, the President, through the Attorney General, may authorize electronic surveillance without a court order under this subchapter to acquire foreign intelligence information for periods of up to one year if the Attorney General certifies in writing under oath that–

(A) the electronic surveillance is solely directed at–

(i) the acquisition of the contents of communications transmitted by means of communications used exclusively between or among foreign powers, as defined in section 1801(a)(1), (2), or (3) of this title; or

(ii) the acquisition of technical intelligence, other than the spoken communications of individuals, from property or premises under the open and exclusive control of a foreign power, as defined in section 1801(a)(1), (2), or (3) of this title;

(B) there is no substantial likelihood that the surveillance will acquire the contents of any communication to which a United States person is a party; and

(C) the proposed minimization procedures with respect to such surveillance meet the definition of minimization procedures under section 1801(h) of this title; and if the Attorney General reports such minimization procedures and any changes thereto to the House Permanent Select Committee on Intelligence and the Senate Select Committee on Intelligence at least thirty days prior to their effective date, unless the Attorney General determines immediate action is required and notifies the committees immediately of such minimization procedures and the reason for their becoming effective immediately.

(2) An electronic surveillance authorized by this subsection may be conducted only in accordance with the Attorney General's certification and the minimization procedures adopted by him. The Attorney General shall assess compliance with such procedures and shall report such assessments to the House Permanent Select Committee on Intelligence and the Senate Select Committee on Intelligence under the provisions of section 1808(a) of this title.

(3) The Attorney General shall immediately transmit under seal to the court established under section 1803(a) of this title a copy of his certification. Such certification shall be maintained under security measures established by the Chief Justice with the concurrence of the Attorney General, in consultation with the Director of National Intelligence, and shall remain sealed unless–

    (A) an application for a court order with respect to the surveillance is made under sections 1801(h)(4) and 1804 of this title; or

    (B) the certification is necessary to determine the legality of the surveillance under section 1806(f) of this title.

(4) With respect to electronic surveillance authorized by this subsection, the Attorney General may direct a specified communication common carrier to–

    (A) furnish all information, facilities, or technical assistance necessary to accomplish the electronic surveillance in such a manner as will protect its secrecy and produce a minimum of interference with the services that such carrier is providing its customers; and

    (B) maintain under security procedures approved by the Attorney General and the Director of National Intelligence any records concerning the surveillance or the aid furnished which such carrier wishes to retain.

The Government shall compensate, at the prevailing rate, such carrier for furnishing such aid.

(b) Applications for a court order under this subchapter are authorized if the President has, by written authorization, empowered the Attorney General to approve applications to the court having jurisdiction under section 1803 of this title, and a judge to whom an application is made may, notwithstanding any other law, grant an order, in conformity with section 1805 of this title, approving electronic surveillance of a foreign power or an agent of a foreign power for the purpose of obtaining foreign intelligence information, except that the court shall not have jurisdiction to grant any order approving electronic surveillance directed solely as described in paragraph (1)(A) of subsection (a) of this section unless such surveillance may involve the acquisition of communications of any United States person.

§ 1803. Designation of Judges

(a) *Court to Hear Applications and Grant Orders; Record of Denial; Transmittal to Court of Review.*

(1) The Chief Justice of the United States shall publicly designate 11 district court judges from at least seven of the United States judicial circuits of whom no fewer than 3 shall reside within 20 miles of the District of Columbia who shall constitute a court which shall have jurisdiction to hear applications for and grant orders approving electronic surveillance anywhere within the United States under the procedures set forth in this chapter, except that no judge designated under this subsection (except when sitting en banc under paragraph (2)) shall hear the same application for electronic surveillance under this chapter which has been denied previously by another judge designated under this subsection. If any judge so designated denies an application for an order authorizing electronic surveillance under this chapter, such judge shall provide immediately for the record a written statement of each reason for his decision and, on motion of the United States, the record shall be transmitted, under seal, to the court of review established in subsection (b) of this section.

(2) (A) The court established under this subsection may, on its own initiative, or upon the request of the Government in any proceeding or a party under section 1861(f) of this title or paragraph (4) or (5) of section 1881a(h) of this title, hold a hearing or rehearing, en banc, when ordered by a majority of the judges that constitute such court upon a determination that–

(i) en banc consideration is necessary to secure or maintain uniformity of the court's decisions; or

(ii) the proceeding involves a question of exceptional importance.

(B) Any authority granted by this chapter to a judge of the court established under this subsection may be exercised by the court en banc. When exercising such authority, the court en banc shall comply with any requirements of this chapter on the exercise of such authority.

(C) For purposes of this paragraph, the court en banc shall consist of all judges who constitute the court established under this subsection.

(b) *Court of Review; Record, Transmittal to Supreme Court.* The Chief Justice shall publicly designate three judges, one of whom shall be publicly designated as the presiding judge, from the United States district courts or courts of appeals who together shall comprise a court of review which shall have jurisdiction to review the denial of any application made under this chapter. If such court determines that the application was properly denied, the court shall immediately provide for the record a written statement of each reason for its decision and, on petition of the United States for a writ of certiorari, the record shall be transmitted under seal to the Supreme Court, which shall have jurisdiction to review such decision.

(c) *Expeditious Conduct of Proceedings; Security Measures for Maintenance of Records.* Proceedings under this chapter shall be conducted as expeditiously as possible. The record of proceedings under this chapter, including applications made and orders granted, shall be maintained under security measures established by the Chief Justice in consultation with the Attorney General and the Director of National Intelligence.

(d) *Tenure.* Each judge designated under this section shall so serve for a maximum of seven years and shall not be eligible for redesignation, except that the judges first designated under subsection (a) of this section shall be designated for terms of from one to seven years so that one term expires each year, and that judges first designated under subsection (b) of this section shall be designated for terms of three, five, and seven years.

(e) (1) Three judges designated under subsection (a) of this section who reside within 20 miles of the District of Columbia, or, if all of such judges are unavailable, other judges of the court established under subsection (a) of this section as may be designated by the presiding judge of such court, shall comprise a pe-

tition review pool which shall have jurisdiction to review petitions filed pursuant to section 1861(f)(1) or 1881a(h)(4) of this title.

(2) Not later than 60 days after March 9, 2006, the court established under subsection (a) of this section shall adopt and, consistent with the protection of national security, publish procedures for the review of petitions filed pursuant to section 1861(f)(1) or 1881a(h)(4) of this title by the panel established under paragraph (1). Such procedures shall provide that review of a petition shall be conducted in camera and shall also provide for the designation of an acting presiding judge.

(2) The authority described in paragraph (1) shall apply to an order entered under any provision of this chapter.

(g) (2) The rules and procedures established under paragraph (1), and any modifications of such rules and procedures, shall be recorded, and shall be transmitted to the following:

(A) All of the judges on the court established pursuant to subsection (a) of this section.

(B) All of the judges on the court of review established pursuant to subsection (b) of this section.

(C) The Chief Justice of the United States.

(D) The Committee on the Judiciary of the Senate.

(E) The Select Committee on Intelligence of the Senate.

(F) The Committee on the Judiciary of the House of Representatives.

(G) The Permanent Select Committee on Intelligence of the House of Representatives.

(3) The transmissions required by paragraph (2) shall be submitted in unclassified form, but may include a classified annex.

§ 1804. Applications for Court Orders

(a) *Submission by Federal Officer; Approval of Attorney General; Contents.* Each application for an order approving electronic surveillance under this subchapter shall be made by a Federal officer in writing upon oath or affirmation to a judge having jurisdiction under section 1803 of this title. Each application shall require the approval of the Attorney General based upon his finding that it satisfies the criteria and requirements of such application as set forth in this subchapter. It shall include–

(1) the identity of the Federal officer making the application;

(2) the identity, if known, or a description of the specific target of the electronic surveillance;

(3) a statement of the facts and circumstances relied upon by the applicant to justify his belief that–

(A) the target of the electronic surveillance is a foreign power or an agent of a foreign power; and

(B) each of the facilities or places at which the electronic surveillance is directed is being used, or is about to be used, by a foreign power or an agent of a foreign power;

(4) a statement of the proposed minimization procedures;

(5) a description of the nature of the information sought and the type of communications or activities to be subjected to the surveillance;

(6) a certification or certifications by the Assistant to the President for National Security Affairs, an executive branch official or officials designated by the President from among those executive officers employed in the area of national security or defense and appointed by the President with the advice and consent of the Senate, or the Deputy Director of the Federal Bureau of Investigation, if designated by the President as a certifying official–

(A) that the certifying official deems the information sought to be foreign intelligence information;

(B) that a significant purpose of the surveillance is to obtain foreign intelligence information;

(C) that such information cannot reasonably be obtained by normal investigative techniques;

(D) that designates the type of foreign intelligence information being sought according to the categories described in section 1801(e) of this title; and

(E) including a statement of the basis for the certification that—

(i) the information sought is the type of foreign intelligence information designated; and

(ii) such information cannot reasonably be obtained by normal investigative techniques;

(7) a summary statement of the means by which the surveillance will be effected and a statement whether physical entry is required to effect the surveillance;

(8) a statement of the facts concerning all previous applications that have been made to any judge under this subchapter involving any of the persons, facilities, or places specified in the application, and the action taken on each previous application; and

(9) a statement of the period of time for which the electronic surveillance is required to be maintained, and if the nature of the intelligence gathering is such that the approval of the use of electronic surveillance under this subchapter should not automatically terminate when the described type of information has first been obtained, a description of facts supporting the belief that additional information of the same type will be obtained thereafter.

(d) *Personal Review by Attorney General.*

(1)(A) Upon written request of the Director of the Federal Bureau of Investigation, the Secretary of Defense, the Secretary of State, the Director of National Intelligence, or the Director of the Central Intelligence Agency, the Attorney General shall personally review under subsection (a) of this section an application under that subsection for a target described in section 1801(b)(2) of this title.

(B) Except when disabled or otherwise unavailable to make a request referred to in subparagraph (A), an official referred to in that subparagraph may not delegate the authority to make a request referred to in that subparagraph.

(C) Each official referred to in subparagraph (A) with authority to make a request under that subparagraph shall take appropriate actions in advance to ensure that delegation of such authority is clearly established in the event such official is disabled or otherwise unavailable to make such request.

§ 1805. Issuance of Order

(a) *Necessary Findings.* Upon an application made pursuant to section 1804 of this title, the judge shall enter an ex parte order as requested or as modified approving the electronic surveillance if he finds that–

(1) the application has been made by a Federal officer and approved by the Attorney General;

(2) on the basis of the facts submitted by the applicant there is probable cause to believe that—

(A) the target of the electronic surveillance is a foreign power or an agent of a foreign power: *Provided,* That no United States person may be considered a foreign power or an agent of a foreign power solely upon the basis of activities protected by the first amendment to the Constitution of the United States; and

(B) each of the facilities or places at which the electronic surveillance is directed is being used, or is about to be used, by a foreign power or an agent of a foreign power;

(3) the proposed minimization procedures meet the definition of minimization procedures under section 1801(h) of this title; and

(4) the application which has been filed contains all statements and certifications required by section 1804 of this title and, if the target is a United States person, the certification or certifications are not clearly erroneous on the basis of the statement made under section 1804(a)(7)(E) of this title and any other information furnished under section 1804(d) of this title.

(b) *Determination of Probable Cause.* In determining whether or not probable cause exists for purposes of an order under subsection (a)(2) of this section, a judge may consider past activities of the target, as well as facts and circumstances relating to current or future activities of the target.

(c) *Specifications and Directions of Orders.*

(1) Specifications

An order approving an electronic surveillance under this section shall specify–

(A) the identity, if known, or a description of the specific target of the electronic surveillance identified or described in the application pursuant to section 1804(a)(3) of this title;

(B) the nature and location of each of the facilities or places at which the electronic surveillance will be directed, if known;

(C) the type of information sought to be acquired and the type of communications or activities to be subjected to the surveillance;

(D) the means by which the electronic surveillance will be effected and whether physical entry will be used to effect the surveillance; and

(E) the period of time during which the electronic surveillance is approved.

(2) Directions

An order approving an electronic surveillance under this section shall direct–

(A) that the minimization procedures be followed;

(B) that, upon the request of the applicant, a specified communication or other common carrier, landlord, custodian, or other specified person, or in circumstances where the Court finds, based upon specific facts provided in the application, that the actions of the target of the application may have the effect of thwarting the identification of a specified person, such other persons, furnish the applicant forthwith all information, facilities, or technical assistance necessary to accomplish the electronic surveillance in such a manner as will protect its secrecy and produce a minimum of interference with the services that such carrier, landlord, custodian, or other person is providing that target of electronic surveillance;

(C) that such carrier, landlord, custodian, or other person maintain under security procedures approved by the Attorney General and the Director of National Intelligence any records concerning the surveillance or the aid furnished that such person wishes to retain; and

(D) that the applicant compensate, at the prevailing rate, such carrier, landlord, custodian, or other person for furnishing such aid.

(3) Special directions for certain orders

An order approving an electronic surveillance under this section in circumstances where the nature and location of each of the facilities or places at which the surveillance will be directed is unknown shall direct the applicant to provide notice to the court within ten days after the date on which surveillance begins to be directed at any new facility or place, unless the court finds good cause to justify a longer period of up to 60 days, of–

(A) the nature and location of each new facility or place at which the electronic surveillance is directed;

(B) the facts and circumstances relied upon by the applicant to justify the applicant's belief that each new facility or place at which the electronic surveillance is directed is or was being used, or is about to be used, by the target of the surveillance;

(C) a statement of any proposed minimization procedures that differ from those contained in the original application or order, that may be necessitated by a change in the facility or place at which the electronic surveillance is directed; and

(D) the total number of electronic surveillances that have been or are being conducted under the authority of the order.

(d) *Duration of Order; Extensions; Review of Circumstances Under Which Information was Acquired, Retained or Disseminated.*

(1) An order issued under this section may approve an electronic surveillance for the period necessary to achieve its purpose, or for ninety days, whichever is less, except that (A) an order under this section shall approve an electronic surveillance targeted against a foreign power, as defined in section 1801(a)(1), (2), or (3) of this title, for the period specified in the application or for one year, whichever is less, and (B) an order under this chapter for a surveillance targeted

against an agent of a foreign power who is not a United States person may be for the period specified in the application or for 120 days, whichever is less.

(2) Extensions of an order issued under this subchapter may be granted on the same basis as an original order upon an application for an extension and new findings made in the same manner as required for an original order, except that (A) an extension of an order under this chapter for a surveillance targeted against a foreign power, as defined in paragraph (5), (6), or (7) of section 1801(a) of this title, or against a foreign power as defined in section 1801(a)(4) of this title that is not a United States person, may be for a period not to exceed one year if the judge finds probable cause to believe that no communication of any individual United States person will be acquired during the period, and (B) an extension of an order under this chapter for a surveillance targeted against an agent of a foreign power who is not a United States person may be for a period not to exceed 1 year.

(3) At or before the end of the period of time for which electronic surveillance is approved by an order or an extension, the judge may assess compliance with the minimization procedures by reviewing the circumstances under which information concerning United States persons was acquired, retained, or disseminated.

(e) (1) Notwithstanding any other provision of this subchapter, the Attorney General may authorize the emergency employment of electronic surveillance if the Attorney General–

    (A) reasonably determines that an emergency situation exists with respect to the employment of electronic surveillance to obtain foreign intelligence information before an order authorizing such surveillance can with due diligence be obtained;

    (B) reasonably determines that the factual basis for the issuance of an order under this subchapter to approve such electronic surveillance exists;

    (C) informs, either personally or through a designee, a judge having jurisdiction under section 1803 of this title at the time of such authorization that the decision has been made to employ emergency electronic surveillance; and

    (D) makes an application in accordance with this subchapter to a judge having jurisdiction under section 1803 of this title as soon as practicable, but not later than 7 days after the Attorney General authorizes such surveillance.

(2) If the Attorney General authorizes the emergency employment of electronic surveillance under paragraph (1), the Attorney General shall require that the minimization procedures required by this subchapter for the issuance of a judicial order be followed.

(3) In the absence of a judicial order approving such electronic surveillance, the surveillance shall terminate when the information sought is obtained, when the application for the order is denied, or after the expiration of 7 days from the time of authorization by the Attorney General, whichever is earliest.

(4) A denial of the application made under this subsection may be reviewed as provided in section 1803 of this title.

(5) In the event that such application for approval is denied, or in any other case where the electronic surveillance is terminated and no order is issued approving the surveillance, no information obtained or evidence derived from such surveillance shall be received in evidence or otherwise disclosed in any trial, hearing, or other proceeding in or before any court, grand jury, department, office, agency, regulatory body, legislative committee, or other authority of the United States, a State, or political subdivision thereof, and no information concerning any United States person acquired from such surveillance shall subsequently be used or disclosed in any other manner by Federal officers or employees without the consent of such person, except with the approval of the Attorney General if the information indicates a threat of death or serious bodily harm to any person.

(g) *Retention of Certifications, Applications and Orders.* Certifications made by the Attorney General pursuant to section 1802(a) of this title and applications made and orders granted under this subchapter shall be retained for a period of at least ten years from the date of the certification or application.

(h) *Release from Liability.* No cause of action shall lie in any court against any provider of a wire or electronic communication service, landlord, custodian, or other person (including any officer, employee, agent, or other specified person thereof) that furnishes any information, facilities, or technical assistance in accordance with a court order or request for emergency assistance under this chapter for electronic surveillance or physical search.

(i) In any case in which the Government makes an application to a judge under this subchapter to conduct electronic surveillance involving communications and the judge grants such application, upon the request of the applicant, the judge shall also authorize the installation and use of pen registers and trap and trace devices, and direct the disclosure of the information set forth in section 1842(d)(2) of this title.

Executive Order 12139—Foreign Intelligence Electronic Surveillance of May 23, 1979

By the authority vested in me as President by Sections 102 and 104 of the Foreign Intelligence Surveillance Act of 1978 (50 U.S.C. 1802 and 1804), in order to provide as set forth in that Act for the authorization of electronic surveillance for foreign intelligence purposes, it is hereby ordered as follows:

1-101. Pursuant to Section 102(a)(1) of the Foreign Intelligence Surveillance Act of 1978 (50 U.S.C. 1802(a)), the Attorney General is authorized to approve electronic surveillance to acquire foreign intelligence information without a court order, but only if the Attorney General makes the certifications required by that Section.

1-102. Pursuant to Section 102(b) of the Foreign Intelligence Act of 1978 (50 U.S.C. 1802(b)), the Attorney General is authorized to approve applications to the court having jurisdiction under Section 103 of that Act to obtain orders for electronic surveillance for the purpose of obtaining foreign intelligence information.

1-103. Pursuant to Section 104(a)(7) of the Foreign Intelligence Surveillance Act of 1978 (50 U.S.C. 1804(a)(7)), the following officials, each of whom is employed in the area of national security or defense, is designated to make the certifications required by Section 104(a)(7) of the Act in support of applications to conduct electronic surveillance:

(a) Secretary of State.
(b) Secretary of Defense.
(c) Director of Central Intelligence.
(d) Director of the Federal Bureau of Investigation.
(e) Deputy Secretary of State.
(f) Deputy Secretary of Defense.
(g) Deputy Director of Central Intelligence.

None of the above officials, nor anyone officially acting in that capacity, may exercise the authority to make the above certifications, unless that official has been appointed by the President with the advice and consent of the Senate.

Executive Order 12333, United States Intelligence Activities, December 4, 1981

Timely and accurate information about the activities, capabilities, plans, and intentions of foreign powers, organizations, and persons and their agents, is essential to the national security of the United States. All reasonable and lawful means must be used to ensure that the United States will receive the best intelligence available. For that purpose, by virtue of the authority vested in me by the Constitution and statutes of the United States of America, including the National Security Act of 1947, as amended, and as President of the United States of America, in order to provide for the effective conduct of United States intelligence activities and the protection of constitutional rights, it is hereby ordered as follows:

PART 1

1.2 The National Security Council.

(a) *Purpose.* The National Security Council (NSC) was established by the National Security Act of 1947 to advise the President with respect to the integration of domestic, foreign and military policies relating to the national security. The NSC shall act as the highest Executive Branch entity that provides review of, guidance for and direction to the conduct of all national foreign intelligence, counterintelligence, and special activities, and attendant policies and programs.

(b) ...The NSC, or a committee established by it, shall consider and submit to the President a policy recommendation, including all dissents, on each special activity and shall review proposals for other sensitive intelligence operations.

1.3 National Foreign Intelligence Advisory Groups.

(a) *Establishment and Duties.* The Director of Central Intelligence shall establish such boards, councils, or groups as required for the purpose of obtaining advice from within the Intelligence Community concerning:

(1) Production, review and coordination of national foreign intelligence;
(2) Priorities for the National Foreign Intelligence Program budget;
(3) Interagency exchanges of foreign intelligence information;
(4) Arrangements with foreign governments on intelligence matters;
(5) Protection of intelligence sources and methods;
(6) Activities of common concern; and

1.5 Director of Central Intelligence.

In order to discharge the duties and responsibilities prescribed by law, the Director of Central Intelligence shall be responsible directly to the President and the NSC and shall:

(a) Act as the primary adviser to the President and the NSC on national foreign intelligence and provide the

President and other officials in the Executive Branch with national foreign intelligence;

(b) Formulate policies concerning foreign intelligence and counterintelligence arrangements with foreign governments, coordinate foreign intelligence and counterintelligence relationships between agencies of the Intelligence Community and the intelligence or internal security services of foreign governments, and establish procedures governing the conduct of liaison by any department or agency with such services on narcotics activities;

(c) Participate in the development of procedures approved by the Attorney General governing criminal narcotics intelligence activities abroad to ensure that these activities are consistent with foreign intelligence programs;

(d) Ensure the establishment by the Intelligence Community of common security and access standards for managing and handling foreign intelligence systems, information, and products;

(e) Ensure that programs are developed which protect intelligence sources, methods, and analytical procedures;

(f) Establish uniform criteria for the determination of relative priorities for the transmission of critical national foreign intelligence, and advise the Secretary of Defense concerning the communications requirements of the Intelligence Community for the transmission of such intelligence;

(g) Have full responsibility for production and dissemination of national foreign intelligence, and authority to levy analytic tasks on departmental intelligence production organizations, in consultation with those organizations, ensuring that appropriate mechanisms for competitive analysis are developed so that diverse points of view are considered fully and differences of judgment within the Intelligence Community are brought to the attention of national policymakers;

(h) Ensure the timely exploitation and dissemination of data gathered by national foreign intelligence collection means, and ensure that the resulting intelligence is disseminated immediately to appropriate government entities and military commands;

1.8 The Central Intelligence Agency.

All duties and responsibilities of the CIA shall be related to the intelligence functions set out below. As authorized by this Order; the National Security Act of 1947, as amended; the CIA Act of 1949, as amended; appropriate directives or other applicable law, the CIA shall:

(a) Collect, produce and disseminate foreign intelligence and counterintelligence, including information not otherwise obtainable. The collection of foreign intelligence or counterintelligence within the United States shall be coordinated with the FBI as required by procedures agreed upon by the Director of Central Intelligence and the Attorney General;

(b) Collect, produce and disseminate intelligence on foreign aspects of narcotics production and trafficking;

(c) Conduct counterintelligence activities outside the United States and, without assuming or performing any internal security functions, conduct counterintelligence activities within the United States in coordination with the FBI as required by procedures agreed upon by the Director of Central Intelligence and the Attorney General;

(d) Coordinate counterintelligence activities and the collection of information not otherwise obtainable when conducted outside the United States by other departments and agencies;

1.9 The Department of State.

The Secretary of State shall:

(a) Overtly collect information relevant to United States foreign policy concerns;

(b) Produce and disseminate foreign intelligence relating to United States foreign policy as required for the execution of the Secretary's responsibilities;

(c) Disseminate, as appropriate, reports received from United States diplomatic and consular posts;

(d) Transmit reporting requirements of the Intelligence Community to the Chiefs of United States Missions abroad; and

(e) Support Chiefs of Missions in discharging their statutory responsibilities for direction and coordination of mission activities.

1.10 The Department of the Treasury.

The Secretary of the Treasury shall:

(a) Overtly collect foreign financial and monetary information;

(b) Participate with the Department of State in the overt collection of general foreign economic information;

(c) Produce and disseminate foreign intelligence relating to United States economic policy as required for the execution of the Secretary's responsibilities; and

(d) Conduct, through the United States Secret Service, activities to determine the existence and capability of surveillance equipment being used against the President of the United States, the Executive Office of the

President, and, as authorized by the Secretary of the Treasury or the President, other Secret Service protectees and United States officials. No information shall be acquired intentionally through such activities except to protect against such surveillance, and those activities shall be conducted pursuant to procedures agreed upon by the Secretary of the Treasury and the Attorney General.

1.11 The Department of Defense.

The Secretary of Defense shall:

(a) Collect national foreign intelligence and be responsive to collection tasking by the Director of Central Intelligence;

(b) Collect, produce and disseminate military and military-related foreign intelligence and counterintelligence as required for execution of the Secretary's responsibilities;

(c) Conduct programs and missions necessary to fulfill national, departmental and tactical foreign intelligence requirements;

(d) Conduct counterintelligence activities in support of Department of Defense components outside the United States in coordination with the CIA, and within the United States in coordination with the FBI pursuant to procedures agreed upon by the Secretary of Defense and the Attorney General;

(e) Conduct, as the executive agent of the United States Government, signals intelligence and communications security activities, except as otherwise directed by the NSC;

(h) Protect the security of Department of Defense installations, activities, property, information, and employees by appropriate means, including such investigations of applicants, employees, contractors, and other persons with similar associations with the Department of Defense as are necessary;

(i) Establish and maintain military intelligence relationships and military intelligence exchange programs with selected cooperative foreign defense establishments and international organizations, and ensure that such relationships and programs are in accordance with policies formulated by the Director of Central Intelligence;

1.13 The Department of Energy.

The Secretary of Energy shall:

(a) Participate with the Department of State in overtly collecting information with respect to foreign energy matters;

(b) Produce and disseminate foreign intelligence necessary for the Secretary's responsibilities;

(c) Participate in formulating intelligence collection and analysis requirements where the special expert capability of the Department can contribute; and

(d) Provide expert technical, analytical and research capability to other agencies within the Intelligence Community.

1.14 The Federal Bureau of Investigation.

Under the supervision of the Attorney General and pursuant to such regulations as the Attorney General may establish, the Director of the FBI shall:

(a) Within the United States conduct counterintelligence and coordinate counterintelligence activities of other agencies within the Intelligence Community. When a counterintelligence activity of the FBI involves military or civilian personnel of the Department of Defense, the FBI shall coordinate with the Department of Defense;

(b) Conduct counterintelligence activities outside the United States in coordination with the CIA as required by procedures agreed upon by the Director of Central Intelligence and the Attorney General;

(c) Conduct within the United States, when requested by officials of the Intelligence Community designated by the President, activities undertaken to collect foreign intelligence or support foreign intelligence collection requirements of other agencies within the Intelligence Community, or, when requested by the Director of the National Security Agency, to support the communications security activities of the United States Government;

(d) Produce and disseminate foreign intelligence and counterintelligence; and

PART 2 CONDUCT OF INTELLIGENCE ACTIVITIES

2.3 Collection of Information.

Agencies within the Intelligence Community are authorized to collect, retain or disseminate information concerning United States persons only in accordance with procedures established by the head of the agency concerned and approved by the Attorney General, consistent with the authorities provided by Part 1 of this Order. Those procedures shall permit collection, retention and dissemination of the following types of information:

(a) Information that is publicly available or collected with the consent of the person concerned;

(b) Information constituting foreign intelligence or counterintelligence, including such information concerning corporations or other commercial organizations. Collection within the United States of foreign intelligence not otherwise obtainable shall be undertaken by the FBI or, when significant foreign intelligence is sought, by other authorized agencies of the Intelligence Community, provided that no foreign intelligence collection by such agencies may be undertaken for the purpose of acquiring information concerning the domestic activities of United States persons;

(c) Information obtained in the course of a lawful foreign intelligence, counterintelligence, international narcotics or international terrorism investigation;

(d) Information needed to protect the safety of any persons or organizations, including those who are targets, victims or hostages of international terrorist organizations;

(e) Information needed to protect foreign intelligence or counterintelligence sources or methods from unauthorized disclosure...

(f) Information concerning persons who are reasonably believed to be potential sources or contacts for the purpose of determining their suitability or credibility;

(g) Information arising out of a lawful personnel, physical or communications security investigation;

(h) Information acquired by overhead reconnaissance not directed at specific United States persons;

(i) Incidentally obtained information that may indicate involvement in activities that may violate federal, state, local or foreign laws...

2.4 Collection Techniques.

Agencies within the Intelligence Community shall use the least intrusive collection techniques feasible within the United States or directed against United States persons abroad. Agencies are not authorized to use such techniques as electronic surveillance, unconsented physical search, mail surveillance, physical surveillance, or monitoring devices unless they are in accordance with procedures established by the head of the agency concerned and approved by the Attorney General. Such procedures shall protect constitutional and other legal rights and limit use of such information to lawful governmental purposes. These procedures shall not authorize:

(a) The CIA to engage in electronic surveillance within the United States except for the purpose of training,

testing, or conducting countermeasures to hostile electronic surveillance;

(b) Unconsented physical searches in the United States by agencies other than the FBI, except for:

(1) Searches by counterintelligence elements of the military services directed against military personnel within the United States or abroad for intelligence purposes, when authorized by a military commander empowered to approve physical searches for law enforcement purposes, based upon a finding of probable cause to believe that such persons are acting as agents of foreign powers; and

(2) Searches by CIA of personal property of non-United States persons lawfully in its possession.

(c) Physical surveillance of a United States person in the United States by agencies other than the FBI, except for: (1) Physical surveillance of present or former employees, present or former intelligence agency contractors or their present of former employees, or applicants for any such employment or contracting; and (2) Physical surveillance of a military person employed by a nonintelligence element of a military service.

(d) Physical surveillance of a United States person abroad to collect foreign intelligence, except to obtain significant information that cannot reasonably be acquired by other means.

2.5 Attorney General Approval.

The Attorney General hereby is delegated the power to approve the use for intelligence purposes, within the United States or against a United States person abroad, of any technique for which a warrant would be required if undertaken for law enforcement purposes, provided that such techniques shall not be undertaken unless the Attorney General has determined in each case that there is probable cause to believe that the technique is directed against a foreign power or an agent of a foreign power. Electronic surveillance, as defined in the Foreign Intelligence Surveillance Act of 1978, shall be conducted in accordance with that Act, as well as this Order.

2.6 Assistance to Law Enforcement Authorities.

Agencies within the Intelligence Community are authorized to:

(a) Cooperate with appropriate law enforcement agencies for the purpose of protecting the employees, information, property and facilities of any agency within the Intelligence Community;

2.9 Undisclosed Participation in Organizations Within the United States.

No one acting on behalf of agencies within the Intelligence Community may join or otherwise participate in any organization in the United States on behalf of any agency within the Intelligence Community without disclosing his intelligence affiliation to appropriate officials of the organization, except in accordance with procedures established by the head of the agency concerned and approved by the Attorney General. Such participation shall be authorized only if it is essential to achieving lawful purposes as determined by the agency head or designee. No such participation may be undertaken for the purpose of influencing the activity of the organization or its members except in cases where:

(a) The participation is undertaken on behalf of the FBI in the course of a lawful investigation; or

(b) The organization concerned is composed primarily of individuals who are not United States persons and is reasonably believed to be acting on behalf of a foreign power.

2.10 Human Experimentation.

No agency within the Intelligence Community shall sponsor, contract for or conduct research on human subjects except in accordance with guidelines issued by the Department of Health and Human Services. The subject's informed consent shall be documented as required by those guidelines.

2.11 Prohibition on Assassination.

No person employed by or acting on behalf of the United States Government shall engage in, or conspire to engage in, assassination.

2.12 Indirect Participation.

No agency of the Intelligence Community shall participate in or request any person to undertake activities forbidden by this Order.

3.4 Definitions.

For the purposes of this Order, the following terms shall have these meanings:

(a) Counterintelligence means information gathered and activities conducted to protect against espionage, other intelligence activities, sabotage, or assassinations conducted for or on behalf of foreign powers, organizations or persons, or international terrorist activities, but not including personnel, physical, document or communications security programs.

(b) Electronic surveillance means acquisition of a nonpublic communication by electronic means without the consent of a person who is a party to an electronic communication or, in the case of a nonelectronic communication, without the consent of a person who is visibly present at the place of communication, but not including the use of radio direction-finding equipment solely to determine the location of a transmitter.

(c) Employee means a person employed by, assigned to or acting for an agency within the Intelligence Community.

(d) Foreign intelligence means information relating to the capabilities, intentions and activities of foreign powers, organizations or persons, but not including counterintelligence except for information on international terrorist activities.

(e) Intelligence activities means all activities that agencies within the Intelligence Community are authorized to conduct pursuant to this Order.

(f) Intelligence Community and agencies within the Intelligence Community refer to the following agencies or organizations:

(1) The Central Intelligence Agency (CIA);

(2) The National Security Agency (NSA);

(3) The Defense Intelligence Agency (DIA);

(4) The offices within the Department of Defense for the collection of specialized national foreign intelligence through reconnaissance programs;

(5) The Bureau of Intelligence and Research of the Department of State;

(6) The intelligence elements of the Army, Navy, Air Force, and Marine Corps, the Federal Bureau of Investigation (FBI), the Department of the Treasury, and the Department of Energy; and

(7) The staff elements of the Director of Central Intelligence.

(h) Special activities means activities conducted in support of national foreign policy objectives abroad which are planned and executed so that the role of the United States Government is not apparent or acknowledged publicly, and functions in support of such activities, but which are not intended to influence United States political processes, public opinion, policies, or media and do not include diplomatic activities or the collection and production of intelligence or related support functions.

(i) United States person means a United States citizen, an alien known by the intelligence agency concerned to be a permanent resident alien, an unincorporated association substantially composed of United States citizens or permanent resident aliens, or a corporation incorporated in the United States, except for a corporation directed and controlled by a foreign government or governments.

3.6 Revocation.

Executive Order No. 12036 of January 24, 1978, as amended, entitled "United States Intelligence Activities," is revoked.

Electronic Communications Privacy Act of 1986, 18 USC 2510 et. seq.[17]

§ 2511. Interception and Disclosure of Wire, Oral, or Electronic Communications Prohibited

(1) Except as otherwise specifically provided in this chapter any person who–

  (a) intentionally intercepts, endeavors to intercept, or procures any other person to intercept or endeavor to intercept, any wire, oral, or electronic communication;

  (b) intentionally uses, endeavors to use, or procures any other person to use or endeavor to use any electronic, mechanical, or other device to intercept any oral communication when–

    (i) such device is affixed to, or otherwise transmits a signal through, a wire, cable, or other like connection used in wire communication; or

    (ii) such device transmits communications by radio, or interferes with the transmission of such communication; or

    (iii) such person knows, or has reason to know, that such device or any component thereof has been sent through the mail or transported in interstate or foreign commerce; or

    (iv) such use or endeavor to use (A) takes place on the premises of any business or other commercial establishment the operations of which affect interstate or foreign commerce; or (B) obtains or is for the purpose of obtaining information relating to the operations of any business or other commercial establishment the operations of which affect interstate or foreign commerce; or

    (v) such person acts in the District of Columbia, the Commonwealth of Puerto Rico, or any territory or possession of the United States;

  (c) intentionally discloses, or endeavors to disclose, to any other person the contents of any wire, oral, or electronic communication, knowing or having reason to know that the information was obtained through the interception of a wire, oral, or electronic communication in violation of this subsection;

  (d) intentionally uses, or endeavors to use, the contents of any wire, oral, or electronic communication, knowing or having reason to know that the information was obtained through the interception of a wire, oral, or electronic communication in violation of this subsection; or

  (e) (i) intentionally discloses, or endeavors to disclose, to any other person the contents of any wire, oral, or electronic communication, intercepted by means authorized by sections 2511(2)(a)(ii), 2511(2)(b)-(c), 2511(2)(e), 2516, and 2518 of this chapter, (ii) knowing or having reason to know that the information was obtained through the interception of such a communication in connection with a criminal investigation, (iii) having obtained or received the information in connection with a criminal investigation, and (iv) with intent to improperly obstruct, impede, or interfere with a duly authorized criminal investigation, shall be punished as provided in subsection (4) or shall be subject to suit as provided in subsection (5).

(2) (a) (ii) Notwithstanding any other law, providers of wire or electronic communication service, their officers, employees, and agents, landlords, custodians, or other persons, are authorized to provide information, facilities, or technical assistance to persons authorized by law to intercept wire, oral, or electronic communications or to conduct electronic surveillance, as defined in section 101 of the Foreign Intelligence Surveillance Act of 1978, if such provider, its officers, employees, or agents, landlord, custodian, or other specified person, has been provided with–

  (A) a court order directing such assistance or a court order pursuant to section 704 of the Foreign Intelligence Surveillance Act of 1978 signed by the authorizing judge, or

  (B) a certification in writing by a person specified in section 2518(7) of this title or the Attorney General of the United States that no warrant or court order is required by law, that all statutory requirements have been met, and that the specified assistance is required...

    No provider of wire or electronic communication service, officer, employee, or agent thereof, or landlord, custodian, or other specified person shall disclose the existence of any interception or surveillance or the device used to accomplish the interception or surveillance with respect to which the person has been furnished a court order or certification under this chapter, except as may otherwise be required by legal process and then only after prior notification to the Attorney General or to the principal prosecuting attorney of a State or any political subdivision of a State, as may be appropriate. Any such disclosure, shall render such person liable for the civil damages provided for in section 2520. No cause of action shall lie in any court against any provider of wire or electronic communication service, its officers, employees, or agents, landlord, custodian, or other specified person for providing information, facilities, or assistance in accordance with the terms of a court order, statutory authorization, or certification under this chapter.

(iii) If a certification under subparagraph (ii)(B) for assistance to obtain foreign intelligence information is based on statutory authority, the certification shall identify the specific statutory provision and shall certify that the statutory requirements have been met.

§ 2515. Prohibition of Use as Evidence of Intercepted Wire or Oral Communications

Whenever any wire or oral communication has been intercepted, no part of the contents of such communication and no evidence derived therefrom may be received in evidence in any trial, hearing, or other proceeding in or before any court, grand jury, department, officer, agency, regulatory body, legislative committee, or other authority of the United States, a State, or a political subdivision thereof if the disclosure of that information would be in violation of this chapter.

§ 2516. Authorization for Interception of Wire, Oral, or Electronic Communications

(1) The Attorney General, Deputy Attorney General, Associate Attorney General, or any Assistant Attorney General, any acting Assistant Attorney General, or any Deputy Assistant Attorney General or acting Deputy Assistant Attorney General in the Criminal Division or National Security Division specially designated by the Attorney General, may authorize an application to a Federal judge of competent jurisdiction for, and such judge may grant in conformity with section 2518 of this chapter an order authorizing or approving the interception of wire or oral communications by the Federal Bureau of Investigation, or a Federal agency having responsibility for the investigation of the offense as to which the application is made, when such interception may provide or has provided evidence of–

(a) any offense punishable by death or by imprisonment for more than one year...

(b) a violation of section 186 or section 501(c) of title 29, United States Code (dealing with restrictions on payments and loans to labor organizations), or any offense which involves murder, kidnapping, robbery, or extortion, and which is punishable under this title;

(c) any offense which is punishable under the following sections of this title:

(d) any offense involving counterfeiting punishable under section 471, 472, or 473 of this title;

(e) any offense involving fraud connected with a case under title 11 or the manufacture, importation, receiving, concealment, buying, selling, or otherwise dealing in narcotic drugs, marihuana, or other dangerous drugs, punishable under any law of the United States;

(f) any offense including extortionate credit transactions under sections 892, 893, or 894 of this title;

(g) a violation of section 5322 of title 31, United States Code (dealing with the reporting of currency transactions), or section 5324 of title 31, United States Code (relating to structuring transactions to evade reporting requirement prohibited);

(h) any felony violation of sections 2511 and 2512 (relating to interception and disclosure of certain communications and to certain intercepting devices) of this title;

(i) any felony violation of chapter 71 (relating to obscenity) of this title;

(j) any violation of section 60123(b) (relating to destruction of a natural gas pipeline...

(k) any criminal violation of section 2778 of title 22 (relating to the Arms Export Control Act);

(l) the location of any fugitive from justice from an offense described in this section;

(m) a violation of section 274, 277, or 278 of the Immigration and Nationality Act (8 U.S.C. 1324, 1327, or 1328) (relating to the smuggling of aliens);

(n) any felony violation of sections 922 and 924 of title 18, United States Code (relating to firearms);

(o) any violation of section 5861 of the Internal Revenue Code of 1986 (relating to firearms);

(p) a felony violation of section 1028 (relating to production of false identification documents)...

(q) any criminal violation of section 229 (relating to chemical weapons...

(r) any criminal violation of section 1 (relating to illegal restraints of trade or commerce)...

(s) any conspiracy to commit any offense described in any subparagraph of this paragraph.

(2) The principal prosecuting attorney of any State, or the principal prosecuting attorney of any political subdivision thereof, if such attorney is authorized by a statute of that State to make application to a State court judge of competent jurisdiction for an order authorizing or approving the interception of wire, oral, or electronic communications, may apply to such judge for, and such judge may grant in conformity with section 2518 of this chapter and with the applicable State statute an order authorizing, or approving the interception of wire, oral, or electronic communications by investigative or law enforcement officers having responsibility for the investigation of the offense as to which the application is made, when such interception may provide or has provided evidence of the commission of the offense of murder, kidnapping, gambling, robbery, bribery, extortion, or dealing in narcotic drugs, marihuana or other dangerous drugs, or other crime dangerous to life, limb, or property, and punishable by imprisonment for more than one year, designated in any applicable State statute authorizing such interception, or any conspiracy to commit any of the foregoing offenses.

(3) Any attorney for the Government (as such term is defined for the purposes of the Federal Rules of Criminal Procedure) may authorize an application to a Federal judge of competent jurisdiction for, and such judge may grant, in conformity with section 2518 of this title, an order authorizing or approving the interception of electronic communications by an investigative or law enforcement officer having responsibility for the investigation of the offense as to which the application is made, when such interception may provide or has provided evidence of any Federal felony.

§ 2518. Procedure for Interception of Wire, Oral, or Electronic Communications

(1) Each application for an order authorizing or approving the interception of a wire, oral, or electronic communication under this chapter shall be made in writing upon oath or affirmation to a judge of competent jurisdiction and shall state the applicant's authority to make such application. Each application shall include the following information:

(a) the identity of the investigative or law enforcement officer making the application, and the officer authorizing the application;

(b) a full and complete statement of the facts and circumstances relied upon by the applicant, to justify his belief that an order should be issued, including (i) details as to the particular offense that has been, is being, or is about to be committed, (ii) except as provided in subsection (11), a particular description of the nature and location of the facilities from which or the place where the communication is to be intercepted, (iii) a particular description of the type of communications sought to be intercepted, (iv) the identity of the person, if known, committing the offense and whose communications are to be intercepted;

(c) a full and complete statement as to whether or not other investigative procedures have been tried and failed or why they reasonably appear to be unlikely to succeed if tried or to be too dangerous;

(d) a statement of the period of time for which the interception is required to be maintained. If the nature of the investigation is such that the authorization for interception should not automatically terminate when the described type of communication has been first obtained, a particular description of facts establishing probable cause to believe that additional communications of the same type will occur thereafter;

(e) a full and complete statement of the facts concerning all previous applications known to the individual authorizing and making the application, made to any judge for authorization to intercept, or for approval of interceptions of, wire, oral, or electronic communications involving any of the same persons, facilities or places specified in the application, and the action taken by the judge on each such application; and

(f) where the application is for the extension of an order, a statement setting forth the results thus far obtained from the interception, or a reasonable explanation of the failure to obtain such results.

(2) The judge may require the applicant to furnish additional testimony or documentary evidence in support of the application.

(3) Upon such application the judge may enter an ex parte order, as requested or as modified, authorizing or approving interception of wire, oral, or electronic communications within the territorial jurisdiction of the court in which the judge is sitting (and outside that jurisdiction but within the United States in the case of a mobile interception device authorized by a Federal court within such jurisdiction), if the judge determines on the basis of the facts submitted by the applicant that—

(a) there is probable cause for belief that an individual is committing, has committed, or is about to commit a particular offense enumerated in section 2516 of this chapter;

(b) there is probable cause for belief that particular communications concerning that offense will be obtained through such interception;

(c) normal investigative procedures have been tried and have failed or reasonably appear to be unlikely to succeed if tried or to be too dangerous;

(d) except as provided in subsection (11), there is probable cause for belief that the facilities from which, or the place where, the wire, oral, or electronic communications are to be intercepted are being used, or are about to be used, in connection with the commission of such offense, or are leased to, listed in the name of, or commonly used by such person.

(4) Each order authorizing or approving the interception of any wire, oral, or electronic communication under this chapter shall specify–

(a) the identity of the person, if known, whose communications are to be intercepted;

(b) the nature and location of the communications facilities as to which, or the place where, authority to intercept is granted;

(c) a particular description of the type of communication sought to be intercepted, and a statement of the particular offense to which it relates;

(d) the identity of the agency authorized to intercept the communications, and of the person authorizing the application; and

(e) the period of time during which such interception is authorized, including a statement as to whether or not the interception shall automatically terminate when the described communication has been first obtained.

An order authorizing the interception of a wire, oral, or electronic communication under this chapter shall, upon request of the applicant, direct that a provider of wire or electronic communication service, landlord, custodian or other person shall furnish the applicant forthwith all information, facilities, and technical assistance necessary to accomplish the interception unobtrusively and with a minimum of interference with the services that such service provider, landlord, custodian, or person is according the person whose communications are to be intercepted. Any provider of wire or electronic communication service, landlord, custodian or other person furnishing such facilities or technical assistance shall be com-

pensated therefor by the applicant for reasonable expenses incurred in providing such facilities or assistance. Pursuant to section 2522 of this chapter, an order may also be issued to enforce the assistance capability and capacity requirements under the Communications Assistance for Law Enforcement Act.

(5) No order entered under this section may authorize or approve the interception of any wire, oral, or electronic communication for any period longer than is necessary to achieve the objective of the authorization, nor in any event longer than thirty days. Such thirty-day period begins on the earlier of the day on which the investigative or law enforcement officer first begins to conduct an interception under the order or ten days after the order is entered. Extensions of an order may be granted, but only upon application for an extension made in accordance with subsection (1) of this section and the court making the findings required by subsection (3) of this section.

(7) Notwithstanding any other provision of this chapter, any investigative or law enforcement officer, specially designated by the Attorney General, the Deputy Attorney General, the Associate Attorney General, or by the principal prosecuting attorney of any State or subdivision thereof acting pursuant to a statute of that State, who reasonably determines that–

(a) an emergency situation exists that involves–

(i) immediate danger of death or serious physical injury to any person,

(ii) conspiratorial activities threatening the national security interest, or

(iii) conspiratorial activities characteristic of organized crime, that requires a wire, oral, or electronic communication to be intercepted before an order authorizing such interception can, with due diligence, be obtained, and

(b) there are grounds upon which an order could be entered under this chapter to authorize such interception, may intercept such wire, oral, or electronic communication if an application for an order approving the interception is made in accordance with this section within forty-eight hours after the interception has occurred, or begins to occur. In the absence of an order, such interception shall immediately terminate when the communication sought is obtained or when the application for the order is denied, whichever is earlier. In the event such application for approval is denied, or in any other case where the interception is terminated without an order having been issued, the contents of any wire, oral, or electronic communication intercepted shall be treated as having been obtained in violation of this chapter, and an inventory shall be served as provided for in subsection (d) of this section on the person named in the application.

(8) (a) The contents of any wire, oral, or electronic communication intercepted by any means authorized by this chapter shall, if possible, be recorded on tape or wire or other comparable device.

(b) Applications made and orders granted under this chapter shall be sealed by the judge. Custody of the applications and orders shall be wherever the judge directs. Such applications and orders shall be disclosed only upon a showing of good cause before a judge of competent jurisdiction and shall not be destroyed except on order of the issuing or denying judge, and in any event shall be kept for ten years.

(c) Any violation of the provisions of this subsection may be punished as contempt of the issuing or denying judge.

(d) Within a reasonable time but not later than ninety days after the filing of an application for an order of approval under section 2518(7)(b) which is denied or the termination of the period of an order or extensions thereof, the issuing or denying judge shall cause to be served, on the persons named in the order or the application, and such other parties to intercepted communications as the judge may determine in his discretion that is in the interest of justice, an inventory which shall include notice of–

(1) the fact of the entry of the order or the application;

(2) the date of the entry and the period of authorized, approved or disapproved interception, or the denial of the application; and

(3) the fact that during the period wire, oral, or electronic communications were or were not intercepted.

The judge, upon the filing of a motion, may in his discretion make available to such person or his counsel for inspection such portions of the intercepted communications, applications and orders as the judge determines to be in the interest of justice. On an ex parte showing of good cause to a judge of competent jurisdiction the serving of the inventory required by this subsection may be postponed.

(9) The contents of any wire, oral, or electronic communication intercepted pursuant to this chapter or evidence derived therefrom shall not be received in evidence or otherwise disclosed in any trial, hearing, or other proceeding in a Federal or State court unless each party, not less than ten days before the trial, hearing, or proceeding, has been furnished with a copy of the court order, and accompanying application, under which the interception was authorized or approved. . .

(10) (a) Any aggrieved person in any trial, hearing, or proceeding in or before any court, department, officer, agency, regulatory body, or other authority of the United States, a State, or a political subdivision thereof, may move to suppress the contents of any wire or oral communication intercepted pursuant to this chapter, or evidence derived therefrom, on the grounds that–

(i) the communication was unlawfully intercepted;

(ii) the order of authorization or approval under which it was intercepted is insufficient on its face; or

(iii) the interception was not made in conformity with the order of authorization or approval.

Such motion shall be made before the trial, hearing, or proceeding unless there was no opportunity to make such motion or the person was not aware of the grounds of the motion. If the motion is granted, the contents of the intercepted wire or oral communication, or evidence derived therefrom, shall be treated as having been obtained in violation of this chapter. The judge, upon the filing of such motion by the aggrieved person, may in his discretion make available to the aggrieved person or his counsel for inspection such portions of the intercepted communication or evidence derived therefrom as the judge determines to be in the interests of justice.

(b) In addition to any other right to appeal, the United States shall have the right to appeal from an order granting a motion to suppress made under paragraph (a) of this subsection, or the denial of an application for an order of approval, if the United States attorney shall certify to the judge or other official granting such motion or denying such application that the appeal is not taken for purposes of delay. Such appeal shall be taken within thirty days after the date the order was entered and shall be diligently prosecuted.

(c) The remedies and sanctions described in this chapter with respect to the interception of electronic communications are the only judicial remedies and sanctions for nonconstitutional violations of this chapter involving such communications.

(11) The requirements of subsections (1)(b)(ii) and (3)(d) of this section relating to the specification of the facilities from which, or the place where, the communication is to be intercepted do not apply if–

(a) in the case of an application with respect to the interception of an oral communication–

(i) the application is by a Federal investigative or law enforcement officer and is approved by the Attorney General, the Deputy Attorney General, the Associate Attorney General, an Assistant Attorney General, or an acting Assistant Attorney General;

(ii) the application contains a full and complete statement as to why such specification is not practical and identifies the person committing the offense and whose communications are to be intercepted; and

(iii) the judge finds that such specification is not practical; and

(b) in the case of an application with respect to a wire or electronic communication–

(i) the application is by a Federal investigative or law enforcement officer and is approved by the Attorney General, the Deputy Attorney General, the Associate Attorney General, an Assistant Attorney General, or an acting Assistant Attorney General;

(ii) the application identifies the person believed to be committing the offense and whose communications are to be intercepted and the applicant makes a showing that there is probable cause to believe that the person's actions could have the effect of thwarting interception from a specified facility;

(iii) the judge finds that such showing has been adequately made; and

(iv) the order authorizing or approving the interception is limited to interception only for such time as it is reasonable to presume that the person identified in the application is or was reasonably proximate to the instrument through which such communication will be or was transmitted.

(12) An interception of a communication under an order with respect to which the requirements of subsections (1)(b)(ii) and (3)(d) of this section do not apply by reason of subsection (11)(a) shall not begin until the place where the communication is to be intercepted is ascertained by the person implementing the

interception order. A provider of wire or electronic communications service that has received an order as provided for in subsection (11)(b) may move the court to modify or quash the order on the ground that its assistance with respect to the interception cannot be performed in a timely or reasonable fashion. The court, upon notice to the government, shall decide such a motion expeditiously.

§ 2522. Enforcement of the Communications Assistance for Law Enforcement Act

(a) *Enforcement by Court Issuing Surveillance Order.* If a court authorizing an interception under this chapter, a State statute, or the Foreign Intelligence Surveillance Act of 1978 (50 U.S.C. 1801 et seq.) or authorizing use of a pen register or a trap and trace device under Chapter 206 or a State statute finds that a telecommunications carrier has failed to comply with the requirements of the Communications Assistance for Law Enforcement Act, the court may, in accordance with section 108 of such Act, direct that the carrier comply forthwith and may direct that a provider of support services to the carrier or the manufacturer of the carrier's transmission or switching equipment furnish forthwith modifications necessary for the carrier to comply.

(b) *Enforcement Upon Application by Attorney General.* The Attorney General may, in a civil action in the appropriate United States district court, obtain an order, in accordance with section 108 of the Communications Assistance for Law Enforcement Act, directing that a telecommunications carrier, a manufacturer of telecommunications transmission or switching equipment, or a provider of telecommunications support services comply with such Act.

(c) *Civil Penalty.*

(1) **IN GENERAL.—** A court issuing an order under this section against a telecommunications carrier, a manufacturer of telecommunications transmission or switching equipment, or a provider of telecommunications support services may impose a civil penalty of up to $10,000 per day for each day in violation after the issuance of the order or after such future date as the court may specify.

Computer Matching and Privacy Act of 1988, 5 U.S.C. § 552a

§ 552a. Records Maintained on Individuals

(a) *Definitions.* For purposes of this section–

(4) the term "record" means any item, collection, or grouping of information about an individual that is maintained by an agency, including, but not limited to,

his education, financial transactions, medical history, and criminal or employment history and that contains his name, or the identifying number, symbol, or other identifying particular assigned to the individual, such as a finger or voice print or a photograph;

(5) the term "system of records" means a group of any records under the control of any agency from which information is retrieved by the name of the individual or by some identifying number, symbol, or other identifying particular assigned to the individual;

(6) the term "statistical record" means a record in a system of records maintained for statistical research or reporting purposes only and not used in whole or in part in making any determination about an identifiable individual, except as provided by section 8 of title 13;

(b) *Conditions of Disclosure.* No agency shall disclose any record which is contained in a system of records by any means of communication to any person, or to another agency, except pursuant to a written request by, or with the prior written consent of, the individual to whom the record pertains, unless disclosure of the record would be–

(1) to those officers and employees of the agency which maintains the record who have a need for the record in the performance of their duties;

(2) required under section 552 of this title;

(3) for a routine use as defined in subsection (a)(7) of this section and described under subsection (e)(4)(D) of this section;

(4) to the Bureau of the Census for purposes of planning or carrying out a census or survey or related activity pursuant to the provisions of title 13;

(5) to a recipient who has provided the agency with advance adequate written assurance that the record will be used solely as a statistical research or reporting record, and the record is to be transferred in a form that is not individually identifiable;

(6) to the National Archives and Records Administration as a record which has sufficient historical or other value to warrant its continued preservation by the United States Government, or for evaluation by the Archivist of the United States or the designee of the Archivist to determine whether the record has such value;

(7) to another agency or to an instrumentality of any governmental jurisdiction within or under the control of the United States for a civil or criminal law enforcement activity if the activity is authorized by law, and if the head of the agency or instrumentality has made a written request to the agency which maintains the record specifying the particular portion desired and the law enforcement activity for which the record is sought;

(8) to a person pursuant to a showing of compelling circumstances affecting the health or safety of an individual if upon such disclosure notification is transmitted to the last known address of such individual;

(9) to either House of Congress, or, to the extent of matter within its jurisdiction, any committee or subcommittee thereof, any joint committee of Congress or subcommittee of any such joint committee;

(10) to the Comptroller General, or any of his authorized representatives, in the course of the performance of the duties of the Government Accountability Office;

(11) pursuant to the order of a court of competent jurisdiction; or

(12) to a consumer reporting agency in accordance with section 3711(e) of title 31.

USA Patriot Act, October 26, 2001

TITLE II—ENHANCED SURVEILLANCE PROCEDURES

Sec. 201. Authority to Intercept Wire, Oral, and Electronic Communications Relating to Terrorism

Section 2516(1) of title 18, United States Code, is amended—

(2) by inserting after paragraph (p). . . the following new paragraph:

'(q) any criminal violation of section 229 (relating to chemical weapons); or sections 2332, 2332a, 2332b, 2332d, 2339A, or 2339B of this title (relating to terrorism);

[This list of statutes simply added to the list for which the government may seek "an order authorizing or approving the interception of wire or oral communications."]

Sec. 202. Authority to Intercept Wire, Oral, and Electronic Communications Relating to Computer Fraud and Abuse Offenses

Section 2516(1)(c) of title 18, United States Code, is amended by striking 'and section 1341 (relating to mail fraud),' and inserting 'section 1341 (relating to mail fraud), a felony violation of section 1030 (relating to computer fraud and abuse),'. . .

[As in section 201, this statute added another crime for which the government may seek "an order authorizing or approving the interception of wire or oral communications."]

Sec. 203. Authority to Share Criminal Investigative Information

(a) *Authority to Share Grand Jury Information.*

(1) IN GENERAL— Rule 6(e)(3)(C) of the Federal Rules of Criminal Procedure is amended to read as follows:

'(C)(i) Disclosure otherwise prohibited by this rule of matters occurring before the grand jury may also be made—

'(III) when the disclosure is made by an attorney for the government to another Federal grand jury;

'(IV) when permitted by a court at the request of an attorney for the government, upon a showing that such matters may disclose a violation of State criminal law, to an appropriate official of a State or subdivision of a State for the purpose of enforcing such law; or

'(V) when the matters involve foreign intelligence or counterintelligence (as defined in section 3 of the National Security Act of 1947 (50 U.S.C. 401a)), or foreign intelligence information (as defined in clause (iv) of this subparagraph), to any Federal law enforcement, intelligence, protective, immigration, national defense, or national security official in order to assist the official receiving that information in the performance of his official duties.

'(iii) Any Federal official to whom information is disclosed pursuant to clause (i)(V) of this subparagraph may use that information only as necessary in the conduct of that person's official duties subject to any limitations on the unauthorized disclosure of such information. Within a reasonable time after such disclosure, an attorney for the government shall file under seal a notice with the court stating the fact that such information was disclosed and the departments, agencies, or entities to which the disclosure was made.

'(iv) In clause (i)(V) of this subparagraph, the term 'foreign intelligence information' means–

'(I) information, whether or not concerning a United States person, that relates to the ability of the United States to protect against–

'(aa) actual or potential attack or other grave hostile acts of a foreign power or an agent of a foreign power;

'(bb) sabotage or international terrorism by a foreign power or an agent of a foreign power; or

'(cc) clandestine intelligence activities by an intelligence service or network of a foreign power or by an agent of foreign power; or

'(II) information, whether or not concerning a United States person, with respect to a foreign power or foreign territory that relates to–

'(aa) the national defense or the security of the United States; or

'(bb) the conduct of the foreign affairs of the United States.'

(b) *Authority to Share Electronic, Wire, and Oral Interception Information.*

(1) LAW ENFORCEMENT.— Section 2517 of title 18, United States Code, is amended by inserting at the end the following:

'(6) Any investigative or law enforcement officer, or attorney for the Government, who by any means authorized by this chapter, has obtained knowledge of the contents of any wire, oral, or electronic communication, or evidence derived therefrom, may disclose such contents to any other Federal law enforcement, intelligence, protective, immigration, national defense, or national security official to the extent that such contents include foreign intelligence or counterintelligence (as defined in section 3 of the National Security Act of 1947 (50 U.S.C. 401a)), or foreign intelligence information (as defined in subsection (19) of section 2510 of this title), to assist the official who is to receive that information in the performance of his official duties. Any Federal official who receives information pursuant to this provision may use that information only as necessary in the conduct of that person's official duties subject to any limitations on the unauthorized disclosure of such information.'

(2) DEFINITION.— Section 2510 of title 18, United States Code, is amended by–

(C) by inserting at the end the following:

'(19)' foreign intelligence information' means–

'(A) information, whether or not concerning a United States person, that relates to the ability of the United States to protect against–

'(i) actual or potential attack or other grave hostile acts of a foreign power or an agent of a foreign power;

'(ii) sabotage or international terrorism by a foreign power or an agent of a foreign power; or

'(iii) clandestine intelligence activities by an intelligence service or network of a foreign power or by an agent of a foreign power; or

'(B) information, whether or not concerning a United States person, with respect to a foreign power or foreign territory that relates to–

'(i) the national defense or the security of the United States; or

'(ii) the conduct of the foreign affairs of the United States.'

(d) *Foreign Intelligence Information.*

(1) IN GENERAL.— Notwithstanding any other provision of law, it shall be lawful for foreign intelligence or counter-intelligence (as defined in section 3 of the National Security Act of 1947 (50 U.S.C. 401a)) or foreign intelligence information obtained as part of a criminal investigation to be disclosed to any Federal law enforcement, intelligence, protective, immigration, national defense, or national security official in order to assist the official receiving that information in the performance of his official duties. Any Federal official who receives information pursuant to this provision may use that information only as necessary in the conduct of that person's official duties subject to any limitations on the unauthorized disclosure of such information.

Sec. 206. Roving Surveillance Authority under the Foreign Intelligence Surveillance Act of 1978

Section 105(c)(2)(B) of the Foreign Intelligence Surveillance Act of 1978 (50 U.S.C. 1805(c)(2)(B)) is amended by inserting ', or in circumstances where the Court finds that the actions of the target of the application may have the effect of thwarting the identification of a specified person, such other persons,' after 'specified person'.

["...Where circumstances suggest that a target's actions may prevent identification of a specified person, this new language appears to permit the Foreign Intelligence Surveillance Court to require a service provider, other common carrier, landlord, custodian or other persons to provide necessary assistance to the applicant for a FISA order for electronic surveillance. The heading to Section 6 of P.L. 107-56 refers to this as "roving surveillance authority." H. Rept. 107-328 calls this a "multipoint" wiretap. . ."[18]]

Sec. 207. Duration of FISA Surveillance of Non-United States Persons who are Agents of a Foreign Power

(a) *Duration.*

(1) SURVEILLANCE.— Section 105(e)(1) of the Foreign Intelligence Surveillance Act of 1978 (50 U.S.C. 1805(e)(1)) is amended by–

(B) inserting before the period the following: ', and (B) an order under this Act for a surveillance targeted against an agent of a foreign power, as defined in section 101(b)(1)(A) may be for the period specified in the application or for 120 days, whichever is less'.

(2) PHYSICAL SEARCH.— Section 304(d)(1) of the Foreign Intelligence Surveillance Act of 1978 (50 U.S.C. 1824(d)(1)) is amended by–

(C) inserting before the period the following: ', and (B) an order under this section for a physical search targeted against an agent of a foreign power as defined in section 101(b)(1)(A) may be for the period specified in the application or for 120 days, whichever is less'.

(b) *Extension.*

(1) IN GENERAL.— Section 105(d)(2) of the Foreign Intelligence Surveillance Act of 1978 (50 U.S.C. 1805(d)(2)) is amended by–

(B) inserting before the period the following: ', and (B) an extension of an order under this Act for a surveillance targeted against an agent of a foreign power as defined in section 101(b)(1)(A) may be for a period not to exceed 1 year'.

(2) DEFINED TERM.— Section 304(d)(2) of the Foreign Intelligence Surveillance Act of 1978 (50 U.S.C. 1824(d)(2) is amended by inserting after 'not a United States person,' the following: 'or against an agent of a foreign power as defined in section 101(b)(1)(A),'.

Sec. 208. Designation of Judges

Section 103(a) of the Foreign Intelligence Surveillance Act of 1978 (50 U.S.C. 1803(a)) is amended by–

(1) striking 'seven district court judges' and inserting '11 district court judges'; and

(2) inserting 'of whom no fewer than 3 shall reside within 20 miles of the District of Columbia' after 'circuits'.

Sec. 209. Seizure of Voice-Mail Messages Pursuant to Warrants

Title 18, United States Code, is amended–

(1) (1) in section 2510–

(A) in paragraph (1), by striking beginning with 'and such' and all that follows through 'communication'; and

(B) in paragraph (14), by inserting 'wire or' after 'transmission of'; and

(2) in subsections (a) and (b) of section 2703–

(A) by striking 'CONTENTS OF ELECTRONIC' and inserting 'CONTENTS OF WIRE OR ELECTRONIC' each place it appears;

(B) by striking 'contents of an electronic' and inserting 'contents of a wire or electronic' each place it appears; and

(C) by striking 'any electronic' and inserting 'any wire or electronic' each place it appears.

Sec. 212. Emergency Disclosure of Electronic Communications to Protect Life and Limb

(a) *Disclosure of Contents.*

(1) IN GENERAL.— Section 2702 of title 18, United States Code, is amended–

(A) by striking the section heading and inserting the following:

'Sec. 2702. Voluntary disclosure of customer communications or records';

(B) in subsection (a)–(iii) by inserting after paragraph (2) the following:

'(3) a provider of remote computing service or electronic communication service to the public shall not knowingly divulge a record or other information pertaining to a subscriber to or customer of such service (not including the contents of communications covered by paragraph (1) or (2)) to any governmental entity.';

(iii) by adding after subparagraph (B) the following:

'(C) if the provider reasonably believes that an emergency involving immediate danger of death or serious physical injury to any person requires disclosure of the information without delay.'; and

(E) by inserting after subsection (b) the following:

(c) *Exceptions For Disclosure Of Customer Records.* A provider described in subsection (a) may divulge a record or other information pertaining to a subscriber to or customer of such service (not including the contents of communications covered by subsection (a)(1) or (a)(2))–

'(1) as otherwise authorized in section 2703;

'(2) with the lawful consent of the customer or subscriber;

'(3) as may be necessarily incident to the rendition of the service or to the protection of the rights or property of the provider of that service;

'(4) to a governmental entity, if the provider reasonably believes that an emergency involving immediate danger of death or serious physical injury to any person justifies disclosure of the information;..

Sec. 213. Authority for Delaying Notice of the Execution of a Warrant

Section 3103a of title 18, United States Code, is amended–
(2) by adding at the end the following:

(b) *Delay.* With respect to the issuance of any warrant or court order under this section, or any other rule of law, to search for and seize any property or material that constitutes evidence of a criminal offense in violation of the laws of the United States, any notice required, or that may be required, to be given may be delayed if–

'(1) the court finds reasonable cause to believe that providing immediate notification of the execution of the warrant may have an adverse result (as defined in section 2705);

'(2) the warrant prohibits the seizure of any tangible property, any wire or electronic communication (as defined in section 2510), or, except as expressly provided in Chapter 121, any stored wire or electronic information, except where the court finds reasonable necessity for the seizure; and

'(3) the warrant provides for the giving of such notice within a reasonable period of its execution, which period may thereafter be extended by the court for good cause shown.'

Sec. 214. Pen Register and Trap and Trace Authority Under FISA

(a) *Applications and Orders.* Section 402 of the Foreign Intelligence Surveillance Act of 1978 (50 U.S.C. 1842) is amended–

(1) in subsection (a)(1), by striking 'for any investigation to gather foreign intelligence information or information concerning international terrorism' and inserting 'for any investigation to obtain foreign intelligence information not concerning a United States person or to protect against international terrorism or clandestine intelligence activities, provided that such investigation of a United States person is not conducted solely upon the basis of activities protected by the first amendment to the Constitution';

(2) by amending subsection (c)(2) to read as follows:

'(2) a certification by the applicant that the information likely to be obtained is foreign intelligence information not concerning a United States person or is relevant to an ongoing investigation to protect against international terrorism or clandestine intelligence activities, provided that such investigation of a United States person is not conducted solely upon the basis of activities protected by the first amendment to the Constitution.';

(4)   by amending subsection (d)(2)(A) to read as follows:

'(A)   shall specify–

'(i)   the identity, if known, of the person who is the subject of the investigation;

'(ii)   the identity, if known, of the person to whom is leased or in whose name is listed the telephone line or other facility to which the pen register or trap and trace device is to be attached or applied;

'(iii)   the attributes of the communications to which the order applies, such as the number or other identifier, and, if known, the location of the telephone line or other facility to which the pen register or trap and trace device is to be attached or applied and, in the case of a trap and trace device, the geographic limits of the trap and trace order.'.

(b) *Authorization During Emergencies.* Section 403 of the Foreign Intelligence Surveillance Act of 1978 (50 U.S.C. 1843) is amended–

(1)   in subsection (a), by striking 'foreign intelligence information or information concerning international terrorism' and inserting 'foreign intelligence information not concerning a United States person or information to protect against international terrorism or clandestine intelligence activities, provided that such investigation of a United States person is not conducted solely upon the basis of activities protected by the first amendment to the Constitution'; and

(2)   in subsection (b)(1), by striking 'foreign intelligence information or information concerning international terrorism' and inserting 'foreign intelligence information . . . [same words as in (1)(a), above.]

Sec. 215. Access to Records and Other Items Under the Foreign Intelligence Surveillance Act

Title V of the Foreign Intelligence Surveillance Act of 1978 (50 U.S.C. 1861 et seq.) is amended by striking sections 501 through 503 and inserting the following:

'Sec. 501. Access to Certain Business Records for Foreign Intelligence and International Terrorism Investigations

'(a)(1)   The Director of the Federal Bureau of Investigation or a designee of the Director (whose rank shall be no lower than Assistant Special Agent in Charge) may make an application for an order requiring the production of any tangible things (including books, records, papers, documents, and other items) for an investigation to protect against international terrorism or clandestine intelligence activities, provided that such investigation of a United States person is not conducted solely upon the basis of activities protected by the first amendment to the Constitution.

'(2)   An investigation conducted under this section shall–

'(A)   be conducted under guidelines approved by the Attorney General under Executive Order 12333 (or a successor order); and

'(B)   not be conducted of a United States person solely upon the basis of activities protected by the first amendment to the Constitution of the United States.

'(b)   Each application under this section–

'(1)   shall be made to–

'(A)   a judge of the court established by section 103(a); or

'(B)   a United States Magistrate Judge under Chapter 43 of title 28, United States Code, who is publicly designated by the Chief Justice of the United States to have the power to hear applications and grant orders for the production of tangible things under this section on behalf of a judge of that court; and

'(2)   shall specify that the records concerned are sought for an authorized investigation conducted in accordance with subsection (a)(2) to obtain foreign intelligence information not concerning a United States person or to protect against international terrorism or clandestine intelligence activities.

'(c)(1)   Upon an application made pursuant to this section, the judge shall enter an ex parte order as requested, or as modified, approving the release of records if the judge finds that the application meets the requirements of this section.

'(2)   An order under this subsection shall not disclose that it is issued for purposes of an investigation described in subsection (a).

'(d)   No person shall disclose to any other person (other than those persons necessary to produce the tangible things under this section) that the Federal Bureau of Investigation has sought or obtained tangible things under this section.

'(e)   A person who, in good faith, produces tangible things under an order pursuant to this section shall not be liable to any other person for such production. Such production shall not be deemed to constitute a waiver of any privilege in any other proceeding or context.

Sec. 216. Modification of Authorities Relating to Use of Pen Registers and Trap and Trace Devices

(a) *General Limitations.* Section 3121(c) of title 18, United States Code, is amended–

(1) by inserting 'or trap and trace device' after 'pen register';

(2) by inserting, 'routing, addressing,' after 'dialing'; and

(3) by striking 'call processing' and inserting 'the processing and transmitting of wire or electronic communications so as not to include the contents of any wire or electronic communications'.

(b) *Issuance of Orders.*

(1) IN GENERAL.— Section 3123(a) of title 18, United States Code, is amended to read as follows:
'*(a) IN GENERAL.*

'(1) *ATTORNEY FOR THE GOVERNMENT—* Upon an application made under section 3122(a)(1), the court shall enter an ex parte order authorizing the installation and use of a pen register or trap and trace device anywhere within the United States, if the court finds that the attorney for the Government has certified to the court that the information likely to be obtained by such installation and use is relevant to an ongoing criminal investigation. The order, upon service of that order, shall apply to any person or entity providing wire or electronic communication service in the United States whose assistance may facilitate the execution of the order. Whenever such an order is served on any person or entity not specifically named in the order, upon request of such person or entity, the attorney for the Government or law enforcement or investigative officer that is serving the order shall provide written or electronic certification that the order applies to the person or entity being served.

'(2) *STATE INVESTIGATIVE OR LAW ENFORCE-MENT OFFICER—* Upon an application made under section 3122(a)(2), the court shall enter an ex parte order authorizing the installation and use of a pen register or trap and trace device within the jurisdiction of the court, if the court finds that the State law enforcement or investigative officer has certified to the court that the information likely to be obtained by such installation and use is relevant to an ongoing criminal investigation.

'(3)(A) Where the law enforcement agency implementing an ex parte order under this subsection seeks to do so by installing and using its own pen register or trap and trace device on a packet-switched data network of a provider of electronic communication service to the public, the agency shall ensure that a record will be maintained which will identify–

'(i) any officer or officers who installed the device and any officer or officers who accessed the device to obtain information from the network;

'(ii) the date and time the device was installed, the date and time the device was uninstalled, and the date, time, and duration of each time the device is accessed to obtain information;

'(iii) the configuration of the device at the time of its installation and any subsequent modification thereof; and

'(iv) any information which has been collected by the device.
    To the extent that the pen register or trap and trace device can be set automatically to record this information electronically, the record shall be maintained electronically throughout the installation and use of such device.

'(B) The record maintained under subparagraph (A) shall be provided ex parte and under seal to the court which entered the ex parte order authorizing the installation and use of the device within 30 days after termination of the order (including any extensions thereof).'.

(2) CONTENTS OF ORDER.— Section 3123(b)(1) of title 18, United States Code, is amended–

(A) (A) in subparagraph (A)–

(B) (B) by striking subparagraph (C) and inserting the following:

'(C) the attributes of the communications to which the order applies, including the number or other identifier and, if known, the location of the telephone line or other facility to which the pen register or trap and trace device is to be attached or applied, and, in the case of an order authorizing installation and use of a trap and trace device under subsection (a)(2), the geographic limits of the order; and'.

(c) *Definitions.*

(1) COURT OF COMPETENT JURISDICTION.— Section 3127(2) of title 18, United States Code, is amended by striking subparagraph (A) and inserting the following:

'(A) any district court of the United States (including a magistrate judge of such a court) or any United States court of appeals having jurisdiction over the offense being investigated; or'.

(2) PEN REGISTER.— Section 3127(3) of title 18, United States Code, is amended–

(A) by striking 'electronic or other impulses' and all that follows through 'is attached' and inserting 'dialing, routing, addressing, or signaling information transmitted by an instrument or facility from which a wire or electronic communication is transmitted, provided, however, that such information shall not include the contents of any communication'; . . .

Sec. 219. Single-Jurisdiction Search Warrants For Terrorism

Rule 41(a) of the Federal Rules of Criminal Procedure is amended by inserting after 'executed' the following: 'and (3) in an investigation of domestic terrorism or international terrorism (as defined in section 2331 of title 18, United States Code), by a Federal magistrate judge in any district in which activities related to the terrorism may have occurred, for a search of property or for a person within or outside the district'.

Sec. 223. Civil Liability for Certain Unauthorized Disclosures

(a) Section 2520 of title 18, United States Code, is amended–

(3) by adding a new subsection (g), as follows:

'(g) IMPROPER DISCLOSURE IS VIOLATION.—Any willful disclosure or use by an investigative or law enforcement officer or governmental entity of information beyond the extent permitted by section 2517 is a violation of this chapter for purposes of section 2520(a).'

Sec. 225. Immunity for Compliance with FISA Wiretap

Section 105 of the Foreign Intelligence Surveillance Act of 1978 (50 U.S.C. 1805) is amended by inserting after subsection (g) the following:

'(h) No cause of action shall lie in any court against any provider of a wire or electronic communication service, landlord, custodian, or other person (including any officer, employee, agent, or other specified person thereof) that furnishes any information, facilities, or technical assistance in accordance with a court order or request for emergency assistance under this Act.'

TITLE IX—IMPROVED INTELLIGENCE

Sec. 905. Disclosure to Director of Central Intelligence of Foreign Intelligence-Related Information with Respect to Criminal Investigations

(a) IN GENERAL.— Title I of the National Security Act of 1947 (50 U.S.C. 402 et seq.) is amended–

(2) by inserting after section 105A the following new section 105B:

"DISCLOSURE OF FOREIGN INTELLIGENCE ACQUIRED IN CRIMINAL INVESTIGATIONS; NOTICE OF CRIMINAL INVESTIGATIONS OF FOREIGN INTELLIGENCE SOURCES

Sec. 105B. (a) Disclosure of Foreign Intelligence

"(1) Except as otherwise provided by law and subject to paragraph (2), the Attorney General, or the head of any other department or agency of the Federal Government with law enforcement responsibilities, shall expeditiously disclose to the Director of Central Intelligence, pursuant to guidelines developed by the Attorney General in consultation with the Director, foreign intelligence acquired by an element of the Department of Justice or an element of such department or agency, as the case may be, in the course of a criminal investigation.

E-Government Act Of 2002, December 17, 2002[19]

Sec. 2. Findings and Purposes

(b) *Purposes.* The purposes of this Act are the following:

(1) To provide effective leadership of Federal Government efforts to develop and promote electronic Government services and processes by establishing an Administrator of a new Office of Electronic Government within the Office of Management and Budget.

(2) To promote use of the Internet and other information technologies to provide increased opportunities for citizen participation in Government.

(3) To promote interagency collaboration in providing electronic Government services, where this collaboration would improve the service to citizens by integrating related functions, and in the use of internal electronic Government processes, where this collaboration would improve the efficiency and effectiveness of the processes.

(4) To improve the ability of the Government to achieve agency missions and program performance goals.

(5) To promote the use of the Internet and emerging technologies within and across Government agencies to provide citizen-centric Government information and services.

(6) To reduce costs and burdens for businesses and other Government entities.

(7) To promote better informed decisionmaking by policy makers.

(8) To promote access to high quality Government information and services across multiple channels.

(9) To make the Federal Government more transparent and accountable.

(10) To transform agency operations by utilizing, where appropriate, best practices from public and private sector organizations.

(11) To provide enhanced access to Government information and services in a manner consistent with laws regarding protection of personal privacy, national security, records retention, access for persons with disabilities, and other relevant laws.

TITLE I—OFFICE OF MANAGEMENT AND BUDGET ELECTRONIC GOVERNMENT SERVICES

Sec. 101. Management and Promotion of Electronic Government Services

(a) IN GENERAL.— Title 44, United States Code, is amended by inserting after Chapter 35 the following:...

Sec. 3602. Office of Electronic Government

'(a) There is established in the Office of Management and Budget an Office of Electronic Government.

'(b) There shall be at the head of the Office an Administrator who shall be appointed by the President.

'(c) The Administrator shall assist the Director...

Sec. 3603. Chief Information Officers Council

'(a) There is established in the executive branch a Chief Information Officers Council.

'(d) The Council is designated the principal interagency forum for improving agency practices related to the design, acquisition, development, modernization, use, operation, sharing, and performance of Federal Government information resources...

Intelligence Reform And Terrorism Prevention Act of 2004 (IRTPA)

[The Intelligence Reform and Terrorism Prevention Act of 2004 amended the National Security Act of 1947 to provide for a Director of National Intelligence (DNI) to assume some of the responsibilities formerly fulfilled by the Director of Central Intelligence. The Director of the Central Intelligence Agency serves as the head of the Central Intelligence Agency and reports to the Director of National Intelligence.]

SEC. 1. SHORT TITLE; TABLE OF CONTENTS

(a) **SHORT TITLE.**—This Act may be cited as the "Intelligence Reform and Terrorism Prevention Act of 2004".

TITLE I—REFORM OF THE INTELLIGENCE COMMUNITY

SEC. 1001. SHORT TITLE

This title may be cited as the "National Security Intelligence Reform Act of 2004".

Subtitle A—Establishment of Director of National Intelligence

SEC. 1011. REORGANIZATION AND IMPROVEMENT OF MANAGEMENT OF INTELLIGENCE COMMUNITY

(a) **IN GENERAL.**— Title I of the National Security Act of 1947 (50 U.S.C. 402 et seq.) is amended by striking sections 102 through 104 and inserting the following new sections:

"DIRECTOR OF NATIONAL INTELLIGENCE

Sec. 102.

"(a) DIRECTOR OF NATIONAL INTELLIGENCE.—

"(1) There is a Director of National Intelligence who shall be appointed by the President, by and with the advice and consent of the Senate. Any individual nominated for appointment as Director of National Intelligence shall have extensive national security expertise.

"(2) The Director of National Intelligence shall not be located within the Executive Office of the President.

"(b) **PRINCIPAL RESPONSIBILITY.**— Subject to the authority, direction, and control of the President, the Director of National Intelligence shall—

"(1) serve as head of the intelligence community;

"(2) act as the principal adviser to the President, to the National Security Council, and the Homeland Security

Council for intelligence matters related to the national security; and

"(3) consistent with section 1018 of the National Security Intelligence Reform Act of 2004, oversee and direct the implementation of the National Intelligence Program.

"(c) PROHIBITION ON DUAL SERVICE.— The individual serving in the position of Director of National Intelligence shall not, while so serving, also serve as the Director of the Central Intelligence Agency or as the head of any other element of the intelligence community.

"RESPONSIBILITIES AND AUTHORITIES OF THE DIRECTOR OF NATIONAL INTELLIGENCE

Sec. 102A.

"(a) PROVISION OF INTELLIGENCE.—

(1) The Director of National Intelligence shall be responsible for ensuring that national intelligence is provided—

"(A) to the President;

"(B) to the heads of departments and agencies of the executive branch;

"(C) to the Chairman of the Joint Chiefs of Staff and senior military commanders;

"(D) to the Senate and House of Representatives and the committees thereof; and

"(E) to such other persons as the Director of National Intelligence determines to be appropriate.

"(2) Such national intelligence should be timely, objective, independent of political considerations, and based upon all sources available to the intelligence community and other appropriate entities.

"(b) ACCESS TO INTELLIGENCE.— Unless otherwise directed by the President, the Director of National Intelligence shall have access to all national intelligence and intelligence related to the national security which is collected by any Federal department, agency, or other entity, except as otherwise provided by law or, as appropriate, under guidelines agreed upon by the Attorney General and the Director of National Intelligence. . . .

"(2) The Director of National Intelligence shall oversee the National Counterterrorism Center and may establish such other national intelligence centers as the Director determines necessary.

"(iv) ensure that the personnel of the intelligence community are sufficiently diverse for purposes of the collection and analysis of intelligence through the recruitment and training of women, minorities, and individuals with diverse ethnic, cultural, and linguistic backgrounds;

"(v) make service in more than one element of the intelligence community a condition of promotion to such positions within the intelligence community as the Director shall specify;. . .

"(4) The Director of National Intelligence shall ensure compliance with the Constitution and laws of the United States by the Central Intelligence Agency and shall ensure such compliance by other elements of the intelligence community through the host executive departments that manage the programs and activities that are part of the National Intelligence Program.

"(g) INTELLIGENCE INFORMATION SHARING.— (1) The Director of National Intelligence shall have principal authority to ensure maximum availability of and access to intelligence information within the intelligence community consistent with national security requirements. The Director of National Intelligence shall—

"(C) ensure development of information technology systems that include multi-level security and intelligence integration capabilities;

"(D) establish policies and procedures to resolve conflicts between the need to share intelligence information and the need to protect intelligence sources and methods;

"(h) ANALYSIS.— To ensure the most accurate analysis of intelligence is derived from all sources to support national security needs, the Director of National Intelligence shall—
Procedures. "(1) implement policies and procedures—

"(A) to encourage sound analytic methods and tradecraft throughout the elements of the intelligence community;

"(B) to ensure that analysis is based upon all sources available; and

"(C) to ensure that the elements of the intelligence community regularly conduct competitive analysis of analytic products, whether such products are produced by or disseminated to such elements;

"(3) ensure that differences in analytic judgment are fully considered and brought to the attention of policymakers; and

"(4) ensure that sufficient relationships are established between intelligence collectors and analysts to facilitate greater understanding of the needs of analysts.

"(i) PROTECTION OF INTELLIGENCE SOURCES AND METHODS.—

(1) The Director of National Intelligence shall protect intelligence sources and methods from unauthorized disclosure.

"(2) Consistent with paragraph (1), in order to maximize the dissemination of intelligence, the Director of National Intelligence shall establish and implement guidelines for the intelligence community for the following purposes:

"(A) Classification of information under applicable law, Executive orders, or other Presidential directives.

"(B) Access to and dissemination of intelligence, both in final form and in the form when initially gathered.

"(C) Preparation of intelligence products in such a way that source information is removed to allow for dissemination at the lowest level of classification possible or in unclassified form to the extent practicable.

"(j) UNIFORM PROCEDURES FOR SENSITIVE COMPARTMENTED INFORMATION.— The Director of National Intelligence, subject to the direction of the President, shall—

"(1) establish uniform standards and procedures for the grant of access to sensitive compartmented information to any officer or employee of any agency or department of the United States and to employees of contractors of those agencies or departments;

"(3) ensure that security clearances granted by individual elements of the intelligence community are recognized by all elements of the intelligence community, and under contracts entered into by those agencies; and

"(4) ensure that the process for investigation and adjudication of an application for access to sensitive compartmented information is performed in the most expeditious manner possible consistent with applicable standards for national security.

"(k)   COORDINATION   WITH   FOREIGN GOVERNMENTS.— Under the direction of the President and in a manner consistent with section Guidelines.

. . .the Director of National Intelligence shall oversee the coordination of the relationships between elements of the intelligence community and the intelligence or security services of foreign governments or international organizations on all matters involving intelligence related to the national security or involving intelligence acquired through clandestine means.

Sec. 103.

"(a) OFFICE OF DIRECTOR OF NATIONAL INTELLIGENCE.— There is an Office of the Director of National Intelligence.

"(b) FUNCTION.— The function of the Office of the Director of National Intelligence is to assist the Director of National Intelligence in carrying out the duties and responsibilities of the Director under this Act, the National Security Act of 1947 (50 U.S.C. 401 et seq.), and other applicable provisions of law, and to carry out such other duties as may be prescribed by the President or by law.

"(c) COMPOSITION.— The Office of the Director of National Intelligence is composed of the following:

"(1) The Director of National Intelligence.

"(2) The Principal Deputy Director of National Intelligence.

"(3) Any Deputy Director of National Intelligence appointed under section 103A.

"(4) The National Intelligence Council.

"(5) The General Counsel.

"(6) The Civil Liberties Protection Officer.

"(7) The Director of Science and Technology.

"(8) The National Counterintelligence Executive (including the Office of the National Counterintelligence Executive).

"(e) LIMITATION ON CO-LOCATION WITH OTHER ELEMENTS OF INTELLIGENCE COMMUNITY.— Commencing as of October 1, 2008, the Office of the Director of National Intelligence may not be co-located with any other element of the intelligence community.

"NATIONAL INTELLIGENCE COUNCIL

Sec. 103B.

"(a) NATIONAL INTELLIGENCE COUNCIL.— There is a National Intelligence Council.

"(b) COMPOSITION.— (1) The National Intelligence Council shall be composed of senior analysts within the intelligence community and substantive experts from the public and private sector, who shall be appointed by, report to, and serve at the pleasure of, the Director of National Intelligence.

"(c) DUTIES AND RESPONSIBILITIES.— (1) The National Intelligence Council shall—

"(A) produce national intelligence estimates for the United States Government, including alternative views held by elements of the intelligence community and other information as specified in paragraph (2);

"(B) evaluate community-wide collection and production of intelligence by the intelligence community and the requirements and resources of such collection and production; and

"(C) otherwise assist the Director of National Intelligence in carrying out the responsibilities of the Director under section 102A.

"(d) SERVICE AS SENIOR INTELLIGENCE ADVISERS.— Within their respective areas of expertise and under the direction of the Director of National Intelligence, the members of the National Intelligence Council shall constitute the senior intelligence advisers of the intelligence community for purposes of representing the views of the intelligence community within the United States Government.

"DIRECTOR OF SCIENCE AND TECHNOLOGY

Sec. 103E.

"(a) DIRECTOR OF SCIENCE AND TECHNOLOGY.— There is a Director of Science and Technology within the Office of the Director of National Intelligence who shall be appointed by the Director of National Intelligence.

"(d) DIRECTOR OF NATIONAL INTELLIGENCE SCIENCE AND TECHNOLOGY COMMITTEE.— (1) There is within the Office of the Director of Science and Technology a Director of National Intelligence Science and Technology Committee.

"(2) The Committee shall be composed of the principal science officers of the National Intelligence Program.

"(3) The Committee shall—

"(A) coordinate advances in research and development related to intelligence; and

"NATIONAL COUNTERINTELLIGENCE EXECUTIVE

Sec. 103F.

"(a) NATIONAL COUNTERINTELLIGENCE EXECUTIVE.— The National Counterintelligence Executive under section 902 of the Counterintelligence Enhancement Act of 2002 (title IX of Public Law 107–306;

50 U.S.C. 402b et seq.) is a component of the Office of the Director of National Intelligence.

"(b) DUTIES.— The National Counterintelligence Executive shall perform the duties provided in the Counterintelligence Enhancement Act of 2002. . .

"CENTRAL INTELLIGENCE AGENCY

Sec. 104.

"(a) CENTRAL INTELLIGENCE AGENCY.— There is a Central Intelligence Agency.

"(b) FUNCTION.— The function of the Central Intelligence Agency is to assist the Director of the Central Intelligence Agency in carrying out the responsibilities specified in section 104A(c).

"DIRECTOR OF THE CENTRAL INTELLIGENCE AGENCY

Sec. 104A.

"(a) DIRECTOR OF CENTRAL INTELLIGENCE AGENCY.— There is a Director of the Central Intelligence Agency who shall be appointed by the President, by and with the advice and consent of the Senate.

"(b) SUPERVISION.— The Director of the Central Intelligence Agency shall report to the Director of National Intelligence regarding the activities of the Central Intelligence Agency.

"(c) DUTIES.— The Director of the Central Intelligence Agency shall—

"(1) serve as the head of the Central Intelligence Agency; and

"(2) carry out the responsibilities specified in subsection (d).

"(d) RESPONSIBILITIES.— The Director of the Central Intelligence Agency shall—

"(1) collect intelligence through human sources and by other appropriate means, except that the Director of the Central Intelligence Agency shall have no police, subpoena, or law enforcement powers or internal security functions;

"(2) correlate and evaluate intelligence related to the national security and provide appropriate dissemination of such intelligence;

"(3) provide overall direction for and coordination of the collection of national intelligence outside the United States through human sources by elements of the intelligence community authorized to undertake such collection and, in coordination with other departments, agencies, or elements of the United States Government which are authorized to undertake such collection, ensure that the most effective use is made of resources and that appropriate account is taken of the risks to the United States and those involved in such collection; and

"(f) COORDINATION WITH FOREIGN GOVERNMENTS.— Under the direction of the Director of National Intelligence and in a manner direction of the Director of National Intelligence and in a manner consistent with section 207 of the Foreign Service Act of 1980 (22 U.S.C. 3927), the Director of the Central Intelligence Agency shall coordinate the relationships between elements of the intelligence community and the intelligence or security services of foreign governments or international organizations on all matters involving intelligence related to the national security or involving intelligence acquired through clandestine means.".

(c) TRANSFORMATION OF CENTRAL INTELLIGENCE AGENCY.— The Director of the Central Intelligence Agency shall, in accordance with standards developed by the Director in consultation with the Director of National Intelligence—

(1) enhance the analytic, human intelligence, and other capabilities of the Central Intelligence Agency;

(2) develop and maintain an effective language program within the Agency;

(3) emphasize the hiring of personnel of diverse backgrounds for purposes of improving the capabilities of the Agency;

(4) establish and maintain effective relationships between human intelligence and signals intelligence within the Agency at the operational level; and

(5) achieve a more effective balance within the Agency with respect to unilateral operations and liaison operations.

SEC. 1012. REVISED DEFINITION OF NATIONAL INTELLIGENCE.

Paragraph (5) of section 3 of the National Security Act of 1947 (50 U.S.C. 401a) is amended to read as follows:

"(5) The terms 'national intelligence' and 'intelligence related to national security' refer to all intelligence, regardless of the source from which derived and including information gathered within or outside the United States, that—

"(A) pertains, as determined consistent with any guidance issued by the President, to more than one United States Government agency; and

"(B) that involves—

"(i) threats to the United States, its people, property, or interests;

"(ii) the development, proliferation, or use of weapons of mass destruction; or

"(iii) any other matter bearing on United States national or homeland security.".

SEC. 1013. JOINT PROCEDURES FOR OPERATIONAL COORDINATION BETWEEN DEPARTMENT OF DEFENSE AND CENTRAL INTELLIGENCE AGENCY

(a) DEVELOPMENT OF PROCEDURES.— The Director of National Intelligence, in consultation with the Secretary of Defense and the Director of the Central Intelligence Agency, shall develop joint procedures to be used by the Department of Defense and the Central Intelligence Agency to improve the coordination and deconfliction of operations that involve elements of both the Armed Forces and the Central Intelligence Agency...

SEC. 1016. INFORMATION SHARING

(a) DEFINITIONS.—In This Section:

(1) *INFORMATION SHARING COUNCIL.—* The term "Information Sharing Council" means the Information Systems Council established by Executive Order 13356, or any successor body designated by the President, and referred to under subsection (g).

(2) *INFORMATION SHARING ENVIRONMENT; ISE.—* The terms "information sharing environment" and "ISE" mean an approach that facilitates the sharing of terrorism information, which approach may include any methods determined necessary and appropriate for carrying out this section.

(4) *TERRORISM INFORMATION.—* The term "terrorism information" means all information, whether collected,

produced, or distributed by intelligence, law enforcement, military, homeland security, or other activities relating to—

(A) the existence, organization, capabilities, plans, intentions, vulnerabilities, means of finance or material support, or activities of foreign or international terrorist groups or individuals, or of domestic groups or individuals involved in transnational terrorism;

(B) threats posed by such groups or individuals to the United States, United States persons, or United States interests, or to those of other nations;

(C) communications of or by such groups or individuals; or

(D) groups or individuals reasonably believed to be assisting or associated with such groups or individuals.

(b) INFORMATION SHARING ENVIRONMENT.

(1) *ESTABLISHMENT.—The President shall—*

(A) create an information sharing environment for the sharing of terrorism information in a manner consistent with national security and with applicable legal standards relating to privacy and civil liberties;

(B) designate the organizational and management structures that will be used to operate and manage the ISE; and

(2) ATTRIBUTES.— The President shall, through the structures described in subparagraphs (B) and (C) of paragraph (1), ensure that the ISE provides and facilitates the means for sharing terrorism information among all appropriate Federal, State, local, and tribal entities, and the private sector through the use of policy guidelines and technologies. The President shall, to the greatest extent practicable, ensure that the ISE provides the functional equivalent of, or otherwise supports, a decentralized, distributed, and coordinated environment that—

(A) connects existing systems, where appropriate, provides no single points of failure, and allows users to share information among agencies, between levels of government, and, as appropriate, with the private sector;

(B) ensures direct and continuous online electronic access to information;

(C) facilitates the availability of information in a form and manner that facilitates its use in analysis, investigations and operations;

(D) builds upon existing systems capabilities currently in use across the Government;

(E) employs an information access management approach that controls access to data rather than

just systems and networks, without sacrificing security;

(F) facilitates the sharing of information at and across all levels of security;

(G) provides directory services, or the functional equivalent, for locating people and information;

(H) incorporates protections for individuals' privacy and civil liberties; and

(I) incorporates strong mechanisms to enhance accountability and facilitate oversight, including audits, authentication, and access controls.

SEC. 1017. ALTERNATIVE ANALYSIS OF INTELLIGENCE BY THE INTELLIGENCE COMMUNITY

(a) IN GENERAL.— ... the Director of National Intelligence shall establish a process and assign an individual or entity the responsibility for ensuring that, as appropriate, elements of the intelligence community conduct alternative analysis (commonly referred to as "red-team analysis") of the information and conclusions in intelligence products.

Subtitle B—National Counterterrorism Center, National Counter Proliferation Center, and National Intelligence Centers

SEC. 1021. NATIONAL COUNTERTERRORISM CENTER

Title I of the National Security Act of 1947 (50 U.S.C. 402 et seq.) is amended by adding at the end the following new section:

"NATIONAL COUNTERTERRORISM CENTER

Sec. 119.

"(a) ESTABLISHMENT OF CENTER.— There is within the Office of the Director of National Intelligence a National Counterterrorism Center.

"(b) DIRECTOR OF NATIONAL COUNTERTERRORISM CENTER.— (1) There is a Director of the National Counterterrorism Center, who shall be the head of the National Counterterrorism Center, and who shall be appointed by the President, by and with the advice and consent of the Senate.

"(d) PRIMARY MISSIONS.— The primary missions of the National Counterterrorism Center shall be as follows:

"(1) To serve as the primary organization in the United States Government for analyzing and integrating all intelligence possessed or acquired by the United States Government pertaining to terrorism and counterterrorism, excepting intelligence pertaining exclusively to domestic terrorists and domestic counterterrorism.

"(2) To conduct strategic operational planning for counterterrorism activities, integrating all instruments of national power, including diplomatic, financial, military, intelligence, homeland security, and law enforcement activities within and among agencies.

"(3) To assign roles and responsibilities as part of its strategic operational planning duties to lead Departments or agencies, as appropriate, for counterterrorism activities that are consistent with applicable law and that support counterterrorism strategic operational plans, but shall not direct the execution of any resulting operations.

"(4) To ensure that agencies, as appropriate, have access to and receive all-source intelligence support needed to execute their counterterrorism plans or perform independent, alternative analysis.

"(5) To ensure that such agencies have access to and receive intelligence needed to accomplish their assigned activities.

"(6) To serve as the central and shared knowledge bank on known and suspected terrorists and international terror groups, as well as their goals, strategies, capabilities, and networks of contacts and support.

"(e) DOMESTIC COUNTERTERRORISM INTELLIGENCE.— (1) The Center may, consistent with applicable law, the direction of the President, and the guidelines referred to in section 102A(b), receive intelligence pertaining exclusively to domestic counterterrorism from any Federal, State, or local government or other source necessary to fulfill its responsibilities and retain and disseminate such intelligence.

"(f) DUTIES AND RESPONSIBILITIES OF DIRECTOR.— (1) The Director of the National Counterterrorism Center shall—

"(A) serve as the principal adviser to the Director of National Intelligence on intelligence operations relating to counterterrorism;

"(B) provide strategic operational plans for the civilian and military counterterrorism efforts of the United States Government and for the effective integration of counterterrorism intelligence and operations across agency boundaries, both inside and outside the United States;

"(C) advise the Director of National Intelligence on the extent to which the counterterrorism program recommendations and budget proposals of the departments, agencies, and elements of the United States Government conform to the priorities established by the President;

"(D) disseminate terrorism information, including current terrorism threat analysis, to the President, the Vice President, the Secretaries of State, Defense, and Homeland Security, the Attorney General, the Director of the Central Intelligence Agency, and other officials of the executive branch as appropriate, and to the appropriate committees of Congress;

"(E) support the Department of Justice and the Department of Homeland Security, and other appropriate agencies, in fulfillment of their responsibilities to disseminate terrorism information, consistent with applicable law, guidelines referred to in section 102A(b), Executive orders and other Presidential guidance, to State and local government officials, and other entities, and coordinate dissemination of terrorism information to foreign governments as approved by the Director of National Intelligence;

"(F) develop a strategy for combining terrorist travel intelligence operations and law enforcement planning and operations into a cohesive effort to intercept terrorists, find terrorist travel facilitators, and constrain terrorist mobility;

"(G) have primary responsibility within the United States Government for conducting net assessments of terrorist threats;

"(g) LIMITATION.— The Director of the National Counterterrorism Center may not direct the execution of counterterrorism operations.

"(i) DIRECTORATE OF INTELLIGENCE.— The Director of the National Counterterrorism Center shall establish and maintain within the National Counterterrorism Center a Directorate of Intelligence which shall have primary responsibility within the United States Government for analysis of terrorism and terrorist organizations (except for purely domestic terrorism and domestic terrorist organizations) from all sources of intelligence, whether collected inside or outside the United States.

"(j) DIRECTORATE OF STRATEGIC OPERATIONAL PLANNING.— (1) The Director of the National Counterterrorism Center shall establish and maintain within the National Counterterrorism Center a Directorate of Strategic Operational Planning which shall provide strategic operational plans for counterterrorism operations conducted by the United States Government.

SEC. 1023. NATIONAL INTELLIGENCE CENTERS

Title I of the National Security Act of 1947, as amended by section 1022 of this Act, is further amended by adding at the end the following new section:

"NATIONAL INTELLIGENCE CENTERS

Sec. 119B.

"**(a) AUTHORITY TO ESTABLISH.**— The Director of National Intelligence may establish one or more national intelligence centers to address intelligence priorities, including, but not limited to, regional issues.

"**(d) MISSION OF CENTERS.**— Pursuant to the direction of the Director of National Intelligence, each national intelligence center under subsection (a) may, in the area of intelligence responsibility assigned to such center—

"(1) have primary responsibility for providing all-source analysis of intelligence based upon intelligence gathered both domestically and abroad;

"(2) have primary responsibility for identifying and proposing to the Director of National Intelligence intelligence collection and analysis and production requirements; and

"(3) perform such other duties as the Director of National Intelligence shall specify.

Subtitle C—Joint Intelligence Community Council

SEC. 1031. JOINT INTELLIGENCE COMMUNITY COUNCIL.

Title I of the National Security Act of 1947 (50 U.S.C. 402 et seq.) is amended by inserting after section 101 the following new section:

"JOINT INTELLIGENCE COMMUNITY COUNCIL

Sec. 101A.

"**(a) JOINT INTELLIGENCE COMMUNITY COUNCIL.**— There is a Joint Intelligence Community Council.

"**(c) FUNCTIONS.**— The Joint Intelligence Community Council shall assist the Director of National Intelligence in developing and implementing a joint, unified national intelligence effort to protect national security by—

"(1) advising the Director on establishing requirements, developing budgets, financial management, and monitoring and evaluating the performance of the intelligence community, and on such other matters as the Director may request;

Subtitle E—Additional Improvements of Intelligence Activities

SEC. 1051. SERVICE AND NATIONAL LABORATORIES AND THE INTELLIGENCE COMMUNITY

The Director of National Intelligence, in cooperation with the Secretary of Defense and the Secretary of Energy, should seek to ensure that each service laboratory of the Department of Defense and each national laboratory of the Department of Energy may, acting through the relevant Secretary and in a manner consistent with the missions and commitments of the laboratory—

(1) assist the Director of National Intelligence in all aspects of technical intelligence, including research, applied sciences, analysis, technology evaluation and assessment, and any other aspect that the relevant Secretary considers appropriate;

TITLE II—FEDERAL BUREAU OF INVESTIGATION

SEC. 2001. IMPROVEMENT OF INTELLIGENCE CAPABILITIES OF THE FEDERAL BUREAU OF INVESTIGATION

(b) IMPROVEMENT OF INTELLIGENCE CAPABILITIES.— The Director of the Federal Bureau of Investigation shall continue efforts to improve the intelligence capabilities of the Federal Bureau of Investigation and to develop and maintain within the Bureau a national intelligence workforce.

(c) NATIONAL INTELLIGENCE WORKFORCE.—

(1) In developing and maintaining a national intelligence workforce under subsection (b), the Director of the Federal Bureau of Investigation shall, develop and maintain a specialized and integrated national intelligence workforce consisting of agents, analysts, linguists, and surveillance specialists who are recruited, trained, and rewarded in a manner which ensures the existence within the Federal Bureau of Investigation

an institutional culture with substantial expertise in, and commitment to, the intelligence mission of the Bureau.

(2) Each agent employed by the Bureau after the date of the enactment of this Act shall receive basic training in both criminal justice matters and national intelligence matters.

(3) Each agent employed by the Bureau after the date of the enactment of this Act shall, to the maximum extent practicable, be given the opportunity to undergo, during such agent's early service with the Bureau, meaningful assignments in criminal justice

(7) Commencing as soon as practicable after the date of the enactment of this Act, each direct supervisor of a Field Intelligence Group, and each Bureau Operational Manager at the Section Chief and Assistant Special Agent in Charge (ASAC) level and above, shall be a certified intelligence officer.

(d) FIELD OFFICE MATTERS.— (1) In improving the intelligence capabilities of the Federal Bureau of Investigation under subsection (b), the Director of the Federal Bureau of Investigation shall ensure that each Field Intelligence Group reports directly to a field office senior manager responsible for intelligence matters.

SEC. 2002. DIRECTORATE OF INTELLIGENCE OF THE FEDERAL BUREAU OF INVESTIGATION

(a) DIRECTORATE OF INTELLIGENCE OF FEDERAL BUREAU OF INVESTIGATION— The element of the Federal Bureau of Investigation known as of the date of the enactment of this Act as the Office of Intelligence is hereby redesignated as the Directorate of Intelligence of the Federal Bureau of Investigation.

(b) HEAD OF DIRECTORATE— The head of the Directorate of Intelligence shall be the Executive Assistant Director for Intelligence of the Federal Bureau of Investigation.

(c) RESPONSIBILITIES— The Directorate of Intelligence shall be responsible for the following:

(1) Supervision of all national intelligence programs, projects, and activities of the Bureau.

(2) The discharge by the Bureau of the requirements in section 105B of the National Security Act of 1947 (50 U.S.C. 403–5b).

(3) The oversight of Bureau field intelligence operations.

(6) Strategic analysis.

(7) Intelligence program and budget management.

(8) The intelligence workforce.

TITLE VI—TERRORISM PREVENTION

Subtitle A—Individual Terrorists as Agents of Foreign Powers

SEC. 6001. INDIVIDUAL TERRORISTS AS AGENTS OF FOREIGN POWERS.

(a) IN GENERAL—Section 101(b)(1) of the Foreign Intelligence Surveillance Act of 1978 (50 U.S.C. 1801(b)(1)) is amended by adding at the end the following new subparagraph:

"(C) engages in international terrorism or activities in preparation therefore; or".

[This change expands the definition of "agent of a foreign power."]

Implementing Recommendations of the 9/11 Commission Act of 2007, August 3, 2007

TITLE VI—CONGRESSIONAL OVERSIGHT OF INTELLIGENCE

SEC. 603. SENSE OF THE SENATE REGARDING A REPORT ON THE 9/11 COMMISSION RECOMMENDATIONS WITH RESPECT TO INTELLIGENCE REFORM AND CONGRESSIONAL INTELLIGENCE OVERSIGHT REFORM

(a) FINDINGS.— Congress makes the following findings:

(2) In its final report, the 9/11 Commission found that—

(A) congressional oversight of the intelligence activities of the United States is dysfunctional;

(B) under the rules of the Senate and the House of Representatives in effect at the time the report was completed, the committees of Congress charged with oversight of the intelligence activities lacked the power, influence, and sustained capability to meet the daunting challenges faced by the intelligence community of the United States;

(C) as long as such oversight is governed by such rules of the Senate and the House of Representatives, the people of the United States will not get the security they want and need;

(D) a strong, stable, and capable congressional committee structure is needed to give the intelligence community of the United States appropriate oversight, support, and leadership; and

(E) the reforms recommended by the 9/11 Commission in its final report will not succeed if congressional oversight of the intelligence community in the United States is not changed.

(3) The 9/11 Commission recommended structural changes to Congress to improve the oversight of intelligence activities.

(4) Congress has enacted some of the recommendations made by the 9/11 Commission and is considering implementing additional recommendations of the 9/11 Commission.

(5) The Senate adopted Senate Resolution 445 in the 108th Congress to address some of the intelligence oversight recommendations of the 9/11 Commission by abolishing term limits for the members of the Select Committee on Intelligence, clarifying jurisdiction for intelligence-related nominations, and streamlining procedures for the referral of intelligence-related legislation, but other aspects of the 9/11 Commission recommendations regarding intelligence oversight have not been implemented.

Protect America Act of 2007, August 5, 2007

SEC. 2. ADDITIONAL PROCEDURE FOR AUTHORIZING CERTAIN ACQUISITIONS OF FOREIGN INTELLIGENCE INFORMATION

The Foreign Intelligence Surveillance Act of 1978 (50 U.S.C. 1801 et seq.) is amended by inserting after section 105 the following:

"CLARIFICATION OF ELECTRONIC SURVEILLANCE OF PERSONS OUTSIDE THE UNITED STATES

Sec. 105A.

"Nothing in the definition of electronic surveillance under section 101(f) shall be construed to encompass surveillance directed at a person reasonably believed to be located outside of the United States.

"ADDITIONAL PROCEDURE FOR AUTHORIZING CERTAIN ACQUISITIONS CONCERNING PERSONS LOCATED OUTSIDE THE UNITED STATES

Sec. 105B.

"(a) Notwithstanding any other law, the Director of National Intelligence and the Attorney General, may for periods of up to one year authorize the acquisition of foreign intelligence information concerning persons reasonably believed to be outside the United States if the Director of National Intelligence and the Attorney General determine, based on the information provided to them, that–

'(1) there are reasonable procedures in place for determining that the acquisition of foreign intelligence information under this section concerns persons reasonably believed to be located outside the United States, and such procedures will be subject to review of the Court pursuant to section 105C of this Act;

'(2) the acquisition does not constitute electronic surveillance;

'(3) the acquisition involves obtaining the foreign intelligence information from or with the assistance of a communications service provider, custodian, or other person (including any officer, employee, agent, or other specified person of such service provider, custodian, or other person) who has access to communications, either as they are transmitted or while they are stored, or equipment that is being or may be used to transmit or store such communications;

'(4) a significant purpose of the acquisition is to obtain foreign intelligence information; and

'(5) the minimization procedures to be used with respect to such acquisition activity meet the definition of minimization procedures under section 101(h).

Executive Order 13462 of February 29, 2008, President's Intelligence Advisory Board and Intelligence Oversight Board

Sec 1. Policy

It is the policy of the United States to ensure that the President and other officers of the United States with responsibility for the security of the Nation and the advancement of its interests have access to accurate, insightful, objective, and timely information concerning the capabilities, intentions, and activities of foreign powers.

Sec. 3. Establishment of the President's Intelligence Advisory Board

(a) There is hereby established, within the Executive Office of the President and exclusively to advise and assist the President as set forth in this order, the President's Intelligence Advisory Board (PIAB).

(b) The PIAB shall consist of not more than 16 members appointed by the President from among individuals who are not employed by the Federal Government.

(d) Members of the PIAB and the Intelligence Oversight Board (IOB) established in section 5 of this order:

  (i) shall serve without any compensation for their work on the PIAB or the IOB; and

  (ii) while engaged in the work of the PIAB or the IOB, may be allowed travel expenses, including per diem in lieu of subsistence. . .

Sec. 4. Functions of the PIAB

Consistent with the policy set forth in section 1 of this order, the PIAB shall have the authority to, as the PIAB determines appropriate, or shall, when directed by the President:

(a) assess the quality, quantity, and adequacy of intelligence collection, of analysis and estimates, and of counterintelligence and other intelligence activities, assess the adequacy of management, personnel and organization in the intelligence community, and review the performance of all agencies of the Federal Government that are engaged in the collection, evaluation, or production of intelligence or the execution of intelligence policy and report the results of such assessments or reviews:

  (i) to the President, as necessary but not less than twice each year; and

  (ii) to the Director of National Intelligence (DNI) and the heads of departments concerned when the PIAB determines appropriate; and

(b) consider and make appropriate recommendations to the President, the DNI, or the head of the department concerned with respect to matters identified to the PIAB by the DNI or the head of a department concerned.

Sec. 5. Establishment of Intelligence Oversight Board

(a) There is hereby established a committee of the PIAB to be known as the Intelligence Oversight Board.

(b) The IOB shall consist of not more than five members of the PIAB who are designated by the President from among members of the PIAB to serve on the IOB.

Sec. 6. Functions of the IOB

Consistent with the policy set forth in section 1 of this order, the IOB shall:

(b) inform the President of intelligence activities that the IOB believes:

  (i) (A) may be unlawful or contrary to Executive Order or presidential directive; and (B) are not being

adequately addressed by the Attorney General, the DNI, or the head of the department concerned; or

  (ii) should be immediately reported to the President.

(c) review and assess the effectiveness, efficiency, and sufficiency of the processes by which the DNI and the heads of departments concerned perform their respective functions under this order and report thereon as necessary, together with any recommendations, to the President and, as appropriate, the DNI and the head of the department concerned;

(d) receive and review information submitted by the DNI under subsection 7(c) of this order and make recommendations thereon, including for any needed corrective action, with respect to such information, and the intelligence activities to which the information relates, as necessary, but not less than twice each year, to the President, the DNI, and the head of the department concerned; and

(e) conduct, or request that the DNI or the head of the department concerned, as appropriate, carry out and report to the IOB the results of, investigations of intelligence activities that the IOB determines are necessary to enable the IOB to carry out its functions under this order.

Sec. 10. Revocation. Executive Order 12863 is Revoked.

FISA Amendments Act of 2008 July 10, 2008

An act to amend the Foreign Intelligence Surveillance Act of 1978 to establish a procedure for authorizing certain acquisitions of foreign intelligence, and for other purposes.

SEC. 1. SHORT TITLE; TABLE OF CONTENTS

(a) **SHORT TITLE.**— This Act may be cited as the "Foreign Intelligence Surveillance Act of 1978 Amendments Act of 2008" or the "FISA Amendments Act of 2008".

TITLE I—FOREIGN INTELLIGENCE SURVEILLANCE

SEC. 101. ADDITIONAL PROCEDURES REGARDING CERTAIN PERSONS OUTSIDE THE UNITED STATES

(a) **IN GENERAL.**— The Foreign Intelligence Surveillance Act of 1978 (50 U.S.C. 1801 et seq.) is amended–

(1) by striking title VII; and

(2) by adding at the end the following:

TITLE VII—ADDITIONAL PROCEDURES REGARDING CERTAIN PERSONS OUTSIDE THE UNITED STATES

Sec. 702. Procedures For Targeting Certain Persons Outside the United States Other than United States Persons

"**(a) AUTHORIZATION.—** Notwithstanding any other provision of law, upon the issuance of an order in accordance with subsection (i)(3) or a determination under subsection (c)(2), the Attorney General and the Director of National Intelligence may authorize jointly, for a period of up to 1 year from the effective date of the authorization, the targeting of persons reasonably believed to be located outside the United States to acquire foreign intelligence information.

"**(b) LIMITATIONS.—** An acquisition authorized under subsection (a)–

"(1) may not intentionally target any person known at the time of acquisition to be located in the United States;

"(2) may not intentionally target a person reasonably believed to be located outside the United States if the purpose of such acquisition is to target a particular, known person reasonably believed to be in the United States;

"(3) may not intentionally target a United States person reasonably believed to be located outside the United States;

"(4) may not intentionally acquire any communication as to which the sender and all intended recipients are known at the time of the acquisition to be located in the United States; and

"(5) shall be conducted in a manner consistent with the fourth amendment to the Constitution of the United States.

Sec. 703. Certain Acquisitions Inside the United States Targeting United States Persons Outside the United States

"**(a)** *Jurisdiction of the Foreign Intelligence Surveillance Court.*

"**(1) IN GENERAL.—** The Foreign Intelligence Surveillance Court shall have jurisdiction to review an application and to enter an order approving the targeting of a United States person reasonably believed to be located outside the United States to acquire foreign intelligence information, if the acquisition constitutes electronic surveillance or the acquisition of stored electronic communications or stored electronic data that requires an order under this Act, and such acquisition is conducted within the United States.

"**(2) LIMITATION.—** If a United States person targeted under this subsection is reasonably believed to be located in the United States during the effective period of an order issued pursuant to subsection (c), an acquisition targeting such United States person under this section shall cease unless the targeted United States person is again reasonably believed to be located outside the United States while an order issued pursuant to subsection (c) is in effect.

"**(b)** *Application.*

"**(1) IN GENERAL.—** Each application for an order under this section shall be made by a Federal officer in writing upon oath or affirmation to a judge having jurisdiction under subsection (a)(1). Each application shall require the approval of the Attorney General. . . and shall include–

"(A) the identity of the Federal officer making the application;

"(B) the identity, if known, or a description of the United States person who is the target of the acquisition;

"(C) a statement of the facts and circumstances relied upon to justify the applicant's belief that the United States person who is the target of the acquisition is–

"(i) a person reasonably believed to be located outside the United States; and

"(ii) a foreign power, an agent of a foreign power, or an officer or employee of a foreign power;

"(D) a statement of proposed minimization procedures. . .

"(E) a description of the nature of the information sought and the type of communications or activities to be subjected to acquisition;

"(F) a certification made by the Attorney General. . . that–

"(i) the certifying official deems the information sought to be foreign intelligence information;

"(ii) a significant purpose of the acquisition is to obtain foreign intelligence information;

"(iii) such information cannot reasonably be obtained by normal investigative techniques;

"(G) a summary statement of the means by which the acquisition will be conducted and whether physical entry is required to effect the acquisition;

"(H) the identity of any electronic communication service provider necessary to effect the acquisition, that the application is not required to identify the specific facilities, places, premises, or property at which the acquisition authorized under this section will be directed or conducted;

"(I) a statement of the facts concerning any previous applications. . .; and

"(J) a statement of the period of time for which the acquisition is required to be maintained, provided that such period of time shall not exceed 90 days per application.

"(2) PROBABLE CAUSE.— In determining whether or not probable cause exists for purposes of paragraph (1)(B), a judge having jurisdiction under subsection (a)(1) may consider past activities of the target and facts and circumstances relating to current or future activities of the target. No United States person may be considered a foreign power, agent of a foreign power, or officer or employee of a foreign power solely upon the basis of activities protected by the first amendment to the Constitution of the United States.

"(d) *Emergency Authorization.*

"(1) AUTHORITY FOR EMERGENCY AUTHORIZATION.— Notwithstanding any other provision of this Act, if the Attorney General reasonably determines that–

"(A) an emergency situation exists with respect to the acquisition of foreign intelligence information for which an order may be obtained under subsection (c) before an order authorizing such acquisition can with due diligence be obtained. . .

"(3) TERMINATION OF EMERGENCY AUTHORIZATION.— In the absence of a judicial order approving an acquisition under paragraph (1), such acquisition shall terminate when the information sought is obtained, when the application for the order is denied, or after the expiration of 7 days from the time of authorization by the Attorney General, whichever is earliest.

"(e) *Release From Liability.* No cause of action shall lie in any court against any electronic communication service provider for providing any information, facilities, or assistance in accordance with an order or request for emergency assistance. . .

Sec. 704. Other Acquisitions Targeting United States Persons Outside the United States

"(a) *Jurisdiction and Scope.*

"(2) SCOPE.— No element of the intelligence community may intentionally target, for the purpose of acquiring foreign intelligence information, a United States person reasonably believed to be located outside the United States under circumstances in which the targeted United States person has a reasonable expectation of privacy and a warrant would be required if the acquisition were conducted inside the United States for law enforcement purposes, unless a judge of the Foreign Intelligence Surveillance Court has entered an order with respect to such targeted United States person or the Attorney General has authorized an emergency acquisition pursuant to subsection (c) or (d), respectively, or any other provision of this Act.

"(3) LIMITATIONS.

"(A) *MOVING OR MISIDENTIFIED TARGETS.—* If a United States person targeted under this subsection is reasonably believed to be located in the United States during the effective period of an order issued pursuant to subsection (c), an acquisition targeting such United States person under this section shall cease unless the targeted United States person is again reasonably believed to be located outside the United States during the effective period of such order.

Sec. 705. Joint Applications and Concurrent Authorizations

"(a) *Joint Applications and Orders.* If an acquisition targeting a United States person under section 703 or 704 is proposed to be conducted both inside and outside the United States, a judge having jurisdiction under section 703(a)(1) or 704(a)(1) may issue simultaneously, upon the request of the Government in a joint application complying with the requirements of sections 703(b) and 704(b), orders under sections 703(c) and 704(c), as appropriate.

TITLE VII—ADDITIONAL PROCEDURES REGARDING CERTAIN PERSONS OUTSIDE THE UNITED STATES

SEC. 102. STATEMENT OF EXCLUSIVE MEANS BY WHICH ELECTRONIC SURVEILLANCE AND INTERCEPTION OF CERTAIN COMMUNICATIONS MAY BE CONDUCTED

(a) *Statement of Exclusive Means.* Title I of the Foreign Intelligence Surveillance Act of 1978 (50 U.S.C. 1801 et seq.) is amended by adding at the end the following new section:

"statement of exclusive means by which electronic surveillance and interception of certain communications may be conducted. . ."

"Sec. 112. (a) Except as provided in subsection (b), the procedures of chapters 119, 121, and 206 of title 18,

United States Code, and this Act shall be the exclusive means by which electronic surveillance and the interception of domestic wire, oral, or electronic communications may be conducted.

SEC. 107. AMENDMENTS FOR PHYSICAL SEARCHES

(a) *Applications.* Section 303 of the Foreign Intelligence Surveillance Act of 1978 (50 U.S.C. 1823) is amended–

"(e)(1) Notwithstanding any other provision of this title, the Attorney General may authorize the emergency employment of a physical search if the Attorney General–

"(A) reasonably determines that an emergency situation exists ... before an order authorizing such physical search can with due diligence be obtained;

SEC. 108. AMENDMENTS FOR EMERGENCY PEN REGISTERS AND TRAP AND TRACE DEVICES

Section 403 of the Foreign Intelligence Surveillance Act of 1978 (50 U.S.C. 1843) is amended—

(1) in subsection (a)(2), by striking "48 hours" and inserting "7 days"; and

(2) (2) in subsection (c)(1)(C), by striking "48 hours" and inserting "7 days".

TITLE II—PROTECTIONS FOR ELECTRONIC COMMUNICATION SERVICE PROVIDERS

SEC. 201. PROCEDURES FOR IMPLEMENTING STATUTORY DEFENSES UNDER THE FOREIGN INTELLIGENCE SURVEILLANCE ACT OF 1978

The Foreign Intelligence Surveillance Act of 1978 (50 U.S.C. 1801 et seq.), as amended by section 101, is further amended by adding at the end the following new title:

TITLE VIII—PROTECTION OF PERSONS ASSISTING THE GOVERNMENT

Sec. 802. Procedures For Implementing Statutory Defenses

"**(a)** *Requirement for Certification.* Notwithstanding any other provision of law, a civil action may not lie or be maintained in a Federal or State court against any person for providing assistance to an element of the intelligence community, and shall be promptly dismissed, if the Attorney General certifies to the district court of the United States in which such action is pending that–

"(1) any assistance by that person was provided pursuant to an order of the court established under section 103(a) directing such assistance;

"(2) any assistance by that person was provided pursuant to a certification in writing under section 2511(2)(a)(ii)(B) or 2709(b) of title 18, United States Code;

"(3) any assistance by that person was provided pursuant to a directive under section 102(a)(4), 105B(e), as added by section 2 of the Protect America Act of 2007 (Public Law 110-55), or 702(h) directing such assistance;

"(4) in the case of a covered civil action, the assistance alleged to have been provided by the electronic communication service provider was–

"(A) in connection with an intelligence activity involving communications that was–

"(i) authorized by the President during the period beginning on September 11, 2001, and ending on January 17, 2007; and

"(ii) designed to detect or prevent a terrorist attack, or activities in preparation for a terrorist attack, against the United States; and

"(B) the subject of a written request or directive, or a series of written requests or directives, from the Attorney General or the head of an element of the intelligence community (or the deputy of such person) to the electronic communication service provider indicating that the activity was–

"(i) authorized by the President; and

"(ii) determined to be lawful; or

"(5) the person did not provide the alleged assistance.

Sec. 803. Preemption

"**(a) IN GENERAL.**— No State shall have authority to–

"(1) conduct an investigation into an electronic communication service provider's alleged assistance to an element of the intelligence community;

"(2) require through regulation or any other means the disclosure of information about an electronic communication service provider's alleged assistance to an element of the intelligence community;

"(3)   impose any administrative sanction on an electronic communication service provider for assistance to an element of the intelligence community; or

"(4)   commence or maintain a civil action or other proceeding to enforce a requirement that an electronic communication service provider disclose information concerning alleged assistance to an element of the intelligence community.

"(b)   SUITS BY THE UNITED STATES.—The United States may bring suit to enforce the provisions of this section.

Executive Order 13475 Of October 7, 2008
Further Amendments To Executive Orders 12139
And 12949 In Light Of The Foreign Intelligence
Surveillance Act Of 1978, Amendments Act Of 2008

SEC. 1.

Section 1–103 of Executive Order 12139 of May 23, 1979, as amended, is further amended by:

(b)   adding after subsection (h) "(i) Deputy Director of the Federal Bureau of Investigation."; and

(c)   by adding after the sentence that begins "None of the above officials . . .", a new sentence to read "The requirement of the preceding sentence that the named official must be appointed by the President with the advice and consent of the Senate does not apply to the Deputy Director of the Federal Bureau of Investigation."

SEC. 2.

Section 3 of Executive Order 12949 of February 9, 1995, as amended, is further amended by:

(d)   adding after subsection (h) "(i) Deputy Director of the Federal Bureau of Investigation."; and

(e)   by adding after the sentence that begins "None of the above officials . . .", a new sentence to read "The requirement of the preceding sentence that the named official must be appointed by the President with the advice and consent of the Senate does not apply to the Deputy Director of the Federal Bureau of Investigation."

The National Intelligence Strategy August 2009

VISION FOR THE INTELLIGENCE COMMUNITY
The United States Intelligence Community must constantly

strive for and exhibit three characteristics essential to our effectiveness. The IC must be *integrated*: a team making the whole greater than the sum of its parts. We must also be *agile*: an enterprise with an adaptive, diverse, continually learning, and mission-driven intelligence workforce that embraces innovation and takes initiative. Moreover, the IC must *exemplify America's values*: operating under the rule of law, consistent with Americans' expectations for protection of privacy and civil liberties, respectful of human rights, and in a manner that retains the trust of the American people.

GOALS AND OBJECTIVES The Intelligence Community has four strategic goals. In order to meet them, we must operate effectively regardless of where the intelligence resides, with a clear legal framework to guide us. The first two goals, supported by six Mission Objectives (MOs), speak to the missions we must accomplish. The third and fourth goals, supported by seven Enterprise Objectives (EOs), describe what we will achieve as an intelligence enterprise to support our Mission Objectives.

- *Enable wise national security policies* by continuously monitoring and assessing the international security environment to warn policymakers of threats and inform them of opportunities. . .
- *Support effective national security action.* The IC will deliver actionable intelligence to support diplomats, military units, interagency organizations in the field, and domestic law enforcement organizations at all levels. . .
- Deliver balanced and improving capabilities that leverage the diversity of the Community's unique competencies and evolve to support new missions and operating concepts. . .
- Operate as a single integrated team, employing collaborative teams that leverage the full range of IC capabilities to meet the requirements of our users, from the President to deployed military units.

MISSION OBJECTIVES

MO 1: Combat Violent Extremism

Understand, monitor, and disrupt violent extremist groups..

- *Provide warning.*
- *Disrupt plans.*
- *Prevent WMD terrorism.*
- *Counter radicalization.*

MO 2: Counter WMD Proliferation

- *Enhance dissuasion.*

- *Support prevention.*
- *Enable rollback.* Identify opportunities and levers that the United States and its allies can use to end or roll back WMD or capabilities that raise serious concerns.
- *Enhance deterrence.*

MO 3: Provide Strategic Intelligence and Warning

Warn of strategic trends and events so that policymakers, military officials, and civil authorities can effectively deter, prevent, or respond to threats and take advantage of opportunities. . .

In particular, the IC must:

- *Broaden expertise.*
- *Deepen understanding.*
- *Enhance outreach.*
- *Improve collaboration.*
- *Increase language skills.*

MO 4: Integrate Counterintelligence

Our CI community must build on its current efforts and focus in four areas:

- *Detect insider threats.*
- *Penetrate foreign services. . .*
- *Integrate CI with cyber.*
- *Assure the supply chain.*

MO 5: Enhance Cybersecurity

- *Leverage partnerships.*
- *Protect U.S. infrastructure.*
- *Combat cyber threats to non-traditional targets.*
- *Manage the cyber mission.*

MO 6: Support Current Operations

Support ongoing diplomatic, military, and law enforcement operations, especially counterinsurgency; security, stabilization, transition, and reconstruction; international counternarcotics; and border security.

. . . Three areas deserve focus:

- *Monitor time-sensitive targets.*
- *Forward deploy collection and analytic presence.* Embed Community analysts in operational settings as part and parcel of an integrated enterprise approach.
- *Share information.*

ENDNOTES

1. U.S. Constitution, Amendments. http://www.law.cornell.edu/constitution/constitution.table.html#amendments.
2. National Security Act of 1947, (Chapter 343; 61 Stat. 496; approved July 26, 1947) [As Amended Through P.L. 110–53, Enacted August 3, 2007], Unofficial Version. http://intelligence.senate.gov/nsaact1947.pdf.
3. Title III of the Omnibus Crime Control and Safe Streets Act of 1968, Wiretapping and Electronic Surveillance, P.L. 90–351, June 19, 1968. http://www.fcc.gov/Bureaus/OSEC/library/legislative_histories/1615.pdf.
4. Executive Order 12139–Foreign intelligence electronic surveillance of May 23, 1979, 44 FR 30311, 3 CFR, 1979 Comp., p. 397, unless otherwise noted. http://www.archives.gov/federal-register/codification/executive-order/12139.html.
5. Executive Order 12333–United States intelligence activities, Dec. 4, 1981, 46 FR 59941, 3 CFR, 1981 Comp., p. 200, unless otherwise noted. https://www.cia.gov/about-cia/eo12333.html.
6. Electronic Communications Privacy Act of 1986, Public law 99–508, 18 U.S.C. § 2510–22, Title 18, Part 1, Chapter 119—Wire And Electronic Communications Interception And Interception Of Oral Communications, October 21, 1986. E-Government Act of 2002.
7. Patriot Act, 2001, October 26, 2001. http://thomas.loc.gov/cgi-bin/bdquery/z?d107:hr03162:%5D.
8. E-Government Act of 2002, Public Law 107–347. http://thomas.loc.gov/cgi-bin/query/z?c107:H.R.2458.ENR.
9. Intelligence Reform and Terrorism Prevention Act Of 2004, (IRTPA), December 17, 2004, Public Law 108–458. http://frwebgate.access.gpo.gov/cgi-bin/getdoc.cgi?dbname=108_cong_public_laws&docid=f:publ458.108.pdf.
10. Implementing Recommendations Of The 9/11 Commission Act Of 2007, August 3, 2007, Public Law 110–53. http://www.nctc.gov/docs/ir-of-the-9-11-comm-act-of- 2007.pdf.
11. Protect America Act of 2007, August 5, 2007, Public Law 110–55. http://intelligence.senate.gov/laws/pl11055.pdf.
12. Executive Order 13462 of February 29, 2008, President's Intelligence Advisory Board and Intelligence Oversight Board, Federal Register, Vol. 73, No. 43. http://edocket.access.gpo.gov/2008/pdf/08-970.pdf.
13. FISA Amendments Act of 2008, July 10, 2008. http://frwebgate.access.gpo.gov/cgi-bin/getdoc.cgi?dbname=110_cong_public_laws&docid=f:publ261.110.
14. Executive Order 13475 of October 7, 2008, Further Amendments to Executive Orders 12139 And 12949 In Light of the Foreign Intelligence Surveillance Act of 1978, Amendments Act of 2008, Federal Register,

Vol. 73, No. 198. http://www.fas.org/irp/offdocs/eo-13475.htm.

15. The National Intelligence Strategy, August 2009. http://www.dni.gov/reports/2009_NIS.pdf.

16. U.S. Constitution, Amendments, 1791. http://www.law.cornell.edu/constitution/constitution.table.html#amendments.

17. Electronic Communications Privacy Act of 1986, Public Law 99–508, 18 U.S.C. § 2510–22, Title 18, Part 1, Chapter 119—Wire And Electronic Communications Interception And Interception Of Oral Communications, October 21, 1986.

18. "The Foreign Intelligence Surveillance Act: An Overview of the Statutory Framework and Recent Judicial Decisions," Updated September 22, 2004, by Elizabeth B. Bazan, CRS RL30465. http://www.fas.org/irp/crs/RL30465.pdf.

19. E-Government Act of 2002. http://thomas.loc.gov/cgi-bin/query/z?c107:H.R.2458.ENR.

ADDITIONAL RESOURCES

"Not a Suicide Pact, The Constitution in a Time of National Emergency," by Richard A. Posner, Oxford University Press, 2006.

The Federation of American Scientists maintains a webpage with extensive reporting about FISA and its amendments. It includes references to numerous Congressional Research Service publications, ACLU motions in legal challenges to FISA amendments and the Government's responses, congressional hearings and individual statements, and more. http://www.fas.org/irp/agency/doj/fisa.

The American Civil Liberties Union maintains a website with a great deal of information about National Security Letters and related issues. http://www.aclu.org/ safefree/ nationalsecurityletters/index.html.

Duke University also maintains a comprehensive website with the heading Civil Liberties Online. It has sections entitled Civil Liberties in Wartime, Surveillance Power, Prosecutorial Tools, Institutional Capacity, Civil Liberties Safeguards, Financial Reporting, Border Control, Beyond the PATRIOT Act, and others. For FISA, there are separate analyses for Surveillance of Wire Communication, Oral Communication and Electronic Communications, Access to Communications, Access to Business Records Held in Third Party Storage, Physical Searches, Other Surveillance Provisions, Streamlining Surveillance Powers, and Reporting Requirements related to the Government's Use of its USA PATRIOT Act Powers. http://www.law.duke.edu/publiclaw/civil/index.php?action=showtopic&topicid=2.

The Center for National Security Studies maintains a website devoted to FISA that includes hearings, committee reports, lists and descriptions of FISA amendments, and FISA Court rulings. http://www.cnss.org/fisa.htm.

2009 Intelligence Community Legal Reference Book, Office of the Director of National Intelligence/Office of General Counsel,

[large file]. This more than 900 page book is an 'everything in one place' resource. Summer 2009. http://www.dni.gov/ reports/IC_Legal_Ref_2009.pdf

"Government Collection of Private Information: Background and Issues Related to the USA PATRIOT Act Reauthorization," by Anna C. Henning, Elizabeth B. Bazan, Charles Doyle, and Edward C. Liu, December 23, 2009, Congressional Research Service R40980. http://opencrs.com/document/R40980/.

FBI Domestic Investigations and Operations Guide (DIOG). www.fbi.gov. The DIOG establishes the FBI's internal rules and procedures to implement the *Attorney General's Guidelines for Domestic FBI Operations* (AGG-Dom), which are posted on the Department of Justice's website, www.usdoj.gov. September 25, 2009.

"This briefing book attempts to provide you with the foundation to improve your knowledge of intelligence issues. The memos in this book give you important basic information about the Intelligence Community and outline the central issues you will likely encounter during your time in Congress..." Introductory letter from Bob Graham. "Confrontation or Collaboration? Congress and the Intelligence Community," Eric Rosenbach and Aki J. Peritz, Harvard Kennedy School, John F. Kennedy School of Government, Belfer Center for Science and International Affairs, September 2009. http://belfercenter.ksg.harvard.edu/files/IC-book-finalasof12JUNE.pdf.

"Intelligence Community Legal Reference Book," Office of the Director of National Intelligence and the Office of General Counsel. This 900 + page book has most if not all intelligence related resources in one place. http://www.dni.gov/reports/IC_Legal_Ref_2009.pdf.

US Attorneys Manual, 9-7.000 Electronic Surveillance. http://www.usdoj.gov/usao/eousa/foia_reading_room/usam/title9/7mcrm.htm.

"Security, At What Cost? Quantifying People's Trade-offs Across Liberty, Privacy and Security," by Neil Robinson, Dimitris Potoglou, Chong Woo Kim, Peter Burge, Richard Warnes, Rand Corporation, 2010. http://rand.org/pubs/ technical_reports/2010/RAND_TR664.pdf.

"Amendments to the Foreign Intelligence Surveillance Act Set to Expire in 2009," by Anna C. Henning and Edward C. Liu, Congressional Research Service, R40138, October 29, 2009. http://opencrs.com/document/R40138/.

"National Security Letters: Proposed Amendments in the 111th Congress," Charles Doyle, Congressional Research Service, R40887, October 28, 2009. http://opencrs.com/document/R40887/.

"Improving Homeland Security at the State Level - Needed: State-level, Integrated Intelligence Enterprises," by James E. Steiner, Central Intelligence Agency, September 2009, Studies in Intelligence, Vol. 53, no. 3. https://www.cia.gov/library/center-for-the-study-of-intelligence/csi-publications/csi-studies/studies/vol.-53-no.-3/index.html.

"The U.S. Intelligence Community and Foreign Policy: Getting Analysis Right," Kenneth G. Lieberthal, The Brookings Institution, September 2009. http://www.brookings.edu/papers/2009/09_intelligence_community_lieberthal.aspx.

For a particularly detailed and thorough (87 page) examination of FISA and the amendments see "The Foreign Intelligence Surveillance Act: An Overview of the Statutory Framework and Recent Judicial Decisions," Updated September 22, 2004, by Elizabeth B. Bazan, CRS RL30465. http://www.fas.org/irp/crs/RL30465.pdf.

For a less detailed review (5 pages), see "The USA PATRIOT Act: A Sketch," April 18, 2002, by Charles Doyle, CRS RS21203. http://www.fas.org/irp/crs/RS21203.pdf.

"What Really Is At Stake With The FISA Amendments Act Of 2008 And Ideas For Future Surveillance Reform," by Stephanie Cooper Blum, 18 B.U. Pub. Int. L.J. 269, 2009.

"Improving Development and Utilization of U.S. Air Force Intelligence Officers," by Marygail K. Brauner, Hugh G. Massey, S. Craig Moore, Darren D. Medlin, Rand, 2009. http://www.rand.org/pubs/technical_reports/2009/RAND_TR628.pdf.

"Intelligence Issues for Congress," Richard A. Best Jr., July 24, 2009, Congressional Research Service, RL33539. http://opencrs.com/document/RL33539/2009-07-24/.

"Confrontation or Collaboration?: Congress and the Intelligence Community, Background Memos on the Intelligence Community, July 2009," Belfer Center for Science and International Affairs. http://belfercenter.ksg.harvard.edu/publication/19201/confrontation_or_collaboration_congress_and_the_intelligence_community.html.

"The "Overview of the Privacy Act of 1974" is a discussion of the Privacy Act's disclosure prohibitions, its access and amendment provisions, and its agency recordkeeping requirements. . ." "Overview of the Privacy Act of 1974," United States Department of Justice, Office of Privacy and Civil Liberties. http://www.usdoj.gov/opcl/1974privacyact-overview.htm.

"The National Security Council: An Organizational Assessment," by Richard A. Best Jr., June 8, 2009, Congressional Research Service, RL30840. http://www.fas.org/sgp/crs/natsec/RL30840.pdf.

"The State Secrets Privilege and Other Limits on Litigation Involving Classified Information," Edward C. Liu, CRS, May 28, 2009, R40603. http://opencrs.com/document/R40603/.

DHS Press Release.

"Homeland Security Secretary Janet Napolitano announced yesterday that she will kill a controversial Bush administration program to expand the use of spy satellites by domestic law enforcement and other agencies.

Napolitano said she acted after state and local law enforcement officials said that access to secret overhead imagery was not a priority.

Two years ago, President George W. Bush's top intelligence and homeland security officials authorized the National Applications Office (NAO) to expand sharing of satellite data with domestic agencies. But congressional Democrats barred funding for what they said could become a new platform for domestic surveillance that would raise privacy and civil liberties concerns.

Earlier this month, House Democrats expressed surprise that Obama included funding for the program in the classified portion of the Department of Homeland Security's 2010 budget, and they threatened to kill the office.

"The Secretary's decision is an endorsement of this Committee's long-held position," Rep. Bennie G. Thompson (D-Miss.), chairman of the House Homeland Security Committee, said in a statement.

Wednesday, June 24th [2009] Morning Roundup - Featured News and Public Events, "From the Washington Post, on Secretary Napolitano's decision to end the National Applications Office program:" http://www.dhs.gov/journal/theblog/2009_06_01_archive.html.

Defending the City: NYPD's Counterterrorism Operations, June 23, 2009, The Washington Institute for Near East Policy. http://www.washingtoninstitute.org/templateC07.php?CID=469.

"Global Metropolitan Policing: An Emerging Trend in Intelligence Sharing," John P. Sullivan and James J. Wirtz, Homeland Security Journal, Vol. V, No. 2, May 2009. http://www.hsaj.org/?fullarticle=5.2.4.

Second Circuit Partially Invalidates National Security Letters Section of the Patriot Act on First Amendment Grounds, Author: José Mauro Decoussau Machado, February 2, 2009, Stanford Law School, The Center for Internet and Society. http://cyberlaw.stanford.edu/packet/200902/second-circuit-partially-invalidates-national-security-letters-section.

"Homeland Security Intelligence: Perceptions, Statutory Definitions, and Approaches," Mark A. Randol, January 14, 2009, CRS RL33616. http://fas.org/sgp/crs/intel/RL33616.pdf.

"Court Rules Patriot Act's "National Security Letter" Gag Provisions Unconstitutional," (12/15/2008), American Civil Liberties Union. http://www.aclu.org/safefree/nsaspying/38113prs20081215.html.

"National Security Letters in Foreign Intelligence Investigations: A Glimpse of the Legal Background and Recent Amendments," by Charles Doyle, March 28, 2008, CRS RS22406. http://fas.org/sgp/crs/intel/RS22406.pdf.

"US Intelligence Community Reform Studies Since 1947," Michael Warner and J. Kenneth Mcdonald, Strategic Management Issues Office, Center for the Study of Intelligence, Washington, DC, April 2005. https://www.cia.gov/library/center-for-the-study-of-intelligence/csi-publications/books-and-monographs/US%20Intelligence%20Community%20Reform%20Studies%20Since%201947.pdf.

5

THE DEPARTMENT OF HOMELAND SECURITY

The Department of Homeland Security's overriding and urgent mission is to lead the unified national effort to secure the country and preserve our freedoms.[1]

The Department of Homeland Security (DHS) was created by the Homeland Security Act of 2002. It is a vast and powerful agency with extraordinary responsibility. DHS incorporated FEMA and 24 other preexisting agencies, or parts of them, and more than 180,000 employees. Because of its size and because every agency brought its own culture and equipment, DHS has had growing pains.[2,3,4] This chapter follows its statutory creation and describes its mandate and limitations.

SOURCES

- Road Map for National Security: Imperative for Change, February 15, 2001[5]
- Homeland Security Act of 2002, November 25, 2002[6]
- USA PATRIOT Improvement and Reauthorization Act of 2005[7]
- Executive Order 13397—Responsibilities of the Department of Homeland Security With Respect to Faith-Based and Community Initiatives, Thursday, March 9, 2006[8]
- The Post-Katrina Emergency Management Reform Act of 2006[9]
- U.S. Department Of Homeland Security Strategic Plan, Fiscal Years 2008–2013[10]

Foundations of Homeland Security: Law and Policy, First Edition. Martin J. Alperen.
© 2011 John Wiley & Sons, Inc. Published 2011 by John Wiley & Sons, Inc.

Road Map for National Security: Imperative For Change, February 15, 2001

Executive Summary. After our examination of the new strategic environment of the next quarter century (Phase I) and of a strategy to address it (Phase II), this Commission concludes that *significant changes must be made in the structures and processes of the U.S. national security apparatus*. Our institutional base is in decline and must be rebuilt. Otherwise, the United States risks losing its global influence and critical leadership role.

Securing the National Homeland. The combination of unconventional weapons proliferation with the persistence of international terrorism will end the relative invulnerability of the U.S. homeland to catastrophic attack. A direct attack against American citizens *on American soil* is likely over the next quarter century.

We therefore recommend the creation of an independent National Homeland Security Agency (NHSA) with responsibility for planning, coordinating, and integrating various U.S. government activities involved in homeland security. NHSA would be built upon the Federal Emergency Management Agency, with the three organizations currently on the front line of border security—the Coast Guard, the Customs Service, and the Border Patrol—transferred to it. NHSA would not only protect American lives, but also assume responsibility for overseeing the protection of the nation's critical infrastructure, including information technology.

The NHSA Director would have Cabinet status and would be a statutory advisor to the National Security Council. The legal foundation for the National Homeland Security Agency would rest firmly within the array of Constitutional guarantees for civil liberties.

The potentially catastrophic nature of homeland attacks necessitates our being prepared to use the extensive resources of the Department of Defense (DoD). Therefore, the department needs to pay far more attention to this mission in the future. *We recommend that a new office of Assistant Secretary for Homeland Security be created to oversee DoD activities in this domain and to ensure that the necessary resources are made available.*

New priorities also need to be set for the U.S. armed forces in light of the threat to the homeland. *We urge, in particular, that the National Guard be given homeland security as a primary mission, as the U.S. Constitution itself ordains.* The National Guard should be reorganized, trained, and equipped to undertake that mission.

Recapitalizing America's Strengths in Science and Education. Americans are living off the economic and security benefits of the last three generations' investment in science and education, but we are now consuming capital. Our systems of basic scientific research and education are in serious crisis, while other countries are redoubling their efforts. In the next quarter century, we will likely see ourselves surpassed, and in relative decline, unless we make a conscious national commitment to maintain our edge.

Institutional Redesign. The dramatic changes in the world since the end of the Cold War have not been accompanied by any major institutional changes in the Executive Branch of the U.S. government. Serious deficiencies exist that only a significant organizational redesign can remedy...

Most troublesome is the lack of an overarching strategic framework guiding U.S. national security policymaking and resource allocation. Clear goals and priorities are rarely set. Budgets are prepared and appropriated as they were during the Cold War...

The Department of State, in particular, is a crippled institution, starved for resources by Congress because of its inadequacies, and thereby weakened further...

For this and other reasons, the power to determine national security policy has steadily migrated toward the National Security Council (NSC) staff. The staff now assumes policymaking roles that many observers have warned against. Yet the NSC staff's role as policy coordinator is more urgently needed than ever, given the imperative of integrating the many diverse strands of policymaking.

Meanwhile, the U.S. intelligence community is adjusting only slowly to the changed circumstances of the post-Cold War era...

Finally, the Department of Defense needs to be overhauled. The growth in staff and staff activities has created mounting confusion and delay. The failure to outsource or privatize many defense support activities wastes huge sums of money. The programming and budgeting process is not guided by effective strategic planning. The weapons acquisition process is so hobbled by excessive laws, regulations, and oversight strictures that it can neither recognize nor seize opportunities for major innovation, and its procurement bureaucracy weakens a defense industry that is already in a state of financial crisis...

To reflect how central economics has become in U.S. national security policy, *we recommend that the Secretary of Treasury be named a statutory member of the National Security Council...*

Critical to the future success of U.S. national security policies is a fundamental restructuring of the State Department. Reform must ensure that responsibility and accountability are clearly established, regional and functional activities are closely integrated, foreign assistance programs are centrally planned and implemented, and strategic planning is emphasized and linked to the allocation of resources...

The Role of Congress. While Congress has mandated many changes to a host of Executive Branch departments and agencies over the years, it has not fundamentally reviewed its own role in national security policy. Moreover, it has not reformed its own structure since 1949. At present, for example, every major defense program must be voted upon no fewer than eighteen times each year by an array of committees and subcommittees. This represents a very poor use of time for busy members of the Executive and Legislative Branches...

Homeland Security Act of 2002, November 25, 2002

Sec. 2. Definitions.

In this Act, the following definitions apply:

> (5) The term "Department" means the Department of Homeland Security.
>
> (13) The term "Secretary" means the Secretary of Homeland Security.

TITLE I—DEPARTMENT OF HOMELAND SECURITY

Sec. 101. Executive Department; Mission.

(a) *Establishment.* There is established a Department of Homeland Security, as an executive department of the United States...

(b) *Mission.*

(1) IN GENERAL.— The primary mission of the Department is to—

> (A) prevent terrorist attacks within the United States;
>
> (B) reduce the vulnerability of the United States to terrorism;

(C) minimize the damage, and assist in the recovery, from terrorist attacks that do occur within the United States;

(D) carry out all functions of entities transferred to the Department, including by acting as a focal point regarding natural and manmade crises and emergency planning;

(E) ensure that the functions of the agencies and subdivisions within the Department that are not related directly to securing the homeland are not diminished or neglected except by a specific explicit Act of Congress;

(F) ensure that the overall economic security of the United States is not diminished by efforts, activities, and programs aimed at securing the homeland; and

(G) monitor connections between illegal drug trafficking and terrorism, coordinate efforts to sever such connections, and otherwise contribute to efforts to interdict illegal drug trafficking.

(2) RESPONSIBILITY FOR INVESTIGATING AND PROSECUTING TERRORISM.— Except as specifically provided by law with respect to entities transferred to the Department under this Act, primary responsibility for investigating and prosecuting acts of terrorism shall be vested not in the Department, but rather in Federal, State, and local law enforcement agencies with jurisdiction over the acts in question.

Sec. 102. Secretary; Functions.

(a) *Secretary.*

(1) IN GENERAL.— There is a Secretary of Homeland Security, appointed by the President, by and with the advice and consent of the Senate.

(2) HEAD OF DEPARTMENT.— The Secretary is the head of the Department and shall have direction, authority, and control over it.

(3) FUNCTIONS VESTED IN SECRETARY.— All functions of all officers, employees, and organizational units of the Department are vested in the Secretary.

(d) *Meetings of National Security Council.* The Secretary may, subject to the direction of the President, attend and participate in meetings of the National Security Council.

(f) *Special Assistant to the Secretary.* The Secretary shall appoint a Special Assistant to the Secretary who shall be responsible for—

(1) creating and fostering strategic communications with the private sector to enhance the primary mission of the Department to protect the American homeland;

(2) advising the Secretary on the impact of the Department's policies, regulations, processes, and actions on the private sector;

(3) interfacing with other relevant Federal agencies with homeland security missions to assess the impact of these agencies' actions on the private sector;

(4) creating and managing private sector advisory councils composed of representatives of industries and associations designated by the Secretary to—

(A) advise the Secretary on private sector products, applications, and solutions as they relate to homeland security challenges; and

(B) advise the Secretary on homeland security policies, regulations, processes, and actions that affect the participating industries and associations;

(5) working with Federal laboratories, federally funded research and development centers, other federally funded organizations, academia, and the private sector to develop innovative approaches to address homeland security challenges to produce and deploy the best available technologies for homeland security missions;

(6) promoting existing public-private partnerships and developing new public-private partnerships to provide for collaboration and mutual support to address homeland security challenges; and

(7) assisting in the development and promotion of private sector best practices to secure critical infrastructure.

Sec. 103. Other Officers.

(a) *Deputy Secretary; Under Secretaries.* There are the following officers, appointed by the President, by and with the advice and consent of the Senate:

(1) A Deputy Secretary of Homeland Security, who shall be the Secretary's first assistant for purposes of subchapter III of Chapter 33 of title 5, United States Code.

(2) An Under Secretary for Information Analysis and Infrastructure Protection.

(3) An Under Secretary for Science and Technology.

(4) An Under Secretary for Border and Transportation Security.

(5) An Under Secretary for Emergency Preparedness and Response.

(6) A Director of the Bureau of Citizenship and Immigration Services.

(7) An Under Secretary for Management.

(8) Not more than 12 Assistant Secretaries.

(9) A General Counsel, who shall be the chief legal officer of the Department.

(c) Commandant of the Coast Guard. To assist the Secretary in the performance of the Secretary's functions, there is a Commandant of the Coast Guard...who shall report directly to the Secretary. In addition to such duties as may be provided in this Act and as assigned to the Commandant by the Secretary, the duties of the Commandant shall include those required by section 2 of title 14, United States Code.

TITLE II—INFORMATION ANALYSIS AND INFRASTRUCTURE PROTECTION

Subtitle A—Directorate for Information Analysis and Infrastructure Protection; Access to Information

[See Homeland Security Act Sec. 201 *et. seq.* in Chapter 11, "Critical Infrastructure Protection" for development of DHS in the area of critical infrastructure.]

Sec. 231 Office of Science and Technology.

(a) (1) There is hereby established within the Department of Justice an Office of Science and Technology (hereinafter the "Office").

Sec. 232. Mission Of Office; Duties.

(a) Mission. The mission of the Office shall be—

(1) to serve as the national focal point for work on law enforcement technology; and

(2) to carry out programs that, through the provision of equipment, training, and technical assistance, improve the safety and effectiveness of law enforcement technology and improve access to such technology by Federal, State, and local law enforcement agencies.

(b) Duties. In carrying out its mission, the Office shall have the following duties:

(1) To provide recommendations and advice to the Attorney General.

(2) To establish and maintain advisory groups ... to assess the law enforcement technology needs of Federal, State, and local law enforcement agencies.

(3) To establish and maintain performance standards in accordance with the National Technology Transfer and Advancement Act of 1995 (Public Law 104–113) for, and test and evaluate law enforcement technologies...

(4) To establish and maintain a program to certify, validate, and mark or otherwise recognize law enforcement technology products that conform to standards established and maintained by the Office in accordance with the National Technology Transfer and Advancement Act of 1995 (Public Law 104–113). The program may, at the discretion of the Office, allow for supplier's declaration of conformity with such standards.

(5) To work with other entities within the Department of Justice, other Federal agencies, and the executive office of the President to establish a coordinated Federal approach on issues related to law enforcement technology.

(6) To carry out research, development, testing, evaluation, and cost-benefit analyses in fields that would improve the safety, effectiveness, and efficiency of law enforcement technologies used by Federal, State, and local law enforcement agencies, including, but not limited to—

(A) weapons capable of preventing use by unauthorized persons, including personalized guns;

(B) protective apparel;

(C) bullet-resistant and explosion-resistant glass;

(D) monitoring systems and alarm systems capable of providing precise location information;

(E) wire and wireless interoperable communication technologies;

(F) tools and techniques that facilitate investigative and forensic work, including computer forensics;

(G) equipment for particular use in counterterrorism, including devices and technologies to disable terrorist devices;

(H) guides to assist State and local law enforcement agencies;

(I) DNA identification technologies; and

(J) tools and techniques that facilitate investigations of computer crime.

(7) To administer a program of research, development, testing, and demonstration to improve the interoperability of voice and data public safety communications.

(8) To serve on the Technical Support Working Group of the Department of Defense, and on other relevant interagency panels, as requested.

(9) To develop, and disseminate to State and local law enforcement agencies, technical assistance and training materials for law enforcement personnel, including prosecutors.

(10) To operate the regional National Law Enforcement and Corrections Technology Centers and, to the extent necessary, establish additional centers through a competitive process.

(11) To administer a program of acquisition, research, development, and dissemination of advanced investigative analysis and forensic tools to assist State and local law enforcement agencies in combating cybercrime.

(12) To support research fellowships in support of its mission.

(13) To serve as a clearinghouse for information on law enforcement technologies.

(14) To represent the United States and State and local law enforcement agencies, as requested, in international activities concerning law enforcement technology.

(15) To enter into contracts and cooperative agreements and provide grants, which may require in-kind or cash matches from the recipient, as necessary to carry out its mission. . .

(c) *Competition required.* Except as otherwise expressly provided by law, all research and development carried out by or through the Office shall be carried out on a competitive basis.

Sec. 235. National Law Enforcement And Corrections Technology Centers.

(a) *In General.* The Director of the Office shall operate and support National Law Enforcement and Corrections Technology Centers (hereinafter in this section referred to as "Centers") and, to the extent necessary, establish new centers through a meritbased, competitive process.

TITLE III—SCIENCE AND TECHNOLOGY IN SUPPORT OF HOMELAND SECURITY

Sec. 301. Under Secretary for Science and Technology.

There shall be in the Department a Directorate of Science and Technology headed by an Under Secretary for Science and Technology

Sec. 302. Responsibilities And Authorities Of The Under Secretary For Science And Technology.

The Secretary. . . shall have the responsibility for—

(1) advising the Secretary regarding research and development efforts and priorities in support of the Department's missions;

(2) developing. . .a national policy and strategic plan for, identifying priorities, goals, objectives and policies

for, and coordinating the Federal Government's civilian efforts to identify and develop countermeasures to chemical, biological, radiological, nuclear, and other emerging terrorist threats, including the development of comprehensive, research-based definable goals for such efforts and development of annual measurable objectives and specific targets to accomplish and evaluate the goals for such efforts;

(3) supporting the Under Secretary for Information Analysis and Infrastructure Protection, by assessing and testing homeland security vulnerabilities and possible threats;

(4) conducting basic and applied research, development, demonstration, testing, and evaluation activities that are relevant to any or all elements of the Department, through both intramural and extramural programs, except that such responsibility does not extend to human health-related research and development activities;

(5) establishing priorities for, directing, funding, and conducting national research, development, test and evaluation, and procurement of technology and systems for—

(A) preventing the importation of chemical, biological, radiological, nuclear, and related weapons and material; and

(B) detecting, preventing, protecting against, and responding to terrorist attacks;

(6) establishing a system for transferring homeland security developments or technologies to Federal, State, local government, and private sector entities;

(7) entering into work agreements, joint sponsorships, contracts, or any other agreements with the Department of Energy regarding the use of the national laboratories or sites and support of the science and technology base at those facilities;. . .

(9) collaborating with the Secretary of Health and Human Services and the Attorney General in determining any new biological agents and toxins that shall be listed as "select agents" in Appendix A of part 72 of title 42, Code of Federal Regulations, pursuant to section 351A of the Public Health Service Act (42 U.S.C. 262a);

(10) supporting United States leadership in science and technology;

(11) establishing and administering the primary research and development activities of the Department, including the long-term research and development needs and capabilities for all elements of the Department;

(12) coordinating and integrating all research, development, demonstration, testing, and evaluation activities of the Department;

(13) coordinating with other appropriate executive agencies in developing and carrying out the science and technology agenda of the Department to reduce duplication and identify unmet needs; and

(14) developing and overseeing the administration of guidelines for merit review of research and development projects throughout the Department, and for the dissemination of research conducted or sponsored by the Department.

Sec. 307. Homeland Security Advanced Research Projects Agency.

(a) *Definitions.* In this section: . . .

(2) HOMELAND SECURITY RESEARCH.— The term "homeland security research" means research relevant to the detection of, prevention of, protection against, response to, attribution of, and recovery from homeland security threats, particularly acts of terrorism.

(3) HSARPA.— The term "HSARPA" means the Homeland Security Advanced Research Projects Agency established in subsection (b).

(b) *Homeland Security Advanced Research Projects Agency.*

(1) ESTABLISHMENT.— There is established the Homeland Security Advanced Research Projects Agency. . ..

(3) RESPONSIBILITIES.— The Director shall administer the Fund to award competitive, merit-reviewed grants, cooperative agreements or contracts to public or private entities, including businesses, federally funded research and development centers, and universities. The Director shall administer the Fund to—

(A) support basic and applied homeland security research to promote revolutionary changes in technologies that would promote homeland security;

(B) advance the development, testing and evaluation, and deployment of critical homeland security technologies; and

(C) accelerate the prototyping and deployment of technologies that would address homeland security vulnerabilities.

(2) UNIVERSITY-BASED CENTERS FOR HOMELAND SECURITY.—

(A) *ESTABLISHMENT.—* The Secretary, acting through the Under Secretary for Science and Technology, shall establish within 1 year of the date of enactment of this Act a university-based center or centers for homeland security. The purpose of this center or centers shall be to establish a coordinated,

university-based system to enhance the Nation's homeland security.

(B) CRITERIA FOR SELECTION.— In selecting colleges or universities as centers for homeland security, the Secretary shall consider the following criteria:

(i) Demonstrated expertise in the training of first responders.

(ii) Demonstrated expertise in responding to incidents involving weapons of mass destruction and biological warfare.

(iii) Demonstrated expertise in emergency medical services.

(iv) Demonstrated expertise in chemical, biological, radiological, and nuclear countermeasures.

(v) Strong affiliations with animal and plant diagnostic laboratories.

(vi) Demonstrated expertise in food safety.

(vii) Affiliation with Department of Agriculture laboratories or training centers.

(viii) Demonstrated expertise in water and wastewater operations.

(ix) Demonstrated expertise in port and waterway security.

(x) Demonstrated expertise in multi-modal transportation.

(xi) Nationally recognized programs in information security.

(xii) Nationally recognized programs in engineering.

(xiii) Demonstrated expertise in educational outreach and technical assistance.

(xiv) Demonstrated expertise in border transportation and security.

(xv) Demonstrated expertise in interdisciplinary public policy research and communication outreach regarding science, technology, and public policy. . . .

Sec. 310. Transfer Of Plum Island Animal Disease Center, Department Of Agriculture.

(a) *In General.* In accordance with title XV, the Secretary of Agriculture shall transfer to the Secretary of Homeland Security the Plum Island Animal Disease Center of the Department of Agriculture, including the assets and liabilities of the Center.

Sec. 311. Homeland Security Science and Technology Advisory Committee.

(a) *Establishment.* There is established within the Department a Homeland Security Science and Technology Advisory Committee (in this section referred to as the "Advisory Committee"). The Advisory Committee shall make recommendations with respect to the activities of the Under Secretary for Science and Technology, including identifying research areas of potential importance to the security of the Nation.

Sec. 312. Homeland Security Institute.

(a) *Establishment.* The Secretary shall establish a federally funded research and development center to be known as the "Homeland Security Institute" (in this section referred to as the "Institute").

(b) *Administration.* The Institute shall be administered as a separate entity by the Secretary.

(c) *Duties.* The duties of the Institute shall be determined by the Secretary, and may include the following:

(1) Systems analysis, risk analysis, and simulation and modeling to determine the vulnerabilities of the Nation's critical infrastructures and the effectiveness of the systems deployed to reduce those vulnerabilities.

(2) Economic and policy analysis to assess the distributed costs and benefits of alternative approaches to enhancing security.

(3) Evaluation of the effectiveness of measures deployed to enhance the security of institutions, facilities, and infrastructure that may be terrorist targets.

(4) Identification of instances when common standards and protocols could improve the interoperability and effective utilization of tools developed for field operators and first responders.

(5) Assistance for Federal agencies and departments in establishing testbeds to evaluate the effectiveness of technologies under development and to assess the appropriateness of such technologies for deployment.

(6) Design of metrics and use of those metrics to evaluate the effectiveness of homeland security programs throughout the Federal Government, including all national laboratories.

(7) Design of and support for the conduct of homeland security-related exercises and simulations.

(8) Creation of strategic technology development plans to reduce vulnerabilities in the Nation's critical infrastructure and key resources.

Sec. 313. Technology Clearinghouse To Encourage And Support Innovative Solutions to Enhance Homeland Security.

(a) *Establishment of Program.* The Secretary…shall establish and promote a program to encourage technological innovation in facilitating the mission of the Department (as described in section 101).

TITLE V—EMERGENCY PREPAREDNESS AND RESPONSE

Sec. 501. Under Secretary for Emergency Preparedness and Response.

There shall be in the Department a Directorate of Emergency Preparedness and Response headed by an Under Secretary for Emergency Preparedness and Response.

Sec. 502. Responsibilities.

The Secretary, acting through the Under Secretary for Emergency Preparedness and Response, shall include—

(1) helping to ensure the effectiveness of emergency response providers to terrorist attacks, major disasters, and other emergencies;

(2) with respect to the Nuclear Incident Response Team…
   (A) establishing standards and certifying when those standards have been met;
   (B) conducting joint and other exercises and training and evaluating performance; and
   (C) providing funds to the Department of Energy and the Environmental Protection Agency, as appropriate, for homeland security planning, exercises and training, and equipment;

(3) providing the Federal Government's response to terrorist attacks and major disasters, including—
   (A) managing such response;
   (B) directing the Domestic Emergency Support Team, the Strategic National Stockpile, the National Disaster Medical System, and…the Nuclear Incident Response Team;
   (C) overseeing the Metropolitan Medical Response System; and
   (D) coordinating other Federal response resources in the event of a terrorist attack or major disaster;

(4) aiding the recovery from terrorist attacks and major disasters;

(5) building a comprehensive national incident management system with Federal, State, and local government personnel, agencies, and authorities, to respond to such attacks and disasters;

(6) consolidating existing Federal Government emergency response plans into a single, coordinated national response plan; and

(7) developing comprehensive programs for developing interoperative communications technology, and helping to ensure that emergency response providers acquire such technology.

Sec. 504. Nuclear Incident Response.

(a) *In General.* At the direction of the Secretary (in connection with an actual or threatened terrorist attack, major disaster, or other emergency in the United States), the Nuclear Incident Response Team shall operate as an organizational unit of the Department. While so operating, the Nuclear Incident Response Team shall be subject to the direction, authority, and control of the Secretary.

USA Patriot Improvement and Reauthorization Act of 2005

Sec. 503. Secretary of Homeland Security in Presidential Line of Succession.

Section 19(d)(1) of title 3, United States Code, is amended by inserting, 'Secretary of Homeland Security' after 'Secretary of Veterans Affairs'.

Executive Order 13397—Responsibilities of the Department of Homeland Security With Respect to Faith-Based and Community Initiatives, Thursday, March 9, 2006

Sec. 1. Establishment of a Center for Faith-Based and Community Initiatives at the Department of Homeland Security.

(a) The Secretary of Homeland Security (Secretary) shall establish within the Department of Homeland Security (Department) a Center for Faith-Based and Community Initiatives (Center).

The Post-Katrina Emergency Management Reform Act of 2006

Sec. 845. Homeland Security Education Program.

"(a) *Establishment.* The Secretary, acting through the Administrator, shall establish a graduate-level Homeland Security Education Program in the National Capital Region to provide educational opportunities to senior Federal officials and selected State and local officials with homeland security and emergency management responsibilities. The Administrator shall appoint an individual to administer the activities under this section.

"(c) *Student Enrollment.*

"(1) SOURCES.— The student body of the Program shall include officials from Federal, State, local, and tribal governments, and from other sources designated by the Administrator.

U.S. Department Of Homeland Security Strategic Plan, Fiscal Years 2008–2013

I. *Introduction.* This Department of Homeland Security's overriding and urgent mission is to lead the unified national effort to secure the country and preserve our freedoms. While the Department was created to secure our country against those who seek to disrupt the American way of life, our charter also includes preparation for and response to all hazards and disasters...

The *2008 Strategic Plan* serves to focus the Department's mission and sharpen operational effectiveness, particularly in delivering services in support of Department-wide initiatives and the other mission goals. It identifies the goals and objectives by which we continually assess our performance. The Department uses performance measures at all levels to monitor our strategic progress and program success. This process also keeps the Department's priorities aligned, linking programs and operations to performance measures, mission goals, resource priorities, and strategic objectives.

II. *Vision.* A secure America, a confident public, and a strong and resilient society and economy.

III. *Mission.* We will lead the unified national effort to secure America. We will prevent and deter terrorist attacks and protect against and respond to threats and hazards to the Nation. We will secure our national borders while welcoming lawful immigrants, visitors, and trade.

V. *Guiding Principles.*

Protect Constitutional Rights and American Values.
Use an All-Hazards Approach.
Build Trust through Collaboration and Partnerships.
Apply Risk Management.
Develop a Culture of Preparedness.
Ensure Accountability.
Capitalize on Emerging Technologies.
Work as an Integrated Response Team.
Be Flexible.

VI. *Goals and Objectives.*

(1) Protect Our Nation from Dangerous People
(2) Protect Our Nation from Dangerous Goods
(3) Protect Critical Infrastructure
(4) Strengthen Our Nation's Preparedness and Emergency Response Capabilities
(5) Strengthen and Unify DHS Operations and Management

ENDNOTES

1. One Team, One Mission, Securing Our Homeland. U.S. Department Of Homeland Security Strategic Plan. Fiscal Years 2008–2013. http://www.dhs.gov/xlibrary/assets/DHS_StratPlan_FINAL_spread.pdf.

2. "DHS was bureaucratically set up to fail... [it incorporated] agencies that were broken to begin with..." Dr. Stephen Flynn, lecture at John Hopkins University, Applied Physics Lab, 2009 Unrestricted Warfare Symposium, March 24, 2009.

3. "Since the Department of Homeland Security was created in 2002, the Department has had 7 of its core components spread out among 85 buildings in 53 separate locations. As one would assume, this separation has adversely affected the need for cohesive communication, coordination, and cooperation across Department component agencies as the Department seeks to fulfill its mission. It has also had an impact on the Department's ability to create the "One DHS" culture that Secretary Napolitano referred to in her testimony last month before the full committee... A single unified headquarters that houses the Secretary, senior Department leadership, component heads, and program managers, will significantly aid the Department in fulfilling its mission." Statement of Chairman Bennie G. Thompson, "Consolidating the Department: An Update on the St. Elizabeths Project" March 26, 2009 (Washington), Committee on Homeland Security. http://homeland.house.gov/Hearings/index.asp?ID=182.

4. "Before the establishment of the Department of Homeland Security, homeland security activities were spread across more than 40 federal agencies and an estimated 2,000 separate Congressional appropriations accounts." "Brief Documentary History of the Department of Homeland Security: 2001–2008." http://www.dhs.gov/xlibrary/assets/brief_documentary_history_of_dhs_2001_2008.pdf.

5. "Road Map for National Security: Imperative for Change," The Phase III Report of the U.S. Commission on National Security/21st Century, February 15, 2001. http://www.au.af.mil/au/awc/awcgate/nssg/phaseIIIfr.pdf.

6. Homeland Security Act of 2002, November 25, 2002. http://www.dhs.gov/xlibrary/assets/hr_5005_enr.pdf.

7. USA PATRIOT Improvement and Reauthorization Act of 2005. http://thomas.loc.gov/cgi-bin/query/z?c109:H.R.3199:

8. Executive Order 13397—Responsibilities of the Department of Homeland Security with Respect to Faith-Based and Community Initiatives, Federal Register Vol. 71, No. 46 Thursday, March 9, 2006. http://edocket.access.gpo.gov/2006/pdf/06-2362.pdf.

9. PKEMRA, (October 4, 2006), http://frwebgate.access.gpo.gov/cgi-bin/getdoc.cgi?dbname=109_cong_public_laws&docid=f:publ295.109.pdf.

10. The order Presidential of succession is: President; Vice President; Speaker of the House of Representatives; President pro tempore of the Senate; Secretary of State; Secretary of the Treasury; Secretary of Defense; Attorney General; Secretary of the Interior; Secretary of Agriculture; Secretary of Commerce; Secretary of Labor; Secretary of Health and Human Services; Secretary of Housing and Urban Development; Secretary of Transportation; Secretary of Energy; Secretary of Education; Secretary of Veterans Affairs; Secretary of Homeland Security. 3 USC 19.

ADDITIONAL RESOURCES

"Major Management Challenges Facing the Department of Homeland Security," Department of Homeland Security Inspector General OIG-10-16, Nov. 2009. http://www.dhs.gov/xoig/assets/mgmtrpts/OIG_10-16_Nov09.pdf.

Homeland Security Advisory System: Task force Report and Recommendations, September 2009. http://www.dhs.gov/xlibrary/assets/hsac_final_report_09_15_09.pdf.

"On July 22nd, 2004, the 9/11 Commission released its official report on the September 11 terrorist attacks, detailing the circumstances and our preparedness regarding the attacks themselves, but also providing recommendations on how best to guard against future attacks. So, it's five years later. Where are we, as a department, on implementing those recommendations, and how do we plan to move forward? Secretary Napolitano today released a report outlining the department's progress on the Commission's recommendations...." "Department Of Homeland Security: Progress In Implementing 9/11 Commission Recommendations," DHS, July 22, 2009. http://www.dhs.gov/xlibrary/assets/dhs_5_year_progress_for_9_11_commission_report.pdf.

"The DHS Directorate of Science and Technology: Key Issues for Congress," Dana A. Shea and Daniel Morgan, CRS, June 22, 2009, RL34356. http://www.opencrs.cdt.org/document/RL34356.

Privacy and Civil Liberties Policy Guidance Memorandum, Department of Homeland Security, June 5, 2009. http://www.dhs.gov/xlibrary/assets/privacy/privacy_crcl_guidance_ise_2009-01.pdf.

"German and U.S. Domestic Counterterrorism Responses: Only Half a World Apart," By Dorle Hellmuth, American Institute for Contemporary German Studies, at Johns Hopkins University, June 2009. http://www.aicgs.org/documents/pubs/hellmuth.atp09.pdf.

"The Department of Homeland Security Intelligence Enterprise: Operational Overview and Oversight Challenges for Congress," Mark A. Randol, CRS May 27, 2009, R40602. http://www.fas.org/sgp/crs/homesec/R40602.pdf.

Data Privacy and Integrity Advisory Committee, Final White Paper on Department of Homeland Security Information Sharing and Access Agreements, Department of Homeland Security, May 14, 2009. http://www.dhs.gov/xlibrary/assets/privacy/privacy_dpiac_issa_final_recs_may2009.pdf.

"The Secretary of the Department of Homeland Security has taken to heart Barack Obama's campaign pledges of "change" and "hope." Unfortunately, the changes she has effected seem generally to be to dismantle sensible Bush-era internal security policies and practices, replacing them with politically correct nostrums and generally inadequate programs." "Department of Insecurity: Making America less safe from 'man-caused disasters," Center for Security Policy May 11, 2009, Frank Gaffney, Jr. http://www.centerforsecuritypolicy.org/p18050.xml?genre_id=1.

"As many as 108 different congressional committees provide some level of oversight to DHS." Greg Bruno, Overhauling Homeland Security, Council on Foreign Relations, March 2, 2009. http://www.cfr.org/publication/18658/overhauling_homeland_security.html.

"Brief Documentary History of the Department of Homeland Security: 2001–2008." "This compilation tells the story of the creation and the organizational history of the first five years of the Department of Homeland Security through its founding documents. These documents include legislation, executive orders, commission reports and recommendations, reorganization plans, presidential directives, speeches, and organization charts. Access to most of the documents is through links. Organization charts and select documents are included in the actual text." http://www.dhs.gov/xlibrary/assets/brief_documentary_history_of_dhs_2001_2008.pdf.

"Top Ten Challenges Facing the Next Secretary of Homeland Security," Homeland Security Advisory Council, September 11, 2008. http://www.dhs.gov/xinfoshare/committees/editorial_0331.shtm.

6

THE FEDERAL EMERGENCY MANAGEMENT AGENCY

The Federal Emergency Management Agency (FEMA) is the Federal Government's emergency management agency employing highly skilled pre-event planners, emergency managers, and first responders. It coordinates the national response and is the primary federal agency responsible for preventing, mitigating, responding to, and recovering from disasters in the United States. FEMA used to be a stand-alone agency but was absorbed into the Department of Homeland Security (DHS) concurrent with DHS's formation in 2002 by the Homeland Security Act.

The Disaster Relief Act of 1974 established the procedures for presidential disaster declarations. FEMA was created during the administration of President Jimmy Carter in 1979. It consolidated under one agency the approximately 100 disaster management functions that previously were scattered among several independent agencies.[1,2]

The Robert T. Stafford Disaster Relief and Emergency Assistance Act,[3] 1988, or the Stafford Act, amended and incorporated the Disaster Relief Act of 1974. The Stafford Act now "constitutes the statutory authority for most Federal disaster response activities especially as they pertain to FEMA and FEMA programs."[4] The Stafford Act is codified at 42 USC sec. 5121 *et seq.*, with associated regulations at 44 CFR sec. 206 *et seq.*

This chapter includes a great deal of information from the Select Bipartisan Committee to Investigate Preparation & Response to Hurricane Katrina because there is no better analysis of FEMA's, and ultimately DHS's failure during that catastrophe. If Katrina had been a practice exercise, it would have been a complete success because it demonstrated so many sources of failure. The Post-Katrina Emergency Management Reform Act addressed many of these problem areas.

Foundations of Homeland Security: Law and Policy, First Edition. Martin J. Alperen.
© 2011 John Wiley & Sons, Inc. Published 2011 by John Wiley & Sons, Inc.

SOURCES

- Executive Order 12148–Federal Emergency Management, July 20, 1979[5]
- The Homeland Security Act Of 2002[6]
- Select Bipartisan Committee to Investigate Preparation & Response to Hurricane Katrina[7]
- The Post-Katrina Emergency Management Reform Act of 2006[8]
- Pets Evacuation and Transportation Standards Act of 2006[9]

Executive Order 12148–Federal Emergency Management, July 20, 1979[10]

Sec. 1. Transfers or Reassignments

1-1. *Transfer or Reassignment of Existing Functions.*

1-101. All functions vested in the President that have been delegated or assigned to the Defense Civil Preparedness Agency, Department of Defense, are transferred or reassigned to the Director of the Federal Emergency Management Agency.

1-102. All functions vested in the President that have been delegated or assigned to the Federal Disaster Assistance Administration, Department of Housing and Urban Development, are transferred or reassigned to the Director of the Federal Emergency Management Agency, including any of those functions redelegated or reassigned to the Department of Commerce with respect to assistance to communities in the development of readiness plans for severe weather-related emergencies.

1-103. All functions vested in the President that have been delegated or assigned to the Federal Preparedness Agency,

General Services Administration, are transferred or reassigned to the Director of the Federal Emergency Management Agency.

1-104. All functions vested in the President by the Earthquake Hazards Reduction Act of 1977 (42 U.S.C. 7701 *et seq.*), including those functions performed by the Office of Science and Technology Policy, are delegated, transferred, or reassigned to the Director of the Federal Emergency Management Agency.

Sec. 2. Management of Emergency Planning and Assistance

2-1. *General.*

2-101. The Director of the Federal Emergency Management Agency shall establish Federal policies for, and coordinate, all civil defense and civil emergency planning, management, mitigation, and assistance functions of Executive agencies...

The Homeland Security Act of 2002

SEC. 503

In accordance with title XV, there shall be transferred to the Secretary [of the Department of Homeland Security] the functions, personnel, assets, and liabilities of the following entities:

(1) The Federal Emergency Management Agency, including the functions of the Director of the Federal Emergency Management Agency relating thereto...

SEC. 507. ROLE OF FEDERAL EMERGENCY MANAGEMENT AGENCY

(a) IN GENERAL.— The functions of the Federal Emergency Management Agency include the following:

(1) All functions and authorities prescribed by the Robert T. Stafford Disaster Relief and Emergency Assistance Act (42 U.S.C. 5121 et seq.).

(2) Carrying out its mission to reduce the loss of life and property and protect the Nation from all hazards by leading and supporting the Nation in a comprehensive, risk-based emergency management program...

  (A) of mitigation, by taking sustained actions to reduce or eliminate long-term risk to people and property from hazards and their effects...

  (B) of planning for building the emergency management profession to prepare effectively for, mitigate against, respond to, and recover from any hazard...

  (C) of response, by conducting emergency operations to save lives and property through positioning emergency equipment and supplies, through evacuating potential victims, through providing food, water, shelter, and medical care to those in need, and through restoring critical public services...

  (D) of recovery, by rebuilding communities so individuals, businesses, and governments can function on their own, return to normal life, and protect against future hazards; and

  (E) of increased efficiencies, by coordinating efforts relating to mitigation, planning, response, and recovery.

(b) FEDERAL RESPONSE PLAN

(1) *ROLE OF FEMA.*— Notwithstanding any other provision of this Act, the Federal Emergency Management Agency shall remain the lead agency for the Federal Response Plan[11] established under Executive Order No. 12148 (44 Fed. Reg. 43239) and Executive Order No. 12656 (53 Fed. Reg. 47491).

Hurricane Katrina

"If 9/11 was a failure of imagination, then Katrina was a failure of initiative."[7] Hurricane Katrina made landfall in the United States Gulf Coast August 29, 2005. Because of the abysmal local, state, and federal response, on September 15, 2005, the House of Representatives created the Select Bipartisan Committee to Investigate the Preparation for and Response to Hurricane Katrina.

The failings of our pre-storm, after-storm, and even long-term responses exposed life-threatening inadequacies. The Committee Report discusses the National Response Plan (now the National Response Framework), Emergency Service Functions, FEMA, the Department of Defense, communications, continuity of operations, housing, medical care, and more.

Select Bipartisan Committee to Investigate the Preparation for and Response to Hurricane Katrina[12]

"Two months before [the Select Bipartisan Committee to Investigate the Preparation for and Response to Hurricane Katrina] was established, former Speaker of the House Newt Gingrich testified before a Government Reform subcommittee about the need to move the government to an "entrepreneurial" model and away from its current "bureaucratic" model, so that we can get government to move with Information Age speed and effectiveness.

'Implementing policy effectively,' Speaker Gingrich said, "is ultimately as important as *making* the right policy...

... in the tragic aftermath of Katrina, America was ... confronted with the vast divide between policy creation and policy implementation. With the life-and-death difference between theory and practice...

... Katrina was a national failure, an abdication of the most solemn obligation to provide for the common welfare. At every level – individual, corporate, philanthropic, and governmental – we failed to meet the challenge... A National Response Plan is not enough. What's needed is a National Action Plan. Not a plan that says Washington will do everything, but one that says, when all else fails, the federal government must do something, whether it's formally requested or not.

... Our system of federalism wisely relies on those closest to the people to meet immediate needs... But faith in federalism alone cannot sanctify a dysfunctional system in which DHS and FEMA simply wait for requests for aid that state and local officials may be unable or unwilling to convey...

... This report is a story about the National Response Plan, and how its 15 Emergency Support Functions (ESFs) were implemented with Katrina. ...

... the Select Committee has matched what was *supposed* to happen under federal, state, and local plans against what *actually* happened.

... It remains difficult to understand how government could respond so ineffectively to a disaster that was anticipated for years, and for which specific dire warnings had been issued for days. This crisis was not only predictable, it was predicted..."[13]

"... We must recognize that we are woefully incapable of storing, moving, and accessing information – especially in times of crisis.

... Many of the problems we have identified can be categorized as "information gaps" ... or failures to act decisively because information was sketchy ...

... we found that while a national emergency management system that relies on state and local governments to identify needs and request resources is adequate for most disasters, a catastrophic disaster like Katrina can and did overwhelm most aspects of the system for an initial period of time... No one anticipated the degree and scope of the destruction the storm would cause, even though many could and should have...

... The failure of local, state, and federal governments to respond more effectively to Katrina — which had been predicted in theory for many years, and forecast with startling accuracy for five days — demonstrates that whatever improvements have been made to our capacity to respond to natural or man-made disasters, four and half years after 9/11, we are still not fully prepared.

... Local first responders were largely overwhelmed and unable to perform their duties, and the National Response Plan did not adequately provide a way for federal assets to quickly supplement or, if necessary, supplant first responders.

... The failure of initiative was also a failure of agility. Response plans at all levels of government lacked flexibility and adaptability.

.... Officials at all levels seemed to be waiting for the disaster that fit their plans, rather than planning and building scalable capacities to meet whatever Mother Nature threw at them. We again encountered the risk averse culture that pervades big government, and again recognized the need for organizations as agile and responsive as the 21st century world in which we live.

... Ours was a response that could not adequately accept civilian and international generosity...

Responsibilities for levee operations and maintenance were diffuse.

The lack of a warning system for breaches and other factors delayed repairs to the levees.

The failure of complete evacuations led to preventable deaths, great suffering, and further delays in relief.

Despite adequate warning 56 hours before landfall, Governor Blanco and Mayor Nagin delayed ordering a mandatory evacuation in New Orleans until 19 hours before landfall.

The failure to order timely mandatory evacuations, Mayor Nagin's decision to shelter but not evacuate the remaining population, and decisions of individuals led to an incomplete evacuation.

The incomplete pre-landfall evacuation led to deaths, thousands of dangerous rescues, and horrible conditions for those who remained.

Federal, state, and local officials' failure to anticipate the post-landfall conditions delayed post-landfall evacuation and support.

It does not appear the President received adequate advice and counsel from a senior disaster professional.

Given the well-known consequences of a major hurricane striking New Orleans, the Secretary should have designated an Incident of National Significance no later than Saturday, two days prior to landfall, when the National Weather Service predicted New Orleans would be struck by a Category 4 or 5 hurricane and President Bush declared a federal emergency.

The Secretary should have convened the Interagency Incident Management Group on Saturday, two days prior to landfall, or earlier to analyze Katrina's potential consequences and anticipate what the federal response would need to accomplish.

The Secretary should have designated the Principal Federal Official on Saturday, two days prior to landfall, from the roster of PFOs who had successfully completed the required training, unlike then-FEMA Director Michael Brown. Considerable confusion was caused by the Secretary's PFO decisions.

The Secretary should have invoked the Catastrophic Incident Annex to direct the federal response posture to fully switch from a reactive to proactive mode of operations.

The Homeland Security Operations Center failed to provide valuable situational information to the White House and key operational officials during the disaster.

The White House failed to deconflict varying damage assessments and discounted information that ultimately proved accurate.

Federal agencies, including DHS, had varying degrees of unfamiliarity with their roles and responsibilities under the National Response Plan and National Incident Management System.

Once activated, the Emergency Management Assistance Compact enabled an unprecedented level of mutual aid assistance to reach the disaster area in a timely and effective manner.

Earlier presidential involvement might have resulted in a more effective response.

Despite extensive preparedness initiatives, DHS was not prepared. . .

DHS and FEMA lacked adequate trained and experienced staff for the Katrina response.

The readiness of FEMA's national emergency response teams was inadequate and reduced the effectiveness of the federal response.

Massive communications damage and a failure to adequately plan for alternatives impaired response efforts, command and control, and situational awareness.

Massive inoperability had the biggest effect on communications, limiting command and control, situational awareness, and federal, state, and local officials' ability to address unsubstantiated media reports.

The National Communication System met many of the challenges posed by Hurricane Katrina, enabling critical communication during the response, but gaps in the system did result in delayed response and inadequate delivery of relief supplies.

Command and control was impaired at all levels, delaying relief.

Lack of communications and situational awareness paralyzed command and control.

Ineffective command and control delayed many relief efforts.

The military played an invaluable role, but coordination was lacking.

The National Response Plan's Catastrophic Incident Annex as written would have delayed the active duty military response, even if it had been implemented.

DOD/DHS coordination was not effective during Hurricane Katrina.

DOD, FEMA, and the state of Louisiana had difficulty coordinating with each other, which slowed the response.

National Guard and DOD response operations were comprehensive, but perceived as slow.

The Coast Guard's response saved many lives, but coordination with other responders could improve.

The Army Corps of Engineers provided critical resources to Katrina victims, but pre-landfall contracts were not adequate.

DOD has not yet incorporated or implemented lessons learned from joint exercises in military assistance to civil authorities that would have allowed for a more effective response to Katrina.

The lack of integration of National Guard and active duty forces hampered the military response.

Northern Command[14] does not have adequate insight into state response capabilities or adequate interface with governors, which contributed to a lack of mutual understanding and trust during the Katrina response.

Even DOD lacked situational awareness of post-landfall conditions, which contributed to a slower response.

DOD lacked an information sharing protocol that would have enhanced joint situational awareness and communications between all military components.

Joint Task Force Katrina command staff lacked joint training, which contributed to the lack of coordination between active duty components.

Joint Task Force Katrina, the National Guard, Louisiana, and Mississippi lacked needed communications equipment and the interoperability required for seamless on-the-ground coordination.

EMAC processing, pre-arranged state compacts, and Guard equipment packages need improvement.

Equipment, personnel, and training shortfalls affected the National Guard response.

Search and rescue operations were a tremendous success, but coordination and integration between the military services, the National Guard, the Coast Guard, and other rescue organizations was lacking.

The collapse of local law enforcement and lack of effective public communications led to civil unrest and further delayed relief.

A variety of conditions led to lawlessness and violence in hurricane stricken areas.

The New Orleans Police Department was ill-prepared for continuity of operations and lost almost all effectiveness.

The lack of a government public communications strategy and media hype of violence exacerbated public concerns and further delayed relief.

EMAC and military assistance were critical for restoring law and order.

Federal law enforcement agencies were also critical to restoring law and order and coordinating activities.

Medical care and evacuations suffered from a lack of advance preparations, inadequate communications, and difficulties coordinating efforts.

Deployment of medical personnel was reactive, not proactive.

Poor planning and pre-positioning of medical supplies and equipment led to delays and shortages.

New Orleans was unprepared to provide evacuations and medical care for its special needs population and dialysis patients, and Louisiana officials lacked a common definition of "special needs."

Most hospital and Veterans Affairs Medical Center emergency plans did not offer concrete guidance about if or when evacuations should take place.

New Orleans hospitals, Veterans Affairs Medical Center, and medical first responders were not adequately prepared for a full evacuation of medical facilities.

The government did not effectively coordinate private air transport capabilities for the evacuation of medical patients.

Hospital and Veterans Affairs Medical Center emergency plans did not adequately prepare for communication needs.

Following Hurricane Katrina, New Orleans Veterans Affairs Medical Center and hospitals' inability to communicate impeded their ability to ask for help.

Medical responders did not have adequate communications equipment or operability.

Evacuation decisions for New Orleans nursing homes were subjective and, in one case, led to preventable deaths.

Lack of electronic patient medical records contributed to difficulties and delays in medical treatment of evacuees.

Top officials at the Department at Health and Human Services and the National Disaster Medical System do not share a common understanding of who controls the National Disaster Medical System under Emergency Support Function-8.

Lack of coordination led to delays in recovering dead bodies.

Deployment confusion, uncertainty about mission assignments, and government red tape delayed medical care.

Long-standing weaknesses and the magnitude of the disaster overwhelmed FEMA's ability to provide emergency shelter and temporary housing.

Relocation plans did not adequately provide for shelter. Housing plans were haphazard and inadequate.

State and local governments made inappropriate selections of shelters of last resort. The lack of a regional database of shelters contributed to an inefficient and ineffective evacuation and sheltering process.

There was inappropriate delay in getting people out of shelters and into temporary housing – delays that officials should have foreseen due to manufacturing limitations.

FEMA failed to take advantage of the Department of Housing and Urban Development's expertise in largescale housing challenges.

FEMA logistics and contracting systems did not support a targeted, massive, and sustained provision of commodities.

FEMA management lacked situational awareness of existing requirements and of resources in the supply chain. An overwhelmed logistics system made it challenging to get supplies, equipment, and personnel where and when needed.

Procedures for requesting federal assistance raised numerous concerns.

The failure at all levels to enter into advance contracts led to chaos and the potential for waste and fraud as acquisitions were made in haste.

Before Katrina, FEMA suffered from a lack of sufficiently trained procurement professionals. DHS procurement continues to be decentralized and lacking a uniform approach, and its procurement office was understaffed given the volume and dollar value of work.

Ambiguous statutory guidance regarding local contractor participation led to ongoing disputes over procuring debris removal and other services.

Attracting emergency contractors and corporate support could prove challenging given the scrutiny that companies have endured.

Contributions by charitable organizations assisted many in need, but the American Red Cross and others faced challenges due to the size of the mission, inadequate logistics capacity, and a disorganized shelter process.

> "We were abandoned. City officials did nothing to protect us. We were told to go to the Superdome, the Convention Center, the interstate bridge for safety. We did this more than once. In fact, we tried them all for every day over a week. We saw buses, helicopters and FEMA trucks, but no one stopped to help us. We never felt so cut off in all our lives. When you feel like this you do one of two things, you either give up or go into survival mode. We chose the latter. This is how we made it. We slept next to dead bodies, we slept on streets at least four times next to human feces and urine. There was garbage everywhere in the city. Panic and fear had taken over."
>
> Patricia Thompson, New Orleans Citizen and Evacuee, Select Committee Hearing, December 6, 2005.[15]

To address these problems, in 2006, Congress enacted the Post-Katrina Emergency Management Reform Act[16] (PKEMRA). It made major changes to FEMA. Parts of the statute are reprinted below.

Also included is the Pets Evacuation and Transportation Standards Act of 2006 that integrated pets in emergency planning.

Summary of PKEMRA

The Act reestablished FEMA[17] as an agency within DHS and made changes to FEMA. It describes what functions were transferred; describes management of 10 regional offices; establishes the National Advisory Council and lists its responsibilities; creates the National Integration Center; discusses credentialing of FEMA workers; and establishes the National Infrastructure Simulation and Analysis Center.

It directs the creation of evacuation plans and exercises; creates the position of Disability Coordinator; creates the

National Operations Center; creates the position of Chief Medical Officer; discusses nuclear response; promotes the use of private sector networks in emergency response; promotes the use of commercially available technology; promotes procurement of a national strategic stockpile; promotes workforce development, the creation of a human capital plan, a gap analysis, defined career paths, recruitment and retention bonuses.

It establishes a homeland security education program; promotes creation of a surge capacity force; promotes development of state catastrophic indexes; offers evacuation development assistance; creates emergency response teams; discusses urban search and rescue teams; suggests prepositioning equipment; establishes a Katrina and Rita Recovery Office; and outlines a plan to teach basic first aid to children.

PKEMRA promotes training; promotes development of assessment capability to monitor whether capabilities actually improve; establishes reporting requirements for almost every activity; requires that an inventory be created of federal response capabilities; discusses measuring federal preparedness; provides Emergency Management Assistance Compact grants; establishes emergency communications priorities and strategies including creating of a National Communication Plan, Regional Communication Coordinator, an Emergency Communication Preparedness Center, and interoperability research and coordination.

It creates a National Disaster Recovery Strategy, a National Disaster Housing Strategy, a Child Locater Center, a Family Register; it provides for transportation assistance, case management services, a small states and rural area advocate; and promotes the use of local businesses; among other things.

Post-Katrina Emergency Management Reform Act Of 2006

SEC. 601. SHORT TITLE

This title may be cited as the "Post-Katrina Emergency Management Reform Act of 2006".

SEC. 602. DEFINITIONS

In this title—

(1) the term "Administrator" means the Administrator of the Agency;

(2) the term "Agency" means the Federal Emergency Management Agency;

(5) the term "Department" means the Department of Homeland Security;

(7) the term "emergency management" means the governmental function that coordinates and integrates all activities necessary to build, sustain, and improve the capability to prepare for, protect against, respond to, recover from, or mitigate against threatened or actual natural disasters, acts of terrorism, or other man-made disasters;

(9) the term "Federal coordinating officer" means a Federal coordinating officer as described in section 302 of the Robert T. Stafford Disaster Relief and Emergency Assistance Act (42 U.S.C. 5143);

(14) the term "Secretary" means the Secretary of Homeland Security;

(15) the term "surge capacity" means the ability to rapidly and substantially increase the provision of search and rescue capabilities, food, water, medicine, shelter and housing, medical care, evacuation capacity, staffing (including disaster assistance employees), and other resources necessary to save lives and protect property during a catastrophic incident;

SEC. 611. STRUCTURING THE FEDERAL EMERGENCY MANAGEMENT AGENCY

Title V of the Homeland Security Act of 2002 (6 U.S.C. 311 et seq.) is amended—

(11) by inserting after section 502, as redesignated and transferred by paragraph (9) of this section, the following:

SEC. 503. FEDERAL EMERGENCY MANAGEMENT AGENCY

"(a) IN GENERAL.— There is in the Department the Federal Emergency Management Agency, headed by an Administrator.

"(b) MISSION.

"(1) *PRIMARY MISSION.*— The primary mission of the Agency is to reduce the loss of life and property and protect the Nation from all hazards, including natural disasters, acts of terrorism, and other man-made disasters, by leading and supporting the Nation in a risk-based, comprehensive emergency management system of preparedness, protection, response, recovery, and mitigation.

"(2) *SPECIFIC ACTIVITIES.*— In support of the primary mission of the Agency, the Administrator shall—

"(A) lead the Nation's efforts to prepare for, protect against, respond to, recover from, and mitigate against the risk of natural disasters, acts of terrorism, and other man-made disasters, including catastrophic incidents;

"(B) partner with State, local, and tribal governments and emergency response providers, with other Federal agencies, with the private sector, and with non-governmental organizations to build a national system of emergency management that can effectively and efficiently utilize the full measure of the Nation's resources to respond to natural disasters, acts of terrorism, and other manmade disasters, including catastrophic incidents;

"(C) develop a Federal response capability that, when necessary and appropriate, can act effectively and rapidly to deliver assistance essential to saving lives or protecting or preserving property or public health and safety in a natural disaster, act of terrorism, or other man-made disaster;

"(D) integrate the Agency's emergency preparedness, protection, response, recovery, and mitigation responsibilities to confront effectively the challenges of a natural disaster, act of terrorism, or other man-made disaster;

"(E) develop and maintain robust Regional Offices that will work with State, local, and tribal governments, emergency response providers, and other appropriate entities to identify and address regional priorities;

"(F) under the leadership of the Secretary, coordinate with the Commandant of the Coast Guard, the Director of Customs and Border Protection, the Director of Immigration and Customs Enforcement, the National Operations Center, and other agencies and offices in the Department to take full advantage of the substantial range of resources in the Department;

"(G) provide funding, training, exercises, technical assistance, planning, and other assistance to build tribal, local, State, regional, and national capabilities (including communications capabilities), necessary to respond to a natural disaster, act of terrorism, or other man-made disaster; and

"(H) develop and coordinate the implementation of a risk-based, all-hazards strategy for preparedness that builds those common capabilities necessary to respond to natural disasters, acts of terrorism, and other man-made disasters while also building the unique capabilities necessary to respond to specific types of incidents that pose the greatest risk to our Nation.

"(c) ADMINISTRATOR

"(1) *IN GENERAL.*— The Administrator shall be appointed by the President, by and with the advice and consent of the Senate.

"(2) *QUALIFICATIONS.*— The Administrator shall be appointed from among individuals who have—

"(A) a demonstrated ability in and knowledge of emergency management and homeland security; and

"(B) not less than 5 years of executive leadership and management experience in the public or private sector.

"(4) PRINCIPAL ADVISOR ON EMERGENCY MANAGEMENT

"(A) *IN GENERAL.*— The Administrator is the principal advisor to the President, the Homeland Security Council, and the Secretary for all matters relating to emergency management in the United States.

(12) in section 504, as redesignated by paragraph (8) of this section—

(B) by striking the matter preceding paragraph (1) and inserting the following:

"(a) *IN GENERAL.*— The Administrator shall provide Federal leadership necessary to prepare for, protect against, respond to, recover from, or mitigate against a natural disaster, act of terrorism, or other man-made disaster, including—";

(D) by striking paragraph (7) and inserting the following:

"(7) helping ensure the acquisition of operable and interoperable communications capabilities by Federal, State, local, and tribal governments and emergency response providers;

"(8) assisting the President in carrying out the functions under the Robert T. Stafford Disaster Relief and Emergency Assistance Act (42 U.S.C. 5121 et seq.) and carrying out all functions and authorities given to the Administrator under that Act;

"(9) carrying out the mission of the Agency to reduce the loss of life and property and protect the Nation from all hazards by leading and supporting the Nation in a risk-based, comprehensive emergency management system of—

"(A) mitigation, by taking sustained actions to reduce or eliminate long-term risks to people and property from hazards and their effects;

"(B) preparedness, by planning, training, and building the emergency management profession to prepare effectively for, mitigate against, respond to, and recover from any hazard;

"(C) response, by conducting emergency operations to save lives and property through positioning emergency equipment, personnel, and supplies, through evacuating potential victims, through providing food, water, shelter, and medical care to those in need, and through restoring critical public services; and

"(D) recovery, by rebuilding communities so individuals, businesses, and governments can function on their own, return to normal life, and protect against future hazards;

"(10) increasing efficiencies, by coordinating efforts relating to preparedness, protection, response, recovery, and mitigation;

"(11) helping to ensure the effectiveness of emergency response providers in responding to a natural disaster, act of terrorism, or other man-made disaster;

"(12) supervising grant programs administered by the Agency;

"(13) administering and ensuring the implementation of the National Response Plan, including coordinating and ensuring the readiness of each emergency support function under the National Response Plan;

"(14) coordinating with the National Advisory Council established under section 508;

"(15) preparing and implementing the plans and programs of the Federal Government for—

"(A) continuity of operations;

"(B) continuity of government; and

"(C) continuity of plans;

"(16) minimizing, to the extent practicable, overlapping planning and reporting requirements applicable to State, local, and tribal governments and the private sector;

"(17) maintaining and operating within the Agency the National Response Coordination Center or its successor;

"(18) developing a national emergency management system that is capable of preparing for, protecting against, responding to, recovering from, and mitigating against catastrophic incidents;

"(19) assisting the President in carrying out the functions under the national preparedness goal and the national preparedness system and carrying out all functions and authorities of the Administrator under the national preparedness System;

"(20) carrying out all authorities of the Federal Emergency Management Agency and the Directorate of Preparedness of the Department as transferred under section 505; and

"(21) otherwise carrying out the mission of the Agency as described in section 503(b).

"(b) *ALL-HAZARDS APPROACH.—* In carrying out the responsibilities under this section, the Administrator shall coordinate the implementation of a risk-based, all-hazards strategy that builds those common capabilities necessary to prepare for, protect against, respond to, recover from, or mitigate against natural disasters, acts of terrorism, and other man-made disasters, while also building the unique capabilities necessary to prepare for, protect against, respond to, recover from, or mitigate against the risks of specific types of incidents that pose the greatest risk to the Nation."; and (13) by inserting after section 504, as redesignated by paragraph (8) of this section, the following:

SEC. 505. FUNCTIONS TRANSFERRED

"(a) *IN GENERAL.—* Except as provided in subsection (b), there are transferred to the Agency the following:

"(1) All functions of the Federal Emergency Management Agency, including existing responsibilities for emergency alert systems and continuity of operations and continuity of government plans and programs as constituted on June 1, 2006, including all of its personnel, assets, components, authorities, grant programs, and liabilities, and including the functions of the Under Secretary for Federal Emergency Management relating thereto.

"(2) The Directorate of Preparedness, as constituted on June 1, 2006, including all of its functions, personnel, assets, components, authorities, grant programs, and liabilities, and including the functions of the Under Secretary for Preparedness relating thereto.

SEC. 506. PRESERVING THE FEDERAL EMERGENCY MANAGEMENT AGENCY

"(a) DISTINCT ENTITY.— The Agency shall be maintained as a distinct entity within the Department.

"(b) REORGANIZATION.— Section 872[18] shall not apply to the Agency, including any function or organizational unit of the Agency.

"(c) PROHIBITION ON CHANGES TO MISSIONS.

"(1) *IN GENERAL.—* The Secretary may not substantially or significantly reduce the authorities, responsibilities, or functions of the Agency or the capability of the Agency to perform those missions, authorities, responsibilities, except as otherwise specifically provided in an Act enacted after the date of enactment of the Post-Katrina Emergency Management Reform Act of 2006.

"(2) *CERTAIN TRANSFERS PROHIBITED.—* No asset, function, or mission of the Agency may be diverted to the principal and continuing use of any other organization, unit, or entity of the Department, except for details or assignments that do not reduce the capability of the Agency to perform its missions.

SEC. 507. REGIONAL OFFICES

"(a) IN GENERAL.— There are in the Agency 10 regional offices, as identified by the Administrator.

"(e) REGIONAL ADVISORY COUNCIL.

"(1) *ESTABLISHMENT.—* Each Regional Administrator shall establish a Regional Advisory Council.

"(f) REGIONAL OFFICE STRIKE TEAMS.

"(1) *IN GENERAL.—* In coordination with other relevant Federal agencies, each Regional Administrator shall oversee multiagency strike teams authorized under section 303 of the Robert T. Stafford Disaster Relief and Emergency Assistance Act (42 U.S.C. 5144)...

"(5) *PREPAREDNESS.—* Each Regional Office strike team shall be trained as a unit on a regular basis and equipped and staffed to be well prepared to respond to natural dsasters, acts of terrorism, and other man-made disasters, including catastrophic incidents.

SEC. 508. NATIONAL ADVISORY COUNCIL

"(a) ESTABLISHMENT.— Not later than 60 days after the date of enactment of the Post-Katrina Emergency Management Reform Act of 2006, the Secretary shall establish an advisory body under section 871(a)[19] to ensure effective and ongoing coordination of Federal preparedness, protection, response, recovery, and mitigation for natural disasters, acts of terrorism, and other man-made disasters, to be known as the National Advisory Council.

"(b) RESPONSIBILITIES.— The National Advisory Council shall advise the Administrator on all aspects of emergency management...

SEC. 509. NATIONAL INTEGRATION CENTER

"(a) IN GENERAL.— There is established in the Agency a National Integration Center.

"(b) RESPONSIBILITIES.

"(1) *IN GENERAL.—* The Administrator, ... shall ensure ongoing management and maintenance of the National Incident Management System, the National Response Plan, and any successor to such system or plan.

"(c) INCIDENT MANAGEMENT.

"(1) *IN GENERAL.*

"(A) *NATIONAL RESPONSE PLAN.—* The Secretary, ... shall ensure that the National Response Plan provides for a clear chain of command to lead and coordinate the Federal response to any natural disaster, act of terrorism, or other man-made disaster.

"(B) *ADMINISTRATOR.—* The chain of the command specified in the National Response Plan shall—

"(i) provide for a role for the Administrator consistent with the role of the Administrator as the principal emergency management advisor to the President, the Homeland Security Council, and the Secretary under section 503(c)(4) and the responsibility of the Administrator under the Post-Katrina Emergency Management Reform Act of 2006, and the amendments made by that Act, relating to natural disasters, acts of terrorism, and other man-made disasters; and

SEC. 511. THE NATIONAL INFRASTRUCTURE SIMULATION AND ANALYSIS CENTER

"(a) DEFINITION.— In this section, the term 'National Infrastructure Simulation and Analysis Center' means the National Infrastructure Simulation and Analysis Center established under section 1016(d) of the USA PATRIOT Act (42 U.S.C. 5195c(d)).

"(b) AUTHORITY.

"(1) *IN GENERAL.—* There is in the Department the National Infrastructure Simulation and Analysis Center which shall serve as a source of national expertise to address critical infrastructure protection and continuity through support for activities related to—

"(A) counterterrorism, threat assessment, and risk mitigation; and

"(B) a natural disaster, act of terrorism, or other manmade disaster.

SEC. 512. EVACUATION PLANS AND EXERCISES

"(a) IN GENERAL.— Notwithstanding any other provision of law, and subject to subsection (d), grants made to States or local or tribal governments by the Department through the State Homeland Security Grant Program or the Urban Area Security Initiative may be used to—

(1) establish programs for the development and maintenance of mass evacuation plans under subsection (b) in the event of a natural disaster, act of terrorism, or other manmade disaster;

(2) prepare for the execution of such plans, including the development of evacuation routes and the purchase and stockpiling of necessary supplies and shelters; and

(3) conduct exercises of such plans.

SEC. 513. DISABILITY COORDINATOR

"**(a) IN GENERAL.**— After consultation with organizations representing individuals with disabilities, the National Council on Disabilities, and the Interagency Coordinating Council on Preparedness and Individuals with Disabilities, established under Executive Order No. 13347 (6 U.S.C. 312 note), the Administrator shall appoint a Disability Coordinator. The Disability Coordinator shall report directly to the Administrator, in order to ensure that the needs of individuals with disabilities are being properly addressed in emergency preparedness and disaster relief.

SEC. 515. NATIONAL OPERATIONS CENTER

"**(a) DEFINITION.**— In this section, the term 'situational awareness' means information gathered from a variety of sources that, when communicated to emergency managers and decision makers, can form the basis for incident management decisionmaking.

"**(b) ESTABLISHMENT.**— The National Operations Center is the principal operations center for the Department and shall—

"(1) provide situational awareness and a common operating picture for the entire Federal Government, and for State, local, and tribal governments as appropriate, in the event of a natural disaster, act of terrorism, or other man-made disaster; and

"(2) ensure that critical terrorism and disaster-related information reaches government decision-makers.

SEC. 621. WORKFORCE DEVELOPMENT

(a) IN GENERAL.— Subpart I of part III of title 5, United States Code, is amended by adding at the end the following:

"CHAPTER 101—FEDERAL EMERGENCY MANAGEMENT AGENCY PERSONNEL

SEC. 624. SURGE CAPACITY FORCE

(a) ESTABLISHMENT.

(1) *IN GENERAL.*— Not later than 6 months after the date of enactment of this Act, the Administrator shall prepare and submit to the appropriate committees of Congress a plan to establish and implement a Surge Capacity Force for deployment of individuals to respond to natural disasters, acts of terrorism, and other man-made disasters, including catastrophic incidents.

SEC. 632. EVACUATION PREPAREDNESS TECHNICAL ASSISTANCE

The Administrator, . . . shall provide evacuation preparedness technical assistance to State, local, and tribal governments, including the preparation of hurricane evacuation studies and technical assistance in developing evacuation plans, assessing storm surge estimates, evacuation zones, evacuation clearance times, transportation capacity, and shelter capacity.

SEC. 633. EMERGENCY RESPONSE TEAMS

Section 303 of the Robert T. Stafford Disaster Relief and Emergency Assistance Act (42 U.S.C. 5144) is amended—

(1) by striking "sec. 303." and all that follows through "The President shall" and inserting the following:

SEC. 303. EMERGENCY SUPPORT AND RESPONSE TEAMS

"**(a) EMERGENCY SUPPORT TEAMS.**— The President shall"; and

(2) by adding at the end the following:

"**(b) EMERGENCY RESPONSE TEAMS.**

"(1) *ESTABLISHMENT.*— In carrying out subsection (a), the President, acting through the Director of the Federal Emergency Management Agency, shall establish—

"(A) at a minimum 3 national response teams; and . . .

"(B) sufficient regional response teams, including Regional Office strike teams under section 507 of the Homeland Security Act of 2002; and

"(C) other response teams as may be necessary to meet the incident management responsibilities of the Federal Government.

"(2) *TARGET CAPABILITY LEVEL.*— The Director shall ensure that specific target capability levels, as defined pursuant to the guidelines established under section 646(a) of the Post-Katrina Emergency Management Reform Act of 2006, are established for Federal emergency response teams.

SEC. 634. URBAN SEARCH AND RESCUE RESPONSE SYSTEM

(a) IN GENERAL.— There is in the Agency a system known as the Urban Search and Rescue Response System.

SEC. 637. PREPOSITIONED EQUIPMENT PROGRAM

(a) IN GENERAL.— The Administrator shall establish a prepositioned equipment program to preposition standardized emergency equipment in at least 11 locations to sustain and replenish critical assets used by State, local, and tribal governments in response to (or rendered inoperable by the effects of) natural disasters, acts of terrorism, and other manmade disasters.

SEC. 639. BASIC LIFE SUPPORTING FIRST AID AND EDUCATION

The Administrator shall enter into agreements with organizations to provide funds to emergency response providers to provide education and training in life supporting first aid to children.

Subtitle D—Emergency Communications

SEC. 671. EMERGENCY COMMUNICATIONS

(a) SHORT TITLE.— This section may be cited as the "21st Century Emergency Communications Act of 2006".

(b) IN GENERAL.— The Homeland Security Act of 2002 (6 U.S.C. 101 et seq.) is amended by adding at the end the following new title:

TITLE XVIII—EMERGENCY COMMUNICATIONS

SEC. 1801. OFFICE OF EMERGENCY COMMUNICATIONS

"(a) IN GENERAL.— There is established in the Department an Office of Emergency Communications.

"(b) DIRECTOR.— The head of the office shall be the Director for Emergency Communications. The Director shall report to the Assistant Secretary for Cybersecurity and Communications.

"(c) RESPONSIBILITIES.— The Director for Emergency Communications shall—

"(1) assist the Secretary in developing and implementing the program described in section 7303(a)(1) of the Intelligence Reform and Terrorism Prevention Act of 2004 (6 U.S.C. 194(a)(1)), except as provided in section 314;

"(2) administer the Department's responsibilities and authorities relating to the SAFECOM[20] Program, excluding elements related to research, development, testing, and evaluation and standards;

"(3) administer the Department's responsibilities and authorities relating to the Integrated Wireless Network program;

"(4) conduct extensive, nationwide outreach to support and promote the ability of emergency response providers and relevant government officials to continue to communicate in the event of natural disasters, acts of terrorism, and other manmade disasters;

"(5) conduct extensive, nationwide outreach and foster the development of interoperable emergency communications capabilities by State, regional, local, and tribal governments and public safety agencies, and by regional consortia thereof;

"(6) provide technical assistance to State, regional, local, and tribal government officials with respect to use of interoperable emergency communications capabilities;

"(7) coordinate with the Regional Administrators regarding the activities of Regional Emergency Communications Coordination Working Groups under section 1805;

"(8) promote the development of standard operating procedures and best practices with respect to use of interoperable emergency communications capabilities for incident response, and facilitate the sharing of information on such best practices for achieving, maintaining, and enhancing interoperable emergency communications capabilities for such response;

"(9) coordinate, in cooperation with the National Communications System, the establishment of a national response capability with initial and ongoing planning, implementation, and training for the deployment of communications equipment for relevant State, local, and tribal governments and emergency response providers in the event of a catastrophic loss of local and regional emergency communications services;

"(10) assist the President, the National Security Council, the Homeland Security Council, and the Director of the Office of Management and Budget in ensuring the continued operation of the telecommunications functions and responsibilities of the Federal Government, excluding spectrum management;

"(11) establish, in coordination with the Director of the Office for Interoperability and Compatibility, requirements for interoperable emergency communications capabilities, which shall be nonproprietary where standards for such capabilities exist, for all public safety radio and data communications systems and equipment purchased using homeland security assistance administered by the Department, excluding any alert and warning device, technology, or system;

"(12) review, in consultation with the Assistant Secretary for Grants and Training, all interoperable emergency communications plans of Federal, State, local, and tribal governments, including Statewide and tactical interoperability plans, developed pursuant to homeland security assistance administered by the Department, but excluding spectrum allocation and management related to such plans;

"(13) develop and update periodically, as appropriate, a National Emergency Communications Plan under section 1802;

SEC. 1802. NATIONAL EMERGENCY COMMUNICATIONS PLAN

"(a) IN GENERAL.— The Secretary, ... shall, ... develop not later than 180 days after the completion of the baseline assessment under section 1803, and periodically update, a National Emergency Communications Plan to provide recommendations regarding how the United States should—

"(1) support and promote the ability of emergency response providers and relevant government officials to continue to communicate in the event of natural disasters, acts of terrorism, and other man-made disasters; and

"(2) ensure, accelerate, and attain interoperable emergency communications nationwide.

SEC. 1805. REGIONAL EMERGENCY COMMUNICATIONS COORDINATION

"(a) IN GENERAL.— There is established in each Regional Office a Regional Emergency Communications Coordination Working Group (in this section referred to as an 'RECC Working Group').

"(d) DUTIES.— The duties of each RECC Working Group shall include—

"(1) assessing the survivability, sustainability, and interoperability of local emergency communications systems to meet the goals of the National Emergency Communications Plan;

SEC. 1806. EMERGENCY COMMUNICATIONS PREPAREDNESS CENTER

"(a) ESTABLISHMENT.— There is established the Emergency Communications Preparedness Center (in this section referred to as the 'Center').

"(c) FUNCTIONS.— The Center shall—

"(1) serve as the focal point for interagency efforts and as a clearinghouse with respect to all relevant intergovernmental information to support and promote (including specifically by working to avoid duplication, hindrances, and counteractive efforts among the participating Federal departments and agencies)—

"(A) the ability of emergency response providers and relevant government officials to continue to communicate in the event of natural disasters, acts of terrorism, and other man-made disasters; and

"(B) interoperable emergency communications;

SEC. 1807. URBAN AND OTHER HIGH RISK AREA COMMUNICATIONS CAPABILITIES

"(a) IN GENERAL.— The Secretary, ... shall provide technical guidance, training, and other assistance, as appropriate, to support the rapid establishment of consistent, secure, and effective interoperable emergency communications capabilities in the event of an emergency in urban and other areas determined by the Secretary to be at consistently high levels of risk from natural disasters, acts of terrorism, and other man-made disasters.

"(b) MINIMUM CAPABILITIES.— The interoperable emergency communications capabilities established under subsection (a) shall ensure the ability of all levels of government, emergency response providers, the private sector, and other organizations with emergency response capabilities—

"(1) to communicate with each other in the event of an emergency;

"(2) to have appropriate and timely access to the Information Sharing Environment described in section 1016 of the National Security Intelligence Reform Act of 2004 (6 U.S.C. 321);

SEC. 673. EMERGENCY COMMUNICATIONS INTEROPERABILITY RESEARCH AND DEVELOPMENT

(a) IN GENERAL.— Title III of the Homeland Security Act of 2002 (6 U.S.C. 181 et seq.), as amended by this Act, is amended by adding at the end the following:

SEC. 315. EMERGENCY COMMUNICATIONS INTEROPERABILITY RESEARCH AND DEVELOPMENT

"(a) *IN GENERAL*.— The Under Secretary for Science and Technology, . . . shall establish a comprehensive research and development program to support and promote—

"(1) the ability of emergency response providers and relevant government officials to continue to communicate in the event of natural disasters, acts of terrorism, and other manmade disasters; and

"(2) interoperable emergency communications capabilities among emergency response providers and relevant government officials, including by—

"(A) supporting research on a competitive basis, including through the Directorate of Science and Technology and Homeland Security Advanced Research Projects Agency; and

"(B) considering the establishment of a Center of Excellence under the Department of Homeland Security Centers of Excellence Program focused on improving emergency response providers' communication capabilities.

SEC. 674. 911 AND E911 SERVICES REPORT

Not later than 180 days after the date of enactment of this Act, the Chairman of the Federal Communications Commission shall submit a report to Congress on the status of efforts of State, local, and tribal governments to develop plans for rerouting 911 and E911 services in the event that public safety answering points are disabled during natural disasters, acts of terrorism, and other man-made disasters.

SEC. 683. NATIONAL DISASTER HOUSING STRATEGY

(a) IN GENERAL.— The Administrator, . . . shall develop, coordinate, and maintain a National Disaster Housing Strategy.

(b) CONTENTS.— The National Disaster Housing Strategy shall—

"(1) outline the most efficient and cost effective Federal programs that will best meet the short-term and long-term housing needs of individuals and households affected by a major disaster;

SEC. 689. INDIVIDUALS WITH DISABILITIES

(a) GUIDELINES.— Not later than 90 days after the date of enactment of this Act. . . the Administrator shall develop guidelines to accommodate individuals with disabilities, which shall include guidelines for—

(1) the accessibility of, and communications and programs in, shelters, recovery centers, and other facilities; and

(2) devices used in connection with disaster operations, including first aid stations, mass feeding areas, portable payphone stations, portable toilets, and temporary housing.

(b) ESSENTIAL ASSISTANCE.— Section 403(a) of the Robert T. Stafford Disaster Relief and Emergency Assistance Act (42 U.S.C. 5170b(a)) is amended—

(1) in paragraph (C) in subparagraph (I), by striking the period and inserting "; and"; and

(D) by adding at the end the following:

"(J) provision of rescue, care, shelter, and essential needs—

"(i) to individuals with household pets and service animals; and

"(ii) to such pets and animals.".

SEC. 689b. REUNIFICATION

(a) DEFINITIONS.— In this section:

(1) *CHILD LOCATOR CENTER.—* The term "Child Locator Center" means the National Emergency Child Locator Center established under subsection (b).

(2) *DECLARED EVENT.—* The term "declared event" means a major disaster or emergency.

(3) *DISPLACED ADULT.—* The term "displaced adult" means an individual 21 years of age or older who is displaced from the habitual residence of that individual as a result of a declared event.

(4) *DISPLACED CHILD.—* The term "displaced child" means an individual under 21 years of age who is displaced from the habitual residence of that individual as a result of a declared event.

(b) NATIONAL EMERGENCY CHILD LOCATOR CENTER.

(1) *IN GENERAL.*— Not later than 180 days after the date of enactment of this Act, the Administrator, . . . shall establish within the National Center for Missing and Exploited Children the National Emergency Child Locator Center. In establishing the National Emergency Child Locator Center, the Administrator shall establish procedures to make all relevant information available to the National Emergency Child Locator Center in a timely manner to facilitate the expeditious identification and reunification of children with their families.

SEC. 689c. NATIONAL EMERGENCY FAMILY REGISTRY AND LOCATOR SYSTEM

(a) DEFINITIONS.— In this section—

(1) the term "displaced individual" means an individual displaced by an emergency or major disaster; and

(2) the term "National Emergency Family Registry and Locator System" means the National Emergency Family Registry and Locator System established under subsection (b).

(b) ESTABLISHMENT.— Not later than 180 days after the date of enactment of this Act, the Administrator shall establish a National Emergency Family Registry and Locator System to help reunify families separated after an emergency or major disaster.

SEC. 689e. DISASTER RELATED INFORMATION SERVICES

Subtitle A of title VI of the Robert T. Stafford Disaster Relief and Emergency Assistance Act (42 U.S.C. 5195 et seq.) is amended by adding at the end the following:

SEC. 616. DISASTER RELATED INFORMATION SERVICES

"(a) IN GENERAL.— Consistent with section 308(a), the Director of Federal Emergency Management Agency shall—

"(1) identify, in coordination with State and local governments, population groups with limited English proficiency and take into account such groups in planning for an emergency or major disaster;

"(2) ensure that information made available to individuals affected by a major disaster or emergency is made

available in formats that can be understood by—

"(A) population groups identified under paragraph (1); and

"(B) individuals with disabilities or other special needs; and

SEC. 689g. DESIGNATION OF SMALL STATE AND RURAL ADVOCATE

(a) IN GENERAL.— Title III of the Robert T. Stafford Disaster Relief and Emergency Assistance Act (15 U.S.C. 5141 et seq.) is amended by adding at the end the following:

SEC. 326. DESIGNATION OF SMALL STATE AND RURAL ADVOCATE

"(a) *IN GENERAL.*— The President shall designate in the Federal Emergency Management Agency a Small State and Rural Advocate.

"(b) *RESPONSIBILITIES.*— The Small State and Rural Advocate shall be an advocate for the fair treatment of small States and rural communities in the provision of assistance under this Act.

"(c) *DUTIES.*— The Small State and Rural Advocate shall—

"(1) participate in the disaster declaration process under section 401 and the emergency declaration process under section 501, to ensure that the needs of rural communities are being addressed;

SEC. 691. ADVANCE CONTRACTING

(a) INITIAL REPORT.

(1) *IN GENERAL.*— Not later than 180 days after the date of enactment of this Act, the Administrator shall submit a report under paragraph (2) identifying—

(A) recurring disaster response requirements, including specific goods and services, for which the Agency is capable of contracting for in advance of a natural disaster or act of terrorism or other man-made disaster in a cost effective manner;

(B) recurring disaster response requirements, including specific goods and services, for which the Agency can not contract in advance of a natural disaster or act of terrorism or other man-made disaster in a cost effective manner; and

(C) a contracting strategy that maximizes the use of advance contracts to the extent practical and cost-effective.

SEC. 307. USE OF LOCAL FIRMS AND INDIVIDUALS

"(a) CONTRACTS OR AGREEMENTS WITH PRIVATE ENTITIES.

"(1) *IN GENERAL.—* In the expenditure of Federal funds for debris clearance, distribution of supplies, reconstruction, and other major disaster or emergency assistance activities which may be carried out by contract or agreement with private organizations, firms, or individuals, preference shall be given, to the extent feasible and practicable, to those organizations, firms, and individuals residing or doing business primarily in the area affected by such major disaster or emergency.

SEC. 697. REGISTRY OF DISASTER RESPONSE CONTRACTORS

(1) IN GENERAL.— The Administrator shall establish and maintain a registry of contractors who are willing to perform debris removal, distribution of supplies, reconstruction, and other disaster or emergency relief activities.

Pets Evacuation and Transportation Standards Act of 2006

SEC. 1. SHORT TITLE

This Act may be cited as the 'Pets Evacuation and Transportation Standards Act of 2006'.

SEC. 2. STANDARDS FOR STATE AND LOCAL EMERGENCY PREPAREDNESS OPERATIONAL PLANS

Section 613 of the Robert T. Stafford Disaster Relief and Emergency Assistance Act (42 U.S.C. 5196b) is amended–

(2) by inserting after subsection (f) the following:

'(g) Standards for State and Local Emergency Preparedness Operational Plans- In approving standards for State and local emergency preparedness operational plans pursuant to subsection (b)(3), the Director shall ensure that such plans take into account the needs of individuals with household pets and service animals prior to, during, and following a major disaster or emergency.'.

SEC. 4. PROVIDING ESSENTIAL ASSISTANCE TO INDIVIDUALS WITH HOUSEHOLD PETS AND SERVICE ANIMALS FOLLOWING A DISASTER

Section 403(a)(3) of the Robert T. Stafford Disaster Relief and Emergency Assistance Act (42 U.S.C. 5170b(a)(3)) is amended–in subparagraph (I), by striking the period and inserting '; and'; and (3) by adding at the end the following:

'(J) provision of rescue, care, shelter, and essential needs–

'(i) to individuals with household pets and service animals; and

'(ii) to such pets and animals.'.

ENDNOTES

1. "FEMA can trace its beginnings to the Congressional Act of 1803. . . .considered the first piece of disaster legislation, provided assistance to a New Hampshire town following an extensive fire. In the century that followed, ad hoc legislation was passed more than 100 times in response to hurricanes, earthquakes, floods and other natural disasters.

   By the 1930s, when the federal approach to problems became popular, the Reconstruction Finance Corporation was given authority to make disaster loans for repair and reconstruction of certain public facilities following an earthquake, and later, other types of disasters. In 1934, the Bureau of Public Roads was given authority to provide funding for highways and bridges damaged by natural disasters. The Flood Control Act, which gave the U.S. Army Corps of Engineers greater authority to implement flood control projects, was also passed. This piecemeal approach to disaster assistance was problematic and it prompted legislation that required greater cooperation between federal agencies and authorized the President to coordinate these activities. . .

   However, emergency and disaster activities were still fragmented. When hazards associated with nuclear power plants and the transportation of hazardous substances were added to natural disasters, more than 100 federal agencies were involved in some aspect of disasters, hazards and emergencies. . .

   President Carter's 1979 executive order merged many of the [approximately one hundred] separate disaster-related responsibilities into the Federal Emergency Management Agency (FEMA). . . ." http://www.fema.gov/about/history.shtm.

2. "The Federal Emergency Management Agency (FEMA) has had a bumpy history almost since its inception. . . created. . . in 1979 after state governors pressed for a better federal response in handling disasters. FEMA endured scandal and often became a parking lot for political appointees. In the Katrina catastrophe, critics say FEMA appeared dysfunctional and they point to several reasons, including FEMA's move into the Department of Homeland Security (DHS) in 2003 and director Michael Brown's inexperience in disaster management.". . .

   "Commenting here are: Jane Bullock, FEMA chief of staff (1993–2001); Tom Ridge, secretary, Department of Homeland Security (2002–2005); Richard Falkenrath, Homeland Security adviser (2001–2005); Michael Brown, FEMA director (2003–2005); and James Lee Witt, FEMA director (1993–2001)." http://www.pbs.org/wgbh/pages/frontline/storm/themes/fema.html.

3. The Stafford Act. http://www.fema.gov/about/stafact.shtm.

4. http://www.fema.gov/about/stafact.shtm.

5. Executive Order 12148–Federal Emergency Management, July 20, 1979. http://www.archives.gov/federal-register/codification/executive-order/12148.html.

6. Homeland Security Act, 2002. http://www.dhs.gov/xabout/laws/law_regulation_rule_0011.shtm.

7. Select Bipartisan Committee to Investigate the Preparation for and Response to Hurricane Katrina. p. xi. http://www.gpoaccess.gov/serialset/creports/katrina.html.

8. PKEMRA, (October 4, 2006). http://frwebgate.access.gpo.gov/cgi-bin/getdoc.cgi?dbname=109_cong_public_laws&docid=f:publ295.109.pdf.

9. Pets Evacuation and Transportation Standards Act of 2006. http://frwebgate.access.gpo.gov/cgi-bin/getdoc.cgi?dbname=109_cong_public_laws&docid=f:publ308.109.pdf.

10. Executive Order 12148–Federal Emergency Management, July 20, 1979, President Jimmy Carter. http://www.archives.gov/federal-register/codification/executive-order/12148.html.

11. "Under the Homeland Security Act, FEMA was explicitly given continued responsibility for the FRP [Federal Response Plan, section 507(b)(1), above] . Notwithstanding the clear language of the statute, the Secretary of Homeland Security initially removed responsibility from FEMA for drafting the FRP and changed the name of this document to the National Response Plan (NRP)... The initial version of the DHS NRP was criticized as too bureaucratic, overly complicated, and as confusing the Federal chain of command. The defects in this plan became clear after the inadequate response by the Federal government to Hurricane Katrina, and even DHS acknowledged the shortcomings." http://transportation.house.gov/hearings/hearingdetail.aspx?NewsID=298

12. Select Bipartisan Committee To Investigate The Preparation For And Response To Hurricane Katrina. http://www.Gpoaccess.Gov/Serialset/Creports/Katrina.Html (pp. ix–xi), http://www.gpoaccess.gov/serialset/creports/pdf/hr109-377/execsummary.pdf (pp. 1–5).

13. Select Bipartisan Committee to Investigate the Preparation for and Response to Hurricane Katrina. http://www.gpoaccess.gov/serialset/creports/pdf/hr109-377/preface.pdf (pp. ix–xi).

14. "U.S. Northern Command (USNORTHCOM) was established October 1, 2002 to provide command and control of Department of Defense (DoD) homeland defense efforts and to coordinate defense support of civil authorities." http://www.northcom.mil/About/index.html.

15. Select Bipartisan Committee to Investigate the Preparation for and Response to Hurricane Katrina. http://www.gpoaccess.gov/serialset/creports/pdf/hr109-377/execsummary.pdf (pp. 1–5).

16. Post Katrina Emergency Management Reform Act, 2006 (October 4, 2006). http://frwebgate.access.gpo.gov/cgi-bin/getdoc.cgi?dbname=109_cong_public_laws&docid=f:publ295.109.pdf.

17. ".... a goal of the Post-Katrina Emergency Management Reform Act was to create a new FEMA, a professional organization that has the expertise, responsibility, authority, and capability to prepare for and manage all aspects of disasters and emergencies. Specifically, [PKEMRA] ... required the FEMA Administrator and Regional Administrators to have professional emergency management qualifications ..." 'Subcommittee on Economic Development, Public Buildings, and Emergency Management - Readiness in the Post-Katrina and Post-9/11 World' report dated September 11, 2007. http://transportation.house.gov/hearings/hearingdetail.aspx?NewsID=298.

18. Section 872 of the Homeland Security Act. "The Secretary may allocate or reallocate functions among the officers of the Department, and may establish, consolidate, alter, or discontinue organizational units within the Department, ...

19. Homeland Security Act of 2002, sec 871(a): "The Secretary may establish, appoint members of, and use the services of, advisory committees, as the Secretary may deem necessary..."

20. "SAFECOM is a communications program of the Department of Homeland Security. SAFECOM provides research, development, testing and evaluation, guidance, tools, and templates on interoperable communications-related issues to local, tribal, state, and Federal emergency response agencies." http://www.safecomprogram.gov/SAFECOM/.

ADDITIONAL INFORMATION

The New Orleans Hurricane Protection System: Assessing Pre-Katrina Vulnerability and Improving Mitigation and Preparedness, 2009, [download is free but registration is required]. http://books.nap.edu/catalog.php?record_id=12647.

"Who's in Charge? Who Should Be? The Role of the Federal Government in Megadisasters: Based on Lessons from Hurricane Katrina," by Richard P. Nathan and Marc Landy, June 2, 2009, The Rockefeller Institute of Government. http://www.rockinst.org/pdf/disaster_recovery/gulfgov/gulfgov_reports/2009-06-02-Whos_in_Charge.PDF.

FEMA in General

Urban Area Security Initiative: FEMA Lacks Measures to Assess How Regional Collaboration Efforts Build Preparedness Capabilities, July 2009, GAO-09-651. http://www.gao.gov/new.items/d09651.pdf.

"Federal Disaster Relief in the U.S.: The Role of Political Partisanship and Preference in Presidential Disaster Declarations and Turndowns," Richard S. Salkowe and Jayajit Chakraborty, (2009) *Journal of Homeland Security and Emergency Management*: Vol. 6, Iss. 1, Article 28. http://www.bepress.com/jhsem/vol6/iss1/28/?sending=10643.

"Challenges Facing FEMA's Disaster Contract Management," Department of Homeland Security Office of Inspector General, OIG-09-70, May 2009. http://www.dhs.gov/xoig/assets/mgmtrpts/OIG_09-70_May09.pdf.

"During the past fifty years, federal disaster policy in the United States has been shaped by an ongoing conflict between proponents who favor federal intervention following a disaster and those who believe disaster response should be the responsibility of state and local governments and charity. This article explores the existing federal disaster policy landscape within the United States with a focus on the Stafford Act, the cultural and political forces that produced it, and how the current system is ill equipped to aid in the response and recovery from major catastrophes.

The Stafford Act defines how federal disasters are declared, determines the types of assistance to be provided by the federal government, and establishes cost sharing arrangements among federal, state, and local governments. The Federal Emergency Management Agency (FEMA) carries out the provisions of the Stafford Act and distributes much of the assistance provided by the Act. With the establishment of the U.S. Department of Homeland Security, the threat of domestic terrorism, and large-scale natural disasters like Hurricane Katrina, the limits of the Stafford Act and FEMA have been shown. We look at several areas where the shortcomings of the Stafford Act have emerged and propose directions for reform."

Moss, Mitchell; Schellhamer, Charles; and Berman, David A. (2009) "The Stafford Act and Priorities for Reform," *Journal of Homeland Security and Emergency Management*: Vol. 6, Iss. 1, Article 13. http://www.bepress.com/jhsem/vol6/iss1/13.

"National Preparedness, FEMA Has Made Progress, but Needs to Complete and Integrate Planning, Exercise, and Assessment Efforts," GAO-09-369, Aparil 2009. http://gao.gov/new.items/d09369.pdf.

FEMA Should Be Independent of DHS

Russel L. Honore, LTG, USA (RET). Testimony Before the House Subcommittee on Transportation and Infrastructure, May 14, 2009. http://transportation.house.gov/Media/file/Full%20Committee/20090514/Honore.pdf.

"An Independent FEMA: Restoring the Nation's Capabilities for Effective Emergency Management and Disaster Response." Testimony, Association of State Floodplain Managers, Inc., before the House Committee on Transportation and Infrastructure, May 14, 2009. http://transportation.house.gov/Media/file/Full%20Committee/20090514/Larson.pdf.

"An Independent FEMA: A Step Toward Rebuilding Federal Emergency Management Capabilities." Testimony of Jerome M. Hauer Before the House Subcommittee on Transportation and Infrastructure, May 14, 2009.

http://transportation.house.gov/Media/file/Full%20Committee/20090514/Hauer.pdf.

"An Independent FEMA: Restoring the Nation's Capabilities for Effective Emergency Management and Disaster Response." Testimony of Larry Gispert, Immediate Past President, International Association of Emergency Managers (USA) Before the House Subcommittee on Transportation and Infrastructure, May 14, 2009. http://transportation.house.gov/Media/file/Full%20Committee/20090514/Gispert.pdf.

Mitchell L. Moss, Henry Hart Rice Professor of Urban Policy and Planning,

Robert F. Wagner Graduate School of Public Service, New York University, Testimony

Before the House Subcommittee on Transportation and Infrastructure, May 14, 2009. http://transportation.house.gov/Media/file/Full%20Committee/20090514/Moss.pdf.

7

NATIONAL SECURITY STRATEGY OF THE UNITED STATES OF AMERICA, MARCH 2006[1]

The strategy emphasizes America's support for democracy as a means of ending tyranny, because, it states, democratic regimes are the most stable and will provide the most security for the United States.

OVERVIEW OF AMERICA'S NATIONAL SECURITY STRATEGY

It is the policy of the United States to seek and support democratic movements and institutions in every nation and culture, with the ultimate goal of ending tyranny in our world. In the world today, the fundamental character of regimes matters as much as the distribution of power among them. The goal of our statecraft is to help create a world of democratic, well-governed states that can meet the needs of their citizens and conduct themselves responsibly in the international system. This is the best way to provide enduring security for the American people.

Achieving this goal is the work of generations... Yet a new totalitarian ideology now threatens, an ideology grounded not in secular philosophy but in the perversion of a proud religion. Its content may be different from the ideologies of the last century, but its means are similar: intolerance, murder, terror, enslavement, and repression.

... The United States must:

- Champion aspirations for human dignity;
- Strengthen alliances to defeat global terrorism and work to prevent attacks against us and our friends;

- Work with others to defuse regional conflicts;
- Prevent our enemies from threatening us, our allies, and our friends with weapons of mass destruction (WMD);
- Ignite a new era of global economic growth through free markets and free trade;
- Expand the circle of development by opening societies and building the infrastructure of democracy;
- Develop agendas for cooperative action with other main centers of global power;
- Transform America's national security institutions to meet the challenges and opportunities of the 21st century; and
- Engage the opportunities and confront the challenges of globalization ....

C. The Way Ahead

The United States has long championed freedom because doing so reflects our values and advances our interests. It reflects our values because we believe the desire for freedom lives in every human heart and the imperative of human dignity transcends all nations and cultures.

Championing freedom advances our interests because the survival of liberty at home increasingly depends on the success of liberty abroad. Governments that honor their citizens' dignity and desire for freedom tend to uphold responsible conduct toward other nations, while governments that brutalize their people also threaten the peace and stability of other nations. Because democracies are the most responsible members of the international system, promoting democracy is the most effective long-term measure for strengthening international stability; reducing regional conflicts; countering

Foundations of Homeland Security: Law and Policy, First Edition. Martin J. Alperen.
© 2011 John Wiley & Sons, Inc. Published 2011 by John Wiley & Sons, Inc.

terrorism and terror-supporting extremism; and extending peace and prosperity.

To protect our Nation and honor our values, the United States seeks to extend freedom across the globe by leading an international effort to end tyranny and to promote effective democracy.

1. Explaining the Goal: Ending Tyranny. Tyranny is the combination of brutality, poverty, instability, corruption, and suffering, forged under the rule of despots and despotic systems. People living in nations such as the Democratic People's Republic of Korea (DPRK), Iran, Syria, Cuba, Belarus, Burma, and Zimbabwe know firsthand the meaning of tyranny; . . .

Though tyranny has few advocates, it needs more adversaries. In today's world, no tyrant's rule can survive without the support or at least the tolerance of other nations . . .

An end to tyranny will not mark an end to all global ills . . . Yet tyranny must not be tolerated – it is a crime of man, not a fact of nature.

2. Explaining the Goal: Promoting Effective Democracies. As tyrannies give way, we must help newly free nations build effective democracies: states that are respectful of human dignity, accountable to their citizens, and responsible towards their neighbors. Effective democracies:

- Honor and uphold basic human rights, including freedom of religion, conscience, speech, assembly, association, and press;
- Are responsive to their citizens, submitting to the will of the people, especially when people vote to change their government;
- Exercise effective sovereignty and maintain order within their own borders, protect independent and impartial systems of justice, punish crime, embrace the rule of law, and resist corruption; and
- Limit the reach of government, protecting the institutions of civil society, including the family, religious communities, voluntary associations, private property, independent business, and a market economy . . .

In effective democracies, freedom is indivisible. Political, religious, and economic liberty advance together and reinforce each other . . .

Elections are the most visible sign of a free society . . .

Participation in elections by individuals or parties must include their commitment to the equality of all citizens; minority rights; civil liberties; voluntary and peaceful transfer of power; and the peaceful resolution of differences. Effective democracy also requires institutions that can protect individual liberty and ensure that the government is responsive and accountable to its citizens. There must be an independent media . . .

There must be political associations and political parties that can freely compete. Rule of law must be reinforced by an independent judiciary, a professional legal establishment, and an honest and competent police force.

3. How We Will Advance Freedom: Principled in Goals and Pragmatic in Means. We have a responsibility to promote human freedom. Yet freedom cannot be imposed; it must be chosen. The form that freedom and democracy take in any land will reflect the history, culture, and habits unique to its people . . .

C. The Way Ahead

From the beginning, the War on Terror has been both a battle of arms and a battle of Ideas . . .

While the War on Terror is a battle of ideas, it is not a battle of religions. The transnational terrorists confronting us today exploit the proud religion of Islam to serve a violent political vision: the establishment, by terrorism and subversion, of a totalitarian empire that denies all political and religious freedom. These terrorists distort the idea of jihad into a call for murder against those they regard as apostates or unbelievers – including Christians, Jews, Hindus, other religious traditions, and all Muslims who disagree with them. Indeed, most of the terrorist attacks since September 11 have occurred in Muslim countries – and most of the victims have been Muslims.

To wage this battle of ideas effectively, we must be clear-eyed about what does and does not give rise to terrorism:

- Terrorism is not the inevitable by-product of poverty. Many of the September 11 hijackers were from middle-class backgrounds, and many terrorist leaders, like bin Laden, are from privileged upbringings.
- Terrorism is not simply a result of hostility to U.S. policy in Iraq. The United States was attacked on September 11 and earlier, well before we toppled the Saddam Hussein regime. Moreover, countries that stayed out of the Iraq war have not been spared from terror attack.
- Terrorism is not simply a result of Israeli-Palestinian issues. Al-Qaida plotting for the September 11 attacks began in the 1990s, during an active period in the peace process.
- Terrorism is not simply a response to our efforts to prevent terror attacks. The al-Qaida network targeted the United States long before the United States targeted al-Qaida. Indeed, the terrorists are emboldened more by perceptions of weakness than by demonstrations of resolve. Terrorists lure recruits by telling them that we

are decadent and easily intimidated and will retreat if attacked.[2]

The terrorism we confront today springs from:

- *Political alienation.* Transnational terrorists are recruited from people who have no voice in their own government and see no legitimate way to promote change in their own country. Without a stake in the existing order, they are vulnerable to manipulation by those who advocate a perverse vision based on violence and destruction.
- *Grievances that can be blamed on others.* The failures the terrorists feel and see are blamed on others, and on perceived injustices from the recent or sometimes distant past. The terrorists' rhetoric keeps wounds associated with this past fresh and raw, a potent motivation for revenge and terror.
- *Sub-cultures of conspiracy and misinformation.* Terrorists recruit more effectively from populations whose information about the world is contaminated by falsehoods and corrupted by conspiracy theories. The distortions keep alive grievances and filter out facts that would challenge popular prejudices and self-serving propaganda.
- *An ideology that justifies murder.* Terrorism ultimately depends upon the appeal of an ideology that excuses or even glorifies the deliberate killing of innocents. A proud religion – the religion of Islam – has been twisted and made to serve an evil end, as in other times and places other religions have been similarly abused.

Defeating terrorism in the long run requires that each of these factors be addressed. The genius of democracy is that it provides a counter to each.

- In place of alienation, democracy offers an ownership stake in society, a chance to shape one's own future.
- In place of festering grievances, democracy offers the rule of law, the peaceful resolution of disputes, and the habits of advancing interests through compromise.
- In place of a culture of conspiracy and misinformation, democracy offers freedom of speech, independent media, and the marketplace of ideas, which can expose and discredit falsehoods, prejudices, and dishonest propaganda.
- In place of an ideology that justifies murder, democracy offers a respect for human dignity that abhors the deliberate targeting of innocent civilians.

Democracy is the opposite of terrorist tyranny, which is why the terrorists denounce it and are willing to kill the innocent to stop it. Democracy is based on empowerment, while the terrorists' ideology is based on enslavement. Democracies expand the freedom of their citizens, while the terrorists seek to impose a single set of narrow beliefs. Democracy sees individuals as equal in worth and dignity, having an inherent potential to create and to govern themselves . . .

The strategy to counter the lies behind the terrorists' ideology is to empower the very people the terrorists most want to exploit: the faithful followers of Islam. We will continue to support political reforms that empower peaceful Muslims to practice and interpret their faith. The most vital work will be done within the Islamic world itself, and Jordan, Morocco, and Indonesia have begun to make important strides in this effort.

Responsible Islamic leaders need to denounce an ideology that distorts and exploits Islam for destructive ends and defiles a proud religion.

Many of the Muslim faith are already making this commitment at great personal risk. They realize they are a target of this ideology of terror. Everywhere we have joined in the fight against terrorism, Muslim allies have stood beside us, becoming partners in this vital cause. Pakistan and Saudi Arabia have launched effective efforts to capture or kill the leadership of the al-Qaida network . . .

The advance of freedom and human dignity through democracy is the long-term solution to the transnational terrorism of today. To create the space and time for that long-term solution to take root, there are four steps we will take in the short term . . .

- **Prevent attacks by terrorist networks before they occur.**
- **Deny WMD to rogue states and to terrorist allies who would use them without hesitation.**
- **Deny terrorist groups the support and sanctuary of rogue states.**

The United States and its allies in the War on Terror make no distinction between those who commit acts of terror and those who support and harbor them, because they are equally guilty of murder. Any government that chooses to be an ally of terror, such as Syria or Iran, has chosen to be an enemy of freedom, justice, and peace. The world must hold those regimes to account.

- **Deny the terrorists control of any nation that they would use as a base and launching pad for terror** . . .

C. The Way Ahead

Regional conflicts can arise from a wide variety of causes, including poor governance, external aggression, competing claims, internal revolt, tribal rivalries, and ethnic or religious hatreds. If left unaddressed, however, these different causes lead to the same ends: failed states, humanitarian disasters, and ungoverned areas that can become safe havens for terrorists.

The Administration's strategy for addressing regional conflicts includes three levels of engagement: conflict prevention and resolution; conflict intervention; and post-conflict stabilization and reconstruction . . .

1. *Conflict Prevention and Resolution.* The most effective long-term measure for conflict prevention and resolution is the promotion of democracy. Effective democracies may still have disputes, but they are equipped to resolve their differences peacefully, either bilaterally or by working with other regional states or international institutions.

2. *Conflict Intervention.* Some conflicts pose such a grave threat to our broader interests and values that conflict intervention may be needed to restore peace and stability . . .

3. *Post-Conflict Stabilization and Reconstruction.* Once peace has been restored, the hard work of post-conflict stabilization and reconstruction must begin.

4. *Genocide.* Patient efforts to end conflicts should not be mistaken for tolerance of the intolerable.

Genocide is the intent to destroy in whole or in part a national, ethnic, racial, or religious group. The world needs to start honoring a principle that many believe has lost its force in parts of the international community in recent years: genocide must not be tolerated.

C. The Way Ahead

We are committed to keeping the world's most dangerous weapons out of the hands of the world's most dangerous people.

1. *Nuclear Proliferation.* The proliferation of nuclear weapons poses the greatest threat to our national security.

Nuclear weapons are unique in their capacity to inflict instant loss of life on a massive scale . . . Therefore, our strategy focuses on controlling fissile material with two priority objectives: first, to keep states from acquiring the capability to produce fissile material suitable for making nuclear weapons; and second, to deter, interdict, or prevent any transfer of that material from states that have this capability to rogue states or to terrorists . . .

2. *Biological Weapons.* Biological weapons also pose a grave WMD threat because of the risks of contagion that would spread disease across large populations and around the globe. Unlike nuclear weapons, biological weapons do not require hard-to-acquire infrastructure or materials.

This makes the challenge of controlling their spread even greater.

3. *Chemical Weapons.* Chemical weapons are a serious proliferation concern and are actively sought by terrorists, including al-Qaida. Much like biological weapons, the threat from chemical weapons increases with advances in technology, improvements in agent development, and ease in acquisition of materials and equipment.

4. *The Need for Action.* The new strategic environment requires new approaches to deterrence and defense. Our deterrence strategy no longer rests primarily on the grim premise of inflicting devastating consequences on potential foes. Both offenses and defenses are necessary to deter state and non-state actors, through denial of the objectives of their attacks and, if necessary, responding with overwhelming force.

VI. Ignite a New Era of Global Economic Growth through Free Markets and Free Trade. . . .

VII. Expand the Circle of Development by Opening Societies and Building the Infrastructure of Democracy.

VIII. Develop Agendas for Cooperative Action with the Other Main Centers of Global Power. . . .

1. *The Western Hemisphere.* These principles guide our relations within our own Hemisphere, the frontline of defense of American national security. Our goal remains a hemisphere fully democratic, bound together by good will, security cooperation, and the opportunity for all our citizens to prosper . . . Countries in the Hemisphere must be helped to the path of sustained political and economic development. The deceptive appeal of anti-free market populism must not be allowed to erode political freedoms and trap the Hemisphere's poorest in cycles of poverty. If America's nearest neighbors are not secure and stable, then Americans will be less secure.

2. *Africa.* Africa holds growing geo-strategic importance and is a high priority of this Administration . . . Our goal is an African continent that knows liberty, peace, stability, and increasing prosperity.

3. *Middle East.* The Broader Middle East continues to command the world's attention. For too long, too many nations of the Middle East have suffered from a freedom deficit. Repression has fostered corruption, imbalanced or stagnant economies, political resentments, regional conflicts, and religious extremism . . . Yet the peoples of the Middle East share the same desires as people in the rest of the world: liberty, opportunity, justice, order, and peace. These desires are now being expressed in movements for reform. The United States is committed to supporting the efforts of reformers to realize a better life for themselves and their region.

4. *Europe.* The North Atlantic Treaty Organization remains a vital pillar of U.S. foreign policy. The Alliance has been strengthened by expanding its membership and now acts beyond its borders as an instrument for peace and stability in many parts of the world. It has also established partnerships with other key European states, including Russia, Ukraine, and others, further extending NATO's historic transformation . . .

5. *Russia.* The United States seeks to work closely with Russia on strategic issues of common interest and to manage issues on which we have differing interest. By reason of geography and power, Russia has great influence not only in Europe and its own immediate neighborhood, but also in many other regions of vital interest to us: the broader Middle East, South and Central Asia, and East Asia. We must encourage Russia to respect the values of freedom and democracy at home and not to impede the cause of freedom and democracy in these regions. Strengthening our relationship will depend on the policies, foreign and domestic, that Russia adopts. Recent trends regrettably point toward a diminishing commitment to democratic freedoms and institutions. We will work to try to persuade the Russian Government to move forward, not backward, along freedom's path.

6. *South and Central Asia.* South and Central Asia is a region of great strategic importance where American interests and values are engaged as never before. India is a great democracy, and our shared values are the foundation of our good relations. We are eager to see Pakistan move along a stable, secure, and democratic path. Our goal is for the entire region of South and Central Asia to be democratic, prosperous, and at peace.

7. *East Asia.* East Asia is a region of great opportunities and lingering tensions. Over the past decade, it has been a source of extraordinary economic dynamism and also of economic turbulence. Few regional economies have more effectively harnessed the engines of future prosperity: technology and globalized trade. Yet few regions have had greater difficulty overcoming the suspicions of the past.

ENDNOTES

1. National Security Strategy of the United States of America, March 2006. http://www.strategicstudies institute.army.mil/pdffiles/nss.pdf.

2. Radicalization, and the creation of new recruits is not at all this simple, and varies according to the recruit's circumstances including where the recruit is from. For one view, see below, Dr. Michael Doran, "The Four Pillars of Anti-Extremist Operations," 2008 Unrestricted Warfare Symposium, John's Hopkins University, Jet Propulsion Laboratory, p. 289–90. http://www.jhuapl.edu/urw_ symposium/Proceedings/2008/Authors/Doran.pdf.

"While it is difficult to profile terrorists in demographic terms, it is possible to profile them in psychopathological terms. The ideology is attractive to people, particularly young men, at times in their lives when an interlocking set of psychological issues besets them. I have been influenced here by David Kenning, an expert in branding. Al Qaeda's ideology gives a single, simple focus to individuals from different personal backgrounds and different countries who are troubled by a wide array of issues. For instance, the ideology provides a narrative and a method of resolving the grievances felt by someone who is frustrated with his own national government because he cannot get a job . . . The ideology has a nice way of taking all of those complex feelings that young men have—in particular, young Muslim men and often young Muslim men in Europe as well as in the Middle East—and channeling them all towards anti-Americanism. America becomes the symbol for all that is frustrating in their lives. *Dr. Mike Doran is the Deputy Assistant Secretary of Defense for Support to Public Diplomacy, responsible for policy, public diplomacy, and strategic communication to promote U.S. national security interests.*

8

NATIONAL STRATEGY FOR COMBATING TERRORISM, SEPTEMBER, 2006[1]

The National Strategy for Combating Terrorism notes that terrorists are not a monolithic group and then sets forth both short-term and long-term approaches for dealing with terrorism.

The National Strategy for Combating Terrorism describes "Today's Terrorist Enemy" as follows:

> This transnational movement is not monolithic. Although al-Qaida functions as the movement's vanguard and remains, along with its affiliate groups and those inspired by them, the most dangerous present manifestation of the enemy, the movement is not controlled by any single individual, group, or state. What unites the movement is a common vision, a common set of ideas about the nature and destiny of the world, and a common goal of ushering in totalitarian rule. What unites the movement is the ideology of oppression, violence, and hate.

The strategy next lays out a strategic vision for the War on Terror. For the short term, the

> "fight involves the application of all instruments of national power and influence to kill or capture the terrorists; deny them safe haven and control of any nation; prevent them from gaining access to WMD; render potential terrorist targets less attractive by strengthening security; and cut off their sources of funding and other resources they need to operate and survive."

In the long run, winning the War on Terror means winning the battle of ideas. Ideas can transform the embittered and

disillusioned either into murderers willing to kill innocents, or into free peoples living harmoniously in a diverse society. The battle of ideas helps to define the strategic intent of our National Strategy for Combating Terrorism. The United States will continue to lead an expansive international effort in pursuit of a two-pronged vision:

- The defeat of violent extremism as a threat to our way of life as a free and open society; and
- The creation of a global environment inhospitable to violent extremists and all who support them.[2]

Strategy for Winning the War on Terror

Long-Term Approach: Advancing Effective Democracy
The long-term solution for winning the War on Terror is the advancement of freedom and human dignity through effective democracy. . . .

The terrorism we confront today springs from:

- *Political alienation.*
- *Grievances that can be blamed on others.*
- *Subcultures of conspiracy and misinformation.*
- *An ideology that justifies murder.*

. . . Democracy is the antithesis of terrorist tyranny, which is why the terrorists denounce it and are willing to kill the innocent to stop it. Democracy is based on empowerment, while the terrorists' ideology is based on enslavement. Democracies expand the freedom of their citizens, while the terrorists seek to impose a single set of narrow beliefs. Democracy sees individuals as equal in worth and dignity, having an

Foundations of Homeland Security: Law and Policy, First Edition. Martin J. Alperen.
© 2011 John Wiley & Sons, Inc. Published 2011 by John Wiley & Sons, Inc.

inherent potential to create, govern themselves, and exercise basic freedoms of speech and conscience. The terrorists see individuals as objects to be exploited, and then to be ruled and oppressed. . . .

Over the Short Term: Four Priorities of Action The advance of freedom, opportunity, and human dignity through democracy is the long-term solution to the transnational terror movement of today. To create the space and time for this long-term solution to take root, we are operating along four priorities of action in the short term.

Prevent Attacks by Terrorist Networks. . . .

- *Deny terrorists entry to the United States and disrupt their travel internationally . . .*
- *Defend potential targets of attack . . .*

Deny WMD to Rogue States and Terrorist Allies Who Seek to Use Them . . . Our comprehensive approach for addressing WMD terrorism hinges on six objectives . . .

- *Determine terrorists' intentions, capabilities, and plans to develop or acquire WMD.*
- *Deny terrorists access to the materials, expertise, and other enabling capabilities required to develop WMD . . .*
- *Deter terrorists from employing WMD.*
- *Detect and disrupt terrorists' attempted movement of WMD-related materials, weapons, and personnel . . .*
- *Prevent and respond to a WMD-related terrorist attack . . .*
- *Define the nature and source of a terrorist-employed WMD device*
- *End state sponsorship of terrorism.*
- *Disrupt the flow of resources from rogue states to terrorists. . . .*

Deny Terrorists Control of Any Nation They Would Use as a Base and Launching Pad for Terror . . .

Institutionalizing Our Strategy for Long-term Success

- *Establish and maintain international standards of accountability . . .*
- *Strengthen coalitions and partnerships . . .*
- *Enhance government architecture and interagency collaboration . . .*
- *Foster intellectual and human capital. . . .*

ENDNOTES

1. National Strategy for Combating Terrorism, September 2006. http://merln.ndu.edu/archivepdf/terrorism/WH/nsct 2006.pdf.
2. National Strategy for Combating Terrorism, September 2006, p. 7. http://merln.ndu.edu/archivepdf/terrorism/WH/nsct2006.pdf.

ADDITIONAL RESOURCES

Operation TRIPWIRE is designed to improve the FBI's intelligence base with a specific goal to aid in identifying potential terrorist sleeper cells within the U.S. It puts in place a roadmap for developing intelligence and collection requirements targeting terrorist training, financing, recruiting, logistical support, and pre-attack preparation within the U.S." Report to the National Commission on Terrorist Attacks upon the United States: The FBI's Counterterrorism Program Since September 2001, U.S. Department of Justice, Federal Bureau of Investigation, April 2004. http://www.fbi.gov/publications/commission/9-11commissionrep.pdf

For example, seeking tips from businesses, a tripwire would be someone buying large amounts of materials that can be used to make explosives, or large amounts of weapons or ammunition.

9

NATIONAL STRATEGY FOR HOMELAND SECURITY, OCTOBER 2007

"The purpose of our Strategy is to guide, organize, and unify our Nation's homeland security efforts. It provides a common framework by which our entire Nation should focus its efforts on the following four goals: Prevent and disrupt terrorist attacks; Protect the American people, our critical infrastructure, and key resources; Respond to and recover from incidents that do occur; and Continue to strengthen the foundation to ensure our long-term success."

SOURCES

- Seeking a National Strategy: A Concert for Preserving Security... April 15, 2000[1]
- National Strategy for Homeland Security, October 2007[2]

Seeking A National Strategy: A Concert for Preserving Security and Promoting Freedom, April 15, 2000

...Thinking about Strategy

This Commission's Phase I report pointed to two contradictory trends ahead: a tide of economic, technological, and intellectual forces that is integrating a global community, amid powerful forces of social and political fragmentation. While no one knows what the mix of these trends will produce, the new world coming will be dramatically different in significant respects. Governments are under pressure from below, by forces of ethnic separatism and violence, and from

above, by economic, technological, and cultural forces beyond any government's full control. We are witnessing a transformation of human society on the magnitude of that between the agricultural and industrial epochs - and in a far more compressed period of time.

Such circumstances put a special premium on strategic wisdom, particularly for a country of the size and character of the United States. In this Commission's view, the essence of American strategy must compose a balance between two key aims. The first is to reap the benefits of a more integrated world in order to expand freedom, security, and prosperity for Americans and for others. But, second, American strategy must also strive to dampen the forces of global instability so that those benefits can endure. Freedom is the quintessential American value, but without security, and the relative stability that results therefrom, it can be evanescent. American strategy should seek both security and freedom, and it must seek them increasingly in concert with others. Hence our title: A Concert for Preserving Security and Promoting Freedom....

[See portions of Phase I of the Report, "New World Coming," in Chapter 2, "Strategic Environment."]

National Strategy for Homeland Security, October 2007

America is at war with terrorist enemies who are intent on attacking our Homeland and destroying our way of life. The lives and livelihoods of the American people also remain at risk from natural catastrophes, including naturally occurring infectious diseases and hazards such as hurricanes and earthquakes, and man-made accidents. Our National Strategy for Homeland Security recognizes that while we must continue

Foundations of Homeland Security: Law and Policy, First Edition. Martin J. Alperen.
© 2011 John Wiley & Sons, Inc. Published 2011 by John Wiley & Sons, Inc.

to focus on the persistent and evolving terrorist threat, we also must address the full range of potential catastrophic events, including man-made and natural disasters, due to their implications for homeland security.

The purpose of our Strategy is to guide, organize, and unify our Nation's homeland security efforts. It provides a common framework by which our entire Nation should focus its efforts on the following four goals:

- Prevent and disrupt terrorist attacks;
- Protect the American people, our critical infrastructure, and key resources;
- Respond to and recover from incidents that do occur; and
- Continue to strengthen the foundation to ensure our long-term success.

While the first three goals help to organize our national efforts, the last goal entails creating and transforming our homeland security principles, systems, structures, and institutions. This includes applying a comprehensive approach to risk management, building a culture of preparedness, developing a comprehensive Homeland Security Management System, improving incident management, better utilizing science and technology, and leveraging all instruments of national power and influence. . . .

Shared Responsibility "Throughout the evolution of our homeland security paradigm, one feature most essential to our success has endured: the notion that homeland security is a shared responsibility built upon a foundation of partnerships. Federal, State, local, and Tribal governments, the private and non-profit sectors, communities, and individual citizens all share common goals and responsibilities – as well as accountability – for protecting and defending the Homeland. . ."

In order to complete this truly national effort, we also must encourage and draw upon an informed and active citizenry. . .

Progress in Homeland Security and Beyond Next, the Strategy outlines progress that has been made. . . ."Since September 11, we have made extraordinary progress, with most of our important successes in the War on Terror and in the full range of homeland security activities having been achieved through effective national and international partnerships. . .

- We have greatly increased worldwide counterterrorism efforts..
- We have instituted an active, multi-layered approach to securing the Homeland that integrates the capabilities of local, Tribal, State, and Federal governments, as well as those of the private and non-profit sectors. . .

- We have made our borders more secure and developed an effective system of layered defense by strengthening the screening of people and goods overseas. . .
- We have strengthened . . . our homeland security and counterterrorism architecture ..
- The Federal Bureau of Investigation (FBI) and the Department of Justice (DOJ) have made the prevention of terrorist attacks their highest priority. . .
- . . . we have enhanced State, local, and Tribal homeland security training and equipment, emergency management capabilities, and the interoperability of communications.
- We have taken a series of historic steps to address biological threats. . .
- We have created a full-scale, comprehensive National Exercise Program. . .

Challenges in Homeland Security and Beyond While America is safer, we are not yet safe. . .significant challenges remain, including:

- The War on Terror remains a generational struggle, and our entire Nation must be engaged and prepared to participate in this effort.
- Terrorists have declared their intention to acquire and use weapons of mass destruction..
- Our vast land and maritime borders make it difficult to completely deny terrorists and their weapons access to the Homeland.
- The United States is not immune to the emergence of homegrown radicalization. . .
- We must counter potential waning in the sense of urgency and levels of international cooperation. . .
- We must guard against complacency. . .
- Although we have substantially improved our cooperation and partnership. . . we must continue to strengthen efforts to achieve full unity of effort through a stronger and further integrated national approach to homeland security.
- . . . we must enhance our ability to measure risk in a consistent and commonly accepted fashion and allocate finite resources accordingly.
- We must make additional reforms to the Foreign Intelligence Surveillance Act. . .
- The Congress must better align its oversight and committee structure in order to reflect the need for streamlined and effective legislative action that supports a unified approach to securing the Nation.

Our Vision and Strategy for Homeland Security We are a Nation blessed with unprecedented liberty, opportunity, and openness – foundations of the American way of life. Our principal terrorist enemies – al-Qaida, its affiliates, and those inspired by them – seek to destroy this way of life...

The United States, through a concerted national effort that galvanizes the strengths and capabilities of Federal, State, local, and Tribal governments; the private and non-profit sectors; and regions, communities, and individual citizens – along with our partners in the international community – will work to achieve a secure Homeland that sustains our way of life as a free, prosperous, and welcoming America.

In order to realize this vision, the United States will use all instruments of national power and influence . . .to achieve our goals to prevent and disrupt terrorist attacks; protect the American people, critical infrastructure, and key resources; and respond to and recover from incidents that do occur. We also will continue to create, strengthen, and transform the principles, systems, structures, and institutions we need to secure our Nation over the long term.

This is our strategy for homeland security."

Prevent and Disrupt Terrorist Attacks ... Over the short term we are working to prevent attacks by terrorist networks, deny weapons of mass destruction (WMD) to rogue states and terrorists who seek to use them, deny terrorists the support and sanctuary of rogue states, and deny terrorists control of any nation they would use as a base and launching pad for terror..

This *National Strategy for Homeland Security* is a companion to the *National Strategy for Combating Terrorism*, and the sections in both on preventing and disrupting terrorist attacks are complementary and mutually reinforcing...

Deny Terrorists, Their Weapons, and Other Terror-Related Materials Entry to the Homeland

- *Prevent terrorist use of illicit pathways into the Homeland.*

Disrupt Terrorists and Their Capacity to Operate in the United States...

- *Disrupt terrorists and their activities and networks.*

Prevent Violent Islamic Extremist Radicalization in the United States

- *Engage key communities as partners in the War on Terror.*
- *Identify and counter the sources of radicalization.*
- *Enhance Federal, State, local, and Tribal government capacities to address radicalization...*

Respond to and Recover from Incidents

... Given the certainty of catastrophes on our soil – no matter how unprecedented or extraordinary – it is our collective duty to provide the best response possible... As the Nation responds based on the scope and nature of the incident, we must begin to lay the foundation not only for a strong recovery over the short term but also for the rebuilding and revitalization of affected communities and regions over the long term...

Incident Management Versus Response

The homeland security community has used the terms "incident management" and "response" in complementary and occasionally interchangeable manners. Within this *Strategy*, "response" refers to actions taken in the immediate aftermath of an incident to save lives, meet basic human needs, and reduce the loss of property. "Incident management," however, is a broader concept that refers to how we manage incidents and mitigate consequences across all homeland security activities, including prevention, protection, and response and recovery. This concept, including the role of the National Incident Management System (NIMS), is discussed" [in the chapter entitled NIMS].

Strengthen the Foundation for an Effective National Response

- *Clarify how national roles and responsibilities are fulfilled across all levels of government and the private and non-profit sectors.* Disaster response has traditionally been handled by State, local, and Tribal governments, with the Federal Government and private and non-profit sectors playing supporting and *ad hoc* roles, respectively
- *Strengthen doctrine to guide the national response...* NIMS forms the backbone of this doctrine and includes, among other things, an Incident Command System as the overall management structure for responding to an incident as well as the concept of Unified Command, which provides for and enables joint decisions and action based on mutually agreed-upon objectives, priorities, and plans among all homeland partners involved in the response effort without affecting individual agency authority, responsibility, or accountability.

Roles and Responsibilities

In today's dynamic threat environment, we must strive for a national response based on engaged partnerships at and across all levels that enable us to anticipate where we should increase or reduce support based on changing circumstances.

Success starts with understanding the following fundamental roles:

Community Response. *One of the fundamental response principles is that all incidents should be handled at the lowest jurisdictional level possible.* The initial response to the majority of incidents typically is handled by local responders within a single jurisdiction. . .

State Response. *State governments have the primary responsibility for assisting local governments to respond to and recover from disasters and emergencies.*

Federal Response. *The Federal Government maintains a wide array of capabilities and resources that may be made available to States and local governments.*

Private and Non-Profit Sector. *The private and non-profit sectors fulfill key roles and work closely with communities, States, and the Federal Government.*

Special Circumstances. *There are special circumstances where the Federal Government exercises a larger, more proactive role.* This includes catastrophic incidents when local and State governments require significant support, and incidents where Federal interests are directly implicated, such as those involving primary Federal jurisdiction or authorities. For example, the Federal Government will lead response efforts to render safe weapons of mass destruction and coordinate related activities with State and local partners, as appropriate.

Assess Situation and Take Initial Action

. . . Our Nation must acknowledge the critical role of first responders to rapidly assess ongoing and emerging incidents. This includes effectively prioritizing and coordinating initial actions, mobilizing and deploying resources and capabilities, and anticipating additional support that may be needed.

Prioritize and coordinate initial actions to mitigate consequences. . .

Examples of Federal Field Teams

Since September 11, the Federal Government has strengthened deployable teams to help respond to natural and manmade disasters. These teams support the emergent needs of State, local, and Tribal jurisdictions or exercise Federal statutory responsibilities by providing specialized expertise and capabilities, establishing emergency response facilities, and supporting overall incident management.

- Emergency Response Teams (ERT) – to be replaced by the Federal Incident Response Support Teams (FIRST) and Incident Management Assistance Teams (IMAT)
- Damage Assessment Teams

- Nuclear Incident Response Team (NIRT)
- Disaster Medical Assistance Teams (DMATs)
- Department of Health and Human Services' Incident Response Coordination Team – formerly the Secretary's Emergency Response Team
- Department of Labor/Occupational Safety and Health Administration's Specialized Response Teams
- National Veterinary Response Teams (NVRT) – formerly the Veterinarian Medical Assistance Teams (VMATs)
- Disaster Mortuary Operational Response Teams (DMORTs)
- Medical Emergency Radiological Response Team (MERRT)
- National Medical Response Teams (NMRTs)
- Scientific and Technical Advisory and Response Teams (STARTs)
- Donations Coordination Teams
- Urban Search and Rescue (US&R) Task Forces
- Incident Management Teams (IMTs)
- Domestic Emergency Support Team (DEST)
- Domestic Animal and Wildlife Emergency Response Teams and Mitigation Assessment Team.

Commence Short-Term Recovery Actions to Stabilize the Affected Area and Demobilize Assets

Ensuring Long-Term Success

Risk Management The assessment and management of risk underlies the full spectrum of our homeland security activities, including decisions about when, where, and how to invest in resources that eliminate, control, or mitigate risks. In the face of multiple and diverse catastrophic possibilities, we accept that risk – a function of threats, vulnerabilities, and consequences – is a permanent condition. We must apply a risk-based framework across all homeland security efforts in order to identify and assess potential hazards (including their downstream effects), determine what levels of relative risk are acceptable, and prioritize and allocate resources among all homeland security partners, both public and private, to prevent, protect against, and respond to and recover from all manner of incidents. . .

Culture of Preparedness Our entire Nation shares common responsibilities in homeland security. In order to help prepare the Nation to carry out these responsibilities, we will continue to foster a Culture of Preparedness that permeates all levels of our society. . .This Culture rests on four principles.

The first principle of our Culture of Preparedness is a shared acknowledgement that creating a prepared Nation will be an enduring challenge. . .

The second principle is the importance of individual and collective initiative to counter fundamental biases toward reactive responses and approaches. . .

The third principle is that individual citizens, communities, the private sector, and non-profit organizations each perform a central role in homeland security. . .

The fourth principle of our Culture of Preparedness is the responsibility of each level of government. . . our Culture must continue to embrace the notion of partnership among all levels of government. . .

Homeland Security Management System . . . we will establish and institutionalize a comprehensive Homeland Security Management System that incorporates all stakeholders. . .

. . . This new Homeland Security Management System will involve a continuous, mutually reinforcing cycle of activity across four phases.

- *Phase One: Guidance*. . . .homeland security guidance . . .is the foundation of our system, and it must be grounded in clearly articulated and up-to-date homeland and relevant national security policies, with coordinated supporting strategies, doctrine, and planning guidance flowing from and fully synchronizing with these policies. . .

- *Phase Two: Planning*. The second phase is a deliberate and dynamic system that translates our policies, strategies, doctrine, and planning guidance into a family of strategic, operational, and tactical plans. . .

- *Phase Three: Execution*. The third phase . . . encompasses the execution of operational and tactical-level plans. This may occur as actual operations in response to real-world events or may happen as part of an exercise. . .

- *Phase Four: Assessment and Evaluation*. The fourth phase involves the continual assessment and evaluation of both operations and exercises. This phase of the system will produce lessons learned and best practices that must be incorporated back into all phases of the Homeland Security Management System.

Incident Management . . . Decision-making during crises and periods of heightened concern, however, is different from decision-making during a steady-state of activity, and we must develop a comprehensive approach that will help Federal, State, local, and Tribal authorities manage incidents across all homeland security efforts.

Our approach will build upon the current National Incident Management System (NIMS). . .

Incident management rests on a core set of common principles and requirements. The first of these is an Incident Command System, which provides the overall structure for managing an incident. . . Unified Command is a sec-

ond core principle. . .Crisis action planning is a third key principle.. They also must be able to provide resources – a fourth requirement – in support of their plans and activities, and we call on all stakeholders to have predetermined capabilities available on a short deployment timeline. . . The maintenance of situational awareness through timely and accurate information is a fifth core principle integral to incident management. . . In order to help facilitate situational awareness and decision-making, we must prioritize incident information – a sixth requirement. . . A seventh requirement of incident management consists of the various multiagency coordination centers that exist throughout all levels of government. . . People exist at the heart of our refocused incident management approach, and deploying people with the skills necessary to manage each incident is the eighth key principle. . .

Science and Technology The United States derives much of its strength from its advantage in the realm of science and technology (S&T), and we must continue to use this advantage and encourage innovative research and development to assist in protecting and defending against the range of natural and man-made threats confronting the Homeland. . .

Legislative Branch Homeland security at the Federal level is not the sole purview of the executive branch of government. The Congress also must take bold steps to fulfill its responsibilities in the national effort to secure the Homeland and protect the American people. The current committee structure, for example, creates competing initiatives and requirements and fails to establish clear and consistent priorities or provide optimal oversight. Accordingly, both houses of the Congress should take action to further streamline the organization and structure of those committees that authorize and appropriate homeland security-related funds and otherwise oversee homeland security missions. The Congress also should fully embrace a risk-based funding approach so that we best prioritize our limited resources to meet our most critical homeland security goals and objectives first, as opposed to distributing funds and making decisions based on political considerations. . .

ENDNOTES

1. "Seeking a National Strategy: A Concert for Preserving Security and Promoting Freedom," The Phase II Report on a U.S. National Security Strategy for the 21st Century, The United States Commission on National Security/21st Century, April 15, 2000, pp. 5–6. http://www.au.af.mil/au/awc/awcgate/nssg/phaseII.pdf.

2. National Strategy for Homeland Security, October 2007. http://www.dhs.gov/xlibrary/assets/nat_strat_homelandsecurity_2007.pdf.

10

BORDER SECURITY

This chapter presents border security legislation and policy documents. It includes the Northern border legislation of the Patriot Act, sections of the Homeland Security Act, and the Artic Region policy of HSPD-25.

SOURCES

- Patriot Act, 2001[1]
- Homeland Security Act of 2002[2]
- Intelligence Reform and Terrorism Prevention Act of 2004, Advanced Technology Northern Border Security Pilot Program, December 17, 2004[3]
- Appropriations, Public Law 109–295, Title V, October 4, 2006[4]
- Arctic Region Policy, NSPD-66/HSPD-25, January 9, 2009[5]
- National Southwest Border Counternarcotics Strategy, June 2009[6]

Patriot Act

SEC. 402. NORTHERN BORDER PERSONNEL

There are authorized to be appropriated—

(1) such sums as may be necessary to triple the number of Border Patrol personnel (from the number authorized under current law), and the necessary personnel and facilities to support such personnel, in each State along the Northern Border;

(2) such sums as may be necessary to triple the number of Customs Service personnel (from the number authorized under current law), and the necessary personnel and facilities to support such personnel, at ports of entry in each State along the Northern Border;

(3) such sums as may be necessary to triple the number of INS inspectors (from the number authorized on the date of the enactment of this Act), and the necessary personnel and facilities to support such personnel, at ports of entry in each State along the Northern Border; and

(4) an additional $50,000,000 each to the Immigration and Naturalization Service and the United States Customs Service for purposes of making improvements in technology for monitoring the Northern Border and acquiring additional equipment at the Northern Border.

SEC. 403. ACCESS BY THE DEPARTMENT OF STATE AND THE INS TO CERTAIN IDENTIFYING INFORMATION IN THE CRIMINAL HISTORY RECORDS OF VISA APPLICANTS AND APPLICANTS FOR ADMISSION TO THE UNITED STATES

(a) AMENDMENT OF THE IMMIGRATION AND NATIONALITY ACT.— Section 105 of the Immigration and Nationality Act (8 U.S.C. 1105) is amended–(4) by adding at the end the following:

'(b)(1) The Attorney General and the Director of the Federal Bureau of Investigation shall provide the Department of

Foundations of Homeland Security: Law and Policy, First Edition. Martin J. Alperen.
© 2011 John Wiley & Sons, Inc. Published 2011 by John Wiley & Sons, Inc.

State and the Service access to the criminal history record information contained in the National Crime Information Center's Interstate Identification Index (NCIC-III), Wanted Persons File, and to any other files maintained by the National Crime Information Center that may be mutually agreed upon by the Attorney General and the agency receiving the access, for the purpose of determining whether or not a visa applicant or applicant for admission has a criminal history record indexed in any such file.

'(2) Such access shall be provided by means of extracts of the records for placement in the automated visa lookout or other appropriate database, and shall be provided without any fee or charge.

'(4) Access to an extract does not entitle the Department of State to obtain the full content of the corresponding automated criminal history record. To obtain the full content of a criminal history record, the Department of State shall submit the applicant's fingerprints and any appropriate fingerprint processing fee authorized by law to the Criminal Justice Information Services Division of the Federal Bureau of Investigation.

(c) TECHNOLOGY STANDARD TO CONFIRM IDENTITY

(1) *IN GENERAL.*— The Attorney General and the Secretary of State jointly, through the National Institute of Standards and Technology (NIST)... shall within 2 years after the date of the enactment of this section, develop and certify a technology standard that can be used to verify the identity of persons applying for a United States visa or such persons seeking to enter the United States pursuant to a visa for the purposes of conducting background checks, confirming identity, and ensuring that a person has not received a visa under a different name or such person seeking to enter the United States pursuant to a visa.

(2) *INTEGRATED.*— The technology standard developed pursuant to paragraph (1), shall be the technological basis for a cross-agency, cross-platform electronic system that is a cost-effective, efficient, fully integrated means to share law enforcement and intelligence information necessary to confirm the identity of such persons applying for a United States visa or such person seeking to enter the United States pursuant to a visa.

Homeland Security Act Of 2002

SEC. 401. UNDER SECRETARY FOR BORDER AND TRANSPORTATION SECURITY

There shall be in the Department a Directorate of Border and Transportation Security headed by an Under Secretary for Border and Transportation Security.

SEC. 402. RESPONSIBILITIES

The Secretary, acting through the Under Secretary for Border and Transportation Security, shall be responsible for the following:

(1) Preventing the entry of terrorists and the instruments of terrorism into the United States.

(2) Securing the borders, territorial waters, ports, terminals, waterways, and air, land, and sea transportation systems of the United States, including managing and coordinating those functions transferred to the Department at ports of entry.

(3) Carrying out the immigration enforcement functions vested by statute in, or performed by, the Commissioner of Immigration and Naturalization (or any officer, employee, or component of the Immigration and Naturalization Service) immediately before the date on which the transfer of functions specified under section 441 takes effect.

(4) Establishing and administering rules, in accordance with section 428, governing the granting of visas or other forms of permission, including parole, to enter the United States to individuals who are not a citizen or an alien lawfully admitted for permanent residence in the United States.

(5) Establishing national immigration enforcement policies and priorities.

(6) Except as provided in subtitle C, administering the customs laws of the United States.

(7) Conducting the inspection and related administrative functions of the Department of Agriculture transferred to the Secretary of Homeland Security under section 421.

(8) In carrying out the foregoing responsibilities, ensuring the speedy, orderly, and efficient flow of lawful traffic and commerce.

Intelligence Reform and Terrorism Prevention Act of 2004, Advanced Technology Northern Border Security Pilot Program, December 17, 2004

SEC. 5101. ESTABLISHMENT

The Secretary of Homeland Security may carry out a pilot program to test various advanced technologies that will improve border security between ports of entry along the northern border of the United States.

SEC. 5102. PROGRAM REQUIREMENTS

(a) REQUIRED FEATURES.— The Secretary of Homeland Security shall design the pilot program under this subtitle to have the following features:

(1) Use of advanced technological systems, including sensors, video, and unmanned aerial vehicles, for border surveillance.

(2) Use of advanced computing and decision integration software for—

  (A) evaluation of data indicating border incursions;

  (B) assessment of threat potential; and

  (C) rapid real-time communication, monitoring, intelligence gathering, deployment, and response.

(3) Testing of advanced technology systems and software to determine best and most cost-effective uses of advanced technology to improve border security.

(4) Operation of the program in remote stretches of border lands with long distances between 24-hour ports of entry with a relatively small presence of United States border patrol officers.

(5) Capability to expand the program upon a determination by the Secretary that expansion would be an appropriate and cost-effective means of improving border security.

(b) COORDINATION WITH OTHER AGENCIES. The Secretary of Homeland Security shall ensure that the operation of the pilot program under this subtitle—

(1) is coordinated among United States, State, local, and Canadian law enforcement and border security agencies; and

(2) includes ongoing communication among such agencies.

SEC. 5201. BORDER SURVEILLANCE

(a) IN GENERAL.— Not later than 6 months after the date of enactment of this Act, the Secretary of Homeland Security shall submit to the President and the appropriate committees of Congress a comprehensive plan for the systematic surveillance of the southwest border of the United States by remotely piloted aircraft.

(b) CONTENTS.— The plan submitted under subsection (a) shall include

(1) recommendations for establishing command and control centers, operations sites, infrastructure, maintenance, and procurement;

(2) cost estimates for the implementation of the plan and ongoing operations;

(3) recommendations for the appropriate agent within the Department of Homeland Security to be the executive agency for remotely piloted aircraft operations;

(4) the number of remotely piloted aircraft required for the plan;

(5) the types of missions the plan would undertake, including—

  (A) protecting the lives of people seeking illegal entry into the United States;

  (B) interdicting illegal movement of people, weapons, and other contraband across the border;

  (C) providing investigative support to assist in the dismantling of smuggling and criminal networks along the border;

  (D) using remotely piloted aircraft to serve as platforms for the collection of intelligence against smugglers and criminal networks along the border; and

SEC. 5202. INCREASE IN FULL-TIME BORDER PATROL AGENTS

In each of the fiscal years 2006 through 2010, the Secretary of Homeland Security shall, subject to the availability of appropriations for such purpose, increase by not less than 2,000 the number of positions for full-time active-duty border patrol agents within the Department of Homeland Security above the number of such positions for which funds were allotted for the preceding fiscal year. In each of the fiscal years 2006 through 2010, in addition to the border patrol agents assigned along the northern border of the United States during the previous fiscal year, the Secretary shall assign a number of border patrol agents equal to not less than 20 percent of the net increase in border patrol agents during each such fiscal year.

SEC. 5203. INCREASE IN FULL-TIME IMMIGRATION AND CUSTOMS ENFORCEMENT INVESTIGATORS

In each of fiscal years 2006 through 2010, the Secretary of Homeland Security shall, subject to the availability of appropriations for such purpose, increase by not less than 800 the number of positions for full-time active duty investigators within the Department of Homeland Security investigating violations of immigration laws. . .above the number of such positions for which funds were made available during the preceding fiscal year.

SEC. 5204. INCREASE IN DETENTION BED SPACE

(a) IN GENERAL.— Subject to the availability of appropriated funds, the Secretary of Homeland Security shall increase by not less than 8,000, in each of the fiscal years 2006 through 2010, the number of beds available for immigration detention and removal operations of the Department of Homeland Security above the number for which funds were allotted for the preceding fiscal year.

Subtitle C—Visa Requirements

SEC. 5301. IN PERSON INTERVIEWS OF VISA APPLICANTS

(a) **REQUIREMENT FOR INTERVIEWS.**— Section 222 of the Immigration and Nationality Act (8 U.S.C. 1202) is amended by adding at the end the following new subsection:

"(h) Notwithstanding any other provision of this Act, the Secretary of State shall require every alien applying for a nonimmigrant visa—

"(1) who is at least 14 years of age and not more than 79 years of age to submit to an in person interview with a consular officer unless the requirement for such interview is waived. . .

Appropriations, Public Law 109–295, Title V, Oct. 4, 2006

SEC. 551

(a) CONSTRUCTION OF BORDER TUNNEL OR PASSAGE.—

Chapter 27 of title 18, United States Code, is amended by adding at the end the following:

§ 554. Border Tunnels and Passages

"(a) Any person who knowingly constructs or finances the construction of a tunnel or subterranean passage that crosses the international border between the United States and another country, other than a lawfully authorized tunnel or passage known to the Secretary of Homeland Security and subject to inspection by Immigration and Customs Enforcement, shall be fined under this title and imprisoned for not more than 20 years.

"(b) Any person who knows or recklessly disregards the construction or use of a tunnel or passage described in subsection (a) on land that the person owns or controls shall be fined under this title and imprisoned for not more than 10 years.

"(c) Any person who uses a tunnel or passage described in subsection (a) to unlawfully smuggle an alien, goods (in violation of section 545), controlled substances, weapons of mass destruction (including biological weapons), or a member of a terrorist organization (as defined in section 2339B(g)(6)) shall be subject to a maximum term of imprisonment that is twice the maximum term of imprisonment that would have otherwise been applicable had the unlawful activity not made use of such a tunnel or passage.".

Arctic Region Policy, NSPD-66 / HSPD-25, January 9, 2009

I. PURPOSE

(A) This directive establishes the policy of the United States with respect to the Arctic region and directs related implementation actions. This directive supersedes Presidential Decision Directive/NSC-26 (PDD-26; issued 1994) with respect to Arctic policy but not Antarctic policy; PDD-26 remains in effect for Antarctic policy only.

(B) This directive shall be implemented in a manner consistent with the Constitution and laws of the United States, with the obligations of the United States under the treaties and other international agreements to which the United States is a party, and with customary international law as recognized by the United States, including with respect to the law of the sea.

II. BACKGROUND

(A) The United States is an Arctic nation, with varied and compelling interests in that region. This directive takes into account several developments, including, among others:

Altered national policies on homeland security and defense;

The effects of climate change and increasing human activity in the Arctic region;

The establishment and ongoing work of the Arctic Council; and

A growing awareness that the Arctic region is both fragile and rich in resources.

III. POLICY

(A) It is the policy of the United States to:

Meet national security and homeland security needs relevant to the Arctic region;

Protect the Arctic environment and conserve its biological resources;

Ensure that natural resource management and economic development in the region are environmentally sustainable;

Strengthen institutions for cooperation among the eight Arctic nations (the United States, Canada, Denmark, Finland, Iceland, Norway, the Russian Federation, and Sweden);

Involve the Arctic's indigenous communities in decisions that affect them; and

Enhance scientific monitoring and research into local, regional, and global environmental issues.

(B) National Security and Homeland Security Interests in the Arctic

The United States has broad and fundamental national security interests in the Arctic region and is prepared to operate either independently or in conjunction with other states to safeguard these interests. These interests include such matters as missile defense and early warning; deployment of sea and air systems for strategic sealift, strategic deterrence, maritime presence, and maritime security operations; and ensuring freedom of navigation and overflight.

The United States also has fundamental homeland security interests in preventing terrorist attacks and mitigating those criminal or hostile acts that could increase the United States vulnerability to terrorism in the Arctic region.

The Arctic region is primarily a maritime domain; as such, existing policies and authorities relating to maritime areas continue to apply, including those relating to law enforcement.[1] Human activity in the Arctic region is increasing and is projected to increase further in coming years. This requires the United States to assert a more active and influential national presence to protect its Arctic interests and to project sea power throughout the region.

([1] These policies and authorities include Freedom of Navigation (PDD/NSC-32), the U.S. Policy on Protecting the Ocean Environment (PDD/NSC-36), Maritime Security Policy (NSPD-41/HSPD-13), and the National Strategy for Maritime Security (NSMS).)

The United States exercises authority in accordance with lawful claims of United States sovereignty, sovereign rights, and jurisdiction in the Arctic region, including sovereignty within the territorial sea, sovereign rights and jurisdiction within the United States exclusive economic zone and on the continental shelf, and appropriate control in the United States contiguous zone.

Freedom of the seas is a top national priority. The Northwest Passage is a strait used for international navigation, and the Northern Sea Route includes straits used for international navigation; the regime of transit passage applies to passage through those straits. Preserving the rights and duties relating to navigation and overflight in the Arctic region supports our ability to exercise these rights throughout the world, including through strategic straits.

Implementation:
In carrying out this policy as it relates to national security and homeland security interests in the Arctic, the Secretaries of State, Defense, and Homeland Security, in coordination with heads of other relevant executive departments and agencies, shall:

Develop greater capabilities and capacity, as necessary, to protect United States air, land, and sea borders in the Arctic region;

Increase Arctic maritime domain awareness in order to protect maritime commerce, critical infrastructure, and key resources;

Preserve the global mobility of United States military and civilian vessels and aircraft throughout the Arctic region;

Project a sovereign United States maritime presence in the Arctic in support of essential United States interests; and

Encourage the peaceful resolution of disputes in the Arctic region.

(F) Maritime Transportation in the Arctic Region

The United States priorities for maritime transportation in the Arctic region are:

To facilitate safe, secure, and reliable navigation;
To protect maritime commerce; and
To protect the environment.

Safe, secure, and environmentally sound maritime commerce in the Arctic region depends on infrastructure to support shipping activity, search and rescue capabilities, short- and long-range aids to navigation, high-risk area vessel-traffic management, iceberg warnings and other sea ice information, effective shipping standards, and measures to protect the marine environment. In addition, effective search and rescue in the Arctic will require local, State, Federal, tribal, commercial, volunteer, scientific, and multinational cooperation.

Implementation:
Commensurate with the level of human activity in the region, establish a risk-based capability to address hazards in the Arctic environment. Such efforts shall advance work on pollution prevention and response standards; determine basing and logistics support requirements, including necessary airlift and icebreaking capabilities; and improve plans and cooperative agreements for search and rescue;

Develop Arctic waterways management regimes in accordance with accepted international standards, including vessel traffic-monitoring and routing; safe navigation standards; accurate and standardized charts; and accurate and timely environmental and navigational information; and

Evaluate the feasibility of using access through the Arctic for strategic sealift and humanitarian aid and disaster relief.

National Southwest Border Counternarcotics Strategy, June 2009

Chapter 1: Intelligence and Information Sharing

STRATEGIC GOAL Substantially reduce the flow of illicit drugs, drug proceeds, and associated instruments of violence across the Southwest border.

STRATEGIC OBJECTIVES Enhance intelligence capabilities associated with the Southwest border.

(1) Interdict drugs, drug proceeds, and associated instruments of violence at the ports of entry, between the ports of entry, and in the air and maritime domains along the Southwest border.

(2) Ensure the prosecution of all significant drug trafficking, money laundering, bulk currency, and weapons smuggling/trafficking cases.

(3) Disrupt and dismantle drug trafficking organizations.

(4) Enhance counterdrug technologies for drug detection and interdiction along the Southwest border.

(5) Enhance U.S.–Mexico cooperation regarding joint counterdrug efforts.

BACKGROUND The United States faces "a range of interrelated challenges on the Southwest border, including drug and human smuggling into the United States, associated violence, and the transit of arms and bulk cash from the United States to Mexico." Over the next few years, the focus of these intelligence programs will be on improving and integrating the flow of timely and relevant intelligence and analysis—as well as the process of information sharing and coordination—among the Federal, State, local, tribal, and territorial agencies dedicated to protecting the Southwest border from the illicit flow of drugs and associated threats."

SUPPORTING ACTIONS

(1) **Enhance coordination and, where possible, harmonization of intelligence and information collection, analysis, and dissemination among the Intelligence Community and law enforcement agencies with Southwest border counterdrug intelligence responsibilities.**

Re-establish the Interagency Working Group on Intelligence Coordination (IWG-IC) to facilitate implementation of all actions in this Chapter....

Enhance coordination of existing intelligence requirements processes among law enforcement and Intelligence Community organizations.

Enhance coordination and, where practicable, integration of Southwest border related intelligence

collection programs and activities carried out by both law enforcement and Intelligence Community organizations.

Enhance coordination of intelligence assessment production among law enforcement and Intelligence Community elements.

Enhance activities to link intelligence efforts and products to operational needs and capabilities.

(2) **Enhance intelligence and information sharing collaboration.**

Enhance intelligence coordination and sharing among Federal law enforcement, Department of Defense, and Intelligence Community elements and "centers."

Enhance intelligence coordination and sharing between Federal agencies/activities and border related State, local and tribal entities.

Enhance coordination of intelligence sharing with Mexico, including information provided to and received from Mexican agencies.

Chapter 2: At the Ports of Entry

SUPPORTING ACTIONS

(1) **Use state-of-the-art detection technology, resources, and training to interdict drugs and other contraband.**

Expand use of drug detection technology by frontline officers.

Expand K-9 unit capabilities for drug detection at ports of entry.

Upgrade and standardize communications on the Southwest border.

Disrupt counterintelligence operations.

(2) **Improve targeting of border threats.**

Increase use of advance information.

Improve and integrate border databases.

Enhance identity management and document security.

Enhance use of trade information.

Increase focus on cargo containers.

Promote the development of intelligence-based targeting.

Chapter 3: Between the Ports of Entry

STRATEGIC GOAL Substantially reduce the flow of illicit drugs, drug proceeds, and associated instruments of violence across the Southwest border.

STRATEGIC OBJECTIVES

(1) Enhance intelligence capabilities associated with the Southwest border.

(2) Interdict drugs, drug proceeds, and associated instruments of violence at the ports of entry, between the ports of entry, and in the air and maritime domains along the Southwest border.

(3) Ensure the prosecution of all significant drug trafficking, money laundering, bulk currency, and weapons smuggling/trafficking cases.

(4) Disrupt and dismantle drug trafficking organizations.

(5) Enhance counterdrug technologies for drug detection and interdiction along the Southwest border.

(6) Enhance U.S.–Mexico cooperation regarding joint counterdrug efforts.

SUPPORTING ACTIONS

(1) **Expand the operational capabilities of U.S. personnel at or near the border**.

Enhance patrol and interdiction capabilities.

Enhance capability to assess suspects.

(2) **Improve coordinated operations and partnerships on the Southwest border**.

Enhance capability of task force initiatives.

Upgrade collaboration with non-Federal agencies.

Continue to improve coordination.

Develop multi-agency and bilateral tunnel detection operations.

Chapter 4: Air and Marine

SUPPORTING ACTIONS

(1) **Sustain the air and marine presence along the Southwest border**.

Optimize detection and response capabilities.

(2) **Enhance bilateral air cooperation**.

Expand liaison and information sharing activities with Mexico.

(3) **Collect comprehensive information on the air and maritime threat**.

Modernize sensors and other collection mechanisms

Establish a common operating picture (COP).

Chapter 5: Investigations and Prosecutions

BACKGROUND Today, four major organizations control the flow of drugs across the Southwest border: the Arellano-Felix Organization on the West Coast, the Gulf Cartel on the Gulf Coast, and the Juarez Cartel and the Sinaloa Cartel/Federation in the Central Region.

SUPPORTING ACTIONS

(1) **Increase the presence of U.S. law enforcement liaisons in Mexico.**

Expedite expansion of U.S. law enforcement liaison presence in Mexico.

Use joint and coordinated efforts among U.S. law enforcement agencies and the Department of the Treasury'sOffice of Foreign Assets Control (OFAC) to disrupt and dismantle drug trafficking organizations operating along the Southwest border.

(2) **Enhance intelligence support to investigations.**

Ensure that State and local investigators have the necessary clearances

Fully utilize threat assessments and other interagency intelligence products.

Standardize assessment of the impact of law enforcement operations.

(3) **Increase prosecutorial and judicial resources dedicated to investigations relating to Mexico and the Southwest border.**

Increase the capacities of U.S. Attorneys Offices to handle Southwest border drug investigations and prosecutions.

Increase the capacities of other criminal justice components to support Southwest border drug investigations and prosecutions.

Enhance the capacities of investigative agencies and U.S. Attorneys Offices to dismantle the financial infrastructure of Southwest border drug trafficking organizations.

(4) **Increase judicial cooperation with Mexico.**

Utilize Merida Initiative activities to build cooperation.

(5) **Attack corruption involving domestic public officials along the Southwest border.**

Conduct integrity awareness training for U.S. law enforcement agencies working along the Southwest border.

Increase the focus on connections between public corruption and threats to U.S. national security.

(6) **Attack foreign official corruption that supports drug trafficking and related crimes.**

Utilize and support the Department of State's anti-Kleptocracy program, specifically visa denials/

revocations through the framework of Presidential Proclamation 7750 (PP7750).

Chapter 8: Technology

SUPPORTING ACTIONS

(1) **Employ state-of-the-art detection technology to interdict drugs and other contraband.**

Improve the ability of law enforcement personnel to detect and identify narcotics and other contraband.

(2) **Develop capabilities to detect, identify, track, and interdict small vessels, including self-propelled semi-submersible boats.**

ENDNOTES

1. Patriot Act, 2001. http://thomas.loc.gov/cgi-bin/bdquery/z?d107:hr03162:%5D.
2. Homeland Security Act of 2002. http://www.dhs.gov/xabout/laws/law_regulation_rule_0011.shtm.
3. Title V, Intelligence Reform and Terrorism Prevention Act of 2004, BORDER PROTECTION, IMMIGRATION, AND VISA MATTERS, Subtitle A—Advanced Technology Northern Border Security Pilot Program, Public Law 108–458—December 17, 2004. http://www.nctc.gov/docs/pl108_458.pdf.
4. Public Law 109–295, Title V, October 4, 2006. http://frwebgate.access.gpo.gov/cgi-bin/getdoc.cgi?dbname=109_cong_public_laws&docid=f:publ295.109.pdf.
5. Arctic Region Policy, NSPD-66/HSPD-25, January 9, 2009. http://www.fas.org/irp/offdocs/nspd/nspd-66.htm.
6. National Southwest Border Counternarcotics Strategy, White House. Office of National Drug Control Strategy, June 2009. "consistent with the provisions of Section 1110 of the Office of National Drug Control Policy Reauthorization Act of 2006 (Public Law 109-469)." http://www.whitehousedrugpolicy.gov/publications/swb_counternarcotics_strategy09/swb_counternarcotics_strategy09.pdf.

ADDITIONAL RESOURCES

Border Security generally

US-VISIT Air and Sea Exit, Notice of Proposed Rulemaking. Establishes biometric exit procedures at all U.S. air and sea ports of departure for most non-U.S. citizens.

US-VISIT Final Rule: Enrollment of Additional Aliens, Additional Biometric Data and Expansion to More Land Ports. This final rule expands the population of aliens who will be subject to US-VISIT requirements to nearly all aliens, including lawful permanent residents.

"Protecting the U.S. Perimeter: Border Searches Under the Fourth Amendment," Yule Kim, June 29, 2009, Congressional Research Service, RL31826. http://opencrs.com/document/RL31826/.

"U.S. Border Security: Realities and Challenges for the Obama Administration," The Heritage Foundation, by Matt A. Mayer, June 17, 2009. http://www.heritage.org/Research/Immigration/upload/bg_2285.pdf.

"Apprehensions by the U.S. Border Patrol: 2005–2008," Department of Homeland Security, by Nancy Rytina and John Simanski, June 2009.

http://www.dhs.gov/xlibrary/assets/statistics/publications/ois_apprehensions_fs_2005-2008.pdf.

FY 2009 Operation Stonegarden (OPSG), Purpose: The intent of FY 2009 OPSG is to enhance law enforcement preparedness and operational readiness along the borders of the United States. Total Funding Available in FY 2009: $60 Million. June 4, 2009. http://www.fema.gov/government/grant/opsg/index.shtm.

Why does the information about Operation Stonegarden come from FEMA? Does the purpose of OPSG fit within FEMA's mission statement?

"Securing the Borders and America's Points of Entry, What Remains to Be Done," Senate Judiciary Committee, Subcommittee on Immigration, Border Security and Citizenship, May 20, 2009. http://judiciary.senate.gov/hearings/hearing.cfm?id=3859.

"Border Security and Military Support: Legal Authorizations and Restrictions," by Stephen R. Viña, CRS RS22443, Updated May 23, 2006. http://www.fas.org/sgp/crs/homesec/RS22443.pdf.

Northern Border

"Toward a New Frontier Improving the U.S.-Canadian Border, The Brookings Institute, 2009. http://www.brookings.edu/~/media/Files/rc/reports/2009/0713_canada_sands/0713_canada_report.pdf.

The United States and Canada: Toward a Better Border," The Brookings Institution, June 19, 2009. http://www.brookings.edu/reports/2009/0527_us_canada.aspx.

Shiprider Program Demonstrates U.S.–Canadian Cooperation, by Dean Lenuik and Jena Baker McNeill, The Heritage Foundation, August 4, 2009. http://www.heritage.org/Research/HomelandSecurity/upload/wm_2576.pdf.

"Framework Agreement On Integrated Cross-Border Maritime Law Enforcement Operations Between The Government Of The United States Of America And The Government Of Canada," May 26, 2009. http://www.dhs.gov/xlibrary/assets/shiprider_agreement.pdf.

"The Shiprider concept involves law enforcement officials from both countries operating together in integrated teams. Utilizing Royal Canadian Mounted Police (RCMP) and U.S. Coast Guard vessels, they combat smuggling, organized drug crime, gun trade and other criminal activity in shared waterways," said Minister Van Loan. "This agreement sends a strong message to criminals that illegal activity will not be tolerated. . .Shiprider enables the RCMP and the U.S. Coast Guard to cross-train, share resources and personnel and utilize each others' vessels in the waters of both countries. . ." Press Release May 26, 2009. http://www.dhs.gov/ynews/releases/pr_1243354565323.shtm.

Canada-United States Framework For The Movement Of Goods And People Across The Border During And Following An Emergency, May 2009. http://www.dhs.gov/xlibrary/assets/border_management_framework_2009-05-27.pdf.

Southern Border

Statement by Homeland Security Secretary Janet Napolitano on the Death of Border Patrol Agent Robert Rosas. http://www.dhs.gov/ynews/releases/pr_1248450509082.shtm.

"U.S. Department of Homeland Security (DHS) Secretary Janet Napolitano announced today the formation of the Homeland Security Advisory Council (HSAC) Southwest Border Task Force, a diverse group of national security experts charged with examining the Department's efforts along the U.S.-Mexico border and providing advice and recommendations directly to the Secretary." June 4, 2009. http://www.dhs.gov/ynews/releases/pr_1244145382319.shtm.

"Southern Border Violence: Homeland Security Threats, Vulnerabilities, and Responsibilities," Congress. Senate. Homeland Security and Governmental Affairs Committee, March 25, 2009. http://hsgac.senate.gov/public/index.cfm?Fuseaction=Hearings.Detail&HearingID=c90839b0-9167-4819-b943-332988b403b1.

"Problems at the Southern Border," NorthCom chief: [Southern] Border violence threatens U.S. security, March 17, 2009.

http://www.gazette.com/articles/renuart_50111__article.html/security_drug.html.

11

CRITICAL INFRASTRUCTURE PROTECTION

This chapter discusses our critical infrastructure and its protection and planning, chronologically, beginning with Executive Order 13231 of October 18, 2001. The National Strategy for the Physical Protection of Critical Infrastructures and Key Assets describes some of our critical infrastructure, the challenges facing those areas, and initiatives to address them.

Critical Infrastructure, usually accompanied by the term "Key Resources" and sometimes abbreviated CI/KR, occupies a unique position in the homeland security arena. Although nothing is more important than saving lives, saving lives requires infrastructure. Take, for example, emergency medical first responders. They rely upon a radio communications dispatcher to tell them where to go and what the problem may be. They require communications to relay back that they have arrived on the scene, and this is what it looks like from here. They rely on communications for advice or to request specific or additional help. Communications requires radios. Radios require electricity, computers, and antenna towers. All of this, including the first responders and the 911 operators are part of the infrastructure.

Our lives are intertwined with infrastructure and one infrastructure is itself intertwined with other infrastructures. If the electricity fails, the fire department will not have water pressure to pump water to put out a fire. Cascading failures occur when one piece of equipment fails causing another to fail. Supervisory Control and Data Acquisition (SCADA) provides a good example. SCADA is the remote computer control for infrastructure such as water and power distribution control valves and switches, dam control valves, pipeline valves, etc. SCADA requires telephone lines or in some cases radios to transmit these SCADA controls. If communications go down,

SCADA goes down and the valves or switches don't operate. The next-level consequence is whatever happens because the valve or switch did not operate.[1]

The National Strategy for the Protection of Critical Infrastructure and Key Resources is a detailed strategy that begins by discussing the nature of possible attacks. It lists three general categories. They are "direct," referring to the particular infrastructure attacked, "indirect," referring to the cascading disruption that might occur by destroying one infrastructure and the effect of that on other infrastructures plus the resulting financial consequences. The last category is "exploitive," and refers to taking advantage of the disruption caused by an attack on infrastructure number one to attack target number two.

This strategy discusses our country's technological sophistication, our reliance on technology, and how it presents many targets. For example, there are 87,000 separate local government jurisdictions in this country, almost 2 million farms, 87,000 food processing plants, and 590,000 highway bridges. Approximately 85% of the country's infrastructure is privately owned, raising the question of who has the right to mandate safety upgrades and who pays for it.

The strategy talks about importance of forming partnerships between the private sector and local, state, and federal authorities. It lists every partner's responsibilities and addresses the importance of modeling to facilitate planning. The Homeland Security Act created a Directorate for Information Analysis and Infrastructure protection. It discusses information sharing and created the Critical Infrastructure Information Act that protects disclosure of critical infrastructure information given by the private sector to the government. The Homeland Security Act also created the Homeland Security Sharing Act to oversee the sharing of this information.

Foundations of Homeland Security: Law and Policy, First Edition. Martin J. Alperen.
© 2011 John Wiley & Sons, Inc. Published 2011 by John Wiley & Sons, Inc.

HSPD 7 established a national policy for the Federal Government to identify and prioritize the Nation's critical infrastructure. It also lists 31 policy statements. HSPD 19 discusses countering the threat of explosives. The National Strategy for Homeland Security discusses CI/KR resiliency and the National Infrastructure Protection Plan.

SOURCES

- Executive Order 13231—Critical Infrastructure Protection in the Information Age, October 18, 2001[2]
- Patriot Act, October 26, 2001[3]
- National Strategy for the Physical Protection of Critical Infrastructures and Key Assets, February, 2002[4]
- Homeland Security Act, November 25, 2002[5]
- HSPD 7. Critical Infrastructure, December 17, 2003[6]
- 9/11 Commission Implementation Act of 2004[7]
- Post-Katrina Emergency Management Reform Act of 2006[8]
- HSPD 19. Combating Terrorist Use of Explosives in the United States, February 12, 2007[9]
- Implementing Recommendations of The 9/11 Commission Act, August 3, 2007[10]
- National Strategy for Homeland Security (2007)[11]
- Critical Infrastructure Key Resource Training Program (CIKRTP)[12]
- National Infrastructure Protection Plan (NIPP) (2009)[13]

Executive Order 13231—Critical Infrastructure Protection In The Information Age, October 18, 2001[14]

Sec. 1. Policy

(a) The information technology revolution has changed the way business is transacted, government operates, and national defense is conducted. Those three functions now depend on an interdependent network of critical information infrastructures. The protection program authorized by this order shall consist of continuous efforts to secure information systems for critical infrastructure, including emergency preparedness communications, and the physical assets that support such systems. Protection of these systems is essential to the telecommunications, energy, financial services, manufacturing, water, transportation, health care, and emergency services sectors.

(b) It is the policy of the United States to protect against disruption of the operation of information systems for critical infrastructure and . . . to ensure that any disruptions that occur are infrequent, of minimal duration, and manageable, and cause the least damage possible.

Sec. 2. Scope

To achieve this policy, there shall be a senior executive branch board to coordinate and have cognizance of Federal efforts and programs that relate to protection of information systems and involve:

(a) cooperation with and protection of private sector critical infrastructure, State and local governments' critical infrastructure, and supporting programs in corporate and academic organizations;

(b) protection of Federal departments' and agencies' critical infrastructure; and

(c) related national security programs.

Sec. 3. Establishment

I hereby establish the "President's Critical Infrastructure Protection Board" (the 'Board").

Sec. 4. Continuing Authorities

(a) *Executive Branch Information Systems Security.* The Director of the Office of Management and Budget (OMB) has the responsibility to develop and oversee the implementation of government-wide policies, principles, standards, and guidelines for the security of information systems that support the executive branch departments and agencies, except those noted in section 4(b) of this order. . .

(b) *National Security Information Systems.* The Secretary of Defense and the Director of Central Intelligence (DCI) shall have responsibility to oversee, develop, and ensure implementation of policies, principles, standards, and guidelines for the security of information systems that support the operations under their respective control. . .

Sec. 5. Board Responsibilities

. . .Among its activities to implement these responsibilities, the Board shall:

(a) Outreach to the Private Sector and State and Local Governments.

(b) Information Sharing.

(c) Incident Coordination and Crisis Response.

(d) Recruitment, Retention, and Training Executive Branch Security Professionals.

(e) Research and Development.

(f) Law Enforcement Coordination with National Security Components.

(g) International Information Infrastructure Protection.

(h) Coordination with Office of Homeland Security.

(b) *NIAC.* There is hereby established the National Infrastructure Advisory Council, which shall provide the President advice on the security of information systems for critical infrastructure supporting other sectors of the economy: banking and finance, transportation, energy, manufacturing, and emergency government services. The NIAC shall be composed of not more than 30 members appointed by the President...

(iii) Executive Order 13130 of July 14, 1999, is hereby revoked.

Sec. 11. National Communications System

Changes in technology are causing the convergence of much of telephony, data relay, and internet communications networks into an interconnected network of networks. The NCS and its National Coordinating Center shall support use of telephony, converged information, voice networks, and next generation networks for emergency preparedness and national security communications functions assigned to them in Executive Order 12472.

Patriot Act, October 26, 2001

Sec. 701. Expansion of Regional Information Sharing System To Facilitate Federal-State-Local Law Enforcement Response Related To Terrorist Attacks

Section 1301 of title I of the Omnibus Crime Control and Safe Streets Act of 1968 (42 U.S.C. 3796h) is amended—

(4) establishing and operating secure information sharing systems to enhance the investigation and prosecution abilities of participating enforcement agencies in addressing multi-jurisdictional terrorist conspiracies and activities; and

Sec. 801. Terrorist Attacks and Other Acts of Violence Against Mass Transportation Systems [This statute criminalizes acts against mass transportation systems.]

Sec. 1016. Critical Infrastructures Protection

(a) SHORT TITLE.— This section may be cited as the "Critical Infrastructures Protection Act of 2001".

(c) POLICY OF THE UNITED STATES.— It is the policy of the United States—

(1) that any physical or virtual disruption of the operation of the critical infrastructures of the United States be rare, brief, geographically limited in effect, manageable, and minimally detrimental to the economy, human and government services, and national security of the United States;

(2) that actions necessary to achieve the policy stated in paragraph (1) be carried out in a public-private part-

nership involving corporate and non-governmental organizations; and

(3) to have in place a comprehensive and effective program to ensure the continuity of essential Federal Government functions under all circumstances.

(d) ESTABLISHMENT OF NATIONAL COMPETENCE FOR CRITICAL INFRASTRUCTURE PROTECTION.—
(1) Support of critical infrastructure protection and continuity by national infrastructure simulation and analysis center.—There shall be established the National Infrastructure Simulation and Analysis Center (NISAC) to serve as a source of national competence to address critical infrastructure protection and continuity through support for activities related to counterterrorism, threat assessment, and risk mitigation.

(e) CRITICAL INFRASTRUCTURE DEFINED.— In this section, the term "critical infrastructure" means systems and assets, whether physical or virtual, so vital to the United States that the incapacity or destruction of such systems and assets would have a debilitating impact on security, national economic security, national public health or safety, or any combination of those matters.

National Strategy for the Physical Protection of Critical Infrastructures and Key Assets, February 2002

...THE NATURE OF POSSIBLE ATTACKS

Terrorists target critical infrastructure and key assets to achieve effects that fall into three general categories:

- **Direct infrastructure effects:** Cascading disruption or arrest of the functions of critical infrastructures or key assets through direct attacks on a critical node, system, or function. The immediate damage to facilities and disruption of services that resulted from the attack on the World Trade Center towers, which housed critical assets of the financial services sector, are examples of direct infrastructure effects.

- **Indirect infrastructure effects:** Cascading disruption and financial consequences for government, society, and economy through public- and private-sector reactions to an attack.[15]

  Public disengagement from air travel and other facets of the economy as a result of the September 11 attacks exemplifies this effect. Mitigating the potential consequences from these types of attacks will require careful assessment of policy and regulatory responses, understanding the psychology of their impacts, and appropriately weighing the costs and benefits of specific actions in response to small-scale attacks.

- **Exploitation of infrastructure:** Exploitation of elements of a particular infrastructure to disrupt or destroy another target. On September 11, terrorists exploited elements of the aviation infrastructure to attack the World Trade Center and the Pentagon, which represented seats of U.S. economic and military power. Determining the potential cascading and cross-sector consequences of this type of attack is extremely difficult.

The New Front Lines Our technologically sophisticated society and institutions present a wide array of potential targets for terrorist exploitation. Our critical infrastructure industries change rapidly to reflect the demands of the markets they serve. Much of the expertise required for planning and taking action to protect critical infrastructures and key assets lies outside the federal government, including precise knowledge of what needs to be protected. In effect, the front lines of defense in this new type of battle have moved into our communities and the individual institutions that make up our critical infrastructure sectors.

Private industry owns and operates approximately 85 percent of our critical infrastructures and key assets. Facility operators have always been responsible for protecting their physical assets against unauthorized intruders. These measures, however conventionally effective, generally have not been designed to cope with significant military or terrorist threats, or the cascading economic and psychological impact they may entail.

The unique characteristics of critical infrastructures and key assets, their continuing—often rapid—evolution, and the significant impediments complicating their protection will require an unprecedented level of key public- and private-sector cooperation and coordination. Our country has more than 87,000 jurisdictions of local governance alone. The challenge ahead is to develop a coordinated and complementary system that reinforces protection efforts rather than duplicates them, and that meets mutually identified essential requirements. In addition, many of our critical infrastructures also span national borders and, therefore, must be protected within the context of international cooperation.

Our open society, highly creative and responsive economic markets, and system of values that engenders individual recognition and freedom have created wealth for our nation, built a strong national security system, and instilled a sense of national confidence in the future. Destruction of our traditions, values, and way of life represents a key objective of our terrorist enemies. Ironically, the tenets of American society that make us free also create an environment that facilitates terrorist operations.

As we strive to understand the nature of terrorism and identify appropriate means to defend against it, we will require new collaborative structures and mechanisms for working together. During the Cold War era, many government and private organizations isolated parts of their physical and information infrastructures into "stovepipes" to assure their protection. This approach is no longer adequate to protect our homeland from determined terrorists. Stimulating voluntary, rapidly adaptive protection activities requires a culture of trust and ongoing collaboration among relevant public- and private-sector stakeholders, rather than more traditional systems of command and control.

Security investments made by all levels of government and private industry have increased since the September 11 attacks. As terrorism continues to evolve, so must the way in which we protect country and ourselves. The costs of protection—including expenditures to develop new technologies, tools, and procedures—will weigh heavily on all levels of government and private industry. Consequently, an effective protection strategy must incorporate well planned and highly coordinated approaches that have been developed by the best minds in our country through innovation and sharing of information, best practices, and shared resources.

[SOME STATISTICS]

Agriculture and Food 1,912,000 farms; 87,000 food-processing plants
Water 1,800 federal reservoirs; 1,600 municipal waste water facilities
Public Health 5,800 registered hospitals
Emergency Services 87,000 U.S. localities
Defense Industrial Base 250,000 firms in 215 distinct industries
Telecommunications 2 billion miles of cable

ENERGY
Electricity 2,800 power plants
Oil and Natural Gas 300,000 producing sites

TRANSPORTATION
Aviation 5,000 public airports
Passenger Rail and Railroads 120,000 miles of major railroads
Highways, Trucking, and Busing 590,000 highway bridges
Pipelines 2 million miles of pipelines
Maritime 300 inland/costal ports
Mass Transit 500 major urban public transit operators

Banking and Finance 26,600 FDIC insured institutions

Chemical Industry and Hazardous Materials 66,000 chemical plants

Postal and Shipping 137 million delivery sites

KEY ASSETS

National Monuments and Icons 5,800 historic buildings
Nuclear Power Plants 104 commercial nuclear power plants
Dams 80,000 dams

Government Facilities 3,000 government owned/operated facilities

Commercial Assets 460 skyscrapers

*These are approximate figures.

Statement of National Policy This document reaffirms our Nation's longstanding policy regarding critical infrastructure and key asset protection. It also delineates a set of guiding principles that underpins our strategy for action to protect our Nation's critical infrastructures and key assets from terrorist attack. As a Nation, we are committed to protecting our critical infrastructures and key assets from acts of terrorism that would:

- Impair the federal government's ability to perform essential national security missions and ensure the general public's health and safety;
- Undermine state and local government capacities to maintain order and to deliver minimum essential public services;
- Damage the private sector's capability to ensure the orderly functioning of the economy and the delivery of essential services; and
- Undermine the public's morale and confidence in our national economic and political institutions.

As a Nation, we must utilize every tool at our disposal and work collaboratively to develop and implement the protective measures that this policy entails. The strategic objectives discussed in the Introduction will focus and drive this effort.

Guiding Principles

1. Assure public safety, public confidence, and services
2. Establish responsibility and accountability
3. Encourage and facilitate partnering among all levels of government and between government and industry
4. Encourage market solutions whenever possible; compensate for market failure with focused government intervention
5. Facilitate meaningful information sharing
6. Foster international security cooperation
7. Develop technologies and expertise to combat terrorist threats
8. Safeguard privacy and constitutional freedoms

ORGANIZING AND PARTNERING FOR CRITICAL INFRASTRUCTURE AND KEY ASSET PROTECTION

Implementing a comprehensive national critical infrastructure and key asset protection strategy requires clear and uni-fying organization, clarity of purpose, common understanding of roles and responsibilities, accountability, and a set of well-understood coordinating processes. A solid organizational scheme sets the stage for effective engagement and interaction between the public and private sectors. . .

The work of providing a clearly defined and unifying organizational framework began with the publication of the President's National Strategy for Homeland Security and continues in this document. This chapter clarifies public-and private-sector roles and responsibilities for critical infrastructure and key asset protection. Ultimately, success lies in our ability to draw effectively and efficiently upon the unique core competencies and resources of each stakeholder. Given the range and complexity of required protection activities and the number of entities involved, clearly defined authority, accountability, and coordinating processes will provide the foundation for a successful and sustainable national protection effort.

Overlapping federal, state, and local governance and the ownership structure of our critical infrastructures and key assets present significant protection challenges. The entities involved are diverse, and the level of understanding of protection roles and responsibilities differs accordingly. Furthermore, these organizations and individuals represent systems, operations, and institutional cultures that are complex and diverse. The range of protective activities that each must undertake is vast and varies from one enterprise to the next. Finally, overlapping protection authorities across federal, state, and local jurisdictions vary greatly. Success in implementing this Strategy's wide range of protection activities lies in establishing a unifying organizational framework that allows the development of complementary, collaborative relationships and efficiently aligns our Nation's protection resources.

In our federalist system of government, federal, state, and local governments and private industry have specific roles and perform certain functions that must be integrated to assure protection. Additionally, each critical infrastructure owner/operator possesses unique capabilities, expertise, and resources that, when integrated appropriately, can contribute to a comprehensive national protection effort.

Federal Government Responsibilities The federal government has fundamental, clearly defined responsibilities under the Constitution. Providing for the common defense and promoting the general welfare of our country are among them. The federal government alone has the capability to use military, intelligence, and diplomatic assets to defend America's interests outside its borders. Closer to home, with support from state and local governments, the federal government has also traditionally led the effort to maintain the security of our borders. To prevent terrorists from entering the U.S., the federal government employs several tools unique to its arsenal, including: military, diplomatic, and intelligence gathering activities; immigration and naturalization functions; and border agents, customs inspectors, and port and air terminal security.

The federal law enforcement apparatus consists of mechanisms that allow it to coordinate multijurisdictional approaches to security threats and incidents and the pursuit of perpetrators across state lines and overseas. . .

Beyond such critical services and functions, the federal government has the capacity to organize, convene, and coordinate across governmental jurisdictions and the private sector. It therefore has the responsibility to develop coherent national policies, strategies, and programs. In the context of homeland security, the federal government will coordinate the complementary efforts and capabilities of government and private institutions to raise our level of protection over the long term for each of our critical infrastructures and key assets.

Every terrorist event has national impact. The federal government will therefore take the lead to insure that the three principal objectives[16] . . . are met. . .

As custodian of many of our Nation's key assets, such as some of our most treasured icons and monuments, and as the owner and operator of mission-critical facilities, the federal government also has significant, direct protection responsibilities.

Federal Lead Departments and Agencies Each critical infrastructure sector has unique security challenges. The National Strategy for Homeland Security provides a sector-based organizational scheme for protecting America's critical infrastructures and key assets. This organizational scheme identifies the federal lead departments and agencies charged with coordinating protection activities and cultivating long-term collaborative relationships with their sector counterparts.

Department of Homeland Security The organizational model of federal lead departments and agencies provides a focused leadership structure for national-level protection coordination and planning. The newly created Department of Homeland Security (DHS) will significantly enhance the effectiveness of this model by providing overall cross-sector coordination. In this role, DHS will serve as the primary liaison and facilitator for cooperation among federal departments and agencies, state and local governments, and the private sector.

As the cross-sector coordinator, DHS will also be responsible for the detailed refinement and implementation of the core elements of this Strategy. This charter includes building and maintaining a complete, current, and accurate assessment of national-level critical assets, systems, and functions, as well as assessing vulnerabilities and protective postures across the critical infrastructure sectors. DHS will use this information to assess threats, provide timely warnings to

threatened infrastructures, and build "red team" capabilities to evaluate preparedness across sectors and government jurisdictions. Furthermore, DHS will collaborate with other federal departments and agencies, state and local governments, and the private sector to define and implement complementary structures and coordination processes for critical infrastructure and key asset protection. . .

Office of Homeland Security The Office of Homeland Security (OHS) will continue to act as the President's principal policy advisory staff and coordinating body for major interagency policy issues related to Homeland Security, including the critical infrastructure and key asset protection mission area. The functions of OHS will be to advise and assist the President in the coordination of the Executive Branch's efforts to detect, prepare for, prevent, protect against, respond to, and recover from terrorist attacks within the United States. . .

State and Local Government Responsibilities The 50 states, 4 territories, and 87,000 local jurisdictions that comprise this Nation have an important and unique role to play in the protection of our critical infrastructures and key assets. All U.S. states and territories have established homeland security liaison offices to manage their counter-terrorism and infrastructure protection efforts. In addition, the states have law enforcement agencies, National Guard units, and other critical services that can be employed to protect their communities.

Like the federal government, states should identify and secure the critical infrastructures and key assets under their control . . . States should further facilitate coordinated planning and preparedness by applying unified criteria for determining criticality, prioritizing protection investments, and exercising preparedness within their jurisdictions. . .

Many states have well-organized relationships with one another through various organizations, such as the National Emergency Managers Association and the National Governors Association, as well as through mutual support agreements. Coordinating with one another, they can capitalize on their mutual capabilities through regional approaches to protection. As proven during September 11 response efforts, mutual aid agreements and other such successful cooperative processes for crisis management demonstrate the competence of various jurisdictions and organizations to plan and work together.

At the onset, every disruption or attack is a local problem. Regardless of who owns and operates the affected infrastructure, each requires an immediate response by local authorities and communities who must support the initial burden of action before the incident escalates to a national event.

Local governments represent the front lines of protection and the face of public services to the American people. Their core competencies must include knowledge of their communities, residents, landscapes, and existing critical services for maintaining public health, safety, and order. Communities look to local leadership to assure safety, economic opportunities, and quality of life. Public confidence, therefore, starts locally and is dependent upon how well communities plan and are able to protect their citizens, respond to emergencies, and establish order from chaos...

For this reason, local communities play critical roles in preparing their citizens for emergencies and engaging their public and private leadership in the development of coordinated local and regional plans to assure the protection of residents and businesses. State and local governments look to the federal government for support and resources when national requirements exceed their capabilities to fulfill them.

Protecting critical infrastructures and key assets will require a particularly close and well-organized partnership among all levels of government. DHS, in particular, will provide a single point of coordination for state and local governments for homeland security issues...

Private-Sector Responsibilities The lion's share of our critical infrastructures and key assets are owned and operated by the private sector. Customarily, private companies prudently engage in risk management planning. They also invest in security as a necessary component of their business operations and to assure customer confidence. In the present threat environment, the private sector remains the first line of defense for its own facilities. Consequently, private-sector owners and operators should reassess and adjust their planning, assurance, and investment programs to accommodate the increased risk presented by deliberate acts of terrorism...

Partnership will provide the foundation for developing and implementing coordinated protection strategies. True partnerships require continuous interaction and, above all, trust. Currently, however, there are barriers impeding the public and private sectors from achieving a relationship of this level. Many current attitudes and institutional relationships, processes, and structures are products of a bygone era. Safeguarding our critical infrastructures and key assets from terrorism in today's fluid marketplace and threat environment requires a new, more cooperative set of institutional relationships and attitudes. The need for partnering is clear.

* * *

PROTECTING KEY ASSETS

Key assets represent a broad array of unique facilities, sites, and structures whose disruption or destruction could have significant consequences across multiple dimensions. One category of key assets comprises the diverse array of national monuments, symbols, and icons that represent our Nation's heritage, traditions and values, and political power. They include a wide variety of sites and structures, such as prominent historical attractions, monuments, cultural icons, and centers

of government and commerce. The sites and structures that make up this key asset category typically draw large amounts of tourism and frequent media attention factors that impose additional protection challenges.

Another category of key assets includes facilities and structures that represent our national economic power and technological advancement. Many of them house significant amounts of hazardous materials, fuels, and chemical catalysts that enable important production and processing functions. Disruption of these facilities could have significant impact on public health and safety, public confidence, and the economy.

A third category of key assets includes such structures as prominent commercial centers, office buildings, and sports stadiums, where large numbers of people regularly congregate to conduct business or personal transactions, shop, or enjoy a recreational pastime.

Given the national-level fame of these sites and facilities and the potential human consequences that could result from their attack, protecting them is important in terms of both preventing fatalities and preserving public confidence.

* * *

Homeland Security Act, November 25, 2002[17]

Sec. 201. Directorate For Information Analysis And Infrastructure Protection

(a) *Under Secretary Of Homeland Security For Information Analysis And Infrastructure Protection.*

(1) IN GENERAL.— There shall be in the Department a Directorate for Information Analysis and Infrastructure Protection headed by an Under Secretary for Information Analysis and Infrastructure Protection, who shall be appointed by the President...

(d) *Responsibilities Of Under Secretary.* Subject to the direction and control of the Secretary, the responsibilities of the Under Secretary for Information Analysis and Infrastructure Protection shall be as follows:

(1) To access, receive, and analyze law enforcement information, intelligence information, and other information from agencies of the Federal Government, State and local government agencies (including law enforcement agencies), and private sector entities, and to integrate such information in order to—

(A) identify and assess the nature and scope of terrorist threats to the homeland;

(B) detect and identify threats of terrorism against the United States; and

(C) understand such threats in light of actual and potential vulnerabilities of the homeland.

(2) To carry out comprehensive assessments of the vulnerabilities of the key resources and critical infrastructure of the United States, including the performance of risk assessments to determine the risks posed by particular types of terrorist attacks within the United States (including an assessment of the probability of success of such attacks and the feasibility and potential efficacy of various countermeasures to such attacks).

(3) To integrate relevant information, analyses, and vulnerability assessments (whether such information, analyses, or assessments are provided or produced by the Department or others) in order to identify priorities for protective and support measures...

(4) To ensure, pursuant to section 202, the timely and efficient access by the Department to all information necessary to discharge the responsibilities under this section, including obtaining such information from other agencies of the Federal Government.

(5) To develop a comprehensive national plan for securing the key resources and critical infrastructure of the United States, including power production, generation, and distribution systems, information technology and telecommunications systems (including satellites), electronic financial and property record storage and transmission systems, emergency preparedness communications systems, and the physical and technological assets that support such systems.

(6) To recommend measures necessary to protect the key resources and critical infrastructure of the United States in coordination with other agencies of the Federal Government and in cooperation with State and local government agencies and authorities, the private sector, and other entities.

(7) To administer the Homeland Security Advisory System, including—

   (A) exercising primary responsibility for public advisories related to threats to homeland security; and

   (B) in coordination with other agencies of the Federal Government, providing specific warning information, and advice about appropriate protective measures and countermeasures, to State and local government agencies and authorities, the private sector, other entities, and the public.

(8) To review, analyze, and make recommendations for improvements in the policies and procedures governing the sharing of law enforcement information, intelligence information, intelligence-related information, and other information relating to homeland security within the Federal Government and between the Federal Government and State and local government agencies and authorities.

(9) To disseminate, as appropriate, information analyzed by the Department within the Department, to other agencies of the Federal Government with responsibilities relating to homeland security, and to agencies of State and local governments and private sector entities with such responsibilities in order to assist in the deterrence, prevention, preemption of, or response to, terrorist attacks against the United States.

(10) To consult with the Director of Central Intelligence and other appropriate intelligence, law enforcement, or other elements of the Federal Government to establish collection priorities and strategies for information, including law enforcement-related information, relating to threats of terrorism against the United States through such means as the representation of the Department in discussions regarding requirements and priorities in the collection of such information.

(11) To consult with State and local governments and private sector entities to ensure appropriate exchanges of information, including law enforcement-related information, relating to threats of terrorism against the United States.

(12) To ensure that—

   (A) any material received pursuant to this Act is protected from unauthorized disclosure and handled and used only for the performance of official duties; and

   (B) any intelligence information under this Act is shared, retained, and disseminated consistent with the authority of the Director of Central Intelligence to protect intelligence sources and methods under the National Security Act of 1947 (50 U.S.C. 401 et seq.) and related procedures and, as appropriate, similar authorities of the Attorney General concerning sensitive law enforcement information.

(13) To request additional information from other agencies of the Federal Government, State and local government agencies, and the private sector relating to threats of terrorism in the United States, or relating to other areas of responsibility assigned by the Secretary, including the entry into cooperative agreements through the Secretary to obtain such information.

(14) To establish and utilize, in conjunction with the chief information officer of the Department, a secure communications and information technology infrastructure, including datamining and other advanced analytical tools, in order to access, receive, and analyze data and information in furtherance of the responsibilities under this section, and to disseminate information acquired and analyzed by the Department, as appropriate.

(15) To coordinate training and other support to the elements and personnel of the Department, other agencies of the Federal Government, and State and local governments that provide information to the Department, or are consumers of information provided by the Department, in order to facilitate the identification and sharing of information revealed in their ordinary duties and the optimal utilization of information received from the Department.

(16) To coordinate with elements of the intelligence community and with Federal, State, and local law enforcement agencies, and the private sector, as appropriate.

(17) To provide intelligence and information analysis and support to other elements of the Department.

(g) _Functions Transferred._ In accordance with title XV, there shall be transferred to the Secretary, for assignment to the Under Secretary for Information Analysis and Infrastructure Protection under this section, the functions, personnel, assets, and liabilities of the following:

(1) The National Infrastructure Protection Center of the Federal Bureau of Investigation (other than the Computer Investigations and Operations Section), including the functions of the Attorney General relating thereto.

(2) The National Communications System of the Department of Defense, including the functions of the Secretary of Defense relating thereto.

(3) The Critical Infrastructure Assurance Office of the Department of Commerce, including the functions of the Secretary of Commerce relating thereto.

(4) The National Infrastructure Simulation and Analysis Center of the Department of Energy and the energy security and assurance program and activities of the Department, including the functions of the Secretary of Energy relating thereto.

(5) The Federal Computer Incident Response Center of the General Services Administration, including the functions of the Administrator of General Services relating thereto.

Subtitle B—Critical Infrastructure Information

SEC. 211. SHORT TITLE.

This subtitle may be cited as the "Critical Infrastructure Information Act of 2002".

SEC. 212. DEFINITIONS.

(3) CRITICAL INFRASTRUCTURE INFORMATION.— The term "critical infrastructure information" means information not customarily in the public domain and related to the security of critical infrastructure or protected systems—

SEC. 214. PROTECTION OF VOLUNTARILY SHARED CRITICAL INFRASTRUCTURE INFORMATION.

(a) _Protection._

(1) IN GENERAL.— Notwithstanding any other provision of law, critical infrastructure information (including the identity of the submitting person or entity) that is voluntarily submitted to a covered Federal agency for use by that agency regarding the security of critical infrastructure and protected systems, analysis, warning, interdependency study, recovery, reconstitution, or other informational purpose, when accompanied by an express statement specified in paragraph (2)—

(A) shall be exempt from disclosure under section 552 of title 5, United States Code (commonly referred to as the Freedom of Information Act);

(B) shall not be subject to any agency rules or judicial doctrine regarding ex parte communications with a decision making official;

(C) shall not, without the written consent of the person or entity submitting such information, be used directly by such agency, any other Federal, State, or local authority, or any third party, in any civil action arising under Federal or State law if such information is submitted in good faith;

(D) shall not, without the written consent of the person or entity submitting such information, be used or disclosed by any officer or employee of the United States for purposes other than the purposes of this subtitle, except—

(i) in furtherance of an investigation or the prosecution of a criminal act; or

(ii) when disclosure of the information would be—

(I) to either House of Congress, or to the extent of matter within its jurisdiction, any committee or subcommittee thereof, any joint committee thereof or subcommittee of any such joint committee; or

(II) to the Comptroller General, or any authorized representative of the Comptroller General, in the course of the performance of the duties of the General Accounting Office.

(E) shall not, if provided to a State or local government or government agency—

   (i) be made available pursuant to any State or local law requiring disclosure of information or records;

   (ii) otherwise be disclosed or distributed to any party by said State or local government or government agency without the written consent of the person or entity submitting such information; or

   (iii) be used other than for the purpose of protecting critical infrastructure or protected systems, or in furtherance of an investigation or the prosecution of a criminal act; and

(F) does not constitute a waiver of any applicable privilege or protection provided under law, such as trade secret protection.

(2) EXPRESS STATEMENT.— For purposes of paragraph (1), the term "express statement", with respect to information or records, means—

(A) in the case of written information or records, a written marking on the information or records substantially similar to the following: "This information is voluntarily submitted to the Federal Government in expectation of protection from disclosure as provided by the provisions of the Critical Infrastructure Information Act of 2002."; or

(B) in the case of oral information, a similar written statement submitted within a reasonable period following the oral communication. . .

(f) *Penalties.* Whoever, being an officer or employee of the United States or of any department or agency thereof, knowingly publishes, divulges, discloses, or makes known in any manner or to any extent not authorized by law, any critical infrastructure information protected from disclosure by this subtitle coming to him in the course of this employment or official duties or by reason of any examination or investigation made by, or return, report, or record made to or filed with, such department or agency or officer or employee thereof, shall be fined under title 18 of the United States Code, imprisoned not more than 1 year, or both, and shall be removed from office or employment.

(g) *Authority To Issue Warnings.* The Federal Government may provide advisories, alerts, and warnings to relevant companies, targeted sectors, other governmental entities, or the general public regarding potential threats to critical infrastructure as appropriate. In issuing a warning, the Federal Government shall take appropriate actions to protect from disclosure—

(1) the source of any voluntarily submitted critical infrastructure information that forms the basis for the warning; or

(2) information that is proprietary, business sensitive, relates specifically to the submitting person or entity, or is otherwise not appropriately in the public domain.

SEC. 221. PROCEDURES FOR SHARING INFORMATION.

The Secretary shall establish procedures on the use of information shared under this title that—

(1) limit the redissemination of such information to ensure that it is not used for an unauthorized purpose;

(2) ensure the security and confidentiality of such information;

(3) protect the constitutional and statutory rights of any individuals who are subjects of such information; and

(4) provide data integrity through the timely removal and destruction of obsolete or erroneous names and information.

SEC. 891. SHORT TITLE; FINDINGS; AND SENSE OF CONGRESS.

SHORT TITLE.— This subtitle may be cited as the "Homeland Security Information Sharing Act".

(b) FINDINGS.— Congress finds the following:

(1) The Federal Government is required by the Constitution to provide for the common defense, which includes terrorist attack.

(2) The Federal Government relies on State and local personnel to protect against terrorist attack.

(3) The Federal Government collects, creates, manages, and protects classified and sensitive but unclassified information to enhance homeland security.

(4) Some homeland security information is needed by the State and local personnel to prevent and prepare for terrorist attack.

(5) The needs of State and local personnel to have access to relevant homeland security information to combat terrorism must be reconciled with the need to preserve the protected status of such information and to protect the sources and methods used to acquire such information.

(6) Granting security clearances to certain State and local personnel is one way to facilitate the sharing of

information regarding specific terrorist threats among Federal, State, and local levels of government.

(7) Methods exist to declassify, redact, or otherwise adapt classified information so it may be shared with State and local personnel without the need for granting additional security clearances.

(8) State and local personnel have capabilities and opportunities to gather information on suspicious activities and terrorist threats not possessed by Federal agencies.

(9) The Federal Government and State and local governments and agencies in other jurisdictions may benefit from such information.

(10) Federal, State, and local governments and intelligence, law enforcement, and other emergency preparation and response agencies must act in partnership to maximize the benefits of information gathering and analysis to prevent and respond to terrorist attacks.

(11) Information systems, including the National Law Enforcement Telecommunications System and the Terrorist Threat Warning System, have been established for rapid sharing of classified and sensitive but unclassified information among Federal, State, and local entities.

(12) Increased efforts to share homeland security information should avoid duplicating existing information systems.

(c) SENSE OF CONGRESS.— It is the sense of Congress that Federal, State, and local entities should share homeland security information to the maximum extent practicable, with special emphasis on hard-to-reach urban and rural communities.

SEC. 1001. INFORMATION SECURITY.

(a) SHORT TITLE.— This title may be cited as the "Federal Information Security Management Act of 2002".

(b) INFORMATION SECURITY.

(1) *IN GENERAL.—* Subchapter II of chapter 35 of title 44, United States Code, is amended to read as follows:
    "SUBCHAPTER II—INFORMATION SECURITY

§ **3531. Purposes**

"The purposes of this subchapter are to—
    "(1) provide a comprehensive framework for ensuring the effectiveness of information security controls over information resources that support Federal operations and assets;
    "(2) recognize the highly networked nature of the current Federal computing environment and provide effective

government-wide management and oversight of the related information security risks, including coordination of information security efforts throughout the civilian, national security, and law enforcement communities;
    "(3) provide for development and maintenance of minimum controls required to protect Federal information and information systems;
    "(4) provide a mechanism for improved oversight of Federal agency information security programs;
    "(5) acknowledge that commercially developed information security products offer advanced, dynamic, robust, and effective information security solutions, reflecting market solutions for the protection of critical information infrastructures important to the national defense and economic security of the nation that are designed, built, and operated by the private sector; and
    "(6) recognize that the selection of specific technical hardware and software information security solutions should be left to individual agencies from among commercially developed products."

HSPD 7. Critical Infrastructure, December 17, 2003

SUBJECT: CRITICAL INFRASTRUCTURE IDENTIFICATION, PRIORITIZATION, AND PROTECTION

Purpose

1. This directive establishes a national policy for Federal departments and agencies to identify and prioritize United States critical infrastructure and key resources and to protect them from terrorist attacks.

Background

2. Terrorists seek to destroy, incapacitate, or exploit critical infrastructure and key resources across the United States to threaten national security, cause mass casualties, weaken our economy, and damage public morale and confidence.

3. America's open and technologically complex society includes a wide array of critical infrastructure and key resources that are potential terrorist targets. The majority of these are owned and operated by the private sector and State or local governments. These critical infrastructures and key resources are both physical and cyber-based and span all sectors of the economy.

4. Critical infrastructure and key resources provide the essential services that underpin American society. The Nation possesses numerous key resources, whose exploitation or destruction by terrorists could cause catastrophic health effects or mass casualties comparable to those from the use of a weapon of mass destruction, or could profoundly affect our national prestige and morale. In addition, there is critical infrastructure so vital that its incapacitation, exploitation, or destruction, through terrorist attack, could have a debilitating effect on security and economic well-being.

5. While it is not possible to protect or eliminate the vulnerability of all critical infrastructure and key resources throughout the country, strategic improvements in security can make it more difficult for attacks to succeed and can lessen the impact of attacks that may occur. In addition to strategic security enhancements, tactical security improvements can be rapidly implemented to deter, mitigate, or neutralize potential attacks.

Definitions

6. In this directive:

a. The term "critical infrastructure" has the meaning given to that term in section 1016(e) of the USA PATRIOT Act of 2001 (42 U.S.C. 5195c(e)).[18]

b. The term "key resources" has the meaning given that term in section 2(9) of the Homeland Security Act of 2002 (6 U.S.C. 101(9)).[19]

c. The term "the Department" means the Department of Homeland Security. . . .

Policy

7. It is the policy of the United States to enhance the protection of our Nation's critical infrastructure and key resources against terrorist acts. . .

12. In carrying out the functions assigned in the Homeland Security Act of 2002, the Secretary shall be responsible for coordinating the overall national effort to enhance the protection of the critical infrastructure and key resources of the United States. The Secretary shall serve as the principal Federal official to lead, integrate, and coordinate implementation of efforts among Federal departments and agencies, State and local governments, and the private sector to protect critical infrastructure and key resources.

15. The Secretary shall coordinate protection activities for each of the following critical infrastructure sectors: information technology; telecommunications; chemical; transportation systems, including mass transit, aviation, maritime, ground/surface, and rail and pipeline systems; emergency services; and postal and shipping. The Department shall coordinate with appropriate departments and agencies to ensure the protection of other key resources including dams, government facilities, and commercial facilities. . . .

16. The Secretary will continue to maintain an organization to serve as a focal point for the security of cyberspace . . . The organization's mission includes analysis, warning, information sharing, vulnerability reduction, mitigation, and aiding national recovery efforts for critical infrastructure information systems. . . .

Roles and Responsibilities of Sector-Specific Federal Agencies

18. Recognizing that each infrastructure sector possesses its own unique characteristics and operating models, there are designated Sector-Specific Agencies, including:

a. Department of Agriculture—agriculture, food (meat, poultry, egg products);

b. Health and Human Services—public health, healthcare, and food (other than meat, poultry, egg products);

c. Environmental Protection Agency—drinking water and water treatment systems;

d. Department of Energy—energy, including the production refining, storage, and distribution of oil and gas, and electric power except for commercial nuclear power facilities;

e. Department of the Treasury—banking and finance;

f. Department of the Interior—national monuments and icons; and

g. Department of Defense—defense industrial base.

Roles and Responsibilities of Other Departments, Agencies, and Offices

22. In addition to the responsibilities given the Department and Sector-Specific Agencies, there are special functions of various Federal departments and agencies and components of the Executive Office of the President related to critical infrastructure and key resources protection.

a. The Department of State, in conjunction with the Department, and the Departments of Justice, Commerce, Defense, the Treasury and other appropriate agencies, will work with foreign countries and international organizations to strengthen the protection of United States critical infrastructure and key resources.

b. The Department of Justice, including the Federal Bureau of Investigation, will reduce domestic terrorist threats, and investigate and prosecute actual or attempted terrorist attacks on, sabotage of, or disruptions of critical infrastructure and key resources. . . .

c. The Department of Commerce, in coordination with the Department, will work with private sector, research, academic, and government organizations to improve technology for cyber systems and promote other critical infrastructure efforts, including using its authority under the Defense Production Act[20] to assure the timely availability of industrial products, materials, and services to meet homeland security requirements.

25. . . . [DHS] and the Sector-Specific Agencies will collaborate with appropriate private sector entities and continue to encourage the development of information sharing and analysis mechanisms. Additionally, [DHS] and Sector-Specific Agencies shall collaborate with the private sector and continue to support sector-coordinating mechanisms:

a. to identify, prioritize, and coordinate the protection of critical infrastructure and key resources; and

b. to facilitate sharing of information about physical and cyber threats, vulnerabilities, incidents, potential protective measures, and best practices.

National Special Security Events

26. The Secretary, after consultation with the Homeland Security Council, shall be responsible for designating events as "National Special Security Events" (NSSEs). This directive supersedes language in previous presidential directives regarding the designation of NSSEs that is inconsistent herewith.

Implementation

27. Consistent with the Homeland Security Act of 2002, the Secretary shall produce a comprehensive, integrated National Plan for Critical Infrastructure and Key Resources Protection[21] to outline national goals, objectives, milestones, and key initiatives within 1 year...

28. The Secretary, consistent with the Homeland Security Act of 2002 and other applicable legal authorities and presidential guidance, shall establish appropriate systems, mechanisms, and procedures to share homeland security information relevant to threats and vulnerabilities in national critical infrastructure and key resources with other Federal departments and agencies, State and local governments, and the private sector in a timely manner.

29. The Secretary will continue to work with the Nuclear Regulatory Commission and, as appropriate, the Department of Energy in order to ensure the necessary protection of:

a. commercial nuclear reactors for generating electric power and non-power nuclear reactors used for research, testing, and training;

b. nuclear materials in medical, industrial, and academic settings and facilities that fabricate nuclear fuel; and

c. the transportation, storage, and disposal of nuclear materials and waste.

31. The Secretary...[shall] develop a program,...to geospatially map, image, analyze, and sort critical infrastructure and key resources by utilizing commercial satellite and airborne systems, and existing capabilities within other agencies. National technical means should be considered as an option of last resort. ...

32. The Secretary will utilize existing, and develop new, capabilities as needed to model comprehensively the potential implications of terrorist exploitation of vulnerabilities in critical infrastructure and key resources, placing specific focus on densely populated areas. Agencies with relevant modeling capabilities shall cooperate with the Secretary...

37. This directive supersedes Presidential Decision Directive/NSC-63 of May 22, 1998 ("Critical Infrastructure Protection"), and any Presidential directives issued prior to this directive to the extent of any inconsistency...[22, 23]

9/11 Commission Implementation Act Of 2004

SEC. 7306. CRITICAL INFRASTRUCTURE AND READINESS ASSESSMENTS.

(a) FINDINGS.— Congress makes the following findings:

(1) Under section 201 of the Homeland Security Act of 2002 (6 U.S.C 121), the Department of Homeland Security, through the Under Secretary for Information Analysis and Infrastructure Protection, has the responsibility—

(A) to carry out comprehensive assessments of the vulnerabilities of the key resources and critical infrastructure of the United States, including the performance of risk assessments to determine the risks posed by particular types of terrorist attacks within the United States;

(B) to identify priorities for protective and supportive measures; and

(C) to develop a comprehensive national plan for securing the key resources and critical infrastructure of the United States.

(2) Under Homeland Security Presidential Directive 7, issued on December 17, 2003, the Secretary of Homeland Security was given 1 year to develop a comprehensive plan to identify, prioritize, and coordinate the protection of critical infrastructure and key resources.

(3) The report of the National Commission on Terrorist Attacks Upon the United States recommended that the Secretary of Homeland Security should—

(A) identify those elements of the United States' transportation, energy, communications, financial, and other institutions that need to be protected;

(B) develop plans to protect that infrastructure; and

(C) exercise mechanisms to enhance preparedness.

SEC. 7403. STUDY REGARDING NATIONWIDE EMERGENCY NOTIFICATION SYSTEM.

(a) STUDY.— The Secretary of Homeland Security ... shall conduct a study to determine whether it is cost-effective, efficient, and feasible to establish and implement an emergency telephonic alert notification system that will—

(1) alert persons in the United States of imminent or current hazardous events caused by acts of terrorism; and

(2) provide information to individuals regarding appropriate measures that may be undertaken to alleviate

or minimize threats to their safety and welfare posed by such events.

(b) TECHNOLOGIES TO CONSIDER.— In conducting the study, the Secretary shall consider the use of the telephone, wireless communications, and other existing communications networks to provide such notification.

SEC. 7404. PILOT STUDY TO MOVE WARNING SYSTEMS INTO THE MODERN DIGITAL AGE.

(a) PILOT STUDY.— The Secretary of Homeland Security, from funds made available for improving the national system to notify the general public in the event of a terrorist attack . . . shall conduct a pilot study under which the Secretary of Homeland Security may issue public warnings regarding threats to homeland security using a warning system that is similar to the AMBER Alert communications network.

Post-Katrina Emergency Management Reform Act, The National Infrastructure Simulation and Analysis Center

SEC. 511.

"**(a)** *Definition.* In this section, the term 'National Infrastructure Simulation and Analysis Center' means the National Infrastructure Simulation and Analysis Center established under section 1016(d) of the USA PATRIOT Act (42 U.S.C. 5195c(d)).

"**(b)** *Authority.*

"**(1) IN GENERAL.—** There is in the Department the National Infrastructure Simulation and Analysis Center which shall serve as a source of national expertise to address critical infrastructure protection and continuity through support for activities related to—
    "(A) counterterrorism, threat assessment, and risk mitigation; and
    "(B) a natural disaster, act of terrorism, or other manmade disaster.

"**(2) INFRASTRUCTURE MODELING.**

"(A) *PARTICULAR SUPPORT.—* The support provided under paragraph (1) shall include modeling, simulation, and analysis of the systems and assets comprising critical infrastructure, in order to enhance preparedness, protection, response, recovery, and mitigation activities.

"(B) *RELATIONSHIP WITH OTHER AGENCIES.—* Each Federal agency and department with critical infrastructure responsibilities under Homeland Security Presidential Directive 7, or any successor to such directive, shall establish a formal relationship, including an agreement regarding information sharing, between the elements of such agency or department and the National Infrastructure Simulation and Analysis Center, through the Department.

"(C) *PURPOSE.*

    "(i) *IN GENERAL.—* The purpose of the relationship under subparagraph (B) shall be to permit each Federal agency and department described in subparagraph (B) to take full advantage of the capabilities of the National Infrastructure Simulation and Analysis Center (particularly vulnerability and consequence analysis), consistent with its work load capacity and priorities, for real-time response to reported and projected natural disasters, acts of terrorism, and other manmade disasters.

    "(ii) *RECIPIENT OF CERTAIN SUPPORT.—* Modeling, simulation, and analysis provided under this subsection shall be provided to relevant Federal agencies and departments, including Federal agencies and departments with critical infrastructure responsibilities under Homeland Security Presidential Directive 7, or any successor to such directive.

HSPD 19. Combating Terrorist Use of Explosives in The United States, February 12, 2007

Policy

(4) "It is the policy of the United States to counter the threat of explosive attacks aggressively by coordinating Federal, State, local, territorial, and tribal government efforts and collaborating with the owners and operators of critical infrastructure and key resources to deter, prevent, detect, protect against, and respond to explosive attacks, including the following:

   (a) applying techniques of psychological and behavioral sciences in the analysis of potential threats of explosive attack;

   (b) using the most effective technologies, capabilities, and explosives search procedures, and applications thereof, to detect, locate, and render safe explosives before they detonate or function as part of an explosive attack, including detection of explosive materials and precursor chemicals used to make improvised explosive or incendiary mixtures;

   (c) applying all appropriate resources to pre-blast or pre-functioning search and explosives render-safe procedures, and to post-blast or post-functioning investigatory and search activities, in order to detect secondary and tertiary explosives and for the purposes of attribution;

(d) employing effective capabilities, technologies, and methodologies, including blast mitigation techniques, to mitigate or neutralize the physical effects of an explosive attack on human life, critical infrastructure, and key resources; and

(5) ... the Attorney General... shall submit to the President... a report, including a national strategy and recommendations, on how more effectively to deter, prevent, detect, protect against, and respond to explosive attacks, including the coordination of Federal Government efforts with State, local, territorial, and tribal governments, first responders, and private sector organizations. The report shall include the following:

(a) a descriptive list of all Federal statutes, regulations, policies, and guidance that (i) set forth agency authorities and responsibilities relating to the prevention or detection of, protection against, or response to explosive attacks, or (ii) govern the use of the assets and capabilities described in paragraph (b) of this section;

(b) an inventory and description of all current Federal Government assets and capabilities specifically relating to the detection of explosives or the protection against or response to explosive attacks, catalogued by geographic location, including the asset's transportability and, to the extent feasible, similar assets and capabilities of State, local, territorial, and tribal governments;

(c) an inventory and description of current research, development, testing, and evaluation initiatives relating to the detection of and protection against explosives and anticipated advances in capabilities for reducing the threat of explosive attacks, and recommendations for the best means of disseminating the results of such initiatives to and among Federal, State, local, territorial, and tribal governments and first responders, as appropriate;

(d) for the purpose of identifying needed improvements in our homeland security posture, an assessment of our ability to deter, prevent, detect, protect against, and respond to an explosive attack based on a review of risk and the list, inventories, and descriptions developed pursuant to paragraphs (a), (b), and (c) of this section, and recommendations to address any such needed improvements;

(e) recommendations for improved detection of explosive chemical compounds, precursor chemicals used to make improvised explosive chemical compounds, and explosive device components;

(f) recommendations for developing a comprehensive understanding of terrorist training and construc-

tion methods relating to explosive attacks and the production of explosive and incendiary materials;

(g) recommendations for protecting critical infrastructure and key resources against an explosive attack that can be used to inform sector-specific plans developed pursuant to the NIPP, including specific actions applicable to each of the critical infrastructure and key resources sectors;

(h) a recommended draft incident annex to the National Response Plan [now National Response Framework] developed pursuant to [HSPD 5], February 28, 2003 (Management of Domestic Incidents), for explosive attacks, detailing specific roles and responsibilities of agencies and heads of agencies through all phases of incident management from prevention and protection through response and recovery;

(i) an assessment of the effectiveness of, and, as necessary, recommendations for improving Federal Government training and education initiatives relating to explosive attack detection, including canine training and performance standards;

(j) recommended components of a national public awareness and vigilance campaign regarding explosive attacks; and

(k) a recommendation on whether any additional Federal Government entity should be established to coordinate Federal Government explosive attack prevention, detection, protection, and response efforts and collaboration with State, local, territorial, and tribal government officials, first responders, and private sector organizations. ...

Roles and Responsibilities

(7) The Attorney General... shall maintain and make available... a web-based secure portal that includes information on incidents involving the suspected criminal misuse of explosives, including those voluntarily reported by State, local, territorial, and tribal authorities.

(8) The Secretary of Homeland Security... shall maintain secure information-sharing systems that make available to law enforcement agencies, and other first responders at the discretion of the Secretary of Homeland Security, information, including lessons learned and best practices, concerning the use of explosives as a terrorist weapon and related insurgent war fighting tactics, both domestically and internationally, for use in enhancing the preparedness of ... personnel to deter, prevent, detect, protect against, and respond to explosive attacks in the United States."

Improving Critical Infrastructure Security, Title X, Implementing Recommendations of The 9/11 Commission Act, August 3, 2007

SEC. 1001. NATIONAL ASSET DATABASE.

(a) IN GENERAL.— Subtitle A of title II of the Homeland Security Act of 2002, as amended by title V, is further amended by adding at the end the following new section:

"SEC. 210E. NATIONAL ASSET DATABASE.

"(a) *ESTABLISHMENT.*

"(1) *NATIONAL ASSET DATABASE.—* The Secretary shall establish and maintain a national database of each system or asset that—

"(A) the Secretary, in consultation with appropriate homeland security officials of the States, determines to be vital and the loss, interruption, incapacity, or destruction of which would have a negative or debilitating effect on the economic security, public health, or safety of the United States, any State, or any local government; or

"(B) the Secretary determines is appropriate for inclusion in the database.

"(2) *PRIORITIZED CRITICAL INFRASTRUCTURE LIST.—* In accordance with Homeland Security Presidential Directive–7, as in effect on January 1, 2007, the Secretary shall establish and maintain a single classified prioritized list of systems and assets included in the database under paragraph (1) that the Secretary determines would, if destroyed or disrupted, cause national or regional catastrophic effects.

"(f) *NATIONAL INFRASTRUCTURE PROTECTION CONSORTIUM.—* The Secretary may establish a consortium to be known as the 'National Infrastructure Protection Consortium'. The Consortium may advise the Secretary on the best way to identify, generate, organize, and maintain any database or list of systems and assets established by the Secretary, including the database established under subsection

(a)(1) and the list established under subsection (a)(2)...

SEC. 1003. SENSE OF CONGRESS REGARDING THE INCLUSION OF LEVEES IN THE NATIONAL INFRASTRUCTURE PROTECTION PLAN.

It is the sense of Congress that the Secretary should ensure that levees are included in one of the critical infrastructure and key resources sectors identified in the National Infrastructure Protection Plan.

National Strategy for Homeland Security, October 2007

Protect the American People, Critical Infrastructure, and Key Resources ... Safeguarding the American people also includes the preservation of the Nation's critical infrastructure and key resources (CI/KR). As set forth in the 2006 National Infrastructure Protection Plan (NIPP), critical infrastructure includes the assets, systems, and networks, whether physical or virtual, so vital to the United States that their incapacitation or destruction would have a debilitating effect on security, national economic security, public health or safety, or any combination thereof. Key resources are publicly or privately controlled resources essential to the minimal operations of the economy and government. By protecting CI/KR, we further protect the American people and build a safer, more secure, and more resilient Nation.

...Terrorist actors can be deterred and dissuaded from conducting attacks if they perceive that they are not likely to achieve their objectives or that the costs of their efforts are too high. The counterterrorism and homeland security activities... are part of our deterrent strategy – making it increasingly difficult for our enemies to achieve their objective of an attack in the Homeland by denying them and their weapons entry to the United States, denying them the ability to operate effectively within our borders, and denying them future recruits by preventing homegrown radicalization.... As a protective function, this concept of "deterrence through denial" requires additional actions, including increased defensive postures at potential sites of attack.

... Additionally, the use of both active and passive countermeasures as well as their unpredictable application will help ensure greater effectiveness. We also must promote public awareness of our increased security practices so terrorists understand that we are increasing the likelihood that they will not succeed.

Protection and Risk Management Despite our best efforts, achieving a complete state of CI/KR protection is not possible in the face of the numerous and varied catastrophic possibilities that could challenge the security of America today. Recognizing that the future is uncertain and that we cannot envision or prepare for every potential threat, we must understand and accept a certain level of risk as a permanent condition....

Changing motivational calculus. Terrorist actors also can be deterred or dissuaded from conducting attacks if they fear potential consequences for their actions. Since September 11, the United States has made it clear that we and our partners in the War on Terror make no distinction between those who commit acts of terror and those who support and harbor them. Any government that chooses to be an ally of terror has chosen to be an enemy of freedom, justice, and peace, and we, along with our international partners, will hold our terrorist enemies to account.

The National Infrastructure Protection Plan Guiding our efforts to protect the Nation's CI/KR is the 2006 National Infrastructure Protection Plan (NIPP) and its supporting Sector-Specific Plans, which were developed pursuant to Homeland Security Presidential Directive-7...

Mitigate Vulnerabilities We will not be able to deter all terrorist threats, and it is impossible to deter or prevent natural catastrophes. We can, however, mitigate the Nation's vulnerability... by ensuring the structural and operational resilience of our critical infrastructure and key resources and by further protecting the American people through medical preparedness.

Ensuring CI/KR Structural Resilience While the devastation of even one sector of our critical infrastructure or key resources would have a debilitating effect on our national security and possibly damage the morale and confidence of the American people, interdependencies make the protection of CI/KR particularly essential. A failure in one area, such as our water supply system, can adversely affect not only public health but also the ability of first responders to provide emergency services. Accordingly, ensuring the survivability of our CI/KR assets, systems, and networks requires that we continue to accurately model their interdependencies and better assess and understand the potential cascading effects that could impact and impede operations in interconnected infrastructures.

For each CI/KR sector, we must collectively work to ensure the ability of power, communications, and other life sustaining systems to survive an attack by terrorists, a natural disaster, and other assessed risks or hazards. In the past, investments in redundant and duplicative infrastructure were used to achieve this objective. We must now focus on the resilience of the system as a whole – an approach that centers on investments that make the system better able to absorb the impact of an event without losing the capacity to function. While this might include the building of redundant assets, resilience often is attained through the dispersal of key functions across multiple service providers and flexible supply chains and related systems. Resilience also includes the protection and physical survivability of key national assets and structures.

Additionally, an important aspect of promoting resilience includes seismic retrofitting and adherence to stricter building codes, as appropriate. Flood mitigation activities are also important and include the maintenance of flood plains.... Many of our CI/KR assets are intertwined with a global infrastructure that has evolved to support modern economies.

While this global system brings efficiencies and benefits, it also creates vulnerabilities and challenges...

Critical Infrastructure and Key Resources Our Nation has identified 17 sectors of critical infrastructure and key resources, each with cross-cutting physical, cyber, and human elements: Agriculture and Food; Banking and Finance; Chemical; Commercial Facilities; Commercial Nuclear Reactors, Materials, and Waste; Dams; Defense Industrial Base; Drinking Water and Water Treatment Systems; Emergency Services; Energy; Government Facilities; Information Technology; National Monuments and Icons; Postal and Shipping; Public Health and Health Care; Telecommunications; Transportation Systems.

Cyber Security: A Special Consideration Many of the Nation's essential and emergency services, as well as our critical infrastructure, rely on the uninterrupted use of the Internet and the communications systems, data, monitoring, and control systems that comprise our cyber infrastructure. A cyber attack could be debilitating to our highly interdependent CI/KR and ultimately to our economy and national security.

Ensuring Operational Resilience Mitigating the vulnerability of government and private sector operations to... disasters depends not only on the structural resilience of our assets, systems, and networks but also on operational resilience. First, we will continue to maintain comprehensive and effective continuity programs, including those that integrate continuity of operations and continuity of government programs, to ensure the preservation of our government under the Constitution and the continuing performance of national essential functions – those government roles that are necessary to lead and sustain the Nation during and following a catastrophic emergency.... Likewise, we strongly encourage the private sector to conduct business continuity planning that recognizes interdependencies and complements governmental efforts – doing so not only helps secure the United States, but also makes good long-term business sense for individual companies.

Protecting the American people through medical preparedness.... Our population, however, requires additional protective measures. We must reduce the vulnerability of the American populace... Reducing the Nation's vulnerability to public health threats requires that we continue to build sustainable systems for prevention, detection, reporting, investigation, control, and recovery... In order to facilitate our efforts, we will continue to upgrade our systems for clinical surveillance and environmental monitoring, as well as ensure the effective and timely integration and sharing of data, conclusions, and other information with State, local, and Tribal authorities and other appropriate homeland security partners...

. . . we must ensure that we have access to the necessary medical countermeasures. . . establishing appropriate levels of medical stockpiles and the systems that can rapidly distribute medical countermeasures to large, at-risk populations. Finally, we must assist communities as they develop medical systems that are able to sustain delivery of situation-appropriate care in the setting of catastrophic events. Like other homeland security activities, protecting the health of citizens is a shared responsibility –. . . collaborative community and regional planning is essential for the protection of the American people.

National Infrastructure Protection Plan, 2009

[T]he overarching goal of the National Infrastructure Protection Plan (NIPP) is to: "[b]uild a safer, more secure, and more resilient America by preventing, deterring, neutralizing, or mitigating the effects of deliberate efforts by terrorists to destroy, incapacitate, or exploit elements of our Nation's CIKR [Critical Infrastructure and Key Resources] and to strengthen national preparedness, timely response, and rapid recovery of CIKR in the event of an attack, natural disaster, or other emergency."

The NIPP provides the unifying structure for the integration of existing and future CIKR protection efforts and resiliency strategies into a single national program to achieve this goal. The NIPP framework supports the prioritization of protection and resiliency initiatives and investments across sectors to ensure that government and private sector resources are applied where they offer the most benefit for mitigating risk by lessening vulnerabilities, deterring threats, and minimizing the consequences of terrorist attacks and other manmade and natural disasters. The NIPP risk management framework recognizes and builds on existing public and private sector protective programs and resiliency strategies in order to be cost-effective and to minimize the burden on CIKR owners and operators. . .

. . . The Homeland Security Act of 2002 provides the basis for Department of Homeland Security (DHS) responsibilities in the protection of the Nation's CIKR. The act assigns DHS the responsibility for developing a comprehensive national plan for securing CIKR and for recommending the "measures necessary to protect the key resources and critical infrastructure of the United States. . .The national approach for CIKR protection is provided through the unifying framework established in Homeland Security Presidential Directive 7 (HSPD-7). This directive establishes the U.S. policy for "enhancing protection of the Nation's CIKR" and mandates a national plan to actuate that policy. In HSPD-7, the President designates the Secretary of Homeland Security as the "principal Federal official to lead CIKR protection efforts. . .

Managing Risk   The cornerstone of the NIPP is its risk analysis and management framework. . . that establishes the processes for combining consequence, vulnerability, and threat information to produce assessments of national or sector risk. The risk management framework is structured to promote continuous improvement to enhance CIKR protection by focusing activities on efforts to: set goals and objectives; identify assets, systems, and networks; assess risk based on consequences, vulnerabilities, and threats; establish priorities based on risk assessments and, increasingly, on return-on-investment for mitigating risk; implement protective programs and resiliency strategies; and measure effectiveness. The results of these processes drive CIKR risk-reduction and management activities. . .

Organizing and Partnering for CIKR Protection   The enormity and complexity of the Nation's CIKR, the distributed character of our national protective architecture, and the uncertain nature of the terrorist threat and other manmade or natural disasters make the effective implementation of protection and resiliency efforts a great challenge. To be effective, the NIPP must be implemented using organizational structures and partnerships committed to sharing and protecting the information needed to achieve the NIPP goal and supporting objectives. . . Sector-specific planning and coordination are addressed through coordinating councils that are established for each sector. Sector Coordinating Councils (SCCs) comprise the representatives of owners and operators, generally from the private sector.

Government Coordinating Councils (GCCs) comprise the representatives of the SSAs; other Federal departments and agencies; and State, local, tribal, and territorial governments. These councils create a structure through which representative groups from all levels of government and the private sector can collaborate or share existing approaches to CIKR protection and work together to advance capabilities. . .

. . .NIPP implementation relies on CIKR information provided voluntarily by owners and operators. Much of this is sensitive business or security information that could cause serious damage to private firms, the economy, public safety, or security through unauthorized disclosure or access. The Federal Government has a statutory responsibility to safeguard CIKR protection-related information. DHS and other Federal agencies use a number of programs and procedures, such as the Protected Critical Infrastructure Information (PCII) Program, to ensure that security-related information is properly safeguarded.

The CIKR protection activities defined in the NIPP are guided by legal requirements such as those described in the Privacy Act of 1974 and are designed to achieve both security and protection of civil rights and liberties.

. . .The NIPP, the National Preparedness Guidelines (NPG), and the National Response Framework (NRF) together provide a comprehensive, integrated approach to the homeland security mission. The NIPP establishes the overall risk-informed approach that defines the Nation's CIKR protection posture, while the NRF provides the approach for domestic incident management. The NPG sets forth national priorities, doctrine, and roles and responsibilities for building capabilities across the prevention, protection, response, and recovery mission areas...

The NRF is implemented to guide overall coordination of domestic incident management activities. NIPP partnerships and processes provide the foundation for the CIKR dimension of the NRF, facilitating threat and incident management across a spectrum of activities... Implementation of the NIPP is both a national preparedness priority and a framework with which to achieve protection capabilities as defined by the NPG.

The NIPP provides the framework for the unprecedented cooperation that is needed to develop, implement, and maintain a coordinated national effort to bring together government at all levels, the private sector, nongovernmental organizations, and international partners. The NIPP depends on supporting SSPs [sector specific plans] for full implementation of this frame-work within and across CIKR sectors. SSPs are developed by the Federal Sector-Specific Agencies (SSAs) designated in... HSPD-7... Together, the NIPP and SSPs provide the mechanisms for: identifying critical assets, systems, and networks, and their associated functions; understanding threats to CIKR; identifying and assessing vulnerabilities and consequences; prioritizing protection initiatives and investments based on costs and benefits so that they are applied where they offer the greatest mitigation of risk; and enhancing information-sharing mech-anisms and protection and resiliency within and across CIKR sectors.

The NIPP considers a full range of physical, cyber, and human risk elements within and across sectors. In accordance with the policy direction established in HSPD-7, the National Strategy for the Physical Protection of Critical Infrastructures and Key Assets, and the National Strategy to Secure Cyberspace, the NIPP includes a special focus on the unique and potentially catastrophic impact of terrorist attacks...The NIPP addresses ongoing and future activities within each of the CIKR sectors identified in HSPD-7...

Critical Infrastructure Key Resource Training Program

This course is designed to establish a reference point and standard of performance for federal, state, and local critical infrastructure protection personnel by providing common references, processes and tools to facilitate consistency within the community tasked with Critical Infrastructure Key Resource (CI/KR) protection. The target audience of this course is the security specialists, program managers, inspectors, investigators, and offices charged with NIPP implementation, compliance, and information sharing; specifically the federal workforce charged with CI/KR protection duties identified in HSPD-7.

This course was developed in accordance with the National Infrastructure Protection Plan (NIPP) with a main goal of developing baseline training for personnel that deal with the nation's "critical infrastructure"...

ENDNOTES

1. For an excellent discussion of critical infrastructure and critical infrastructure protection, see "Critical Infrastructure Protection in Homeland Security: Defending a Networked Nation" by Ted G. Lewis, John Wiley & Sons, 2006.

   For excellent descriptions of several existing, real world, cascading failures waiting to happen, see, "The Edge of Disaster, Building a Resilient Nation," Stephen Flynn, 2007.

   For much more information specifically on SCADA, see Sandia National Labs, The Center For SCADA Security. http://www.sandia.gov/scada/history.htm.

2. Executive Order 13231—Critical Infrastructure Protection in the Information Age, October 18, 2001. http://frwebgate.access.gpo.gov/cgi-bin/getdoc.cgi?dbname=2001_register&docid=fr18oc01-139.pdf.

3. Patriot Act. October 26, 2001. http://thomas.loc.gov/cgi-bin/bdquery/z?d107:hr03162:%5D.

4. National Strategy for the Physical Protection of Critical Infrastructures and Key Assets, February, 2002. http://www.dhs.gov/xlibrary/assets/Physical_Strategy.pdf.

5. Homeland Security Act, November 25, 2002. http://www.dhs.gov/xlibrary/assets/hr_5005_enr.pdf.(accessed 03/15/09).

6. HSPD 7. http://www.dhs.gov/xabout/laws/gc_1214597989952.shtm.

7. TITLE VII—Implementation Of 9/11 Commission Recommendations, Intelligence Reform and Terrorism Prevention Act of 2004, Subtitle C—National Preparedness, Public Law 108–458—December 17, 2004. http://www.nctc.gov/docs/pl108_458.pdf.

8. Public Law 109–295, Title VI, Post-Katrina Emergency Management Reform Act, 2006 (October 4, 2006). http://frwebgate.access.gpo.gov/cgi-bin/getdoc.cgi?dbname=109_cong_public_laws&docid=f:publ295.109.pdf.

9. HSPD 19. http://www.dhs.gov/xabout/laws/gc_1219260981698.shtm.

10. Improving Critical Infrastructure Security, Title X, Implementing Recommendations Of The 9/11 Commission Act, August 3, 2007. http://www.nctc.gov/docs/ir-of-the-9-11-comm-act-of-2007.pdf.

11. National Strategy for Homeland Security, Homeland Security Council, October, 2007, pp. 25–37. http://www.dhs.gov/xlibrary/assets/nat_strat_homelandsecurity_2007.pdf. (accessed March 28, 2009).

12. Critical Infrastructure Key Resource Training Program (CIKRTP). http://www.fletc.gov/training/programs/counterterrorism-division/critical-infrastructure-key-resource-protection-qualification-training-program-cikrtp (accessed March 19, 2009).

13. NIPP. http://www.dhs.gov/xlibrary/assets/NIPP_Plan.pdf, http://www.dhs.gov/xprevprot/programs/editorial_0827.shtm.

14. http://thomas.loc.gov/cgi-bin/bdquery/z?d107:hr03162:%5D.

15. "The September 11 attacks inflicted casualties and material damages on a far greater scale than any other terrorist aggression in recent history. Lower Manhattan lost approximately 30 percent of its office space and a number of businesses ceased to exist. Close to 200,000 jobs were destroyed or relocated out of New York City, at least temporarily. The destruction of physical assets was estimated in the national accounts to amount to $14 billion for private businesses, $1.5 billion for state and local government enterprises and $0.7 billion for federal enterprises. Rescue, cleanup and related costs have been estimated to amount to at least $11 billion for a total direct cost of $27.2 billion." Center for Contemporary Conflict, August 2002. http://www.ccc.nps.navy.mil/si/aug02/homeland.asp.

16. The *National Strategy for Homeland Security* defines "homeland security" and identifies a strategic framework based on three national objectives. In order of priority, these are (1) preventing terrorist attacks within the United States, (2) reducing America's vulnerability to terrorism, and (3) minimizing the damage and recovering from attacks that do occur.

17. http://www.dhs.gov/xlibrary/assets/hr_5005_enr.pdf.

18. "In this section, the term 'critical infrastructure' means systems and assets, whether physical or virtual, so vital to the United States that the incapacity or destruction of such systems and assets would have a debilitating impact on security, national economic security, national public health or safety, or any combination of those matters."

19. "The term "key resources" means publicly or privately controlled resources essential to the minimal operations of the economy and government."

20. The actual statute is available at Pub. L. No. 81-774 (1950); codified at 50 U.S.C. App. §§2061 et. seq. "As outlined in Title III of the Defense Production Act of 1950, the mission of the DPA Title III Program is to create assured, affordable, and commercially viable production capabilities and capacities for items essential for national defense. See the Defense Production Act Title III Homepage at http://www.acq.osd.mil/ott/dpatitle3/index.htm.(accessed March 19, 2009).

    Also see SourceWatch discussion, The Defense Production Act of 1950 (Public Law 81-774) was enacted due to "Rising wages and prices during the Korean War [which] caused serious economic difficulties within the United States. In an effort to expand production and insure economic stability, the Defense Production Act of 1950 (Public Law 81-774) authorized Governmental activities in various areas, including requisition of property for national defense, expansion of productive capacity and supply, wage and price stabilization, settlement of labor disputes, control of consumer and real estate credit, and establishment of contract priorities and materials allocation designed to aid the national defense. Under section 712, the Joint Committee on Defense Production was established to serve as a 'watchdog' over Federal agencies administering the various programs authorized by the act. The members of the committee were drawn from the Senate and House Committees on Banking and Currency." http://www.sourcewatch.org/index.php?title= Defense_Production_Act_of_1950.

21. HSPD 19(5)(g) "...the Attorney General, in coordination with the Secretary of Homeland Security...shall submit to the President...a report,...on how more effectively to deter, prevent, detect, protect against, and respond to explosive attacks,...The report shall include the following: (g) recommendations for protecting critical infrastructure and key resources against an explosive attack..."

22. See Presidential Decisions Directives in general. http://ftp.fas.org/irp/offdocs/pdd-63.htm. See White Paper on PDD 63. http://ftp.fas.org/irp/offdocs/paper598.htm.

23. Critical Infrastructure Key Resource Training Program (CIKRTP). http://www.fletc.gov/training/programs/counterterrorism-division/critical-infrastructure-key-resource-protection-qualification-training-program-cikrtp.

ADDITIONAL RESOURCES

Websites

National Infrastructure Protection Center FBI. http://www.calea.org/online/newsletter/No75/The%20National%20Infrastructure%20Protection%20Center.htm.

National Infrastructure Simulation and Analysis Center (NISAC). http://www.sandia.gov/nisac/.

Center For Infrastructure Protection at George Mason University School of Law. http://cip. gmu.edu/.

DHS Daily Open Source Infrastructure Report is collected each weekday as a summary of open-source published information concerning significant critical infrastructure issues. http://www.dhs.gov/xinfoshare/programs/editorial_0542.shtm.

Center for Nonproliferation Studies. http://cns.miis.edu/. NPT Briefing Book (MCIS/CNS) 2009, Interim Annecy Edition.

The most comprehensive source of background and reference material on the Nuclear Nonproliferation Treaty and

its associated regime is now available online. http://cns.
miis.edu/treaty_npt/npt_briefing_book_2009/index.htm.

Books and Articles

American Society of Civil Engineers, America's Infrastructure 2009
Report Card, March 25, 2009. http://s3.amazonaws.com/ ascere-
portcard/sites/default/files/RC2009_full_report.pdf.

"The Edge of Disaster, Rebuilding a Resilient Nation," by Stephen
Flynn, Random House 2007.

"Critical Infrastructure Protection in Homeland Security: Defending a Networked Nation" by Ted G. Lewis, Wiley, 2006.

"Unconquerable Nation, Knowing Our Enemy Strengthening Ourselves," by Brian Michael Jenkins, Rand, 2006. Includes an
extensive reading list.

"Critical Path, A Brief History of Critical infrastructure Protection
in the United States," by Kathi Ann Brown, 2006, Spectrum
Publishing Group.

"Critical Infrastructure Protection, OMB Leadership Needed to
Strengthen Agency Planning Efforts to Protect Federal Cyber Assets," GAO-10-148, October 2009. http://www.gao.gov/
new.items/d10148.pdf.

"EMP and you," by Frank Gaffney, Jr., Center for Security Policy, September 07, 2009. http://www.centerforsecuritypolicy.
org/p18167.xml?genre_id=1.

"Chemical Facility Security: Reauthorization, Policy Issues,
and Options for Congress," by Dana A. Shea, Congressional Research Service, September 3, 2009, R40695.
http://ftp.fas.org/sgp/crs/homesec/R40695.pdf.

CIP Report, Biosafety and Biosecurity, An Overview of Biosafety
and Biosecurity, by Donald F. Thompson, Center for Infrastructure Protection, September 2009. http://cip.gmu.edu/
archive/cip_report_8.2.pdf.

CIP Report, "America's Infrastructure," Center for Infrastructure
Protection, by Andrew W. Herrmann, October 2009. http://cip.
gmu.edu/archive/cip_report_8.3.pdf.

"American Association of State Highway and Transportation Officials: Working Toward Reviving our Aging Bridges and
Structures," by Kelley Rehm, *CIP Report,* Center for Infrastructure Protection, October 2009. http://cip.gmu.edu/archive/
cip_report_8.3.pdf.

"Chemical Sector Security: Success through Collaboration," *CIP
Report,* Chemical Sector, Center for Infrastructure Protection
November 2009. http://cip.gmu.edu/archive/cip_report_8.4.pdf.

The Critical Infrastructure Protection Report," Center for Infrastruc-
ture Protection, August 2009, Vol. 8, no. 2. http://cip.gmu.edu/
archive/cip_report_8.1.pdf. Focus: National Monuments and
Icons; NMI Sector Overview; US Secret Service; National
Mall Plan; Statue of Liberty; Legal Insights; Cyber Conflict
Perspectives.

Effectively Transforming Our Electric Delivery System to a Smart
Grid, Subcommittee on Energy & Environment, July 23, 2009.
http://science.house.gov/publications/hearings_markups_details.
aspx?NewsID=2553.

American Society of Civil Engineers, Guiding Principles for the
Nation's Critical Infrastructure, 2009. http://content.asce.org/
files/pdf/GuidingPrinciplesFinalReport.pdf.

Government Accountability Office, Defense Critical Infrastructure: Actions Needed to Improve the Consistency, Reliability, and Usefulness of DOD's Tier 1 Task Critical Asset List,
GAO-09-740R, July 17, 2009. http://www.gao.gov/new.items/
d09740r.pdf.

Securing the Modern Electric Grid from Physical and Cyber Attacks, Subcommittee on Emerging Threats, Cybersecurity, and Science and Technology, Tuesday, July 21, 2009.
http://homeland.house.gov/Hearings/index.asp?ID=206.

"Chemical Facility Security: Reauthorization, Policy Issues,
and Options for Congress," Dana A. Shea, July 13, 2009,
Congressional Research Service, R40695. http://www.fas.org/
sgp/crs/homesec/R40695.pdf.

Engineering Security: Protective Design for High Risk Buildings,
2009, New York City Police Department. http://www.nyc.gov/
html/nypd/html/counterterrorism/engineeringsecurity.shtml.

The Department of Homeland Security's (DHS) Critical Infrastructure Protection Cost-Benefit Report, GAO-09-654R, June 26,
2009. http://www.gao.gov/new.items/d09654r.pdf.

Congressional Hearing: MARKUP of H.R. 2868 - "The Chemical Facility Antiterrorism Act of 2009," June 23, 2009.
http://homeland. house.gov/Hearings/index.asp?ID=200.

Department of Homeland Security Privacy Impact Assessments (PIA), Chemical Facility Anti-Terrorism Standards
(CFATS) Update, June 11, 2009. http://www.dhs.gov/ xli-
brary/assets/privacy/privacy_pia_nppd_cfatschemsupdate.pdf.

"The Chemical Facility Antiterrorism Act of 2009," Testimony
before Congress, House, Homeland Security Committee, June
16, 2009. http://homeland. house.gov/Hearings/index.asp?ID=
199.

"Terrorism and Security Issues Facing the Water Infrastructure
Sector," Claudia Copeland, May 26, 2009, CRS RL32189.
http://opencrs.com/document/RL32189.

"Fragility: Next Wave in Critical Infrastructure Protection," Journal
of Strategic Security May 2009, Vol. 2, no. 2. http://www.henley-
putnam.edu/652-267.htm. [free download but registration re-
quired]

Critical Infrastructure Protection Program [George Mason
University]*CIP Report*, Vol. 7, no. 9, April 2009.
http://cip.gmu.edu/archive/cip_report_7.9.pdf Maritime and Port
Security.

Protected Critical Infrastructure Information (PCII) Program Procedures Manual, DHS. http://www.dhs.gov/xlibrary/
assets/pcii_program_procedures_manual.pdf.

Siobhan Gorman, Electricity Grid in U.S. Penetrated By Spies,
Wall Street Journal, April 8, 2009. http://online.wsj.com/
article/SB123914805204099085.html.

Highway Infrastructure, Federal Efforts to Strengthen Security
Should Be Better Coordinated and Targeted on the Nation's
Most Critical Highway Infrastructure. http://www.gao.gov/
new.items/d0957.pdf.

National Infrastructure Protection Plan Critical Manufacturing Sector. http://www.dhs.gov/xlibrary/assets/nipp_snapshot_
criticalmanufacturing.pdf. National Academies Press 2009.

Countering Terrorism: Biological Agents, Transportation Networks, and Energy Systems. Summary of a U.S.-Russian

Workshop, National Academies Press 2009. http://www.nap. edu/catalog.php?record_id=12490. [free download but registration required]

"Strengthening Our Infrastructure for a Sustainable Future," by Darren Springer and Greg Dierkersk, National Governors Association, 2009. http://www.nga.org/Files/pdf/ 0902INFRASTRUC-TUREVISION.PDF.

"The Global Nuclear Detection Architecture,"by Dana A. Shea, March 25, 2009, CRS RL34574. http://opencrs.com/document/RL34574/.

"Nuclear Powerplant Security and Vulnerabilities," by Mark Holt and Anthony Andrews, RL34331, March 18, 2009. http://www.fas.org/sgp/crs/homesec/RL34331.pdf.

"Better Oversight Needed to Ensure That Security Improvements at Lawrence Livermore National Laboratory Are Fully Implemented and Sustained." GAO-09-321, March 16, 2009. http://www.gao.gov/new.items/d09321.pdf.

"Nuclear Cooperation With Other Countries, A Primer," by Paul Kerr and Mary Beth Nikitin, March 9, 2009, CRS RS22937. http://www.fas.org/sgp/crs/nuke/RS22937.pdf.

Nuclear Nonproliferation: Strengthened Oversight Needed to Address Proliferation and Management Challenges in IAEA's Technical Cooperation Program. GAO-09-275, March 5, 2009. http://www.gao.gov/new.items/d09275.pdf.

Patrick J. Massey,"Generational Hazards," Homeland Security Affairs III, no. 3, September 2007. http://www.hsaj.org/?article=3.3.3.

See "The Edge of Disaster," by Stephen Flynn, 2007, for several well described existing and predictable infrastructure failures.

From Protection to Resiliance, Homeland Security Advisory Council, Summary of Meeting Held on June 23, 2005, 2. Critical Infrastructure Task Force. http://www.dhs.gov/xlibrary/assets/HSAC_MtgMinutes_June23-05.pdf.

Canada

Canadian Defence and Foreign Affairs Institute (CDFAI), Resource Industries and Security Issues in Northern Alberta, June 2009. http://www.cdfai.org/PDF/Resource%20Industries%20and%20Security%20Issues%20in%20Northern%20Alberta.pdf.

12

CYBER SECURITY

This chapter describes our actions to protect cyber security. The Patriot Act of 2001 included directives for expanded information sharing and the development of increased cyber forensics capabilities. The chapter reviews actions mandated by the Patriot Act, the Homeland Security Act of 2002, the Cyber Security Research and Development Act of 2002, the National Strategy to Secure Cyberspace, 2003, and HSPD 23 of 2008.

SOURCES

- Patriot Act, 2001[1]
- Homeland Security Act of 2002[2]
- Cyber Security Research and Development Act, November 27, 2002[3]
- The National Strategy to Secure Cyberspace, February 2003[4]
- HSPD – 23: National Cyber Security Initiative, January 8, 2008. Classified

INTRODUCTION

"A successful cyber attack against a major financial service provider could severely impact the national economy, while cyber attacks against physical infrastructure computer systems such as those that control power grids or oil refineries have the potential to disrupt services for hours to weeks."[5]

"Federal agencies report increasing cyber-intrusions into government computer networks, perpetrated by a range of known and unknown actors.

Like other national security challenges in the post-9/11 era, the cyber threat is multi-faceted and lacks clearly delineated boundaries. Some cyber attackers operate through foreign nations' military or intelligence-gathering operations, whereas others have connections to terrorist groups or operate as individuals. Some cyber threats might be viewed as international or domestic criminal enterprises."[6]

Patriot Act, 2001

SEC. 816. DEVELOPMENT AND SUPPORT OF CYBERSECURITY FORENSIC CAPABILITIES.

(a) IN GENERAL.— The Attorney General shall establish such regional computer forensic laboratories as the Attorney General considers appropriate, and provide support to existing computer forensic laboratories, in order that all such computer forensic laboratories have the capability–

(1) to provide forensic examinations with respect to seized or intercepted computer evidence relating to criminal activity (including cyberterrorism);

(2) to provide training and education for Federal, State, and local law enforcement personnel and prosecutors regarding investigations, forensic analyses, and prosecutions of computer-related crime (including cyberterrorism);

(3) to assist Federal, State, and local law enforcement in enforcing Federal, State, and local criminal laws relating to computer-related crime;

Foundations of Homeland Security: Law and Policy, First Edition. Martin J. Alperen.
© 2011 John Wiley & Sons, Inc. Published 2011 by John Wiley & Sons, Inc.

(4) to facilitate and promote the sharing of Federal law enforcement expertise and information about the investigation, analysis, and prosecution of computer-related crime with State and local law enforcement personnel and prosecutors, including the use of multijurisdictional task forces...

Homeland Security Act of 2002

SEC. 225. CYBER SECURITY ENHANCEMENT ACT OF 2002.

(a) SHORT TITLE.— This section may be cited as the "Cyber Security Enhancement Act of 2002".

(b) AMENDMENT OF SENTENCING GUIDELINES RELATING TO CERTAIN COMPUTER CRIMES.

(1) *DIRECTIVE TO THE UNITED STATES SENTENCING COMMISSION.—* Pursuant to its authority under section 994(p) of title 28, United States Code, and in accordance with this subsection, the United States Sentencing Commission shall review and, if appropriate, amend its guidelines and its policy statements applicable to persons convicted of an offense under section 1030 of title 18, United States Code.

(2) *REQUIREMENTS.—* In carrying out this subsection, the Sentencing Commission shall—

(A) ensure that the sentencing guidelines and policy statements reflect the serious nature of the offenses described in paragraph (1), the growing incidence of such offenses, and the need for an effective deterrent and appropriate punishment to prevent such offenses;

(B) consider the following factors and the extent to which the guidelines may or may not account for them—

(i) the potential and actual loss resulting from the offense;

(ii) the level of sophistication and planning involved in the offense;

(iii) whether the offense was committed for purposes of commercial advantage or private financial benefit;

(iv) whether the defendant acted with malicious intent to cause harm in committing the offense;

(v) the extent to which the offense violated the privacy rights of individuals harmed;

(vi) whether the offense involved a computer used by the government in furtherance of national defense, national security, or the administration of justice;

(vii) whether the violation was intended to or had the effect of significantly interfering with or disrupting a critical infrastructure; and

(viii) whether the violation was intended to or had the effect of creating a threat to public health or safety, or injury to any person;

(C) assure reasonable consistency with other relevant directives and with other sentencing guidelines;

(D) account for any additional aggravating or mitigating circumstances that might justify exceptions to the generally applicable sentencing ranges;

Cyber Security Research and Development Act, November 27, 2002

SEC. 2. FINDINGS.

The Congress finds the following:

(1) Revolutionary advancements in computing and communications technology have interconnected government, commercial, scientific, and educational infrastructures—including critical infrastructures for electric power, natural gas and petroleum production and distribution, telecommunications, transportation, water supply, banking and finance, and emergency and government services—in a vast, interdependent physical and electronic network.

(2) Exponential increases in interconnectivity have facilitated enhanced communications, economic growth, and the delivery of services critical to the public welfare, but have also increased the consequences of temporary or prolonged failure.

(3) A Department of Defense Joint Task Force concluded after a 1997 United States information warfare exercise that the results "clearly demonstrated our lack of preparation for a coordinated cyber and physical attack on our critical military and civilian infrastructure"...

SEC. 4. NATIONAL SCIENCE FOUNDATION RESEARCH.

(a) COMPUTER AND NETWORK SECURITY RESEARCH GRANTS.
(1) *IN GENERAL.—* The Director shall award grants for basic research on innovative approaches to the structure of computer and network hardware and software that are aimed at enhancing computer security...

(b) COMPUTER AND NETWORK SECURITY RESEARCH CENTERS.
(1) *IN GENERAL.—* The Director shall award multiyear grants, subject to the availability of appropriations, to

institutions of higher education, nonprofit research institutions, or consortia thereof to establish multidisciplinary Centers for Computer and Network Security Research...

SEC. 5. NATIONAL SCIENCE FOUNDATION COMPUTER AND NETWORK SECURITY PROGRAMS.

(a) COMPUTER AND NETWORK SECURITY CAPACITY BUILDING GRANTS.

(1) *IN GENERAL.*— The Director shall establish a program to award grants to institutions of higher education (or consortia thereof) to establish or improve undergraduate and master's degree programs in computer and network security, to increase the number of students, including the number of students from groups historically underrepresented in these fields, who pursue undergraduate or master's degrees in fields related to computer and network security, and to provide students with experience in government or industry related to their computer and network security studies.

(c) GRADUATE TRAINEESHIPS IN COMPUTER AND NETWORK SECURITY RESEARCH.

(1) *IN GENERAL.*— The Director shall establish a program to award grants to institutions of higher education to establish traineeship programs for graduate students who pursue computer and network security research leading to a doctorate degree by providing funding and other assistance, and by providing graduate students with research experience in government or industry related to the students' computer and network security studies.

(e) CYBER SECURITY FACULTY DEVELOPMENT TRAINEESHIP PROGRAM.

(1) *IN GENERAL.*— The Director shall establish a program to award grants to institutions of higher education to establish traineeship programs to enable graduate students to pursue academic careers in cyber security upon completion of doctoral degrees.

SEC. 8. NATIONAL INSTITUTE OF STANDARDS AND TECHNOLOGY PROGRAMS.

(a) RESEARCH PROGRAM.— The National Institute of Standards and Technology Act (15 U.S.C. 271 et seq.) is amended—

(2) by inserting after section 21 the following new section:
"SEC. 22. RESEARCH PROGRAM ON SECURITY OF COMPUTER SYSTEMS

"(a) ESTABLISHMENT.— The Director shall establish a program of assistance to institutions of higher education that enter into partnerships with for-profit entities to support research to improve the security of computer systems. The partnerships may also include government laboratories and nonprofit research institutions...

SEC. 12. NATIONAL ACADEMY OF SCIENCES STUDY ON COMPUTER AND NETWORK SECURITY IN CRITICAL INFRASTRUCTURES.

(a) STUDY.— Not later than 3 months after the date of the enactment of this Act, the Director of the National Institute of Standards and Technology shall enter into an arrangement with the National Research Council of the National Academy of Sciences to conduct a study of the vulnerabilities of the Nation's network infrastructure and make recommendations for appropriate improvements...

The National Strategy to Secure Cyberspace, February 2003

Our Nation's critical infrastructures consist of the physical and cyber assets of public and private institutions in several sectors: agriculture, food, water, public health, emergency services, government, defense industrial base, information and telecommunications, energy, transportation, banking and finance, chemicals and hazardous materials, and postal and shipping. Cyberspace is the nervous system of these infrastructures—the control system of our country. Cyberspace comprises hundreds of thousands of interconnected computers, servers, routers, switches, and fiber optic cables that make our critical infrastructures work. Thus, the healthy functioning of cyberspace is essential to our economy and our national security.

...This National Strategy to Secure Cyberspace is part of an overall effort to protect the Nation. It is an implementing component of the National Strategy for Homeland Security and is complemented by the National Strategy for the Physical Protection of Critical Infrastructures and Key Assets. The purpose of this document is to engage and empower Americans to secure the portions of cyberspace that they own, operate, or control, or with which they interact...

A Unique Problem, a Unique Process Most critical infrastructures, and the cyberspace on which they rely, are privately owned and operated. The technologies that create and support cyberspace evolve rapidly from private sector and academic innovation. Government alone cannot sufficiently secure cyberspace...

[The President] has called for voluntary partnerships among government, industry, academia, and nongovernmental groups to secure and defend cyberspace ... In recognition of this need for partnership, the process to develop the National Strategy to Secure Cyberspace included soliciting views from both the public and private sectors. To do so, the White House sponsored town hall meetings on cyberspace security in ten metropolitan areas. Consequently, individual sectors (e.g., higher education, state and local government, banking and finance) formed workgroups to create initial sector-specific cyberspace security strategies. Additionally, the White House created a Presidential advisory panel, the National Infrastructure Advisory Council, consisting of leaders from the key sectors of the economy, government, and academia...

The *National Strategy to Secure Cyberspace* articulates five national priorities...

Priority I: A National Cyberspace Security Response System

Rapid identification, information exchange, and remediation can often mitigate the damage caused by malicious cyberspace activity.

Priority II: A National Cyberspace Security Threat and Vulnerability Reduction Program

...A National Cyberspace Security Threat and Vulnerability reduction program will include coordinated national efforts conducted by governments and the private sector to identify and remediate the most serious cyber vulnerabilities through collaborative activities, such as sharing best practices and evaluating and implementing new technologies...

Priority III: A National Cyberspace Security Awareness and Training Program

Many information-system vulnerabilities exist because of a lack of cyberspace security Awareness...

Priority IV: Securing Governments' Cyberspace

Priority V: National Security and International Cyberspace Security Cooperation

Threat and Vulnerability: A Five-Level Problem

Level 1, the Home User/Small Business

Though not a part of a critical infrastructure the computers of home users can become part of networks of remotely controlled machines that are then used to attack critical infrastructures...

Level 2, Large Enterprises
Level 3, Critical Sectors/Infrastructures
Level 4, National Issues and Vulnerabilities
Level 5, Global

The worldwide web is a planetary information grid of systems. Internationally shared standards enable interoperability among the world's computer systems. This interconnectedness, however, also means that problems on one continent have the potential to affect computers on another.

National Policy and Guiding Principles ...It is the policy of the United States to prevent or minimize disruptions to critical information infrastructures and thereby protect the people, the economy, the essential human and government services, and the national security of the United States. Disruptions that do occur should be infrequent, of minimal duration and manageable and cause the least damage possible.

[The objectives are to]

- Prevent cyber attacks against our critical infrastructures;
- Reduce our national vulnerabilities to cyber attack; and,
- Minimize the damage and recovery time from cyber attacks that do occur.

Department of Homeland Security and Cyberspace Security DHS unites 22 federal entities for the common purpose of improving homeland security. The Department also creates a focal point for managing cyberspace incidents that could impact the federal government or even the national information infrastructures...

Designation of Coordinating Agencies To facilitate and enhance this collaborative structure, the government has designated a "Lead Agency" for each of the major sectors of the economy vulnerable to infrastructure attack. In addition, the Office of Science and Technology Policy (OSTP) coordinates research and development to support critical infrastructure protection. The Office of Management and Budget (OMB) oversees the implementation of governmentwide policies, principles, standards, and guidelines for federal government computer security programs. The Department of State coordinates international outreach on cybersecurity. The Director of Central Intelligence is responsible for assessing the foreign threat to U.S. networks and information systems. The Department of Justice (DOJ) and the Federal Bureau of Investigation (FBI) lead the national effort to investigate and prosecute cybercrime.

The National Cyberspace Security Response System ...is a public-private architecture, coordinated by the Department of Homeland Security, for analyzing and warning; managing incidents of national significance; promoting continuity in government systems and private sector infrastructures; and increasing information sharing across and between organizations to improve cyberspace security.

1. ANALYSIS a. Provide for the Development of Tactical and Strategic Analysis of Cyber Attacks and Vulnerability Assessments...

2. WARNING a. Encourage the Development of a Private Sector Capability to Share a Synoptic View of the Health of Cyberspace...

b. Expand the Cyber Warning and Information
. . .Network to Support DHS's Role in Coordinating Crisis
Management for Cyberspace

4. RESPONSE AND RECOVERY a. Create Processes to
Coordinate the Voluntary Development of National Public-
Private Continuity and Contingency Plans . . .

1. Secure the Mechanisms of the Internet
    . . .securing the protocols on which the Internet is
    based, ensuring the security of the routers that direct
    the flow of data, and implementing effective manage-
    ment practices.
    a. Improve the Security and Resilience of Key In-
    ternet Protocols
        . . . three key protocols: the Internet Protocol
        (IP), the Domain Name System (DNS), and the
        Border Gateway Protocol (BGP). . .
    b. Promote Improved Internet Routing
2. Foster Trusted Digital Control Systems/Supervisory
    Control and Data Acquisition Systems
        . . .digital control systems (DCS) and supervi-
    sory control and data acquisition systems (SCADA).
    DCS/SCADA are computer-based systems that are
    used by many infrastructures and industries to re-
    motely control sensitive processes and physical func-
    tions that once had to be controlled manually. DCS
    and SCADA are present in almost every sector of the
    economy including water, transportation, chemicals,
    energy, and manufacturing, among others.
        Increasingly DCS/SCADA systems use the Inter-
    net to transmit data rather than the closed networks
    used in the past. Securing DCS/SCADA is a national
    priority. . .
3. Reduce and Remediate Software Vulnerabilities. . .
4. Understand Infrastructure Interdependency and Im-
    prove Physical Security of Cyber Systems and
    Telecommunications. . .

**Priority III: A National Cyberspace Security Awareness
and Training Program**

Priority IV: Securing Governments' Cyberspace
. . .OMB's first report to Congress on government information security reform in February 2002 identified six common government-wide security performance gaps.
These weaknesses included:

(1) Lack of senior management attention;
(2) Lack of performance measurement;
(3) Poor security education and awareness;
(4) Failure to fully fund and integrate security into capital
    planning and investment control;

(5) Failure to ensure that contractor services are ade-
    quately secure; and
(6) Failure to detect, report, and share information on
    vulnerabilities.

**Priority V: National Security and International
Cyberspace Security Cooperation**

1. Strengthen Counterintelligence Efforts in Cyberspace
2. Improve Attack Attribution and Prevention Capabil-
    ities
3. Improve Coordination for Responding to Cyber At-
    tacks within the United States National Security
    Community
4. Reserve the Right to Respond in an Appropriate
    Manner

**HSPD – 23: National Cyber Security Initiative,
January 8, 2008**

This HSPD and its corresponding NSPD 54, remains classified. There have been a few pieces of information released.

"In January 2008, the President approved . . . the Comprehensive National Cybersecurity Initiative (CNCI) –
that establishes the policy, strategy and guidelines to secure federal systems. The directive provides a comprehensive approach that anticipates future cyber threats and
technologies. . .Under CNCI, DHS leverages the National
Cyber Security Division (NCSD) and the U.S. Computer
Emergency Readiness Team (US-CERT), a 24-hour watch,
warning, and response operations center. . .

. . . NCSD has greatly reduced the number of Internet access points throughout the federal government and will be deploying EINSTEIN 2 systems to those locations. EINSTEIN
and EINSTEIN 2 are intrusion detection devices deployed
by US-CERT to collect relevant data that enable analysts
to detect potentially malicious cyber activities on federal
networks. The EINSTEIN 2 system achieved Initial Operational Capability on December 5, 2008. EINSTEIN 2 was
developed to collect, analyze and share computer security information across the federal government. NCSD has begun
deployment of EINSTEIN 2, which will provide comprehensive, real-time intrusion detection capabilities and a single
point of situational awareness across all executive branch
agencies. This system and other DHS-developed cyber components are incorporated in the National Cybersecurity &
Protection Program, which represents the integrated system
architecture.

. . .The department has also engaged private sector partners under the NIPP Partnership Framework to define the
federal role for extending cybersecurity into critical infrastructure domains. In addition, the Secret Service currently
maintains 24 Electronic Crimes Task Forces to prevent,

detect, mitigate and aggressively investigate cyber attacks on our nation's financial and critical infrastructures. . ."[7]

"Our military and civilian information infrastructure is highly vulnerable. And our military forces are highly dependent on this infrastructure, so this is the Achilles' heel of our otherwise overwhelming military might. There is a growing awareness about advanced cyber threats, but scant real progress to better secure our information infrastructure against those threats. Of particular concern is the vulnerability of our space assets to cyber attack, not only satellites but also ground stations."[8]

On February 9, 2009, President Obama ordered a sixty-day review of the Country's cyber security. The completed report is available.[9]

ENDNOTES

1. Patriot Act, 2001. http://thomas.loc.gov/cgi-bin/bdquery/z?d107:hr03162:%5D.
2. Homeland Security Act of 2002, Title II Information Analysis And Infrastructure Protection, Subtitle C—Information Security, November 25, 2002. http://www.dhs.gov/xabout/laws/law_regulation_rule_0011.shtm.
3. Cyber Security Research and Development Act, Public Law 107–305, November 27, 2002. http://www.nist.gov/director/ocla/Public_Laws/PL107-305.pdf.
4. The National Strategy to Secure Cyberspace, February 2003. http://www.dhs.gov/xlibrary/assets/National_Cyberspace_Strategy.pdf.
5. Dennis C. Blair, Director of National Intelligence, February 12, 2009, Annual Threat Assessment of the Intelligence Community for the Senate Select Committee on Intelligence, p. 38. http://www.dni.gov/testimonies/20090212_testimony.pdf.

   "We assess that a number of nations, including Russia and China, have the technical capabilities to target and disrupt elements of the US information infrastructure and for intelligence collection. Nation states and criminals target our government and private sector information networks to gain competitive advantage in the commercial sector. Terrorist groups, including al-Qaida, HAMAS, and Hizballah, have expressed the desire to use cyber means to target the United States. Criminal elements continue to show growing sophistication in technical capability and targeting and today operate a pervasive, mature on-line service economy in illicit cyber capabilities and services available to anyone willing to pay. . .

   We expect disruptive cyber activities to be the norm in future political or military conflicts. The Distributed Denial of Service (DDoS) attacks and Web defacements that targeted Georgia in 2008 and Estonia in 2007 dis-

rupted government, media, and banking Web sites. DDoS attacks and Web defacements targeted Georgian government Web sites, including that of Georgian President Saakishvili, intermittently disrupting online access to the official Georgian perspective of the conflict and some Georgian Government functions but did not affect military action." DNI, P. 39.

6. John Rollins and Anna C. Henning, "Comprehensive National Cybersecurity Initiative: Legal Authorities and Policy Considerations" Summary. CRS R40427, March 10, 2009. http://assets.opencrs.com/rpts/R40427_20090310.pdf.
7. Fact Sheet: DHS End-of-Year Accomplishments, Release Date: December 18, 2008, For Immediate Release, Office of the Press Secretary. http://www.dhs.gov/xnews/releases/pr_1229609413187.shtm.
8. DOD, Defense Science Board, "Defense Imperatives for the New Administration." August 2008, p. 3. http://www.acq.osd.mil/dsb/reports/2008-11-Defense_Imperatives.pdf.
9. Hathaway, Melissa, Cybersecurity Chief at the National Security Council, "Securing Our Digital future," May 29, 2009. http://www.whitehouse.gov/cyberreview/.

ADDITIONAL RESOURCES

"Securing Cyberspace for the 44th Presidency," Center for Strategic & International Studies, December 2009. http://csis.org/files/media/csis/pubs/081208_securingcyberspace_44.pdf.

"Homeland Security: DHS's Progress and Challenges in Key Areas of Maritime, Aviation, and Cybersecurity," Government Accountability Office, GAO-10-106, December 2009. http://www.gao.gov/new.items/d10106.pdf.

"Cyberspace Leadership: Towards New Culture, Conduct, and Capabilities," by Gen. Kevin P. Chilton, USAF, Air & Space Power Journal, Fall 2009, Vol. 23, no. 3. http://www.airpower.maxwell.af.mil/airchronicles/apj/apj09/fal09.htm.

"Significant Cyber Events Since 2006," Center for Strategic & International Studies (CSIS), November 9, 2009. http://csis.org/files/publication/091109_cyber_events_since_2006.pdf.

"Capability of the People's Republic of China to Conduct Cyber Warfare and Computer Network Exploitation." The US-China Economic and Security Review Commission, October 9, 2009. http://www.uscc.gov/researchpapers/2009/NorthropGrumman_PRC_Cyber_Paper_FINAL_Approved%20Report_16Oct2009.pdf.

"Federal Cybersecurity Report: Danger on the Front Lines," CDW Government, Inc., 2009. http://webobjects.cdw.com/webobjects/media/pdf/Newsroom/2009-CDWG-Federal-Cybersecurity-Report-1109.pdf.

Critical Infrastructure Protection: Current Cyber Sector-Specific Planning Approach Needs Reassessment, GAO-09-969, September, 2009. http://www.gao.gov/new.items/d09969.pdf.

"Significant Cyber Events Since 2006" [May 2006 – August 2009] October 14, 2009, Center for Strategic & International Studies. http://csis.org/files/publication/091016_cyber_events_since_2006.pdf.

"Cyberdeterrence and Cyberwar," by Martin C. LibiCki, 2009, Rand. http://www.rand.org/pubs/monographs/2009/RAND_MG877.pdf.

"Vulnerabilities Highlight the Need for More Effective Web Security Management," (Redacted), Department of Homeland Security Inspector General OIG-09-101, September 2009. http://www.dhs.gov/xoig/assets/mgmtrpts/OIG_09-101_Sep09.pdf.

"Cyber Attacks: Protecting Industry Against Growing Threats," September 14, 2009. http://hsgac.senate.gov/public/index.cfm?FuseAction=Hearings.Hearing&Hearing_ID=c643f97a-0814-4770-8121-ba20ce4d90db.

For detailed computer security information going back to 1995, see, "Special Publications in the 800 series present documents of general interest to the computer security community. The Special Publication 800 series was established in 1990 to provide a separate identity for information technology security publications. This Special Publication 800 series reports on ITL's research, guidelines, and outreach efforts in computer security, and its collaborative activities with industry, government, and academic organizations." National Institutes of Standards and Technology, Information Technology Laboratory, Computer Security Division, Computer Security Resource Center. http://csrc.nist.gov/publications/PubsSPs.html.

"Critical Infrastructure Protection Cybersecurity – Recent Strategies and Policies: An Analysis," by Elgin Brunner, Anna Michalkova, Manuel Suter, Myriam Dunn Cavelty, Center for Security Studies, Focal Report 3: August 2009, Zurich. http://www.isn.ethz.ch/isn/Digital-Library/Publications/Detail/?lng=en&id=108743.

"The Department of Homeland Security and the Information Technology Sector Coordinating Council today released the IT Sector Baseline Risk Assessment to identify and prioritize national-level risks to critical sector-wide IT functions while outlining strategies to mitigate those risks and enhance national and economic security." August 25, 2009. http://www.dhs.gov/ynews/releases/pr_1251249275263.shtm.

"Securing Cyberspace: Guarding the New Frontier," by Richard Mereand, Association of the United States Army. http://www.ausa.org/publications/ilw/ilw_pubs/NSW/Documents/SecuringCyberspace0909.pdf.

Partnership for Public Service, Cyber IN-Security: Strengthening the Federal Cybersecurity Workforce, July 2009, Booz, Allen, Hamilton. http://ourpublicservice.org/OPS/publications/download.php?id=135.

Denial of Service Attacks on US and South Korean Governments, July 4th weekend, 2009. New York Times, July 8, 2009. http://www.nytimes.com/2009/07/09/technology/09cyber.html.

The Guardian (UK) July 8, 2009. http://www.guardian.co.uk/world/2009/jul/08/south-korea-cyber-attack.

Department of Homeland Security Privacy Impact Assessments (PIA), Federal Information Security Issues, June 30, 2009, GAO-09-817R. http://www.gao.gov/new.items/d09817r.pdf.

Cybersecurity: Continued Federal Efforts Are Needed to Protect Critical Systems and Information, GAO-09-835T [testimony], June 25, 2009. http://www.gao.gov/new.items/d09835t.pdf.

Congressional Hearing: "Assessing Cybersecurity Activities at NIST and DHS," June 25, 2009. http://science.house.gov/publications/hearings_markups_details.aspx?NewsID=2514.

"Privacy and the White House Cyberspace Policy Review," Center for Democracy & Technology June 2009. http://www.cdt.org/security/20090619_cybersec_actions.pdf.

The United States Department of Defense has established USCYBERCOM as a unified command subordinate to the Strategic Command. The purpose is to "…develop a comprehensive approach to DoD cyberspace operations." Secretary of Defense Memorandum to Secretaries of Military Departments, June 23, 2009." https://www.chds.us/… (accessed June 24, 2009).

"Computer Science Research Funding: How Much Is Too Little?" by Eli Zimet, Stuart Starr, Clifford Lau, and Anup Ghosh, Center for Technology and National Security Policy, National Defense University, June 2009. http://www.ndu.edu/ctnsp/Def_Tech/DTP%2064%20Computer%20Science%20Research%20Funding.pdf.

"Defense Secretary Robert M. Gates … ordered the creation of the military's first headquarters designed to coordinate Pentagon efforts in the emerging battlefield of cyberspace and computer-network security… Mr. Gates intends to nominate Lt. Gen. Keith Alexander, currently director of the National Security Agency, for a fourth star and to take on the top job at the new organization, to be called Cybercom.

The new command's mission will be to coordinate the day-to-day operation—and protection—of military and Pentagon computer networks. Currently, the Defense Department operates 15,000 separate computer networks and more than seven million individual computers or information-technology devices, officials said."

New Military Command for Cyberspace, by Thom Shanke, The New York Times, June 23, 2009. http://www.nytimes.com/2009/06/24/technology/24cyber.html.

"The Confluence of Cyber Crime and Terrorism," by Steven P. Bucci, Ph.D, Heritage Foundation, Lecture #1123, June 12, 2009. http://www.heritage.org/Research/NationalSecurity/hl1123.cfm.

Woodley, Shawn, Henry L. Stimson, "The Global Challenge of Securing Cyberspace," May 18, 2009. http://www.stimson.org/pub.cfm?ID=805.

"Cyberspace Policy Review: Assuring a Trusted and Resilient Information and Communications Infrastructure," White House, April 17, 2009. http://www.whitehouse.gov/assets/documents/Cyberspace_Policy_Review_final.pdf.

Technology, Policy, Law, and Ethics Regarding U.S. Acquisition and Use of Cyberattack Capabilities, 2009. http://www.nap.edu/catalog.php?record_id=12651.

"Critical Issues for Cyber Assurance Policy Reform: An Industry Assessment," Intelligence and National Security Alliance (INSA). http://www.insaonline.org/assets/files/INSA_CyberAssurance_Assessment.pdf.

Electronic Frontier Foundation. EFF is the leading civil liberties group defending your rights in the digital world. http://www.eff.org/.

Lolita C. Baldor, "Pentagon says it spent $100 million in last 6 months to repair, respond to cyber attacks" NewsDay.com., April 7, 2009. http://www.newsday.com/news/politics/wire/sns-ap-pentagon-cyber,0,2867965.story.

Tracking GhostNet: Investigating a Cyber Espionage Network, March 31, 2009. http://www.hsdl.org/hslog/?q=node/4787.

Dearth of technical experts leaves US open to cyber attack, panel says. By Jeff Bliss, Bloomberg, March 20, 2009. http://www.boston.com/news/nation/articles/2009/03/20/dearth_of_technical_experts_leaves_us_open_to_cyber_attack_panel_says?mode=PF. (accessed March 20, 2009).

John Rollins, Anna C. Henning, "Comprehensive National Cybersecurity Initiative: Legal Authorities and Policy Implications," March 10, 2009, Congressional Research Service, R40427. http://www.fas.org/sgp/crs/natsec/R40427.pdf.

Cybersecurity Chief Resigns, March 7, 2009. http://online.wsj.com/article/SB123638468860758145.html.

Center for Strategic & International Studies (CSIS), Innovation and Cybersecurity Regulation March 2009. http://www.csis.org/media/csis/pubs/090327_lewis_innovation_cybersecurity.pdf.

Cyberspace and the National Security of the United Kingdom: Threats and Responses. Royal Institute of International Affairs, March 2009. http://www.chathamhouse.org.uk/publications/papers/download/-/id/726/file/13679_r0309cyberspace.pdf.

"DHS/Office of Intelligence and Analysis (I&A) judges that a number of emerging trends point to leftwing extremists maturing and expanding their cyber attack capabilities over the next decade with the aim of attacking targets in the United States. . ." "Leftwing Extremists Likely to Increase Use of Cyber Attacks over the Coming Decade" 26 January 2009, Prepared by the Strategic Analysis Group, Homeland Environment and Threat Analysis Division. http://www.fas.org/irp/eprint/leftwing.pdf. (accessed April 15, 2009).

US CERT. Computer Emergency Response Teams.

US-CERT is charged with providing response support and defense against cyber attacks for the Federal Civil Executive Branch (.gov) and information sharing and collaboration with state and local government, industry and international partners. http://www.us-cert.gov/.

"Cyber Analysis and Warning, DHS Faces Challenges In Establishing A Comprehensive National Capability," United States Government Accountability Office, Report to the Subcommittee on Emerging Threats, Cybersecurity, and Science and Technology, Committee on Homeland Security, House of Representatives. July 2008. GAO 08-588. http://www.gao.gov/new.items/d08588.pdf.

Council of Europe Convention on Cybercrime, Budapest, November 23, 2001. http://conventions.coe.int/Treaty/Commun/QueVoulezVous.asp?NT=185&CL=ENG.

Council of Europe Convention on Cybercrime, Computer Crime & Intellectual Property Section, United States Department of Justice. http://www.usdoj.gov/criminal/cybercrime/COEFAQs.htm.

13

AGRICULTURE AND FOOD

In this chapter we recognize how large the "farm to table" system is and how many points there are in this system for disruption. It describes our efforts to improve safety.

> "When we discuss food safety issues, we must consider the important role each link of the food chain plays in ensuring a safe food supply. The entire chain includes growers, packers, shippers, food handlers, processors, retailers and consumers. If a link in that chain is broken, it threatens the safety and integrity of our food supply. That's why we must work together to improve how we communicate public health messages to the entire food chain. . ."[1]

The section of the National Strategy for the Physical Protection of Critical Infrastructure and Key Assets included here discusses the agricultural sector in general by noting the vastness of the farm to table system. It identifies the agencies with roles in this sector as the Department of Health and Human Services (DHS) and the Department of Agriculture.

The Homeland Security Act transferred to DHS certain agricultural inspection responsibilities that were formerly under the purview of the Department of Agriculture. They are listed in the Homeland Security Act, sec. 421(b). Section 421 does not provide any direction or set goals and priorities.

The next document, HSPD 9, was the beginning of major changes to the country's food safety monitoring and provides more specific guidance. It sets forth the duties and responsibilities of the various federal and state actors in the missions of Awareness and Warning, Vulnerability Assessments, Mitigation Strategies, Response Planning and Recovery, and Research and Development. HSPD 9 established the National Veterinary Stockpile and the National Plant Disease

Recovery System. Like other sections of homeland security documents, this HSPD promotes the development of higher education facilities to meet the country's needs in this area.

SOURCES

- National Strategy for the Physical Protection of Critical Infrastructures and Key Assets, February 2002[2]
- Public Health Security and Bioterrorism Preparedness and Response Act of June 12, 2002[3]
- Homeland Security Act, November 25, 2002, Sec. 421[4]
- HSPD 9, Defense of United States Agriculture and Food, January 30, 2004[5]

National Strategy for the Physical Protection of Critical Infrastructures and Key Assets, February 2002

". . . From farm to table, our Nation's agriculture and food systems are among the most efficient and productive in the world. These industries are a source of essential commodities in the U.S., and they account for close to one-fifth of the Gross Domestic Product. A significant percentage of that figure also contributes to our export economy, as the U.S. exports approximately one quarter of its farm and ranch products.

The Agriculture and Food Sectors include:

- The supply chains for feed, animals, and animal products;
- Crop production and the supply chains of seed, fertilizer, and other necessary related materials; and
- The post-harvesting components of the food supply chain, from processing, production, and packaging

Foundations of Homeland Security: Law and Policy, First Edition. Martin J. Alperen.
© 2011 John Wiley & Sons, Inc. Published 2011 by John Wiley & Sons, Inc.

through storage and distribution to retail sales, institutional food services, and restaurant or home consumption.

Agriculture and Food Sector Challenges The fundamental need for food, as well as great public sensitivity to food safety makes assuring the security of food production and processing a high priority.

Our food and agriculture industries have been developed over several decades and are unique with respect to their structures and processes. The greatest threats to the food and agricultural systems are disease and contamination, in which case, sector decentralization represents a challenge to assuring their protection...

Because of the food system's many points of entry, detection is a critical tool for securing the agriculture and food sectors. There is an urgent need to improve and validate analytical methods for detecting bioterrorist agents in food products, as well as a need for enhanced laboratory capabilities and capacities...

Additionally, we must expand our system of laboratories... We must also increase the number of qualified personnel (veterinarians and lab technicians) and laboratories with the ability to diagnose and treat animal disease outbreaks and crop contamination...

Moving and processing crops and animals require transporting them over long distances. During transport, these resources spend time in storage areas and facilities where they may come in contact with other products. Accordingly, the agriculture and food sectors depend on transportation system owners and operators, particularly regarding trucks and containers, to meet the safety and security standards necessary to protect food products in transit. We must improve mechanisms designed to track the movement of animals and commodities in transit and enable officials to pinpoint where an outbreak or contamination originates.

Rapid acquisition and use of threat information could help to prevent an attack from spreading beyond individual facilities or local communities to become a regional or national problem. Unfortunately, serious institutional barriers and disincentives for sharing such information exist within the sectors and their structures. For instance, there are significant, direct economic disincentives associated with reporting problems or suspected contamination in food processing.

Meanwhile, the agriculture and food markets are highly competitive, and many parts of the food system operate within slim profit margins. As a result, some companies may be more likely to hold onto information related to incidents involving suspected contamination in order to prevent the potential financial consequences of what might be a false alarm.

Protecting the public from an outbreak or contamination incident requires timely reporting of information for prompt decision-making and action. In the current environ-ment, when crops or animals must be culled or preventively killed to deal with disease or contamination, the fear of a negative public response and attendant economic implications to the sector may impede the needed levels of response in the agriculture and food sectors.

Deliberate contaminations by terrorists aim to harm people or animals to the greatest extent possible. Another principal objective is to create panic and inflict economic damage. Because of the influence the media has on how the public responds to incidents, clear and accurate communication of information to news outlets is essential. Official spokespersons at state, regional, and national levels should be pre-assigned. Although food regulators routinely communicate with industry on food-safety issues, planning for public communications in the event of a deliberate contamination should also be a priority, as should defining stakeholder responsibilities within those plans.

Public Health Security and Bioterrorism Preparedness and Response Act of 2002

TITLE III—PROTECTING SAFETY AND SECURITY OF FOOD AND DRUG SUPPLY

Subtitle A—Protection of Food Supply

SEC. 301. FOOD SAFETY AND SECURITY STRATEGY.

(a) IN GENERAL.— The President's Council on Food Safety (as established by Executive Order No. 13100) shall . . . develop a crisis communications and education strategy with respect to bioterrorist threats to the food supply. Such strategy shall address threat assessments; technologies and procedures for securing food processing and manufacturing facilities and modes of transportation; response and notification procedures; and risk communications to the public.

SEC. 302. PROTECTION AGAINST ADULTERATION OF FOOD.

(a) INCREASING INSPECTIONS FOR DETECTION OF ADULTERATION OF FOOD.— Section 801 of the Federal Food, Drug, and Cosmetic Act (21 U.S.C. 381) is amended by adding at the end the following subsection:

"(h)(1) The Secretary shall give high priority to increasing the number of inspections under this section for the purpose of enabling the Secretary to inspect food offered for import at ports of entry into the United States, with the greatest priority given to inspections to detect the intentional adulteration of food.".

SEC. 303. ADMINISTRATIVE DETENTION.

(a) EXPANDED AUTHORITY.— Section 304 of the Federal Food, Drug, and Cosmetic Act (21 U.S.C. 334) is amended by adding at the end the following subsection:

"(h) *ADMINISTRATIVE DETENTION OF FOODS.*

"*(1)* ***DETENTION AUTHORITY.*** "(A) IN GENERAL.— An officer or qualified employee of the Food and Drug Administration may order the detention,...of any article of food that is found during an inspection, examination, or investigation under this Act if the officer... has credible evidence or information indicating that such article presents a threat of serious adverse health consequences or death to humans or animals.

(c) TEMPORARY HOLDS AT PORTS OF ENTRY.— Section 801 of the Federal Food, Drug, and Cosmetic Act, as amended by section 302(d)of this Act, is amended by adding at the end the following:

"(j)(1) If an officer or qualified employee of the Food and Drug Administration has credible evidence or information indicating that an article of food presents a threat of serious adverse health consequences or death to humans or animals, and such officer or qualified employee is unable to inspect, examine, or investigate such article upon the article being offered for import at a port of entry into the United States, the officer... shall request the Secretary of Treasury to hold the food at the port of entry for a reasonable period of time, not to exceed 24 hours, for the purpose of enabling the Secretary to inspect, examine, or investigate the article as appropriate.

SEC. 305. REGISTRATION OF FOOD FACILITIES.

(a) IN GENERAL.— Chapter IV of the Federal Food, Drug, and Cosmetic Act (21 U.S.C. 341 et seq.) is amended by adding at the end the following:
"SEC. 415. REGISTRATION OF FOOD FACILITIES.

"(a) *REGISTRATION.—*

"*(1) IN GENERAL.—* The Secretary shall by regulation require that any facility engaged in manufacturing, processing, packing, or holding food for consumption in the United States be registered with the Secretary...

SEC. 306. MAINTENANCE AND INSPECTION OF RECORDS FOR FOODS.

(a) IN GENERAL.— Chapter IV of the Federal Food, Drug, and Cosmetic Act, as amended by section 305 of this Act, is amended by inserting before section 415 the following section:

"SEC. 414. MAINTENANCE AND INSPECTION OF RECORDS.

"(b) REGULATIONS CONCERNING RECORDKEEPING.— The Secretary...may by regulation establish requirements regarding the establishment and maintenance, for not longer than two years, of records by persons (excluding farms and restaurants) who manufacture, process, pack, transport, distribute, receive, hold, or import food, which records are needed by the Secretary for inspection to allow the Secretary to identify the immediate previous sources and the immediate subsequent recipients of food, including its packaging, in order to address credible threats of serious adverse health consequences or death to humans or animals.

SEC. 307. PRIOR NOTICE OF IMPORTED FOOD SHIPMENTS.

(a) IN GENERAL.— Section 801 of the Federal Food, Drug, and Cosmetic Act, as amended by section 305(c) of this Act, is amended by adding at the end the following subsection:

"(m)(1) In the case of an article of food that is being imported or offered for import into the United States, the Secretary, after consultation with the Secretary of the Treasury, shall by regulation require, for the purpose of enabling such article to be inspected at ports of entry into the United States, the submission to the Secretary of a notice providing the identity of each of the following: The article; the manufacturer and shipper of the article; if known within the specified period of time that notice is required to be provided, the grower of the article; the country from which the article originates; the country from which the article is shipped; and the anticipated port of entry for the article. An article of food imported or offered for import without submission of such notice in accordance with the requirements under this paragraph shall be refused admission into the United States. Nothing in this section may be construed as a limitation on the port of entry for an article of food.

SEC. 313. SURVEILLANCE OF ZOONOTIC DISEASES.

The Secretary of Health and Human Services shall coordinate the surveillance of zoonotic diseases.

SEC. 333. BIOSECURITY UPGRADES AT THE DEPARTMENT OF AGRICULTURE.

There is authorized to be appropriated for fiscal year 2002, $180,000,000 for the purpose of enabling the Agricultural

Research Service to conduct building upgrades to modernize existing facilities, of which (1) $100,000,000 shall be allocated for renovation, updating, and expansion of the Biosafety Level 3 laboratory and animal research facilities at the Plum Island Animal Disease Center (Greenport, New York), and of which (2) $80,000,000 shall be allocated for the Agricultural Research Service/Animal and Plant Health Inspection Service facility in Ames, Iowa. There are authorized to be appropriated such sums as may be necessary for fiscal years 2003 through 2006 for the purpose described in the preceding sentence, for the planning and design of an Agricultural Research Service biocontainment laboratory for poultry research in Athens, Georgia, and for the planning, updating, and renovation of the Arthropod-Borne Animal Disease Laboratory in Laramie, Wyoming.

SEC. 334. AGRICULTURAL BIOSECURITY.

(a) *Security at Colleges and Universities.*

(1) GRANTS.— The Secretary of Agriculture (referred to in this section as the "Secretary") may award grants to covered entities to review security standards and practices at their facilities in order to protect against bioterrorist attacks.

(b) *Guidelines for Agricultural Biosecurity.*

(1) IN GENERAL.— The Secretary may award grants to associations of food producers or consortia of such associations for the development and implementation of educational programs to improve biosecurity on farms in order to ensure the security of farm facilities against potential bioterrorist attacks.

SEC. 335. AGRICULTURAL BIOTERRORISM RESEARCH AND DEVELOPMENT.

(a) IN GENERAL.— The Secretary of Agriculture . . . may utilize existing research authorities and research programs to protect the food supply of the United States by conducting and supporting research activities to–

(1) enhance the capability of the Secretary to respond in a timely manner to emerging or existing bioterrorist threats. . .;

(2) develop new and continue partnerships with institutions of higher education. . .;

(3) strengthen coordination with the intelligence. . .;

(4) expand the involvement of the Secretary with international organizations dealing with plant and animal disease control;

(5) continue research to develop rapid detection field test. . .;

(6) develop an agricultural bioterrorism early warning surveillance system . . .; and

TITLE IV—DRINKING WATER SECURITY AND SAFETY

SEC. 401. TERRORIST AND OTHER INTENTIONAL ACTS.

The Safe Drinking Water Act (title XIV of the Public Health Service Act) is amended by inserting the following new section after section 1432:
    "SEC. 1433. TERRORIST AND OTHER INTENTIONAL ACTS.

"(a) VULNERABILITY ASSESSMENTS.— (1) Each community water system serving a population of greater than 3,300 persons shall conduct an assessment of the vulnerability of its system to a terrorist attack or other intentional acts intended to substantially disrupt the ability of the system to provide a safe and reliable supply of drinking water. . .

"(b) EMERGENCY RESPONSE PLAN.— Each community water system serving a population greater than 3,300 shall prepare or revise, where necessary, an emergency response plan that incorporates the results of vulnerability assessments that have been completed. . .
    The emergency response plan shall include, but not be limited to, plans, procedures, and identification of equipment that can be implemented or utilized in the event of a terrorist or other intentional attack on the public water system. The emergency response plan shall also include actions, procedures, and identification of equipment which can obviate or significantly lessen the impact of terrorist attacks or other intentional actions on the public health and the safety and supply of drinking water provided to communities and individuals. Community water systems shall, to the extent possible, coordinate with existing Local Emergency Planning Committees established under the Emergency Planning and Community Right-to-Know Act (42 U.S.C. 11001 et seq.) when preparing or revising an emergency response plan under this subsection.

"(d) GUIDANCE TO SMALL PUBLIC WATER SYSTEMS.– The Administrator shall provide guidance to community water systems serving a population of less than 3,300 persons on how to conduct vulnerability assessments, prepare emergency response plans, and address threats from terrorist attacks or other intentional.

SEC. 402. OTHER SAFE DRINKING WATER ACT AMENDMENTS.

The Safe Drinking Water Act (title XIV of the Public Health Service Act) is amended by inserting the following new sections after section 1433 (as added by section 401 of this Act):

SEC. 1434. CONTAMINANT PREVENTION, DETECTION AND RESPONSE.

"(a) IN GENERAL.– The Administrator . . . shall review (or enter into contracts or cooperative agreements to provide for a review of) current and future methods to prevent, detect and respond to the intentional introduction of chemical, biological or radiological contaminants into community water systems and source water for community water systems, including each of the following:

Homeland Security Act, 2002

SEC. 421. TRANSFER OF CERTAIN AGRICULTURAL INSPECTION FUNCTIONS OF THE DEPARTMENT OF AGRICULTURE.

(a) TRANSFER OF AGRICULTURAL IMPORT AND ENTRY INSPECTION FUNCTIONS.— There shall be transferred to the Secretary [of DHS] the functions of the Secretary of Agriculture relating to agricultural import and entry inspection activities under the laws specified in subsection (b).

(b) COVERED ANIMAL AND PLANT PROTECTION LAWS.— The laws referred to in subsection (a) are the following:

(1) The Act commonly known as the Virus-Serum-Toxin Act (the eighth paragraph under the heading "Bureau of Animal Industry" in the Act of March 4, 1913; 21 U.S.C. 151 et seq.).

(2) Section 1 of the Act of August 31, 1922 (commonly known as the Honeybee Act; 7 U.S.C. 281).

(3) Title III of the Federal Seed Act (7 U.S.C. 1581 et seq.).

(4) The Plant Protection Act (7 U.S.C. 7701 et seq.).

(5) The Animal Health Protection Act (subtitle E of title X of Public Law 107–171; 7 U.S.C. 8301 et seq.).

(6) The Lacey Act Amendments of 1981 (16 U.S.C. 3371 et seq.).

(7) Section 11 of the Endangered Species Act of 1973 (16 U.S.C. 1540).

HSPD 9. Defense of United States Agriculture and Food, January 30, 2004

Purpose

1. This directive establishes a national policy to defend the agriculture and food system against terrorist attacks, major disasters, and other emergencies. . . .

Policy

4. It is the policy of the United States to protect the agriculture and food system from terrorist attacks, major disasters, and other emergencies. . .

Roles and Responsibilities

6. As established in . . . HSPD-7 [12], the Secretary of Homeland Security is responsible for coordinating the overall national effort to enhance the protection of the critical infrastructure and key resources of the United States. . . . This directive shall be implemented in a manner consistent with HSPD-7.

Awareness and Warning

8. The Secretaries of . . . shall build upon and expand current monitoring and surveillance programs to:

a. develop robust, comprehensive, and fully coordinated surveillance and monitoring systems, including international information, for animal disease, plant disease, wildlife disease, food, public health, and water quality that provides early detection and awareness of disease, pest, or poisonous agents;

b. develop systems that, as appropriate, track specific animals and plants, as well as specific commodities and food; and

c. develop nationwide laboratory networks for food, veterinary, plant health, and water quality that integrate existing Federal and State laboratory resources, are interconnected, and utilize standardized diagnostic protocols and procedures.

9. The Attorney General . . . shall develop and enhance intelligence operations and analysis capabilities focusing on the agriculture, food, and water sectors. . .

10. The Secretary of Homeland Security shall . . . create a new biological threat awareness capacity that will enhance detection and characterization of an attack. This new capacity will build upon the improved and upgraded surveillance systems described in paragraph 8 and integrate and analyze domestic and international surveillance and monitoring data collected from human health, animal health, plant health, food, and water quality systems. . .

Vulnerability Assessments

11. The Secretaries of . . . shall expand and continue vulnerability assessments of the agriculture and food sectors.

These vulnerability assessments should identify requirements of the National Infrastructure Protection Plan developed by the Secretary of Homeland Security...

Response Planning and Recovery

14. The Secretary of Homeland Security... will ensure that the combined Federal, State, and local response capabilities are adequate to respond quickly and effectively to a terrorist attack, major disease outbreak, or other disaster affecting the national agriculture or food infrastructure...

15. The Secretary of Homeland Security... shall develop a coordinated agriculture and food-specific standardized response plan that will be integrated into the National Response Plan. This plan will ensure a coordinated response to an agriculture or food incident and will delineate the appropriate roles of Federal, State, local, and private sector partners, and will address risk communication for the general public.

16. The Secretaries of Agriculture and Health and Human Services... shall enhance recovery systems that are able to stabilize agriculture production, the food supply, and the economy, rapidly remove and effectively dispose of contaminated agriculture and food products or infected plants and animals, and decontaminate premises.

18. The Secretary of Agriculture... shall work with State and local governments and the private sector to develop:

    a. A National Veterinary Stockpile (NVS) containing sufficient amounts of animal vaccine, antiviral, or therapeutic products to appropriately respond to the most damaging animal diseases affecting human health and the economy and that will be capable of deployment within 24 hours of an outbreak...

    b. A National Plant Disease Recovery System (NPDRS) capable of responding to a high-consequence plant disease with pest control measures and the use of resistant seed varieties within a single growing season to sustain a reasonable level of production for economically important crops. The NPDRS will utilize the genetic resources contained in the U.S. National Plant Germplasm System, as well as the scientific capabilities of the Federal-State-industry agricultural research and extension system. The NPDRS shall include emergency planning for the use of resistant seed varieties and pesticide control measures to prevent, slow, or stop the spread of a high-consequence plant disease, such as wheat smut or soybean rust.

Outreach and Professional Development

19. The Secretary of Homeland Security... shall work with appropriate private sector entities to establish an effective information sharing and analysis mechanism for agriculture and food.

20. The Secretaries of... shall support the development of and promote higher education programs for the protection of animal, plant, and public health.

21. The Secretaries of... shall support the development of and promote a higher education program to address protection of the food supply.

22. The Secretaries... shall establish opportunities for professional development and specialized training in agriculture and food protection...

Research and Development

23. The Secretaries of... will accelerate and expand development of current and new countermeasures against the intentional introduction or natural occurrence of catastrophic animal, plant, and zoonotic diseases...

24. The Secretaries of... will develop a plan to provide safe, secure, and state-of-the-art agriculture biocontainment laboratories that research and develop diagnostic capabilities for foreign animal and zoonotic diseases.

25. The Secretary of Homeland Security... shall establish university-based centers of excellence in agriculture and food security...."

ENDNOTES

1. FoodSafety.gov quoting from the California Department of Food & Agriculture web site: http://www.foodsafety.gov/~fsg/fsgweb.html.
2. National Strategy for the Physical Protection of Critical Infrastructures and Key Assets, February 2002. http://www.dhs.gov/xlibrary/assets/Physical_Strategy.pdf.
3. Public Health Security and Bioterrorism Preparedness and Response Act of 2002. P.L. 107-188, June 12, 2002. http://frwebgate.access.gpo.gov/cgi-bin/getdoc.cgi?dbname=107_cong_public_laws&docid=f:publ188.107.
4. Homeland Security Act, 2002. http://www.dhs.gov/xlibrary/assets/hr_5005_enr.pdf.
5. HSPD 9. http://www.dhs.gov/xabout/laws/gc_121744954 7663.shtm. (accessed March 19, 2009).
6. The National Food Safety Information Network. http://www.foodsafety.gov/~fsg/network.html.
7. Food Safety From Farm To Table: A National Food Safety Initiative Report To The President May 1997. http://www.cfsan.fda.gov/~dms/fsreport.html.

ADDITIONAL RESOURCES

The National Food Safety Information Network[6] one of the initiatives in the May 1997 National Food Safety Initiative Report to the President[7], brings together the Federal Government's primary mechanisms for providing food safety information to the public. The "Network's" goal is to increase the effectiveness and efficiency of the government's food safety information dissemination activities. The "Network" consists of:

USDA Meat and Poultry Hotline: a toll-free telephone service that helps consumers prevent foodborne illness, specifically by answering questions about safe storage, handling, and preparation of meat and poultry products.

Center for Food Safety and Applied Nutrition (CFSAN) Outreach and Information Center: a toll-free telephone service that helps provide information to the public and answers consumer and industry questions about food (excluding meat and poultry), seafood, and cosmetics.

FoodSafety.gov web site: a gateway to federal, state and local government food safety information. It is maintained by FDA's Center for Food Safety and Applied Nutrition, listed above.

EdNet, the National Food Safety Educator's Network: the federal government's (FDA, USDA, CDC) electronic network for providing food safety information to educators. The "Network" members share information and cooperate on joint initiatives designed to increase the effectiveness and efficiency of the federal government's efforts to provide and respond to the public's need for up-to-date, scientifically based, food safety information.

USDA, Food Safety and Inspection Service. http://www.fsis.usda.gov/.

Countering Bioterrorism and Other Threats to the Food Supply. http://www.foodsafety.gov/~fsg/bioterr.html. This site has links to: Federal Government Web Sites; Federal Government/Private Sector Partnerships; State and Local Government Web Sites; International Web Sites.

USDA, Food Defense and Emergency Response. http://www.fsis.usda.gov/Food_Defense_&_Emergency_Response/index.asp.

Food Defense Awareness Training:

Food defense training kit for first-line employees in the food and agriculture industry.

Podcasts on Food Defense; Meat, Poultry and Egg Product Inspection

Food Defense podcasts. Streaming video is also available to address food defense topics.

Information regarding FSIS' assessment of vulnerabilities in the food supply along with industry food defense guidance, such as developing food defense plans.

Learn how FSIS is monitoring the food supply to detect acts of intentional contamination.

Information about FSIS' emergency operations and response activities, along with model State emergency response plans.

Information on FSIS' work with states, the media, and guidance on disposal and decontamination following an incident of intentional contamination of the food supply.

USDA, Homeland Security. This site has links to: http://www.usda.gov/wps/portal/!ut/p/_s.7_0_A/7_0_CJ?navid=HOMELANDSECU&navtype=CO.

Guidelines to help agricultural producers enhance security at the farm level. These practical measures help to protect against natural disasters, as well as the unintentional or intentional introduction of plant or animal diseases.

USDA will likely be called upon again to assist in responding to natural and intentional disasters. The Incident Command System video provides information on the types of disasters that USDA may be called upon to assist with and provides background on how USDA utilizes the Incident Command System.

Strategic Partnership Program Agroterrorism (SPPA). DHS, USDA, FDA, FBI will collaborate with private industry and the States in a joint initiative, the Strategic Partnership Program Agroterrorism (SPPA) Initiative. The SPPA Initiative will be a true partnership program, where an industry member or trade association or State may volunteer to participate. http://www.usda.gov/wps/portal/?contentidonly=true&contentid=content_sppa.html.

"Food Safety: Agencies Need to Address Gaps in Enforcement and Collaboration to Enhance Safety of Imported Food," September 2009, GAO-09-873. http://www.gao.gov/new.items/d09873.pdf.

"Crops, ponds destroyed in quest for food safety," by Carolyn Lochhead, San Francisco Chronicle, July 13, 2009. http://www.sfgate.com/cgi-bin/article.cgi?f=/c/a/2009/07/13/MN0218DVJ8.DTL.

"Keeping America's Food Safe: A Blueprint For Fixing The Food Safety System At The U.S. Department Of Health And Human Services." The Robert Wood Johnson Foundation. Keeping America's Food Safe: A Blueprint for Fixing the Food Safety System at the U.S. Department of Health and Human Services, March 2009. http://healthyamericans.org/assets/files/2009FoodSafetyReport.pdf. (accessed March 31, 2009).

"To Say That Food Safety In This Country Is A Patchwork System Is Giving It Too Much Credit. Food Safety In America Has Become A Hit-Or-Miss Gamble, And That Is Truly Frightening. It's Time To Find The Gaps In The System And Remedy Them." Keeping America's Food Safe: p. 1, quoting Sen.Tom Harkin, Chairman Of The Senate Committee On Agriculture, Nutrition And Forestry. Remarks during Senate Agriculture Committee. Washington, D.C., February 5, 2009. http://healthyamericans.org/assets/files/2009FoodSafetyReport.pdf.

Food safety involves oversight by the U.S. Department of Health and Human Services, the U.S. Department of Agriculture, and the U.S. Environmental Protection Agency. "Currently, according to a 2007 GAO report, "the federal oversight of food safety is fragmented, with 15 agencies collectively administering at least 30 laws related to food safety." Among the problems listed in the report are antiquated laws, fractured and uncoordinated management, inadequate, consolidated federal oversight and leadership. The main recommendation is to consolidate the food safety functions under one agency. Keeping America's Food Safe: p. 2, quoting Robinson, R.A. *Food Safety and Security, Fundamental Changes Needed to Ensure Safe Food.* Washington, D.C.: U.S. General Accounting Office, October 2001. http://healthyamericans.org/assets/files/2009FoodSafetyReport.pdf.

Center for State Homeland Security, recent articles on Biodefense and Agriculture. http://cshs-us.org/CSHS_Home.htm.

14

TRANSPORTATION SECURITY

The Transportation Security chapter begins with an overview provided by, first, those portions of the National Strategy for the Physical Protection of Critical Infrastructures and Key Assets related to transportation. This Strategy discusses aviation, passenger rail and railroads, highway trucking and bussing, maritime, and mass transit systems. The National Strategy for Transportation Security directs the creation of a Modal Security Plan for Aviation. Title XII of the Implementing Recommendations of the 9/11 Commission Act Of 2007 directs transportation security information sharing and creates a National Transportation Security Center of Excellence. Public transportation security is discussed in the National Transit Systems Security Act of 2007 that directs creation of a national strategy for public transportation. Title XV of the Implementing Recommendations of the 9/11 Commission Act of 2007 discusses security for busses and railroads.

Each of the following specific sectors is discussed individually. As will be seen, while there is a great deal of legislation regarding aviation and maritime security, there is much less in the rail, trucking, and bus sectors.

Foundations of Homeland Security: Law and Policy, First Edition. Martin J. Alperen.
© 2011 John Wiley & Sons, Inc. Published 2011 by John Wiley & Sons, Inc.

A. OVERVIEW

SOURCES

- National Strategy Physical Protection Critical Infrastructures Key Assets, February 2002[1]
- National Strategy for Transportation Security, December 17, 2004[2]
- Executive Order 13416—Strengthening Surface Transportation Security, December, 2006[3]
- Title XII, Implementing Recommendations of the 9/11 Commission Act Of 2007[4]
- Title XIV, Implementing Recommendations of the 9/11 Commission Act Of 2007[5]
- Title XV, Implementing Recommendations of the 9/11 Commission Act of 2007[6]

National Strategy For The Physical Protection Of Critical Infrastructures And Key Assets, February 2002

Transportation The transportation sector consists of several key modes: aviation, maritime traffic, rail, pipelines, highways, trucking and busing, and public mass transit. The diversity and size of the transportation sector makes it vital to our economy and national security, including military mobilization and deployment. As a whole, its infrastructure is robust, having been developed over decades of both private and public investment. Together the various transportation modes provide mobility of our population and contribute to our much-cherished individual freedom. The transportation infrastructure is also convenient. Americans rely on its easy access and reliability in their daily lives.

Aviation The aviation mode is vast, consisting of thousands of entry points.

The Nation's aviation system consists of two main parts:

- Airports and the associated assets needed to support their operations, including the aircraft that they serve; and
- Aviation command, control, communications, and information systems needed to support and maintain safe use of our national airspace.

Before September 11, the security of airports and their associated assets was the responsibility of private carriers and state and local airport owners and operators. In the months following the September 11 attacks, Congress passed legislation establishing the Transportation Security Administration as the responsible authority for assuring aviation security.

AVIATION MODE CHALLENGES ... Its distribution and open access through thousands of entry points at home and abroad make it difficult to secure. Furthermore, components of the aviation infrastructure are not only attractive terrorist targets, but also serve as potential weapons to be exploited ...

Additional unique protection challenges for aviation include:

- *Volume*: U.S. air carriers transport millions of passengers every day and at least twice as many bags and other cargo.
- *Limited capabilities and available space*: Current detection equipment and methods are limited in number, capability, and ease of use.
- *Time-sensitive cargo*: "Just-in-time" delivery of valuable cargo is essential for many businesses—any significant time delay in processing and transporting such cargo would negatively affect the U.S. economy.
- *Security versus convenience*: Maintaining security while limiting congestion and delays complicates the task of security and has important financial implications.
- *Accessibility*: Most airports are open to the public; their facilities are close to public roadways for convenience and to streamline access for vehicles delivering passengers to terminals.

Passenger Rail and Railroads ...Trains carry 40 percent of intercity freight—a much larger portion than is moved by any other single mode of transportation. About 20 percent of that freight is coal, a critical resource for the generation of electricity. More than 20 million intercity travelers use the rail system annually, and 45 million passengers ride trains and subways operated by local transit authorities...

RAIL MODE CHALLENGES Our Nation's railway system is vast and complex, with multiple points of entry. Differences in design, structure, and purpose of railway stations complicate the sector's overall protection framework. The size and breadth of the sector make it difficult to react to threats effectively or efficiently in all scenarios. This fact complicates protection efforts, but it also offers certain mitigating potential in the event of a terrorist attack. For example, trains are confined to specific routes and are highly controllable. If hijacked, a train can be shunted off the mainline and rendered less of a threat. Similarly, the loss of a bridge or tunnel can impact traffic along major corridors; however, the potential for national-level disruptions is limited.

The greater risk is associated with rail transport of hazardous materials.

Security solutions to the container shipping challenge should recognize that, in many cases, commerce, including essential national security materials, must continue to flow. Stifling commerce to meet security needs simply swaps one consequence of a security threat for another...

An additional area of concern is the marking of container cars to indicate the specific type of hazardous materials being transported... Planners must take care, however, to devise a system of markings that terrorists cannot easily decipher...

Railroads have well-developed contingency plans and backups for dispatch, control, and communications equipment that are sufficient for localized or minor disruptions...

Highway Trucking and Bussing The trucking and busing industry is a fundamental component of our national transportation infrastructure. Without the sector's resources, the movement of people, goods, and services around the country would be greatly impeded. Components of this infrastructure include highways, roads, inter-modal terminals, bridges, tunnels, trucks, buses, maintenance facilities, and roadway border crossings.

HIGHWAYS, TRUCKING, AND BUSING MODE CHALLENGES Because of its heterogeneity in size and operations and the multitude of owners and operators nationwide, the trucking and busing infrastructure is highly resilient, flexible, and responsive to market demand. For the same reason, the sector is fractionated and regulated by multiple jurisdictions at state, federal, and—sometimes—local levels.

Transportation choke points (e.g., bridges and tunnels, inter-modal terminals, border crossings, and highway interchanges) present unique protection challenges...

...Given the number of public and private small-business owners and operators in this sector, the cost of infrastructure protection is also a major challenge...

...Another challenge is the way in which sector security incidents are handled across multiple jurisdictions.

Pipelines The United States has a vast pipeline industry, consisting of many hundreds of thousands of miles of pipelines, many of which are buried underground. These lines move a variety of substances such as crude oil, refined petroleum products, and natural gas.

Pipeline facilities already incorporate a variety of stringent safety precautions that account for the potential effects a disaster could have on surrounding areas. Moreover, most elements of pipeline infrastructures can be quickly repaired or bypassed to mitigate localized disruptions. Destruction of one or even several of its key components would not disrupt the entire system. As a whole, the response and recovery capabilities of the pipeline industry are well proven, and most large control-center operators have established extensive contingency plans and backup protocols.

PIPELINE MODE CHALLENGES ...Several hundred thousand miles of pipeline span the country, and it is not realistic to expect total security for all facilities. As such, protection efforts focus on infrastructure components whose impairment would have significant effects on the energy markets and the economy as a whole...

Maritime The maritime shipping infrastructure includes ports and their associated assets, ships and passenger transportation systems, coastal and inland waterways, locks, dams and canals, and the network of railroads and pipelines that connect these waterborne systems to other transportation networks. There are 361 seaports in the United States, and their operations range widely in size and characteristics...

MARITIME MODE CHALLENGES The size, diversity, and complexity of this infrastructure make the inspection of all vessels and cargo that passes through our ports an extremely difficult undertaking...

Major portions of the maritime industry's operations are international in nature and are governed by international agreements and multinational authorities, such as the International Maritime Organization...

DoT currently recommends guidelines for passenger vessel and terminal security, including passenger and baggage screening and training of crews...

Mass Transit Systems Each year passengers take approximately 9.5 billion trips on public transit. In fact, mass transit carries more passengers in a single day than air or rail transportation.

Mass transit systems are designed to be publicly accessible. Most are owned and operated by state and local agencies. A city relies on its mass transit system to serve a significant portion of its workforce in addition to being a means of evacuation in case of emergency...

MASS TRANSIT MODE CHALLENGES Mass transit is regulated by various agencies...

Mass transit systems were designed for openness and ease of public access, which makes monitoring points of entry and exit difficult. Protecting them is also expensive...

National Strategy For Transportation Security, Intelligence Reform and Terrorism Prevention Act of 2004

TITLE IV—TRANSPORTATION SECURITY, DECEMBER 17, 2004

SEC. 4001. NATIONAL STRATEGY FOR TRANSPORTATION SECURITY.

(a) IN GENERAL.— Section 114 of title 49, United States Code, is amended by adding at the end the following:

"(t) TRANSPORTATION SECURITY STRATEGIC PLANNING.

"(1) *IN GENERAL.—* The Secretary of Homeland Security shall develop, prepare, implement, and update, as needed—

"(A) a National Strategy for Transportation Security; and

"(B) transportation modal security plans.

"(3) *CONTENTS OF NATIONAL STRATEGY FOR TRANSPORTATION SECURITY.—* The National Strategy for Transportation Security shall include the following:

"(A) An identification and evaluation of the transportation assets in the United States that, in the interests of national security and commerce, must be protected from attack or disruption by terrorist or other hostile forces, including modal security plans for aviation, bridge and tunnel, commuter rail and ferry, highway, maritime, pipeline, rail, mass transit, over-the-road bus, and other public transportation infrastructure assets that could be at risk of such an attack or disruption.

"(B) The development of risk-based priorities across all transportation modes and realistic deadlines for addressing security needs associated with those assets referred to in subparagraph (A).

"(C) The most appropriate, practical, and cost-effective means of defending those assets against threats to their security.

"(D) A forward-looking strategic plan that sets forth the agreed upon roles and missions of Federal,

State, regional, and local authorities and establishes mechanisms for encouraging private sector cooperation and participation in the implementation of such plan.

"(E) A comprehensive delineation of response and recovery responsibilities and issues regarding threatened and executed acts of terrorism within the United States.

"(F) A prioritization of research and development objectives that support transportation security needs, giving a higher priority to research and development directed toward protecting vital transportation assets.

"(5) *PRIORITY STATUS.*

"*(A) IN GENERAL.—* The National Strategy for Transportation Security shall be the governing document for Federal transportation security efforts...

(b) AVIATION SECURITY PLANNING; OPERATIONAL CRITERIA.— Section 44904 of title 49, United States Code, is amended—

(2) by inserting after subsection (b) the following:

"(c) MODAL SECURITY PLAN FOR AVIATION.— In addition to the requirements set forth in subparagraphs (B) through (F) of section 114(t)(3), the modal security plan for aviation prepared under section 114(t) shall—

"(1) establish a damage mitigation and recovery plan for the aviation system in the event of a terrorist attack; and

"(2) include a threat matrix document that outlines each threat to the United States civil aviation system and the corresponding layers of security in place to address such threat.

Executive Order 13416—Strengthening Surface Transportation Security, December, 2006

By the authority vested in me as President...it is hereby ordered as follows:

Sec. 1. Policy.

The security of our Nation's surface transportation systems is a national priority, vital to our economy, and essential to the security of our Nation. Federal, State, local, and tribal governments, the private sector, and the public share responsibility for the security of surface transportation. It is the policy of the United States to protect the people, property, and territory of the United States by facilitating the

implementation of a comprehensive, coordinated, and efficient security program to protect surface transportation systems within and adjacent to the United States against terrorist attacks.

Sec. 3. Functions of the Secretary of Homeland Security.

The Secretary is the principal Federal official responsible for infrastructure protection activities for surface transportation. To implement the policy set forth in section 1 of this order, the Secretary shall...

(a) assess the security of each surface transportation mode and evaluate the effectiveness and efficiency of current Federal Government surface transportation security initiatives;

(b) building upon current security initiatives, not later than December 31, 2006, develop a comprehensive transportation systems sector specific plan, as defined in the NIPP;

(c) not later than 90 days after the comprehensive transportation systems sector specific plan is completed, develop an annex to such plan that addresses each surface transportation mode, which shall also include, at a minimum—

(i) an identification of existing security guidelines and security requirements and any security gaps, a description of how the transportation systems sector specific plan will be implemented for such mode, and the respective roles, responsibilities, and authorities of Federal, State, local, and tribal governments and the private sector;

(ii) schedules and protocols for annual reviews of the effectiveness of surface transportation security-related information sharing mechanisms in bringing about the timely exchange of surface transportation security information among Federal, State, local, and tribal governments and the private sector, as appropriate; and

(d) develop, implement, and lead a process ... to coordinate research, development, testing, and evaluation of technologies (including alternative uses for commercial off-the-shelf technologies and products) relating to the protection of surface transportation, including—

(iii) not later than 180 days after the date of this order ... establishing and making available to Federal, State, local, and tribal government entities, and private sector owners and operators of surface transportation systems, lists of available technologies and products relating to the protection of surface transportation; and

Title XII, Implementing Recommendations of the 9/11 Commission Act of 2007, Transportation Security Planning and Information Sharing, August 3, 2007[7]

SEC. 1203. TRANSPORTATION SECURITY INFORMATION SHARING.

(a) IN GENERAL.— Section 114 of title 49, United States Code, is amended by adding at the end the following:

"(u) TRANSPORTATION SECURITY INFORMATION SHARING PLAN.

"(2) *ESTABLISHMENT OF PLAN.—* The Secretary of Homeland Security... shall establish a Transportation Security Information Sharing Plan...

"(3) *PURPOSE OF PLAN.—* The Plan shall promote sharing of transportation security information between the Department of Homeland Security and public and private stakeholders.

"(4) *CONTENT OF PLAN.—* The Plan shall include—

"(A) a description of how intelligence analysts within the Department of Homeland Security will coordinate their activities within the Department and with other Federal, State, and local agencies, and tribal governments, including coordination with existing modal information sharing centers and the center described in section 1410 of the Implementing Recommendations of the 9/11 Commission Act of 2007;

"(B) the establishment of a point of contact, which may be a single point of contact within the Department of Homeland Security, for each mode of transportation for the sharing of transportation security information with public and private stakeholders...

SEC. 1205. NATIONAL TRANSPORTATION SECURITY CENTER OF EXCELLENCE.

(a) ESTABLISHMENT.— The Secretary shall establish a National Transportation Security Center of Excellence to conduct research and education activities, and to develop or provide professional security training, including the training of transportation employees and transportation professionals.

SEC. 1304. SURFACE TRANSPORTATION SECURITY INSPECTORS.

(a) IN GENERAL.— The Secretary, acting through the Administrator of the Transportation Security Administration, is authorized to train, employ, and utilize surface transportation security inspectors.

SEC. 1307. NATIONAL EXPLOSIVES DETECTION CANINE TEAM TRAINING PROGRAM.

(a) DEFINITIONS.— For purposes of this section, the term "explosives detection canine team" means a canine and a canine handler that are trained to detect explosives, radiological materials, chemical, nuclear or biological weapons, or other threats as defined by the Secretary.

(b) IN GENERAL.—
(1) *INCREASED CAPACITY.—* the Secretary of Homeland Security shall—

(A) begin to increase the number of explosives detection canine teams certified by the Transportation Security Administration for the purposes of transportation-related security by up to 200 canine teams annually by the end of 2010; and

(B) encourage State, local, and tribal governments and private owners of high-risk transportation facilities to strengthen security through the use of highly trained explosives detection canine teams.

(2) *EXPLOSIVES DETECTION CANINE TEAMS.—* The Secretary of Homeland Security shall increase the number of explosives detection canine teams by—

(A) using the Transportation Security Administration's National Explosives Detection Canine Team Training Center, including expanding and upgrading existing facilities, procuring and breeding additional canines, and increasing staffing and oversight commensurate with the increased training and deployment capabilities;

(B) partnering with other Federal, State, or local agencies, nonprofit organizations, universities, or the private sector to increase the training capacity for canine detection teams;

(C) procuring explosives detection canines trained by nonprofit organizations, universities, or the private sector... or

(D) a combination of subparagraphs (A), (B), and (C), as appropriate.

(d) DEPLOYMENT.— The Secretary shall—

(1) use the additional explosives detection canine teams as part of the Department's efforts to strengthen security across the Nation's transportation network, and

may use the canine teams on a more limited basis to support other homeland security missions, as determined appropriate by the Secretary...

SEC. 1309. PROHIBITION OF ISSUANCE OF TRANSPORTATION SECURITY CARDS TO CONVICTED FELONS.

(a) IN GENERAL.— Section 70105 of title 46, United States Code, is amended—

(2) in subsection (c), by amending paragraph (1) to read as follows:

"(1) *DISQUALIFICATIONS.*

"(A) *PERMANENT DISQUALIFYING CRIMINAL OFFENSES.*— Except as provided under paragraph (2), an individual is permanently disqualified from being issued a biometric transportation security card under subsection (b) if the individual has been convicted, or found not guilty by reason of insanity, in a civilian or military jurisdiction of any of the following felonies:

"(i) Espionage or conspiracy to commit espionage.

"(ii) Sedition or conspiracy to commit sedition.

"(iii) Treason or conspiracy to commit treason.

"(iv) A Federal crime of terrorism (as defined in section 2332b(g) of title 18), a crime under a comparable State law, or conspiracy to commit such crime.

"(v) A crime involving a transportation security incident.

"(vi) Improper transportation of a hazardous material in violation of section 5104(b) of title 49, or a comparable State law.

"(vii) Unlawful possession, use, sale, distribution, manufacture, purchase, receipt, transfer, shipment, transportation, delivery, import, export, or storage of, or dealing in, an explosive or explosive device...

"(viii) Murder.

"(ix) Making any threat, or maliciously conveying false information knowing the same to be false, concerning the deliverance, placement, or detonation of an explosive or other lethal device in or against a place of public use, a State or other government facility, a public transportation system, or an infrastructure facility.

"(x) A violation of Chapter 96 of title 18, popularly known as the Racketeer Influenced and Corrupt Organizations Act, or a comparable State law, if one of the predicate acts found by a jury or admitted by the defendant consists of one of the crimes listed in this subparagraph.

"(xi) Attempt to commit any of the crimes listed in clauses (i) through (iv).

"(xii) Conspiracy or attempt to commit any of the crimes described in clauses (v) through (x).

National Transit Systems Security Act of 2007, Implementing Recommendations of the 9/11 Commission Act of 2007, Title XIV, Public Transportation Security, August 3, 2007[8]

SEC. 1401. SHORT TITLE.

This title may be cited as the "National Transit Systems Security Act of 2007".

(4) FRONTLINE EMPLOYEE.— The term "frontline employee" means an employee of a public transportation agency who is a transit vehicle driver or operator, dispatcher, maintenance and maintenance support employee, station attendant, customer service employee, security employee, or transit police, or any other employee who has direct contact with riders on a regular basis, and any other employee of a public transportation agency that the Secretary determines should receive security training under section 1408.

SEC. 1403. FINDINGS.

Congress finds that—

(1) 182 public transportation systems throughout the world have been primary targets of terrorist attacks;

(2) more than 6,000 public transportation agencies operate in the United States;

(3) people use public transportation vehicles 33,000,000 times each day;

(4) the Federal Transit Administration has invested $93,800,000,000 since 1992 for construction and improvements;

(5) the Federal investment in transit security has been insufficient; and

(6) greater Federal investment in transit security improvements per passenger boarding is necessary to better protect the American people, given transit's vital importance in creating mobility and promoting our Nation's economy.

SEC. 1404. NATIONAL STRATEGY FOR PUBLIC TRANSPORTATION SECURITY.

(a) NATIONAL STRATEGY.— Not later than 9 months after the date of enactment of this Act...the Secretary...shall develop and implement the modal plan for public transportation, entitled the "National Strategy for Public Transportation Security".

(b) PURPOSE.

(1) *GUIDELINES.*— In developing the National Strategy for Public Transportation Security, the Secretary shall establish guidelines for public transportation security that—

(A) minimize security threats to public transportation systems; and

(B) maximize the abilities of public transportation systems to mitigate damage resulting from terrorist attack or other major incident.

SEC. 1405. SECURITY ASSESSMENTS AND PLANS.

(b) BUS AND RURAL PUBLIC TRANSPORTATION SYSTEMS.— The Secretary shall—

(1) conduct security assessments, based on a representative sample, to determine the specific needs of—

(A) local bus-only public transportation systems; and

(B) public transportation systems that receive funds under section 5311 of title 49, United States Code; and

(c) SECURITY PLANS.

(1) *REQUIREMENT FOR PLAN.*

(A) HIGH RISK AGENCIES.— The Secretary shall require public transportation agencies determined by the Secretary to be at high risk for terrorism to develop a comprehensive security plan...

SEC. 1406. PUBLIC TRANSPORTATION SECURITY ASSISTANCE.

(a) SECURITY ASSISTANCE PROGRAM.

(1) *IN GENERAL.*— The Secretary shall establish a program for making grants to eligible public transportation agencies for security improvements...

(2) *ELIGIBILITY.*— A public transportation agency is eligible for a grant under this section if the Secretary has performed a security assessment or the agency has developed a security plan under section 1405...

SEC. 1407. SECURITY EXERCISES.

(a) IN GENERAL.— The Secretary shall establish a program for conducting security exercises for public transportation agencies for the purpose of assessing and improving the capabilities of entities described in subsection (b) to prevent, prepare for, mitigate against, respond to, and recover from acts of terrorism...

SEC. 1408. PUBLIC TRANSPORTATION SECURITY TRAINING PROGRAM.

(a) IN GENERAL.— ...the Secretary shall develop and issue detailed final regulations, for a public transportation security training program to prepare public transportation employees, including frontline employees, for potential security threats and conditions...

SEC. 1409. PUBLIC TRANSPORTATION RESEARCH AND DEVELOPMENT.

(a) ESTABLISHMENT OF RESEARCH AND DEVELOPMENT PROGRAM.— The Secretary shall carry out a research and development program for the purpose of improving the security of public transportation systems....

SEC. 1410. INFORMATION SHARING.

(a) INTELLIGENCE SHARING.— The Secretary shall ensure that the Department of Transportation receives appropriate and timely notification of all credible terrorist threats against public transportation assets in the United States.

(b) INFORMATION SHARING ANALYSIS CENTER.

(1) AUTHORIZATION.— The Secretary shall provide for the reasonable costs of the Information Sharing and Analysis Center for Public Transportation (referred to in this subsection as the "ISAC")...

SEC. 1411. THREAT ASSESSMENTS.

Not later than 1 year after the date of enactment of this Act, the Secretary shall complete a name-based security background check against the consolidated terrorist watchlist and an immigration status check for all public transportation frontline employees...

Title XV, Implementing Recommendations of the 9/11 Commission Act of 2007, August 3, 2007[9]

SEC. 1501. DEFINITIONS.

In this title, the following definitions apply:

(13) SECURITY-SENSITIVE MATERIAL.— The term "security-sensitive material" means a material, or a group or class of material, in a particular amount and form that the Secretary, in consultation with the Secretary of Transportation, determines, through a rulemaking with opportunity for public comment, poses a significant risk to national security while being transported in commerce due to the potential use of the material in an act of terrorism. In making such a designation, the Secretary shall, at a minimum, consider the following:

(A) Class 7 radioactive materials.

(B) Division 1.1, 1.2, or 1.3 explosives.

(C) Materials poisonous or toxic by inhalation, including Division 2.3 gases and Division 6.1 materials.

(D) A select agent or toxin regulated by the Centers for Disease Control and Prevention under part 73 of title 42, Code of Federal Regulations.

ADDITIONAL RESOURCES

The Department of Transportation's Office of Hazardous Materials Safety "is the Federal safety authority for ensuring the safe transport of hazardous materials by air, rail, highway, and water." http://www.phmsa.dot.gov/hazmat

"Homeland Security: DHS's Progress and Challenges in Key Areas of Maritime, Aviation, and Cybersecurity," Government Accountability Office, GAO-10-106, Dec. 2009, http://www.gao.gov/new.items/d10106.pdf

Mineta Transportation Institute, The Role of Transportation in Campus Emergency Planning, June 2009, http://transweb.sjsu.edu/mtiportal/research/publications/documents/Role20of20Transportation20(Complete20with20Cover).pdf

"Transportation Security: Issues for the 111 Congress," May 15, 2009, David Randall Peterman, John Frittelli, Bart Elias, Congressional Research Service RL33512, http://opencrs.com/document/RL33512

"Interagency Coordination. The impressions of the mass transit sector since the creation of the Department of Homeland Security are that while we, as an industry infrastructure have made some gains in establishing working relationships with the various DHS Directorates, we continue to see examples of competition, strained relationships and silos within the Department...A similar condition is seen to exist between the DHS and the DOT... Similarly, it is the impression of the mass transit sector that while we have seen some strengthening of the outreach and partnering between DHS and this sector through activities such as the "Coordinating Councils", we continue to see DHS proceed on critical activities such as security technology research and development unilaterally and without seeking industry input." "On Transit Security Funding for Fiscal Year (FY) 2010," Testimony Of William W. Millar, President, American Public Transportation Association, Submitted To The House Appropriations Subcommittee on Homeland Security. April 16, 2009. http://www.apta.com/government_affairs/aptatest/testimony090416.cfm

Transportation Research Board's National Cooperative Highway Research Program (NCHRP) Synthesis 392: Transportation's Role in Emergency Evacuation and Reentry. March 30, 2009. http://trb.org/news/blurb_detail.asp?id=10106

Commercial Vehicle Security: Risk-Based Approach Needed to Secure the Commercial Vehicle Sector, Report to the Chairman, Committee on Homeland Security, House of Representatives, February 2009, GAO-09-85, https://www.hsdl.org/homesec/docs/gao/nps46-033109-07.pdf&code=7c43e2f4b70822dd875eb14876f72b8f

DHS' Plan for Implementing Secure Systems of Transportation, Department of Homeland Security Office of Inspector General, OIG-09-03, October 2008, http://www.dhs.gov/xoig/assets/mgmtrpts/OIG_09-03_Oct08.pdf

"Transportation for Tomorrow," Report of the National Surface Transportation Policy and Revenue Study Commission, December 2007, http://transportationfortomorrow.org/final_report/pdf/final_report.pdf

"New Strategies to Protect America: Terrorism and Mass Transit after London and Madrid," August 10, 2005, Bill Johnstone, The Center for American Progress, http://www.americanprogress.org/kf/transit_security.pdf

Terrorism And Transit Security: 12 Recommendations For Progress, August 10, 2005, Brian D. Taylor, AICP, http://www.americanprogress.org/kf/taylor_transit_security.pdf

"Terrorism, Transit and Public Safety, Evaluating the Risks," By Todd Litman, Victoria (British Columbia) Transport Policy Institute, 18 July 2005. http://www.counteract.eu/Pages/05072020-20Victoria20Police20Institute20Study.pdf

"Intermodal Transportation Safety and Security Issues: Training against Terrorism," Ronald W. Tarr, Vicki McGurk, and Carol Jones, University of Central Florida, Journal of Public Transportation, Vol. 8, No. 4, 2005, http://www.nctr.usf.edu/jpt/pdf/JPT208-4S20Tarr.pdf

"Improving Public Surface Transportation Security: What Do We Do Now?" Brian Jenkins, February 27, 2003. www.lexingtoninstitute.org/docs/500.pdf

B. AVIATION SECURITY

The Aviation and Transportation Security Act created the Transportation Security Administration (TSA), which is responsible for security in all modes of transportation (including civil aviation) that are overseen by the Department of Trans-portation. This act discusses the use of biometrics for iden-tification of airport personnel, law enforcement travel where the officers retain their weapon, advanced airline passenger screening explosives detection, and air marshals.

The Intelligence Reform and Terrorism Prevention Act of 2004 directs security of air cargo in general, and investigation of blast-resistant baggage containers. HSPD 16 describes a vision of aviation security and creates a national strategy for aviation security.

The National Strategy for Aviation Security describes the national strategy. Its "supporting plans address the following areas: aviation transportation system security; aviation op-erational threat response; aviation transportation system re-covery; air domain surveillance and intelligence integration; domestic outreach; and international outreach."

SOURCES

- Aviation and Transportation Security Act, November. 19, 2001[10]
- Intelligence Reform and Terrorism Prevention Act of 2004, Air Cargo Security[11]
- NSPD 47/HSPD 16, Aviation Security Policy, June 22, 2006[12]
- Security and Accountability for Every Port Act Of 2006[13]
- National Strategy for Aviation Security, March 26, 2007[14]
- Aviation Transportation System Security Plan, March 26, 2007[15]
- Air Domain Surveillance and Intelligence Integration Plan, March 26, 2007[16]
- Aviation Operational Threat Response Plan, March 26, 2007[17]
- Domestic Outreach Plan, March 26, 2007[18]
- International Outreach Plan, March 26, 2007[19]

Creation of the Transportation Security Administration (TSA), The Aviation and Transportation Security Act, November 19, 2001

An Act To improve aviation security, and for other purposes. *Be it enacted by the Senate and House of Representatives of the United States of America in Congress assembled,*

SEC. 1. SHORT TITLE.

This Act may be cited as the "Aviation and Transportation Security Act."

TITLE I—AVIATION SECURITY

SEC. 101. TRANSPORTATION SECURITY ADMINISTRATION.

(a) IN GENERAL.— Chapter 1 of title 49, United States Code, is amended by adding at the end the following:

§ 114. Transportation Security Administration

"(a) *IN GENERAL.—* The Transportation Security Admin-istration shall be an administration of the Department of Transportation.

"(b) *UNDER SECRETARY.*

"(1)*APPOINTMENT.—* The head of the Administration shall be the Under Secretary of Transportation for Security. The Under Secretary shall be appointed by the President, by and with the advice and consent of the Senate.

"(d) *FUNCTIONS.—* The Under Secretary shall be respon-sible for security in all modes of transportation...

"(e) *SCREENING OPERATIONS.—* The Under Secretary shall—

"(1) be responsible for day-to-day Federal security screen-ing operations for passenger air transportation and intrastate air transportation...

"(2) develop standards for the hiring and retention of se-curity screening personnel;

"(3) train and test security screening personnel; and

"(4) be responsible for hiring and training personnel to provide security screening at all airports in the United States where screening is required...

"(f) *ADDITIONAL DUTIES AND POWERS.—* In addition to carrying out the functions specified in subsections (d) and (e), the Under Secretary shall—

"(1) receive, assess, and distribute intelligence informa-tion related to transportation security;

"(2) assess threats to transportation;

"(3) develop policies, strategies, and plans for dealing with threats to transportation security;

"(4) make other plans related to transportation security, including coordinating countermeasures with appro-priate departments, agencies, and instrumentalities of the United States Government;

"(5) serve as the primary liaison for transportation security to the intelligence and law enforcement communities;

"(6) on a day-to-day basis, manage and provide operational guidance to the field security resources of the Administration, including Federal Security Managers. . .

"(7) enforce security-related regulations and requirements;

"(8) identify and undertake research and development activities necessary to enhance transportation security;

"(9) inspect, maintain, and test security facilities, equipment, and systems;

"(10) ensure the adequacy of security measures for the transportation of cargo;

"(11) oversee the implementation, and ensure the adequacy, of security measures at airports and other transportation facilities;

"(12) require background checks for airport security screening personnel, individuals with access to secure areas of airports, and other transportation security personnel;

"(13) work in conjunction with the Administrator of the Federal Aviation Administration with respect to any actions or activities that may affect aviation safety or air carrier operations;

"(14) work with the International Civil Aviation Organization and appropriate aeronautic authorities of foreign governments. . .to address security concerns on passenger flights by foreign air carriers in foreign air transportation. . .

"(h) *MANAGEMENT OF SECURITY INFORMATION. . . the Under Secretary shall—*

"(1) enter into memoranda of understanding with Federal agencies or other entities to share or otherwise cross-check as necessary data on individuals identified on Federal agency databases who may pose a risk to transportation or national security;

"(2) establish procedures for notifying the Administrator of the Federal Aviation Administration, appropriate State and local law enforcement officials, and airport or airline security officers of the identity of individuals known to pose, or suspected of posing, a risk of air piracy or terrorism or a threat to airline or passenger safety;

"(3) . . . establish policies and procedures requiring air carriers—

"(A) to use information from government agencies to identify individuals on passenger lists who may be a threat to civil aviation or national security; and

"(B) if such an individual is identified, notify appropriate law enforcement agencies, prevent the in-

dividual from boarding an aircraft, or take other appropriate action with respect to that individual; and

"(4) consider requiring passenger air carriers to share passenger lists with appropriate Federal agencies for the purpose of identifying individuals who may pose a threat to aviation safety or national security.

(g) *TRANSITION PROVISIONS.—* . . .

*(4) **TRANSFER OF OWNERSHIP.**—* In recognition of the assumption of the financial costs of security screening of passengers and property at airports, and as soon as practical after the date of enactment of this Act, air carriers may enter into agreements with the Under Secretary to transfer the ownership, at no cost to the United States Government, of any personal property, equipment, supplies, or other material associated with such screening, regardless of the source of funds used to acquire the property, that the Secretary determines to be useful for the performance of security screening of passengers and property at airports.

SEC. 104. IMPROVED FLIGHT DECK INTEGRITY MEASURES.

(a) **IN GENERAL.—** As soon as possible after the date of enactment of this Act, the Administrator of the Federal Aviation Administration shall—

(1) issue an order (without regard to the provisions of chapter 5 of title 5, United States Code)—

(A) prohibiting access to the flight deck of aircraft engaged in passenger air transportation or intrastate air transportation that are required to have a door between the passenger and pilot compartments under title 14, Code of Federal Regulations, except to authorized persons;

(B) requiring the strengthening of the flight deck door and locks on any such aircraft operating in air transportation or intrastate air transportation that has a rigid door in a bulkhead between the flight deck and the passenger area to ensure that the door cannot be forced open from the passenger compartment;

(C) requiring that such flight deck doors remain locked while any such aircraft is in flight except when necessary to permit access and egress by authorized persons; and

(D) prohibiting the possession of a key to any such flight deck door by any member of the flight crew who is not assigned to the flight deck; and

(2) take such other action, including modification of safety and security procedures and flight deck re-design, as may be necessary to ensure the safety and security of the aircraft.

(b) IMPLEMENTATION OF OTHER METHODS.— As soon as possible after such date of enactment, the Administrator of the Federal Aviation Administration may develop and implement methods—

(1) to use video monitors or other devices to alert pilots in the flight deck to activity in the cabin, except that the use of such monitors or devices shall be subject to nondisclosure requirements applicable to cockpit video recordings under section 1114(c);

(2) to ensure continuous operation of an aircraft transponder in the event of an emergency; and

(3) to revise the procedures by which cabin crews of aircraft can notify flight deck crews of security breaches and other emergencies, including providing for the installation of switches or other devices or methods in an aircraft cabin to enable flight crews to discreetly notify the pilots in the case of a security breach occurring in the cabin.

SEC. 105. DEPLOYMENT OF FEDERAL AIR MARSHALS.

(a) IN GENERAL.— Subchapter I of chapter 449 of title 49, United States Code, is amended by adding at the end the following:

§ 44917. Deployment of Federal Air Marshals

"(a) *IN GENERAL.—* The Under Secretary of Transportation for Security under the authority provided by section 44903(d)—

"(1) may provide for deployment of Federal air marshals on every passenger flight of air carriers in air transportation or intrastate air transportation;

"(2) shall provide for deployment of Federal air marshals on every such flight determined by the Secretary to present high security risks;

"(4) shall require air carriers providing flights described in paragraph (1) to provide seating for a Federal air marshal on any such flight without regard to the availability of seats on the flight and at no cost to the United States Government or the marshal;

"(6) may enter into agreements with Federal, State, and local agencies under which appropriately-trained law enforcement personnel from such agencies, when

traveling on a flight of an air carrier, will carry a firearm and be prepared to assist Federal air marshals;

"(7) shall establish procedures to ensure that Federal air marshals are made aware of any armed or unarmed law enforcement personnel on board an aircraft; and

"(8) may appoint—

"(A) an individual who is a retired law enforcement officer;

"(B) an individual who is a retired member of the Armed Forces; and

"(C) an individual who has been furloughed from an air carrier crew position in the 1-year period beginning on September 11, 2001, as a Federal air marshal, regardless of age, if the individual otherwise meets the background and fitness qualifications required for Federal air marshals.

SEC. 106. IMPROVED AIRPORT PERIMETER ACCESS SECURITY.

(a) IN GENERAL.— Section 44903 of title 49, United States Code, is amended by adding at the end the following:

"(h) IMPROVED AIRPORT PERIMETER ACCESS SECURITY.

"(4) *AIRPORT PERIMETER SCREENING.—*The Under Secretary—

"(A) shall require, as soon as practicable after the date of enactment of this subsection, screening or inspection of all individuals, goods, property, vehicles, and other equipment before entry into a secured area of an airport in the United States described in section 44903(c);

"(C) shall establish procedures to ensure the safety and integrity of—

"(i) all persons providing services with respect to aircraft providing passenger air transportation or intrastate air transportation and facilities of such persons at an airport in the United States described in section 44903(c);

"(ii) all supplies, including catering and passenger amenities, placed aboard such aircraft, including the sealing of supplies to ensure easy visual detection of tampering; and

"(iii) all persons providing such supplies and facilities of such persons;

"(D) shall require vendors having direct access to the airfield and aircraft to develop security programs; and

"(E) may provide for the use of biometric or other technology that positively verifies the identity of each employee and law enforcement officer who enters a secure area of an airport.".

SEC. 107. CREW TRAINING.

(a) IN GENERAL.— Subchapter I of chapter 449 of title 49, United States Code, is amended by adding at the end the following:

§ 44918. Crew Training

"(a) *IN GENERAL.—* Not later than 60 days after the date of enactment of the Aviation and Transportation Security Act, the Administrator of the Federal Aviation Administration, in consultation with . . . shall develop detailed guidance for a scheduled passenger air carrier flight and cabin crew training program to prepare crew members for potential threat conditions.

"(b) *PROGRAM ELEMENTS.—* The guidance shall require such a program to include, at a minimum, elements that address the following:

"(1) Determination of the seriousness of any occurrence.

"(2) Crew communication and coordination.

"(3) Appropriate responses to defend oneself.

"(4) Use of protective devices assigned to crew members (to the extent such devices are required by the Administrator or Under Secretary).

"(5) Psychology of terrorists to cope with hijacker behavior and passenger responses.

"(6) Live situational training exercises regarding various threat conditions.

"(7) Flight deck procedures or aircraft maneuvers to defend the aircraft.

SEC. 108. SECURITY SCREENING BY PRIVATE COMPANIES.

(a) IN GENERAL.— Subchapter I of chapter 449 of title 49, United States Code, is amended by adding at the end the following:

§ 44919. Security Screening Pilot Program

"(a) *ESTABLISHMENT OF PROGRAM.—* The Under Secretary shall establish a pilot program under which, upon approval of an application submitted by an operator of an airport, the screening of passengers and property at the airport under section 44901 will be carried out by the screening personnel of a qualified private screening company under a contract entered into with the Under Secretary.

SEC. 110. SCREENING.

(b) PASSENGERS AND PROPERTY.— Section 44901 of title 49,United States Code, is amended—

(2) by striking subsections (a) and (b) and inserting the following:

"(a) *IN GENERAL.—* The Under Secretary of Transportation for Security shall provide for the screening of all passengers and property, including United States mail, cargo, carry-on and checked baggage, and other articles, that will be carried aboard a passenger aircraft operated by an air carrier or foreign air carrier in air transportation or intrastate air transportation. In the case of flights and flight segments originating in the United States, the screening shall take place before boarding and shall be carried out by a Federal Government employee (as defined in section 2105 of title 5, United States Code), except as otherwise provided in section 44919 or 44920 and except for identifying passengers and baggage for screening under the CAPPS and known shipper programs and conducting positive bag-match programs.

"(b) *SUPERVISION OF SCREENING.—* All screening of passengers and property at airports in the United States where screening is required under this section shall be supervised by uniformed Federal personnel of the Transportation Security Administration who shall have the power to order the dismissal of any individual performing such screening.

"(c) *CHECKED BAGGAGE.—* A system must be in operation to screen all checked baggage at all airports in the United States as soon as practicable but not later than the 60th day following the date of enactment of the Aviation and Transportation Security Act.

"(d) *EXPLOSIVE DETECTION SYSTEMS.*

"*(1) IN GENERAL.—* The Under Secretary of Transportation for Security shall take all necessary action to ensure that—

"(A) explosive detection systems are deployed as soon as possible to ensure that all United States airports described in section 44903(c) have sufficient explosive detection systems to screen all checked baggage no later than December 31, 2002, and that as soon as such systems are in place at an airport, all checked baggage at the airport is screened by those systems; and

"(B) all systems deployed under subparagraph (A) are fully utilized; and

"(C) if explosive detection equipment at an airport is unavailable, all checked baggage is screened by an alternative means.

"(f) *CARGO DEADLINE.*— A system must be in operation to screen, inspect, or otherwise ensure the security of all cargo that is to be transported in all-cargo aircraft in air transportation and intrastate air transportation as soon as practicable after the date of enactment of the Aviation and Transportation Security Act.

"(g) *DEPLOYMENT OF ARMED PERSONNEL.*

"*(1) IN GENERAL.*— The Under Secretary shall order the deployment of law enforcement personnel authorized to carry firearms at each airport security screening location to ensure passenger safety and national security.

"*(2) MINIMUM REQUIREMENTS.* . . the Under Secretary shall order the deployment of at least 1 law enforcement officer at each airport security screening location..

SEC. 111. TRAINING AND EMPLOYMENT OF SECURITY SCREENING

(a) IN GENERAL.— Section 44935 of title 49, United States Code, is amended—

(2) by striking subsection (e) and inserting the following:

"(f) EMPLOYMENT STANDARDS FOR SCREENING PERSONNEL.

"(2) *VETERANS PREFERENCE.*— The Under Secretary shall provide a preference for the hiring of an individual as a security screener if the individual is a member or former member of the armed forces and if the individual is entitled, under statute, to retired, retirement, or retainer pay on account of service as a member of the armed forces.

SEC. 112. RESEARCH AND DEVELOPMENT.

(b) ADDITIONAL MATTERS REGARDING RESEARCH AND DEVELOPMENT.

(1) *ADDITIONAL PROGRAM REQUIREMENTS.*— Subsection (a) of section 44912 of title 49, United States Code, is amended

(3) *SCIENTIFIC ADVISORY PANEL.*— Subsection (c) of that section is amended to read as follows:

"**(c) SCIENTIFIC ADVISORY PANEL.**— (1) The Administrator shall establish a scientific advisory panel, as a

subcommittee of the Research, Engineering, and Development Advisory Committee, to review, comment on, advise the progress of, and recommend modifications in, the program established under subsection (a) of this section, including the need for long-range research programs to detect and prevent catastrophic damage to commercial aircraft, commercial aviation facilities, commercial aviation personnel and passengers, and other components of the commercial aviation system by the next generation of terrorist weapons. . .

SEC. 113. FLIGHT SCHOOL SECURITY.

(a) IN GENERAL.— Subchapter II of chapter 449 of title 49, United States Code, is amended by adding at the end the following new section:

§ 44939. Training to Operate Certain Aircraft

"(a) *WAITING PERIOD.*— A person subject to regulation under this part may provide training in the operation of any aircraft . . . to an alien . . . or to any other individual specified by the Under Secretary of Transportation for Security only if— "(1) that person has first notified the Attorney General that the individual has requested such training and furnished the Attorney General with that individual's identification..

"(d) *SECURITY AWARENESS TRAINING FOR EMPLOYEES.*— The Under Secretary shall require flight schools to conduct a security awareness program for flight school employees to increase their awareness of suspicious circumstances and activities of individuals enrolling in or attending flight school.".

SEC. 114. INCREASED PENALTIES FOR INTERFERENCE WITH SECURITY PERSONNEL.

(a) IN GENERAL.— Chapter 465 of title 49, United States Code, is amended by inserting after section 46502 the following:

§ 46503. Interference with Security Screening Personnel

"An individual in an area within a commercial service airport in the United States who, by assaulting a Federal, airport, or air carrier employee who has security duties within the airport, interferes with the performance of the duties of the employee or lessens the ability of the employee to perform those duties, shall be fined under title 18, imprisoned for not more than 10 years, or both. If the individual used a dangerous weapon in committing the assault or interference, the individual may be imprisoned for any term of years or life imprisonment.".

SEC. 115. PASSENGER MANIFESTS.

Section 44909 is amended by adding at the end the following:
  "(c) FLIGHTS IN FOREIGN AIR TRANSPORTATION TO THE UNITED STATES.

"(1) IN GENERAL.— Not later than 60 days after the date of enactment of the Aviation and Transportation Security Act, each air carrier and foreign air carrier operating a passenger flight in foreign air transportation to the United States shall provide to the Commissioner of Customs by electronic transmission a passenger and crew manifest containing the information specified in paragraph (2

"(2) INFORMATION.— A passenger and crew manifest for a flight required under paragraph (1) shall contain the following information:

  "(A) The full name of each passenger and crew member.
  "(B) The date of birth and citizenship of each passenger and crew member.
  "(C) The sex of each passenger and crew member.
  "(D) The passport number and country of issuance of each passenger and crew member if required for travel.
  "(E) The United States visa number or resident alien card number of each passenger and crew member, as applicable.

SEC. 118. SECURITY SERVICE FEE.

(a) IN GENERAL.— Subchapter II of chapter 449 is amended by adding at the end the following:

§ 44940. Security Service Fee

"(a) *GENERAL AUTHORITY.*

  "(1) *PASSENGER FEES.—* The Under Secretary of Transportation for Security shall impose a uniform fee, on passengers of air carriers and foreign air carriers in air transportation and intrastate air transportation originating at airports in the United States, to pay for the following costs of providing civil aviation security services:...

"(c) *LIMITATION ON FEE.—* Fees imposed under subsection (a)(1) may not exceed $2.50 per enplanement in air transportation or intrastate air transportation that originates at an airport in the United States, except that the total amount of such fees may not exceed $5.00 per one-way trip.

SEC. 125. ENCOURAGING AIRLINE EMPLOYEES TO REPORT SUSPICIOUS ACTIVITIES.

(a) IN GENERAL.— Subchapter II of chapter 449 of title 49, United States Code, is amended by inserting at the end the following:

§ 44941. Immunity for Reporting Suspicious Activities

"(a) *IN GENERAL.—* Any air carrier or foreign air carrier or any employee of an air carrier or foreign air carrier who makes a voluntary disclosure of any suspicious transaction relevant to a possible violation of law or regulation, relating to air piracy, a threat to aircraft or passenger safety, or terrorism, as defined by section 3077 of title 18, United States Code, to any employee or agent of the Department of Transportation, the Department of Justice, any Federal, State, or local law enforcement officer, or any airport or airline security officer shall not be civilly liable to any person under any law or regulation of the United States, any constitution, law, or regulation of any State or political subdivision of any State, for such disclosure.

SEC. 126. LESS-THAN-LETHAL WEAPONRY FOR FLIGHT DECK CREWS.

(a) NATIONAL INSTITUTE OF JUSTICE STUDY.— The National Institute of Justice shall assess the range of less-than-lethal weaponry available for use by a flight deck crewmember temporarily to incapacitate an individual who presents a clear and present danger to the safety of the aircraft, its passengers, or individuals on the ground . . .

SEC. 128. FLIGHT DECK SECURITY.

The pilot of a passenger aircraft operated by an air carrier in air transportation or intrastate air transportation is authorized to carry a firearm into the cockpit if—

  (1) the Under Secretary of Transportation for Security approves;
  (2) the air carrier approves;
  (3) the firearm is approved by the Under Secretary; and
  (4) the pilot has received proper training for the use of the firearm, as determined by the Under Secretary.

SEC. 136. SHORT-TERM ASSESSMENT AND DEPLOYMENT OF EMERGING SECURITY TECHNOLOGIES AND PROCEDURES.

Section 44903 of title 49, United States Code, is amended by adding at the end the following:

"(i) SHORT-TERM ASSESSMENT AND DEPLOYMENT OF EMERGING SECURITY TECHNOLOGIES AND PROCEDURES.

"(1) IN GENERAL.— The Under Secretary of Transportation for Security shall recommend to airport operators, within 6 months after the date of enactment of the Aviation and Transportation Security Act, commercially available measures or procedures to prevent access to secure airport areas by unauthorized persons. As part of the 6-month assessment, the Under Secretary for Transportation Security shall—

"(A) review the effectiveness of biometrics systems currently in use at several United States airports, including San Francisco International;

"(B) review the effectiveness of increased surveillance at access points;

"(C) review the effectiveness of card- or keypad-based access systems;

"(D) review the effectiveness of airport emergency exit systems and determine whether those that lead to secure areas of the airport should be monitored or how breaches can be swiftly responded to; and

"(E) specifically target the elimination of the "piggybacking" phenomenon, where another person follows an authorized person through the access point. The 6-month assessment shall include a 12-month deployment strategy for currently available technology at all category X airports . . . Not later than 18 months after the date of enactment of this Act, the Secretary of Transportation shall conduct a review of reductions in unauthorized access at these airports.

"(2) COMPUTER-ASSISTED PASSENGER PRESCREENING SYSTEM.

"(A) *IN GENERAL.—* The Secretary of Transportation shall ensure that the Computer-Assisted Passenger Prescreening System, or any successor system—

"(i) is used to evaluate all passengers before they board an aircraft; and

"(ii) includes procedures to ensure that individuals selected by the system and their carry-on and checked baggage are adequately screened.

SEC. 144. LIMITATION ON LIABILITY FOR ACTS TO THWART CRIMINAL VIOLENCE OR AIRCRAFT PIRACY.

Section 44903 is amended by adding at the end the following:

"(h) LIMITATION ON LIABILITY FOR ACTS TO THWART CRIMINAL VIOLENCE OR AIRCRAFT PIRACY.—An individual shall not be liable for damages in any action brought in a Federal or State court arising out of the acts of the individual in attempting to thwart an act of criminal violence or piracy on an aircraft if that individual reasonably believed that such an act of criminal violence or piracy was occurring or was about to occur.'

Title IV, Intelligence Reform and Terrorism Prevention Act, Aviation Security, December 17, 2004[20]

SEC. 4012. ADVANCED AIRLINE PASSENGER PRESCREENING.

(a) IN GENERAL.

(1) *DOMESTIC FLIGHTS.—* Section 44903(j)(2) of title 49, United States Code, is amended by adding at the end the following:

"(C) ADVANCED AIRLINE PASSENGER PRESCREENING.

"(i) *COMMENCEMENT OF TESTING.—* Not later than January 1, 2005, the Assistant Secretary of Homeland Security (Transportation Security Administration) . . . shall commence testing of an advanced passenger prescreening system that will allow the Department of Homeland Security to assume the performance of comparing passenger information . . . to the automatic selectee and no fly lists, utilizing all appropriate records in the consolidated and integrated terrorist watchlist maintained by the Federal Government.

"(ii) *ASSUMPTION OF FUNCTION.—* Not later than 180 days after completion of testing under clause (i), the Assistant Secretary . . . shall begin to assume the performance of the passenger prescreening function of comparing passenger information to the automatic selectee and no fly lists and utilize all appropriate records in the consolidated and integrated terrorist watchlist maintained by the Federal Government in performing that function.

"(iii) *REQUIREMENTS.—* In assuming performance of the function under clause (ii), the Assistant Secretary shall—

"(I) establish a procedure to enable airline passengers, who are delayed or prohibited from boarding a flight because the advanced passenger prescreening system determined that they might pose a security threat, to appeal such determination and correct information contained in the system;

"(II) ensure that Federal Government databases that will be used to establish the identity of a passenger under the system will not produce a large number of false positives;

"(III) establish an internal oversight board to oversee and monitor the manner in which the system is being implemented;

"(IV) establish sufficient operational safeguards to reduce the opportunities for abuse;

"(V) implement substantial security measures to protect the system from unauthorized access;

"(VI) adopt policies establishing effective oversight of the use and operation of the system; and

"(VII) ensure that there are no specific privacy concerns with the technological architecture of the system.

"(D) SCREENING OF EMPLOYEES AGAINST WATCHLIST.— The Assistant Secretary of Homeland Security . . . shall ensure that individuals are screened against all appropriate records in the consolidated and integrated terrorist watchlist maintained by the Federal Government before—

"(i) being certificated by the Federal Aviation Administration;

"(ii) being granted unescorted access to the secure area of an airport; or

"(iii) being granted unescorted access to the air operations area . . . of an airport.

"*(iii)* **NO FLY AND AUTOMATIC SELECTEE LISTS**.— The Secretary of Homeland Security, in consultation with the Terrorist Screening Center, shall design and review, as necessary, guidelines, policies, and operating procedures for the collection, removal, and updating Applicability of data maintained, or to be maintained, in the no fly and automatic selectee lists.

"(G) APPEAL PROCEDURES.

"(i) *IN GENERAL*.— The Assistant Secretary shall establish a timely and fair process for individuals identified as a threat under one or more of subparagraphs (C), (D), and (E) to appeal to the Transportation Security Administration the determination and correct any erroneous information.

"(ii) *RECORDS*.— The process shall include the establishment of a method by which the Assistant Secretary will be able to maintain a record of air passengers and other individuals who have been misidentified and have corrected erroneous information. To prevent repeated delays of misidentified passengers and other individuals, the Transportation Security Administration record shall contain information determined by the Assistant Secretary to authenticate the identity of such a passenger or individual.

SEC. 4013. DEPLOYMENT AND USE OF DETECTION EQUIPMENT AT AIRPORT SCREENING CHECKPOINTS.

(a) IN GENERAL.— Subchapter I of chapter 449, of title 49, United States Code, is amended by adding at the end the following:

§ 44925. Deployment and Use of Detection Equipment at Airport Screening Checkpoints

"(a) *WEAPONS AND EXPLOSIVES*.— The Secretary of Homeland Security shall give a high priority to developing, testing, improving, and deploying, at airport screening checkpoints, equipment that detects nonmetallic, chemical, biological, and radiological weapons, and explosives, in all forms, on individuals and in their personal property. The Secretary shall ensure that the equipment alone, or as part of an integrated system, can detect under realistic operating conditions the types of weapons and explosives that terrorists would likely try to smuggle aboard an air carrier aircraft.

SEC. 4016. FEDERAL AIR MARSHALS.

(a) FEDERAL AIR MARSHAL ANONYMITY.— The Director of the Federal Air Marshal Service of the Department of Homeland Security shall continue operational initiatives to protect the anonymity of Federal air marshals.

SEC. 4022. IMPROVED PILOT LICENSES.

(a) IN GENERAL.— Not later than one year after the date of enactment of this Act, the Administrator of the Federal Aviation Administration shall begin to issue improved pilot licenses consistent with the requirements of title 49, United States Code, and title 14, Code of Federal Regulations.

(b) REQUIREMENTS.— Improved pilots licenses issued under subsection
(a) shall—

(1) be resistant to tampering, alteration, and counterfeiting;

(2) include a photograph of the individual to whom the license is issued; and

(3) be capable of accommodating a digital photograph, a biometric identifier, or any other unique identifier that the Administrator considers necessary.

(c) TAMPERING.— To the extent practical, the Administrator shall develop methods to determine or reveal whether any component or security feature of a license issued under subsection (a) has been tampered, altered, or counterfeited.

SEC. 4025. PROHIBITED ITEMS LIST.

Not later than 60 days after the date of enactment of this Act, the Assistant Secretary for Homeland Security (Transportation Security Administration) shall complete a review of the list of items prohibited from being carried aboard a passenger aircraft operated by an air carrier or foreign air carrier in air transportation or intrastate air transportation set forth in section 1540 of title 49, Code of Federal Regulations, and shall release a revised list that includes—

(1) butane lighters; and

(2) any other modification that the Assistant Secretary considers appropriate.

SEC. 4026. MAN-PORTABLE AIR DEFENSE SYSTEMS (MANPADS).

(a) UNITED STATES POLICY ON NONPROLIFERATION AND EXPORT CONTROL.

(1) *TO LIMIT AVAILABILITY AND TRANSFER OF MANPADS.*— The President shall pursue, on an urgent basis, further strong international diplomatic and cooperative efforts, including bilateral and multilateral treaties, in the appropriate forum to limit the availability, transfer, and proliferation of MANPADSs worldwide.

(b) FAA AIRWORTHINESS CERTIFICATION OF MISSILE DEFENSE SYSTEMS FOR COMMERCIAL AIRCRAFT.

(1) *IN GENERAL.*— As soon as practicable, but not later than the date of completion of Phase II of the Department of Homeland Security's counter-man-portable air defense system (MANPADS) development and demonstration program, the Administrator of the Federal Aviation Administration shall establish a process for conducting airworthiness and safety certification of missile defense systems for commercial aircraft certified as effective and functional by the Department of Homeland Security. The process shall require a certification by the Administrator that such systems can be safely integrated into aircraft systems and ensure airworthiness and aircraft system integrity.

(2) *CERTIFICATION ACCEPTANCE.*— Under the process, the Administrator shall accept the certification of the Department of Homeland Security that a missile defense system is effective and functional to defend commercial aircraft against MANPADSs.

(3) *EXPEDITIOUS CERTIFICATION.*— Under the process, the Administrator shall expedite the airworthiness and safety certification of missile defense systems for commercial aircraft certified by the Department of Homeland Security...

Air Cargo Security, December 17, 2004

SEC. 4051. PILOT PROGRAM TO EVALUATE USE OF BLAST RESISTANT CARGO AND BAGGAGE CONTAINERS.

(a) IN GENERAL.— Beginning not later than 180 days after the date of enactment of this Act, the Assistant Secretary of Homeland Security (Transportation Security Administration) shall carry out a pilot program to evaluate the use of blast-resistant containers for cargo and baggage on passenger aircraft to minimize the potential effects of detonation of an explosive device.

Aviation Security Policy, NSPD 47/HSPD 16, June 22, 2006[21]

NSPD-47/HSPD-16 details a strategic vision for aviation security while recognizing ongoing efforts, and directs the production of a National Strategy for Aviation Security and supporting plans. The supporting plans address the following areas: aviation transportation system security; aviation operational threat response; aviation transportation system recovery; air domain surveillance and intelligence integration; domestic outreach; and international outreach.

National Strategy for Aviation Security: An over-arching national strategy is necessary to optimize the coordination and integration of government-wide aviation security efforts. The Strategy sets forth U.S. Government agency roles and responsibilities, establishes planning and operations coordination requirements, and builds on current strategies, tools, and resources...

Security and Accountability for Every Port Act of 2006

SEC. 701. SECURITY PLAN FOR ESSENTIAL AIR SERVICE AND SMALL COMMUNITY AIRPORTS.

(a) IN GENERAL.— ...the Transportation Security Administration shall submit to Congress a security plan for—

(1) Essential Air Service airports in the United States; and

(2) airports whose community or consortia of communities receive assistance under the Small Community Air Service Development Program authorized under section 41743 of title 49, United States Code, and maintain, resume, or obtain scheduled passenger air carrier service with assistance from that program in the United States.

National Strategy For Aviation Security, March 26, 2007

The United States has a vital national interest in protecting its people, infrastructure, and other interests from threats in the Air Domain...

The Aviation Transportation System[2] comprises a broad spectrum of private and public sector elements, including: aircraft and airport operators; over 19,800 private and public use airports; the aviation sector; and a dynamic system of facilities, equipment, services, and airspace...

Three broad principles provide overarching guidance to the Strategy, its objectives, and its actions. First, the Nation must use the full range of its assets and capabilities to prevent the Air Domain from being exploited by terrorist groups, hostile nation-states, and criminals to commit acts against the United States, its people, its infrastructure, and its other interests. Second, the Nation must ensure the safe and efficient use of the Air Domain. Third, the Nation must continue to facilitate travel and commerce.

Threats to the Air Domain Threats to the Air Domain are numerous, complex, and adaptive...Threats focused on the Air Domain can be analyzed in two ways: by originator and by targets and tactics.

Threat Originators There are three main originators of threats: terrorist groups; hostile nation-states; and other criminals.

Terrorist Groups... Their ultimate goal in the Air Domain is to conduct multiple, simultaneous, catastrophic attacks exploiting the Aviation Transportation System ... Terrorist groups, best typified by al-Qa'ida and its affiliates, pose several threats to the Air Domain.

Targets and Tactics There are three primary categories of threats: to and from aircraft; to the Aviation Transportation System infrastructure; and from hostile exploitation of cargo.

Threats to and from Aircraft. Aircraft can be disaggregated into four categories of threats:

- large passenger aircraft;
- large all-cargo aircraft;
- small aircraft, such as aircraft used primarily to transport small numbers of people or to provide unique services, including light private and corporate aircraft, and helicopters; and
- non-traditional aircraft, such as unmanned aerial vehicles (UAVs), ultra-light aircraft, gliders, and aerial-application aircraft.

Threats to the Aviation Transportation System Infrastructure. Reported threats to Aviation Transportation System infrastructure, which comprises airports and those facilities and systems that are used to provide Air Navigation Services (ANS) and other important related services needed to support air operations in U.S. airspace, are relatively few. In part, this is due to the relatively low public profile of ANS infrastructure such as Air Traffic Control facilities and systems, the robustness and resilience of these systems due to many layers of redundancies, and the Nation's likely capacity to recover rapidly and thus limit the psychological or economic impact of any attack...

Threats from Hostile Exploitation of Cargo. The air-cargo industry is highly dynamic and encompasses a wide range of users, making it subject to potential exploitation by terrorists...

Aviation Transportation System Security Plan, Supporting Plan to the National Strategy for Aviation Security, March 26, 2007

Executive Summary ... The Aviation Transportation System Security Plan (Plan) continues, expands, and enhances efforts to further reduce vulnerabilities in all critical system areas. This Plan directs aggressive efforts to: (1) ensure that anyone entering or using the Aviation Transportation System has been identified and vetted or screened; (2) ensure the United States Government is taking all reasonable measures to detect and prevent the use of weapons against elements of the Air Domain, or to use the Aviation Transportation System to transport, become a weapon, or serve as a means of dispersal of weapons including Chemical, Biological, Radiological, Nuclear, or High-Yield Explosives (CBRNE)2, as well as liquid explosives; and (3) harden the critical elements of the Aviation Transportation System infrastructure against other forms of attack, such as Man-Portable Air Defense Systems (MANPADS) and stand-off weapons or cyber attack.

This Plan, along with the Aviation Operational Threat Response (AOTR) and Aviation Transportation System Recovery (ATSR) plans, addresses enhancements to the national-level Air Domain prevention-response-recovery capabilities of the United States Government. As such, these three plans are aligned in function. An examination of threats, vulnerabilities, and consequences has driven the generation of this Plan's components, with designation of lead agencies to address each major element. Although the ATSS, AOTR, and ATSR are separate and distinct plans, there is an anticipation of overlap in their execution. The ATSS, focusing on measures to prevent a terrorist attack, is expected to continue in effect even if an attack occurs...

Strategic Goals and Objectives This Plan supports five broad strategic actions from the National Strategy for Aviation Security:

- Maximize domain awareness
- Deploy layered security

---

[2] The Aviation Transportation System is defined as U.S. airspace, all manned and unmanned aircraft operating in that airspace, all U.S. aviation operators, airports, airfields, air navigation services, and related infrastructure, and all aviation-related industry.

- Promote a safe, efficient, and secure Aviation Transportation System
- Enhance international cooperation
- Assure continuity of the Aviation Transportation System. . .
- Although the focus of this Plan is on preventing a successful attack through reducing vulnerabilities, all recommendations or plan components must take into account all three components of risk: threat, vulnerabilities, and consequences.
- The ability to prevent a wide range of events/attacks with a scalable, flexible set of protective measures will help build resiliency into the Aviation Transportation System.
- Recognition that as a multi-layered system of systems, any one of the current or recommended measures in our layered security system can potentially be compromised, but together provide greatly enhanced security. The United States Government will address, enhance, and further strengthen all major layers and systems critical to risk reduction in aviation security.

Air Domain Surveillance and Intelligence Integration Plan, Supporting Plan to the National Strategy for Aviation Security, March 26, 2007

Executive Summary Air Domain awareness is the effective understanding of threats associated with the Air Domain that could impact the security, safety, or economy of the United States. Achieving such understanding requires close coordination across the United States Government to better integrate intelligence, information, and surveillance data, and analysis related to the Air Domain to facilitate a shared situational awareness across Federal, State, local, and tribal governments and private entities and foreign partners that have aviation security responsibilities. This Air Domain awareness supports a multitude of users across the full spectrum of aviation security and defense activities, including the prevention, response, and recovery activities described in the Aviation Transportation System Security, Aviation Operational Threat Response, and Aviation Transportation System Recovery plans. . . .

Scope This Plan directs the following:

- maximizing Air Domain awareness by improving and developing new capabilities that enable persistent and effective monitoring of all aircraft, cargo, people, and infrastructure in identified areas of interest and at designated times, consistent with the protection of civil liberties and privacy;
- collection and analysis of appropriate data, as well as methods for distributing these to a range of policy-makers and operational users, to inform their decision-making about threats emerging either at home or abroad;
- an approach that addresses the threats identified in NSPD-47/HSPD-16. . .

Aviation Operational Threat Response Plan, Supporting Plan To The National Strategy For Aviation Security, March 26, 2007

Executive Summary The Aviation Operational Threat Response Plan (Plan) directs the coordination, as appropriate, of the United States Government operational response to terrorist, criminal, and hostile state threats to, or attacks against, the United States and its interests in the Air Domain. This Plan is part of an active, layered, aviation security and defense in-depth. This Plan enhances our existing capabilities by directing the coordination, collaboration, and integration of United States Government national-level agency command centers, which includes for the purposes of this plan, operations centers. It enhances our capability to achieve coordinated, unified, timely, and effective planning and mission accomplishment to counter those threats that require immediate aviation response actions. This Plan supports the strategic objectives listed in NSPD-47/HSPD-16.

To execute the coordination requirements and response activities more effectively, this Plan directs lead and supporting Federal department and agency roles and responsibilities based on the following criteria: existing law, desired United States Government outcome, greatest potential impact of the threat, the response capabilities required, assets on-scene, and authority to act. This Plan directs immediate actions, generally short duration in nature, to counter the full range of airborne and ground-based aviation security threats. These threats include, but are not limited to, those identified in NSPD-47/HSPD-16: attacks using aircraft as weapons against ground-based targets; attacks against aircraft, including hijacking and air piracy; attacks using standoff weapons, including Man Portable Air Defense Systems (MANPADS) or weapons of mass destruction (WMD); and attacks against Aviation Transportation System (ATS) infrastructure.

For the purposes of this plan, Aviation Operational Threat Response (AOTR) execution begins when intelligence or other information is received that an incident is occurring and that an immediate response is necessary. AOTR execution concludes when the threat has been defeated or otherwise resolved. Specific operational response activities include, but are not limited to, the following: airborne interception and surface-to-air operations; onboard law enforcement response; aviation law enforcement ground interdiction and response and counterterrorism operations; interdiction and disposition of designated tracks of interest; and operational response to a domestic attack, or threat of attack, using standoff weapons such as MANPADS. This Plan does not address steady-state security actions taken during ambiguous or generalized periods of threat or vulnerability, conducted in accordance with the ATS Security plan. It also does not include post-attack incident response activities, conducted in accordance with the ATS Recovery plan.

This Plan, together with the ATS Security and ATS Recovery plans, address the national-level prevention-response-recovery aspects of the United States Government efforts to counter direct threats to, and attacks on, the United States in the Air Domain. As such, these three plans are synchronized in function, and facilitate and require the further synchronization of prevention-response-recovery execution at the operational and tactical levels.

Domestic Outreach Plan, Supporting Plan To The National Strategy For Aviation Security, March 26, 2007

Executive Summary The United States Government responded to the attacks of September 11, 2001, with an unambiguous, comprehensive increase in measures to enhance aviation security. It was quickly apparent that the active, layered aviation security and defense in-depth, which was the ultimate goal, would rely to a great degree on participation by aviation security partners at the State, local, and tribal levels, as well as within the Federal and private sectors. While there have been efforts to-date to inform and gain support from these organizations to achieve aviation security goals, the Domestic Outreach Plan provides strategic level guidance that will synchronize these efforts. In addition to the primary objective of providing a plan for conducting outreach to implement the other plans developed pursuant to NSPD-47/HSPD-16 more effectively, this plan also provides guidance for outreach in the event of a threat to or attack on the United States or another incident that disrupts in the Aviation Transportation System.

The recently established Aviation Government Coordinating Council (AGCC) and Aviation Sector Coordinating Council (ASCC) will be responsible for conducting outreach during the implementation process of the National Strategy for Aviation Security (National Strategy) and its supporting plans. In order to ensure that all appropriate stakeholders are involved as the plans move toward implementation, it will be important to use the AGCC and ASCC as fora for coordination.

The Plan outlines a framework for incident communications during a potential threat or after an attack on the United States or another incident that disrupts the Aviation Transportation System. This plan provides guidance for communications during aviation incidents for which major elements of the National Response Plan (NRP) are not activated.

Introduction The Domestic Outreach Plan (Plan) outlines a comprehensive engagement strategy that ensures that the interests of State, local, and tribal governments and the private sector are considered in the Federal Government's implementation of NSPD-47/HSPD-16 and future aviation security policy actions, as appropriate.

This Plan directs Federal departments and agencies to involve these stakeholders during the implementation of several of the supporting plans. With leadership from the Secretary of Homeland Security, this Plan relies on coordination with a variety of Federal government and external partners to identify stakeholders and leverage lessons learned through previous efforts included in HSPDs 5, 7, 8, and 13.[2] A key consideration in the implementation of the aviation security supporting plans is the benefits that could potentially be gained by engaging stakeholders in security enhancement efforts.

International Outreach Plan, Supporting Plan To The National Strategy For Aviation Security, March 26, 2007

Executive Summary The support of allies around the world is vital to the security of the nation, as events beyond our borders have an undeniable impact on United States' interests. . .

In accordance with NSPD-47/HSPD-16, the Secretary of State shall lead coordination of the United States' international outreach efforts to secure the Air Domain. The International Outreach Plan (Plan) sets forth a strategy to promote close cooperation with foreign partners, international and regional organizations, and the private sector to solicit international support for an improved global aviation security framework. This Plan advances the policies set forth by President Bush and will help to accomplish the President's vision of a fully coordinated United States Government effort to protect our interests in the Air Domain.

ADDITIONAL RESOURCES

TSA. http://www.tsa.gov/

Secure Flight Program, http://www.tsa.gov/what_we_do/layers/secureflight/index.shtm

FAA. http://www.faa.gov/

"Security of Air Cargo During Ground Transportation (Redacted)," Department of Homeland Security Inspector General OIG-10-09, Nov. 2009, http://www.dhs.gov/xoig/assets/mgmtrpts/OIGr_10-09_Nov09.pdf

"Aviation Security: A National Strategy and Other Actions Would Strengthen TSA's Efforts to Secure Commercial Airport Perimeters and Access Controls," Government Accountability Office, September 2009, GAO-09-399 http://www.gao.gov/new.items/d09399.pdf

[2]HSPD-5: "Management of Domestic Incidents;" HSPD-7: "Critical Infrastructure Identification, Prioritization, and Protection;" HSPD-8: "National Preparedness;" and, HSPD-13: "Maritime Security Policy."

Congress. Senate. Commerce, Science & Transportation Committee. "Aviation Safety: The Hudson River Midair Collision and the Safety Of Air Operations in Congested Space," September 15, 2009, http://commerce.senate.gov/public/index.cfm?FuseAction=Hearings.Hearing&Hearing_ID=524c62a9-f53c-4860-89fd-031c0ae97b06

Congress. House. Homeland Security Committee, General Aviation Security: Assessing Risks and the Road Ahead, July 15, 2009, http://homeland.house.gov/Hearings/index.asp?ID=204

Advanced Information on Private Aircraft Arriving and Departing the United States: Notice of Proposed Rulemaking. The proposed rule will require more detailed information to be filed with CBP's eAPIS system about arriving and departing private aircraft and persons onboard within a timeframe necessary to assess the risks that certain flights may pose to national security.

United States and Spain Formalize Arrangement to Interdict High-Risk Travelers,

July 1, 2009, Madrid, Spain—DHS Secretary Janet Napolitano met with Spanish Interior Minister Alfredo Pérez Rubalcaba today and signed a Declaration of Principles formalizing the Immigration Advisory Program (IAP)—which allows for the identification of high-risk travelers at foreign airports before they board aircraft bound for the United States—at Madrid Barajas International Airport.

The arrangement will help combat the use of fraudulent travel documents, prevent terrorists and other criminals from entering the United States, disrupt alien smuggling and promote cooperation between DHS and the Ministry of the Interior. "Protecting our nation from terrorism requires close coordination with our international allies," said Secretary Napolitano. "This collaboration enhances the capabilities of United States and Spain to facilitate legal travel and deter dangerous people attempting to enter our country."

IAP has operated as an extended pilot program in Madrid since February 11, 2008. Since its implementation, IAP Madrid has identified or prevented the travel of 402 improperly documented travelers, intercepted 23 persons with fraudulent documents, and stopped 10 terrorism-related suspects. http://www.dhs.gov/ynews/releases/pr_1246476969702.shtm

Aviation Safety: Better Data and Targeted FAA Efforts Needed to Identify and Address Safety Issues of Small Air Cargo Carriers, GAO-09-614, June 2009, http:// www.gao.gov/new.items/d09614.pdf

"Aviation Safety: The Role and Responsibility of Commercial Air Carriers and Employees," Testimony before Congress. Senate. Commerce, Science & Transportation Subcommittee, June 17, 2009, http://commerce.senate.gov/public/index.cfm?FuseAction=Hearings.Hearing&Hearing_ID=4e8e64ab-df44-4f79-b1b1-19f691b60d21

"TSA's Role in General Aviation Security," Department of Homeland Security, Office of Inspector General, OIG-09-69, May 27, 2009, http://www.dhs.gov/xoig/assets/mgmtrpts/OIG_09-69_May09.pdf

"Recovering from Transportation Disasters: Draft The National Transportation Recovery Strategy Draft, May 4, 2009." U.S. Department of Transportation, Draft. http://www.iaem.com/committees/GovernmentAffairs/documents/DRAFTNationalTransportationRecoveryStrategy_05-04-091.pdf (accessed 05-22-09).

"Aviation Security, TSA Has Completed Key Activities Associated with Implementing Secure Flight, but Additional Actions Are Needed to Mitigate Risks" Report to Congressional Committees, United States Government Accountability Office, May 2009, **GAO-09-292**, http://www.gao.gov/products/GAO-09-292

"Transportation Security Administration's Known Shipper Program,"Department of Homeland Security Inspector General OIG-09-35–(Redacted). March 2009. http://www.dhs.gov/xoig/assets/mgmtrpts/OIGr_09-35_Mar09.pdf

Transportation Security: Comprehensive Risk Assessments and Stronger Internal Controls Needed to Help Inform TSA Resource Allocation, Report to the Chairman, Committee on Homeland Security, House of Representatives, GAO, GAO-09-492, March 2009, https://www.hsdl.org/homesec/docs/gao/nps43-042309-01.pdf&code=7c43e2f4b70822dd875eb14876f72b8f

"National Aviation Security Policy, Strategy, and Mode-Specific Plans, Background and Considerations for Congress," Bart Elias, February 2, 2009, CRS RL34302. http://www.fas.org/sgp/crs/homesec/RL34302.pdf

C. MARITIME TRANSPORTATION SECURITY

The Maritime Transportation Security Act of 2002 begins with Congressional findings. It discusses port security and mandates the development of both National and Area Maritime Transportation Security Plans. The Intelligence Reform and Terrorism Prevention Act mandates that ship passengers and crew be screened against terrorist watch-lists. HSPD 13 provides a global perspective and defines the term, "maritime domain." The National Strategy for Maritime Security and its supporting plans provide a broad, policy-level analysis emphasizing a global perspective and the integration of worldwide commercial interests.

The Safe Ports Act adds to the existing documents and the Small Vessel Security Strategy closes the circle by involving previously uncontrolled small vessels in our national strategy.

SOURCES

- Maritime Transportation Security Act of 2002, November 25, 2002[22]
- Intelligence Reform and Terrorism Prevention Act, Title IV, Subtitle D, December 17, 2004[23]
- HSPD 13. Maritime Security Policy, December 21, 2004[24]
- Reducing Crime and Terrorism at America's Seaports Act of 2005[25]
- National Strategy for Maritime Security, September 2005[26]

- National Plan to Achieve Maritime Domain Awareness, October 2005[27]
- International Outreach and Coordination Strategy, November 2005[28]
- Maritime Transportation System Security Recommendations [Plan], October 2005[29]
- Maritime Commerce Security Plan, October 2005[30]
- The Maritime Infrastructure Recovery Plan, April 2006[31]
- Security and Accountability for Every Port Act Of 2006[32]
- Small Vessel Security Strategy, April 2008[33]

Maritime Transportation Security Act Of 2002[34]

An Act To amend the Merchant Marine Act, 1936, to establish a program to ensure greater security for United States seaports, and for other purposes.

Be it enacted by the Senate and House of Representatives of the United States of America in Congress assembled,

SEC. 1. SHORT TITLE; TABLE OF CONTENTS.

(a) SHORT TITLE.— This Act may be cited as the "Maritime Transportation Security Act of 2002,"

TITLE I—MARITIME TRANSPORTATION SECURITY

SEC. 101. FINDINGS.

The Congress makes the following findings:

(1) There are 361 public ports in the United States that are an integral part of our Nation's commerce.

(2) United States ports handle over 95 percent of United States overseas trade. The total volume of goods imported and exported through ports is expected to more than double over the next 20 years.

(3) The variety of trade and commerce carried out at ports includes bulk cargo, containerized cargo, passenger transport and tourism, and intermodal transportation systems that are complex to secure.

(4) The United States is increasingly dependent on imported energy for a substantial share of its energy supply, and a disruption of that share of supply would seriously harm consumers and our economy.

(5) The top 50 ports in the United States account for about 90 percent of all the cargo tonnage. Twenty-five United States ports account for 98 percent of all container shipments. Cruise ships visiting foreign destinations embark from at least 16 ports. Ferries in the United States transport 113,000,000 passengers and 32,000,000 vehicles per year.

(6) Ports often are a major locus of Federal crime, including drug trafficking, cargo theft, and smuggling of contraband and aliens.

(7) Ports are often very open and exposed and are susceptible to large scale acts of terrorism that could cause a large loss of life or economic disruption.

(8) Current inspection levels of containerized cargo are insufficient to counter potential security risks. Technology is currently not adequately deployed to allow for the nonintrusive inspection of containerized cargo.

(9) The cruise ship industry poses a special risk from a security perspective.

(10) Securing entry points and other areas of port facilities and examining or inspecting containers would increase security at United States ports.

(11) Biometric identification procedures for individuals having access to secure areas in port facilities are important tools to deter and prevent port cargo crimes, smuggling, and terrorist actions.

(12) United States ports are international boundaries that—

(A) are particularly vulnerable to breaches in security;

(B) may present weaknesses in the ability of the United States to realize its national security objectives; and

(C) may serve as a vector or target for terrorist attacks aimed at the United States.

(13) It is in the best interests of the United States—

(A) to have a free flow of interstate and foreign commerce and to ensure the efficient movement of cargo;

(B) to increase United States port security by establishing improving communication among law enforcement officials responsible for port security;

(C) to formulate requirements for physical port security, recognizing the different character and nature of United States port facilities, and to require the establishment of security programs at port facilities;

(D) to provide financial assistance to help the States and the private sector to increase physical security of United States ports;

(E) to invest in long-term technology to facilitate the private sector development of technology that will assist in the nonintrusive timely detection of crime or potential crime at United States ports;

(F) to increase intelligence collection on cargo and intermodal movements to address areas of potential threat to safety and security; and

(G) to promote private sector procedures that provide for in-transit visibility and support law enforcement efforts directed at managing the security risks of cargo shipments.

(14) On April 27, 1999, the President established the Interagency Commission on Crime and Security in United States Ports to undertake a comprehensive study of the nature and extent of the problem of crime in our ports, as well as the ways in which governments at all levels are responding. The Commission concluded that frequent crimes in ports include drug smuggling, illegal car exports, fraud, and cargo theft. Internal conspiracies are an issue at many ports and contribute to Federal crime. Criminal organizations are exploiting weak security at ports to commit a wide range of cargo crimes. Intelligence and information sharing among law enforcement agencies needs to be improved and coordinated at many ports. A lack of minimum physical and personnel security standards at ports and related facilities leaves many ports and port users very vulnerable. Access to ports and operations within ports is often uncontrolled. Security-related and detection-related equipment, such as small boats, cameras, large-scale x-ray machines, and vessel tracking devices, are lacking at many ports.

(15) The International Maritime Organization and other similar international organizations are currently developing a new maritime security system that contains the essential elements for enhancing global maritime security. Therefore, it is in the best interests of the United States to implement new international instruments that establish such a system.

SEC. 102. PORT SECURITY.

(a) IN GENERAL.— Title 46, United States Code, is amended by adding at the end the following new subtitle:

Subtitle VI—Miscellaneous "Chapter 701—PORT SECURITY."

§ 70101. Definitions

"For the purpose of this chapter:

"(1) The term 'Area Maritime Transportation Security Plan' means an Area Maritime Transportation Security Plan prepared under section 70103(b).

"(2) The term 'facility' means any structure or facility of any kind located in, on, under, or adjacent to any waters subject to the jurisdiction of the United States.

"(6) The term 'transportation security incident' means a security incident resulting in a significant loss of life, environmental damage, transportation system disruption, or economic disruption in a particular area.

§ 70102. United States Facility and Vessel Vulnerability Assessments

"(a) INITIAL ASSESSMENTS.— The Secretary shall conduct an assessment of vessel types and United States facilities on or adjacent to the waters subject to the jurisdiction of the United States to identify those vessel types and United States facilities that pose a high risk of being involved in a transportation security incident.

"(b) FACILITY AND VESSEL ASSESSMENTS.— (1) Based on the information gathered under subsection (a) of this section, the Secretary shall conduct a detailed vulnerability assessment of the facilities and vessels that may be involved in a transportation security incident. . .

§ 70103. Maritime Transportation Security Plans

"(a) NATIONAL MARITIME TRANSPORTATION SECURITY PLAN.— (1) The Secretary shall prepare a National Maritime Transportation Security Plan for deterring and responding to a transportation security incident.

"(2) The National Maritime Transportation Security Plan shall provide for efficient, coordinated, and effective action to deter and minimize damage from a transportation security incident. . .

"(b) AREA MARITIME TRANSPORTATION SECURITY PLANS.— (1) The Federal Maritime Security Coordinator shall—

"(A) submit to the Secretary an Area Maritime Transportation Security Plan for the area; and

"(B) solicit advice from the Area Security Advisory Committee required under this chapter, for the area to assure preplanning of joint deterrence efforts, including appropriate procedures for deterrence of a transportation security incident.

"(c) VESSEL AND FACILITY SECURITY PLANS.— (1) Within 6 months after the prescription of interim final regulations on vessel and facility security plans, an owner or operator of a vessel or facility described in paragraph (2) shall prepare and submit to the Secretary a security plan for the vessel or facility, for deterring a transportation security incident to the maximum extent practicable.

"(d) NONDISCLOSURE OF INFORMATION.— Notwithstanding any other provision of law, information developed under this chapter is not required to be disclosed to the public, including—

"(1) facility security plans, vessel security plans, and port vulnerability assessments; and

"(2) other information related to security plans, procedures, or programs for vessels or facilities authorized under this chapter.

§ 70104. Transportation Security Incident Response

"(a) FACILITY AND VESSEL RESPONSE PLANS.— The Secretary shall—

"(1) establish security incident response plans for vessels and facilities that may be involved in a transportation security incident...

§ 70105. Transportation Security Cards

"(a) PROHIBITION.— (1) The Secretary shall prescribe regulations to prevent an individual from entering an area of a vessel or facility that is designated as a secure area by the Secretary for purposes of a security plan for the vessel or facility ... unless the individual—

"(A) holds a transportation security card issued under this section and is authorized to be in the area in accordance with the plan; or

"(B) is accompanied by another individual who holds a transportation security card issued under this section and is authorized to be in the area in accordance with the plan.

§ 70106. Maritime Safety and Security Teams

"(a) IN GENERAL.— To enhance the domestic maritime security capability of the United States, the Secretary shall establish such maritime safety and security teams as are needed to safeguard the public and protect vessels, harbors, ports, facilities, and cargo in waters subject to the jurisdiction of the United States from destruction, loss or injury from crime, or sabotage due to terrorist activity, and to respond to such activity in accordance with the transportation security plans developed under section 70103.

"(b) MISSION.— Each maritime safety and security team shall be trained, equipped, and capable of being employed to—

"(1) deter, protect against, and rapidly respond to threats of maritime terrorism;

"(2) enforce moving or fixed safety or security zones established pursuant to law;

"(3) conduct high speed intercepts;

"(4) board, search, and seize any article or thing on or at, respectively, a vessel or facility found to present a risk to the vessel or facility, or to a port;

"(5) rapidly deploy to supplement United States armed forces domestically or overseas;

"(6) respond to criminal or terrorist acts within a port so as to minimize, insofar as possible, the disruption caused by such acts;

"(7) assist with facility vulnerability assessments required under this chapter; and

"(8) carry out other security missions as are assigned to it by the Secretary.

§ 70108. Foreign Port Assessment

"(a) IN GENERAL.— The Secretary shall assess the effectiveness of the antiterrorism measures maintained at—

"(1) a foreign port—

"(A) served by vessels documented under Chapter 121 of this title; or

"(B) from which foreign vessels depart on a voyage to the United States; and

"(2) any other foreign port the Secretary believes poses a security risk to international maritime commerce.

§ 70109. Notifying Foreign Authorities

"(a) IN GENERAL.— If the Secretary, after conducting an assessment under section 70108, finds that a port in a foreign country does not maintain effective antiterrorism measures, the Secretary shall notify the appropriate authorities of the government of the foreign country of the finding and recommend the steps necessary to improve the antiterrorism measures in use at the port.

§ 70110. Actions When Foreign Ports Not Maintaining Effective Antiterrorism Measures

"(a) IN GENERAL.— If the Secretary finds that a foreign port does not maintain effective antiterrorism measures, the Secretary—

"(1) may prescribe conditions of entry into the United States for any vessel arriving from that port, or any vessel carrying cargo or passengers originating from or transshipped through that port;

"(2) may deny entry into the United States to any vessel that does not meet such conditions; and

"(3) shall provide public notice for passengers of the ineffective antiterrorism measures.

§ 70113. Maritime Intelligence

"(a) IN GENERAL.— The Secretary shall implement a system to collect, integrate, and analyze information concerning vessels operating on or bound for waters subject to the jurisdiction of the United States, including information related to crew, passengers, cargo, and intermodal shipments.

§ 70114. Automatic Identification Systems

"(a) SYSTEM REQUIREMENTS.— (1) Subject to paragraph (2), the following vessels, while operating on the navigable waters of the United States, shall be equipped with and operate an automatic identification system under regulations prescribed by the Secretary:..

§ 70115. Long-Range Vessel Tracking System

"The Secretary may develop and implement a long-range automated vessel tracking system for all vessels in United States waters that are equipped with the Global Maritime Distress and Safety System or equivalent satellite technology.

Intelligence Reform And Terrorism Prevention Act, Title IV, Subtitle D, December 17, 2004

SEC. 4071. WATCH LISTS FOR PASSENGERS ABOARD VESSELS.

(a) WATCH LISTS.

(1) *IN GENERAL.—* As soon as practicable but not later than 180 days after the date of the enactment of this Act, the Secretary of Homeland Security shall—

    (A) implement a procedure under which the Department of Homeland Security compares information about passengers and crew who are to be carried aboard a cruise ship with a comprehensive, consolidated database containing information about known or suspected terrorists and their associates;

    (B) use the information obtained by comparing the passenger and crew information with the information in the database to prevent known or suspected terrorists and their associates from boarding such ships or to subject them to specific additional security scrutiny, through the use of "no transport" and "automatic selectee" lists or other means.

HSPD 13. Maritime Security Policy, December 21, 2004

I. BACKGROUND

For the purposes of this directive, "Maritime Domain" means all areas and things of, on, under, relating to, adjacent to, or bordering on a sea, ocean, or other navigable waterway, including all maritime-related activities, infrastructure, people, cargo, and vessels and other conveyances. Due to its complex nature and immense size, the Maritime Domain is particularly susceptible to exploitation and disruption by individuals, organizations, and States. The Maritime Domain facilitates a unique freedom of movement and flow of goods while allowing people, cargo, and conveyances to transit with anonymity not generally available by movement over land or by air. Individuals and organizations hostile to the United States have demonstrated a continuing desire to exploit such vulnerabilities.

The United States must deploy the full range of its operational assets and capabilities to prevent the Maritime Domain from being used by terrorists, criminals, and hostile States to commit acts of terrorism and criminal or other unlawful or hostile acts against the United States, its people, economy, property, territory, allies, and friends. . .

II. POLICY

The security of the Maritime Domain is a global issue. The United States, in cooperation with our allies and friends around the world and our State, local, and private sector partners, will work to ensure that lawful private and public activities in the Maritime Domain are protected against attack and criminal and otherwise unlawful or hostile exploitation. . .

It is the policy of the United States to take all necessary and appropriate actions, consistent with U.S. law, treaties and other international agreements to which the United States is a party, and customary international law as determined for the United States by the President, to enhance the security of and protect U.S. interests in the Maritime Domain, including the following:

- Preventing terrorist attacks or criminal acts or hostile acts in, or the unlawful exploitation of, the Maritime Domain, and reducing the vulnerability of the Maritime Domain to such acts and exploitation;

- Enhancing U.S. national security and homeland security by protecting U.S. population centers, critical infrastructure, borders, harbors, ports, and coastal approaches in the Maritime Domain;

- Expediting recovery and response from attacks within the Maritime Domain;

- Maximizing awareness of security issues in the Maritime Domain in order to support U.S. forces and improve United States Government actions in response to identified threats;

- Enhancing international relationships and promoting the integration of U.S. allies and international and private sector partners into an improved global maritime security framework to advance common security interests in the Maritime Domain; and

- Ensuring seamless, coordinated implementation of authorities and responsibilities relating to the security of the Maritime Domain by and among Federal departments and agencies. These actions must be undertaken in a manner that facilitates global commerce and preserves the freedom of the seas for legitimate military and commercial navigation and other legitimate activities as well as civil liberties and the rights guaranteed under the Constitution.

III. POLICY COORDINATION

The Maritime Security Policy Coordinating Committee (MSPCC) is hereby established, consistent with NSPD-1 and HSPD-1. The MSPCC... shall act as the primary forum for interagency coordination of the implementation of this directive... The MSPCC shall provide analysis of new U.S. policies, strategies, and initiatives relating to maritime security for consideration by the Deputies and Principals Committees of the NSC and the HSC, and subsequently by the NSC and the HSC...The MSPCC shall be co-chaired by an NSC staff representative selected by the Assistant to the President for National Security Affairs and an HSC representative selected by the Assistant to the President for Homeland Security...

V. POLICY ACTIONS

In concert with the development of a National Strategy for [M]aritime Security, the following actions shall be taken:

Maritime Domain Awareness (MDA). Maritime Domain Awareness is the effective understanding of anything associated with the global Maritime Domain that could impact the security, safety, economy, or environment of the United States. It is critical that the United States develop an enhanced capability to identify threats to the Maritime Domain as early and as distant from our shores as possible by integrating intelligence, surveillance, observation, and navigation systems into a common operating picture accessible throughout the United States Government.

Global Maritime Intelligence Integration. A robust and coordinated intelligence effort serves as the foundation for effective security efforts in the Maritime Domain. In support of this effort, I direct the Secretaries of Defense and Homeland Security, with the support of the Director of Central Intelligence, and in coordination with the Director of the National Counterterrorism Center (NCTC) and the Director of the Federal Bureau of Investigation (FBI), to use existing intelligence capabilities to integrate all available intelligence on a global basis regarding the location, identity, and operational capabilities and intentions of potential threats to U.S. interests in the Maritime Domain...

Domestic Outreach. A successful strategy to implement this directive must include coordination with State and local authorities and consultation with appropriate private sector persons and entities...

Coordination of International Efforts and International Outreach. Ensuring the security of the Maritime Domain must be a global effort... The Secretary of State shall lead the coordination of United States Government initiatives in the implementation of this directive with regard to activities with foreign governments and international organizations...

Maritime Threat Response. The Secretaries of Defense and Homeland Security... shall develop a comprehensive National Maritime Security Response Plan...

Maritime Infrastructure Recovery. Rapid recovery from an attack or similar disruption in the Maritime Domain is critical to the economic well-being of our Nation... The Secretary of Homeland Security... shall be responsible for the development of recommended minimum Federal standards... for maritime recovery operations, and shall develop comprehensive national maritime infrastructure recovery standards and a plan, ... shall focus on the restoration of physical assets and transportation systems....

Maritime Transportation System Security. The Secretary of Homeland Security... shall develop recommendations for improvements to the national and international regulatory framework with respect to licensing, carriage, communications, safety equipment, and other critical systems for all private vessels, including commercial vessels, operating in the Maritime Domain.

Maritime Commerce Security... the United States must promote global supply chain security practices to reduce the risk of terrorists or criminals acting against the United States from within the Maritime Domain. The Secretary of Homeland Security... shall lead a collaborative interagency effort... to develop a comprehensive international maritime supply chain security plan...

Reducing Crime and Terrorism at America's Seaports Act of 2005

SEC. 302. ENTRY BY FALSE PRETENSES TO ANY SEAPORT.

(a) IN GENERAL.— Section 1036 of title 18, United States Code, is amended–

    (4) ... by ... inserting the following:

...Sec. 26. Definition of Seaport

'As used in this title, the term 'seaport' means all piers, wharves, docks, and similar structures, adjacent to any waters subject to the jurisdiction of the United States, to which a vessel may be secured, including areas of land, water, or land and water under and in immediate proximity to such structures, buildings on or contiguous to such structures, and the equipment and materials on such structures or in such buildings.'.

SEC. 303. CRIMINAL SANCTIONS FOR FAILURE TO HEAVE TO, OBSTRUCTION OF BOARDING, OR PROVIDING FALSE INFORMATION.

(a) OFFENSE.— Chapter 109 of title 18, United States Code, is amended by adding at the end the following:
'Sec. 2237. Criminal sanctions for failure to heave to, obstruction of boarding, or providing false information
'(a)(1) It shall be unlawful for the master, operator, or person in charge of a vessel of the United States, or a vessel subject to the jurisdiction of the United States, to knowingly fail to obey an order by an authorized Federal law enforcement officer to heave to that vessel. . .

SEC. 304. CRIMINAL SANCTIONS FOR VIOLENCE AGAINST MARITIME NAVIGATION, PLACEMENT OF DESTRUCTIVE DEVICES.

(a) PLACEMENT OF DESTRUCTIVE DEVICES.

(1) *IN GENERAL.—* Chapter 111 of title 18, United States Code, as amended by subsection (a), is further amended by adding at the end the following:
'Sec. 2282A. Devices or dangerous substances in waters of the United States likely to destroy or damage ships or to interfere with maritime commerce

'(a) A person who knowingly places, or causes to be placed, in navigable waters of the United States, by any means, a device or dangerous substance which is likely to destroy or cause damage to a vessel or its cargo, cause interference with the safe navigation of vessels, or interference with maritime commerce (such as by damaging or destroying marine terminals, facilities, or any other marine structure or entity used in maritime commerce) with the intent of causing such destruction or damage, interference with the safe navigation of vessels, or interference with maritime commerce shall be fined under this title or imprisoned for any term of years, or for life; or both.
'(b) A person who causes the death of any person by engaging in conduct prohibited under subsection (a) may be punished by death.

(b) VIOLENCE AGAINST MARITIME NAVIGATION.

(1) *IN GENERAL.—* Chapter 111 of title 18, United States Code as amended by subsections (a) and (c), is further amended by adding at the end the following:
'Sec. 2282B. Violence against aids to maritime navigation
'Whoever intentionally destroys, seriously damages, alters, moves, or tampers with any aid to maritime . . . if such act endangers or is likely to endanger the safe navigation of a ship, shall be fined under this title or imprisoned for not more than 20 years, or both.'.

SEC. 305. TRANSPORTATION OF DANGEROUS MATERIALS AND TERRORISTS.

(a) TRANSPORTATION OF DANGEROUS MATERIALS AND TERRORISTS.— Chapter 111 of title 18, as amended by section 305, is further amended by adding at the end the following:
'Sec. 2283. Transportation of explosive, biological, chemical, or radioactive or nuclear materials

'(a) *IN GENERAL.—* Whoever knowingly transports aboard any vessel within the United States and on waters subject to the jurisdiction of the United States or any vessel outside the United States and on the high seas or having United States nationality an explosive or incendiary device, biological agent, chemical weapon, or radioactive or nuclear material, knowing that any such item is intended to be used to commit an offense . . . shall be fined under this title or imprisoned for any term of years or for life, or both.

'(b) *CAUSING DEATH.—* Any person who causes the death of a person by engaging in conduct prohibited by subsection (a) may be punished by death.

Sec. 2284. Transportation of Terrorists

'(a) IN GENERAL.— Whoever knowingly and intentionally transports any terrorist aboard any vessel within the United States and on waters subject to the jurisdiction of the United States or any vessel outside the United States and on the high seas or having United States nationality, knowing that the transported person is a terrorist, shall be fined under this title or imprisoned for any term of years or for life, or both.

Sec. 2292. Imparting or Conveying False Information

'(a) IN GENERAL.— Whoever imparts or conveys or causes to be imparted or conveyed false information, knowing the information to be false, concerning an attempt or alleged attempt being made or to be made, to do any act that would be a crime prohibited by this chapter or by chapter 111 of this title, shall be subject to a civil penalty of not more than

$5,000, which shall be recoverable in a civil action brought in the name of the United States.

'(b) MALICIOUS CONDUCT.— Whoever knowingly, intentionally, maliciously, or with reckless disregard for the safety of human life, imparts or conveys or causes to be imparted or conveyed false information, knowing the information to be false, concerning an attempt or alleged attempt to do any act which would be a crime prohibited by this chapter or by chapter 111 of this title, shall be fined under this title or imprisoned not more than 5 years.

The National Strategy For Maritime Security, September 2005

The safety and economic security of the United States depends upon the secure use of the world's oceans...

Maritime security is best achieved by blending public and private maritime security activities on a global scale into an integrated effort that addresses all maritime threats. The new National Strategy for Maritime Security aligns all Federal government maritime security programs ...

Sec. I Introduction—Maritime Security

...much of what occurs in the maritime domain with respect to vessel movements, activities, cargoes, intentions, or ownership is often difficult to discern. The oceans are increasingly threatened by illegal exploitation of living marine resources and increased competition over nonliving marine resources. Although the global economy continues to increase the value of the oceans' role as highways for commerce and providers of resources, technology and the forces of globalization have lessened their role as barriers. Thus, this continuous domain serves as a vast, ready, and largely unsecured medium for an array of threats by nations, terrorists, and criminals...

Defeating this array of threats to maritime security – including the threat or use of weapons of mass destruction (WMD) – requires a common understanding and a joint effort for action on a global scale.... Nations have a common interest in achieving two complementary objectives: to facilitate the vibrant maritime commerce that underpins economic security, and to protect against ocean-related terrorist, hostile, criminal, and dangerous acts...

Sec. II Threats to Maritime Security

...The maritime domain in particular presents not only a medium by which these threats can move, but offers a broad array of potential targets ... While the variety of actors threatening the maritime domain continues to grow in number and capability, they can be broadly grouped as nation-states, terrorists, and transnational criminals and pirates...

...Successful attacks in the maritime domain provide opportunities to cause significant disruption to regional and global economies ... Terrorists have indicated a strong desire

to use WMD ... Terrorists can also develop effective attack capabilities relatively quickly using a variety of platforms, including explosives-laden suicide boats and light aircraft; merchant and cruise ships as kinetic weapons to ram another vessel, warship, port facility, or offshore platform; commercial vessels as launch platforms for missile attacks; underwater swimmers to infiltrate ports; and unmanned underwater explosive delivery vehicles. Mines are also an effective weapon because they are low-cost, readily available, easily deployed, difficult to counter, and require minimal training. Terrorists can also take advantage of a vessel's legitimate cargo, such as chemicals, petroleum, or liquefied natural gas, as the explosive component of an attack. Vessels can be used to transport powerful conventional explosives or WMD for detonation in a port or alongside an offshore facility.

...Terrorists might attempt cyber attacks to disrupt critical information networks, or attempt to cause physical damage to information systems that are integral to the operation of marine transportation and commerce systems...

Environmental Destruction Intentional acts that result in environmental disasters can have far-reaching, negative effects on the economic viability and political stability of a region...

Sec. III Strategic Objectives

...Three broad principles provide overarching guidance to this Strategy. First, *preserving the freedom of the seas* is a top national priority. The right of vessels to travel freely in international waters, engage in innocent and transit passage, and have access to ports is an essential element of national security. The free, continuing, unthreatened intercourse of nations is an essential global freedom and helps ensure the smooth operation of the world's economy.

Second, the United States Government must *facilitate and defend commerce* to ensure this uninterrupted flow of shipping ... The adoption of a just-in-time delivery approach to shipping by most industries, rather than stockpiling or maintaining operating reserves of energy, raw materials, and key components, means that a disruption or slowing of the flow of almost any item can have widespread implications for the overall market, as well as upon the national economy.

Third, the United States Government must *facilitate the movement of desirable goods and people across our borders, while screening out dangerous people and material* ...

Embed Security into Commercial Practices Embed security into commercial practices to reduce vulnerabilities and facilitate commerce.

...Since 2001, the United States Government has developed and implemented a cargo container security strategy to identify, target, and inspect cargo containers before they reach U.S. ports...

Deploy Layered Security

DEPLOY LAYERED SECURITY TO UNIFY PUBLIC AND PRIVATE SECURITY MEASURES. The ability to achieve maritime security is contingent upon a layered security system that integrates the capabilities of governments and commercial interests throughout the world. The public and private sectors acting in concert can prevent terrorist attacks and criminal acts only by using diverse and complementary measures, rather than relying upon a single point solution.

Physical protection is a fundamental layer of security. Primary protection measures by government agencies include maritime security or enforcement zones, vessel movement control, and the inspection of targeted cargo. Security zones are established and enforced around designated fixed facilities, certain vessels in transit, and sensitive geographic areas to provide an exclusion zone for controlled access and use only by the government. Around these zones, the private sector employs other layers of physical security, such as access barriers, fencing, lighting, surveillance cameras, and guards, along with oversight procedures, to ensure system integrity for the critical infrastructure and key resources that they own and operate...

- The rapid and accurate identification of individuals for access to secure, restricted, and critical areas is a paramount protection measure that must be implemented by the private sector...
- Protection layers also include the positive control of high-interest vessels. Mandatory adherence to a national vessel-movement reporting system is required for all vessels entering and departing U.S. ports...
- Not all maritime assets, facilities, systems, or ports require equal protection...

Physical cargo inspection adds another layer of security. With as many as 30,000 containers entering the United States every day, physical inspection of all cargo would effectively shut down the entire U.S. economy, with ripple effects far beyond the seaports. Inspections on this scale are prohibitively expensive and often ineffective. Using mandatory reporting information provided by the private sector, the United States will screen all inbound cargo and inspect all cargo designated as high-risk and ideally prescreen it before loading. In addition, all inbound cargo will be screened for WMD or their components. Establishment of the Domestic Nuclear Defense Office will contribute to improving the detection of a nuclear device or fissile or radiological material entering the United States through the maritime domain.

Interdiction of personnel and materials Interdiction, whether against terrorist personnel, terrorist materiel support, WMD, or other contraband, will be carefully coordinated to ensure prioritization of intelligence, proper allocation of resources, and, when necessary, swift, decisive action.

The United States, along with its international partners, will monitor those vessels, cargoes, and people of interest from the point of origin, through intervening ports, to the point of entry to ensure the integrity of the transit, to manage maritime traffic routing, and, if necessary, to interdict or divert vessels for inspection and search...

Military and law enforcement response provides a fourth security layer. For maritime security operations on the high seas or in its exclusive economic zones, territorial seas, internal seas, inland rivers, ports, and waterways, the United States must have well-trained, properly equipped, and ready maritime security forces from both the U.S. Armed Forces and national, regional, State, and local law enforcement agencies to detect, deter, interdict, and defeat any potential adversary... maritime security forces must be visible, vigilant, well-trained, well-equipped, mobile, adaptive, and capable of generating effective presence quickly, randomly, and unpredictably.

Assure Continuity of the Marine Transportation System
Assure continuity of the marine transportation system to maintain vital commerce and defense readiness.

The United States will be prepared to maintain vital commerce and defense readiness in the aftermath of any terrorist attack or other similarly disruptive incidents that occur within the maritime domain. The response to such events should not default to an automatic shutdown of the marine transportation system; instead, the United States will be prepared to disengage selectively only designated portions, and immediately implement contingency measures to ensure the public's safety and continuity of commerce...

National Plan To Achieve Maritime Domain Awareness, Of the National Strategy For Maritime Security, October 2005

This Plan supports the strategic objectives and elements of the National Strategy for Maritime Security (NSMS), which emphasizes "the ability to know, so that preemptive or interdiction actions may be taken as early as possible."

Purpose Of The Plan ... The *National Plan to Achieve Maritime Domain Awareness* is a cornerstone for successful execution of the security plans tasked in NSPD-41/HSPD-13. This Plan serves to unify United States Government and support international efforts to achieve MDA across the Federal government, with the private sector and civil authorities within the United States, and with our allies and partners. It directs close coordination of a broad range of federal departments and agencies for this lasting endeavor...

Key Definitions

Maritime Domain is all areas and things of, on, under, relating to, adjacent to, or bordering on a sea, ocean, or other navigable waterway, including all maritime related activities, infrastructure, people, cargo, and vessels and other conveyances.

Maritime Domain Awareness is the effective understanding of anything associated with the maritime domain that could impact the security, safety, economy, or environment of the United States.

Global Maritime Community of Interest (GMCOI) includes, among other interests, the federal, state, and local departments and agencies with responsibilities in the maritime domain. Because certain risks and interests are common to government, business, and citizen alike, community membership also includes public, private and commercial stakeholders, as well as foreign governments and international stakeholders.

The following objectives constitute the MDA Essential Task List, which will guide the development of capabilities that the United States Government will pursue and when executed will provide the GMCOI an effective understanding of the maritime domain.

Guiding Principles The first step towards meeting these principles is to ensure GMCOI stakeholders, at all levels, know what they can do to help, how they can do it and, most importantly why Maritime Domain Awareness is in their collective best interest.

Unity of Effort. MDA requires a coordinated effort within and among the GMCOI...

Information Sharing and Integration. MDA depends upon unparalleled information sharing...The primary method for information sharing is the national maritime common operational picture (COP). The COP is a near-time, dynamically tailorable, networkcentric virtual information grid shared by all U.S. Federal, state, and local agencies with maritime interests and responsibilities...

International Outreach And Coordination Strategy, Of the National Strategy For Maritime Security, November 2005

I. Introduction ...The maritime domain encompasses trade routes, communication links, and natural resources vital to the global economy and the well-being of people in the United States and around the world...

II. Strategic Environment: The United States – A Maritime Nation In A Globalized World Covering 70% of the Earth's surface, the world's oceans and waterways offer all nationstates a network of enormous importance to their security and prosperity. These searoads have been a primary driver in the globalization of commercial interests, allowing all nations to participate in the ever-expanding global marketplace. This maritime transportation system is vast,

serving more than 100,000 ocean-going ships, as well as tens of millions of workboats, fishing vessels and recreational vessels. Every nation, including the United States, depends on an efficient and open maritime transportation system of waterways, ports, and intermodal connections to carry people and cargo to, from and along its shores. More than 40% of the world's merchant fleet enters United States harbors in any one year. Approximately 30,000 containers enter United States ports every day, and nearly 95% of all international commerce enters the United States through the nation's 361 public and private ports. Over 80% of the world's trade travels by water. The Maritime domain plays a critical role in the U.S. and global economies.

III. Strategic Goals To safeguard the maritime domain, the United States must forge cooperative partnerships and alliances with other nations, as well as with public and private stakeholders in the international community...

...this *Strategy* establishes the following Strategic Goals:

A *coordinated policy* for United States government maritime security activities with foreign governments, international and regional organizations, and the private sector.

Enhanced outreach to foreign governments, international and regional organizations, private sector partners, and the public abroad to solicit support for improved global maritime security.

[Appendix B of this document, not included here, lists approximately thirty-five maritime security initiatives as of July 2005.]

Maritime Transportation System Security Recommendations [Plan], October 2005

Executive Summary The Marine Transportation System (MTS) generates nearly $750 billion of the U.S. Gross Domestic Product and handles 95% of all overseas trade.[1] The MTS makes it possible for goods from other countries to be delivered to our front door step. It enables the U.S. to project military presence across the globe, creates jobs that support local economies, and provides a source of recreation for all Americans. Fundamentally, the Nation's economic and military security are closely linked to the health and functionality of the MTS.[2]

Improving security of the MTS while maintaining its functionality will not be an easy task. A complex system, the MTS is geographically diverse and composed of many types of assets, operations, and infrastructure that are operated and influenced by a diverse set of stakeholders, all of which play an

---

[1]American Association of Port Authorities. *America's Ports: Gateways to Global Trade.* Available: http://www.aapa-ports.org/industryinfo/americasports.htm, Last accessed: April 25, 2005.
[2]Interagency Task Force on Coast Guard Roles and Missions. *A Coast Guard for the Twenty First Century: Reportof the Interagency Task Force on U.S. Coast Guard Roles and Missions.* December 1999.

important role in the system. In addition, the MTS is an open system which enables many users to use and benefit from it at minimal cost. The complexity and openness of the MTS make it efficient, however these characteristics also present many challenges to those trying to improve system security.

To overcome these challenges, the cooperation of all stakeholders is paramount and is central to improving security. Envision Maritime Transportation System Security as:

A systems-oriented security regime built upon layers of protection and defense-in-depth that effectively mitigates critical system security risks, while preserving the functionality and efficiency of the MTS. Understanding the most effective security risk management strategies involves cooperation and participation of both domestic and international stakeholders acting at strategic points in the system, the U.S. seeks to improve security through a cooperative and cohesive effort involving all stakeholders.

This vision can further be thought of as a series of security nets providing layers of protection that are actualized by the following strategic recommendations...

A Systems View The MTS is a complex system with many types of assets, operations, and infrastructure as well as a widely diverse set of stakeholders. From a systems perspective, the MTS is a **network** of maritime operations that interface with shoreside operations at intermodal connections as part of overall global supply chains or domestic commercial operations...

Maritime Commerce Security Plan, Of the National Strategy For Maritime Security, October 2005[35]

I. Introduction ...The Maritime Commerce Security Plan contains recommendations to promote international supply chain security...

This is a risk management plan. As such, it is dependent on reliable information and intelligence to evaluate threats and assess risk. For this reason, the National Plan to Achieve Maritime Domain Awareness and the Global Maritime Intelligence Integration Plan are very important to the success of the Maritime Commerce Security Plan.

All of the component plans of the national strategy provide important support for the improvement of supply chain security. None of these plans should be considered as an independent solution, but together they form an integrated strategy.

Containerized cargo has made the maritime transportation process so efficient that transportation costs are no longer a significant barrier to international trade. Low transportation costs combined with free trade agreements have created an explosive growth in global trade, raising our standard of living. This efficient global supply chain now stretches from the far reaches of the planet directly into the heartland of America...

The Challenge ...The maritime transportation system is vulnerable because it could be used as a conduit for terrorists and their weapons...Maritime commerce could be used to transport a wide spectrum of threats...

There is some debate about calculating the economic impact of even a brief closure of a major seaport. Some estimates run into the millions of dollars. Other estimates suggest that the economic cost would be in the billions. Nevertheless, there is agreement that any sustained closure of the United States' major seaports will have a significant and rapidly expanding impact on the economy.[3]

III. The Maritime Commerce Security Plan The Goal The goal of the Maritime Commerce Security Plan is to improve the security of the maritime supply chain...

The End State The desired end state of the Maritime Commerce Security Plan is a fast, safe, efficient, and secure supply chain that transports only authorized persons and cargo.

Scope The Maritime Commerce Security Plan is focused on the maritime component of international supply chain security. As such, the focus is on maritime cargo...

The Framework In its simplest form, maritime commerce security requires that the cargo is secure when it is loaded, and that it remains secure during transit. The framework to achieve this objective is best described in terms of five parts: (1) accurate data, (2) secure cargo, (3) secure vessels/ports, (4) secure transit, and (5) international standards and compatible regulations.

The Maritime Infrastructure Recovery Plan, National Strategy For Maritime Security, April 2006

The MIRP contains procedures for recovery management and provides mechanisms for national, regional, and local decision-makers to set priorities for redirecting commerce, a primary means of restoring domestic cargo flow. This plan is employed when the Secretary of Homeland Security declares an actual or threatened Transportation Security Incident (TSI; 33 CFR 101.105)... to be an Incident of National

---

[3]For further discussion on the economic impact see:

Stephen S. Cohen, *Economic Impact of a West Coast Dock Shutdown*, University of California at Berkeley, January 2002 (http://www.portmod.org/news/2002/May%202/Cohen%20Final%20Jan%202002.pdf);

Organisation for Economic Co-operation and Development, *Security in Maritime Transport: Risk Factors and Economic Impact* Maritime Transport Committee, July 2003 (http://www.oecd.org/dataoecd/63/13/4375896.pdf); and

Peter V. Hall,"We'd Have to Sink the Ships, Impact Studies and the 2002 West Coast Port Lockout," *Economic Development Quarterly*, Vol. 18, No. 4, November 2004.

Significance (INS), in accordance with the criteria set out in the National Response Plan (NRP) and HSPD-5.

Any such TSI declared to be an INS accordingly is referred to as a "national TSI." Additionally, the MIRP reflects the organizational constructs detailed in the NRP . . .

Following an incident that triggers the implementation of this plan, the MIRP is used to guide the designees of the Secretary of Homeland Security in the decision making process to maintain the nation's MTS operational capabilities, and if compromised, to restore transportation capabilities.

Decision-making affecting the nation's entire MTS draws on both domestic and international resources for recovery. The operational decisions to facilitate the diversion of cargo to alternate sites, including foreign ports, will be based on just-in-time information; currently there is no recognized methodology or uniform standards for measuring either domestic or foreign port cargo-handling capacity. Information of this type is necessary to support recovery efforts; however, it is not currently available. The need for port cargo-handling reserve capacity information is addressed in the Next Steps/Recommendations Section of this plan.

Since this plan focuses on maritime transportation capabilities as a system, it only addresses the restoration of individual physical assets to restore the MTS. The vast majority of maritime transportation infrastructure assets are privately owned and operated. The decision to repair, replace, or rebuild private physical assets is a private sector decision. However, the federal government acknowledges that federal assistance may be required to help private industry in restoring critical cargo-handling infrastructure. Additionally, the plan recognizes that further study is needed to determine how the federal government can provide assistance or create incentives to private maritime stakeholders to establish sufficient critical cargo-handling infrastructure . . .

Purpose The purpose of the MIRP is to establish a comprehensive approach to recover from a national TSI.

Objective The primary objective of the MIRP is to provide guidance for federal decision makers to use in restoring maritime transportation . . .

Security and Accountability for Every Port Act of 2006, or Safe Port Act[36]

An Act to improve maritime and cargo security through enhanced layered defenses, and for other purposes. Be it enacted by the Senate and House of Representatives of the United States of America in Congress assembled,

SEC. 1. SHORT TITLE; TABLE OF CONTENTS.

(a) SHORT TITLE.— This Act may be cited as the "Security and Accountability For Every Port Act of 2006" or the "SAFE Port Act".

SEC. 101. AREA MARITIME TRANSPORTATION SECURITY PLAN TO INCLUDE SALVAGE RESPONSE PLAN.

SEC. 104. TRANSPORTATION SECURITY CARD.

(a) IN GENERAL.— Section 70105 of title 46, United States Code, is amended by adding at the end the following:

"(i) *IMPLEMENTATION SCHEDULE.—* In implementing the transportation security card program under this section, the Secretary shall–

"(1) establish a priority for each United States port based on risk, including vulnerabilities assessed under section 70102; and

"(2) implement the program, based upon such risk and other factors as determined by the Secretary, at all facilities regulated under this chapter at–

"(A) the 10 United States ports that the Secretary designates top priority not later than July 1, 2007;

"(B) the 40 United States ports that are next in order of priority to the ports described in subparagraph (A) not later than January 1, 2008; and

"(C) all other United States ports not later than January 1, 2009.

"(j) *TRANSPORTATION SECURITY CARD PROCESSING DEADLINE.—* Not later than January 1, 2009, the Secretary shall process and issue or deny each application for a transportation security card under this section for individuals with current and valid merchant mariners' documents on the date of the enactment of the SAFE Port Act.

"(k) *DEPLOYMENT OF TRANSPORTATION SECURITY CARD READERS.*

"(1) *PILOT PROGRAM.* "(A) In general.—The Secretary shall conduct a pilot program to test the business processes, technology, and operational impacts required to deploy transportation security card readers at secure areas of the marine transportation system.

"(B) Geographic locations.—The pilot program shall take place at not fewer than 5 distinct geographic locations, to include vessels and facilities in a variety of environmental settings.

"(2) Correlation with transportation security cards.–

"(A) In general.—The pilot program described in paragraph (1) shall be conducted concurrently with the issuance of the transportation security cards described in subsection (b) to ensure card and card reader interoperability.

SEC. 108. ESTABLISHMENT OF INTERAGENCY OPERATIONAL CENTERS FOR PORT SECURITY.

(a) IN GENERAL.— Chapter 701 of title 46, United States Code, is amended by inserting after section 70107 the following:

''Sec. 70107A. Interagency operational centers for port security

''(a) *IN GENERAL.*— The Secretary shall establish interagency operational centers for port security at all high-priority ports not later than 3 years after the date of the enactment of the SAFE Port Act.

''(d) *SECURITY INCIDENTS.*— During a transportation security incident on or adjacent to waters subject to the jurisdiction of the United States, the Coast Guard Captain of the Port designated by the Commandant of the Coast Guard in a maritime security command center described in subsection (a) shall act as the incident commander, unless otherwise directed by the President.

SEC. 109. NOTICE OF ARRIVAL FOR FOREIGN VESSELS ON THE OUTER CONTINENTAL SHELF.

(a) NOTICE OF ARRIVAL.— Not later than 180 days after the date of the enactment of this Act, the Secretary of the department in which the Coast Guard is operating shall update and finalize the rulemaking on notice of arrival for foreign vessels on the Outer Continental Shelf.

SEC. 113. PORT SECURITY TRAINING PROGRAM.

(a) IN GENERAL.— The Secretary . . . shall establish a Port Security Training Program (referred to in this section as the ''Training Program'') for the purpose of enhancing the capabilities of each facility required to submit a plan under section 70103(c) of title 46, United States Code, to prevent, prepare for, respond to, mitigate against, and recover from threatened or actual acts of terrorism, natural disasters, and other emergencies.

(b) REQUIREMENTS.— The Training Program shall provide validated training that–

(1) reaches multiple disciplines, including Federal, State, and local government officials, commercial seaport personnel and management, and governmental and nongovernmental emergency response providers;

(2) provides training at the awareness, performance, and management and planning levels;

(3) utilizes multiple training mediums and methods;

(4) addresses port security topics, including–

(A) facility security plans and procedures, how security plans and procedures are adjusted when threat levels increase;

(B) facility security force operations and management;

(C) physical security and access control at facilities;

(D) methods of security for preventing and countering cargo theft;

(E) container security;

(F) recognition and detection of weapons, dangerous substances, and devices;

(G) operation and maintenance of security equipment and systems;

(H) security threats and patterns;

(I) security incident procedures, including procedures for communicating with governmental and nongovernmental emergency response providers; and

(J) evacuation procedures;

(7) addresses security requirements under facility security plans; and

(8) educates, trains, and involves individuals in neighborhoods around facilities required to submit a plan under section 70103(c) of title 46, United States Code, on how to observe and report security risks.

SEC. 115. FACILITY EXERCISE REQUIREMENTS.

The Secretary of the Department in which the Coast Guard is operating shall require each high risk facility to conduct live or full-scale exercises . . . not less frequently than once every 2 years, in accordance with the facility security plan required under section 70103(c) of title 46, United States Code.

Subtitle C—Port Operations

SEC. 121. DOMESTIC RADIATION DETECTION AND IMAGING.

(a) SCANNING CONTAINERS.— Subject to section 1318 of title 19, United States Code, not later than December 31, 2007, all containers entering the United States through the 22 ports through which the greatest volume of containers enter the United States by vessel shall be scanned for radiation. To the extent practicable, the Secretary shall deploy next generation radiation detection technology.

(e) OTHER WEAPONS OF MASS DESTRUCTION THREATS.— Not later than 180 days after the date of the enactment of this Act, the Secretary shall submit to the appropriate congressional committees a report on the feasibility of, and a strategy for, the development of equipment to detect and prevent shielded nuclear and radiological threat material and chemical, biological, and other weapons of mass destruction from entering the United States.

(i) *INTERMODAL RAIL RADIATION DETECTION TEST CENTER.*

(1) ESTABLISHMENT.— In accordance with subsection (b), and in order to comply with this section, the Secretary shall establish an Intermodal Rail Radiation Detection Test Center (referred to in this subsection as the "Test Center").

SEC. 122. INSPECTION OF CAR FERRIES ENTERING FROM ABROAD.

Not later than 120 days after the date of the enactment of this Act, the Secretary . . . shall seek to develop a plan for the inspection of passengers and vehicles before such passengers board, or such vehicles are loaded onto, a ferry bound for a United States facility . . .

SEC. 123. RANDOM SEARCHES OF CONTAINERS.

Not later than 1 year after the date of the enactment of this Act, the Secretary, acting through the Commissioner, shall develop and implement a plan, utilizing best practices for empirical scientific research design and random sampling, to conduct random searches of containers in addition to any targeted or preshipment inspection of such containers required by law or regulation or conducted under any other program conducted by the Secretary . . .

SEC. 128. CENTER OF EXCELLENCE FOR MARITIME DOMAIN AWARENESS.

(a) ESTABLISHMENT.— The Secretary shall establish a university-based Center for excellence for Maritime Domain Awareness . . .

Small Vessel Security Strategy, April 2008

Foreword Since the terrorist attacks of September 11, 2001, maritime security efforts have focused primarily on large commercial vessels, cargoes, and crew. Efforts to address the small vessel[1] environment have largely been limited to

---

[1] Small vessels are characterized as any watercraft regardless of method of propulsion, less than 300 gross tons. Small vessels can include commercial fishing vessels, recreational boats and yachts, towing vessels, uninspected passenger vessels, or any other commercial vessels involved in foreign or U.S. voyages.

traditional safety and basic law enforcement concerns. Small vessels are, however, readily vulnerable to potential exploitation by terrorists, smugglers of weapons of mass destruction (WMDs), narcotics, aliens, and other contraband, and other criminals. Small vessels have also been successfully employed overseas by terrorists to deliver Waterborne Improvised Explosive Devices (WBIEDs). . .

Introduction

PURPOSE OF THE STRATEGY The intent of the *Small Vessel Security Strategy* (SVSS) is to reduce potential security and safety risks from small vessels through the adoption and implementation of a coherent system of regimes, awareness, and security operations that strike the proper balance between fundamental freedoms, adequate security, and continued economic stability. Additionally, the strategy is intended to muster the help of the small vessel community in reducing risks in the maritime domain . . .

SCOPE The SVSS is designed to guide efforts to mitigate the potential security risks arising from small vessels operating in the maritime domain. While guiding DHS efforts, this strategy acknowledges that to effectively reduce risk, all maritime security partners—Federal, state, local, and Tribal partners and the private sector as well as international partners—must work together to develop, implement, and undertake cooperative actions to reduce both security and safety risks from misuse of small vessels.

The following are some of the security concerns presented by small vessels:

- Small vessels operate (of ten routinely and with ease) in close proximity to critical infrastructure (CI) and key resources (KR), as well as major transportation channels and military ships, which may be potential high-profile targets.
- There is a lack of a centralized access to hull identification and vessel registration (owner) data.
- The ability to identify small vessel operators is limited because of unev en requirements for small vessel user certification and documentation.
- There are very limited Advance Notice of Arrival (ANOA) requirements for most recreational small vessels arriving from abroad.[12]
- There is limited awareness among small vessel operators of arrival reporting requirements and limited resources to enforce requirements, making enforceability of the small vessel arrival reporting process difficult.

---

[12] CBP APIS requires all commercial vessels to provide advance manifests of crew and passengers. Within the USCG Seventh District (specifically in southeast Florida) there is a requirement for ANOA on recreational vessels.

- There is limited ability to screen for weapons of mass destruction (WMDs), especially chemical and biological agents.
- Among the large population of small vessel operators, there is a longstanding public expectation of totally unregulated access and use of U.S. waterways.

Offsetting these security concerns are the small vessel community's contributions to security:

- An abundance of geographically dispersed small vessels providing a large number of "eyes on the water" that would be impossible to replace using only government assets.
- An immense population of small vessel operators whose presence on U.S. waters can serve as a deterrent by identifying suspicious activities, given their adequate education and training.
- Willing volunteer partners to assist in providing the initial response capability for maritime incidents.
- A wealth of professional mariners and recreational boaters who understand the local waterways and are willing to assist in developing methods to reduce risk in the maritime domain.

...The four scenarios of gravest concern in using small vessels in terrorist-related attacks have been identified as:

a. Domestic Use of Waterborne Improvised Explosive Devices (WBIEDs);

b. Conveyance for smuggling weapons (including WMDs) into the United States;

c. Conveyance for smuggling terrorists into the United States; and

d. Waterborne platform for conducting a stand-off attack (e.g. Man-Portable Air-Defense System (MANPADS) attacks).

ADDITIONAL RESOURCES

"The Cargo-Screening Clog: Why the Maritime Mandate Needs to Be Re-examined," by Jena Baker McNeill and Jessica Zuckerman, the Heritage Foundation, January 13, 2010, http://s3.amazonaws.com/thf_media/2010/pdf/bg_2357.pdf

"Review of United States Coast Guard's Certification of Maritime Awareness Global Network (MAGNET) (Unclassified Summary)," Department of Homeland Security Inspector General OIG-10-07, October 2009, http://www.dhs.gov/xoig/assets/mgmtrpts/OIG_10-07_Oct09.pdf

"CBP's Ability to Detect Biological and Chemical Threats in Maritime Cargo Containers," (Redacted), The Department of Homeland Security Office of Inspector General, OIG-10-01, October 2009, http://www.dhs.gov/xoig/assets/mgmtrpts/OIG_10-01_Oct09.pdf

Supporting Maritime Interoperability for the Common Defense, Common Defense Quarterly, By Jim Churchill, George Galdorisi and Stephanie Hszieh, July 2009, http://commondefensequarterly.com/CDQ2/maritime.htm

"Navy Role In Irregular Warfare and Counterterrorism: Background and Issues for Congress," Ronald O'Rourke, June 4, 2009, CRS, RS22373. http://www.fas.org/sgp/crs/natsec/RS22373.pdf

...I am proud to introduce the first revision of *Coast Guard Publication 1, U.S. Coast Guard: America's Maritime Guardian* (Pub 1). Since its original printing in 2002, Pub 1 has served as our capstone doctrine. It defines our principles and culture. It describes our history, our missions, our purpose, and our Guardian Ethos. It communicates who and what the Coast Guard is, what we do, and how we accomplish our missions. Commandant's Letter of Promulgation, May 2009. http://www.uscg.mil/top/about/doc/Pub1_May09.pdf

D. RAIL TRANSPORTATION

SOURCES

- DOT Federal Railroad Administration Action Plan for Addressing Critical Railroad Safety Issues, May 16, 2005[37]
- Rail Safety and Security, Testimony of Joseph H. Boardman, Administrator, Federal Railroad Administration, before the Committee on Commerce, Science, and Transportation, United States Senate, January 18, 2007[38]
- Title XV, Implementing Recommendations of the 9/11 Commission Act, August 3, 2007[39]
- DOT Federal Railroad Administration, National Rail Safety Action Plan, Final Report, 2005–2008, May 2008[40]
- Rail Security, Securing Our Nation's Rail Systems, TSA Website[41]
- Fiscal Year 2009 Freight Rail Security Grant Program[42]
- Fiscal Year 2009 Freight Rail Security Grant Program DHS[43]

DOT Federal Railroad Administration, Action Plan, Railroad Safety Issues, May 16, 2005

Introduction The railroad industry's overall safety record has improved over the last decade and most safety trends are moving in the right direction. However, significant train accidents continue to occur, and the train accident rate has not shown substantive improvement in recent years. Moreover, recent train accidents have highlighted specific issues that need prompt government and industry attention, and the strong growth of rail and highway traffic continue to drive up exposure at highway-rail grade crossings. The Federal Railroad Administration (FRA) is aggressively addressing these critical issues and implementing the plan outlined below to improve railroad safety.

The FRA's safety program is increasingly guided by careful analysis of accident, inspection, and other safety data. FRA attempts to direct both its regulatory and compliance efforts toward those areas involving the highest safety risks. This proactive approach to managing risks is constantly being honed and improved. This action plan embodies that approach and will:

- Target the most frequent, highest risk causes of accidents;
- Focus FRA's oversight and inspection resources; and
- Accelerate research efforts that have the potential to mitigate the largest risks.

The FRA's plan includes initiatives in several areas: reducing human factor-caused train accidents; acting to address the serious problem of fatigue among railroad operating employees; improving track safety; enhancing hazardous materials safety and emergency preparedness; better focusing FRA's resources (inspections and enforcement) on areas of greatest safety concern; and improving highway-rail grade crossing safety.

... the great majority of train accidents are caused by track and human factors, and human factor accidents are growing in number. The causes of train accidents are generally grouped into five categories: human factors, track and structures, equipment, signal and train control, and miscellaneous. Two categories of accidents–those caused by defective track and those caused by human factors–comprise more than 70 percent of all train accidents and a very high percentage of serious train accidents are, accordingly, the major target areas for improving the accident rate. In recent years, most of the serious events involving train collisions or derailments resulting in release of hazardous materials, or harm to rail passengers, have been caused by human factor or track causes ...

Addressing Fatigue Fatigue has long been a fact of life for many railroad operating employees, given their long and often unpredictable work hours and fluctuating schedules ...

Improving Track Safety Track-caused accidents comprised 34 percent of all train accidents over the last five years ...

Improving Hazardous Materials Safety and Emergency Response Capability Generally, the rail industry's record on transporting hazardous materials is very impressive ...

Ensure that emergency responders have timely access to hazardous materials information.

Rail Safety and Security, Testimony of Joseph H. Boardman, Administrator, Federal Railroad Administration, before the Committee on Commerce, Science, and Transportation, United States Senate, January 18, 2007

Chairman Inouye, Vice Chairman Stevens, and other members of the Committee, I am pleased to be here today to testify, on behalf of the Secretary of Transportation, about the security of our Nation's passenger and freight railroad network and the efforts that the Department of Transportation (DOT) is making to enhance rail safety and security.[44]

The Federal Railroad Administration's (FRA) primary mission is to promote the safety of the U.S. railroad industry and to reduce the number and severity of accidents and incidents arising from railroad operations. Our railroad safety mission necessarily includes our involvement in railroad security issues.

The U.S. Department of Homeland Security (DHS) and its Transportation Security Administration (TSA) have primary responsibility for transportation security, with FRA providing support in the railroad sector. FRA works closely with TSA and the railroad industry on a daily basis in addressing railroad security and safety issues, participates in the Government Coordinating Council for Rail, and contributed its expertise to the National Strategy for Transportation Security and the National Infrastructure Protection Plan ...

Overview of the Railroad Industry The U.S. railroad network is a vital link in the Nation's transportation system and is critical to the economy, national defense, and public health. Passenger and freight railroads operate over 170,000 route miles of track and employ over 232,000 workers ...

Amtrak, the Alaska Railroad Corporation, and commuter railroads provide passenger rail service to more than 500 million passengers yearly. Passenger operators face many challenges in their efforts to provide a secure public transportation environment. By definition, the systems are open, providing numerous points of access and egress leading to high passenger turnover and making them difficult to monitor effectively. Amtrak, for example, operates as many as 300 trains per day serving over 500 stations in 46 States, and Amtrak trains use tracks owned by freight railroads except for operations in the Northeast Corridor and in Michigan.

Privately-owned freight railroads connect industries and businesses with each other across the country and with markets overseas, moving 42 percent of all intercity freight, measured in ton-miles, including 67 percent of the coal used by electric utilities to produce power, and chemicals used in manufacturing and water purification. Seven Class I railroads haul over 90 percent of the rail cargo in the U.S., with the remaining 10 percent being transported by 30 regional railroads and over 500 local railroads. Typically railroads move about 1.7 to 1.8 million carloads of hazardous materials (hazmat) yearly, with roughly 105,000 of these carloads being toxic inhalation hazard (TIH) materials, such as chlorine and anhydrous ammonia. Over 64 percent of TIH materials are currently transported by rail . . .

Since the September 11th terrorist atrocities, FRA has been actively engaged in the railroad industry's response to the terrorist threat. The railroads have developed their own security plans, and FRA has worked with the railroads, rail labor, and law enforcement personnel to develop the Railway Alert Network, which permits timely distribution of information and intelligence on security issues.

Working with DOT's Federal Transit Administration (FTA), we have participated in security risk assessments on commuter railroads, and we have conducted security risk assessments of Amtrak as well . . .

In September 2004, DOT and DHS entered into a memorandum of understanding (MOU) concerning their respective roles on security issues.

The MOU notes that DHS has primary responsibility for security in all modes of Transportation but also recognizes that DOT has responsibilities in the area of transportation security.

The MOU reflects the agencies' shared commitment to a systems risk-based approach and to development of practical solutions, recognizing that each agency brings core competencies, legal authorities, resources, and expertise to the railroad mission . . .

Freight Railroad Security Railroads have voluntarily developed and adopted security plans based on comprehensive risk analyses, and the national intelligence community's best practices, that address the security of not only hazmat but of freight in general . . .

DHS has provided funding to the Railroad Research Foundation, a nonprofit organization devoted to sustaining a safe and productive railroad industry, to develop a Web-based tool to calculate rail route specific hazmat risks, and assist in route selection decisions. This tool would be available to rail carriers in performing route analysis, and to DOT, TSA, and government emergency planners.

Title XV, Implementing Recommendations of the 9/11 Commission Act, August 3, 2007

SEC. 1511. RAILROAD TRANSPORTATION SECURITY RISK ASSESSMENT AND NATIONAL STRATEGY.

(a) RISK ASSESSMENT.— The Secretary shall establish a Federal task force . . . to complete, within 6 months of the date of enactment of this Act, a nationwide risk assessment of a terrorist attack on railroad carriers.

(b) NATIONAL STRATEGY.

(1) *REQUIREMENT.—* Not later than 9 months after the date of enactment of this Act . . . the Secretary . . . shall develop and implement the modal plan for railroad transportation, entitled the "National Strategy for Railroad Transportation Security".

SEC. 1513. RAILROAD SECURITY ASSISTANCE.

(a) SECURITY IMPROVEMENT GRANTS.— (1) The Secretary . . . is authorized to make grants to railroad carriers, the Alaska Railroad, security-sensitive materials offerors who ship by railroad, owners of railroad cars used in the transportation of security-sensitive materials, State and local governments (for railroad passenger facilities and infrastructure not owned by Amtrak), and Amtrak for intercity passenger railroad and freight railroad security improvements described in subsection (b) as approved by the Secretary . . .

SEC. 1514. SYSTEMWIDE AMTRAK SECURITY UPGRADES.

(a) IN GENERAL.

(1) *GRANTS.—* Subject to subsection (b), the Secretary . . . is authorized to make grants to Amtrak in accordance with the provisions of this section.

(2) *GENERAL PURPOSES.—* The Secretary may make such grants for the purposes of—

- (A) protecting underwater and underground assets and systems;
- (B) protecting high-risk and high-consequence assets identified through systemwide risk assessments;
- (C) providing counterterrorism or security training;
- (D) providing both visible and unpredictable deterrence; and
- (E) conducting emergency preparedness drills and exercises.

(3) SPECIFIC PROJECTS.—The Secretary shall make such grants—

- (A) to secure major tunnel access points and ensure tunnel integrity in New York, New Jersey, Maryland, and Washington, DC;
- (B) to secure Amtrak trains;
- (C) to secure Amtrak stations;
- (D) to obtain a watchlist identification system approved by the Secretary;

(E) to obtain train tracking and interoperable communications systems that are coordinated with Federal, State, and local agencies and tribal governments to the maximum extent possible;

(F) to hire, train, and employ police and security officers, including canine units, assigned to full-time security or counterterrorism duties related to railroad transportation;

(G) for operating and capital costs associated with security awareness, preparedness, and response training, including training under section 1517, and training developed by universities, institutions of higher education, and nonprofit employee labor organizations, for railroad employees, including frontline employees; and

(H) for live or simulated exercises, including exercises described in section 1516.

SEC. 1517. RAILROAD SECURITY TRAINING PROGRAM.

(a) IN GENERAL.— Not later than 6 months after the date of enactment of this Act, the Secretary shall develop and issue regulations for a training program to prepare railroad frontline employees for potential security threats and conditions.

SEC. 1518. RAILROAD SECURITY RESEARCH AND DEVELOPMENT.

(a) ESTABLISHMENT OF RESEARCH AND DEVELOPMENT PROGRAM.— The Secretary . . . shall carry out a research and development program for the purpose of improving the security of railroad transportation systems . . .

SEC. 1519. RAILROAD TANK CAR SECURITY TESTING.

(a) RAILROAD TANK CAR VULNERABILITY ASSESSMENT.

(1) ASSESSMENT.— The Secretary shall assess the likely methods of a deliberate terrorist attack against a railroad tank car used to transport toxic-inhalation-hazard materials, and for each method assessed, the degree to which it may be successful in causing death, injury, or serious adverse effects to human health, the environment, critical infrastructure, national security, the national economy, or public welfare.

Rail Security, Securing Our Nation's Rail Systems, TSA Website

While state and local governments are primarily responsible for rail security, we have taken a number of steps to ensure the security of these crucial assets by working in concert with the Department of Homeland Security, other federal agencies, industry experts, and our local counterparts.

Training Teams and Deploying Manpower and Resources to the Field Federal Air Marshals, Surface Transportation, canine teams, and advanced screening technology working as Visible Intermodal Protection Response, or VIPR Teams, offer the ability to raise the level of security in any mode of transportation anywhere in the country quickly and effectively. http://www.tsa.gov/lawenforcement/index.shtm.

Through the Surface Transportation Security Inspection Program, we have deployed 100 inspectors, assigned to 18 field offices across the country. These inspectors provide support to our nation's largest mass transit systems, and perform frequent inspections of key facilities including stations and terminals for suspicious or unattended items, among others   potential   threats . . . http://www.tsa.gov/approach/people/inspectors.shtm.

Through the Surface Transportation Security Inspection Program, or STSI, we have deployed 100 inspectors assigned to 18 field offices across the country, to provide support to our nation's largest mass transit systems.

Fiscal Year 2009 Freight Rail Security Grant Program

The Freight Rail Security Grant Program (FRSGP) is a component of the Transit Security Grant Program (TSGP), which is one of five grant programs that constitute the Department of Homeland Security (DHS) fiscal year (FY) 2009 focus on infrastructure protection activities . . .

The FRSGP was created as a result of Public Law (PL) 110-53, "Implementing Recommendations of the 9/11 Commission Act of 2007". In FY 2009, the FRSGP will provide $15,000,000 to fund security training for railroad frontline employees, the completion of vulnerability assessments, the development of security plans, and Global Positioning System (GPS) tracking on railroad cars within the Freight Rail industry.

Fiscal Year 2009 Freight Rail Security Grant Program, Department of Homeland Security

. . . DHS will fund security initiatives for freight rail carriers that transport Rail Security-Sensitive Materials (SSM) through designated high population-density areas and freight railroad car owners that transport poisonous by inhalation/toxic inhalation hazardous (TIH) materials.

- Railroad carriers
  - Class I carriers may request funds to support security awareness and emergency response training for frontline employees provided that they have

completed an acceptable vulnerability assessment and security plan.

- Class II and Class III carriers may request funds to conduct a vulnerability assessment and develop a security plan. The carriers may also request funds to support security awareness and emergency response training for frontline employees provided that they have completed an acceptable vulnerability assessment and security plan.

- Freight Rail Class

    Class I – Annual operating revenues more than $319.2 million

    Class II – Annual operating revenues between $25.5 million and $319.2 million

    Class III – Annual operating revenues less than $25.5 million

    (Classifications designated by the Surface Transportation Board)

- Railroad car owners may request funds to acquire and install satellite Global Positioning System (GPS) tracking on railroad cars that transport TIH.

ADDITIONAL RESOURCES

"The Federal Role in Rail Transit Safety," David Randall Peterman and William J. Mallett, July 6, 2009, Congressional Research Service, R40688, http://opencrs.com/document/R40688/

"Transportation Security: Key Actions Have Been Taken to Enhance Mass Transit and Passenger Rail Security, but Opportunities Exist to Strengthen Federal Strategy and Programs," GAO-09-678, June 2009, http://www.gao.gov/new.items/d09678.pdf

"Freight Rail Security: Actions Have Been Taken to Enhance Security, but the Federal Strategy Can Be Strengthened and Security Efforts Better Monitored," GAO-09-243, April 2009. http://www.gao.gov/new.items/d09243.pdf

Improving the Safety and Security of Freight and Passenger Rail in Pennsylvania, 2008 http://www.rand.org/pubs/technical_reports/2008/RAND_TR615.pdf

Rail and Public Transportation Security Act of 2007, Testimony of William W. Millar, President, American Public Transportation Association, Before the House Committee on Homeland Security, March 7, 2007, http://www.apta.com/government_affairs/aptatest/testimony070306.cfm

E. TRUCKING

Patriot Act Section 1012 limits the issuance of HAZMAT licenses to those who do not pose a security risk. The Security and Accountability for Every Port Act of 2006, Section 703, established regulations (first recommended in 2004) requiring legal residency and verification of social security numbers or fingerprints before issuing a commercial driver's license.

SOURCES

- Patriot Act, 2001[45]
- Security and Accountability for Every Port Act of 2006[46], October 13, 2006
- GAO Comments on Commercial Vehicle Security, February 2009[47]

Patriot Act, 2001

SEC. 1012. LIMITATION ON ISSUANCE OF HAZMAT LICENSES.

(a) LIMITATION

(1) *IN GENERAL.*— Chapter 51 of title 49, United States Code, is amended by inserting after section 5103 the following new section:

'Sec. 5103a. Limitation on issuance of hazmat licenses

'(a) *LIMITATION.*

'*(1) ISSUANCE OF LICENSES.*— A State may not issue to any individual a license to operate a motor vehicle transporting in commerce a hazardous material unless the Secretary of Transportation has first determined, upon receipt of a notification under subsection (c)(1)(B), that the individual does not pose a security risk warranting denial of the license.

'(c) *BACKGROUND RECORDS CHECK.*

'*(1) IN GENERAL.*— Upon the request of a State regarding issuance of a license described in subsection (a)(1) to an individual, the Attorney General– '(A) shall carry out a background records check regarding the individual . . .

Security and Accountability for Every Port Act of 2006,[48] October 13, 2006

SEC. 703. TRUCKING SECURITY.

(c) VERIFICATION OF COMMERCIAL MOTOR VEHICLE TRAFFIC.

(1) *GUIDELINES.*— Not later than 18 months after the date of the enactment of this Act, the Secretary . . . shall draft guidelines for Federal, State, and local law enforcement officials, including motor carrier safety enforcement personnel, on how to identify noncompliance with Federal laws uniquely applicable to commercial motor vehicles and commercial motor vehicle operators engaged in cross-border traffic and

communicate such noncompliance to the appropriate Federal authorities. Such guidelines shall be coordinated with the training and outreach activities of the Federal Motor Carrier Safety Administration under section 4139 of SAFETEA-LU (Public Law 109-59).

(2) *VERIFICATION.—* Not later than 18 months after the date of the enactment of this Act, the Administrator of the Federal Motor Carrier Safety Administration shall modify the final rule regarding the enforcement of operating authority (Docket No. FMCSA-2002-13015)[49] to establish a system or process by which a carrier's operating authority can be verified during a roadside inspection.

GAO Comments on Commercial Vehicle Security, February 2009[50]

"Certain characteristics of commercial trucks and buses make them inherently vulnerable to terrorist attacks and therefore difficult to secure . . .

Between 1997 and 2008 there were 510 terrorist-related commercial truck and bus bombing attacks worldwide, killing over 6,000 people, with 106 bombings occurring during 2007 alone, killing over 2,500 people . . .

Terrorists have used a variety of trucks—rental, refrigerator, cement, dump, sewerage, gasoline tanker, trucks with chlorine and propane tanks, and fire engines—to attack a broad range of critical infrastructure, including police and military facilities, playgrounds, childcare centers, hotels, and bridges. Worldwide, commercial buses have also been attacked numerous times, including in Israel, England, Iraq, the Philippines, Lebanon, Sri Lanka, India, Russia, and Pakistan.

In the United States, terrorists used a commercial truck containing fertilizer-based explosives to attack the World Trade Center in 1993, killing 6 and injuring 1,000 people. Two years later, a similar attack occurred at the Alfred P. Murrah Federal Building in Oklahoma City, Oklahoma, killing 168 people and injuring more than 800. Terrorists have also targeted overseas U.S. military personnel with commercial VBIEDs [vehicle borne improvised explosive device] at the Marine barracks in Lebanon (1983), Khobar Towers in Saudi Arabia (1996), and at U.S. embassies in Kuwait (1983), Lebanon (1984), Kenya (1998), and Tanzania (1998) . . ."

TSA has begun conducting risk assessments of the commercial vehicle sector, but has not completed these efforts or fully used the results to support its security strategy . . . TSA developed threat assessments of the commercial vehicle sector, but generally did not identify the likelihood of specific threats as required by the NIPP . . . TSA has begun to conduct industry vulnerability assessments of the commercial vehicle sector, but its efforts are in the early stages . . ."

This report also includes an appendix listing all incidents of truck and bus bombings worldwide between 1997 and 2008.

ADDITIONAL RESOURCES

"[T]he Federal Motor Carrier Safety Administration (FMCSA) has initiated programs to protect the public from terrorists using commercial motor vehicles as weapons or targets. A top priority for commercial vehicle security is protecting the transportation of hazardous materials." http://www.fmcsa.dot.gov/safety-security/security/index.asp

Potential Threat to Homeland Using Heavy Transport Vehicles, July 30, 2004, FBI and DHS, [Minnesota Petroleum Marketers Association]   http://www.mpmaonline.com/Potential%20 Threat%20to%20the%20Homeland%20Using%20Heavy%20 Transport%20Vehicles%2030%20July%2004.pdf

F. BUS

The Implementing Recommendations of the 9/11 Commission Act of 2007 contains a few sections devoted to bus transportation. The statute requires bus operators to complete vulnerability assessments and provides guidance for implementing security plans. It provides for grants for a broad range of security efforts. Finally, there are provisions for security exercises and training programs.

SOURCES

- Implementing Recommendations of the 9/11 Commission Act of 2007[51]

Title XV, Implementing Recommendations of the 9/11 Commission Act of 2007

SEC. 1531. OVER-THE-ROAD BUS SECURITY ASSESSMENTS AND PLANS.

(a) IN GENERAL.— Not later than 18 months after the date of enactment of this Act, the Secretary shall issue regulations that—

(1) require each over-the-road bus operator assigned to a high-risk tier under this section—

(A) to conduct a vulnerability assessment in accordance with subsections (c) and (d); and

(B) to prepare, submit to the Secretary for approval, and implement a security plan . . . (e); and

(2) establish standards and guidelines for developing and implementing the vulnerability assessments and security plans for carriers assigned to high-risk tiers consistent with this section.

(b) NON HIGH-RISK PROGRAMS.— The Secretary may establish a security program for over-the-road bus operators not assigned to a high-risk tier, including—

(1) guidance for such operators in conducting vulnerability assessments and preparing and implementing security plans, as determined appropriate by the Secretary; and

(2) a process to review and approve such assessments and plans, as appropriate.

(c) DEADLINE FOR SUBMISSION.— Not later than 9 months after the date of issuance of the regulations under subsection (a), the vulnerability assessments and security plans required by such regulations for over-the-road bus operators assigned to a high-risk tier shall be completed and submitted to the Secretary for review and approval.

(d) VULNERABILITY ASSESSMENTS.

(1) *REQUIREMENTS.—* The Secretary shall provide technical assistance and guidance to over-the-road bus operators in conducting vulnerability assessments under this section and shall require that each vulnerability assessment of an operator assigned to a high-risk tier under this section includes, as appropriate—

(A) identification and evaluation of critical assets and infrastructure, including platforms, stations, terminals, and information systems;

(B) identification of the vulnerabilities to those assets and infrastructure; and

(C) identification of weaknesses in—

    (i) physical security;

    (ii) passenger and cargo security;

    (iii) the security of programmable electronic devices, computers, or other automated systems which are used in providing over-the-road bus transportation;

    (iv) alarms, cameras, and other protection systems;

    (v) communications systems and utilities needed for over-the-road bus security purposes, including dispatching systems;

    (vi) emergency response planning;

    (vii) employee training; and

    (viii) such other matters as the Secretary determines appropriate.

(2) *THREAT INFORMATION.—* The Secretary shall provide in a timely manner to the appropriate employees of an over-the-road bus operator, as designated by the over-the-road bus operator, threat information that is relevant to the operator when preparing and submitting a vulnerability assessment and security plan, including an assessment of the most likely methods that could be used by terrorists to exploit weaknesses in over-the-road bus security.

(e) SECURITY PLANS.

(1) *REQUIREMENTS.—* The Secretary shall provide technical assistance and guidance to over-the-road bus operators in preparing and implementing security plans under this section and shall require that each security plan of an over-the-road bus operator assigned to a high-risk tier under this section includes, as appropriate—

(A) the identification of a security coordinator having authority—

    (i) to implement security actions under the plan;

    (ii) to coordinate security improvements; and

    (iii) to receive communications from appropriate Federal officials regarding over-the-road bus security;

(B) a list of needed capital and operational improvements;

(C) procedures to be implemented or used by the over-the-road bus operator in response to a terrorist attack, including evacuation and passenger communication plans that include individuals with disabilities, as appropriate;

(D) the identification of steps taken with State and local law enforcement agencies, emergency responders, and Federal officials to coordinate security measures and plans for response to a terrorist attack;

(E) a strategy and timeline for conducting training under section 1534;

(F) enhanced security measures to be taken by the over-the-road bus operator when the Secretary declares a period of heightened security risk;

(G) plans for providing redundant and backup systems required to ensure the continued operation of critical elements of the over-the-road bus operator's system in the event of a terrorist attack or other incident . . .

(2) *SECURITY COORDINATOR REQUIREMENTS.—* The Secretary shall require that the individual serving as the security coordinator identified in paragraph (1)(A) is a citizen of the United States. The Secretary may waive this requirement with respect to an individual if the Secretary determines that it is appropriate to do so based on a background check of the individual and a review of the consolidated terrorist watchlist.

(h) TIER ASSIGNMENT.— The Secretary shall assign each over-the-road bus operator to a risk-based tier established by the Secretary:

(1) *PROVISION OF INFORMATION.—* The Secretary may request, and an over-the-road bus operator shall provide, information necessary for the Secretary to assign an over-the-road bus operator to the appropriate tier under this subsection.

(2) *NOTIFICATION.—* Not later than 60 days after the date an over-the-road bus operator is assigned to a tier under this section, the Secretary shall notify the operator of the tier to which it is assigned and the reasons for such assignment.

(3) *HIGH-RISK TIERS.—* At least one of the tiers established by the Secretary under this section shall be a tier designated for high-risk over-the-road bus operators.

SEC. 1532. OVER-THE-ROAD BUS SECURITY ASSISTANCE.

(a) IN GENERAL.— The Secretary shall establish a program for making grants to eligible private operators providing transportation by an over-the-road bus for security improvements described in subsection (b).

(b) USES OF FUNDS.— A recipient of a grant received under subsection (a) shall use the grant funds for one or more of the following:

(1) Constructing and modifying terminals, garages, and facilities, including terminals and other over-the-road bus facilities owned by State or local governments, to increase their security.

(2) Modifying over-the-road buses to increase their security.

(3) Protecting or isolating the driver of an over-the-road bus.

(4) Acquiring, upgrading, installing, or operating equipment, software, or accessorial services for collection, storage, or exchange of passenger and driver information through ticketing systems or other means and for information links with government agencies, for security purposes.

(5) Installing cameras and video surveillance equipment on over-the-road buses and at terminals, garages, and over-the-road bus facilities.

(6) Establishing and improving an emergency communications system linking drivers and over-the-road buses to the recipient's operations center or linking the operations center to law enforcement and emergency personnel.

(7) Implementing and operating passenger screening programs for weapons and explosives.

(8) Public awareness campaigns for enhanced over-the-road bus security.

(9) Operating and capital costs associated with over-theroad bus security awareness, preparedness, and response training, including training under section 1534 and training developed by institutions of higher education and by nonprofit employee labor organizations, for over-the-road bus employees, including frontline employees.

(10) Chemical, biological, radiological, or explosive detection, including canine patrols for such detection.

(11) Overtime reimbursement, including reimbursement of State, local, and tribal governments for costs, for enhanced security personnel assigned to duties related to over-the-road bus security during periods of high or severe threat levels, National Special Security Events, or other periods of heightened security as determined by the Secretary.

(12) Live or simulated exercises, including those described in section 1533.

(13) Operational costs to hire, train, and employ police and security officers, including canine units, assigned to fulltime security or counterterrorism duties related to over-theroad bus transportation, including reimbursement of State, local, and tribal government costs for such personnel.

(14) Development of assessments or security plans under section 1531.

(15) Such other improvements as the Secretary considers appropriate . . ..

SEC. 1533. OVER-THE-ROAD BUS EXERCISES.

(a) IN GENERAL.— The Secretary shall establish a program for conducting security exercises for over-the-road bus transportation for the purpose of assessing and improving the capabilities of entities described in subsection (b) to prevent, prepare for, mitigate, respond to, and recover from acts of terrorism.

SEC. 1534. OVER-THE-ROAD BUS SECURITY TRAINING PROGRAM.

(a) IN GENERAL.— Not later than 6 months after the date of enactment of this Act, the Secretary shall develop and issue regulations for an over-the-road bus training program to prepare over-the-road bus frontline employees for potential security threats and conditions. The regulations shall take into consideration any current security training requirements or best practices.

(c) PROGRAM ELEMENTS.— The regulations developed under subsection (a) shall require security training programs, to include, at a minimum, elements to address the following, as applicable:

(1) Determination of the seriousness of any occurrence or threat.

(2) Driver and passenger communication and coordination.

(3) Appropriate responses to defend or protect oneself.

(4) Use of personal and other protective equipment.

(5) Evacuation procedures for passengers and over-the-road bus employees, including individuals with disabilities and the elderly.

(6) Psychology, behavior, and methods of terrorists, including observation and analysis.

(7) Training related to psychological responses to terrorist incidents, including the ability to cope with hijacker behavior and passenger responses.

(8) Live situational training exercises regarding various threat conditions, including tunnel evacuation procedures.

(9) Recognition and reporting of dangerous substances, suspicious packages, and situations.

(10) Understanding security incident procedures, including procedures for communicating with emergency response providers and for on-scene interaction with such emergency response providers.

(11) Operation and maintenance of security equipment and systems.

SEC. 1536. MOTOR CARRIER EMPLOYEE PROTECTIONS.

Section 31105 of title 49, United States Code, is amended to read:

"(a) PROHIBITIONS.— (1) A person may not discharge an employee, or discipline or discriminate against an employee regarding pay, terms, or privileges of employment, because—

"(A) (i) the employee, or another person at the employee's request, has filed a complaint or begun a proceeding related to a violation of a commercial motor vehicle safety or security regulation, standard, or order, or has testified or will testify in such a proceeding; or

"(ii) the person perceives that the employee has filed or is about to file a complaint or has begun or is about to begin a proceeding related to a violation of a commercial motor vehicle safety or security regulation, standard, or order;

"(B) the employee refuses to operate a vehicle because—

"(i) the operation violates a regulation, standard, or order of the United States related to commercial motor vehicle safety, health, or security; or

"(ii) the employee has a reasonable apprehension of serious injury to the employee or the public because of the vehicle's hazardous safety or security condition;

"(C) the employee accurately reports hours on duty pursuant to chapter 315;

"(D) the employee cooperates, or the person perceives that the employee is about to cooperate, with a safety or security investigation by the Secretary of Transportation, the Secretary of Homeland Security, or the National Transportation Safety Board; or

"(E) the employee furnishes, or the person perceives that the employee is or is about to furnish, information to the Secretary of Transportation, the Secretary of Homeland Security, the National Transportation Safety Board, or any Federal, State, or local regulatory or law enforcement agency as to the facts relating to any accident or incident resulting in injury or death to an individual or damage to property occurring in connection with commercial motor vehicle transportation.

"(2) Under paragraph (1)(B)(ii) of this subsection, an employee's apprehension of serious injury is reasonable only if a reasonable individual in the circumstances then confronting the employee would conclude that the hazardous safety or security condition establishes a real danger of accident, injury, or serious impairment to health. To qualify for protection, the employee must have sought from the employer, and been unable to obtain, correction of the hazardous safety or security condition . . . .

ADDITIONAL RESOURCES

"Recovering from Disasters: The National Transportation Recovery Strategy," United States. Dept. of Transportation, October 2009, http://www.dot.gov/disaster_recovery/

ENDNOTES

1. National Strategy for the Physical Protection of Critical Infrastructures and Key Assets, February, 2002. http://www.dhs.gov/xlibrary/assets/Physical_Strategy.pdf.

2. National Strategy for Transportation Security, Intelligence Reform and Terrorism Prevention Act of 2004, Title IV—Transportation Security, Subtitle A, Public Law 108–458, December 17, 2004. http:// www. nctc. gov/ docs/ pl108_ 458. pdf.

3. Executive Order 13416—Strengthening Surface Transportation Security, December 2006. http://edocket.access.gpo.gov/2006/pdf/06-9619.pdf.

4. Transportation Security Planning And Information Sharing, Implementing Recommendations Of The 9/11 Commission Act Of 2007, Title XII, August 3, 2007, Public law 110–53. http://www.nctc.gov/docs/ir-of-the-9-11-comm-act-of-2007.pdf.

5. National Transit Systems Security Act of 2007, Implementing Recommendations of The 9/11 Commission Act of 2007, Title XIV, Public Transportation Security, August 3, 2007, Public law 110–53. http://www.nctc.gov/docs/ir-of-the-9-11-comm-act-of-2007.pdf.

6. Surface Transportation Security, Subtitle A—General Provisions, Implementing Recommendations of The 9/11 Commission Act of 2007, TITLE XV, August 3, 2007, Public law 110–53. http://www.nctc.gov/docs/ir-of-the-9-11-comm-act-of-2007.pdf.

7. Transportation Security Planning And Information Sharing, Implementing Recommendations of The 9/11 Commission Act Of 2007, Title XII, August 3, 2007. Http://Www.Nctc.Gov/Docs/Ir-Of-The-9-11-Comm-Act-Of-2007.Pdf.

8. National Transit Systems Security Act of 2007, Implementing Recommendations of The 9/11 Commission Act of 2007, Title XIV, Public Transportation Security, August 3, 2007. Http://Www.Nctc.Gov/Docs/Ir-Of-The-9-11-Comm-Act-Of-2007.Pdf.

9. Surface Transportation Security, Subtitle A—General Provisions, Implementing Recommendations of The 9/11 Commission Act of 2007, TITLE XV, August 3, 2007. Http://Www.Nctc.Gov/Docs/Ir-Of-The-9-11-Comm-Act-Of-2007.Pdf.

10. Aviation and Transportation Security Act. http://www.tsa.gov/assets/pdf/Aviation_and_Transportation_Security_Act_ATSA_Public_Law_107_1771.pdf.

11. Intelligence Reform and Terrorism Prevention Act of 2004, Title IV—Transportation Security, Subtitle C—Air Cargo Security, Public Law 108–458, December 17, 2004. http://www.nctc.gov/docs/pl108_458.pdf.

12. NSPD 47 / HSPD 16, Aviation Security Policy. http://www.dhs.gov/xprevprot/laws/gc_1173113497603.shtm.

13. Security And Accountability For Every Port Act Of 2006, Title VII, (Public Law 109–347), October 13, 2006. http://thomas.loc.gov/cgi-bin/toGPObss/http://frwebgate.access.gpo.gov/cgi-bin/getdoc.cgi?dbname=109_cong_public_laws&docid=f:publ347.109.

14. National Strategy for Aviation Security. http://www.dhs.gov/xlibrary/assets/laws_hspd_aviation_security.pdf.

15. Aviation Transportation System Security Plan, Supporting Plan to the National Strategy for Aviation Security," March 26, 2007. http://www.dhs.gov/xlibrary/assets/hspd16_transsystemsecurityplan.pdf.

16. Air Domain Surveillance and Intelligence Integration Plan, Supporting Plan to the National Strategy for Aviation Security, March 26, 2007. http://www.dhs.gov/xlibrary/assets/hspd16_domsurvintelplan.pdf.

17. Aviation Operational Threat Response Plan, Supporting Plan to the National Strategy for Aviation Security, March 26, 2007. http://www.dhs.gov/xlibrary/assets/hspd16_opthreatrespplan.pdf.

18. Domestic Outreach Plan, Supporting Plan to the National Strategy for Aviation Security, March 26, 2007. http://www.dhs.gov/xlibrary/assets/hspd16_domoutreachplan.pdf.

19. International Outreach Plan, Supporting Plan to the National Strategy for Aviation Security, March 26, 2007. http://www.dhs.gov/xlibrary/assets/hspd16_intloutreachplan.pdf.

20. Intelligence Reform and Terrorism Prevention Act of 2004, Title IV—Transportation Security, Public Law 108–458, December 17, 2004. http://www.nctc.gov/docs/pl108_458.pdf.

21. NSPD 47/HSPD 16, June 22, 2006. http://www.dhs.gov/xprevprot/laws/gc_1173113497603.shtm.

22. Maritime Transportation Security Act of 2002, Public Law 107–295, November 25, 2002. http://www.tsa.dhs.gov/assets/pdf/MTSA.pdf.

23. Intelligence Reform and Terrorism Prevention Act of 2004, Title IV—Transportation Security, Subtitle D—Maritime Security, Public Law 108–458, December 17, 2004. http://www.nctc.gov/docs/pl108_458.pdf.

24. HSPD 13. Maritime Security Policy, December 21, 2004. http://www.dhs.gov/xabout/laws/gc_1217624446873.shtm#1.

25. Reducing Crime and Terrorism at America's Seaports Act of 2005, Title III of the USA PATRIOT Improvement and Reauthorization Act of 2005. http://thomas.loc.gov/cgi-bin/query/z?c109:H.R.3199:.

26. National Strategy for Maritime Security, September 2005. http://www.dhs.gov/xlibrary/assets/HSPD13_MaritimeSecurityStrategy.pdf.

27. National Plan To Achieve Maritime Domain Awareness, October 2005. http://www.dhs.gov/xlibrary/assets/HSPD_MDAPlan.pdf.

28. International Outreach and Coordination Strategy, National Strategy for Maritime Security, November 2005. http://www.dhs.gov/xlibrary/assets/HSPD_IOCPlan.pdf.

29. Maritime Transportation System Security Recommendations [Plan], October 2005. http://www.dhs.gov/xlibrary/assets/HSPD_MTSSPlan.pdf.

30. Maritime Commerce Security Plan, October 2005. http://www.dhs.gov/xlibrary/assets/HSPD_MCSPlan.pdf.

31. The Maritime Infrastructure Recovery Plan, National Strategy for Maritime Security, April 2006. http://www.dhs.gov/xlibrary/assets/HSPD_MIRPPlan.pdf.

32. Security And Accountability For Every Port Act Of 2006 (Public Law 109–347), October 13, 2006. http://thomas. loc.gov/cgi-bin/toGPObss/http://frwebgate.access.gpo. gov/cgi-bin/getdoc.cgi?dbname=109_cong_public_laws &docid=f:publ347.109.

33. Small Vessel Security Strategy, April 2008. http://www. dhs.gov/xlibrary/assets/small-vessel-security-strategy. pdf.

34. Maritime Transportation Security Act of 2002. http:// www.tsa.dhs.gov/assets/pdf/MTSA.pdf.

35. Maritime Commerce Security Plan, National Strategy for Maritime Security, October 2005. http://www.dhs. gov/xlibrary/assets/HSPD_MCSPlan.pdf.

36. Security And Accountability For Every Port Act of 2006 (Public Law 109–347) http://thomas.loc.gov/cgi-bin/ toGPObss/http://frwebgate.access.gpo.gov/cgi-bin/ getdoc.cgi?dbname=109_cong_public_laws&docid= f:publ347.109.

37. DOT Federal Railroad Administration, Action Plan, Railroad Safety Issues, May 16, 2005. http://www.fra. dot.gov/downloads/safety/action_plan_final_051605. pdf.

38. Rail Safety and Security, Senate Committee on Commerce, Science and Transportation Testimony of Joseph H. Boardman, Administrator, Federal Railroad Administration, U.S. Department of Transportation, before the Committee on Commerce, Science, and Transportation, United States Senate, January 18, 2007. http://www.fra. dot.gov/us/content/1787.

39. Surface Transportation Security, Subtitle B—Railroad Security, Implementing Recommendations of The 9/11 Commission Act of 2007, TITLE XV, August 3, 2007. Http://Www.Nctc.Gov/Docs/Ir-Of-The-9-11-Comm-Act-Of-2007.Pdf.

40. DOT Federal Railroad Administration, National Rail Safety Action Plan, Final Report, 2005—2008, May 2008. http://www.fra.dot.gov/downloads/PubAffairs/ final_report_May_2008.pdf.

41. TSA website, Rail Security. http://www.tsa.gov/what_ we_do/rail/index.shtm.

42. Freight Rail Security Grant Program Fiscal Year 2009. http://www.tsa.gov/what_we_do/grants/programs/ frsgp/2009/index.shtm.

43. Fiscal Year 2009 Freight Rail Security Grant Program Department of Homeland Security. http://www.tsa.gov/ assets/pdf/fy09_frsgp_fact_sheet.pdf.

44. Also see, Railway Alert Network, May 5, 2004, Rail Security, House Committee on Transportation and Infrastructure, Testimony of the Honorable Allan Rutter, Administrator, Department of Transportation. http://www. fra.dot.gov/us/content/1649.

45. Patriot Act, 2001. http://thomas.loc.gov/cgi-bin/ bdquery/z?d107:hr03162:5D.

46. Security And Accountability For Every Port Act of 2006, October 13, 2006, (Public Law 109–347). http:// thomas.loc.gov/cgi-bin/toGPObss/http://frwebgate. access.gpo.gov/cgi-bin/getdoc.cgi?dbname=109_cong_ public_laws&docid=f:publ347.109.

47. The Government Accountability Office, Report to the Chairman, Committee on Homeland Security, House of Representatives on Commercial Vehicle Security, February, 2009, GAO-09-85, pages 11,12,22, 23,25. http:// www.gao.gov/new.items/d0985.pdf (internal citations omitted) (accessed March 31, 2009).

48. Security And Accountability For Every Port Act of 2006, October 13, 2006, (Public Law 109–347). http://thomas. loc.gov/cgi-bin/bdquery/z?d109:h.r.04954.

49. Federal Motor Carrier Safety Administration, Rulemakings and Notices – 2002. http://www.fmcsa.dot. gov/rules-regulations/administration/rulemakings/ rules2002.htm.

50. "Risk-Based Approach Needed to Secure the Commercial Vehicle Sector," The Government Accountability Office, Report to the Chairman, Committee on Homeland Security, House of Representatives on Commercial Vehicle Security, February, 2009, GAO-09-85, pages 11,12,22, 23,25. http://www.gao.gov/new.items/ d0985. pdf (internal citations omitted) (accessed March 31, 2009).

51. Title XV, Implementing Recommendations Of The 9/11 Commission Act Of 2007.http://www.nctc.gov/docs/ ir-of-the-9-11-comm-act-of-2007.pdf.

15

WEAPONS OF MASS DESTRUCTION

The gravest danger our Nation faces lies at the crossroads of radicalism and technology[1]

The greatest danger of another catastrophic attack in the United States will materialize if the world's most dangerous terrorists acquire the world's most dangerous weapons[2]

The Commission believes that unless the world community acts decisively and with great urgency, it is more likely than not that a weapon of mass destruction will be used in a terrorist attack somewhere in the world by the end of 2013[3]

The publically available version of HSPD 4, also known as NSPD 17 (National Security Presidential Directive), is America's National Strategy to Combat Weapons of Mass Destruction. It lists three pillars upon which the strategy is based. They are: (1) counterproliferation, described as preparing to deter and defend against WMD; (2) nonproliferation, to prevent terrorists from acquiring WMD; and (3) consequence management—preparation in case WMD is actually used. HSPD 4 elaborates on each of these pillars.

This portion of the National Strategy for Homeland Security describes our WMD strategy as our effort to "deny terrorists and terrorist-related weapons and materials entry into our country and across all international borders, disrupt their ability to operate within our borders, and prevent the emergence of violent Islamic radicalization in order to deny terrorists future recruits and defeat homegrown extremism." This strategy describes each of these areas in detail.

SOURCES

- HSPD-4, National Strategy to Combat Weapons of Mass Destruction, December 2002[4]
- Intelligence Reform and Terrorism Prevention Act of 2004[5]
- HSPD 14/NSPD 43. Domestic Nuclear Detection, April 15, 2005[6]
- Executive Order 13382—Blocking Property of Weapons of Mass Destruction Proliferators and Their Supporters, July 1, 2005[7]
- Domestic Nuclear Detection Office, 2006[8]
- Enhanced Defenses Against Weapons Of Mass Destruction, August 3, 2007[9]
- HSPD 17 / NSPD 48, Nuclear Materials Information Center[10]

HSPD-4 National Strategy To Combat Weapons Of Mass Destruction December 2002

"Weapons of mass destruction (WMD) – nuclear, biological, and chemical – in the possession of hostile states and terrorists represent one of the greatest security challenges facing the United States . . .

Pillars of Our National Strategy Our National Strategy to Combat Weapons of Mass Destruction has three principal pillars:

Counterproliferation We know from experience that we cannot always be successful in preventing and containing the proliferation of WMD to hostile states and terrorists. Therefore, U.S. military and appropriate civilian agencies must possess the full range of operational capabilities to counter

Foundations of Homeland Security: Law and Policy, First Edition. Martin J. Alperen.
© 2011 John Wiley & Sons, Inc. Published 2011 by John Wiley & Sons, Inc.

the threat and use of WMD by states and terrorists against the United States, our military forces, and friends and allies.

INTERDICTION Effective interdiction is a critical part of the U.S. strategy to combat WMD and their delivery means. We must enhance the capabilities of our military, intelligence, technical, and law enforcement communities to prevent the movement of WMD materials, technology, and expertise to hostile states and terrorist organizations.

DETERRENCE Today's threats are far more diverse and less predictable than those of the past. States hostile to the United States and to our friends and allies have demonstrated their willingness to take high risks to achieve their goals, and are aggressively pursuing WMD and their means of delivery as critical tools in this effort. As a consequence, we require new methods of deterrence. A strong declaratory policy and effective military forces are essential elements of our contemporary deterrent posture, along with the full range of political tools to persuade potential adversaries not to seek or use WMD. The United States will continue to make clear that it reserves the right to respond with overwhelming force – including through resort to all of our options – to the use of WMD against the United States, our forces abroad, and friends and allies.

In addition to our conventional and nuclear response and defense capabilities, our overall deterrent posture against WMD threats is reinforced by effective intelligence, surveillance, interdiction, and domestic law enforcement capabilities. Such combined capabilities enhance deterrence both by devaluing an adversary's WMD and missiles, and by posing the prospect of an overwhelming response to any use of such weapons.[11]

DEFENSE AND MITIGATION Because deterrence may not succeed, and because of the potentially devastating consequences of WMD use against our forces and civilian population, U.S. military forces and appropriate civilian agencies must have the capability to defend against WMD-armed adversaries, including in appropriate cases through preemptive measures. This requires capabilities to detect and destroy an adversary's WMD assets before these weapons are used. In addition, robust active and passive defenses and mitigation measures must be in place to enable U.S. military forces and appropriate civilian agencies to accomplish their missions, and to assist friends and allies when WMD are used.

Active defenses disrupt, disable, or destroy WMD en route to their targets. Active defenses include vigorous air defense and effective missile defenses against today's threats. Passive defenses must be tailored to the unique characteristics of the various forms of WMD. The United States must also have the ability rapidly and effectively to mitigate the effects of a WMD attack against our deployed forces.

Our approach to defend against biological threats has long been based on our approach to chemical threats, despite the fundamental differences between these weapons. The United States is developing a new approach to provide us and our friends and allies with an effective defense against biological weapons.

Finally, U.S. military forces and domestic law enforcement agencies as appropriate must stand ready to respond against the source of any WMD attack. The primary objective of a response is to disrupt an imminent attack or an attack in progress, and eliminate the threat of future attacks. As with deterrence and prevention, an effective response requires rapid attribution and robust strike capability. We must accelerate efforts to field new capabilities to defeat WMD-related assets. The United States needs to be prepared to conduct post-conflict operations to destroy or dismantle any residual WMD capabilities of the hostile state or terrorist network. An effective U.S. response not only will eliminate the source of a WMD attack but will also have a powerful deterrent effect upon other adversaries that possess or seek WMD or missiles.

Nonproliferation

ACTIVE NONPROLIFERATION DIPLOMACY The United States will actively employ diplomatic approaches in bilateral and multilateral settings in pursuit of our nonproliferation goals. We must dissuade supplier states from cooperating with proliferant states and induce proliferant states to end their WMD and missile programs. We will hold countries responsible for complying with their commitments. In addition, we will continue to build coalitions to support our efforts, as well as to seek their increased support for nonproliferation and threat reduction cooperation programs. However, should our wide-ranging nonproliferation efforts fail, we must have available the full range of operational capabilities necessary to defend against the possible employment of WMD. . ...

MULTILATERAL REGIMES Existing nonproliferation and arms control regimes play an important role in our overall strategy. The United States will support those regimes that are currently in force, and work to improve the effectiveness of, and compliance with, those regimes. Consistent with other policy priorities, we will also promote new agreements and arrangements that serve our nonproliferation goals. Overall, we seek to cultivate an international environment that is more conducive to nonproliferation. Our efforts will include:

- Nuclear
  - Strengthening of the Nuclear Nonproliferation Treaty and International Atomic Energy Agency (IAEA), including through ratification of an IAEA Additional Protocol by all NPT states parties, assurances that all states put in place full-scope IAEA safeguards agreements, and appropriate increases in funding for the Agency;

- Negotiating a Fissile Material Cut-Off Treaty that advances U.S. security interests; and
- Strengthening the Nuclear Suppliers Group[12] and Zangger Committee[13].
- Chemical and Biological
  - Effective functioning of the Organization for the Prohibition of Chemical Weapons[14];
  - Identification and promotion of constructive and realistic measures to strengthen the BWC[15] and thereby to help meet the biological weapons threat; and
  - Strengthening of the Australia Group[16].
- Missile
  - Strengthening the Missile Technology Control Regime (MTCR)[17], including through support for universal adherence to the International Code of Conduct Against Ballistic Missile Proliferation[18].

NONPROLIFERATION AND THREAT REDUCTION COOPERATION

The United States pursues a wide range of programs, including the Nunn-Lugar program, designed to address the proliferation threat stemming from the large quantities of Soviet-legacy WMD and missile-related expertise and materials. Maintaining an extensive and efficient set of nonproliferation and threat reduction assistance programs to Russia and other former Soviet states is a high priority. We will also continue to encourage friends and allies to increase their contributions to these programs, particularly through the G-8 Global Partnership Against the Spread of Weapons and Materials of Mass Destruction. In addition, we will work with other states to improve the security of their WMD-related materials.

CONTROLS ON NUCLEAR MATERIALS

In addition to programs with former Soviet states to reduce fissile material and improve the security of that which remains, the United States will continue to discourage the worldwide accumulation of separated plutonium and to minimize the use of highly-enriched uranium. As outlined in the National Energy Policy, the United States will work in collaboration with international partners to develop recycle and fuel treatment technologies that are cleaner, more efficient, less waste-intensive, and more proliferation-resistant.

U.S. EXPORT CONTROLS

We must ensure that the implementation of U.S. export controls furthers our nonproliferation and other national security goals, ...

WMD Consequence Management

The National Strategy for Homeland Security discusses U.S. Government programs to deal with the consequences of the use of a chemical, biological, radiological, or nuclear weapon in the United States. A number of these programs offer training, planning, and assistance to state and local governments. To maximize their effectiveness, these efforts need to be integrated and comprehensive. Our first responders must have the full range of protective, medical, and remediation tools to identify, assess, and respond rapidly to a WMD event on our territory. ...

Intelligence Reform and Terrorism Prevention Act of 2004

SEC. 1022. NATIONAL COUNTER PROLIFERATION CENTER.

Title I of the National Security Act of 1947, as amended by section 1021 of this Act, is further amended by adding at the end the following new section:
    "NATIONAL COUNTER PROLIFERATION CENTER

SEC. 119A.

"(a) ESTABLISHMENT.— Not later than 18 months after the date of the enactment of the National Security Intelligence Reform Act of 2004, the President shall establish a National Counter Proliferation Center, taking into account all appropriate government tools to prevent and halt the proliferation of weapons of mass destruction, their delivery systems, and related materials and technologies.

"(b) MISSIONS AND OBJECTIVES.— In establishing the National Counter Proliferation Center, the President shall address the following missions and objectives to prevent and halt the proliferation of weapons of mass destruction, their delivery systems, and related materials and technologies:

"(1) Establishing a primary organization within the United States Government for analyzing and integrating all intelligence possessed or acquired by the United States pertaining to proliferation.

"(2) Ensuring that appropriate agencies have full access to and receive all-source intelligence support needed to execute their counter proliferation plans or activities, and perform independent, alternative analyses.

"(3) Establishing a central repository on known and suspected proliferation activities, including the goals, strategies, capabilities, networks, and any individuals, groups, or entities engaged in proliferation.

"(4) Disseminating proliferation information, including proliferation threats and analyses, to the President, to the appropriate departments and agencies, and to the appropriate committees of Congress.

"(5) Conducting net assessments and warnings about the proliferation of weapons of mass destruction, their delivery systems, and related materials and technologies.

"(6) Coordinating counter proliferation plans and activities of the various departments and agencies of the United States Government to prevent and halt the proliferation of weapons of mass destruction, their delivery systems, and related materials and technologies.

"(7) Conducting strategic operational counter proliferation planning for the United States Government to prevent and halt the proliferation of weapons of mass destruction, their delivery systems, and related materials and technologies.

"(c) NATIONAL SECURITY WAIVER.— The President may waive the requirements of this section, and any parts thereof, if the President determines that such requirements do not materially improve the ability of the United States Government to prevent and halt the proliferation of weapons of mass destruction, their delivery systems, and related materials and technologies. Such waiver shall be made in writing to Congress and shall include a description of how the missions and objectives in subsection (b) are being met.

Executive Order 13382 Blocking Property of Weapons of Mass Destruction Proliferators and Their Supporters, July 1, 2005

By the authority vested in me as President by the Constitution and the laws of the United States of America, including the International Emergency Economic Powers Act (50 U.S.C. 1701 et seq.) (IEEPA), the National Emergencies Act (50 U.S.C. 1601 et seq.), and section 301 of title 3, United States Code, I, George W. Bush, President of the United States of America, in order to take additional steps with respect to the national emergency described and declared in Executive Order 12938 of November 14, 1994, regarding the proliferation of weapons of mass destruction and the means of delivering them, and the measures imposed by that order, as expanded by Executive Order 13094 of July 28, 1998, hereby order:

Sec. 1. (a) Except to the extent provided in section 203(b)(1), (3), and (4) of IEEPA (50 U.S.C. 1702(b)(1), (3), and (4)), or in regulations, orders, directives, or licenses that may be issued pursuant to this order, and notwithstanding any contract entered into or any license or permit granted prior to the effective date of this order, all property and interests in property of the following persons, that are in the United States, that hereafter come within the United States, or that are or hereafter come within the possession or control of United States persons, are blocked and may not be transferred, paid, exported, withdrawn, or otherwise dealt in:

(i) the persons listed in the Annex to this order;

(ii) any foreign person determined by the Secretary of State, in consultation with the Secretary of the Treasury, the Attorney General, and other relevant agencies, to have engaged, or attempted to engage, in activities or transactions that have materially contributed to, or pose a risk of materially contributing to, the proliferation of weapons of mass destruction or their means of delivery (including missiles capable of delivering such weapons), including any efforts to manufacture, acquire, possess, develop, transport, transfer or use such items, by any person or foreign country of proliferation concern;

(iii) any person determined by the Secretary of the Treasury, in consultation with the Secretary of State, the Attorney General, and other relevant agencies, to have provided, or attempted to provide, financial, material, technological or other support for, or goods or services in support of, any activity or transaction described in paragraph (a)(ii) of this section, or any person whose property and interests in property are blocked pursuant to this order; and

(iv) any person determined by the Secretary of the Treasury, in consultation with the Secretary of State, the Attorney General, and other relevant agencies, to be owned or controlled by, or acting or purporting to act for or on behalf of, directly or indirectly, any person whose property and interests in property are blocked pursuant to this order.

(b) Any transaction or dealing by a United States person or within the United States in property or interests in property blocked pursuant to this order is prohibited, including, but not limited to, (i) the making of any contribution or provision of funds, goods, or services by, to, or for the benefit of, any person whose property and interests in property are blocked pursuant to this order, and (ii) the receipt of any contribution or provision of funds, goods, or services from any such person.

(c) Any transaction by a United States person or within the United States that evades or avoids, has the purpose of evading or avoiding, or attempts to violate any of the prohibitions set forth in this order is prohibited.

(d) Any conspiracy formed to violate the prohibitions set forth in this order is prohibited.

Sec. 5. For those persons whose property and interests in property are blocked pursuant to section 1 of this order who might have a constitutional presence in the United States, I find that because of the ability to transfer funds or other assets instantaneously, prior notice to such persons of measures to be taken pursuant to this order would render these measures ineffectual. I therefore determine that for these measures to be effective in addressing the national emergency declared in Executive Order 12938, as amended, there need be no prior notice of a listing or determination made pursuant to section 1 of this order.

HSPD 14/NSPD 43, Domestic Nuclear Detection, April 15, 2005

(1) To protect against the unauthorized importation, possession, storage, transportation, development, or use of a nuclear explosive device, fissile material, or radiological material in the United States, and to protect against attack using such devices or materials against the people, territory, or interests of the United States, it is the policy of the United States to:

    (a) Continue to develop, deploy, and enhance national nuclear and radiological detection capabilities in an effort to better detect, report on, disrupt, and prevent attempts to import, possess, store, transport, develop, or use such devices and materials;

    (b) Continue to enhance the effective integration of nuclear and radiological detection capabilities . . .

    (c) Continue to advance the science of nuclear and radiological detection . . .

(2) To implement the policy set forth in paragraph (1), the Secretary of Homeland Security . . . shall establish a national level Domestic Nuclear Detection Office (DNDO) within the Department of Homeland Security. The DNDO shall include personnel from the departments of Homeland Security (DHS), Defense (DOD), Energy (DOE), State (DOS), Justice (DOJ) . . . The Secretary of Homeland Security shall have authority, direction, and control over the DNDO as provided in section 102 (a) (2) of the Homeland Security Act of 2002.

The DNDO shall:

    (d) Develop . . . an enhanced global nuclear detection architecture with the following implementation: (i) the DNDO will be responsible for the implementation of the domestic portion of the global architecture; (ii) the Secretary of Defense will retain responsibility for implementation of DOD requirements within and outside the United States; and (iii) the Secretaries of State, Defense, and Energy will maintain their respective responsibilities for policy guidance and implementation of the portion of the global architecture outside the United States . . .

    (e) Conduct, support, coordinate, and encourage an aggressive, expedited, *evolutionary, and transformational program of research* and development efforts to support the policy set forth in paragraph (1); . . . [emphasis added] . . . .

Domestic Nuclear Detection Office, 2006

SEC. 501. ESTABLISHMENT OF DOMESTIC NUCLEAR DETECTION OFFICE.

(a) ESTABLISHMENT OF OFFICE.— The Homeland Security Act of 2002 (6 U.S.C. 101 et seq.) is amended by adding at the end the following:

TITLE XVIII–DOMESTIC NUCLEAR DETECTION OFFICE

SEC. 1801. DOMESTIC NUCLEAR DETECTION OFFICE.

"(a) ESTABLISHMENT.— There shall be established in the Department a Domestic Nuclear Detection Office (referred to in this title as the 'Office') . . .

"(b) DIRECTOR.— The Office shall be headed by a Director for Domestic Nuclear Detection, who shall be appointed by the President.

SEC. 1802. MISSION OF OFFICE.

"(a) MISSION.— The Office shall be responsible for coordinating Federal efforts to detect and protect against the unauthorized importation, possession, storage, transportation, development, or use of a nuclear explosive device, fissile material, or radiological material in the United States, and to protect against attack using such devices or materials against the people, territory, or interests of the United States and, to this end, shall—

"(1) serve as the primary entity of the United States Government to further develop, acquire, and support the deployment of an enhanced domestic system to detect and report on attempts to import, possess, store, transport, develop, or use an unauthorized nuclear explosive device, fissile material, or radiological material in the United States, and improve that system over time;

"(2) enhance and coordinate the nuclear detection efforts of Federal, State, local, and tribal governments and the private sector to ensure a managed, coordinated response;

"(3) establish, with the approval of the Secretary and in coordination with the Attorney General, the Secretary of Defense, and the Secretary of Energy, additional protocols and procedures for use within the United States to ensure that the detection of unauthorized nuclear explosive devices, fissile material, or radiological material is promptly reported to the Attorney General, the Secretary, the Secretary of Defense, the Secretary of Energy, and other appropriate officials or their respective designees for appropriate action by law enforcement, military, emergency response, or other authorities;

"(4) develop, with the approval of the Secretary and in coordination with the Attorney General, the Secretary of State, Secretary of Defense, and the Secretary of Energy, an enhanced global nuclear detection architecture with implementation under which–

"(A) the Office will be responsible for the implementation of the domestic portion of the global architecture;

"(B) the Secretary of Defense will retain responsibility for implementation of Department of Defense requirements within and outside the United States; and

"(C) the Secretary of State, the Secretary of Defense, and the Secretary of Energy will maintain their respective responsibilities for policy guidance and implementation of the portion of the global architecture outside the United States, which will be implemented consistent with applicable law and relevant international arrangements;

"(5) ensure that the expertise necessary to accurately interpret detection data is made available in a timely manner for all technology deployed by the Office to implement the global nuclear detection architecture;

"(6) conduct, support, coordinate, and encourage an aggressive, expedited, evolutionary, and transformational program of research and development to generate and improve technologies to detect and prevent the illicit entry, transport, assembly, or potential use within the United States of a nuclear explosive device or fissile or radiological material, and coordinate with the Under Secretary for Science and Technology on basic and advanced or transformational research and development efforts relevant to the mission of organizations;

"(7) carry out a program to test and evaluate technology for detecting a nuclear explosive device and fissile or radiological material, in coordination with the Secretary of Defense and the Secretary of Energy, as appropriate, and establish performance metrics for evaluating the effectiveness of individual detectors and detection systems in detecting such devices or material

"(A) under realistic operational and environmental conditions; and

"(B) against realistic adversary tactics and countermeasures;

"(8) support and enhance the effective sharing and use of appropriate information generated by the intelligence community, law enforcement agencies, counterterrorism community, other government agencies, and foreign governments, as well as provide appropriate information to such entities;

"(9) further enhance and maintain continuous awareness by analyzing information from all Office mission-related detection systems; and

Improving Critical Infrastructure Security, Title XI, Enhanced Defenses Against Weapons Of Mass Destruction, August 3, 2007

SEC. 1101. NATIONAL BIOSURVEILLANCE INTEGRATION CENTER.

(a) IN GENERAL.— Title III of the Homeland Security Act of 2002 (6 U.S.C. et seq.) is amended by adding at the end the following:

"SEC. 316. NATIONAL BIOSURVEILLANCE INTEGRATION CENTER.

"(a) ESTABLISHMENT.— The Secretary shall establish, operate, and maintain a National Biosurveillance Integration Center (referred to in this section as the 'NBIC'), which shall be headed by a Directing Officer, under an office or directorate of the Department that is in existence as of the date of the enactment of this section.

"(b) PRIMARY MISSION.— The primary mission of the NBIC is to—

"(1) enhance the capability of the Federal Government to—

"(A) rapidly identify, characterize, localize, and track a biological event of national concern by integrating and analyzing data relating to human health, animal, plant, food, and environmental monitoring systems (both national and international); and

"(B) disseminate alerts and other information to Member Agencies and, in coordination with (and where possible through) Member Agencies, to agencies of State, local, and tribal governments, as appropriate, to enhance the ability of such agencies to respond to a biological event of national concern; and

"(2) oversee development and operation of the National Biosurveillance Integration System.

"(c) REQUIREMENTS.— The NBIC shall detect, as early as possible, a biological event of national concern that presents a risk to the United States or the infrastructure or key assets of the United States, including by—

"(1) consolidating data from all relevant surveillance systems maintained by Member Agencies to detect biological events of national concern across human, animal, and plant species;

"(2) seeking private sources of surveillance, both foreign and domestic, when such sources would enhance coverage of critical surveillance gaps;

"(3) using an information technology system that uses the best available statistical and other analytical tools to identify and characterize biological events of national concern in as close to real-time as is practicable;

"(4) providing the infrastructure for such integration, including information technology systems and space, and support for personnel from Member Agencies with sufficient expertise to enable analysis and interpretation of data;

"(5) working with Member Agencies to create information technology systems that use the minimum amount of patient data necessary and consider patient confidentiality and privacy issues at all stages of development and apprise the Privacy Officer of such efforts; and

"(6) alerting Member Agencies and, in coordination with (and where possible through) Member Agencies, public health agencies of State, local, and tribal governments regarding any incident that could develop into a biological event of national concern.

"(2) ASSESSMENTS.— The Directing Officer of the NBIC shall—"(A) on an ongoing basis, evaluate available data for evidence of a biological event of national concern; and "(B) integrate homeland security information with NBIC data to provide overall situational awareness and determine whether a biological event of national concern has occurred.

"(3) INFORMATION SHARING.

"(A) *IN GENERAL.*— The Directing Officer of the NBIC shall—

"(i) establish a method of real-time communication with the National Operations Center;

"(ii) in the event that a biological event of national concern is detected, notify the Secretary and disseminate results of NBIC assessments relating to that biological event of national concern to appropriate Federal response entities and, in coordination with relevant Member Agencies, regional, State, local, and tribal governmental response entities in a timely manner;

"(iv) share NBIC incident or situational awareness reports, and other relevant information, consistent with the

information sharing environment established under section 1016 of the Intelligence Reform and Terrorism Prevention Act of 2004 (6 U.S.C. 485) and any policies, guidelines, procedures, instructions, or standards established under that section.

HSPD 17/NSPD 48, Nuclear Materials Information Center

There is no public text of NSPD-48 / HSPD-17; however, the classified directive was discussed in April 2, 2008, testimony before the Senate Homeland Security and Governmental Affairs Committee by Rolf Mowatt-Larssen, Director of the Office of Intelligence and Counterintelligence of the Department of Energy.

"On August 28, 2006, the national-level Nuclear Materials Information Program (NMIP) was established via National and Homeland Security Presidential Directive (NSPD-48/HSPD-17). NMIP is an interagency effort managed by the Department of Energy's Office of Intelligence and Counterintelligence, in close coordination with the Departments of State, Defense, Homeland Security, Justice, the Nuclear Regulatory Commission, and agencies under the Director of National Intelligence.

While the specifics of NMIP are classified, the goal of NMIP is to consolidate information from all sources pertaining to worldwide nuclear materials holdings and their security status into an integrated and continuously updated information management system. This will help us understand the gaps in our current knowledge and ensure that such information is available to support all appropriate Federal departments' and agencies' nonproliferation, counterproliferation and counterterrorism efforts. NMIP also is developing a national registry for identifying and tracking nuclear material samples that are held throughout the U.S. to support the information needs of the United Stated Government."

ENDNOTES

1. President Bush, The National Security Strategy of the United States of America, September 17, 2002, as quoted in HSPD 4 (unclassified version).

2. The 9/11 Commission Report, p. 380. http://www.9-11commission.gov/report/911Report.pdf.

3. World At Risk, The Report of the Commission on the Prevention of WMD Proliferation and Terrorism Vintage books, December 2008. http://documents.scribd.com/docs/15bq1nrl9aerfu0yu9qd.pdf. p. xv.

4. HSPD 4/NSPD 17, National Strategy to Combat Weapons of Mass Destruction, December 2002 [unclassified version], http://www.fas.org/irp/offdocs/nspd/nspd-wmd.pdf.

5. Intelligence Reform and Terrorism Prevention Act Of 2004, (IRTPA), December 17, 2004, Public Law 108–458, http://frwebgate.access.gpo.gov/cgi-bin/getdoc.cgi?dbname=108_cong_public_laws&docid=f:publ458.108.pdf.

6. NSPD 43/HSPD 14. Domestic Nuclear Detection, April 15, 2005. http://www.fas.org/irp/offdocs/nspd/nspd-43.html.

7. Executive Order 13382—Blocking Property of Weapons of Mass Destruction Proliferators and Their Supporters, Federal Register Vol. 70, No. 126, July 1, 2005. http://edocket.access.gpo.gov/2005/pdf/05-13214.pdf.

8. Domestic Nuclear Detection Office, Title V of the Security And Accountability For Every Port Act of 2006 (Public Law 109–347). http://thomas.loc.gov/cgi-bin/toGPObss/http://frwebgate.access.gpo.gov/cgi-bin/getdoc.cgi?dbname=109_cong_public_laws&docid=f:publ347.109.

9. Improving Critical Infrastructure Security, Title XI, Enhanced Defenses Against Weapons Of Mass Destruction, Implementing Recommendations of The 9/11 Commission Act, August 3, 2007. http://www.nctc.gov/docs/ir-of-the-9-11-comm-act-of-2007.pdf.

10. HSPD 17/ NSPD 48, Nuclear Materials Information Center, Testimony Before the Committee on Homeland Security and Governmental Affairs, U.S. Senate, April 2008. http://hsgac.senate.gov/public/_files/040208MowattLarssen.pdf.

11. How do we strike back at an enemy without a home base and without citizens to be responsible for?

    "How can one successfully deter attackers who see their own death as the ultimate (spiritual) gain, who have little they hold dear that we can threaten retaliation against, and who perceive continued restraint as the violation of what they see as a religious duty to alter an unacceptable status quo through violence?" Kevin Chilton, General, USAF, Greg Weaver, "Waging Deterrence in the Twenty-First Century," Strategic Studies Quarterly, Vol. 3, No. 1, Spring, 2009, p. 37. http://www.au.af.mil/au/ssq/2009/Spring/chilton.pdf.

    Subnational actors . . . "act subnationally in order to divest themselves of the obligations that come with legitimacy and sometimes seek to exact control based on a reward system that includes the afterlife . . . Rationality in the international system is based on a this-life reward system." Norton A. Schwartz, General, USAF, Timothy R. Kirk, Lieutenant Colonel, USAF, "Policy and Purpose, The Economy of Deterrence," Strategic Studies Quarterly, Vol. 3, No. 1, Spring, 2009, p. 26. http://www.au.af.mil/au/ssq/2009/Spring/schwartz.pdf.

    "One of the troubling aspects of this problem, for example, concerns the relatively easy issue of biological warfare or dirty bombs. It is not clear what we can do in response to that threat other than the active measures of trying to intercept these weapons before they are deployed. It would be very nice if the people in the general region from which the terrorists come all believed in their gut that if the U.S. or the West were attacked with these weapons, they would be attacked too, even if not in a very straightforward way and not clear how. It would be good if they believed it was inevitable. Unfortunately, I do not think they do." Paul Davis, Deterring Tacit and Direct Support. 2008 Unrestricted Warfare Symposium, Johns Hopkins University, Applied Physics Lab, March 10–11, 2008. Proceedings, p. 233. http://www.jhuapl.edu/urw_symposium/Proceedings/2008/Authors/Davis.pdf.

12. "The Nuclear Suppliers Group is a group of nuclear supplier countries which seeks to contribute to the nonproliferation of nuclear weapons through the implementation of guidelines for nuclear exports." http://www.nuclearsuppliersgroup.org/.

13. "Our Committee, named after its first Chairman Prof. Claude Zangger, was formed following the coming into force of the Nuclear Non-Proliferation Treaty (NPT), to serve as the "faithful interpreter" of its Article III, paragraph 2, to harmonize the interpretation of nuclear export control policies for NPT Parties.

    The Committee has been focussing on what is meant in Article III.2 of the Treaty by "especially designed or prepared equipment or material for the processing, use or production of special fissionable material." The Zangger Committee maintains a Trigger List (triggering safeguards as a condition of supply) of nuclear-related strategic goods to assist NPT Parties in identifying equipment and materials subject to export controls.

    Today the Zangger Committee has 37 members including all the nuclear weapon States. Its Trigger List includes illustrative examples of equipment and materials judged to be within the understandings of the Committee. The Trigger List and the Zangger Committee's understandings are published by the International Atomic Energy Agency (IAEA) in the INFCIRC/209 series." http://www.zanggercommittee.org/Zangger/default.htm (accessed March 18, 2009).

14. "The Organisation for the Prohibition of Chemical Weapons (OPCW) is the implementing body of the Chemical Weapons Convention (CWC or Convention)." http://www.opcw.org/about-opcw/.

15. "The Biological Weapons Convention (BWC) entered into force in 1975. It bans development, production, stockpiling or otherwise acquiring/retaining microbial or other biological agents or toxins whatever their origin that have no justification for prophylactic, protective or other peaceful purposes. It also covers weapons, equipment or means of delivery designed to use biological agents for hostile purposes or in armed conflict. To strengthen efforts to combat the BW threat, States Parties agreed at the November 2002 BWC Review Conference

to have experts meet annually through 2006 to discuss and promote common understanding and effective action on biosecurity, national implementation measures, suspicious outbreaks of disease, disease surveillance and codes of conduct for scientists." US Department of State. http://www.state.gov/t/isn/bw/.

16. "The Australia Group is an informal forum of countries which, through the harmonisation of export controls, seeks to ensure that exports do not contribute to the development of chemical or biological weapons. Coordination of national export control measures assists Australia Group participants to fulfil their obligations under the Chemical Weapons Convention and the Biological and Toxin Weapons Convention to the fullest extent possible." http://www.australiagroup.net/en/index.html.

17. "The Missile Technology Control Regime is an informal and voluntary association of countries which share the goals of non-proliferation of unmanned delivery systems capable of delivering weapons of mass destruction, and which seek to coordinate national export licensing efforts aimed at preventing their proliferation." http://www.mtcr.info/english/index.html.

18. "The [International Code of Conduct Against Ballistic Missile Proliferation] calls for greater restraint in developing, testing, using, and transferring ballistic missiles. It does not prohibit owning missiles or discriminate against their use in conducting peaceful operations in outer space. The key elements of the Code require state signatories to:...ratify, accede, or otherwise abide by the Treaty on Principles Governing the Activities of States in the Exploration and Use of Outer Space, including the Moon and Other Celestial Bodies (1967), the Convention on International Liability for Damage Caused by Space Objects (1972), and the Convention on Registration of Objects Launched into Outer Space (1975); curb and prevent the proliferation of Ballistic Missiles capable of delivering weapons of mass destruction, both at a global and regional level, through multilateral, bilateral and national endeavors..." http://www.nti.org/db/China/icoc.htm (accessed March 18, 2009).

ADDITIONAL RESOURCES

Will Terrorists Go Nuclear, by Brian Michael Jenkins, Prometheus Books, 2008. Includes an extensive reading list.

"Joint Service Chemical and Biological Defense Program FY 08-09 Overview," http://www.acq.osd.mil/cp/cbdreports/cbd0vw08.pdf

"Securing Vulnerable Nuclear Materials: Meeting the Global Challenge," November 2009, By Kenneth N. Luongo, Stanley Foundation, November 2009, http://www.stanleyfoundation.org/publications/pab/Luongo_PAB1109.pdf

"Terrorism and WMD: The Link with the War in Afghanistan," Center for Strategic & International Studies (CSIS), Nov. 9, 2009, http://csis.org/files/publication/091109_Terrorism_WMD.pdf

"The Clock is Ticking: A Progress Report on America's Preparedness to Prevent Weapons of Mass Destruction Proliferation and Terrorism," by the bipartisan Commission on the Prevention of Weapons of Mass Destruction Proliferation and Terrorism. The report is especially concerned with bioterrorism. October 21, 2009, http://www.preventwmd.gov/static/docs/report/WMDRpt10-20Final.pdf

"World at Risk," the Report of the Commission on the Prevention of Weapons of Mass Destruction Proliferation and Terrorism, Vantage Books, December 2008. Also available online at http://www.preventwmd.gov/static/docs/report/worldatrisk_full.pdf

"The authors carry out a scenario analysis and strategic gaming revolving around a catastrophic terrorist attack on the Port of Long Beach." "Considering the Effects of a Catastrophic Terrorist Attack," Charles Meade and Roger C. Molander, Rand 2006, http://www.rand.org/pubs/technical_reports/2006/RAND_TR391.pdf

National Counterproliferation Center

The National Counterproliferation Center (NCPC) was founded on November 21, 2005 in the Office of the Director of National Intelligence to help the United States counter the threats caused by the proliferation of chemical, biological, radiological and nuclear weapons. www.Counterwmd.Gov

Global Security.org has many links regarding Weapons of Mass Destruction, including state-specific links to countries in the news. http://www.globalsecurity.org/index.html

The Domestic Nuclear Detection Office (DNDO) is a jointly staffed office to improve the Nation's capability to detect and report unauthorized attempts to import, possess, store, develop, or transport nuclear or radiological material for use against the Nation... http://www.dhs.gov/xabout/structure/editorial_0766.shtm

"Preventing Nuclear Terrorism: Evolving Forms of the Nuclear Genie," Rolf Mowatt-Larssen, *October 2009, Belfer Center, Harvard University,* http://belfercenter.ksg.harvard.edu/files/Evolving%20Forms%20of%20Nuclear%20Genie.pdf

DOD Bioweapons Report to Congress April 2009 http://www.acq.osd.mil/cp/cbdreports/cbdpreporttocongress2009.pdf

The Federation of American Scientists has an online resource devoted to biological and chemical warfare and another called the Nuclear Information Project. http://www.fas.org/

Export control and treaty compliance. http://www.bis.doc.gov/

Los Alamos National Laboratory is a national security science laboratory. "The Lab works to realize a capabilities-based approach to science for the needs of U.S. national security." http://www.lanl.gov/natlsecurity/index.shtml

"Nuclear Zero: Key Issues to be Addressed," Carnegie Endowment for International Peace, *Security Index Journal,* Vol. 15, No. 3-4 (88-89), Summer/Fall 2009, http://www.carnegieendowment.org/publications/index.cfm?fa=view&id=23719&prog=zgp&proj=znpp

"CBW Magazine: Journal on Chemical and Biological Weapons," Institute for Defence Studies and Analyses, v. 2, no. 4,

July-September 2009, Overview of National Implementation Measures for Use of Micro-organisms - BTWC Concerns; European Union Policy on CBRN security: A Primer; Counter Bio-Terror; An Assessment of Iran's Chemical and Biological Weapons; http://www.idsa.in/publications/cbw/CBW2(4).pdf

Truman National Security Project, Nuclear Weapons: A New Paradigm for the 21st Century, July 30, 2009, http://www.truman project.org/files/backgrounders/Nuclear_Weapons.pdf.

"Nuclear Cooperation with Other Countries: A Primer," by Paul K. Kerr and Mary Beth Nikitin, Congressional Research Service, July 21, 2009 RS 22937, http://www.fas.org/sgp/crs/nuke/RS22937.pdf

"Road to 2010: Addressing the Nuclear Question in the Twenty First Century," Great Britain. Cabinet Office, Presented to Parliament by the Prime Minister, by Command of Her Majesty, http://www.cabinetoffice.gov.uk/reports/roadto2010.aspx

"Toward an Intelligence-based Nuclear Cooperation Regime," by Rens Lee, July 2009, http://www.fpri.org/enotes/200907 .lee.intelligencenuclarcooperation.html

"Some Nuclear Cuts are Feasible, but Big Ones are Dangerous," Loren B. Thompson, Ph.D. Lexington Institute, July 15, 2009, http://lexingtoninstitute.org/1448.shtml

"A Smuggler's Procurement of Nuclear Dual-Use Pressure Transducers for Iran," David Albright, Paul Brannan and Andrea Scheel, Institute for Science and International Security, July 14, 2009, http://isis-online.org/publications/iran/Yadegari_ Iran_illicit_trade_14July2009.pdf

"Smugglers Assist North Korea-Directed Illicit Trade to Myanmar," David Albright, Paul Brannan and Andrea Scheel, July 14, 2009, Institute for Science and International Security, http://isis-online.org/publications/dprk/North_Korea_Myanmar_illicit_ trade_14July2009.pdf

"Are We Prepared?: Four WMD Crises That Could Transform U.S. Security," Center for the Study of Weapons of Mass Destruction (CSWMD), June 2009, http://www.ndu.edu/WMDCenter/docUploaded/Are%20We%20Prepared.pdf

Worst-Case Scenario: Dealing with WMD Must Be Part of Providing for Common Defense, James Jay Carafano, Ph.D. Heritage Foundation. June 29, 2009, http://www.heritage.org/Research/HomelandSecurity/upload/AR05.pdf

Achieving Nonproliferation Goals: Moving From Denial to Technology Governance, June 2009, Stimson Center, http://www .stanleyfoundation.org/publications/pab/TurpenPAB609.pdf

Summary of a Workshop, Assessing Medical Preparedness to Respond to a Terrorist Nuclear Event: [download is free but registration is required], 2009, http://www.nap.edu/catalog.php?record_id=12578

Combating Nuclear Smuggling: Lessons Learned from DHS Testing of Advanced Radiation Detection Portal Monitors, GAO-09-804T [testimony], June 25, 2009, http://www.gao.gov/new.items/d09804t.pdf

The Science of Security: Lessons Learned in Developing, Testing and Operating Advanced Radiation Monitors, June 25, 2009, http://science.house.gov/publications/hearings_markups_details .aspx?NewsID=2513

Joint Chiefs of Staff, JP 3-40, Combating Weapons of Mass Destruction, 10 June 2009 http://www.dtic.mil/doctrine/jel/new_pubs/jp3_40.pdf

Combating Nuclear Smuggling: DHS Improved Testing of Advanced Radiation Detection Portal Monitors, but Preliminary Results Show Limits of the New Technology, GAO-09-655, May 2009, http://www.gao.gov/new.items/d09655.pdf

"America's Strategic Posture, The Final Report of the Congressional Commission on the Strategic Posture of the United States," http://www.usip.org/strategic_posture/final.html.

"From Counterforce to Minimal Deterrence: A New Nuclear Policy on the Path Toward Eliminating Nuclear Weapons." http://www.fas.org/programs/ssp/nukes/doctrine/targeting.pdf p. 1.

"Beyond START: Negotiating the Next Step in U.S. and Russian Strategic Nuclear Arms Reductions," Steven Pifer, Brookings Institute, Policy Paper number 15, May 2009. http://www .brookings.edu/~/media/Files/rc/papers/2009/05_arms_reduction _pifer/05_arms_reduction_pifer.pdf.

"This Policy Outlook by an eminent Dutch scholar argues that nuclear weapons have unintended beneficial consequences. They can make the intended development of a more peaceful global and political order possible. The Carnegie Nonproliferation Program presents this paper in hopes of furthering international dialogue and debate on the nuclear order, including the abolition of nuclear weapons." "The Taming of the Great Nuclear Powers," Godfried van Benthem van den Bergh, Carnegie Endowment, May 2009. http://www.carnegieendowment.org/files/taming_great_powers.pdf

"Nuclear Disarmament: US and Russia Resume Negotiations," No. 53, by Oliver Thränert, International Relations and Security Network, May 2009, http://www.isn.ethz.ch/isn/Digital-Library/Publications/Detail/?lng=en&id=100009

"Building Partner Capacity to Combat Weapons of Mass Destruction," by Jennifer D. P. Moroney and Joe Hogler, with Benjamin Bahney, Kim Cragin, David R. Howell, Charlotte Lynch, S. Rebecca Zimmerman, Rand, 2009. http://www.rand.org/pubs/monographs/MG783/

"Considering the Effects of a Catastrophic Terrorist Attack," by Charles Meade and Roger C. Molander, RAND Center for Terrorism Risk Management Policy, 2006, http://www.rand.org/pubs/technical_reports/2006/RAND_TR391.pdf

"Deterrence and Influence in Counterterrorism: A Component in the War on al Qaeda," by Paul K. Davis and Brian Michael Jenkins, Prepared for the Defense Advanced Research Projects Agency, Rand National Defense Research Institute, 2002, http://www.rand.org/pubs/monograph_reports/MR1619/MR1619.pdf

16

BIODEFENSE AND WMD MEDICAL COUNTERMEASURES

Section 817 of the Patriot Act, entitled "Expansion of The Biological Weapons Statute" creates a new crime in the existing Biological Weapons Statute that prohibits possession of biological agents or toxins.[1] Not included here, the remainder of section 817 adds a new section prohibiting certain persons (felons, fugitives, illegal aliens, etc.) from shipping or transporting certain listed biological agents or toxins.

The Homeland Security Act, Sec. 1708, established a National Bio-Weapons Defense Analysis Center.

The National Strategy for the Physical Protection of Critical Infrastructures and Key Assets, in the section entitled "Public Health," describes the public health sector and lays out the challenges this sector faces. It states the familiar notion that public health workers have traditionally exposed themselves to harm during emergencies, but have not expected to be targets themselves. Most hospitals, it points out, are freely accessible, and while in some circumstances this is good, under other circumstances, such as an epidemic, this is dangerous. One of the more important public health sector initiatives is to dramatically improve communications to the public during emergencies.

HSPD 10 sets forth the four pillars of our Biodefense: Threat Awareness, Prevention and Protection, Surveillance and Detection, and Response and Recovery and elaborates on each of them.

HSPD 18 is devoted to medical countermeasures against weapons of mass destruction. It admits that having the proper resources for all possible threats at all times and in all places is not possible and establishes a two-tiered approach to development of countermeasures. Tier 1 focuses on developing Agent-Specific countermeasures. Tier 2 relates to developing new medical countermeasures. This HSPD addresses biological, chemical, and nuclear threats.

The Implementing Recommendations of the 9/11 Commission Act established the National Biosurveillance Integration Center to "identify, characterize, localize, and track a biological event of national concern." HSPD 21, building upon HSPD 10 three years earlier, established a national Strategy for Public Health and Medical Preparedness and supported establishing a branch of medicine called "disaster medicine."

SOURCES

- Patriot Act, October 26, 2001[2]
  Sec. 817. Expansion Of The Biological Weapons Statute
- Public Health Security and Bioterrorism Preparedness and Response Act of June 12, 2002[3]
- Homeland Security Act, November 25, 2002[4]
  Sec. 1708. National Bio-Weapons Defense Analysis Center
- National Strategy for the Physical Protection of Critical Infrastructures and Key Assets, February 2003[5]
- Executive Order 13295 of April 4, 2003, Revised List of Quarantinable Communicable Diseases[6]
- HSPD 10. Biodefense for the 21st Century, April 28, 2004[7]
- Project BioShield Act of 2004, P.L. 108–276, July 21, 2004[8]
- Post Katrina Emergency Management Reform Act, October 4, 2006[9]
- HSPD 18. Medical Countermeasures against Weapons of Mass Destruction, January 31, 2007[10]

- Implementing Recommendations of the 9/11 Commission Act of August 2007[11]
- HSPD 21. Public Health and Medical Preparedness, October 18, 2007[12]
- DOD National Center for Medical Intelligence, March 2009[13]
- National Strategy for Countering Biological Threats, November 2009[14]

Patriot Act

"18 USC Sec. 175 is amended by inserting:

'(b) ADDITIONAL OFFENSE.— Whoever knowingly possesses any biological agent, toxin, or delivery system of a type or in a quantity that, under the circumstances, is not reasonably justified by a prophylactic, protective, bona fide research, or other peaceful purpose, shall be fined under this title, imprisoned not more than 10 years, or both. In this subsection, the terms 'biological agent' and 'toxin' do not encompass any biological agent or toxin that is in its naturally occurring environment, if the biological agent or toxin has not been cultivated, collected, or otherwise extracted from its natural source..."

Public Health Security and Bioterrorism Preparedness and Response Act of 2002

An act to improve the ability of the United States to prevent, prepare for, and respond to bioterrorism and other public health emergencies.

TITLE I—NATIONAL PREPAREDNESS FOR BIOTERRORISM AND OTHER PUBLIC HEALTH EMERGENCIES

Subtitle A—National Preparedness and Response Planning, Coordinating, and Reporting

SEC. 101. NATIONAL PREPAREDNESS AND RESPONSE.

(a) IN GENERAL.— The Public Health Service Act (42 U.S.C. 201 et seq.) is amended by adding at the end the following title:

"TITLE XXVIII—NATIONAL PREPAREDNESS FOR BIOTERRORISM AND OTHER PUBLIC HEALTH EMERGENCIES

"Subtitle A—National Preparedness and Response Planning, Coordinating, and Reporting

Sec. 2801. National Preparedness Plan.

"(a) IN GENERAL.

"(1) *PREPAREDNESS AND RESPONSE REGARDING PUBLIC HEALTH EMERGENCIES.*— The Secretary shall further develop and implement a coordinated strategy, building upon the core public health capabilities established pursuant to section 319A, for carrying out health-related activities to prepare for and respond effectively to bioterrorism and other public health emergencies, including the preparation of a plan under this section. The Secretary shall periodically thereafter review and, as appropriate, revise the plan.

"(b) PREPAREDNESS GOALS.— The plan under subsection (a) should include provisions in furtherance of the following:

"(1) Providing effective assistance to State and local governments in the event of bioterrorism or other public health emergency.

"(2) Ensuring that State and local governments have appropriate capacity to detect and respond effectively to such emergencies, including capacities for the following:

"(A) Effective public health surveillance and reporting mechanisms at the State and local levels.

"(B) Appropriate laboratory readiness.

"(C) Properly trained and equipped emergency response, public health, and medical personnel.

"(D) Health and safety protection of workers responding to such an emergency.

"(E) Public health agencies that are prepared to coordinate health services (including mental health services) during and after such emergencies.

"(F) Participation in communications networks that can effectively disseminate relevant information in a timely and secure manner to appropriate public and private entities and to the public.

"(3) Developing and maintaining medical countermeasures (such as drugs, vaccines and other biological products, medical devices, and other supplies) against biological agents toxins that may be involved in such emergencies.

"(4) Ensuring coordination and minimizing duplication of Federal, State, and local planning, preparedness, and response activities, including during the investigation of a suspicious disease outbreak or other potential public health emergency.

"(5) Enhancing the readiness of hospitals and other health care facilities to respond effectively to such emergencies.

SEC. 102. ASSISTANT SECRETARY FOR PUBLIC HEALTH EMERGENCY PREPAREDNESS; NATIONAL DISASTER MEDICAL SYSTEM.

(a) IN GENERAL.— Title XXVIII of the Public Health Service Act, as added by section 101 of this Act, is amended by adding at the end the following subtitle:

"Subtitle B—Emergency Preparedness and Response

Sec. 2811. Coordination of Preparedness for and Response to Bioterrorism and Other Public Health Emergencies.

"**(a)** *Assistant Secretary for Public Health Emergency Preparedness.*

"**(1) IN GENERAL.—** There is established within the Department of Health and Human Services the position of Assistant Secretary for Public Health Emergency Preparedness.

"**(b)** *National Disaster Medical System.*

"**(1) IN GENERAL.—** The Secretary shall provide for the operation in accordance with this section of a system to be known as the National Disaster Medical System. The Secretary shall designate the Assistant Secretary for Public Health Emergency Preparedness as the head of the National Disaster Medical System, subject to the authority of the Secretary.

"**(2) FEDERAL AND STATE COLLABORATIVE SYSTEM.**

"**(A)** *IN GENERAL.—* The National Disaster Medical System shall be a coordinated effort by the Federal agencies specified in subparagraph (B), working in collaboration with the States and other appropriate public or private entities, to carry out the purposes described in paragraph (3).

"**(B)** *PARTICIPATING FEDERAL AGENCIES.—* The Federal agencies referred to in subparagraph (A) are the Department of Health and Human Services, the Federal Emergency Management Agency, the Department of Defense, and the Department of Veterans Affairs.

"**(3) PURPOSE OF SYSTEM.**

"**(A)** *IN GENERAL.—* The Secretary may activate the National Disaster Medical System to—

"(i) provide health services, health-related social services, other appropriate human services, and appropriate auxiliary services to respond to the needs of victims of a public health emergency (whether or not determined to be a public health emergency under section 319);. . .

SEC. 103. IMPROVING ABILITY OF CENTERS FOR DISEASE CONTROL AND PREVENTION.

Section 319D of the Public Health Service Act (42 U.S.C. 247d-4) is amended to read as follows:

Sec. 319D. Revitalizing the Centers for Disease Control and Prevention.

"**(a) FACILITIES; CAPACITIES.**

"**(1)** *FINDINGS.—* Congress finds that the Centers for Disease Control and Prevention has an essential role in defending against and combatting public health threats and requires secure and modern facilities, and expanded and improved capabilities related to bioterrorism and other public health emergencies, sufficient to enable such Centers to conduct this important mission.

"**(2)** *FACILITIES.*

"**(A)** *IN GENERAL.—* The Director of the Centers for Disease Control and Prevention may design, construct, equip new facilities, renovate existing facilities (including laboratories, laboratory support buildings, communication facilities, transshipment complexes, secured and isolated parking structures, buildings, and other facilities and infrastructure), and upgrade security of such facilities, in order to better conduct the capacities described in section 319A, and for supporting public health activities.

"**(3)** *IMPROVING THE CAPACITIES OF THE CENTERS FOR DISEASE CONTROL AND PREVENTION.—* The Secretary, taking into account evaluations under section 319B(a), shall expand, enhance, and improve the capabilities of the Centers for Disease Control and Prevention relating to preparedness for and responding effectively to bioterrorism and other public health emergencies.

Activities that may be carried out under the preceding sentence include–

"(A) expanding or enhancing the training of personnel;

"(B) improving communications facilities and networks, including delivery of necessary information to rural areas;

"(C) improving capabilities for public health surveillance and reporting activities, taking into account the integrated system or systems of public health alert communications and surveillance networks under subsection (b); and

"(D) improving laboratory facilities related to bioterrorism and other public health emergencies, increasing the security of such facilities.

"(b) NATIONAL COMMUNICATIONS AND SURVEILLANCE NETWORKS.

"(1) *IN GENERAL.*— The Secretary, directly or through awards of grants, contracts, or cooperative agreements, shall provide for the establishment of an integrated system or systems of public health alert communications and surveillance networks between and among

"(A) Federal, State, and local public health officials;

"(B) public and private health-related laboratories, hospitals, and other health care facilities;

SEC. 104. ADVISORY COMMITTEES AND COMMUNICATIONS; STUDY REGARDING COMMUNICATIONS ABILITIES OF PUBLIC HEALTH AGENCIES.

(a) *In General.* Section 319F of the Public Health Service Act (42 U.S.C. 247d-6) is amended–

(3) by inserting after subsection (a) the following subsections:

"(2) National advisory committee on children and terrorism.

"(A) IN GENERAL.— For purposes of paragraph (1), Secretary shall establish an advisory committee to be known as the National Advisory Committee on Children and Terrorism (referred to in this paragraph as the 'Advisory Committee').

"(B) DUTIES.— The Advisory Committee shall provide recommendations regarding–

"(i) the preparedness of the health care (including mental health care) system to respond to bioterrorism as it relates to children;

"(ii) needed changes to the health care and emergency medical service systems and emergency medical services protocols to meet the special needs of children; and

"(iii) changes, if necessary, to the national stockpile under section 121 of the Public Health Security and Bioterrorism Preparedness and Response Act of 2002 to meet the emergency health security of children.

"(A) *IN GENERAL.*— For purposes of paragraph (1), Secretary shall establish an advisory committee to be known as the Emergency Public Information and Advisory Committee (referred to in this paragraph as the 'EPIC Advisory Committee').

"(B) *DUTIES.*— The EPIC Advisory Committee shall make recommendations to the Secretary and the working group under subsection (a) and report on appropriate ways to communicate public health information regarding bioterrorism and other public health emergencies to the public.

"(C) *STRATEGY FOR COMMUNICATION OF INFORMATION REGARDING BIOTERRORISM AND OTHER PUBLIC HEALTH EMERGENCIES.*— In coordination with working group under subsection (a), the Secretary shall develop a strategy for effectively communicating information regarding bioterrorism and other public health emergencies, and shall develop means by which to communicate such information.

(b) *Study Regarding Communications Abilities of Public Health Agencies.*— The Secretary of Health and Human Services, in consultation with the Federal Communications Commission, the National Telecommunications and Information Administration, and other appropriate Federal agencies, shall conduct a study to determine whether local public health entities have the ability to maintain communications in the event of a bioterrorist attack or other public health emergency.

SEC. 105. EDUCATION OF HEALTH CARE PERSONNEL; TRAINING REGARDING PEDIATRIC ISSUES.

Section 319F(g) of the Public Health Service Act, as redesignated by section 104(a)(2) of this Act, is amended to read as follows:

"(g) Education; Training Regarding Pediatric Issues.

"(1) MATERIALS; CORE CURRICULUM.—The Secretary . . . **shall–**

"(A) develop materials for teaching the elements of a core curriculum for the recognition and identification of potential bioweapons and other agents that may create a public health emergency, and for the care of victims of such emergencies, recognizing the special needs of children and other vulnerable populations, to public health officials, medical professionals, emergency physicians and other emergency department staff, laboratory personnel, and other personnel working in health care facilities (including poison control centers);

"(B) develop a core curriculum and materials for community-wide planning by State and local governments, and other health care facilities, emergency response units, and appropriate public and private sector entities to respond to a bioterrorist attack or other public health emergency;

SEC. 107. EMERGENCY SYSTEM FOR ADVANCE REGISTRATION OF HEALTH PROFESSIONS VOLUNTEERS.

Part B of title III of the Public Health Service Act, as amended by section 106 of this Act, is amended by inserting after section 319H the following section:

Sec. 319I. Emergency System for Advance Registration of Health Professions Volunteers.

"(a) IN GENERAL.— The Secretary shall. . . establish and maintain a system for the advance registration of health professionals for the purpose of verifying the credentials, licenses, accreditations, and hospital privileges of such professionals when, during public health emergencies, the professionals volunteer to provide health services (referred to in this section as the 'verification system'). In carrying out the preceding sentence, the Secretary shall provide for an electronic database for the verification system.

"(d) COORDINATION AMONG STATES.— The Secretary may encourage each State to provide legal authority during a public health emergency for health professionals authorized in another State to provide certain health services to provide such health services in the State.

SEC. 108. WORKING GROUP.
Section 319F of the Public Health Service Act, as amended by section 104(a), is amended by striking subsection (a) and inserting the following:

"(a) *Working Group on Bioterrorism and Other Public Health Emergencies.*

"(1) IN GENERAL.— The Secretary. . . shall establish a working group on the prevention, preparedness, response to bioterrorism and other public health emergencies. Such joint working group,. . . meet . . . for the purpose of consultation on, assisting in, and making recommendations on—

"(A) responding to a bioterrorist attack. . .

"(B) prioritizing countermeasures required to treat, prevent, or identify exposure to a biological agent or toxin pursuant to section 351A;

"(C) facilitation. . . for the development, manufacture, distribution, supply-chain management, and purchase of priority countermeasures;

"(D) research on pathogens likely to be used in a biological threat or attack on the civilian population;

"(E) development of shared standards for equipment to detect and to protect against biological agents and toxins;

"(F) assessment of the priorities for and enhancement of the preparedness of public health institutions, providers of medical care, and other emergency service personnel (including firefighters) to detect, diagnose, and respond (including mental health response) to a biological threat or attack;

"(G) in the recognition that medical and public health professionals are likely to provide much of the first response to such an attack, development and enhancement of the quality of joint planning and training programs that address the public health and medical consequences of a biological threat or attack on the civilian population between–

"(i) local firefighters, ambulance personnel, and public security officers, or other emergency response personnel (including private response contractors); and

"(ii) hospitals, primary care facilities, and public health agencies;

"(H) development of strategies for Federal, State, and local agencies to communicate information to the public regarding biological threats or attacks;

"(I) ensuring that the activities under this subsection address the health security needs of children and other vulnerable populations;

"(J) strategies for decontaminating facilities contaminated as a result of a biological attack. . .

SEC. 121. STRATEGIC NATIONAL STOCKPILE.

(a) *Strategic National Stockpile.*

(1) IN GENERAL.— The Secretary of Health and Human Services (referred to in this section as the "Secretary"), in coordination with the Secretary of Veterans Affairs, shall maintain a stockpile or stockpiles of drugs, vaccines and other biological products, medical devices, and other supplies in such numbers, types, and amounts as are determined by the Secretary to be appropriate and practicable, taking into account other available sources, to provide for the emergency health security of the United States, including the emergency health security of children and other vulnerable populations, in the event of a bioterrorist attack or other public health emergency.

(c) *Disclosures.* No Federal agency shall disclose under section 552, United States Code, any information identifying the location at which materials in the stockpile under subsection (a) are stored.

SEC. 122. ACCELERATED APPROVAL OF PRIORITY COUNTERMEASURES.

(a) IN GENERAL.— The Secretary of Health and Human Services may designate a priority countermeasure as a fast-track product . . .

(b) USE OF ANIMAL TRIALS.— A drug for which approval is sought under section 505(b) of the Federal Food, Drug, and Cosmetic Act or section 351 of the Public Health Service Act on the basis of evidence of effectiveness that is derived from animal studies pursuant to section 123 may be designated as a fast track product for purposes of this section.

SEC. 124. SECURITY FOR COUNTERMEASURE DEVELOPMENT AND PRODUCTION.

Part B of title III of the Public Health Service Act, as amended by section 110 of this Act, is amended by inserting after section 319J the following section:

SEC. 125. ACCELERATED COUNTERMEASURE RESEARCH AND DEVELOPMENT.

Section 319F(h) of the Public Health Service Act, as redesignated by section 104(a)(2) of this Act, is amended to read as follows:

''(h) Accelerated Research and Development on Priority Pathogens and Countermeasures.

''(1) IN GENERAL.— With respect to pathogens of potential use in a bioterrorist attack, and other agents that may cause a public health emergency, the Secretary, taking into consideration any recommendations of the working group under subsection (a), shall conduct, and award grants, contracts, or cooperative agreements for, research, investigations, , demonstrations, and studies in the health sciences relating to–

(A) the epidemiology and pathogenesis of such pathogens;

(B) the sequencing of the genomes, or other DNA analysis, or other comparative analysis, of priority pathogens (as determined by the Director of the National Institutes of Health in consultation with the working group established in subsection (a)),

(C) the development of priority countermeasures; and

''(3) ROLE OF DEPARTMENT OF VETERANS AFFAIRS.— In carrying out paragraph (1), the Secretary shall consider using the biomedical research and development capabilities of the Department of Veterans Affairs, in conjunction with that Department's affiliations with health-professions universities.

''(4) PRIORITY COUNTERMEASURES.— For purposes of this section, the term 'priority countermeasure' means a drug, product, device, vaccine, vaccine adjuvant, or diagnostic test that the Secretary determines to be–

''(A) a priority to treat, identify, or prevent infection by a biological agent or toxin listed pursuant to section 351A(a)(1), or harm from any other agent that may cause a public health emergency; or

''(B) a priority to diagnose conditions that may result in adverse health consequences or death and may be caused by the administering of a drug, biological product, device, vaccine, vaccine adjuvant, antiviral, diagnostic test that is a priority under subparagraph (A).''.

SEC. 126. EVALUATION OF NEW AND EMERGING TECHNOLOGIES REGARDING BIOTERRORIST ATTACK AND OTHER PUBLIC HEALTH EMERGENCIES.

(a) IN GENERAL.— The Secretary of Health and Human Services (referred to in this section as the ''Secretary'') shall promptly carry out a program to periodically evaluate new and emerging technologies. . .

SEC. 127. POTASSIUM IODIDE.

(a) IN GENERAL.— Through the national stockpile under section 121, the President, subject to subsections (b) and (c), shall make available to State and local governments potassium iodide tablets for stockpiling and for distribution as appropriate to public facilities, such as schools and hospitals, in quantities sufficient to provide adequate protection for the population within 20 miles of a nuclear power plant.

Subtitle C—Improving State, Local, and Hospital Preparedness for and Response to Bioterrorism and Other Public Health Emergencies

SEC. 131. GRANTS TO IMPROVE STATE, LOCAL, AND HOSPITAL PREPAREDNESS FOR AND RESPONSE TO BIOTERRORISM AND OTHER PUBLIC HEALTH EMERGENCIES.

(a) IN GENERAL.— Part B of title III of the Public Health Service Act (42 U.S.C. 243 et seq.) is amended by inserting after section 319C the following sections:

Subtitle E—Additional Provisions

SEC. 152. EXPANDED RESEARCH BY SECRETARY OF ENERGY.

(a) *Detection and Identification Research.*

(1) IN GENERAL.— In conjunction with the working group under section 319F(a) of the Public Health Service

Act, the Secretary of Energy and the Administrator of the National Nuclear Security Administration shall expand, enhance, and intensify research relevant to the rapid detection and identification of pathogens likely to be used in a bioterrorism attack or other agents that may cause a public health emergency.

SEC. 154. ENHANCEMENT OF EMERGENCY PREPAREDNESS OF DEPARTMENT OF VETERANS AFFAIRS.

(a) *Readiness of Department Medical Center.* (1) The Secretary of Veterans Affairs shall take appropriate actions to enhance the readiness of Department of Veterans Affairs medical centers to protect the patients and staff of such centers from chemical or biological attack or otherwise to respond to such an attack and so as to enable such centers to fulfil [*sic*] their obligations as part of the Federal response to public health emegencies.

(2) Actions under paragraph (1) shall include–

"(A) the provision of decontamination equipment and personal protection equipment at Department medical centers; and

"(B) the provision of training in the use of such equipment to staff of such centers.

(f) *Mental Health Counseling.* (1) With respect to activities conducted by personnel serving at Department medical centers, the Secretary shall, in consultation with the Secretary of Health and Human Services, the American Red Cross, and the working group under section 319F(a) of the Public Health Service Act, develop and maintain various strategies for providing mental health counseling and assistance, including counseling and assistance for post-traumatic stress disorder, to local and community emergency response providers, veterans, active duty military personnel, and individuals seeking care at Department medical centers following a bioterrorist attack or other public health emergency.

Homeland Security Act, November 25, 2002[15]

Sec. 1708. National Bio-Weapons Defense Analysis Center

There is established in the Department of Defense a National Bio-Weapons Defense Analysis Center. Its mission is to develop countermeasures to potential attacks by terrorists using weapons of mass destruction.

National Strategy for the Physical Protection of Critical Infrastructures and Key Assets, February, 2003

PUBLIC HEALTH. The public health sector is vast and diverse. It consists of state and local health departments, hos-

pitals, health clinics, mental health facilities, nursing homes, blood-supply facilities, laboratories, mortuaries, and pharmaceutical stockpiles.

Hospitals, clinics, and public health systems play a critical role in mitigating and recovering from the effects of natural disasters or deliberate attacks on the homeland. Physical damage to these facilities or disruption of their operations could prevent a full, effective response and exacerbate the outcome of an emergency situation. Even if a hospital or public health facility were not the direct target of a terrorist strike, it could be significantly impacted by secondary contamination involving chemical, radiological, or biological agents.

In addition to established medical networks, the U.S. depends on several highly specialized laboratory facilities and assets, especially those related to disease control and vaccine development and storage, such as the HHS Centers for Disease Control and Prevention, the National Institutes of Health, and the National Strategic Stockpile.

Public Health Sector Challenges. Public health workers are accustomed to placing themselves in harm's way during an emergency. They may be unlikely, however, to view themselves as potential targets of terrorist acts.

Most hospitals and clinics are freely accessible facilities that provide the public with an array of vital services. This free access, however, also makes it difficult to identify potential threats or prevent malicious entry into these facilities. This fact, combined with a lack of means and standards to recognize and detect potentially contaminated individuals, can have an important impact on facility security and emergency operations.

Another significant challenge is the variation in structural and systems design within our hospitals and clinics. On one hand, so-called "immune buildings" have built-in structural design elements that help prevent contamination and the spread of infectious agents to the greatest extent possible. Such features include controlled airflow systems, isolation rooms, and special surfaces that eliminate infectious agents on contact. At the other extreme are buildings with relatively little built-in environmental protection. Protection of this category of facility presents the greatest challenge.

During an epidemic, infectious individuals who continue to operate in the community at large may pose a significant public health risk. The sector needs to develop comprehensive protocols governing the isolation of infectious individuals during a crisis.

Additional public health sector challenges relate to the maintenance, protection, and distribution of stockpiles of critical emergency resources. Currently, other than the National Strategic Stockpile, there are limited resources for rotating and replenishing supplies of critical materials and medicines. Supply chain management for medical materials also requires greater attention to ensure secure and efficient functioning during an emergency. Potential solutions to these problems are impacted by complex legal and tax issues. Currently, the federal government has only limited regulatory authority to request information from companies concerning their available inventory of medical supplies and their capacity to produce them. Since pharmaceutical companies are taxed on their product inventories, they try to avoid stockpiling finished goods and meet demand through "just-in-time" manufacturing.

Executive Order 13295 Of April 4, 2003, Revised List Of Quarantinable Communicable Diseases

Sec. 1. Based upon the recommendation of the Secretary of Health and Human Services (the "Secretary"), in consultation with the Surgeon General, and for the purpose of specifying certain communicable diseases for regulations providing for the apprehension, detention, or conditional release of individuals to prevent the introduction, transmission, or spread of suspected communicable diseases, the following communicable diseases are hereby specified pursuant to section 361(b) of the Public Health Service Act:

(a) Cholera; Diphtheria; infectious Tuberculosis; Plague; Smallpox; Yellow Fever; and Viral Hemorrhagic Fevers (Lassa, Marburg, Ebola, Crimean-Congo, South American, and others not yet isolated or named).

(b) Severe Acute Respiratory Syndrome (SARS), which is a disease associated with fever and signs and symptoms of pneumonia or other respiratory illness, is transmitted from person to person predominantly by the aerosolized or droplet route, and, if spread in the population, would have severe public health consequences.

Sec. 5. Executive Order 12452 of December 22, 1983, is hereby revoked

HSPD 10. April 28, 2004

... Bioterror attacks could mimic naturally-occurring disease, potentially delaying recognition of an attack and creating uncertainty about whether one has even occurred. An attacker may thus believe that he could escape identification and capture or retaliation.

Biological weapons attacks could be mounted either inside or outside the United States and, because some biological weapons agents are contagious, the effects of an initial attack could spread widely. Disease outbreaks, whether natural or deliberate, respect no geographic or political borders.

Preventing and controlling future biological weapons threats will be even more challenging. Advances in biotech-

nology and life sciences – including the spread of expertise to create modified or novel organisms – present the prospect of new toxins, live agents, and bioregulators that would require new detection methods, preventive measures, and treatments. These trends increase the risk for surprise. Anticipating such threats through intelligence efforts is made more difficult by the dual-use nature of biological technologies and infrastructure, and the likelihood that adversaries will use denial and deception to conceal their illicit activities. The stakes could not be higher for our Nation. Attacks with biological weapons could:

- Cause catastrophic numbers of acute casualties, long-term disease and disability, psychological trauma, and mass panic;
- Disrupt critical sectors of our economy and the day-to-day lives of Americans; and
- Create cascading international effects by disrupting and damaging international trade relationships, potentially globalizing the impacts of an attack on United States soil.

Fortunately, the United States possesses formidable capabilities to mount credible biodefenses. We have mobilized our unrivaled biomedical research infrastructure and expanded our international research relationships. In addition, we have an established medical and public health infrastructure that is being revitalized and expanded. These capabilities provide a critical foundation on which to build improved and comprehensive biodefenses ...

Building on these accomplishments, we conducted a comprehensive evaluation of our biological defense capabilities to identify future priorities and actions to support them. The results of that study provide a blueprint for our future biodefense program, Biodefense for the 21st Century, that fully integrates the sustained efforts of the national and homeland security, medical, public health, intelligence, diplomatic, and law enforcement communities. *Specific direction to departments and agencies to carry out this biodefense program is contained in a classified version of this directive.*

Biodefense for the 21st Century. . . . Defending against biological weapons attacks requires us to further sharpen our policy, coordination, and planning to integrate the biodefense capabilities that reside at the Federal, state, local, and private sector levels. We must further strengthen the strong international dimension to our efforts, which seeks close international cooperation and coordination with friends and allies to maximize our capabilities for mutual defense against biological weapons threats.

While the public health philosophy of the 20th Century - emphasizing prevention - is ideal for addressing natural disease outbreaks, it is not sufficient to confront 21st Century threats where adversaries may use biological weapons agents as part of a long-term campaign of aggression and terror. Health care providers and public health officers are among our first lines of defense. Therefore, we are building on the progress of the past three years to further improve the preparedness of our public health and medical systems to address current and future BW threats and to respond with greater speed and flexibility to multiple or repetitive attacks.

Pillars of Our Biodefense Program. The essential pillars of our national biodefense program are: Threat Awareness, Prevention and Protection, Surveillance and Detection, and Response and Recovery.

Threat Awareness.

Biological Warfare Related Intelligence. Timely, accurate, and relevant intelligence enables all aspects of our national biodefense program.[16] Despite the inherent challenges of identifying and characterizing biological weapons programs and anticipating biological attacks, we are improving the Intelligence Community's ability to collect, analyze, and disseminate intelligence ... Among our many initiatives, we are continuing to develop more forward-looking analyses, to include Red Teaming efforts, to understand new scientific trends that may be exploited by our adversaries to develop biological weapons and to help position intelligence collectors ahead of the problem.

Prevention and Protection

Proactive Prevention. Preventing biological weapons attacks is by far the most cost-effective approach to biodefense. Prevention requires the continuation and expansion of current multilateral initiatives to limit the access of agents, technology, and know-how to countries, groups, or individuals seeking to develop, produce, and use these agents.

To address this challenge, we are further enhancing diplomacy, arms control, law enforcement, multilateral export controls, and threat reduction assistance that impede adversaries seeking biological weapons capabilities. Federal departments and agencies with existing authorities will continue to expand threat reduction assistance programs aimed at preventing the proliferation of biological weapons expertise. We will continue to build international coalitions to support these efforts, encouraging increased political and financial support for nonproliferation and threat reduction programs. We will also continue to expand efforts to control access and use of pathogens to strengthen security and prevention.

Critical Infrastructure Protection. Protecting our critical infrastructure from the effects of biological weapons attacks is a priority. A biological weapons attack might deny us access to essential facilities and response capabilities. Therefore, we are working to improve the survivability and en-

sure the continuity and restoration of operations of critical infrastructure sectors following biological weapons attacks. Assessing the vulnerability of this infrastructure, particularly the medical, public health, food, water, energy, agricultural, and transportation sectors, is the focus of current efforts. The Department of Homeland Security, in coordination with other appropriate Federal departments and agencies, leads these efforts, which include developing and deploying biodetection technologies and decontamination methodologies.

Surveillance and Detection

Attack Warning. Early warning, detection, or recognition of biological weapons attacks to permit a timely response to mitigate their consequences is an essential component of biodefense. Through the President's recently proposed biosurveillance initiative, the United States is working to develop an integrated and comprehensive attack warning system to rapidly recognize and characterize the dispersal of biological agents in human and animal populations, food, water, agriculture, and the environment. ...

Attribution. Deterrence is the historical cornerstone of our defense, and attribution – the identification of the perpetrator as well as method of attack - forms the foundation upon which deterrence rests. Biological weapons, however, lend themselves to covert or clandestine attacks that could permit the perpetrator to remain anonymous. We are enhancing our deterrence posture by improving attribution capabilities. We are improving our capability to perform technical forensic analysis and to assimilate all-source information to enable attribution assessments ...

Mass Casualty Care. Following a biological weapons attack, all necessary means must be rapidly brought to bear to prevent loss of life, illness, psychological trauma, and to contain the spread of potentially contagious diseases. Provision of timely preventive treatments such as antibiotics or vaccines saves lives, protects scarce medical capabilities, preserves social order, and is cost effective.

The Administration is working closely with state and local public health officials to strengthen plans to swiftly distribute needed medical countermeasures. Moreover, we are working to expand and, where needed, create new Federal, state, and local medical and public health capabilities for all-hazard mass casualty care.

The Department of Health and Human Services ... is the principal Federal agency responsible for coordinating all Federal-level assets activated to support and augment the state and local medical and public health response to mass casualty events. For those mass casualty incidents that require parallel deployment of Federal assets in other functional areas such as transportation or law enforcement, the Department of Homeland Security will coordinate the overall

Federal response in accordance with its statutory authorities for domestic incident management . . .

Risk Communication. A critical adjunct capability to mass casualty care is effective risk communication. Timely communications with the general public and the medical and public health communities can significantly influence the success of response efforts, including health- and life-sustaining interventions. Efforts will be made to develop communication strategies, plans, products, and channels to reach all segments of our society, including those with physical or language limitations. These efforts will ensure timely domestic and international dissemination of information that educates and reassures the general public and relevant professional sectors before, during, and after an attack or other public health emergency.

Medical Countermeasure Development. Development and deployment of safe, effective medical countermeasures against biological weapons agents of concern remains an urgent priority. The National Institutes of Health (NIH) . . . is working . . . to shape and execute an aggressive research program to develop better medical countermeasures. NIH's work increasingly will reflect the potential for novel or genetically engineered biological weapons agents and possible scenarios that require providing broad-spectrum coverage against a range of possible biological threats to prevent illness even after exposure. Additionally, we have begun construction of new labs . . .

Decontamination. Recovering from a biological weapons attack may require significant decontamination and remediation activities. We are working to improve Federal capabilities to support states and localities in their efforts to rapidly assess, decontaminate, and return to pre-attack activities, and are developing standards and protocols for the most effective approaches for these activities . . ."

Project Bioshield Act of 2004, July 21, 2004

Be it enacted by the Senate and House of Representatives of the United States of America in Congress assembled,

SEC. 2. BIOMEDICAL COUNTERMEASURE RESEARCH AND DEVELOPMENT AUTHORITIES.

(a) IN GENERAL.— Part B of title III of the Public Health Service Act (42 U.S.C. 243 et seq.) is amended by inserting after section 319F the following section:

Sec. 319F–1. Authority for Use of Certain Procedures Regarding Qualified Countermeasure Research and Development Activities.

"(a) *IN GENERAL.*

"(1) *AUTHORITY.*—In conducting and supporting research and development activities regarding countermeasures under section 319F(h), the Secretary may conduct and support such activities in accordance with this section and, in consultation with the Director of the National Institutes of Health, as part of the program under section 446, if the activities concern qualified countermeasures.

"(2) *QUALIFIED COUNTERMEASURE.*— For purposes of this section, the term 'qualified countermeasure' means a drug (as that term is defined by section 201(g)(1) of the Federal Food, Drug, and Cosmetic Act (21 U.S.C. 321(g)(1))), biological product (as that term is defined by section 351(i) of this Act (42 U.S.C. 262(i))), or device (as that term is defined by section 201(h) of the Federal Food, Drug, and Cosmetic Act (21 U.S.C. 321(h))) that the Secretary determines to be a priority (consistent with sections 302(2) and 304(a) of the Homeland Security Act of 2002) to—

"(A) treat, identify, or prevent harm from any biological, chemical, radiological, or nuclear agent that may cause a public health emergency affecting national security; or

"(B) treat, identify, or prevent harm from a condition that may result in adverse health consequences or death and may be caused by administering a drug, biological product, or device that is used as described in subparagraph (A).

"(2) FEDERAL TORT CLAIMS ACT COVERAGE.

"(A) *IN GENERAL.*— A person carrying out a contract under paragraph (1), and an officer, employee, or governing board member of such person, shall, subject to a determination by the Secretary, be deemed to be an employee of the Department of Health and Human Services for purposes of claims under sections 1346(b) and 2672 of title 28, United States Code, for money damages for personal injury, including death, resulting from performance of functions under such contract.

(2) *ADDITIONAL AUTHORITY.*— Section 319F–2 of the Public Health Service Act, as added by paragraph (1), is amended to read as follows:

Sec. 319F–2. Strategic National Stockpile.

"(a) STRATEGIC NATIONAL STOCKPILE.

"(1) *IN GENERAL.*— The Secretary, in coordination with the Secretary of Homeland Security (referred to in this section as the 'Homeland Security Secretary'), shall maintain a stockpile or stockpiles of drugs, vaccines and other biological products, medical devices, and other supplies in such numbers, types, and amounts as are determined by the Secretary to be appropriate and practicable, taking into account other available sources, to provide for the emergency health security of the United States, including the emergency health security of children and other vulnerable populations, in the event of a bioterrorist attack or other public health emergency.

"(b) SMALLPOX VACCINE DEVELOPMENT.

"(1) *IN GENERAL.*— The Secretary shall award contracts, enter into cooperative agreements, or carry out such other activities as may reasonably be required in order to ensure that the stockpile under subsection (a) includes an amount of vaccine against smallpox as determined by such Secretary to be sufficient to meet the health security needs of the United States.

"(iii) AVAILABILITY OF SIMPLIFIED ACQUISITION PROCEDURES.

"(I) *IN GENERAL.*— If the Secretary determines that there is a pressing need for a procurement of a specific countermeasure, the amount of the procurement under this subsection shall be deemed to be below the threshold amount specified in section 4(11) of the Office of Federal Procurement Policy Act (41 U.S.C. 403(11)), for purposes of application to such procurement, pursuant to section 302A(a) of the Federal Property and Administrative Services Act of 1949 (41 U.S.C. 252a(a)). . .

SEC. 4. AUTHORIZATION FOR MEDICAL PRODUCTS FOR USE IN EMERGENCIES.

(a) IN GENERAL.— Section 564 of the Federal Food, Drug, and Cosmetic Act (21 U.S.C. 360bbb–3) is amended to read as follows:

Sec. 564. Authorization for Medical Products for Use in Emergencies.

"(a) IN GENERAL.

"(1) *EMERGENCY USES.*— Notwithstanding sections 505, 510(k), and 515 of this Act and section 351 of the Public Health Service Act, and subject to the provisions of this section, the Secretary may authorize the introduction into interstate commerce, during the effective period of a declaration under subsection (b), of a drug, device, or biological product intended for use in an actual or potential emergency (referred to in this section as an 'emergency use').

"(2) *APPROVAL STATUS OF PRODUCT.*— An authorization under paragraph (1) may authorize an emergency use of a product that—

"(A) is not approved, licensed, or cleared for commercial distribution under a provision of law referred to in such paragraph (referred to in this section as an 'unapproved product'); or

"(B) is approved, licensed, or cleared under such a provision, but which use is not under such provision an

approved, licensed, or cleared use of the product (referred to in this section as an 'unapproved use of an approved product').

"(b) DECLARATION OF EMERGENCY.

"(1) *IN GENERAL.*— The Secretary may declare an emergency justifying the authorization under this subsection for a product on the basis of—

"(A) a determination by the Secretary of Homeland Security that there is a domestic emergency, or a significant potential for a domestic emergency, involving a heightened risk of attack with a specified biological, chemical, radiological, or nuclear agent or agents;

"(B) a determination by the Secretary of Defense that there is a military emergency, or a significant potential for a military emergency, involving a heightened risk to United States military forces of attack with a specified biological, chemical, radiological, or nuclear agent or agents; or

"(C) a determination by the Secretary of a public health emergency under section 319 of the Public Health Service Act that affects, or has a significant potential to affect, national security, and that involves a specified biological, chemical, radiological, or nuclear agent or agents, or a specified disease or condition that may be attributable to such agent or agents . . .

Post Katrina Emergency Management Reform Act, October 4, 2006

SEC. 611. STRUCTURING THE FEDERAL EMERGENCY MANAGEMENT AGENCY.

Title V of the Homeland Security Act of 2002 (6 U.S.C. 311 et seq.) is amended—

(1) by striking the title heading and inserting the following:

Sec. 516. Chief Medical Officer.

"(a) IN GENERAL.— There is in the Department a Chief Medical Officer, who shall be appointed by the President, by and with the advice and consent of the Senate.

"(b) QUALIFICATIONS.— The individual appointed as Chief Medical Officer shall possess a demonstrated ability in and knowledge of medicine and public health.

"(c) RESPONSIBILITIES.— The Chief Medical Officer shall have the primary responsibility within the Department for medical issues related to natural disasters, acts of terrorism, and other manmade disasters, including—

"(1) serving as the principal advisor to the Secretary and the Administrator on medical and public health issues;

"(2) coordinating the biodefense activities of the Department;

"(3) ensuring internal and external coordination of all medical preparedness and response activities of the Department, including training, exercises, and equipment support;

"(4) serving as the Department's primary point of contact with the Department of Agriculture, the Department of Defense, the Department of Health and Human Services, the Department of Transportation, the Department of Veterans Affairs, and other Federal departments or agencies, on medical and public health issues;

"(5) serving as the Department's primary point of contact for State, local, and tribal governments, the medical community, and others within and outside the Department, with respect to medical and public health matters;

"(6) discharging, in coordination with the Under Secretary for Science and Technology, the responsibilities of the Department related to Project Bioshield; and

"(7) performing such other duties relating to such responsibilities as the Secretary may require."

HSPD 18. Medical Countermeasures Against Weapons Of Mass Destruction, January 31, 2007

Biological Threats. The biological threat spectrum can be framed in four distinct categories, each of which presents unique challenges and significant opportunities for developing medical countermeasures:

a. *Traditional Agents:* Traditional agents are naturally occurring microorganisms or toxin products with the potential to be disseminated to cause mass casualties. Examples of traditional agents include *Bacillus anthracis* (anthrax) and *Yersinia pestis* (plague).

b. *Enhanced Agents:* Enhanced agents are traditional agents that have been modified or selected to enhance their ability to harm human populations or circumvent current countermeasures, such as a bacterium that has been modified to resist antibiotic treatment.

c. *Emerging Agents:* Emerging agents are previously unrecognized pathogens that might be naturally occurring and present a serious risk to human populations, such as the virus responsible for Severe Acute Respiratory Syndrome (SARS). Tools to detect and treat these agents might not exist or might not be widely available.

d. *Advanced Agents:* Advanced agents are novel pathogens or other materials of biological nature that have been artificially engineered in the laboratory to bypass traditional countermeasures or produce a more severe or otherwise enhanced spectrum of disease.

Nuclear and Radiological Threats. Threats posed by fissile and other radiological material will persist. Our Nation must improve its biodosimetry capabilities and continue to develop medical countermeasures as appropriate to mitigate the health effects of radiation exposure from the following threats:

e. *Improvised Nuclear Devices:* Improvised nuclear devices incorporate radioactive materials designed to result in the formation of a nuclear-yield reaction. Such devices can be wholly fabricated or can be created by modifying a nuclear weapon.

f. *Radiological Dispersal Devices:* Radiological Dispersal Devices (RDDs) are devices, other than a nuclear explosive device, designed to disseminate radioactive material to cause destruction, damage, or injury.

g. *Intentional Damage or Destruction of a Nuclear Power Plant:* Deliberate acts that cause damage to a reactor core and destruction of the containment facility of a nuclear reactor could contaminate a wide geographic area with radioactive material.

Chemical Threats. Existing and new types of chemicals present a range of threats. Development of targeted medical countermeasures might be warranted for materials in the following categories:

h. *Toxic Industrial Materials and Chemicals:* Toxic Industrial Materials and Chemicals are toxic substances in solid, liquid, or gaseous form that are used or stored for use for military or commercial purposes.

i. *Traditional Chemical Warfare Agents:* Traditional chemical warfare agents encompass the range of blood, blister, choking, and nerve agents historically developed for warfighter use.

j. *Non-traditional Agents:* Non-traditional agents (NTAs) are novel chemical threat agents or toxicants requiring adapted countermeasures.

Creating defenses against a finite number of known or anticipated agents is a sound approach for mitigating the most catastrophic CBRN threats; however, we also must simultaneously employ a broad-spectrum "flexible" approach to address other current and future threats. We must be capable of responding to a wide variety of potential challenges, including a novel biological agent that is highly communicable, associated with a high rate of morbidity or mortality, and without known countermeasure at the time of its discovery. Although significant technological, organizational, and procedural challenges will have to be overcome, such a balanced strategic approach would mitigate current and future CBRN threats and benefit public health.

Policy. It is the policy of the United States to draw upon the considerable potential of the scientific community in the public and private sectors to address our medical countermeasure requirements relating to CBRN threats. Our Nation will use a two tiered approach for development and acquisition of medical countermeasures, which will balance the immediate need to provide a capability to mitigate the most catastrophic of the current CBRN threats with long-term requirements to develop more flexible, broader spectrum countermeasures to address future threats. Our approach also will support regulatory decisions and will permit us to address the broadest range of current and future CBRN threats.

TIER I: FOCUSED DEVELOPMENT OF AGENT-SPECIFIC MEDICAL COUNTERMEASURES. The first tier uses existing, proven approaches for developing medical countermeasures to address challenges posed by select current and anticipated threats, such as traditional CBRN agents. Recognizing that as threats change our countermeasures might become less effective, we will invest in an integrated and multi-layered defense.

TIER II: DEVELOPMENT OF A FLEXIBLE CAPABILITY FOR NEW MEDICAL COUNTERMEASURES. Second tier activities will emphasize the need to capitalize upon the development of emerging and future technologies that will enhance our ability to respond flexibly to anticipated, emerging, and future CBRN threats … Department-level strategic and implementation plans will reflect the following guiding principles and objectives:

k. *Integrate Fundamental Discovery and Medical Development to Realize Novel Medical Countermeasure Capabilities:* We will target some investments to support the development of broad spectrum approaches to surveillance, diagnostics, prophylactics, and therapeutics that utilize platform technologies. This will require targeted, balanced, and sustained investments between fundamental research to discover new technologies and applied research for technology development to deliver new medical capabilities and countermeasures …

l. *Establish a Favorable Environment for Evaluating New Approaches:* We must ensure that our investments lead to products that expand the scientific data base, increase the efficiency with which safety and efficacy can be evaluated, and improve the rate at which products under Investigational New Drug or Investigational Device Exemption status progress through the regulatory or approval process. In addition, we

must continue to use new tools to evaluate and utilize promising candidates in a time of crisis. Examples of such tools include the "Animal Rule" for testing the efficacy of medical countermeasures against threat agents when human trials are not ethically feasible and the Emergency Use Authorization. . .

m. *Integrate the Products of New and Traditional Approaches:* We must address the challenges that will arise from integrating these new approaches with existing processes. We must incorporate the use of non-pharmacological interventions in our response planning. This integration will forge a flexible biodefense capability that aligns our national requirements for medical countermeasures with the concepts of operation that are used in conjunction with other strategies for mitigating the public health impacts of WMD attacks.

In order to achieve our Tier I and II objectives, it will be necessary to facilitate the development of products and technologies that show promise but are not yet eligible for procurement through BioShield or the Strategic National Stockpile.

We will support the advanced development of these products through targeted investments across a broad portfolio, with the understanding that some of these products may be deemed unsuitable for further investment as additional data becomes available, but the expectation that others will become candidates for procurement.

Implementing Recommendations of the 9/11 Commission Act of August 2007

"SEC. 316. NATIONAL BIOSURVEILLANCE INTEGRATION CENTER.

"(a) ESTABLISHMENT.— The Secretary shall establish, operate, and maintain a National Biosurveillance Integration Center (referred to in this section as the 'NBIC'), which shall be headed by a Directing Officer, under an office or directorate of the Department that is in existence as of the date of the enactment of this section.

"(b) PRIMARY MISSION.— The primary mission of the NBIC is to—

"(1) enhance the capability of the Federal Government to—

"(A) rapidly identify, characterize, localize, and track a biological event of national concern by integrating and analyzing data relating to human health, animal, plant, food, and environmental monitoring systems (both national and international); and

"(B) disseminate alerts and other information to Member Agencies and, in coordination with (and where possible through) Member Agencies, to agencies of State, local, and tribal governments, as appropriate, to enhance the ability of such agencies to respond to a biological event of national concern; and

"(2) oversee development and operation of the National Biosurveillance Integration System.

"(c) REQUIREMENTS.— The NBIC shall detect, as early as possible, a biological event of national concern that presents a risk to the United States or the infrastructure or key assets of the United States, including by—

"(1) consolidating data from all relevant surveillance systems maintained by Member Agencies to detect biological events of national concern across human, animal, and plant species;

"(2) seeking private sources of surveillance, both foreign and domestic, when such sources would enhance coverage of critical surveillance gaps;

"(3) using an information technology system that uses the best available statistical and other analytical tools to identify and characterize biological events of national concern in as close to real-time as is practicable;

"(4) providing the infrastructure for such integration, including information technology systems and space, and support for personnel from Member Agencies with sufficient expertise to enable analysis and interpretation of data;

"(5) working with Member Agencies to create information technology systems that use the minimum amount of patient data necessary and consider patient confidentiality and privacy issues at all stages of development and apprise the Privacy Officer of such efforts; and

"(6) alerting Member Agencies and, in coordination with (and where possible through) Member Agencies, public health agencies of State, local, and tribal governments regarding any incident that could develop into a biological event of national concern.

HSPD 21. Public Health and Medical Preparedness,[17] October 18, 2007

"Purpose.

1. This directive establishes a National Strategy for Public Health and Medical Preparedness (Strategy), which builds upon principles set forth in Biodefense for the 21st Century (April 2004) and will transform our national approach to protecting the health of the American people against all disasters. . . .

3. A catastrophic health event, such as a terrorist attack with a weapon of mass destruction (WMD), a naturally-occurring pandemic, or a calamitous meteorological or geological event, could cause tens or hundreds of thousands of casualties or more, weaken our economy, damage public morale and confidence, and threaten our national security. It is therefore critical that we establish a strategic vision that will enable a level of public health and medical preparedness sufficient to address a range of possible disasters.

5. This Strategy draws key principles from the National Strategy for Homeland Security (October 2007), the National Strategy to Combat Weapons of Mass Destruction (December 2002), and Biodefense for the 21st Century (April 2004) that can be generally applied to public health and medical preparedness. Those key principles are the following: (1) preparedness for all potential catastrophic health events; (2) vertical and horizontal coordination across levels of government, jurisdictions, and disciplines; (3) a regional approach to health preparedness; (4) engagement of the private sector, academia, and other nongovernmental entities in preparedness and response efforts; and (5) the important roles of individuals, families, and communities.

6. Present public health and medical preparedness plans incorporate the concept of "surging" existing medical and public health capabilities in response to an event that threatens a large number of lives. *The assumption that conventional public health and medical systems can function effectively in catastrophic health events has, however, proved to be incorrect in real-world situations.* [emphasis added]. Therefore, it is necessary to transform the national approach to health care in the context of a catastrophic health event in order to enable U.S. public health and medical systems to respond effectively to a broad range of incidents.

7. The most effective complex service delivery systems result from rigorous end-to-end system design. A critical and formal process by which the functions of public health and medical preparedness and response are designed to integrate all vertical (through all levels of government) and horizontal (across all sectors in communities) components can achieve a much greater capability than we currently have.

8. The United States has tremendous resources in both public and private sectors that could be used to prepare for and respond to a catastrophic health event. To exploit those resources fully, they must be organized in a rationally designed system that is incorporated into pre-event planning, deployed in a coordinated manner in response to an event, and guided by a constant and timely flow of relevant information during

an event. This Strategy establishes principles and objectives to improve our ability to respond comprehensively to catastrophic health events. It also identifies critical antecedent components of this capability and directs the development of an implementation plan that will delineate further specific actions and guide the process to fruition.

Implementation Actions.

12. Biodefense for the 21st Century provides a foundation for the transformation of our catastrophic health event response and preparedness efforts. Although the four pillars of that framework – Threat Awareness, Prevention and Protection, Surveillance and Detection, and Response and Recovery – were developed to guide our efforts to defend against a bioterrorist attack, they are applicable to a broad array of natural and manmade public health and medical challenges and are appropriate to serve as the core functions of the Strategy for Public Health and Medical Preparedness.

13. To accomplish our objectives, we must create a firm foundation for community medical preparedness. We will increase our efforts to inform citizens and empower communities, buttress our public health infrastructure, and explore options to relieve current pressures on our emergency departments and emergency medical systems so that they retain the flexibility to prepare for and respond to events.

14. Ultimately, the Nation must collectively support and facilitate the establishment of a discipline of disaster health. The specialty of emergency medicine evolved as a result of the recognition of the special considerations in emergency patient care, and similarly the recognition of the unique principles in disaster-related public health and medicine merit the establishment of their own formal discipline.

Critical Components of Public Health and Medical Preparedness.

15. Currently, the four most critical components of public health and medical preparedness are biosurveillance, countermeasure distribution, mass casualty care, and community resilience. Although those capabilities do not address all public health and medical preparedness requirements, they currently hold the greatest potential for mitigating illness and death and therefore will receive the highest priority in our public health and medical preparedness efforts. Those capabilities constitute the focus and major objectives of this Strategy.

16. *Biosurveillance*: The United States must develop a nationwide, robust, and integrated biosurveillance capability, with connections to international disease surveillance systems, in order to provide early warning and ongoing characterization of disease outbreaks in near real-time. Surveillance must use multiple modalities and an in-depth architecture. We must enhance clinician awareness and participation and strengthen laboratory diagnostic capabilities and capacity in order to recognize potential threats as early as possible. Integration of biosurveillance elements and other data (including human health, animal health, agricultural, meteorological, environmental, intelligence, and other data) will provide a comprehensive picture of the health of communities and the associated threat environment for incorporation into the national "common operating picture." A central element of biosurveillance must be an epidemiologic surveillance system to monitor human disease activity across populations. That system must be sufficiently enabled to identify specific disease incidence and prevalence in heterogeneous populations and environments and must possess sufficient flexibility to tailor analyses to new syndromes and emerging diseases. State and local government health officials, public and private sector health care institutions, and practicing clinicians must be involved in system design, and the overall system must be constructed with the principal objective of establishing or enhancing the capabilities of State and local government entities.

17. *Countermeasure Stockpiling and Distribution*: In the context of a catastrophic health event, rapid distribution of medical countermeasures (vaccines, drugs, and therapeutics) to a large population requires significant resources within individual communities. Few if any cities are presently able to meet the objective of dispensing countermeasures to their entire population within 48 hours after the decision to do so. Recognizing that State and local government authorities have the primary responsibility to protect their citizens, the Federal Government will create the appropriate framework and policies for sharing information on best practices and mechanisms to address the logistical challenges associated with this requirement. The Federal Government must work with nonfederal stakeholders to create effective templates for countermeasure distribution and dispensing that State and local government authorities can use to build their own capabilities.

18. *Mass Casualty Care*: The structure and operating principles of our day-to-day public health and medical systems cannot meet the needs created by a catastrophic health event. Collectively, our Nation must

develop a disaster medical capability that can immediately re-orient and coordinate existing resources within all sectors to satisfy the needs of the population during a catastrophic health event. Mass casualty care response must be (1) rapid, (2) flexible, (3) scalable, (4) sustainable, (5) exhaustive (drawing upon all national resources), (6) comprehensive (addressing needs from acute to chronic care and including mental health and special needs populations), (7) integrated and coordinated, and (8) appropriate (delivering the correct treatment in the most ethical manner with available capabilities). We must enhance our capability to protect the physical and mental health of survivors; protect responders and health care providers; properly and respectfully dispose of the deceased; ensure continuity of society, economy, and government; and facilitate long-term recovery of affected citizens.

19. The establishment of a robust disaster health capability requires us to develop an operational concept for the medical response to catastrophic health events that is substantively distinct from and broader than that which guides day-to-day operations. In order to achieve that transformation, the Federal Government will facilitate and provide leadership for key stakeholders to establish the following four foundational elements: Doctrine, System Design, Capacity, and Education and Training. The establishment of those foundational elements must result from efforts within the relevant professional communities and will require many years, but the Federal Government can serve as an important catalyst for this process.

20. *Community Resilience*: The above components address the supply side of the preparedness function, ultimately providing enhanced services to our citizens. The demand side is of equal importance. Where local civic leaders, citizens, and families are educated regarding threats and are empowered to mitigate their own risk, where they are practiced in responding to events, where they have social networks to fall back upon, and where they have familiarity with local public health and medical systems, there will be community resilience that will significantly attenuate the requirement for additional assistance. (emphasis added). The Federal Government must formulate a comprehensive plan for promoting community public health and medical preparedness to assist State and local authorities in building resilient communities in the face of potential catastrophic health events.

Biosurveillance.

21. The Secretary of Health and Human Services shall establish an operational national epidemiologic surveil-

lance system for human health, with international connectivity where appropriate...

23. In accordance with the schedule set forth below, the Secretary of Health and Human Services ... shall develop templates, using a variety of tools and including private sector resources when necessary, that provide minimum operational plans to enable communities to distribute and dispense countermeasures to their populations within 48 hours after a decision to do so. ... The Secretary shall also assist State, local government, and regional entities in tailoring templates to fit differing geographic sizes, population densities, and demographics, and other unique or specific local needs. ...

Mass Casualty Care.

31. The impact of the "worried well" in past disasters is well documented, and it is evident that mitigating the mental health consequences of disasters can facilitate effective response. Recognizing that maintaining and restoring mental health in disasters has not received sufficient attention to date ... the Secretary of Health and Human Services ... shall establish a Federal Advisory Committee for Disaster Mental Health [and] shall submit to the Secretary of Health and Human Services recommendations for protecting, preserving, and restoring individual and community mental health in catastrophic health event settings, including pre-event, intra-event, and post-event.

DOD National Center for Medical Intelligence, March 2009[18]

The Department of Defense established the National Center for Medical Intelligence (NCMI) March 20, 2009. "[M]edical intelligence" is defined as the product of collection, evaluation, and all-source analysis of worldwide health threats and issues, including foreign medical capabilities, infectious disease, environmental health risks, developments in biotechnology and biomedical subjects of national and military importance, and support to force protection."

Based on their definition of medical intelligence, the NCMI would be an extraordinary compliment to DHS's biosurveillance. Although DHS is not mentioned, the Instruction states "... will prepare and coordinate integrated, all-source intelligence for the Department of Defense and other government and international organizations on foreign health threats and other medical issues to protect U.S. interests worldwide."

National Strategy for Countering Biological Threats, November 2009

... Under the *National Strategy for Countering Biological Threats (Strategy)*, we will encourage the alignment of global attitudes against the intentional misuse of the life sciences or derivative materials, techniques, or expertise to harm people, agriculture, or other critical resources.

Our *Strategy* is targeted to reduce biological threats by: (1) improving global access to the life sciences to combat infectious disease regardless of its cause; (2) establishing and reinforcing norms against the misuse of the life sciences; and (3) instituting a suite of coordinated activities that collectively will helpinfluence, identify, inhibit, and/or interdict those who seek to misuse the life sciences.

The *Strategy* provides a framework for future United States Government planning efforts that supports the overall *National Biodefense Strategy* (Homeland Security Presidential Directive (HSPD)-10/National Security Presidential Directive-33), and complements existing White House strategies related to biological threat preparedness and response:

*Management of Domestic Incidents (*HSPD-5*)* and the related *National Response Framework;*

*National Preparedness (*HSPD-8*);*

*National Strategy for Defense of United States Agriculture and Food (*HSPD-9*);*

*Medical Countermeasures against Weapons of Mass Destruction (*HSPD-18*); and*

*Public Health and Medical Preparedness (*HSPD-21*).*

This *Strategy* reflects the fact that the challenges presented by biological threats cannot be addressed by the Federal Government alone, and that planning and participation must include the full range of domestic and international partners. . .

Objective Seven: Transform the international dialogue on biological threats

The life sciences revolution is global in nature and people of all nations can benefit from efforts to reduce the risk of misuse to enable biological threats. Optimal implementation of any effort to manage the risk requires international cooperation and coordination. Currently, the plurality of perspectives in the international community as to the severity of the risk and mitigative actions that nations should take presents a challenge to risk management . . .

Revitalizing the Biological and Toxin Weapons Convention (BWC). The BWC is a uniquely important venue through which we can promote and globally advance our objectives for non-proliferation and risk management of biological threats. The membership of the BWC, however, is not universal and concerns remain that some treaty partners may be developing biological weapons. As the central international forum dedicated to mitigating risks posed by the development and use of biological weapons, the BWC can help focus attention on the evolving nature of biological threats, increase attention to and promote international ef-

forts to prevent proliferation and terrorism, and build tighter linkages between the health and security sectors . . .

Expanding Our International Partnerships and Bio-engagement. Over the past decade, our cooperative partnerships with a number of nations have demonstrably reduced the risks posed by legacy biological weapons programs. By assisting with efforts to redirect former weapons scientists, repurpose or decommission facilities and equipment, develop and implement practices that permit safe and secure work with high-risk pathogens and toxins, build scientific ties, and improve mutual understanding, our security engagement programs have developed a strong track record of effective risk management. We will seek to build upon this record by forging new partnerships that reduce the risks from biological threats by:

Integrating efforts to meet our international obligations

We, and many of our international colleagues, have a number of multilateral and bilateral obligations that lie at the nexus of security, health, and science. We will continue to meet our obligations; however, we will look for opportunities to leverage synergies in activities that are relevant to multiple fora.

ENDNOTES

1. For a recount of a prosecution under this statute, see, Andrew M. Grossman, "When Art Becomes a Crime: A Case Study in Overcriminalization" The Heritage Foundation, No. 39, March 24, 2009. http://www.heritage.org/Research/LegalIssues/upload/lm_39.pdf.

2. Patriot Act. http://thomas.loc.gov/cgi-bin/bdquery/z?d107:hr03162:%5D.

3. Public Health Security and Bioterrorism Preparedness and Response Act of 2002. P.L. 107–188, June 12, 2002. http://frwebgate.access.gpo.gov/cgi-bin/getdoc.cgi?dbname=107_cong_public_laws&docid=f:publ188.107.

4. Homeland Security Act of 2002. http://www.dhs.gov/xabout/laws/law_regulation_rule_0011.shtm.

5. National Strategy for the Physical Protection of Critical Infrastructures and Key Assets, February 2003. http://www.dhs.gov/xlibrary/assets/Physical_Strategy.pdf.

6. Executive Order 13295 of April 4, 2003, Revised List of Quarantinable Communicable Diseases, Federal Register /Vol. 68, No. 68. http://edocket.access.gpo.gov/2003/pdf/03-8832.pdf.

7. HSPD 10. Biodefense for the 21st Century. http://www.dhs.gov/xabout/laws/gc_1217605824325.shtm#1 (accessed March 19, 2009).

8. Project BioShield Act of 2004, P.L. 108–276, July 21, 2004. http://frwebgate.access.gpo.gov/cgi-bin/getdoc.cgi?dbname=108_cong_public_laws&docid=f:publ276.108.pdf.

9. Public Law 109–295, Title VI, Post Katrina Emergency Management Reform Act, October 4, 2006. http://frwebgate.access.gpo.gov/cgi-bin/getdoc.cgi?dbname=109_cong_public_laws&docid=f:publ295.109.pdf.

10. HSPD 18. Medical Countermeasures against Weapons of Mass Destruction, January 31, 2007. http://www.dhs.gov/xabout/laws/gc_1219175362551.shtm.

11. Implementing Recommendations Of The 9/11 Commission Act Of [August] 2007. Http://www.Nctc.Gov/Docs/Ir-Of-The-9-11-Comm-Act-Of-2007.Pdf (accessed April 01, 2009).

12. HSPD 21 Oct. 18, 2007. http://www.dhs.gov/xabout/laws/gc_1219263961449.shtm. (accessed May 02, 2009).

13. DoD Instruction [DODI 6420.01] March 20, 2009, National Center for Medical Intelligence (NCMI). http://www.dtic.mil/whs/directives/corres/pdf/642001p.pdf (accessed March 31, 2009).

14. National Strategy for Countering Biological Threats, National Security Council, November 2009. http:// www.whitehouse.gov/sites/default/files/National_Strategy_for_Countering_BioThreats.pdf.

15. Homeland Security Act. http://www.dhs.gov/xlibrary/assets/hr_5005_enr.pdf.

16. Intelligence enables all aspects of our national security, homeland defense, and homeland security systems, and not just Biodefense.

17. HSPD 21 October 18, 2007. http://www.dhs.gov/xabout/laws/gc_1219263961449.shtm. (accessed March 26, 2009).

18. DoD Instruction [DODI 6420.01] March 20, 2009, National Center for Medical Intelligence (NCMI). http://www.dtic.mil/whs/directives/corres/pdf/642001p. pdf.

ADDITIONAL RESOURCES

Biosurveillance

Joint Program Executive Office for Chemical and Biological Defense, *Chem-Bio Defense Quarterly*, Vol. 6 No. 3, July–September 2009 http://www.jpeocbd.osd.mil/packs/Magazine.aspx

Biological Research: Observations on DHS's Analyses Concerning Whether FMD [Foot-and-mouth disease] Research Can Be Done as Safely on the Mainland as on Plum Island, GAO-09-747, July 30, 2009. http://www.gao.gov/new.items/d09747.pdf

Project BioShield Act: HHS Has Supported Development, Procurement, and Emergency Use of Medical Countermeasures to Address Health Threats, GAO-09-878R, July 24, 2009. http://www.gao.gov/htext/d09878r.html

Testimony Before the Subcommittee on Emerging Threats, Cybersecurity, and Science and Technology, Committee on Homeland Security, House of Representatives ... Preliminary Observations on Department of Homeland Security's Biosurveillance Initiatives, Statement of William O. Jenkins, Jr. Director Homeland Security and Justice Issues, GAO-08-960T, July 16, 2008. http://www.gao.gov/new.items/d08960t.pdf

Project BioShield: Purposes and Authorities, Frank Gottron, July 6, 2009, Congressional Research Service, RS21507, http://www.fas.org/sgp/crs/terror/RS21507.pdf

Dispensing Medical Countermeasures for Public Health Emergencies:, Workshop Summary, National Academies press, 2008, http://www.nap.edu/catalog.php?record_id=12221

The National Biodefense Analysis and Countermeasures Center: Issues for Congress, Updated November 21, 2006, http://italy.usembassy.gov/pdf/other/RL32891.pdf

Pandemic FLU

"Mandatory Vaccinations: Precedent and Current Laws," by Kathleen S. Swendiman, October 26, 2009, Congressional Research Service, RS21414

"The 2009 Influenza A(H1N1) Outbreak: Selected Legal Issues," October 29, 2009, CRS R40560, by Kathleen S. Swendiman, Nancy Lee Jones. http://opencrs.com/document/R40560

"The 2009 Influenza Pandemic: An Overview," Sarah A. Lister, and C. Stephen Redhead, September 10, 2009, Congressional Research Service, R40554, http://opencrs.com/document/R40554/

"Mandatory Vaccinations: Precedent and Current Laws," Kathleen S. Swendiman,

Congressional Research Service, September 8, 2009, RS21414, http://opencrs.com/document/RS21414/

"How Computer Modeling Can Stem the Spread of Influenza," by Joshua M. Epstein, Brookings Institute, August, 2009, http://www.brookings.edu/multimedia/video/2009/0818_modeling_epstein.aspx

"Swine Flu – the Sickly Side of Globalization," Sara Kuepfer, International Relations anad Security Network, http://www.isn.ethz.ch/isn/Current-Affairs/Special-Reports/Preparing-for-a-Pandemic/Globalization-Goes-Viral

United Kingdon Parliament, Pandemic Influenza: Follow-up, July 28, 2009, http://www.publications.parliament.uk/pa/ld200809/ldselect/ldsctech/155/155.pdf

"The Role for Exercises in Senior Policy Pandemic Influenza Preparedness," K. C. Decker and Keith Holtermann, (2009) *Journal of Homeland Security and Emergency Management*: Vol. 6 : Iss. 1, Article 32. http://www.bepress.com/jhsem/vol6/iss1/32/?sending=10643

"Influenza Pandemic: Greater Agency Accountability Needed to Protect Federal Workers in the Event of a Pandemic," GAO-09-783T [testimony] June 16, 2009, http://www.gao.gov/new.items/d09783t.pdf

"Influenza Pandemic: Increased Agency Accountability Could Help Protect Federal Employees Serving the Public in the Event of a Pandemic," GAO-09-404, June 2009, http://www.gao.gov/new.items/d09404.pdf

"Protecting Our Employees: Pandemic Influenza Preparedness and the Federal Workforce," Testimony before Congress. Senate. Homeland Security and Governmental Affairs Committee,

June 16, 2009, http://hsgac.senate.gov/public/index.cfm?Fuseaction=Hearings.Detail&HearingID=b90e817c-49fc-4747-9583-b475632363ed

Homeland Security Should Deploy Bio-Sensors Now, by Daniel Goure, Ph.D., Jun 8, 2009, Lexington Institute, http://lexingtoninstitute.org/1431.shtml

"Pandemic Flu: Closing the Gaps," June 3, 2009. U.S. Senate, Homeland Security and Government Affairs Committee http://hsgac.senate.gov/public/index.cfm?Fuseaction=Hearings.Detail&HearingID=6c228b70-8e79-41af-aa3f-893317c92c86

"Pandemic Flu: Lessons From the Frontlines," June 2009, http://healthyamericans.org/reports/?reportid=64

"Quarantine and Isolation: Selected Legal Issues Relating to Employment," by Nancy Lee Jones and Jon O. Shimabukuro, May 11, 2009, CRS RL33609, http://www.fas.org/sgp/crs/misc/RL33609.pdf

The "Trust for America's Health, the Center for Biosecurity, and the Robert Wood Johnson Foundation analyze the initial response to the H1N1 outbreak... which found that U.S. officials executed strong coordination and communication and an ability to adapt to changing circumstances, but it also how quickly the nation's core public health capacity would be overwhelmed if an outbreak were more severe or widespread. http://healthyamericans.org/reports/?reportid=64

"Summary Of Legal Authorities For Use In Response To An Outbreak Of Pandemic Influenza," Attorney General of the United States, April 25, 2009, http://www.fbiic.gov/public/2009/may/AGMemo.pdf

"An influenza pandemic is projected to have a global impact requiring a sustained, largescale response from the healthcare community to provide care to sick patients. Healthcare workers will be at very high risk of becoming infected when caring for patients with pandemic flu unless adequate health and safety measures are in place, in advance of the pandemic, that will protect them. There is no existing comprehensive federal OSHA standard with mandatory and enforceable provisions that require planning and preparation designed to protect healthcare workers from exposures to pandemic influenza." "Healthcare Workers In Peril: Preparing To Protect Worker Health And Safety During Pandemic Influenza, A Union Survey Report." January 1, 2009. http://www.afscme.org/docs/Health_Care_Workers_In_Peril.pdf

The Pandemic and All-Hazards Preparedness Act (P.L. 109-417): Provisions and changes to Preexisting Law, by Sarah A. Lister and Frank Gottron, March 12, 2007, CRS Report RL33589 http://www.nationalaglawcenter.org/assets/crs/RL33589.pdf

Americans With Disabilities Act

The Americans with Disabilities Act (ADA): Allocation of Scarce Medical Resources During a Pandemic. Nancy Lee Jones, Legislative Attorney, American Law Division. April 21, 2006, CRS Report RL33381. https://www.policyarchive.org/bitstream/handle/10207/2809/RL33381_20060421.pdf?sequence=1

Federal Agencies

School-Based Emergency Preparedness, A National Analysis and Recommended Protocol, http://www.ahrq.gov/prep/schoolprep/ August 2008.

The Center for Bioterrorism Education, a joint endeavor between Creighton University Medical Center and University of Nebraska Medical Center http://www.bioprepare.org/index.htm

Advice for Safeguarding Buildings Against Chemical or Biological Attack http://securebuildings.lbl.gov/

World Health Organization, Epidemic and Pandemic Alert and Response http://www.who.int/csr/disease/influenza/pandemic/en/

HHS Pandemic Influenza Plan http://www.hhs.gov/pandemicflu/plan/

Centers For Disease Control and Prevention http://www.bt.cdc.gov/

U.S. Government avian and pandemic flu information http://www.pandemicflu.gov/

Biomedical Advanced Research and Development Authority (BARDA), U.S. Department of Health and Human Services. http://www.hhs.gov/aspr/barda/index.html

National Institute of Allergy and Infectious Diseases (NIAID) National Institutes of Health (NIH), http://www3.niaid.nih.gov/topics/BiodefenseRelated/

United States Government Accountability Office, Report to Congressional Requesters, Emergency Preparedness, States Are Planning for Medical Surge, but Could Benefit from Shared Guidance for Allocating Scarce Medical Resources, June 2008. GAO-08-668. http://www.gao.gov/new.items/d08668.pdf

United States Government Accountability Office, GAO Report to Congressional Committees, Opportunities Exist to Improve the Management and Oversight of Federally Funded Research and Development Centers October 2008. GAO-09-15 http://www.gao.gov/new.items/d0915.pdf.

The Report of the Commission on the Prevention of WMD Proliferation and Terrorism, WORLD AT RISK, New York, NY, December 2, 2008. http://www.preventwmd.gov/static/docs/report/worldatrisk_full.pdf

Military Resources

Chem-Bio Defense Quarterly Magazine, Vol. 6 No. 1 [2008], Joint Program Executive Office for Chemical and Biological Defense http://www.jpeocbd.osd.mil/packs/Default2.aspx?pg=0

Medical Research & Development, USAMRMC. https://mrmc.amedd.army.mil/mrdindex.asp

Defense Science Board, Department of Defense Biological Safety and Security Program http://www.acq.osd.mil/dsb/reports/2009-05-Bio_Safety.pdf

Educational Institutions

Biodefense Reference Library, *Resources for Strategic Planning & Project Development.* http://www.humanitarian.net/biodefense/

Center for Infectious Disease Research & Policy, University of Minnesota With links to specific hazards: Anthrax, Botulism, Plague, Smallpox, Tularemia, VHF, Biosecurity, Food Safety. http://www.cidrap.umn.edu/cidrap/content/bt/bioprep/news/sep2308contracts-jw.html

The Northeast Biodefense Center. http://www.nbc.columbia.edu/

Western Regional Center of Excellence for Biodefense and Emerging Infectious Diseases. http://www.rcebiodefense.org/rce6/6pub_2_pro.htm

Private Sector

Biodefense news tips. 2009 ASM Biodefense and Emerging Diseases Research Meeting http://www.eurekalert.org/pub_releases/2009-02/asfm-bnt021909.php

"Report: Commission on the Prevention of WMD Proliferation and Terrorism" Summary of this report with comments and link to full report. http://hspolitics.wordpress.com/2008/12/14/report-commission-on-the-prevention-of-wmd-proliferation-and-terrorism/

Strong as the Weakest Link: Medical Response to a Catastrophic Event, Eileen Salinsky, National Health Policy Forum, Background Paper No. 65, Washington, DC, August 8, 2008, http://www.nhpf.org/library/background-papers/BP65_Surge Capacity_08-08-08.pdf

The Federation of American Scientists has an online resource devoted to biological and chemical warfare and another called the Nuclear Information Project. http://www.fas.org/

Oregon lab on front lines of smallpox biodefense. Drug developed in Corvallis lab stands ready to fight smallpox Corvallis lab on front lines of biodefense. Feb. 7, 2009. http://www.homeland1.com/bioterrorism-biodefense-food-safety/articles/453514-Oregon-lab-on-front-lines-of-smallpox-biodefense

European BioSafety Association, http://www.ebsaweb.eu/

Hospitals

"The Center for Biosecurity is an independent, nonprofit organization of the University of Pittsburgh Medical Center (UPMC). The Center works to affect policy and practice in ways that lessen the illness, death, and civil disruption that would follow large-scale epidemics, whether they occur naturally or result from the use of a biological weapon." http://www.upmc-biosecurity.org/.

17

NATIONAL CONTINUITY POLICY

HSPD 20 is the Nation's Continuity Plan. It establishes the policy for continuing our constitutional form of government (COG), and continuity of the government's operations (COOP). The Annex lists the federal agencies and places them into one of the five categories depending on their role in this effort.

SOURCES

- HSPD 20, NATIONAL CONTINUITY POLICY[1]
- HSPD 20, Annex A[2]

HSPD 20. National Continuity Policy, May 9, 2007

Purpose

1. This directive establishes a comprehensive national policy on the continuity of Federal Government structures and operations and a single National Continuity Coordinator responsible for coordinating the development and implementation of Federal continuity policies. This policy establishes "National Essential Functions," prescribes continuity requirements for all executive departments and agencies, and provides guidance for State, local, territorial, and tribal governments, and private sector organizations in order to ensure a comprehensive and integrated national continuity program that will enhance the credibility of our national security posture and enable a more rapid and effective response to and recovery from a national emergency.

Definitions

2. In this directive:
   a. "Continuity of Government," or "COG," means a coordinated effort within the Federal Government's executive branch to ensure that National Essential Functions continue to be performed during a Catastrophic Emergency;
   b. "Continuity of Operations," or "COOP," means an effort within individual executive departments and agencies to ensure that Primary Mission-Essential Functions continue to be performed during a wide range of emergencies, including localized acts of nature, accidents, and technological or attack-related emergencies;
   c. "Enduring Constitutional Government," or "ECG," means a cooperative effort among the executive, legislative, and judicial branches of the Federal Government, coordinated by the President, as a matter of comity with respect to the legislative and judicial branches and with proper respect for the constitutional separation of powers among the branches, to preserve the constitutional framework under which the Nation is governed and the capability of all three branches of government to execute constitutional responsibilities and provide for orderly succession, appropriate transition of leadership, and interoperability and support of the National Essential Functions during a catastrophic emergency;

Foundations of Homeland Security: Law and Policy, First Edition. Martin J. Alperen.
© 2011 John Wiley & Sons, Inc. Published 2011 by John Wiley & Sons, Inc.

d. "National Essential Functions," or "NEFs," means that subset of Government Functions that are necessary to lead and sustain the Nation during a catastrophic emergency and that, therefore, must be supported through COOP and COG capabilities; and

e. "Primary Mission Essential Functions," or "PMEFs," means those Government Functions that must be performed in order to support or implement the performance of NEFs before, during, and in the aftermath of an emergency.

Policy

3. It is the policy of the United States to maintain a comprehensive and effective continuity capability composed of Continuity of Operations and Continuity of Government programs in order to ensure the preservation of our form of government under the Constitution and the continuing performance of National Essential Functions under all conditions.

Implementation Actions

4. Continuity requirements shall be incorporated into daily operations of all executive departments and agencies. As a result of the asymmetric threat environment, adequate warning of potential emergencies that could pose a significant risk to the homeland might not be available, and therefore all continuity planning shall be based on the assumption that no such warning will be received. Emphasis will be placed upon geographic dispersion of leadership, staff, and infrastructure in order to increase survivability and maintain uninterrupted Government Functions. Risk management principles shall be applied to ensure that appropriate operational readiness decisions are based on the probability of an attack or other incident and its consequences.

5. The following NEFs are the foundation for all continuity programs and capabilities and represent the overarching responsibilities of the Federal Government to lead and sustain the Nation during a crisis, and therefore sustaining the following NEFs shall be the primary focus of the Federal Government leadership during and in the aftermath of an emergency that adversely affects the performance of Government Functions:

a. Ensuring the continued functioning of our form of government under the Constitution, including the functioning of the three separate branches of government;

b. Providing leadership visible to the Nation and the world and maintaining the trust and confidence of the American people;

c. Defending the Constitution of the United States against all enemies, foreign and domestic, and preventing or interdicting attacks against the United States or its people, property, or interests;

d. Maintaining and fostering effective relationships with foreign nations;

e. Protecting against threats to the homeland and bringing to justice perpetrators of crimes or attacks against the United States or its people, property, or interests;

f. Providing rapid and effective response to and recovery from the domestic consequences of an attack or other incident;

g. Protecting and stabilizing the Nation's economy and ensuring public confidence in its financial systems; and

h. Providing for critical Federal Government services that address the national health, safety, and welfare needs of the United States.

6. The President shall lead the activities of the Federal Government for ensuring constitutional government. . . .

8. The National Continuity Coordinator . . . will lead the development of a National Continuity Implementation Plan (Plan), which shall include prioritized goals and objectives, a concept of operations, performance metrics by which to measure continuity readiness, procedures for continuity and incident management activities, and clear direction to executive department and agency continuity coordinators, as well as guidance to promote interoperability of Federal Government continuity programs and procedures with State, local, territorial, and tribal governments, and private sector owners and operators of critical infrastructure, as appropriate. . .

9. . . . each branch of the Federal Government is responsible for its own continuity programs, . . .

11. Continuity requirements for the Executive Office of the President (EOP) and executive departments and agencies shall include the following:

a. The continuation of the performance of PMEFs during any emergency must be for a period up to 30 days or until normal operations can be resumed, and the capability to be fully operational at alternate sites as soon as possible after the occurrence of an emergency, but not later than 12 hours after COOP activation;

b. Succession orders and pre-planned devolution of authorities that ensure the emergency delegation of authority must be planned and documented in advance in accordance with applicable law;

c. Vital resources, facilities, and records must be safeguarded, and official access to them must be provided;

d. Provision must be made for the acquisition of the resources necessary for continuity operations on an emergency basis;

e. Provision must be made for the availability and redundancy of critical communications capabilities at alternate sites in order to support connectivity between and among key government leadership, internal elements, other executive departments and agencies, critical partners, and the public;

f. Provision must be made for reconstitution capabilities that allow for recovery from a catastrophic emergency and resumption of normal operations; and

g. Provision must be made for the identification, training, and preparedness of personnel capable of relocating to alternate facilities to support the continuation of the performance of PMEFs.

16. The Secretary of Homeland Security shall:

a. Develop, lead, and conduct a Federal continuity training and exercise program, which shall be incorporated into the National Exercise Program developed pursuant to Homeland Security Presidential Directive-8 of December 17, 2003 ("National Preparedness)...

18. The Secretary of Defense, in coordination with the Secretary of Homeland Security, shall provide secure, integrated, Continuity of Government communications to the President, the Vice President, and, at a minimum, Category I executive departments and agencies.

Homeland Security Presidential Directive 20, Annex A[3]

In accordance with NSPD-51/HSPD-20, National Continuity Policy, executive departments and agencies are assigned to one of four categories commensurate with their COOP/COG/ECG responsibilities during an emergency. These categories shall be used for continuity planning, communications requirements, emergency operations capabilities, and other related requirements.

2. Category I:

a. Department of State
b. Department of the Treasury

c. Department of Defense, including the U.S. Army Corps of Engineers
d. Department of Justice, including the Federal Bureau of Investigation
e. Department of Health and Human Services
f. Department of Transportation
g. Department of Energy
h. Department of Homeland Security, including:
    a. Federal Emergency Management Agency
    b. United States Secret Service
    c. National Communications System
i. Office of the Director of National Intelligence
j. Central Intelligence Agency

3. Category II:

a. Department of the Interior
b. Department of Agriculture
c. Department of Commerce
d. Department of Labor
e. Department of Housing and Urban Development
f. Department of Education
g. Department of Veterans Affairs
h. Environmental Protection Agency
i. Federal Communications Commission
j. Federal Reserve System
k. General Services Administration
l. National Archives and Records Administration
m. Nuclear Regulatory Commission
n. Office of Personnel Management
o. Social Security Administration
p. United States Postal Service

4. Category III:

a. Commodity Futures Trading Commission
b. Export-Import Bank of the United States
c. Farm Credit Administration
d. Federal Deposit Insurance Corporation
e. Federal Mediation and Conciliation Service
f. National Aeronautics and Space Administration
g. National Credit Union Administration
h. National Labor Relations Board
i. National Science Foundation
j. Railroad Retirement Board
k. Securities and Exchange Commission
l. Small Business Administration
m. Tennessee Valley Authority

5. Category IV: All executive branch commissions, boards, bureaus, and members of the Small Agency Council not otherwise identified in Categories I, II, or III.

ENDNOTES

1. HSPD 20. http://www.dhs.gov/xabout/laws/gc_1219245 380392.shtm.
2. HSPD 20, Annex A. http://www.dhs.gov/xabout/laws/gc_1215544078004.shtm.
3. HSPD 20, Annex A. http://www.dhs.gov/xabout/laws/gc_1215544078004.shtm.

ADDITIONAL RESOURCES

Department of Defense Directive Number 3020.26, January 9, 2009, Department of Defense Continuity Programs. This document "Revises continuity policies and assigns responsibilities for developing and maintaining Defense Continuity Programs to enhance the DoD readiness posture. http://www.dtic.mil/whs/directives/corres/pdf/302026p.pdf.

Federal Continuity Directive 1 (FCD 1), Federal Executive Branch National Continuity Program and Requirements, *February 2008.* "The purpose of this FCD is to provide direction for the development of continuity plans and programs for the Federal executive branch." http://www.fema.gov/pdf/about/offices/fcd1.pdf.

Federal Continuity Directive 2 (FCD 2), Federal Executive Branch Mission Essential Function and Primary Mission Essential Function Identification and Submission Process *February 2008.* This document "provides guidance and direction for the departments and agencies in the process for identification of their essential functions, and the Business Process Analysis and Business impact Analysis that support and identify the relationship between these essential functions." http://www.fema.gov/pdf/about/offices/fcd2.pdf.

This workshop "Provide[s] training on the formalized process for . . . submission of potential Primary Mission Essential Functions that support the National Essential Functions . . ." Mission Essential Function (MEF) and Primary Mission Essential Function (PMEF) Workshop Overview for Continuity Coordinators, undated, National Continuity Policy Implementation Plan – Primary Mission Essential Functions http://www.fema.gov/pdf/about/offices/fcd2_b.pdf.

This document provides a "how to" make a COOP plan. Continuity of Operations (COOP) Plan Template Instructions, Federal Emergency Management Agency, undated http://www.fema.gov/doc/government/coop/coop_plan_template_instructions.doc.

This document "assesses the strengths and weaknesses of TSA's COOP Program and its ability to continue mission-essential functions during emergency situations." Portions of the document are redacted (crossed out for security reasons). Transportation Security Administration Continuity of Operations Program Redacted. Office of OIG-06-60. August 2006. http://www.dhs.gov/xoig/assets/mgmtrpts/OIGr_06-60_Aug06.pdf.

This document provides a "how to" for continuity of operations planning for businesses. http://www.ready.gov/business/plan/planning.html.

This document provides a host of FEMA COOP resources including available programs, resources, and education and training. It includes a section on COOP for pandemic flu. http://www.fema.gov/government/coop/index.shtm#2.

This document provides a history of US efforts at CoG. Harold C. Relyea, "Continuity of Government: Current Federal Arrangements and the Future." CRS Report for Congress, Order Code RS21089, January 7, 2005, http://www.globalsecurity.org/military/library/report/crs/rs21089.pdfhttp://www.au.af.mil/au/awc/awcgate/crs/rs21089.pdf.

18

IDENTIFICATION ISSUES

This chapter consolidates some of the issues involving identification. Included is the use of biometrics for terrorism screening. HSPD 2 proposes the use of immigration policies to fight terrorist entry into the United States. It creates the Foreign Terrorist Tracking Task Force to prevent entry of known or suspected terrorists and increases the number of customs and INS Agents. It attempts to stop abuses of student visas and initiates discussions with Mexico and Canada about compatible visa programs. HSPD 6 deals with the use of information about known or suspected terrorists and directs federal agencies to provide all terrorist information to the Terrorist Threat Integration Center. HSPD 11 establishes more detailed screening procedures. HSPD 24 creates the framework to ensure that federal agencies use biometrics to assist with identification, use compatible computer systems, use a layered approach to identification, and share data between agencies.

The statutes in the Real ID Act section present, in chronological order, development of the so-called Real ID. They begin with the Homeland Security Act of 2002 stating, "Nothing in this Act shall be construed to authorize the development of a national identification system or card." In July 2004, the 9/11 Commission Report recommended a better form of identification. Portions of the 9/11 Commission Report Recommendations, including the identification recommendation, were implemented by the Intelligence Reform and Terrorism Prevention Act of 2004. This act establishes standards for identification that would be required for an ID to be acceptable for federal business including admission to federal buildings and entry onto aircraft. "The Western Hemisphere Travel Initiative requires all citizens of the United States, Canada, Mexico, and Bermuda to have a passport or other accepted document that establishes the bearer's identity and nationality to enter or depart the United States from within the Western Hemisphere."

SOURCES

- I. TERRORIST SCREENING: BIOMETRICS FOR IDENTIFICATION.
  - HSPD 2, Combating Terrorism Through Immigration Policies[1]
  - HSPD 6, Screening Information to Protect Against Terrorism[2]
  - HSPD 11, Comprehensive Terrorist-Related Screening[3]
  - HSPD 24, Biometrics for Identification[4]
- II. REAL ID ACT.
  - Homeland Security Act Of 2002[5]
  - Sec. 1514, National Identification System Not Authorized.
  - 9/11 Commission Report Recommendations, July 2004[6]
  - Intelligence Reform and Terrorism Prevention Act of 2004[7]
  - The Western Hemisphere Travel Initiative[8]
- III. COMMON IDENTIFICATION FOR FEDERAL EMPLOYEES
  - HSPD 12. Common Identification for Federal Employees[9]

Foundations of Homeland Security: Law and Policy, First Edition. Martin J. Alperen.
© 2011 John Wiley & Sons, Inc. Published 2011 by John Wiley & Sons, Inc.

I. TERRORIST SCREENING: BIOMETRICS FOR IDENTIFICATION.

HSPD 2. Combating Terrorism Through Immigration Policies, October 29, 2001

SUBJECT: Combating Terrorism Through Immigration Policies

A. NATIONAL POLICY The United States has a long and valued tradition of welcoming immigrants and visitors. But the attacks of September 11, 2001, showed that some come to the United States to commit terrorist acts, to raise funds for illegal terrorist activities, or to provide other support for terrorist operations, here and abroad. It is the policy of the United States to work aggressively to prevent aliens who engage in or support terrorist activity from entering the United States and to detain, prosecute, or deport any such aliens who are within the United States.

1. By November 1, 2001, the Attorney General shall create the Foreign Terrorist Tracking Task Force (Task Force) . . . The Task Force shall ensure that, to the maximum extent permitted by law, Federal agencies coordinate programs to accomplish the following: 1) deny entry into the United States of aliens associated with, suspected of being engaged in, or supporting terrorist activity; and 2) locate, detain, prosecute, or deport any such aliens already present in the United States. . .

2. . . .significantly increase the number of Customs and INS special agents assigned to Joint Terrorism Task Forces. . .

3. The Government shall implement measures to end the abuse of student visas and prohibit certain international students from receiving education and training in sensitive areas, including areas of study with direct application to the development and use of weapons of mass destruction.

4. North American Complementary Immigration Policies The Secretary of State . . . shall promptly initiate negotiations with Canada and Mexico to assure maximum possible compatibility of immigration, customs, and visa policies. . .

HSPD 6. Screening Information to Protect Against Terrorism

"Homeland Security Presidential Directive 6 concerns the use of information about individuals known or suspected to engage in terrorist activities. United States policy is to develop, integrate, and maintain thorough, accurate, and current information about individuals known or appropriately suspected to be or have been engaged in conduct related to terrorism. Such information shall be used to support fed-

eral, state, local, territorial, tribal, foreign-government, and private-sector screening processes, and diplomatic, military, intelligence, law enforcement, immigration, visa, and protective processes. The directive will be implemented in a manner consistent with the provisions of the Constitution and applicable laws, including those protecting the rights of all Americans.

1. The Attorney General shall establish an organization to consolidate the Government's approach to terrorism screening and provide for the appropriate and lawful use of Terrorist Information in screening processes.

2. The heads of executive departments and agencies shall, to the extent permitted by law, provide to the Terrorist Threat Integration Center (TTIC) on an ongoing basis all appropriate Terrorist Information in their possession, custody, or control.

HSPD 11. Comprehensive Terrorist-Related Screening

"HSPD 11 establishes comprehensive terrorist-related screening procedures in order to more effectively detect and interdict individuals known or reasonably suspected to be engaged in terrorist activities. It enhances terrorist-related screening through comprehensive, coordinated procedures that detect, identify, track, and interdict people, cargo, and other entities.

1. In order more effectively to detect and interdict individuals known or reasonably suspected to be or have been engaged in conduct constituting, in preparation for, in aid of, or related to terrorism ("suspected terrorists") and terrorist activities, it is the policy of the United States to:

   a. enhance terrorist-related screening (as defined below) through comprehensive, coordinated procedures that detect, identify, track, and interdict people, cargo, conveyances, and other entities and objects that pose a threat to homeland security, and to do so in a manner that safeguards legal rights, including freedoms, civil liberties, and information privacy guaranteed by Federal law, and builds upon existing risk assessment capabilities while facilitating the efficient movement of people, cargo, conveyances, and other potentially affected activities in commerce; and

   b. implement a coordinated and comprehensive approach to terrorist-related screening – in immigration, law enforcement, intelligence, counterintelligence, and protection of the border, transportation systems, and critical infrastructure – that supports homeland security, at home and abroad.

2. This directive builds upon HSPD-6. . .

3. In this directive, the term "terrorist-related screening" means the collection, analysis, dissemination, and use of information related to people, cargo, conveyances, and other entities and objects that pose a threat to homeland security. Terrorist-related screening also includes risk assessment, inspection, and credentialing.

4. Not later than 75 days after the date of this directive, the Secretary of Homeland Security, . . . shall submit to me, . . . a report setting forth plans and progress in the implementation of this directive

5. The report shall outline a strategy to enhance the effectiveness of terrorist-related screening activities, in accordance with the policy set forth in section 1 of this directive, by developing comprehensive, coordinated, systematic terrorist-related screening procedures and capabilities that also take into account the need to:

   a. maintain no less than current levels of security created by existing screening and protective measures;

   b. encourage innovations that exceed established standards;

   c. ensure sufficient flexibility to respond rapidly to changing threats and priorities;

   d. permit flexibility to incorporate advancements into screening applications and technology rapidly;

   e. incorporate security features, including unpredictability, that resist circumvention to the greatest extent possible;

   f. build upon existing systems and best practices and, where appropriate, integrate, consolidate, or eliminate duplicative systems used for terrorist-related screening;

   g. facilitate legitimate trade and travel, both domestically and internationally;

   h. limit delays caused by screening procedures that adversely impact foreign relations, or economic, commercial, or scientific interests of the United States; and

   i. enhance information flow between various screening programs.

6. The report shall also include the following:

   a. the purposes for which individuals will undergo terrorist-related screening;

   b. a description of the screening opportunities to which terrorist-related screening will be applied;

   c. the information individuals must present, including, as appropriate, the type of biometric identifier or other form of identification or identifying information to be presented, at particular screening opportunities;

   d. mechanisms to protect data, including during transfer of information;

   e. mechanisms to address data inaccuracies, including names inaccurately contained in the terrorist screening data consolidated pursuant to HSPD-6;

   f. the procedures and frequency for screening people, cargo, and conveyances;

   g. protocols to support consistent risk assessment and inspection procedures;

   h. the skills and training required for the screeners at screening opportunities;

   i. the hierarchy of consequences that should occur if a risk indicator is generated as a result of a screening opportunity;

   j. mechanisms for sharing information among screeners and all relevant Government agencies, including results of screening and new information acquired regarding suspected terrorists between screening opportunities;

   k. recommended research and development on technologies designed to enhance screening effectiveness and further protect privacy interests; and

   l. a plan for incorporating known traveler programs into the screening procedures, where appropriate.

HSPD 24. Biometrics for Identification, June 5, 2008

Scope

1. The executive branch has developed an integrated screening capability to protect the Nation against "known and suspected terrorists" (KSTs). The executive branch shall build upon this success, in accordance with this directive, by enhancing its capability to collect, store, use, analyze, and share biometrics to identify and screen KSTs and other persons who may pose a threat to national security.

2. Existing law determines under what circumstances an individual's biometric and biographic information can be collected. This directive requires agencies to use, in a more coordinated and efficient manner, all biometric information associated with persons who may pose a threat to national security, consistent with applicable law, including those laws relating to privacy and confidentiality of personal data.

3. This directive provides a Federal framework for applying existing and emerging biometric technologies to the collection, storage, use, analysis, and sharing of data in identification and screening processes employed by agencies to enhance national security, consistent with applicable law, including information privacy and other legal rights under United States law.

4. The executive branch recognizes the need for a layered approach to identification and screening of individuals, as no single mechanism is sufficient. . . .

8. Many agencies already collect biographic and biometric information in their identification and screening processes. With improvements in biometric technologies, and in light of its demonstrated value as a tool to protect national security, it is important to ensure agencies use compatible methods and procedures in the collection, storage, use, analysis, and sharing of biometric information.

Policy

11. Through integrated processes and interoperable systems, agencies shall, to the fullest extent permitted by law, make available to other agencies all biometric and associated biographic and contextual information associated with persons for whom there is an articulable and reasonable basis for suspicion that they pose a threat to national security.

II. REAL ID.

Homeland Security Act of 2002[10]

SEC. 1514. NATIONAL IDENTIFICATION SYSTEM NOT AUTHORIZED.

"Nothing in this Act shall be construed to authorize the development of a national identification system or card."

9/11 Commission Report Recommendations

According to the dates of various documents, concern about a national identification card existed at least as early as 2002 when the Homeland Security Act contained section 1514, above. The idea that a better form of identification was needed as a matter of homeland security originated at least as early as the July 2004, 9/11 Commission Recommendation, below.

"Secure identification should begin in the United States. The federal government should set standards for the issuance of birth certificates and sources of identification, such as many entry points to vulnerable facilities, including gates for boarding aircraft, sources of identification are the last opportunity to ensure that people are who they say they are and to check whether they are terrorists.[41]"

[footnote 41 reads, On achieving more reliable identification, see Markle Foundation task force report, Creating a Trusted Information Network for Homeland Security (Markle Foundation, 2003), p. 72 (online at www.markle.org)].[11]

Intelligence Reform and Terrorism Prevention Act of 2004

Subtitle B—Terrorist Travel and Effective Screening

SEC. 7201. COUNTERTERRORIST TRAVEL INTELLIGENCE.

(a) FINDINGS.— Consistent with the report of the National Commission on Terrorist Attacks Upon the United States, Congress makes the following findings:

(1) Travel documents are as important to terrorists as weapons since terrorists must travel clandestinely to meet, train, plan, case targets, and gain access to attack sites.

(2) International travel is dangerous for terrorists because they must surface to pass through regulated channels, present themselves to border security officials, or attempt to circumvent inspection points.

(3) Terrorists use evasive, but detectable, methods to travel, such as altered and counterfeit passports and visas, specific travel methods and routes, liaisons with corrupt government officials, human smuggling networks, supportive travel agencies, and immigration and identity fraud.

(4) Before September 11, 2001, no Federal agency systematically analyzed terrorist travel strategies. If an agency had done so, the agency could have discovered the ways in which the terrorist predecessors to al Qaeda had been systematically, but detectably, exploiting weaknesses in our border security since the early 1990s.

(5) Many of the hijackers were potentially vulnerable to interception by border authorities. Analyzing their characteristic travel documents and travel patterns could have allowed authorities to intercept some of the hijackers and a more effective use of information available in government databases could have identified some of the hijackers.

(6) The routine operations of our immigration laws and the aspects of those laws not specifically aimed at protecting against terrorism inevitably shaped al Qaeda's planning and opportunities.

(7) New insights into terrorist travel gained since September 11, 2001, have not been adequately integrated into the front lines of border security.

SEC. 7205. INTERNATIONAL STANDARDS FOR TRANSLITERATION OF NAMES INTO THE ROMAN ALPHABET FOR INTERNATIONAL TRAVEL DOCUMENTS AND NAME-BASED WATCHLIST SYSTEMS.

(a) FINDINGS.—Congress makes the following findings:

(1) The current lack of a single convention for translating Arabic names enabled some of the 19 hijackers of aircraft used in the terrorist attacks against the United States that occurred on September 11, 2001, to vary the spelling of their names to defeat name-based terrorist watchlist systems and to make more difficult any potential efforts to locate them.

(2) Although the development and utilization of terrorist watchlist systems using biometric identifiers will be helpful, the full development and utilization of such systems will take several years, and name-based terrorist watchlist systems will always be useful.

SEC. 7212. DRIVER'S. LICENSES AND PERSONAL IDENTIFICATION CARDS.

(b) *Standards for Acceptance by Federal Agencies.*

(1) IN GENERAL.

(A) *LIMITATION ON ACCEPTANCE.–* No Federal agency may accept, for any official purpose, a driver's license or personal identification card newly issued by a State more than 2 years after the promulgation of the minimum standards under paragraph (2) unless the driver's license or personal identification card conforms to such minimum standards. . .

(2) MINIMUM STANDARDS.— shall include–. . . (D) standards for information to be included on each driver's license or personal identification card, including—

(i) the person's full legal name;

(ii) the person's date of birth;

(iii) the person's gender;

(iv) the person's driver's license or personal identification card number;

(v) a digital photograph of the person;

(vi) the person's address of principal residence; and

(vii) the person's signature;

(E) standards for common machine-readable identity information to be included on each driver's license or personal identification card, including defined minimum data elements;

(F) security standards to ensure that driver's licenses and personal identification cards are–

(i) resistant to tampering, alteration, or counterfeiting; and

(ii) capable of accommodating and ensuring the security of a digital photograph or other unique identifier; and

(G) a requirement that a State confiscate a driver's license or personal identification card if any component or security feature of the license or identification card is compromised."

The Western Hemisphere Travel Initiative

"The Western Hemisphere Travel Initiative (WHTI) requires all citizens of the United States, Canada, Mexico, and Bermuda to have a passport or other accepted document that establishes the bearer's identity and nationality to enter or depart the United States from within the Western Hemisphere.

The travel document requirements make up the departments of State and Homeland Security's Western Hemisphere Travel Initiative. This change in travel document requirements is the result of recommendations made by the 9/11 Commission, which Congress subsequently passed into law in the Intelligence Reform and Terrorism Prevention Act of 2004.

This travel initiative is being implemented in two phases:

Air travel requirements went into effect January 23, 2007 and now all travelers including children must present a passport or secure travel document when entering the United States by air.

Land/Sea requirements are transitioning toward standard and consistent documents for all travelers entering the country with full implementation on June 1, 2009. . .

"WHTI requires travelers to present a passport or other approved secure document denoting citizenship and identity for all land and sea travel into the United States. WHTI establishes document requirements for travelers entering the United States who were previously exempt, including citizens of the U.S., Canada and Bermuda. These document requirements are effective June 1, 2009."

III. COMMON IDENTIFICATION FOR FEDERAL EMPLOYEES

HSPD 12, Common Identification for Federal Employees[12]

Policies for a Common Identification Standard for Federal Employees and Contractors, August 27, 2004

"There are wide variations in the quality and security of identification used to gain access to secure facilities where there is potential for terrorist attacks. In order to eliminate these variations, U.S. policy is to enhance security, increase

Government efficiency, reduce identity fraud, and protect personal privacy by establishing a mandatory, Government-wide standard for secure and reliable forms of identification issued by the Federal Government to its employees and contractors (including contractor employees). This directive mandates a federal standard for secure and reliable forms of identification..."

Implementing Recommendations of the 9/11 Commission Act of 2007[13]

SEC. 409.

(a) IN GENERAL.— Title V of the Homeland Security Act of 2002 (6 U.S.C. 311 et seq.) is amended by adding at the end the following:
"SEC. 522. MODEL STANDARDS AND GUIDELINES FOR CRITICAL INFRASTRUCTURE WORKERS.

"(a) *IN GENERAL.*— Not later than 12 months after the date of enactment of the Implementing Recommendations of the 9/11 Commission Act of 2007 . . . the Administrator shall establish model standards and guidelines for credentialing critical infrastructure workers that may be used by a State to credential critical infrastructure workers that may respond to a natural disaster, act of terrorism, or other manmade disaster.

ENDNOTES

1. HSPD 2. October 29, 2001. http://www.dhs.gov/xabout/laws/gc_1214333907791.shtm.
2. HSPD 6. September 16, 2003. http://www.dhs.gov/xabout/laws/gc_1214594853475.shtm.
3. HSPD 11. August 27, 2004. http://www.dhs.gov/xabout/laws/gc_1217614237097.shtm.
4. HSPD 24. June 5, 2008. http://www.dhs.gov/xabout/laws/gc_1219257118875.shtm.
5. Homeland Security Act Of 2002. November 25, 2002. http://www.dhs.gov/xlibrary/assets/hr_5005_enr.pdf.
6. 9/11 Commission Report Recommendations, July 2004. http://www.9-11commission.gov/report/911Report_Ch 12.htm.
7. Intelligence Reform And Terrorism Prevention Act Of December 17, 2004. http://www.nctc.gov/docs/pl108_458.pdf.
8. Western Hemisphere Travel Initiative. http://www.dhs.gov/xprevprot/programs/gc_1200693579776.shtm.
9. HSPD 12. August 27, 2004. http://www.dhs.gov/xabout/laws/gc_1217616624097.shtm.
10. Homeland Security Act Of 2002. http://www.dhs.gov/xlibrary/assets/hr_5005_enr.pdf.
11. 9/11 Commission Report Recommendations, July 2004. http://www.gpoaccess.gov/911/pdf/fullreport.pdf, p. 390.
12. HSPD 12. http://www.dhs.gov/xabout/laws/gc_1217616 624097.shtm.

13. Strengthening Use Of The Incident Command System, Title IV, Implementing Recommendations of the 9/11 Commission Act of 2007, August 3, 2007. http://www.nctc.gov/docs/ir-of-the-9-11-comm-act-of-2007.pdf.

ADDITIONAL RESOURCES

Real ID Final Rule. The Department of Homeland Security has issued a final rule to establish minimum standards for state-issued driver's licenses and identification cards in accordance with the REAL ID Act of 2005. http://www.dhs.gov/files/laws/gc_1172765386179.shtm

Western Hemisphere Travel Initiative (WHTI). Final rules that require travelers to present a passport or other approved secure document denoting citizenship and identity for all travel into the United States. http://www.dhs.gov/files/laws/gc_118297 7197138.shtm

Changes to the Visa Waiver Program to Implement the Electronic System for Travel Authorization (ESTA) Program: Interim Final Rule. Requires Visa Waiver Program travelers to provide certain biographical information to U.S. Customs and Border Protection (CBP) officers electronically before departing to the United States. http://www.dhs.gov/files/laws/gc_1212505190650.shtm

"A Scorecard on the Post-9/11 Port Worker Background Checks," National Employment Law Project, July, 2009, http://nelp.3cdn.net/2d5508b4cec6e13da6_upm6b20e5.pdf

Privacy Impact Assessments (PIA), Personal Identity Verification, Department of Homeland Security, June 18, 2009, http://www.dhs.gov/xlibrary/assets/privacy/privacy_pia_dhs_pivupdate.pdf

Cynthia Brougher, Legal Analysis of Religious Exemptions for Photo Identification Requirements, Congressional Research Service R40515, April 13, 2009, http://opencrs.com/document/R40515/

National Governor's Association supports legislation that might weaken the REAL ID Act. It is called the PASS ID Act (Providing for Additional Security in State's Identification Act of 2009). See "The Appearance of Security: REAL ID Final Regulations vs. PASS ID Act of 2009," April 2009, by Janice Kephart. Janice Kephart is former counsel to the 9/11 Commission and Director of National Security Policy at the Center for Immigration Studies. http://cis.org/PASSID

"Repealing REAL ID? Rolling Back Driver's License Security," Center for Immigration Studies (CIS), June 2009, http://www.cis.org/articles/2009/realid.pdf

Potentially High Costs and Insufficient Grant Funds Pose a Challenge to REAL ID Implementation, OIG-09-36. March 2009. http://www.dhs.gov/xoig/assets/mgmtrpts/OIG_09-36_Mar09.pdf

Department of State: Undercover Tests Reveal Significant Vulnerabilities in State's Passport Issuance Process, Report to Congressional Requesters United States. Government Accountability Office. March 2009. http://www.gao.gov/new.items/d09447.pdf

"The ID Divide, Addressing the Challenges of Identification and Authentication in American Society," Peter P. Swire and Cassandra Q. Butts, Center for American Progress, June 2008, http://www.americanprogress.org/issues/2008/06/pdf/id_divide.pdf

19

EMERGENCY PREPAREDNESS AND RESPONSE

Executive Order 13,234 establishes the President's Task Force on Citizen Preparedness. HSPD 3 details the Homeland Security Advisory System. The Homeland Security Act creates the Directorate for Information Analysis and Infrastructure Protection where an Undersecretary of the Directorate is directed to establish and administer the Homeland Security Advisory System. The Department of Health and Human Services is required to set priorities for chemical, biological, radiological, and nuclear response strategy. A Directorate of Emergency Preparedness and Response whose responsibilities include developing a program for interoperative communications technology is established. The Nuclear Incident Response Teams are assigned to DHS.

The Implementing Recommendations of the 9/11 Commission Act establishes a grant program for interoperable communications and provides detailed instructions for operating the Advisory system. Another section authorizes DHS to establish a National Domestic Preparedness Consortium to invigorate state and lower level training.

HSPD 21 discusses building community resilience and communities learning and preparing to mitigate their own risk and respond to local problems.

The National Strategy for Homeland Security, in the context of a longer term strategy, discusses developing a "culture of preparedness" and the Homeland Security Management system. In a section entitled "Investing in Intellectual and Human Capital," this document states the need for trained, homeland security professionals. There are then sections on incident management and interoperable communications.

SOURCES

- Executive Order 13234 of November 9, 2001, Presidential Task Force on Citizen Preparedness in the War on Terrorism[1]
- HSPD 3. Homeland Security Advisory System (March 11, 2002)[2]
- Homeland Security Act of 2002 (November 25, 2002)[3]
- 9/11 Commission Implementation Act of 2004[4]
- Post Katrina Emergency Management Reform Act, October 4, 2006[5]
- Public Alert and Warning System, Executive Order 13407 of June 26, 2006[6]
- Warning, Alert, and Response Network Act of October 13, 2006[7]
- Implementing Recommendations of the 9/11 Commission Act, August 3, 2007[8]
- National Strategy for Homeland Security, October 2007[9]

Executive Order 13234 of November 9, 2001, Presidential Task Force on Citizen Preparedness in the War on Terrorism

Sec. 1. Establishment.

There is hereby established the "Presidential Task Force on Citizen Preparedness in the War On Terrorism" (Task Force).

Sec. 3. Mission.

The Task Force shall identify, review, and recommend appropriate means by which the American public can:

(a) prepare in their homes, neighborhoods, schools, places of worship, workplaces, and public places for

Foundations of Homeland Security: Law and Policy, First Edition. Martin J. Alperen.
© 2011 John Wiley & Sons, Inc. Published 2011 by John Wiley & Sons, Inc.

the potential consequences of any possible terrorist attacks within the United States; and

(b) volunteer to assist or otherwise support State and local public health and safety officials and others engaged in the effort to prevent, prepare for, and respond to any possible terrorist attacks within the United States.

Sec. 4. Reporting Requirement.

The Task Force shall submit its recommendations to the President within 40 days from the date of this order.

Sec. 5. Termination of Task Force.

The Task Force shall terminate 30 days after submitting its report to the President.

HSPD 3. Homeland Security Advisory System, March 11, 2002[10]

SUBJECT: Homeland Security Advisory System

Purpose The Nation requires a Homeland Security Advisory System to provide a comprehensive and effective means to disseminate information regarding the risk of terrorist acts to Federal, State, and local authorities and to the American people. Such a system would provide warnings in the form of a set of graduated "Threat Conditions" that would increase as the risk of the threat increases. At each Threat Condition, Federal departments and agencies would implement a corresponding set of "Protective Measures" to further reduce vulnerability or increase response capability during a period of heightened alert.

This system is intended to create a common vocabulary, context, and structure for an ongoing national discussion about the nature of the threats that confront the homeland and the appropriate measures that should be taken in response. It seeks to inform and facilitate decisions appropriate to different levels of government and to private citizens at home and at work.

Homeland Security Advisory System ... There are five Threat Conditions, each identified by a description and corresponding color. From lowest to highest, the levels and colors are:

Low = Green;
Guarded = Blue;
Elevated = Yellow;
High = Orange;
Severe = Red.

The higher the Threat Condition, the greater the risk of a terrorist attack. Risk includes both the probability of an attack occurring and its potential gravity. Threat Conditions shall be assigned by the Attorney General in consultation with the Assistant to the President for Homeland Security.[11]

... Threat Conditions may be assigned for the entire Nation, or they may be set for a particular geographic area or industrial sector.

... The decision whether to publicly announce Threat Conditions shall be made on a case-by-case basis by the Attorney General in consultation with the Assistant to the President for Homeland Security. Every effort shall be made to share as much information Regarding the threat as possible, consistent with the safety of the Nation ...

... A decision on which Threat Condition to assign shall integrate a variety of considerations. This integration will rely on qualitative assessment, not quantitative calculation. Higher Threat Conditions indicate greater risk of a terrorist act, with risk including both probability and gravity. Despite best efforts, there can be no guarantee that, at any given Threat Condition, a terrorist attack will not occur. An initial and important factor is the quality of the threat information itself. The evaluation of this threat information shall include, but not be limited to, the following factors:

1. To what degree is the threat information credible?
2. To what degree is the threat information corroborated?
3. To what degree is the threat specific and/or imminent?
4. How grave are the potential consequences of the threat?"

Homeland Security Act of 2002[12]

SEC. 201. DIRECTORATE FOR INFORMATION ANALYSIS AND INFRASTRUCTURE PROTECTION.

(a)(1) IN GENERAL.— There shall be in the Department a Directorate for Information Analysis and Infrastructure Protection ....

(d) RESPONSIBILITIES OF UNDER SECRETARY.— The responsibilities of the Under Secretary for Information Analysis and Infrastructure Protection shall be as follows:

(7) To administer the Homeland Security Advisory System, including—

(A) exercising primary responsibility for public advisories related to threats to homeland security; and

(B) in coordination with other agencies of the Federal Government, providing specific warning information, and advice about appropriate protective measures and countermeasures, to State and local government agencies and authorities, the private sector, other entities, and the public.

SEC. 304. CONDUCT OF CERTAIN PUBLIC HEALTH-RELATED ACTIVITIES.

(c) ADMINISTRATION OF COUNTERMEASURES AGAINST SMALLPOX.— Section 224 of the Public Health Service Act (42 U.S.C. 233) is amended by adding the following:

"(p)(2)(A)(i) IN GENERAL.—The Secretary [of DHS]may issue a declaration, pursuant to this paragraph, concluding that an actual or potential bioterrorist incident or other actual or potential public health emergency makes advisable the administration of a covered countermeasure to a category or categories of individuals.

"(iii) EFFECTIVE PERIOD.—The Secretary shall specify in such declaration the beginning and ending dates of the effective period of the declaration, . . .

SEC. 501. UNDER SECRETARY FOR EMERGENCY PREPAREDNESS AND RESPONSE.

There shall be in the Department a Directorate of Emergency Preparedness and Response headed by an Under Secretary for Emergency Preparedness and Response.

SEC. 502. RESPONSIBILITIES.

. . . shall include—

(1) helping to ensure the effectiveness of emergency response providers to terrorist atacks, major disasters, and other emergencies;

(2) with respect to the Nuclear Incident Response Team (regardless of whether it is operating as an organizational unit of the Department pursuant to this title)—

   (A) establishing standards and certifying when those standards have been met;

   (B) conducting joint and other exercises and training and evaluating performance; and

   (C) providing funds to the Department of Energy and the Environmental Protection Agency, as appropriate, for homeland security planning, exercises and training, and equipment;

(3) providing the Federal Government's response to terrorist attacks and major disasters, including—

   (A) managing such response;

   (B) directing the Domestic Emergency Support Team, the Strategic National Stockpile, the National Disaster Medical System, and (when operating as an organizational unit of the Department pursuant to this title) the Nuclear Incident Response Team;

   (C) overseeing the Metropolitan Medical Response System; and

   (D) coordinating other Federal response resources in the event of a terrorist attack or major disaster;

(4) aiding the recovery from terrorist attacks and major disasters;

(5) building a comprehensive national incident management system with Federal, State, and local government personnel, agencies, and authorities, to respond to such attacks and disasters;

(6) consolidating existing Federal Government emergency response plans into a single, coordinated national response plan; and

(7) developing comprehensive programs for developing interoperative communications technology, and helping to ensure that emergency response providers acquire such technology.

SEC. 504. NUCLEAR INCIDENT RESPONSE.

(a) IN GENERAL.— At the direction of the Secretary (in connection with an actual or threatened terrorist attack, major disaster, or other emergency in the United States), the Nuclear Incident Response Team shall operate as an organizational unit of the Department. While so operating, the Nuclear Incident Response Team shall be subject to the direction, authority, and control of the Secretary.

9/11 Commission Implementation Act of 2004

SEC. 7301. THE INCIDENT COMMAND SYSTEM.

(a) FINDINGS.— Consistent with the report of the National Commission on Terrorist Attacks Upon the United States, Congress makes the following findings:

(1) The attacks on September 11, 2001, demonstrated that even the most robust emergency response capabilities can be overwhelmed if an attack is large enough.

(2) Teamwork, collaboration, and cooperation at an incident site are critical to a successful response to a terrorist attack.

(3) Key decisionmakers who are represented at the incident command level help to ensure an effective

response, the efficient use of resources, and responder safety.

(4) The incident command system also enables emergency managers and first responders to manage, generate, receive, evaluate, share, and use information.

(5) Regular joint training at all levels is essential to ensuring close coordination during an actual incident.

(6) In Homeland Security Presidential Directive 5, the President directed the Secretary of Homeland Security to develop an incident command system, to be known as the National Incident Management System (NIMS), and directed all Federal agencies to make the adoption of NIMS a condition for the receipt of Federal emergency preparedness assistance by States, territories, tribes, and local governments beginning in fiscal year 2005.

SEC. 7302. NATIONAL CAPITAL REGION MUTUAL AID.

(a) DEFINITIONS.— In this section:

(1) *AUTHORIZED REPRESENTATIVE OF THE FEDERAL GOVERNMENT.—* The term "authorized representative of the Federal Government" means any individual or individuals designated by the President with respect to the executive branch, the Chief Justice with respect to the Federal judiciary, or the President of the Senate and Speaker of the House of Representatives with respect to Congress, or their designees, to request assistance under a mutual aid agreement for an emergency or public service event.

(6) *MUTUAL AID AGREEMENT.—* The term "mutual aid agreement" means an agreement, authorized under subsection (b), for the provision of police, fire, rescue and other public safety and health or medical services to any party to the agreement during a public service event, an emergency, or pre-planned training event.

(7) *NATIONAL CAPITAL REGION OR REGION.—* The term "National Capital Region" or "Region" means the area defined under section 2674(f)(2) of title 10, United States Code, and those counties with a border abutting that area and any municipalities therein.

(9) *PUBLIC SERVICE EVENT.—* The term "public service event"—

(A) means any undeclared emergency, incident or situation in preparation for or response to which ... [an agency] requests or provides assistance under a Mutual Aid Agreement within the National Capital Region; and

(B) includes Presidential inaugurations, public gatherings, demonstrations and protests, and law enforcement, fire, rescue, emergency health and medical services, transportation, communications, public works and engineering, mass care, and other support that require human resources, equipment, facilities or services supplemental to or greater than the requesting jurisdiction can provide.

SEC. 7303. ENHANCEMENT OF PUBLIC SAFETY COMMUNICATIONS INTEROPERABILITY.

(a) COORDINATION OF PUBLIC SAFETY INTEROPERABLE COMMUNICATIONS PROGRAMS.

(1) *PROGRAM.—* The Secretary of Homeland Security... shall establish a program to enhance public safety interoperable communications at all levels of government. Such program shall—

(A) establish a comprehensive national approach to achieving public safety interoperable communications;

(B) coordinate with other Federal agencies in carrying out subparagraph (A);

(C) develop, in consultation with other appropriate Federal agencies and State and local authorities, appropriate minimum capabilities for communications interoperability for Federal, State, and local public safety agencies;

(D) accelerate ... the development of national voluntary consensus standards for public safety interoperable communications, recognizing—

(i) the value, life cycle, and technical capabilities of existing communications infrastructure;

(ii) the need for cross-border interoperability between States and nations;

(iii) the unique needs of small, rural communities; and

(iv) the interoperability needs for daily operations and catastrophic events;

(E) encourage the development and implementation of flexible and open architectures incorporating, where possible, technologies that currently are commercially available, with appropriate levels of security, for short-term and long-term solutions to public safety communications interoperability;

(F) assist other Federal agencies in identifying priorities for research, development, and testing and evaluation with regard to public safety interoperable communications;

(G) identify priorities within the Department of Homeland Security for research, development, and testing and evaluation with regard to public safety interoperable communications;

(I) provide technical assistance to State and local public safety agencies regarding planning, acquisition strategies, interoperability architectures, training, and other functions necessary to achieve public safety communications interoperability;

(J) develop and disseminate best practices to improve public safety communications interoperability; and

(2) *OFFICE FOR INTEROPERABILITY AND COMPATIBILITY.*

(A) *ESTABLISHMENT OF OFFICE.—* The Secretary may establish an Office for Interoperability and Compatibility within the Directorate of Science and Technology to carry out this subsection.

(c) INTERNATIONAL INTEROPERABILITY.— Not later than 18 months after the date of enactment of this Act, the President shall establish a mechanism for coordinating cross-border interoperability issues between—

(1) the United States and Canada; and

(2) the United States and Mexico.

(d) HIGH RISK AREA COMMUNICATIONS CAPABILITIES.— Title V of the Homeland Security Act of 2002 (6 U.S.C. 311 et seq.) is amended by adding at the end the following:
"SEC. 510. URBAN AND OTHER HIGH RISK AREA COMMUNICATIONS CAPABILITIES.

"(a) *IN GENERAL.—* The Secretary . . . shall provide technical guidance, training, and other assistance, as appropriate, to support the rapid establishment of consistent, secure, and effective interoperable communications capabilities in the event of an emergency in urban and other areas determined by the Secretary to be at consistently high levels of risk from terrorist attack.

"(b) *MINIMUM CAPABILITIES.—* The interoperable communications capabilities established under subsection (a) shall ensure the ability of all levels of government agencies, emergency response . . . and other organizations with emergency response capabilities—

"(1) to communicate with each other in the event of an emergency; and

"(2) to have appropriate and timely access to the Information Sharing Environment described in section 1016 of the National Security Intelligence Reform Act of 2004.".

(g) *DEFINITIONS.—* In this section:

(1) *INTEROPERABLE COMMUNICATIONS.—* The term "interoperable communications" means the ability of emergency response providers and relevant Federal, State, and local government agencies to communicate with each other as necessary, through a dedicated public safety network utilizing information technology systems and radio communications systems, and to exchange voice, data, or video with one another on demand, in real time, as necessary.

SEC. 7304. REGIONAL MODEL STRATEGIC PLAN PILOT PROJECTS.

(a) PILOT PROJECTS.— . . .the Secretary of Homeland Security shall establish not fewer than 2 pilot projects in high threat urban areas or regions that are likely to implement a national model strategic plan.

(b) PURPOSES.— The purposes of the pilot projects required by this section shall be to develop a regional strategic plan to foster interagency communication in the area in which it is established and coordinate the gathering of all Federal, State, and local first responders in that area, consistent with the national strategic plan developed by the Department of Homeland Security.

SEC. 7305. PRIVATE SECTOR PREPAREDNESS.

(a) FINDINGS.— Consistent with the report of the National Commission on Terrorist Attacks Upon the United States, Congress makes the following findings:

(1) Private sector organizations own 85 percent of the Nation's critical infrastructure and employ the vast majority of the Nation's workers.

(2) Preparedness in the private sector and public sector for rescue, restart and recovery of operations should include, as appropriate—

(A) a plan for evacuation;

(B) adequate communications capabilities; and

(C) a plan for continuity of operations.

**Post Katrina Emergency Management Reform Act,
October 4, 2006**

SEC. 611. STRUCTURING THE FEDERAL EMERGENCY MANAGEMENT AGENCY.

Title V of the Homeland Security Act of 2002 (6 U.S.C. 311 et seq.) is amended—

(1) by striking the title heading and inserting the following:..

'SEC. 512. EVACUATION PLANS AND EXERCISES.

"(a) IN GENERAL.— Notwithstanding any other provision of law, and subject to subsection (d), grants made to States or local or tribal governments by the Department through the State Homeland Security Grant Program or the Urban Area Security Initiative may be used to—

"(1) establish programs for the development and maintenance of mass evacuation plans under subsection (b) in the event of a natural disaster, act of terrorism, or other manmade disaster;

"(2) prepare for the execution of such plans, including the development of evacuation routes and the purchase and stockpiling of necessary supplies and shelters; and

"(3) conduct exercises of such plans.

"(b) PLAN DEVELOPMENT.— In developing the mass evacuation plans authorized under subsection (a), each State, local, or tribal government shall, to the maximum extent practicable—

"(1) establish incident command and decision making processes;

"(2) ensure that State, local, and tribal government plans, including evacuation routes, are coordinated and integrated;

"(3) identify primary and alternative evacuation routes and methods to increase evacuation capabilities along such routes such as conversion of two-way traffic to one-way evacuation routes;

"(4) identify evacuation transportation modes and capabilities, including the use of mass and public transit capabilities, and coordinating and integrating evacuation plans for all populations including for those individuals located in hospitals, nursing homes, and other institutional living facilities;

"(5) develop procedures for informing the public of evacuation plans before and during an evacuation, including individuals—

"(A) with disabilities or other special needs;

"(B) with limited English proficiency; or

"(C) who might otherwise have difficulty in obtaining such information; and

"(6) identify shelter locations and capabilities.

"(c) ASSISTANCE.

"(2) *REQUESTED ASSISTANCE.—* The Administrator shall make assistance available upon request of a State, local, or tribal government to assist hospitals, nursing homes, and other institutions that house individuals with special needs to establish, maintain, and exercise mass evacuation plans that are coordinated and integrated into the plans developed by that State, local, or tribal government under this section.

"SEC. 513. DISABILITY COORDINATOR.

"(a) IN GENERAL.— After consultation with organizations representing individuals with disabilities, the National Council on Disabilities, and the Interagency Coordinating Council on Preparedness and Individuals with Disabilities, established under Executive Order No. 13347 (6 U.S.C. 312 note), the Administrator shall appoint a Disability Coordinator. . .

"(b) RESPONSIBILITIES.— The Disability Coordinator shall be responsible for—

"(1) providing guidance and coordination on matters related to individuals with disabilities in emergency planning requirements and relief efforts in the event of a natural disaster, act of terrorism, or other manmade disaster;

"(2) interacting with the staff of the Agency, the National Council on Disabilities, the Interagency Coordinating Council on Preparedness and Individuals with Disabilities established under Executive Order No. 13347 (6 U.S.C. 312 note), other agencies of the Federal Government, and State, local, and tribal government authorities regarding the needs of individuals with disabilities in emergency planning requirements and relief efforts in the event of a natural disaster, act of terrorism, or other man-made disaster;

"(3) consulting with organizations that represent the interests and rights of individuals with disabilities about the needs of individuals with disabilities in emergency planning requirements and relief efforts in the event of a natural disaster, act of terrorism, or other man-made disaster;

"(4) ensuring the coordination and dissemination of best practices and model evacuation plans for individuals with disabilities;

"(5) ensuring the development of training materials and a curriculum for training of emergency response providers, State, local, and tribal government officials, and others on the needs of individuals with disabilities;

"(6) promoting the accessibility of telephone hotlines and websites regarding emergency preparedness, evacuations, and disaster relief;

"(7) working to ensure that video programming distributors, including broadcasters, cable operators, and satellite television services, make emergency information accessible to individuals with hearing and vision disabilities;

"(8) ensuring the availability of accessible transportation options for individuals with disabilities in the event of an evacuation;

"(9) providing guidance and implementing policies to ensure that the rights and wishes of individuals with disabilities regarding post-evacuation residency and relocation are respected;

"(10) ensuring that meeting the needs of individuals with disabilities are included in the components of the national preparedness system established under section 644 of the Post-Katrina Emergency Management Reform Act of 2006. . .

Subtitle C—Comprehensive Preparedness System

CHAPTER 1—NATIONAL PREPAREDNESS SYSTEM

SEC. 642. NATIONAL PREPAREDNESS.

In order to prepare the Nation for all hazards, including natural disasters, acts of terrorism, and other man-made disasters, the President . . . shall develop a national preparedness goal and a national preparedness system.

SEC. 643. NATIONAL PREPAREDNESS GOAL.

(a) ESTABLISHMENT.— The President, acting through the Administrator, shall complete, revise, and update, as necessary, a national preparedness goal that defines the target level of preparedness to ensure the Nation's ability to prevent, respond to, recover from, and mitigate against natural disasters, acts of terrorism, and other man-made disasters.

(b) NATIONAL INCIDENT MANAGEMENT SYSTEM AND NATIONAL RESPONSE PLAN.— The national preparedness goal, to the greatest extent practicable, shall be consistent with the National Incident Management System and the National Response Plan.

SEC. 644. ESTABLISHMENT OF NATIONAL PREPAREDNESS SYSTEM.

(a) ESTABLISHMENT.— The President, acting through the Administrator, shall develop a national preparedness system to enable the Nation to meet the national preparedness goal.

(b) COMPONENTS.— The national preparedness system shall include the following components:

(1) Target capabilities and preparedness priorities.

(2) Equipment and training standards.

(3) Training and exercises.

(4) Comprehensive assessment system.

(5) Remedial action management program.

(6) Federal response capability inventory.

(7) Reporting requirements.

(8) Federal preparedness.

(c) NATIONAL PLANNING SCENARIOS.— The national preparedness system may include national planning scenarios.

SEC. 645. NATIONAL PLANNING SCENARIOS.

(a) IN GENERAL.— The Administrator, in coordination with the heads of appropriate Federal agencies and the National Advisory Council, may develop planning scenarios to reflect the relative risk requirements presented by all hazards, including natural disasters, acts of terrorism, and other man-made disasters, in order to provide the foundation for the flexible and adaptive development of target capabilities and the identification of target capability levels to meet the national preparedness goal.

(b) DEVELOPMENT.— In developing, revising, and replacing national planning scenarios, the Administrator shall ensure that the scenarios—

(1) reflect the relative risk of all hazards and illustrate the potential scope, magnitude, and complexity of a broad range of representative hazards; and

(2) provide the minimum number of representative scenarios necessary to identify and define the tasks and target capabilities required to respond to all hazards.

SEC. 646. TARGET CAPABILITIES AND PREPAREDNESS PRIORITIES.

(a) ESTABLISHMENT OF GUIDELINES ON TARGET CAPABILITIES.— Not later than 180 days after the date of enactment of this Act, the Administrator . . . shall complete, revise, and update, as necessary, guidelines to define risk-based target capabilities for Federal, State, local, and tribal government preparedness that will enable the Nation to prevent, respond to, recover from, and mitigate against all hazards, including natural disasters, acts of terrorism, and other man-made disasters.

(d) TERRORISM RISK ASSESSMENT.— With respect to analyzing and assessing the risk of acts of terrorism, the Administrator shall consider—

(1) the variables of threat, vulnerability, and consequences related to population (including transient commuting and tourist populations), areas of high population density, critical infrastructure, coastline, and international borders; and

(2) the most current risk assessment available from the Chief Intelligence Officer of the Department of the threats of terrorism against the United States.

(e) PREPAREDNESS PRIORITIES.— In establishing the guidelines under subsection (a), the Administrator shall establish preparedness priorities that appropriately balance the risk of all hazards, including natural disasters, acts of terrorism, and other man-made disasters, with the resources required to prevent, respond to, recover from, and mitigate against the hazards. . .

Subtitle D—Emergency Communications

SEC. 671. EMERGENCY COMMUNICATIONS.

(a) SHORT TITLE.— This section may be cited as the "21st Century Emergency Communications Act of 2006".

(b) IN GENERAL.— The Homeland Security Act of 2002 (6 U.S.C. 101 et seq.) is amended by adding at the end the following new title:

TITLE XVIII—EMERGENCY COMMUNICATIONS

SEC. 1801. OFFICE OF EMERGENCY COMMUNICATIONS.

"(a) IN GENERAL.— There is established in the Department an Office of Emergency Communications.

"(b) DIRECTOR.— The head of the office shall be the Director for Emergency Communications. . .

"(c) RESPONSIBILITIES.— The Director for Emergency Communications shall—

"(4) conduct extensive, nationwide outreach to support and promote the ability of emergency response providers and relevant government officials to continue to communicate in the event of natural disasters, acts of terrorism, and other manmade disasters;

"(5) conduct extensive, nationwide outreach and foster the development of interoperable emergency communications capabilities by State, regional, local, and tribal governments and public safety agencies, and by regional consortia thereof;

"(8) promote the development of standard operating procedures and best practices with respect to use of interoperable emergency communications capabilities for incident response, and facilitate the sharing of information on such best practices for achieving, maintaining, and enhancing interoperable emergency communications capabilities for such response;

"(11) establish, in coordination with the Director of the Office for Interoperability and Compatibility, requirements for interoperable emergency communications capabilities, which shall be nonproprietary where standards for such capabilities exist, for all public safety radio and data communications systems and equipment purchased using homeland security assistance administered by the Department, excluding any alert and warning device, technology, or system;

SEC. 1802. NATIONAL EMERGENCY COMMUNICATIONS PLAN.

"(a) IN GENERAL.— The Secretary . . . shall . . . develop . . . a National Emergency Communications Plan to provide recommendations regarding how the United States should—

"(1) support and promote the ability of emergency response providers and relevant government officials to continue to communicate in the event of natural disasters, acts of terrorism, and other man-made disasters; and

"(2) ensure, accelerate, and attain interoperable emergency communications nationwide. "(8) recommend goals and timeframes for the deployment of emergency, command-level communications systems based on new and existing equipment across the United States and develop a timetable for the deployment of interoperable emergency communications systems nationwide. . .

SEC. 1805. REGIONAL EMERGENCY COMMUNICATIONS COORDINATION.

"(a) IN GENERAL.— There is established in each Regional Office a Regional Emergency Communications Coordination Working Group (in this section referred to as an 'RECC Working Group'). Each RECC Working Group shall report to the relevant Regional Administrator and coordinate its activities with the relevant Regional Advisory Council.

"(b) MEMBERSHIP.— Each RECC Working Group shall consist of the following:

"(1) *NON-FEDERAL.*— Organizations representing the interests of the following:

"(A) State officials.

"(B) Local government officials, including sheriffs.

"(C) State police departments.

"(D) Local police departments.

"(E) Local fire departments.

"(F) Public safety answering points (9–1–1 services).

"(G) State emergency managers, homeland security directors, or representatives of State Administrative Agencies.

"(H) Local emergency managers or homeland security directors.

"(I) Other emergency response providers as appropriate.

"(2) *FEDERAL.*— Representatives from the Department, the Federal Communications Commission, and other Federal departments and agencies with responsibility for coordinating interoperable emergency communications with or providing emergency support services to State, local, and tribal governments.

"(c) COORDINATION.— Each RECC Working Group shall coordinate its activities with the following:

"(1) Communications equipment manufacturers and vendors (including broadband data service providers).

"(2) Local exchange carriers.

"(3) Local broadcast media.

"(4) Wireless carriers.

"(5) Satellite communications services.

"(6) Cable operators.

"(7) Hospitals.

"(8) Public utility services.

"(9) Emergency evacuation transit services.

"(10) Ambulance services.

"(11) HAM and amateur radio operators.

"(d) DUTIES.— The duties of each RECC Working Group shall include—

"(1) assessing the survivability, sustainability, and interoperability of local emergency communications systems to meet the goals of the National Emergency Communications Plan. . .

SEC. 1806. EMERGENCY COMMUNICATIONS PREPAREDNESS CENTER.

"(a) ESTABLISHMENT.— There is established the Emergency Communications Preparedness Center (in this section referred to as the 'Center').

"(b) OPERATION.— The Secretary, the Chairman of the Federal Communications Commission, the Secretary of Defense, the Secretary of Commerce, the Attorney General of the United States, and the heads of other Federal departments and agencies or their designees shall jointly operate the Center in accordance with the Memorandum of Understanding entitled, 'Emergency Communications Preparedness Center (ECPC) Charter'.

"(c) FUNCTIONS.— The Center shall—

"(1) serve as the focal point for interagency efforts and as a clearinghouse with respect to all relevant intergovernmental information to support and promote (including specifically by working to avoid duplication, hindrances, and counteractive efforts among the participating Federal departments and agencies)—

"(A) the ability of emergency response providers and relevant government officials to continue to communicate in the event of natural disasters, acts of terrorism, and other man-made disasters; and

"(B) interoperable emergency communications. . .

SEC. 1807. URBAN AND OTHER HIGH RISK AREA COMMUNICATIONS CAPABILITIES.

"(a) IN GENERAL.— The Secretary . . . shall provide technical guidance, training, and other assistance, as appropriate, to support the rapid establishment of consistent, secure, and effective interoperable emergency communications capabilities in the event of an emergency in urban and other areas determined by the Secretary to be at consistently high levels of risk from natural disasters, acts of terrorism, and other man-made disasters.

"(b) MINIMUM CAPABILITIES.— The interoperable emergency communications capabilities established under subsection (a) shall ensure the ability of all levels of government, emergency response providers, the private sector, and other organizations with emergency response capabilities—

"(1) to communicate with each other in the event of an emergency;

"(2) to have appropriate and timely access to the Information Sharing Environment. . .

SEC. 672. OFFICE FOR INTEROPERABILITY AND COMPATIBILITY.

(a) IN GENERAL.— Title III of the Homeland Security Act of 2002 (6 U.S.C. 181 et seq.) is amended by adding at the end the following:
"SEC. 314. OFFICE FOR INTEROPERABILITY AND COMPATIBILITY.

"(a) *CLARIFICATION OF RESPONSIBILITIES.—* The Director of the Office for Interoperability and Compatibility shall—

"(1) . . . support the creation of national voluntary consensus standards for interoperable emergency communications;

"(2) establish a comprehensive research, development, testing, and evaluation program for improving interoperable emergency communications;

"(3) establish, in coordination with the Director for Emergency Communications, requirements for interoperable emergency communications capabilities, which shall be nonproprietary where standards for such capabilities exist, for all public safety radio and data communications systems and equipment purchased using homeland security assistance administered by the Department, excluding any alert and warning device, technology, or system;

"(4) conduct pilot projects . . . to test and demonstrate technologies, including data and video, that enhance—

"(A) the ability of emergency response providers and relevant government officials to continue to communicate in the event of natural disasters, acts of terrorism, and other man-made disasters; and

"(B) interoperable emergency communications capabilities.

SEC. 673. EMERGENCY COMMUNICATIONS INTEROPERABILITY RESEARCH AND DEVELOPMENT.

(a) IN GENERAL.— Title III of the Homeland Security Act of 2002 (6 U.S.C. 181 et seq.), as amended by this Act, is amended by adding at the end the following:

"SEC. 315. EMERGENCY COMMUNICATIONS INTEROPERABILITY RESEARCH AND DEVELOPMENT.

"(a) *IN GENERAL.—* The Under Secretary for Science and Technology . . . shall establish a comprehensive research and development program to support and promote—

"(1) the ability of emergency response providers and relevant government officials to continue to communicate in the event of natural disasters, acts of terrorism, and other manmade disasters; and

"(2) interoperable emergency communications capabilities among emergency response providers and relevant government officials response providers' communication capabilities.

"(b) *PURPOSES.—* The purposes of the program established under subsection (a) include—

"(1) supporting research, development, testing, and evaluation on emergency communication capabilities;

"(2) understanding the strengths and weaknesses of the public safety communications systems in use;

"(3) examining how current and emerging technology can make emergency response providers more effective, and how Federal, State, local, and tribal government agencies can use this technology in a coherent and cost-effective manner. . .

SEC. 674. 911 AND E911 SERVICES REPORT.

Not later than 180 days after the date of enactment of this Act, the Chairman of the Federal Communications Commission shall submit a report to Congress on the status of efforts of State, local, and tribal governments to develop plans for rerouting 911 and E911 services in the event that public safety answering points are disabled during natural disasters, acts of terrorism, and other man-made disasters.

SEC. 682. NATIONAL DISASTER RECOVERY STRATEGY.

(a) IN GENERAL.— The Administrator . . . shall develop, coordinate, and maintain a National Disaster Recovery Strategy to serve as a guide to recovery efforts after major disasters and emergencies.

(b) CONTENTS.— The National Disaster Recovery Strategy shall—

(1) outline the most efficient and cost-effective Federal programs that will meet the recovery needs of States,

local and tribal governments, and individuals and households affected by a major disaster;

(2) clearly define the role, programs, authorities, and responsibilities of each Federal agency that may be of assistance in providing assistance in the recovery from a major disaster;

(3) promote the use of the most appropriate and cost effective building materials (based on the hazards present in an area) in any area affected by a major disaster, with the goal of encouraging the construction of disaster-resistant buildings; and

SEC. 683. NATIONAL DISASTER HOUSING STRATEGY.

(a) IN GENERAL.— The Administrator . . . shall develop, coordinate, and maintain a National Disaster Housing Strategy.

(b) CONTENTS.— The National Disaster Housing Strategy shall—

(1) outline the most efficient and cost effective Federal programs that will best meet the short-term and long-term housing needs of individuals and households affected by a major disaster;

(2) clearly define the role, programs, authorities, and responsibilities of each entity in providing housing assistance in the event of a major disaster. . .

(3) describe programs directed to meet the needs of special needs and low-income populations and ensure that a sufficient number of housing units are provided for individuals with disabilities. . .

SEC. 689. INDIVIDUALS WITH DISABILITIES.

(a) GUIDELINES.— . . . the Administrator shall develop guidelines to accommodate individuals with disabilities, which shall include guidelines for—

(1) the accessibility of, and communications and programs in, shelters, recovery centers, and other facilities; and

(2) devices used in connection with disaster operations, including first aid stations, mass feeding areas, portable payphone stations, portable toilets, and temporary housing. . .

SEC. 689B. REUNIFICATION.

(b) NATIONAL EMERGENCY CHILD LOCATOR CENTER.

(1) *IN GENERAL.—* . . .the Administrator . . . shall establish within the National Center for Missing and Exploited Children the National Emergency Child Locator Center. In establishing the National Emergency Child Locator Center, the Administrator shall establish procedures to make all relevant information available to the National Emergency Child Locator Center in a timely manner to facilitate the expeditious identification and reunification of children with their families.

(2) *PURPOSES.—* The purposes of the Child Locator Center are to—

(A) enable individuals to provide to the Child Locator Center the name of and other identifying information about a displaced child or a displaced adult who may have information about the location of a displaced child;

(B) enable individuals to receive information about other sources of information about displaced children and displaced adults; and

(C) assist law enforcement in locating displaced children.

(D) refer reports of displaced adults to—

(i) an entity designated by the Attorney General to provide technical assistance in locating displaced adults; and

(ii) the National Emergency Family Registry and Locator System as defined under section 689c(a);

(E) enter into cooperative agreements with Federal and State agencies and other organizations such as the American Red Cross as necessary to implement the mission of the Child Locator Center. . .

SEC. 689C. NATIONAL EMERGENCY FAMILY REGISTRY AND LOCATOR SYSTEM.

(b) ESTABLISHMENT.— Not later than 180 days after the date of enactment of this Act, the Administrator shall establish a National Emergency Family Registry and Locator System to help reunify families separated after an emergency or major disaster.

(c) OPERATION OF SYSTEM.— The National Emergency Family Registry and Locator System shall—

(1) allow a displaced adult (including medical patients) to voluntarily register (and allow an adult that is the

parent or guardian of a displaced child to register such child), by submitting personal information to be entered into a database (such as the name, current location of residence, and any other relevant information that could be used by others seeking to locate that individual);

(2) be accessible through the Internet and through a tollfree number, to receive reports of displaced individuals. . .

Public Alert and Warning System, Executive Order 13407 of June 26, 2006

Sec. 1. Policy.

It is the policy of the United States to have an effective, reliable, integrated, flexible, and comprehensive system to alert and warn the American people in situations of war, terrorist attack, natural disaster, or other hazards to public safety and well-being (public alert and warning system), taking appropriate account of the functions, capabilities, and needs of the private sector and of all levels of government in our Federal system, and to ensure that under all conditions the President can communicate with the American people.

Sec. 2. Functions of the Secretary of Homeland Security.

(a) To implement the policy set forth in section 1 of this order, the Secretary of Homeland Security shall:

(i) inventory, evaluate, and assess the capabilities and integration with the public alert and warning system of Federal, State, territorial, tribal, and local public alert and warning resources;

(ii) establish or adopt, as appropriate, common alerting and warning protocols, standards, terminology, and operating procedures for the public alert and warning system to enable interoperability and the secure delivery of coordinated messages to the American people through as many communication pathways as practicable, taking account of Federal Communications Commission rules as provided by law;

(iii) ensure the capability to adapt the distribution and content of communications on the basis of geographic location, risks, or personal user preferences, as appropriate;

(iv) include in the public alert and warning system the capability to alert and warn all Americans, including those with disabilities and those without an understanding of the English language;

(v) through cooperation with the owners and operators of communication facilities, maintain, protect, and, if necessary, restore communications facilities and capabilities necessary for the public alert and warning system;

(vi) ensure the conduct of training, tests, and exercises for the public alert and warning system;

(vii) ensure the conduct of public education efforts so that State, territorial, tribal, and local governments, the private sector, and the American people understand the functions of the public alert and warning system and how to access, use, and respond to information from the public alert and warning system;

(viii) consult, coordinate, and cooperate with the private sector, including communications media organizations, and Federal, State, territorial, tribal, and local governmental authorities, including emergency response providers, as appropriate;

(ix) administer the Emergency Alert System (EAS) as a critical component of the public alert and warning system; and

(x) ensure that under all conditions the President of the United States can alert and warn the American people.

Warning, Alert, and Response Network Act, October 13, 2006[13]

TITLE VI—WARNING, ALERT, AND RESPONSE NETWORK ACT.

Commercial Mobile Service Alerts

SEC. 601. SHORT TITLE.

This title may be cited as the "Warning, Alert, and Response Network Act".

SEC. 602. FEDERAL COMMUNICATIONS COMMISSION DUTIES.

(a) *Commercial Mobile Service Alert Regulations.* Within 180 days after the date on which the Commercial Mobile Service Alert Advisory Committee, established pursuant to section 603(a), transmits recommendations to the Federal Communications Commission, the Commission shall complete a proceeding to adopt relevant technical standards, protocols, procedures, and other technical requirements based on the recommendations of such Advisory Committee necessary to enable commercial mobile service alerting capability for commercial mobile service providers that voluntarily elect to transmit emergency alerts. . .

(b) *Commercial Mobile Service Election.*
(1) AMENDMENT OF COMMERCIAL MOBILE SERVICE LICENSE.—Within 120 days after the date on which the Federal Communications Commission adopts

relevant technical standards and other technical requirements pursuant to subsection (a), the Commission shall complete a proceeding–

(A) to allow any licensee providing commercial mobile service . . . to transmit emergency alerts to subscribers to, or users of, the commercial mobile service provided by such licensee;

(B) to require any licensee providing commercial mobile service that elects, in whole or in part, under paragraph (2) not to transmit emergency alerts to provide clear and conspicuous notice at the point of sale of any devices with which its commercial mobile service is included, that it will not transmit such alerts via the service it provides for the device; and

(C) to require any licensee providing commercial mobile service that elects under paragraph (2) not to transmit emergency alerts to notify its existing subscribers of its election.

(2) ELECTION.

(A) **IN GENERAL.**—Within 30 days after the Commission issues its order under paragraph (1), each licensee providing commercial mobile service shall file an election with the Commission with respect to whether or not it intends to transmit emergency alerts.

(B) **TRANSMISSION STANDARDS; NOTIFICA-TION.**—If a licensee providing commercial mobile service elects to transmit emergency alerts via its commercial mobile service, the licensee shall–

(i) notify the Commission of its election; and

(ii) agree to transmit such alerts in a manner consistent with the technical standards, procedures, and other technical requirements implemented by the Commission.

(C) **NO FEE FOR SERVICE.**—A commercial mobile service licensee that elects to transmit emergency alerts may not impose a separate or additional charge for such transmission or capability.

(D) **CONSUMER CHOICE TECHNOLOGY.**—Any commercial mobile service licensee electing to transmit emergency alerts may offer subscribers the capability of preventing the subscriber's device from receiving such alerts, or classes of such alerts, other than an alert issued by the President.

(c) *Digital Television Transmission Towers Retransmission Capability.* Within 90 days after the date on which the Commission adopts relevant technical standards based on recommendations of the Commercial Mobile Service Alert Advisory Committee, established pursuant to section 603(a), the Commission shall complete a proceeding to require licensees

and permittees of noncommercial educational broadcast stations or public broadcast stations . . . to install necessary equipment and technologies on, or as part of, any broadcast television digital signal transmitter to enable the distribution of geographically targeted alerts by commercial mobile service providers that have elected to transmit emergency alerts under this section.

SEC. 605. GRANT PROGRAM FOR REMOTE COMMUNITY ALERT SYSTEMS.

(a) GRANT PROGRAM.— The Under Secretary of Commerce for Oceans and Atmosphere, in consultation with the Secretary of Homeland Security, shall establish a program under which grants may be made to provide for outdoor alerting technologies in remote communities effectively unserved by commercial mobile service . . . for the purpose of enabling residents of those communities to receive emergency alerts.

Implementing Recommendations of the 9/11 Commission Act of 2007
TITLE III—ENSURING COMMUNICATIONS INTEROPERABILITY FOR FIRST RESPONDERS

SEC. 301.

(a) ESTABLISHMENT.— Title XVIII of the Homeland Security Act of 2002 (6 U.S.C. 571 et seq.) is amended by adding at the end the following new section:

INTEROPERABLE EMERGENCY COMMUNICATIONS GRANT PROGRAM
Adding: "SEC. 1809. "(a).—The Secretary shall establish the Interoperable Emergency Communications Grant Program to make grants to States to carry out initiatives to improve local, tribal, statewide, regional, national and, where appropriate, international interoperable emergency communications, including communications in collective response to natural disasters, acts of terrorism, and other man-made disasters."

TITLE XXII—INTEROPERABLE EMERGENCY COMMUNICATIONS

SEC. 2201. INTEROPERABLE EMERGENCY COMMUNICATIONS.

(b) FCC VULNERABILITY ASSESSMENT AND REPORT ON EMERGENCY COMMUNICATIONS BACK-UP SYSTEM.

(1) *IN GENERAL.*— Not later than 180 days after the date of enactment of this Act, the Federal Communications

Commission shall conduct a vulnerability assessment of the Nation's critical communications and information systems infrastructure and shall evaluate the technical feasibility of creating a backup emergency communications system that complements existing communications resources and takes into account next generation and advanced communications technologies. The overriding objective for the evaluation shall be providing a framework for the development of a resilient interoperable communications system for emergency responders in an emergency. The Commission shall consult with the National Communications System and shall evaluate all reasonable options, including satellites, wireless, and terrestrial-based communications systems and other alternative transport mechanisms that can be used in tandem with existing technologies.

(2) *FACTORS TO BE EVALUATED.*— The evaluation under paragraph (1) shall include—

(A) a survey of all Federal agencies that use terrestrial or satellite technology for communications security and an evaluation of the feasibility of using existing systems for the purpose of creating such an emergency back-up public safety communications system;

(B) the feasibility of using private satellite, wireless, or terrestrial networks for emergency communications;

(C) the technical options, cost, and deployment methods of software, equipment, handsets or desktop communications devices for public safety entities in major urban areas, and nationwide; and

(D) the feasibility and cost of necessary changes to the network operations center of terrestrial-based or satellite systems to enable the centers to serve as emergency back-up communications systems.

(c) JOINT ADVISORY COMMITTEE ON COMMUNICATIONS CAPABILITIES OF EMERGENCY MEDICAL AND PUBLIC HEALTH CARE FACILITIES.

(1) *ESTABLISHMENT.*— The Assistant Secretary of Commerce for Communications and Information and the Chairman of the Federal Communications Commission, in consultation with the Secretary of Homeland Security and the Secretary of Health and Human Services, shall establish a joint advisory committee to examine the communications capabilities and needs of emergency medical and public health care facilities. The joint advisory committee shall be composed of individuals with expertise in communications technologies and emergency medical and public health care, including representatives of Federal, State and local governments, industry and non-profit health organizations, and academia and educational institutions.

(2) *DUTIES.*— The joint advisory committee shall—

(A) assess specific communications capabilities and needs of emergency medical and public health care facilities, including the improvement of basic voice, data, and broadband capabilities;

(B) assess options to accommodate growth of basic and emerging communications services used by emergency medical and public health care facilities;

(C) assess options to improve integration of communications systems used by emergency medical and public health care facilities with existing or future emergency communications networks; and

(D) report its findings to the Senate Committee on Commerce, Science, and Transportation and the House of Representatives Committee on Energy and Commerce, within 6 months after the date of enactment of this Act.

(d) AUTHORIZATION OF EMERGENCY MEDICAL AND PUBLIC HEALTH COMMUNICATIONS PILOT PROJECTS.

(1) *IN GENERAL.*— The Assistant Secretary of Commerce for Communications and Information may establish not more than 10 geographically dispersed project grants to emergency medical and public health care facilities to improve the capabilities of emergency communications systems in emergency medical care facilities.

(5) *DEPLOYMENT AND DISTRIBUTION.*— The Assistant Secretary shall seek to the maximum extent practicable to ensure a broad geographic distribution of project sites.

(6) *TRANSFER OF INFORMATION AND KNOWLEDGE.*— The Assistant Secretary shall establish mechanisms to ensure that the information and knowledge gained by participants in the pilot program are transferred among the pilot program participants and to other interested parties, including other applicants that submitted applications.

SEC. 501. HOMELAND SECURITY ADVISORY SYSTEM AND INFORMATION SHARING.

(a) ADVISORY SYSTEM AND INFORMATION SHARING.

(1) *IN GENERAL.*— Subtitle A of title II of the Homeland Security Act of 2002 (6 U.S.C. 121 et seq.) is amended by adding at the end the following:

HOMELAND SECURITY ADVISORY SYSTEM
Adding: "SEC. 203. HOMELAND SECURITY ADVISORY SYSTEM.

"(a) *REQUIREMENT*.— The Secretary shall administer the Homeland Security Advisory System[14] in accordance with this section to provide advisories or warnings regarding the threat or risk that acts of terrorism will be committed on the homeland to Federal, State, local, and tribal government authorities and to the people of the United States, as appropriate. The Secretary shall exercise primary responsibility for providing such advisories or warnings.

"(b) *REQUIRED ELEMENTS*.— In administering the Homeland Security Advisory System, the Secretary shall—

"(1) establish criteria for the issuance and revocation of such advisories or warnings;

"(2) develop a methodology, relying on the criteria established under paragraph (1), for the issuance and revocation of such advisories or warnings;

"(3) provide, in each such advisory or warning, specific information and advice regarding appropriate protective measures and countermeasures that may be taken in response to the threat or risk, at the maximum level of detail practicable to enable individuals, government entities, emergency response providers, and the private sector to act appropriately;

"(4) whenever possible, limit the scope of each such advisory or warning to a specific region, locality, or economic sector believed to be under threat or at risk; and

"(5) not, in issuing any advisory or warning, use color designations as the exclusive means of specifying homeland security threat conditions that are the subject of the advisory or warning.

SEC. 901. PRIVATE SECTOR PREPAREDNESS.

(a) IN GENERAL.— Title V of the Homeland Security Act of 2002 (6 U.S.C. 311 et seq.), as amended by section 409, is further amended by adding at the end the following:

"SEC. 523. GUIDANCE AND RECOMMENDATIONS.

"(a) *IN GENERAL.*— Consistent with their responsibilities and authorities under law, as of the day before the date of the enactment of this section, the Administrator and the Assistant Secretary for Infrastructure Protection, in consultation with the private sector, may develop guidance or recommendations and identify best practices to assist or foster action by the private sector in—

"(1) identifying potential hazards and assessing risks and impacts;

"(2) mitigating the impact of a wide variety of hazards, including weapons of mass destruction;

"(3) managing necessary emergency preparedness and response resources;

"(4) developing mutual aid agreements;

"(5) developing and maintaining emergency preparedness and response plans, and associated operational procedures;

"(6) developing and conducting training and exercises to support and evaluate emergency preparedness and response plans and operational procedures;

"(7) developing and conducting training programs for security guards to implement emergency preparedness and response plans and operations procedures; and

"(8) developing procedures to respond to requests for information from the media or the public. . .

"(c) *SMALL BUSINESS CONCERNS.*— In developing guidance or recommendations or identifying best practices under subsection (a), the Administrator and the Assistant Secretary for Infrastructure Protection shall take into consideration small business concerns . . . including any need for separate guidance or recommendations or best practices, as necessary and appropriate.

"SEC. 524. VOLUNTARY PRIVATE SECTOR PREPAREDNESS ACCREDITATION AND CERTIFICATION PROGRAM.

"(a) ESTABLISHMENT.

"(1) *IN GENERAL.*— The Secretary . . . shall establish and implement the voluntary private sector preparedness accreditation and certification program in accordance with this section.

"(2) *DESIGNATION OF OFFICER.*— The Secretary shall designate an officer responsible for the accreditation and certification program under this section. . . .

"(b) VOLUNTARY PRIVATE SECTOR PREPAREDNESS STANDARDS; VOLUNTARY ACCREDITATION AND CERTIFICATION PROGRAM FOR THE PRIVATE SECTOR.

"(1) *ACCREDITATION AND CERTIFICATION PROGRAM.*— Not later than 210 days after the date of enactment of the Implementing Recommendations of the 9/11 Commission Act of 2007, the designated officer shall—

"(A) begin supporting the development and updating, as necessary, of voluntary preparedness standards. . .

"(i) develop and promote a program to certify the preparedness of private sector entities that voluntarily choose to seek certification under the program; and

"(ii) implement the program. . .

"(2) *PROGRAM ELEMENTS.*

"(A) *IN GENERAL.* "(i) Program.—The program developed and implemented under this subsection shall assess whether a private sector entity complies with voluntary preparedness standards.

"(D) *SMALL BUSINESS CONCERNS.*— The designated officer and any entity with which the designated officer enters into an agreement under paragraph (3)(A) shall establish separate classifications and methods of certification for small business

"(3) *ACCREDITATION AND CERTIFICATION PROCESSES.*—

"(A) *AGREEMENT.*

"(i) *In general.*—Not later than 210 days after the date of enactment of the Implementing Recommendations of the 9/11 Commission Act of 2007, the designated officer shall enter into one or more agreements with a highly qualified nongovernmental entity with experience or expertise in coordinating and facilitating the development and use of voluntary consensus standards and in managing or implementing accreditation and certification programs for voluntary consensus standards, or a similarly qualified private sector entity, to carry out accreditations and oversee the certification process under this subsection. An entity entering into an agreement with the designated officer under this clause (hereinafter referred to in this section as a 'selected entity') shall not perform certifications under this subsection.

"(ii) *Contents.*—A selected entity shall manage the accreditation process and oversee the certification process in accordance with the program established under this subsection and accredit qualified third parties to carry out the certification program established under this subsection. . .

SEC. 1204. NATIONAL DOMESTIC PREPAREDNESS CONSORTIUM.

(a) IN GENERAL.— The Secretary is authorized to establish, operate, and maintain a National Domestic Preparedness Consortium within the Department.

(b) MEMBERS.— Members of the National Domestic Preparedness Consortium shall consist of—

(1) the Center for Domestic Preparedness;

(2) the National Energetic Materials Research and Testing Center, New Mexico Institute of Mining and Technology;

(3) the National Center for Biomedical Research and Training, Louisiana State University;

(4) the National Emergency Response and Rescue Training Center, Texas A&M University;

(5) the National Exercise, Test, and Training Center, Nevada Test Site;

(6) the Transportation Technology Center, Incorporated, in Pueblo, Colorado; and

(7) the National Disaster Preparedness Training Center, University of Hawaii.

(c) DUTIES.— The National Domestic Preparedness Consortium shall identify, develop, test, and deliver training to State, local, and tribal emergency response providers, provide on-site and mobile training at the performance and management and planning levels, and facilitate the delivery of training by the training partners of the Department.

[See HSPD 21(20) in the Resiliency and a Culture of Preparedness chapter.]

National Strategy for Homeland Security, October 2007

"To best protect the American People, homeland security must be a responsibility shared across our entire Nation . . . As we secure the Homeland, however, we cannot simply rely on defensive approaches and well-planned response and recovery measures. We recognize that our efforts must involve offense at home and abroad"[15]

We need a culture of preparedness. ". . .Homeland security is a shared responsibility built on a foundation of partnerships . . . . The private and non-profit sectors must also be full partners in homeland security . . . The non-profit sector, including volunteer and relief groups and faith-based organizations, provides important support services for the nation, including meals and shelter, counseling, and compassion and comfort . . . In order to complete this truly national effort, we also must encourage and draw upon an informed and active citizenry. For instance, citizens should each understand what to do if they observe suspicious behavior in their community[16] and what to do in the event of an attack or natural disaster . . ."[17].

Ensuring Long-Term Success: Risk Management The assessment and management of risk underlies the full spectrum of our homeland security activities, including decisions about when, where, and how to invest in resources that eliminate, control, or mitigate risks. In the face of multiple and diverse catastrophic possibilities, we accept that risk – a function of threats, vulnerabilities, and consequences – is a permanent condition. We must apply a risk-based framework across all homeland security efforts in order to identify and assess potential hazards (including their downstream effects), determine what levels of relative risk are acceptable, and prioritize and allocate resources among all homeland security partners, both public and private, to prevent, protect against, and respond to and recover from all manner of incidents...

Culture of Preparedness ... we will continue to foster a Culture of Preparedness that permeates all levels of our society – from individual citizens, businesses, and non-profit organizations to Federal, State, local, and Tribal government officials and authorities. This Culture rests on four principles.

The first principle of our Culture of Preparedness is a shared acknowledgement that creating a prepared Nation will be an enduring challenge. As individual citizens we must guard against complacency, and as a society we must balance the sense of optimism that is fundamental to the American character with a sober recognition that future catastrophes will occur. The certainty of future calamities should inform and motivate our preparedness...

The second principle is the importance of individual and collective initiative to counter fundamental biases toward reactive responses and approaches. Our Culture, therefore, must encourage and reward innovation and new ways of thinking...

The third principle is that individual citizens, communities, the private sector, and non-profit organizations each perform a central role in homeland security. Citizen and community preparedness are among the most effective means of securing the Homeland... All Americans must share in the full range of homeland security activities, including prevention and protection, but it is particularly important that we all take responsibility for increasing the likelihood that we can survive an incident and care for our own basic needs in the immediate aftermath.[18] As more Americans contribute to homeland security through self-reliance and mutual assistance, we reduce the burden on our emergency responders so they can focus on those most in need...

The fourth principle of our Culture of Preparedness is the responsibility of each level of government in fostering a prepared Nation. Although Federal, State, local, and Tribal governments will have roles and responsibilities unique to each, our Culture must continue to embrace the notion of partnership among all levels of government. Built upon a foundation of partnerships, common goals, and shared responsibility, the creation of our Culture of Preparedness is an enduring touchstone for homeland security.

Homeland Security Management System In order to continue strengthening the foundations of a prepared Nation, we will establish and institutionalize a comprehensive Homeland Security Management System that incorporates all stakeholders... .

... This new Homeland Security Management System ... will involve a continuous, mutually reinforcing cycle of activity across four phases.

Phase One: Guidance. The first phase in our Homeland Security Management System encompasses overarching homeland security guidance. It is the foundation of our system, and it must be grounded in clearly articulated and up-to-date homeland and relevant national security policies, with coordinated supporting strategies, doctrine, and planning guidance flowing from and fully synchronizing with these policies...

Phase Two: Planning. The second phase is a deliberate and dynamic system that translates our policies, strategies, doctrine, and planning guidance into a family of strategic, operational, and tactical plans...

Strategic plans educate and drive resource requirements and capabilities, laying the foundation for more detailed operational and tactical plans. Based on the resource and capability requirements identified in strategic plans, operational and tactical plans prescribe the actions of all applicable stakeholders arranged in time and space in order to achieve specific goals...

Requirements and capabilities within the planning phase of our system also must place particular emphasis on training and education so that homeland security professionals not only acquire the specific functional skills that are needed to successfully execute operational plans but also understand the broader strategic context in which these plans will be executed. Leadership development must be emphasized in this education and training process, because planning and execution across a wide array of communities, organizational structures, and professions requires specific leadership skills. The second phase ultimately culminates in tactical plans by homeland security partners that describe the specific field-level activities they will undertake to fulfill the responsibilities assigned to them in the operational plan.

Phase Three: Execution. The third phase in the Homeland Security Management System encompasses the execution of operational and tactical-level plans.

Phase Four: Assessment and Evaluation. The fourth phase involves the continual assessment and evaluation of both operations and exercises. This phase of the system will produce lessons learned and best practices that must be incorporated back into all phases of the Homeland Security Management System.

Incident Management While our Homeland Security Management System provides a framework for integrating four essential phases in a deliberate process to secure the Homeland, there will be times when incidents force the homeland security community to compress this cycle of activity and assume a more crisis-oriented posture. Decision-making during crises and periods of heightened concern, however, is different from decision-making during a steady-state of activity, and we must develop a comprehensive approach that will help Federal, State, local, and Tribal authorities manage incidents across all homeland security efforts.

Our approach will build upon the current National Incident Management System (NIMS). An outgrowth of Homeland Security Presidential Directive-5 issued on February 28, 2003, NIMS focuses largely on stakeholders in the discipline of response. Incidents, however, are not limited to natural and man-made disasters that strike the Homeland. They also include, for example, threats developing overseas, law enforcement and public health actions and investigations, and even specific protective measures taken at critical infrastructure sites, for example. In order to realize the full intent of HSPD-5, our new approach to incident management must apply not only to response and recovery but also to the prevention and protection phases of an incident as well. Federal efforts must be directed toward coordination of resources across sectors (public, private, and non-profit), disciplines, and among Federal, State, local, and Tribal officials.

Incident management rests on a core set of common principles and requirements. The first of these is an *Incident Command System*, which provides the overall structure for managing an incident. Our current system for incident command has five major functional areas: command, operations, planning, logistics, and finance and administration. Although a sixth area – intelligence – is currently applied on an *ad hoc* basis, we must institutionalize this area throughout our new approach in support of prevention and protection activities. *Unified Command* is a second core principle. The Federal Government must fully adopt and implement this principle, which is commonly used at the State and local levels and provides the basis from which multiple agencies can work together effectively to manage an incident by ensuring that all decisions will be based upon mutually agreed upon objectives and plans, regardless of the number of entities or jurisdictions involved.

Interoperable and Resilient Communications

Our Nation continues to confront two distinct communications challenges: interoperability and survivability. Unimpeded and timely flow of information in varying degrees across multiple operational systems and between different disciplines and jurisdictions is critical to command, control, and coordination of operational activities. To achieve interoperability, we must have compatible equipment, standard operating procedures, planning, mature governance structures, and a collaborative culture that enables all necessary parties to work together seamlessly. Survivable communications infrastructure is even more fundamental. To achieve survivability, our national security and emergency preparedness communications systems must be resilient – either able to withstand destructive forces regardless of cause or sufficiently redundant to suffer damage and remain reliable. Without the appropriate application of interoperable communications technologies, standards, and governance structures, effective and safe incident management will be hindered...

Science and Technology

The United States derives much of its strength from its advantage in the realm of science and technology (S&T), and we must continue to use this advantage and encourage innovative research and development to assist in protecting and defending against the range of natural and man-made threats confronting the Homeland.

Over the past six years, focused partnerships with our Nation's vast and varied research enterprise, which...have yielded significant capabilities that are helping us to better protect the lives and livelihoods of the American people. For instance, the focused application of the Nation's nuclear expertise has produced improved tools for countering the threat of nuclear terrorism against the Homeland. We also have applied biometric technologies and systems to enhance the security of travel documents and inhibit the movement of terrorists internationally and across our borders. The development and application of a variety of chemical, biological, radiological, and nuclear countermeasures are helping to prevent WMD terrorism and address the public health consequences that can stem from a range of natural and man-made disasters. We also have upgraded the technical capabilities of our first responders through the provision of decontamination equipment and protective gear...

...Specifically, we will continue to engage in disciplined dialogue about the threats we face, our strategies to counter them, and how S&T can bridge gaps in approaches or facilitate the more effective and efficient achievement of our objectives. Our collaborative S&T efforts should continue to explore existing or emerging...Research in systems and operations science that will allow the integration of technology into functional capability is of equal importance. For example, a sound scientific knowledge base regarding health and medical response systems could improve our ability to manage the health consequences of disasters. By promoting the evolution of current technologies and fielding new, revolutionary capabilities, S&T will remain an essential and enduring enabler of our *Strategy*.

Legislative Branch

Homeland security at the Federal level is not the sole purview of the executive branch of government. The Congress also must take bold steps to fulfill its responsibilities in the national effort to secure the Homeland and protect the American people. The current committee structure, for example, creates competing initiatives and requirements and fails to establish clear and consistent priorities or provide optimal oversight. Accordingly, both houses of the Congress should take action to further streamline the organization and structure of those committees that authorize and appropriate homeland security-related funds and otherwise oversee homeland security missions. The Congress also should fully embrace a risk-based funding approach so that we best prioritize our limited resources to meet our most critical homeland security goals and objectives first, as opposed to distributing funds and making decisions based on political considerations. In addition, Congress should help ensure that we have the necessary tools to address changing technologies and homeland security threats while protecting privacy and civil liberties. Finally, in the same manner that Congress was an important partner in building an effective national security system during the Cold War and beyond, a strong partnership with Congress will be essential to help secure the Homeland in the years ahead."

ENDNOTES

1. Executive Order 13234 of November 9, 2001, Presidential Task Force on Citizen Preparedness in the War on Terrorism, Federal Register Vol. 66, No. 221. http://frwebgate.access.gpo.gov/cgi-bin/getdoc.cgi?dbname=2001_register&docid=fr15no01-130.pdf.

2. HSPD 3, March 11, 2002. http://www.dhs.gov/xabout/laws/gc_1214508631313.shtm.

3. Homeland Security Act of 2002, Public law 107–296. http://www.dhs.gov/xlibrary/assets/hr_5005_enr.pdf.

4. Title VII—Implementation Of 9/11 Commission Recommendations, Intelligence Reform and Terrorism Prevention Act of 2004, Subtitle C—National Preparedness, Public Law 108–458—December 17, 2004. http://www.nctc.gov/docs/pl108_458.pdf.

5. Public Law 109–295, Title VI, Post Katrina Emergency Management Reform Act, 2006 (October 4, 2006). http://frwebgate.access.gpo.gov/cgi-bin/getdoc.cgi?dbname=109_cong_public_laws&docid=f:publ295.109.pdf.

6. Public Alert and Warning System, Executive Order 13407 of June 26, 2006. http://www.fas.org/irp/offdocs/eo/eo-13407.htm.

7. Warning, Alert, And Response Network Act, Title VI of the Security And Accountability For Every Port Act Of 2006, Public Law 109–347, October 13, 2006. http://thomas.loc.gov/cgi-bin/toGPObss/http://frwebgate.access.gpo.gov/cgi-bin/getdoc.cgi?dbname=109_cong_public_laws&docid=f:publ347.109

8. Implementing Recommendations Of The 9/11 Commission Act Of 2007, August 3, 2007, Public Law 110–53. http://intelligence.senate.gov/laws/pl11053.pdf.

9. National Strategy for Homeland Security, Homeland Security Council, October, 2007. http://www.dhs.gov/xlibrary/assets/nat_strat_homelandsecurity_2007.pdf.

10. HSPD 3. http://www.dhs.gov/xabout/laws/gc_1214508631313.shtm.

11. HSPD 5, at paragraph 24, made a "technical amendment" to HSPD 3 by replacing a sentence and requiring "Except in exigent circumstances, the Secretary of Homeland Security shall seek the views of the Attorney General, and any other federal agency heads the Secretary deems appropriate, including other members of the Homeland Security Council, on the Threat Condition to be assigned." http://www.dhs.gov/xabout/laws/gc_1214592333605.shtm (accessed March 18, 2009).

12. Homeland Security Act of 2002, November 25, 2002, Public Law 107–296. http://www.dhs.gov/xlibrary/assets/hr_5005_enr.pdf.

13. Warning, Alert, And Response Network Act, October 13, 2006, (Public Law 109–347). http://thomas.loc.gov/cgi-bin/toGPObss/http://frwebgate.access.gpo.gov/cgi-bin/getdoc.cgi?dbname=109_cong_public_laws&docid=f:publ347.109.

14. See DHS Chronology of Changes to the Advisory System Color beginning, March 12, 2002. http://www.dhs.gov/xabout/history/editorial_0844.shtm.

15. National Strategy for Homeland Security, October 2007, letter from George W. Bush, October 5, 2007.

16. "IF YOU SEE SOMETHING, SAY SOMETHING. Nevada's 7 Signs of Terrorism" A video prepared by the Institute for Security Studies at the University of Nevada, Las Vegas. http://iss.unlv.edu/.

    Nevada's 7 Signs of Terrorism http://iss.unlv.edu/Media%20Files/SevenSigns.html.

    Arizona' 8 Signs of Terrorism http://8signs.jmhelfgot.com/toc.html.

17. National Strategy for Homeland Security, October 2007, p. 4.

18. 3 Days, 3 Ways, Are You Ready? "a public motivation campaign urging you, your family, and the community to prepare for emergencies and disasters. 3 Days, 3 Ways is more than a campaign; it's a message relying on the participation and action steps each of us takes today. The message is simple, be ready to survive on your own for a minimum of 3 Days following a disaster. For large disasters, you may not receive any government assistance for up to 7 Days. Become prepared in 3 Ways – make a plan, build a kit, and get involved. Any step we take today will put us in a greater position for resiliency, whether from a major earthquake, a winter storm, a terrorist act or a pandemic flu outbreak." King County Washington, Office of Emergency Management, http://www.govlink.org/3days3ways/.

ADDITIONAL RESOURCES

"Project Impact shows [videos] feature local, regional and national experts who talk about disaster and emergency management issues relevant to our area. Topics include information on hazards and disasters, emergency preparedness and response, homeland security..." sponsored by The King County Washington Office of Emergency Management. http://www.kingcounty.gov/safety/prepare/residents_business/PersonalPreparedness/ProjectImpact.aspx#EmerPrep

"Catastrophic Incident Search and Rescue Addendum to the National Search and Rescue Supplement to the International Aeronautical and Maritime Search and Rescue Manual," Version 2.0, November 2009, by Department of Homeland Security, Department of Interior, Department of Commerce, Department of Defense, Department of Transportation, National Aeronautics and Space Administration, and Federal Communications Commission, http://www.uscg.mil/hq/cg5/cg534/nsarc/CISAddendum2.0_Nov09.pdf

"Looking Out for the Very Young, Elderly and Others with Special Needs: Lessons from Katrina and other Major Disasters," October 20, 2009, Subcommittee on Economic Development, Public Buildings, and Emergency Management, House Transportation and Infrastructure Committee, http://transportation.house.gov/hearings/hearingDetail.aspx?NewsID=1030

"The Emergency Alert System (EAS) and All-Hazard Warnings," by Linda K. Moore, Congressional Research Service, August 14, 2009, RL32527, http://opencrs.com/document/RL32527/

"National Level Exercise 2009 (NLE 09) is scheduled for July 27 through July 31, 2009. NLE 09 will be the first major exercise conducted by the United States government that will focus exclusively on terrorism prevention and protection, as opposed to incident response and recovery." http://www.fema.gov/media/fact_sheets/nle09.shtm

Emergency Communications: Vulnerabilities Remain and Limited Collaboration and Monitoring Hamper Federal Efforts, GAO-09-604, June 2009, http://www.gao.gov/new.items/d09604.pdf

AVMA Emergency Preparedness and Response, April 2009, American Veterinary Medical Association, http://www.avma.org/disaster/emerg_prep_resp_guide.pdf

Secretary Napolitano Announces 60-Day Review of Homeland Security Advisory System, July 14, 2009, http://www.dhs.gov/ynews/releases/pr_1247586668272.shtm

"Emergency Communications: The Future of 911," Linda K. Moore, June 16, 2009, Congressional Research Service, RL34755, http://opencrs.com/document/RL34755/

"Are We Ready? A Status Report on Emergency Preparedness for the 2009 Hurricane Season," U.S. Senate Committee on Homeland Security and Governmental Affairs, Ad Hoc Subcommittee on Disaster Recovery. June 4, 2009 testimony of: The Honorable W. Craig Fugate, Administrator, Federal Emergency Management Agency, U.S. Department of Homeland Security; Major General Frank Grass, Director of Operations, United States Northern Command; Mr. George Foresman, Advisory Board Co-Chairman, Corporate Crisis Response Officers Association and former DHS Undersecretary for Preparedness and Emergency Response; Mr. Armond Mascelli, Vice President, Disaster Operations, American Red Cross; Ms. Janet Durden, President, United Way of Northeast Louisiana. http://hsgac.senate.gov/public/index.cfm?Fuseaction=Hearings.Detail&HearingID=66b3873b-8b2d-4cb1-a647-a798fe962c78

FBI Terrorist Watch List. "We found that the FBI failed to nominate many subjects in the terrorism investigations that we sampled, did not nominate many others in a timely fashion, and did not update or remove watchlist records as required." The Federal Bureau of Investigation's Terrorist Watchlist Nomination Practices, U.S. Department of Justice Office of the Inspector General Audit Division Audit Report, 09-25 May 2009, p. iv. http://www.usdoj.gov/oig/reports/FBI/a0925/final.pdf

State and Local Pandemic Preparedness, Congress. House Oversight and Government Reform, [May 20, 2009] http://oversight.house.gov/story.asp?ID=2446

Public Role And Engagement In Counterterrorism Efforts: Implications Of Israeli Practices For The U.S., Final Report, 2 April 2009, Prepared for Department of Homeland, Security, Office of Science and Technology, http://mcfan.org/Documents/Executive%20Summary%20from%20Public_Role_in_CT_Israeli_Practices_Task_08-22.pdf

"The UNISDR Terminology aims to promote common understanding and common usage of disaster risk reduction concepts and to assist the disaster risk reduction efforts of authorities, practitioners and the public." UNISDR Terminology on Disaster Risk Reduction (2009), United Nations International Strategy for Risk Reduction, http://www.unisdr.org/eng/library/UNISDR-terminology-2009-eng.pdf

"Evacuating Large Urban Areas: Challenges for Emergency Management Policies and Concepts," James Kendra, Jack Rozdilsky, David A. McEntire, Journal of Homeland Security and Emergency Management, Berkeley Electronic Press, Vol. 5, Iss. 1, 2008, http://www.bepress.com/jhsem/vol5/iss1/32/. [See Errata list on this web page.]

The Americans with Disabilities Act and Emergency Preparedness and Response Nancy Lee Jones, Legislative Attorney, American Law Division, Updated October 15, 2008, CRS Report RS22254, http://opencrs.com/document/RS22254/

20

NATIONAL INCIDENT MANAGEMENT SYSTEM (NIMS)

HSPD 5 ordered creation of the National Incident Management System (NIMS) and the National Response Plan (NRP) (now called the National Response Framework, NRF). NIMS is intended to improve the ability of different organizations (neighboring cities, counties, states, or federal resources) to work together. This includes such things as using the same terminology (the plain English "message acknowledged" instead of "10-4"), and speaking over interoperable communications.

The NRF integrates all of the federal and local, state, tribal, planning into one "all-discipline, all hazards" plan. The purpose of the NRF, using NIMS, is to "provide the structure and mechanisms for national level policy and operational direction for Federal support to State and local incident managers and for exercising direct Federal authorities and responsibilities, as appropriate."

SOURCES

- HSPD 5, February 28, 2003[1]
- Intelligence Reform and Terrorism Prevention Act of 2004[2]

HSPD 5, February 28, 2003

SUBJECT: MANAGEMENT OF DOMESTIC INCIDENTS

Purpose

1. To enhance the ability of the United States to manage domestic incidents by establishing a sin-

gle, comprehensive national incident management system.

Policy

3. ... the United States Government shall establish a single, comprehensive approach to domestic incident management. The objective of the United States Government is to ensure that all levels of government across the Nation have the capability to work efficiently and effectively together, using a national approach to domestic incident management. In these efforts, with regard to domestic incidents, the United States Government treats crisis management and consequence management as a single, integrated function, rather than as two separate functions.

4. The Secretary of Homeland Security is the principal Federal official for domestic incident management ... responsible for coordinating Federal operations within the United States ... The Secretary shall coordinate the Federal Government's resources utilized in response to or recovery from terrorist attacks, major disasters, or other emergencies if and when any one of the following four conditions applies: (1) a Federal department or agency acting under its own authority has requested the assistance of the Secretary; (2) the resources of State and local authorities are overwhelmed and Federal assistance has been requested by the appropriate State and local authorities; (3) more than one Federal department or agency has become substantially involved in responding to the incident; or (4) the Secretary has been directed to assume responsibility for managing the domestic incident by the President.

Foundations of Homeland Security: Law and Policy, First Edition. Martin J. Alperen.
© 2011 John Wiley & Sons, Inc. Published 2011 by John Wiley & Sons, Inc.

6. ...Initial responsibility for managing domestic incidents generally falls on State and local authorities. The Federal Government will assist State and local authorities when their resources are overwhelmed, or when Federal interests are involved ...

7. The Federal Government recognizes the role that the private and nongovernmental sectors play ... The Secretary will coordinate with the private and nongovernmental sectors to ensure adequate planning, equipment, training, and exercise activities and to promote partnerships to address incident management capabilities.

8. The Attorney General has lead responsibility for criminal investigations of terrorist acts or terrorist threats by individuals or groups inside the United States ...

9. ...The Secretary of Defense shall provide military support to civil authorities for domestic incidents as directed by the President or when consistent with military readiness and appropriate under the circumstances and the law. The Secretary of Defense shall retain command of military forces providing civil support....

10. The Secretary of State has the responsibility, ... to protect our national security, to coordinate international activities related to the prevention, preparation, response, and recovery from a domestic incident, and for the protection of United States citizens and United States interests overseas ...

Tasking

14. The heads of all Federal departments and agencies are directed to provide their full and prompt cooperation ...

15. The Secretary shall develop ... and administer a National Incident Management System (NIMS). This system will provide a consistent nationwide approach for Federal, State, and local governments to work effectively and efficiently together to prepare for, respond to, and recover from domestic incidents, regardless of cause, size, or complexity. To provide for interoperability and compatibility among Federal, State, and local capabilities, the NIMS will include a core set of concepts, principles, terminology, and technologies covering the incident command system; multi-agency coordination systems; unified command; training; identification and management of resources (including systems for classifying types of resources); qualifications and certification; and the collection, tracking, and reporting of incident information and incident resources.

16. The Secretary shall develop ... and administer a National Response Plan (NRP). This plan shall integrate Federal Government domestic prevention, preparedness, response, and recovery plans into one all-discipline, all-hazards plan. The NRP shall be unclassified. [The NRP has been updated by the National Response Framework (NRF).]

   a. The NRP, using the NIMS, shall, with regard to response to domestic incidents, provide the structure and mechanisms for national level policy and operational direction for Federal support to State and local incident managers and for exercising direct Federal authorities and responsibilities, as appropriate.

   b. The NRP will include protocols for operating under different threats or threat levels ...

   c. The NRP will include a consistent approach to reporting incidents, providing assessments, and making recommendations to the President, the Secretary, and the Homeland Security Council.

17. The Secretary shall:

   a. By April 1, 2003, (1) develop and publish an initial version of the NRP ...

   b. By June 1, 2003, develop a national system of standards, guidelines, and protocols to implement the NIMS ...

18. The heads of Federal departments and agencies shall adopt the NIMS within their departments and ... All Federal departments and agencies will use the NIMS in their domestic incident management and emergency prevention, preparedness, response, recovery, and mitigation activities ...

20. Beginning in Fiscal Year 2005, Federal departments and agencies shall make adoption of the NIMS a requirement, to the extent permitted by law, for providing Federal preparedness assistance through grants, contracts, or other activities ...

Intelligence Reform and Terrorism Prevention Act of 2004

Subtitle C—National Preparedness

SEC. 7301. THE INCIDENT COMMAND SYSTEM

(b) SENSE OF CONGRESS.— It is the sense of Congress that—

(1) the United States needs to implement the recommendations of the National Commission on Terrorist Attacks Upon the United States by adopting a unified incident command system and significantly enhancing communications connectivity between and among all

levels of government agencies, emergency response providers (as defined in section 2 of the Homeland Security Act of 2002 (6 U.S.C. 101), and other organizations with emergency response capabilities;

(2) the unified incident command system should enable emergency managers and first responders to manage, generate, receive, evaluate, share, and use information in the event of a terrorist attack or a significant national disaster;

(3) emergency response agencies nationwide should adopt the Incident Command System known as NIMS;

(4) when multiple agencies or multiple jurisdictions are involved, they should follow a unified command system based on NIMS;

(5) the regular use of, and training in, NIMS by States and, to the extent practicable, territories, tribes, and local governments, should be a condition for receiving Federal preparedness assistance; and

(6) the Secretary of Homeland Security should require, as a further condition of receiving homeland security preparedness funds from the Office of State and Local Government Coordination and Preparedness, that grant applicants document measures taken to fully and aggressively implement the Incident Command System and unified command procedures.

ENDNOTES

1. HSPD 5. http://www.dhs.gov/xabout/laws/gc_1214592333605.shtm#1.
2. Intelligence Reform and Terrorism Prevention Act Of 2004, (IRTPA), December 17, 2004, Public Law 108–458. http://frwebgate.access.gpo.gov/cgi-bin/getdoc.cgi?dbname=108_cong_public_laws&docid=f:publ458.108.pdf.

ADDITIONAL REOURCES

The National Emergency Management Institute offers free online courses in NIMS and ICS. http://training.fema.gov/IS/NIMS.asp.

21

NATIONAL RESPONSE FRAMEWORK[1]

The NRF describes itself as a guide to "how the Nation conducts all-hazards response." It is directed towards professional emergency managers and builds on NIMS. The NRF describes who does what in incident response. The "who" means who is involved in each sector of government (local, state, national, and tribal levels). The "what" means what actions are taken. It describes the organization of our emergency response structure, and stresses the importance of planning.

INTRODUCTION

Overview

This *National Response Framework (NRF)* [or *Framework*] is a guide to how the Nation conducts all-hazards response. It is built upon *scalable, flexible, and adaptable coordinating structures* to align key roles and responsibilities *across the Nation*. It describes specific authorities and best practices for managing incidents that range from the serious but purely local, to large-scale terrorist attacks or catastrophic natural disasters.

This document explains the common discipline and structures that have been exercised and matured at the local, tribal, State, and national levels over time. It describes key lessons learned from Hurricanes Katrina and Rita, focusing particularly on how the Federal Government is organized to support communities and States in catastrophic incidents. Most importantly, it builds upon the *National Incident Management System (NIMS)*, which provides a consistent template for managing incidents.

The term "response" as used in this *Framework* includes immediate actions to save lives, protect property and the environment, and meet basic human needs. Response also includes the execution of emergency plans and actions to support short-term recovery. The *Framework* is always in effect, and elements can be implemented as needed on a flexible, scalable basis to improve response.

INTENDED AUDIENCE

The *Framework* is written especially for government executives, private-sector and nongovernmental organization (NGO) leaders, and emergency management practitioners. First, it is addressed to senior elected and appointed leaders, such as Federal department or agency heads, State Governors, mayors, tribal leaders, and city or county officials – those who have a responsibility to provide for effective response. For the Nation to be prepared for any and all hazards, its leaders must have a baseline familiarity with the concepts and mechanics of the *Framework*.

At the same time, the *Framework* informs emergency management practitioners, explaining the operating structures and tools used routinely by first responders and emergency managers at all levels of government. For these readers, the *Framework* is augmented with online access to supporting documents, further training, and an evolving resource for exchanging lessons learned. (fn. To support users of the *Framework*, the Department of Homeland Security has created an online **NRF Resource Center**, available at http://www.fema.gov/NRF.

One of the challenges to effective response is the relatively high turnover and short tenure among elected and appointed officials responsible for response at all levels.

Foundations of Homeland Security: Law and Policy, First Edition. Martin J. Alperen.
© 2011 John Wiley & Sons, Inc. Published 2011 by John Wiley & Sons, Inc.

Effective response hinges upon well-trained leaders and responders who have invested in response preparedness, developed engaged partnerships, and are able to achieve shared objectives. The players' bench is constantly changing, but a concise, common playbook is needed by all . . .

FRAMEWORK UNPACKED

The *Framework* presents the key response principles, participants, roles, and structures that guide the Nation's response operations. The remainder of the *Framework* is organized as follows:

Chapter I – Roles and Responsibilities. This chapter sharpens the focus on *who* is involved with emergency management activities at the local, tribal, State, and Federal levels and with the private sector and NGOs.

Chapter II – Response Actions. This chapter describes *what* we as a Nation collectively do to respond to incidents.

Chapter III – Response Organization. This chapter explains *how* we as a Nation are organized to implement response actions.

Chapter IV – Planning: A Critical Element of Effective Response. This chapter emphasizes the importance of planning and summarizes the elements of national planning structures.

HOW THE FRAMEWORK IS ORGANIZED

The *National Response Framework* is comprised of the core document, the Emergency Support Function (ESF), Support, and Incident Annexes, and the Partner Guides. The core document describes the doctrine that guides our national response, roles and responsibilities, response actions, response organizations, and planning requirements to achieve an effective national response to any incident that occurs.

The following documents provide more detailed information to assist practitioners in implementing the *Framework*:

Emergency Support Function Annexes

Support Annexes

Incident Annexes

Partner Guides

The *National Incident Management System (NIMS)*

These documents are available at the **NRF Resource Center**, http://www.fema.gov/NRF.

RESPONSE: THE *WHO*

An effective, unified national response requires layered, mutually supporting capabilities. The *Framework* systematically incorporates public-sector agencies, the private sector, and NGOs. It also emphasizes the importance of personal preparedness by individuals and households.

Communities, tribes, States, the Federal Government, NGOs, and the private sector should each understand their respective roles and responsibilities, and complement each other in achieving shared goals. Each governmental level plays a prominent role in developing capabilities needed to respond to incidents . . .

It is important that each level of government adapt and apply the general roles outlined in the *Framework*. To do this, organizations should define key leadership and staff functions, adopt capabilities-based planning as the method to build response capabilities, and impose the discipline needed to plan and operate effectively.

Even when a community is overwhelmed by an incident, there is still a core, sovereign responsibility to be exercised at this local level, with unique response obligations to coordinate with State, Federal, and private-sector support teams.

Local Governments. Resilient communities begin with prepared individuals and depend on the leadership and engagement of local government, NGOs, and the private sector. Individuals, families, and caregivers to those with special needs should enhance their awareness of risk and threats, develop household emergency plans that include care for pets and service animals, and prepare emergency supply kits. Individuals can also volunteer in their communities.

States, Territories, and Tribal Governments. States, territories, and tribal governments have responsibility for the public health and welfare of the people in their jurisdiction. State and local governments are closest to those impacted by incidents, and have always had the lead in response and recovery. During response, States play a key role coordinating resources and capabilities throughout the State and obtaining resources and capabilities from other States.

If a State anticipates that its resources may be exceeded, the Governor can request assistance from the Federal Government and/or from other States through mutual aid and assistance agreements such as the Emergency Management Assistance Compact (EMAC).

The Federal Government. The Federal Government maintains a wide array of capabilities and resources that can be made available upon request of the Governor. When an incident occurs that exceeds or is anticipated to exceed State, tribal, or local resources, the Federal Government may provide resources and capabilities to support the State response . . .

Pursuant to the Homeland Security Act of 2002 and Homeland Security Presidential Directive (HSPD) 5, the Secretary of Homeland Security is the principal Federal official for domestic incident management . . .

The Private Sector and NGOs. The private sector and NGOs contribute to response efforts through engaged partnerships with each level of government . . .

Private-sector organizations play an essential role in protecting critical infrastructure systems and implementing plans for the rapid restoration of normal commercial activities and critical infrastructure operations in the event of disruption. The protection of critical infrastructure and the ability to rapidly restore normal commercial activities can mitigate the impact of an incident, improve the quality of life of individuals, and accelerate the pace of recovery for communities and the Nation.

NGOs also serve a vital role at the local, State, and national levels by **performing essential service missions in times of need.** They provide sheltering, emergency food supplies, and other vital support services.

RESPONSE: THE *WHAT* AND THE *HOW*

The *National Response Framework* is always in effect, and elements can be implemented at any level at any time. The *Framework* is capabilities based, which is to say that local governments, tribes, States, and the Federal Government all develop functional capabilities and identify resources that may be required based on hazard identification and risk assessment, threats, and other potential incidents such as those represented by the National Planning Scenarios.

The *Framework* describes *what we do* and *how we respond.* In short, the *National Response Framework* explains how, at all levels, the Nation effectively manages all-hazards response consistent with the *National Strategy for Homeland Security.*

SCOPE

The *Framework* provides structures for implementing nationwide response policy and operational coordination for all types of domestic incidents. It can be partially or fully implemented in the context of a threat, in anticipation of a significant event, or in response to an incident. Selective implementation allows for a scaled response, delivery of the resources needed, and an appropriate level of coordination.

It is not always obvious at the outset whether a seemingly minor event might be the initial phase of a larger, rapidly growing threat. The *Framework* incorporates standardized organizational structures that promote on-scene initiative, innovation, and sharing of essential resources drawn from all levels of government, NGOs, and the private sector. Response must be quickly scalable, flexible, and adaptable.

This *Framework*, therefore, eliminates the Incident of National Significance declaration. No such declaration is required by the *Framework* and none will be made. The authorities of the Secretary of Homeland Security to coordinate large-scale national responses are unaltered by this change. Elimination of this declaration will, however, support a more nimble, scalable, and coordinated response by the entire national emergency management community.

RESPONSE DOCTRINE

Response doctrine defines basic roles, responsibilities, and operational concepts for response across all levels of government and with NGOs and the private sector. The overarching objective of response activities centers upon saving lives and protecting property and the environment. Five key principles of operations define response actions in support of the Nation's response mission. Taken together, these five principles of operation constitute national response doctrine.

Response Doctrine: Five Key Principles
1. Engaged partnership
2. Tiered response
3. Scalable, flexible, and adaptable operational capabilities
4. Unity of effort through unified command
5. Readiness to act

Response doctrine is rooted in America's Federal system and the Constitution's division of responsibilities between Federal and State governments. Because this doctrine reflects the history of emergency management and the distilled wisdom of responders and leaders at all levels, it gives elemental form to the *Framework.*

ENGAGED PARTNERSHIP

Leaders at all levels must communicate and actively support engaged partnerships by developing shared goals and aligning capabilities so that no one is overwhelmed in times of crisis. Layered, mutually supporting capabilities at Federal, State, tribal, and local levels allow for planning together in times of calm and responding together effectively in times of need.

Engaged partnerships are essential to preparedness. Effective response activities begin with a host of preparedness activities conducted well in advance of an incident. Preparedness involves a combination of planning, resources, training, exercising, and organizing to build, sustain, and improve operational capabilities. Preparedness is the process of identifying the personnel, training, and equipment needed for a wide range of potential incidents, and developing jurisdiction-specific plans for delivering capabilities when needed for an incident.

Nationwide preparedness is described in the *National Preparedness Guidelines* and the *National Exercise Program.*

TIERED RESPONSE

Incidents must be managed at the lowest possible jurisdictional level and supported **by additional capabilities when**

needed. It is not necessary that each level be overwhelmed prior to requesting resources from another level.

Incidents begin and end locally, and most are wholly managed at the local level. Many incidents require unified response from local agencies, NGOs, and the private sector, and some require additional support from neighboring jurisdictions or the State. A small number require Federal support.

A basic premise of the *Framework* is that incidents are generally handled at the lowest jurisdictional level possible.

SCALABLE, FLEXIBLE, AND ADAPTABLE OPERATIONAL CAPABILITIES

As incidents change in size, scope, and complexity, the response must adapt to meet requirements. The number, type, and sources of resources must be able to expand rapidly to meet needs associated with a given incident.

UNITY OF EFFORT THROUGH UNIFIED COMMAND

Effective *unified command* is indispensable to response activities and requires a clear understanding of the roles and responsibilities of each participating organization. Success requires *unity of effort*, which respects the chain of command of each participating organization while harnessing seamless coordination across jurisdictions in support of common objectives.

Use of the Incident Command System (ICS) is an important element across multijurisdictional or multiagency incident management activities . . . This *Framework* employs the *NIMS* standardized structures and tools that enable a unified approach to be effective both on scene and at the emergency operations centers.

The Department of Defense (DOD) is a full partner in the Federal response to domestic incidents, and its response is fully coordinated through the mechanisms of this *Framework*.

READINESS TO ACT

Effective response requires readiness to act balanced with an understanding of risk. From individuals, households, and communities to local, tribal, State, and Federal governments, national response depends on the instinct and ability to act.

Once response activities have begun, on-scene actions are based on *NIMS* principles. Acting swiftly and effectively requires clear, focused communication and the processes to support it. Without effective communication, a bias toward action will be ineffectual at best, likely perilous. An effective national response relies on disciplined processes, procedures, and systems to communicate timely, accurate, and accessible information on the incident's cause, size, and current situation to the public, responders, and others. Well-developed public information, education strategies, and communication plans help to ensure that lifesaving measures, evacuation routes, threat and alert systems, and other public safety information are coordinated and communicated to numerous diverse audiences in a consistent, accessible, and timely manner.

PART OF A BROADER STRATEGY

The *National Response Framework* is required by, and integrates under, a larger *National Strategy for Homeland Security* (*Strategy*) that serves to guide, organize, and unify our Nation's homeland security efforts. The *Strategy* reflects our increased understanding of the threats confronting the United States, incorporates lessons learned from exercises and real-world catastrophes, and articulates how we should ensure our long-term success by strengthening the homeland security foundation we have built. It provides a common framework by which our entire Nation should focus its homeland security efforts on achieving the following four goals:

1. Prevent and disrupt terrorist attacks.
2. Protect the American people and our critical infrastructure and key resources.
3. Respond to and recover from incidents that do occur.
4. Continue to strengthen the foundation to ensure our long-term success.

The *Framework* primarily focuses on the third goal: respond to and recover from incidents that do occur.

The *Strategy* calls for a *National Response Framework* that helps to strengthen the foundation for an effective national response, rapidly assess emerging incidents, take initial actions, expand operations as needed, and commence recovery actions to stabilize the area. It also calls for the *Framework* to be clearly written, easy to understand, and designed to be truly national in scope, meeting the needs of State, local, and tribal governments and the private sector and NGOs, as well as the Federal Government. In addition, the *Strategy* underscores the need to ensure that those communities devastated or severely affected by a catastrophic incident are set on a sustainable path for long-term rebuilding and revitalization. The *Framework* is designed to respond to and support the *Strategy* and is intended to be informed by and tie seamlessly to national, State, tribal, and local preparedness activities and investments . . .

ENDNOTE

1. National Response Framework Resource Center, January 2008, pages 1–13. http://www.fema.gov/emergency/nrf/.

22

AUTHORITY TO USE MILITARY FORCE

This chapter lays out the more important authorities regarding the use of military force starting with Congressional and Presidential powers as outlined in the Constitution. It includes the Posse Comitatus Act and the War Powers Resolution. Three actual authorizations to use military force are presented as well as information about Northcom's role in homeland security.

SOURCES

- U.S. Constitution, Article I Section 8 and Article II section 2, 1787[1]
- U.S. Constitution, Amendment III, 1791[2]
- Insurrection Act 1807 (10 USC 331)
- U.S. Constitution, Amendment XIV, 1868[3]
- Posse Comitatus Act 1878 (18 USC 1385)
- War Powers Resolution of 1973[4]
- Military Support for Civilian Law Enforcement, (10 USC 371)
- Authorization for Military Action Against Iraq Resolution, January 14, 1991[5]
- Authorization for Use of Military Force, September 18, 2001[6]
- Patriot Act, October 26, 2001[7]
- Standup of Northern Command, October 1, 2002
  - Northcom Website[8]
  - Global Security Org.[9]
- Authorization for Use of Military Force Against Iraq Resolution of 2002[10]

- Strategy for Homeland Defense and Civil Support, Department of Defense, June 2005[11]
- John Warner National Defense Authorization Act For Fiscal Year 2007[12]
- National Defense Authorization Act For Fiscal Year 2008, January 28, 2008[13]
- Northcom's CBRNE Consequence Management Response Force, October 1, 2008
  - U.S. Air Force News[14]
  - Army Times[15]

U.S. Constitution, Article I Section 8, Congressional Power

Sec. 8.

The Congress shall have power to lay and collect taxes, duties, imposts and excises, to pay the debts and provide for the common defense and general welfare of the United States; but all duties, imposts and excises shall be uniform throughout the United States;

...To declare war, grant letters of marque and reprisal, and make rules concerning captures on land and water;

To raise and support armies, but no appropriation of money to that use shall be for a longer term than two years;

To provide and maintain a navy;

To make rules for the government and regulation of the land and naval forces;

To provide for calling forth the militia to execute the laws of the union, suppress insurrections and repel invasions;

Foundations of Homeland Security: Law and Policy, First Edition. Martin J. Alperen.
© 2011 John Wiley & Sons, Inc. Published 2011 by John Wiley & Sons, Inc.

To provide for organizing, arming, and disciplining, the militia, and for governing such part of them as may be employed in the service of the United States, reserving to the states respectively, the appointment of the officers, and the authority of training the militia according to the discipline prescribed by Congress; . . .

—And

To make all laws which shall be necessary and proper for carrying into execution the foregoing powers, and all other powers vested by this Constitution in the government of the United States, or in any department or officer thereof.

U.S. Constitution, Article II Section 2, Presidential Power

Sec. 2.

The President shall be commander in chief of the Army and Navy of the United States, and of the militia of the several states, when called into the actual service of the United States; he may require the opinion, in writing, of the principal officer in each of the executive departments, upon any subject relating to the duties of their respective offices, and he shall have power to grant reprieves and pardons for offenses against the United States, except in cases of impeachment . . .

U.S. Constitution, Amendment III, 1791

No soldier shall, in time of peace be quartered in any house, without the consent of the owner, nor in time of war, but in a manner to be prescribed by law.

Insurrection Act 1807 (current version, codified at 10 USC § 331 *et. seq.*)

§ 331. Federal Aid for State Governments

Whenever there is an insurrection in any State against its government, the President may, upon the request of its legislature or of its governor if the legislature cannot be convened, call into Federal service such of the militia of the other States, in the number requested by that State, and use such of the armed forces, as he considers necessary to suppress the insurrection.

§ 332. Use of Militia and Armed Forces to Enforce Federal Authority

Whenever the President considers that unlawful obstructions, combinations, or assemblages, or rebellion against the authority of the United States, make it impracticable to enforce the laws of the United States in any State by the ordinary course of judicial proceedings, he may call into Federal service such of the militia of any State, and use such of the armed forces, as he considers necessary to enforce those laws or to suppress the rebellion.

§ 333. Interference with State and Federal Law

The President, by using the militia or the armed forces, or both, or by any other means, shall take such measures as he considers necessary to suppress, in a State, any insurrection, domestic violence, unlawful combination, or conspiracy, if it–

(1) so hinders the execution of the laws of that State, and of the United States within the State, that any part or class of its people is deprived of a right, privilege, immunity, or protection named in the Constitution and secured by law, and the constituted authorities of that State are unable, fail, or refuse to protect that right, privilege, or immunity, or to give that protection; or

(2) opposes or obstructs the execution of the laws of the United States or impedes the course of justice under those laws.

In any situation covered by clause (1), the State shall be considered to have denied the equal protection of the laws secured by the Constitution.

§ 334. Proclamation to Disperse

Whenever the President considers it necessary to use the militia or the armed forces under this chapter, he shall, by proclamation, immediately order the insurgents to disperse and retire peaceably to their abodes within a limited time.

U.S. Constitution, Amendment XIV, 1868

Sec. 1.

All persons born or naturalized in the United States, and subject to the jurisdiction thereof, are citizens of the United States and of the state wherein they reside. No state shall make or enforce any law which shall abridge the privileges or immunities of citizens of the United States; nor shall any state deprive any person of life, liberty, or property, without due process of law; nor deny to any person within its jurisdiction the equal protection of the laws.

Sec. 5.

The Congress shall have power to enforce, by appropriate legislation, the provisions of this article.

Posse Comitatus Act 1878 (18 USC 1385)

Posse Comitatus, Latin, means, "The power or force of the county. The entire population of a county above the age of fifteen, which a sheriff may summon to his assistance in certain cases; as to aid him in keeping the peace, in pursuing and arresting felons, etc."[16] It was intended to prevent the use of federal troops for law enforcement in the former Confederate states. One commentator states its original purpose was to "preclude the presence of soldiers from deterring voters during Reconstruction..."[17]

There are several exemptions to the Posse Comitatus Act including; the Coast guard is not subject to the Act, the National Guard is exempt from the Act when it is operating under state authority pursuant to Title 32 United States Code, and the military may provide equipment and technical assistance in the "War on Drugs." There is also a statutory exemption under the Insurrection Act. The Posse Comitatus Act does not apply when the Insurrection Act is invoked.

18 USC § 1385. Use of Army and Air Force as Posse Comitatus

Whoever, except in cases and under circumstances expressly authorized by the Constitution or Act of Congress, willfully uses any part of the Army or the Air Force as a posse comitatus or otherwise to execute the laws shall be fined under this title or imprisoned not more than two years, or both.

War Powers Resolution of 1973, (50 USC 1541 *et. seq.*)

§ 1541. Purpose and Policy

(a) *Congressional declaration.* It is the purpose of this chapter to fulfill the intent of the framers of the Constitution of the United States and insure that the collective judgment of both the Congress and the President will apply to the introduction of United States Armed Forces into hostilities, or into situations where imminent involvement in hostilities is clearly indicated by the circumstances, and to the continued use of such forces in hostilities or in such situations.

(b) *Congressional legislative power under necessary and proper clause.* Under article I, section 8, of the Constitution, it is specifically provided that the Congress shall have the power to make all laws necessary and proper for carrying into execution, not only its own powers but also all other powers vested by the Constitution in the Government of the United States, or in any department or officer thereof.

(c) *Presidential executive power as Commander-in-Chief; limitation.* The constitutional powers of the President as Commander-in-Chief to introduce United States Armed Forces into hostilities, or into situations where imminent involvement in hostilities is clearly indicated by the circum-

stances, are exercised only pursuant to (1) a declaration of war, (2) specific statutory authorization, or (3) a national emergency created by attack upon the United States, its territories or possessions, or its armed forces.

§ 1542. Consultation; Initial and Regular Consultations

The President in every possible instance shall consult with Congress before introducing United States Armed Forces into hostilities or into situations where imminent involvement in hostilities is clearly indicated by the circumstances, and after every such introduction shall consult regularly with the Congress until United States Armed Forces are no longer engaged in hostilities or have been removed from such situations.

§ 1543. Reporting Requirement

(a) *Written report; time of submission; circumstances necessitating submission; information reported.* In the absence of a declaration of war, in any case in which United States Armed Forces are introduced–

(1) into hostilities or into situations where imminent involvement in hostilities is clearly indicated by the circumstances;

(2) into the territory, airspace or waters of a foreign nation, while equipped for combat, except for deployments which relate solely to supply, replacement, repair, or training of such forces; or

(3) in numbers which substantially enlarge United States Armed Forces equipped for combat already located in a foreign nation;

the President shall submit within 48 hours to the Speaker of the House of Representatives and to the President pro tempore of the Senate a report, in writing, setting forth–

(A) the circumstances necessitating the introduction of United States Armed Forces;

(B) the constitutional and legislative authority under which such introduction took place; and

(C) the estimated scope and duration of the hostilities or involvement.

(b) *Other information reported.* The President shall provide such other information as the Congress may request in the fulfillment of its constitutional responsibilities with respect to committing the Nation to war and to the use of United States Armed Forces abroad.

(c) *Periodic reports; semiannual requirement.* Whenever United States Armed Forces are introduced into hostilities or into any situation described in subsection (a) of this section, the President shall, so long as such armed forces continue to be engaged in such hostilities or situation, report to the Congress periodically on the status of such hostilities or situation as well as on the scope and duration of such hostilities or situation, but in no event shall he report to the Congress less often than once every six months.

§ 1544. Congressional Action

(b) *Termination of use of United States Armed Forces; exceptions; extension period.* Within sixty calendar days after a report is submitted or is required to be submitted pursuant to section 1543(a)(1) of this title, whichever is earlier, the President shall terminate any use of United States Armed Forces with respect to which such report was submitted (or required to be submitted), unless the Congress (1) has declared war or has enacted a specific authorization for such use of United States Armed Forces, (2) has extended by law such sixty-day period, or (3) is physically unable to meet as a result of an armed attack upon the United States. Such sixty-day period shall be extended for not more than an additional thirty days if the President determines and certifies to the Congress in writing that unavoidable military necessity respecting the safety of United States Armed Forces requires the continued use of such armed forces in the course of bringing about a prompt removal of such forces.

(c) *Concurrent resolution for removal by President of United States Armed Forces.* Notwithstanding subsection (b) of this section, at any time that United States Armed Forces are engaged in hostilities outside the territory of the United States, its possessions and territories without a declaration of war or specific statutory authorization, such forces shall be removed by the President if the Congress so directs by concurrent resolution.

Military Support For Civilian Law Enforcement, 10 USC 371 *et. seq.*

§ 371. Use of Information Collected During Military Operations

(a) The Secretary of Defense may, in accordance with other applicable law, provide to Federal, State, or local civilian law enforcement officials any information collected during the normal course of military training or operations that may be relevant to a violation of any Federal or State law within the jurisdiction of such officials.

(b) The needs of civilian law enforcement officials for information shall, to the maximum extent practicable, be taken into account in the planning and execution of military training or operations.

(c) The Secretary of Defense shall ensure, to the extent consistent with national security, that intelligence information held by the Department of Defense and relevant to drug interdiction or other civilian law enforcement matters is provided promptly to appropriate civilian law enforcement officials.

§ 372. Use of Military Equipment and Facilities

(a) IN GENERAL.— The Secretary of Defense may, in accordance with other applicable law, make available any equipment (including associated supplies or spare parts), base facility, or research facility of the Department of Defense to any Federal, State, or local civilian law enforcement official for law enforcement purposes.

(b) EMERGENCIES INVOLVING CHEMICAL AND BIOLOGICAL AGENTS.— (1) In addition to equipment and facilities described in subsection (a), the Secretary may provide an item referred to in paragraph (2) to a Federal, State, or local law enforcement or emergency response agency to prepare for or respond to an emergency involving chemical or biological agents if the Secretary determines that the item is not reasonably available from another source . . .

§ 373. Training and Advising Civilian Law Enforcement Officials

The Secretary of Defense may, in accordance with other applicable law, make Department of Defense personnel available–

(1) to train Federal, State, and local civilian law enforcement officials in the operation and maintenance of equipment, including equipment made available under section 372 of this title; and

(2) to provide such law enforcement officials with expert advice relevant to the purposes of this chapter.

§ 374. Maintenance and Operation of Equipment

(a) The Secretary of Defense may, in accordance with other applicable law, make Department of Defense personnel available for the maintenance of equipment for Federal, State, and local civilian law enforcement officials, including equipment made available under section 372 of this title.

(b)(1) Subject to paragraph (2) and in accordance with other applicable law, the Secretary of Defense may, upon request from the head of a Federal law enforcement agency, make Department of Defense personnel available to operate equipment (including equipment made available under section 372 of this title) with respect to–

(A) a criminal violation of a provision of law specified in paragraph (4)(A);

(B) assistance that such agency is authorized to furnish to a State, local, or foreign government which is involved in the enforcement of similar laws;

(C) a foreign or domestic counter-terrorism operation; or

(D) a rendition of a suspected terrorist from a foreign country to the United States to stand trial.

(2) Department of Defense personnel made available to a civilian law enforcement agency under this subsection may operate equipment for the following purposes:

(A) Detection, monitoring, and communication of the movement of air and sea traffic.

(B) Detection, monitoring, and communication of the movement of surface traffic outside of the geographic boundary of the United States and within the United States not to exceed 25 miles of the boundary if the initial detection occurred outside of the boundary.

(C) Aerial reconnaissance.

(D) Interception of vessels or aircraft detected outside the land area of the United States for the purposes of communicating with such vessels and aircraft to direct such vessels and aircraft to go to a location designated by appropriate civilian officials.

(E) Operation of equipment to facilitate communications in connection with law enforcement programs specified in paragraph (4)(A).

(F) Subject to joint approval by the Secretary of Defense and the Attorney General (and the Secretary of State in the case of a law enforcement operation outside of the land area of the United States)–

(i) the transportation of civilian law enforcement personnel along with any other civilian or military personnel who are supporting, or conducting, a joint operation with civilian law enforcement personnel;

(ii) the operation of a base of operations for civilian law enforcement and supporting personnel; and

(iii) the transportation of suspected terrorists from foreign countries to the United States for trial (so long as the requesting Federal law enforcement agency provides all security for such transportation and maintains custody over the suspect through the duration of the transportation).

(3) Department of Defense personnel made available to operate equipment for the purpose stated in paragraph (2)(D) may continue to operate such equipment into the land area of the United States in cases involving the pursuit of vessels or aircraft where the detection began outside such land area.

(4) In this subsection:

(c) The Secretary of Defense may, in accordance with other applicable law, make Department of Defense personnel available to any Federal, State, or local civilian law enforcement agency to operate equipment for purposes other than described in subsection (b)(2) only to the extent that such support does not involve direct participation by such personnel in a civilian law enforcement operation unless such direct participation is otherwise authorized by law.

§ 375. Restriction on Direct Participation by Military Personnel

The Secretary of Defense shall prescribe such regulations as may be necessary to ensure that any activity (including the provision of any equipment or facility or the assignment or detail of any personnel) under this chapter does not include or permit direct participation by a member of the Army, Navy, Air Force, or Marine Corps in a search, seizure, arrest, or other similar activity unless participation in such activity by such member is otherwise authorized by law.

§ 376. Support Not to Affect Adversely Military Preparedness

Support (including the provision of any equipment or facility or the assignment or detail of any personnel) may not be provided to any civilian law enforcement official under this chapter if the provision of such support will adversely affect the military preparedness of the United States. The Secretary of Defense shall prescribe such regulations as may be necessary to ensure that the provision of any such support does not adversely affect the military preparedness of the United States.

§ 379. Assignment of Coast Guard Personnel to Naval Vessels for Law Enforcement Purposes

(a) The Secretary of Defense and the Secretary of Homeland Security shall provide that there be assigned on board every appropriate surface naval vessel at sea in a drug-interdiction area members of the Coast Guard who are trained in law enforcement and have powers of the Coast Guard under title 14, including the power to make arrests and to carry out searches and seizures.

(b) Members of the Coast Guard assigned to duty on board naval vessels under this section shall perform such law enforcement functions (including drug-interdiction functions)–

(1) as may be agreed upon by the Secretary of Defense and the Secretary of Homeland Security; and

(2) as are otherwise within the jurisdiction of the Coast Guard.

(c) No fewer than 500 active duty personnel of the Coast Guard shall be assigned each fiscal year to duty under this section. However, if at any time the Secretary of Homeland Security, after consultation with the Secretary of Defense, determines that there are insufficient naval vessels available for purposes of this section, such personnel may be assigned other duty involving enforcement of laws listed in section 374(b)(4)(A) of this title.

§ 382. Emergency Situations Involving Chemical or Biological Weapons of Mass Destruction

(a) IN GENERAL.— The Secretary of Defense, upon the request of the Attorney General, may provide assistance in support of Department of Justice activities relating to the enforcement of section 175 or 2332c of title 18 during an emergency situation involving a biological or chemical weapon of mass destruction. Department of Defense resources, including personnel of the Department of Defense, may be used to provide such assistance if–

(1) the Secretary of Defense and the Attorney General jointly determine that an emergency situation exists; and

(2) the Secretary of Defense determines that the provision of such assistance will not adversely affect the military preparedness of the United States.

(b) EMERGENCY SITUATIONS COVERED.—In this section, the term "emergency situation involving a biological or chemical weapon of mass destruction" means a circumstance involving a biological or chemical weapon of mass destruction . . .

(2)(A) Except as provided in subparagraph (B), the regulations may not authorize the following actions:

(i) Arrest.

(ii) Any direct participation in conducting a search for or seizure of evidence related to a violation of section 175 or 2332c of title 18.

(iii) Any direct participation in the collection of intelligence for law enforcement purposes.

(B) The regulations may authorize an action described in subparagraph (A) to be taken under the following conditions:

(i) The action is considered necessary for the immediate protection of human life, and civilian law enforcement officials are not capable of taking the action.

Authorization for Military Action Against Iraq Resolution, January 14, 1991

SEC. 1. SHORT TITLE.

This joint resolution may be cited as the 'Authorization for Use of Military Force Against Iraq Resolution'. Signed by President Bush January 14, 1991.

SEC. 2. AUTHORIZATION FOR USE OF UNITED STATES ARMED FORCES.

(a) AUTHORIZATION.— The President is authorized, subject to subsection (b), to use United States Armed Forces pursuant to United Nations Security Council Resolution 678 (1990) in order to achieve implementation of Security Council Resolutions 660, 661, 662, 664, 665, 666, 667, 669, 670, 674, and 677.

(b) REQUIREMENT FOR DETERMINATION THAT USE OF MILITARY FORCE IS NECESSARY.— Before exercising the authority granted in subsection (a), the President shall make available to the Speaker of the House of Representatives and the President pro tempore of the Senate his determination that–

(1) The United States has used all appropriate diplomatic and other peaceful means to obtain compliance by Iraq with the United Nations Security Council resolutions cited in subsection (a); and

(2) That those efforts have not been and would not be successful in obtaining such compliance.

(c) WAR POWERS RESOLUTION REQUIREMENTS.

(1) *SPECIFIC STATUTORY AUTHORIZATION.—* Consistent with section 8(a)(1) of the War Powers Resolution, the Congress declares that this section is intended to constitute specific statutory authorization within the meaning of section 5(b) of the War Powers Resolution.

(2) *APPLICABILITY OF OTHER REQUIREMENTS.—* Nothing in this resolution supersedes any requirement of the War Powers Resolution.

Authorization For Use Of Military Force, September 18, 2001

To authorize the use of United States Armed Forces against those responsible for the recent attacks launched against the United States.

Whereas, on September 11, 2001, acts of treacherous violence were committed against the United States and its citizens; and

Whereas, such acts render it both necessary and appropriate that the United States exercise its rights to self-defense and to protect United States citizens both at home and abroad; and

Whereas, in light of the threat to the national security and foreign policy of the United States posed by these grave acts of violence; and

Whereas, such acts continue to pose an unusual and extraordinary threat to the national security and foreign policy of the United States; and

Whereas, the President has authority under the Constitution to take action to deter and prevent acts of international terrorism against the United States: Now, therefore, be it Resolved by the Senate and House of Representatives of the United States of America in Congress assembled,

SEC. 1. SHORT TITLE.

This joint resolution may be cited as the 'Authorization for Use of Military Force'.

SEC. 2. AUTHORIZATION FOR USE OF UNITED STATES ARMED FORCES.

(a) IN GENERAL.— That the President is authorized to use all necessary and appropriate force against those nations, organizations, or persons he determines planned, authorized, committed, or aided the terrorist attacks that occurred on September 11, 2001, or harbored such organizations or persons, in order to prevent any future acts of international terrorism against the United States by such nations, organizations or persons.

(b) WAR POWERS RESOLUTION REQUIREMENTS.

(1) *SPECIFIC STATUTORY AUTHORIZATION.—* Consistent with section 8(a)(1) of the War Powers Resolution, the Congress declares that this section is intended to constitute specific statutory authorization within the meaning of section 5(b) of the War Powers Resolution.

(2) *APPLICABILITY OF OTHER REQUIREMENTS.—* Nothing in this resolution supercedes any requirement of the War Powers Resolution.

Patriot Act, October 26, 2001

Sec. 106. Presidential Authority.

Section 203 of the International Emergency Powers Act (50 U.S.C. 1702) is amended—

(D) by inserting at the end the following:

"(C) when the United States is engaged in armed hostilities or has been attacked by a foreign country or foreign nationals, confiscate any property, subject to the jurisdic-tion of the United States, of any foreign person, foreign organization, or foreign country that he determines has planned, authorized, aided, or engaged in such hostilities or attacks against the United States; and all right, title, and interest in any property so confiscated shall vest, when, as, and upon the terms directed by the President, in such agency or person as the President may designate from time to time, and upon such terms and conditions as the President may prescribe, such interest or property shall be held, used, administered, liquidated, sold, or otherwise dealt with in the interest of and for the benefit of the United States, and such designated agency or person may perform any and all acts incident to the accomplishment or furtherance of these purposes."

Sec. 886. Sense of Congress Reaffirming The Continued Importance and Applicability of The Posse Comitatus Act.

(a) FINDINGS.— Congress finds the following:

(1) Section 1385 of title 18, United States Code (commonly known as the "Posse Comitatus Act"), prohibits the use of the Armed Forces as a posse comitatus to execute the laws except in cases and under circumstances expressly authorized by the Constitution or Act of Congress.

(2) Enacted in 1878, the Posse Comitatus Act was expressly intended to prevent United States Marshals, on their own initiative, from calling on the Army for assistance in enforcing Federal law.

(3) The Posse Comitatus Act has served the Nation well in limiting the use of the Armed Forces to enforce the law.

(4) Nevertheless, by its express terms, the Posse Comitatus Act is not a complete barrier to the use of the Armed Forces for a range of domestic purposes, including law enforcement functions, when the use of the Armed Forces is authorized by Act of Congress or the President determines that the use of the Armed Forces is required to fulfill the President's obligations under the Constitution to respond promptly in time of war, insurrection, or other serious emergency.

(5) Existing laws, including chapter 15 of title 10, United States Code (commonly known as the "Insurrection Act"), and the Robert T. Stafford Disaster Relief and Emergency Assistance Act (42 U.S.C. 5121 et seq.), grant the President broad powers that may be invoked in the event of domestic emergencies, including an

attack against the Nation using weapons of mass destruction, and these laws specifically authorize the President to use the Armed Forces to help restore public order.

Standup Of Northern Command, October 1, 2002

NORTHCOM Website

...As authorized by President George W. Bush April 17, 2002, the Department of Defense (DoD) announced the establishment of U.S. Northern Command (USNORTHCOM) to consolidate under a single unified command those existing homeland defense and civil support missions that were previously executed by other military organizations...

Global Security Org.

NORTHCOM's area of operations includes the United States, Canada, Mexico, parts of the Caribbean and the contiguous waters in the Atlantic and Pacific oceans. The commander is responsible for land, aerospace and sea defenses of the United States. He will command U.S. forces that operate within the United States in support of civil authorities. The command will provide civil support not only in response to attacks, but for natural disasters. NORTHCOM takes the homeland defense role from the U.S. Joint Forces Command (JFCOM). JFCOM's Joint Task Force-Civil Support and related activities report to NORTHCOM. The NORTHCOM headquarters has established liaisons with the homeland security directors of each state, and has working ties with related federal and state agencies.

The command's area of responsibility covers the continental United States, Alaska, Canada, Mexico and surrounding water out to 500 miles. The new command is tasked with defense planning and security cooperation for other nations in its area of responsibility. US Southern Command remained responsible for contingency planning, operations, security and force protection for Cuba, Bahamas, British Virgin Islands, and the Turks and Caicos.

The command's mission is the preparation for, prevention of, deterrence of, preemption of, defense against, and response to threats and aggression directed towards U.S. territory, sovereignty, domestic population, and infrastructure; as well as crisis management, consequence management, and other domestic civil support.

Authorization for Use of Military Force Against Iraq Resolution Of 2002, October 16, 2002

Joint Resolution. To authorize the use of United States Armed Forces against Iraq.

Whereas in 1990 in response to Iraq's war of aggression against and illegal occupation of Kuwait, the United States forged a coalition of nations to liberate Kuwait and its people

in order to defend the national security of the United States and enforce United Nations Security Council resolutions relating to Iraq;

Whereas after the liberation of Kuwait in 1991, Iraq entered into a United Nations sponsored cease-fire agreement pursuant to which Iraq unequivocally agreed, among other things, to eliminate its nuclear, biological, and chemical weapons programs and the means to deliver and develop them, and to end its support for international terrorism;

Whereas the efforts of international weapons inspectors, United States intelligence agencies, and Iraqi defectors led to the discovery that Iraq had large stockpiles of chemical weapons and a large scale biological weapons program, and that Iraq had an advanced nuclear weapons development program that was much closer to producing a nuclear weapon than intelligence reporting had previously indicated;

Whereas Iraq, in direct and flagrant violation of the cease-fire, attempted to thwart the efforts of weapons inspectors to identify and destroy Iraq's weapons of mass destruction stockpiles and development capabilities, which finally resulted in the withdrawal of inspectors from Iraq on October 31, 1998;

Whereas in Public Law 105–235 (August 14, 1998), Congress concluded that Iraq's continuing weapons of mass destruction programs threatened vital United States interests and international peace and security, declared Iraq to be in "material and unacceptable breach of its international obligations" and urged the President "to take appropriate action, in accordance with the Constitution and relevant laws of the United States, to bring Iraq into compliance with its international obligations";

Whereas Iraq both poses a continuing threat to the national security of the United States and international peace and security in the Persian Gulf region and remains in material and unacceptable breach of its international obligations by, among other things, continuing to possess and develop a significant chemical and biological weapons capability, actively seeking a nuclear weapons capability, and supporting and harboring terrorist organizations;

Whereas Iraq persists in violating resolution of the United Nations Security Council by continuing to engage in brutal repression of its civilian population thereby threatening international peace and security in the region, by refusing to release, repatriate, or account for non-Iraqi citizens wrongfully detained by Iraq, including an American serviceman, and by failing to return property wrongfully seized by Iraq from Kuwait;

Whereas the current Iraqi regime has demonstrated its capability and willingness to use weapons of mass destruction against other nations and its own people;

Whereas the current Iraqi regime has demonstrated its continuing hostility toward, and willingness to attack, the United States, including by attempting in 1993 to assassinate former President Bush and by firing on many thousands of occasions on United States and Coalition Armed Forces engaged in enforcing the resolutions of the United Nations Security Council;

Whereas members of al Qaida, an organization bearing responsibility for attacks on the United States, its citizens, and interests, including the attacks that occurred on September 11, 2001, are known to be in Iraq;

Whereas Iraq continues to aid and harbor other international terrorist organizations, including organizations that threaten the lives and safety of United States citizens;

Whereas the attacks on the United States of September 11, 2001, underscored the gravity of the threat posed by the acquisition of weapons of mass destruction by international terrorist organizations;

Whereas Iraq's demonstrated capability and willingness to use weapons of mass destruction, the risk that the current Iraqi regime will either employ those weapons to launch a surprise attack against the United States or its Armed Forces or provide them to international terrorists who would do so, and the extreme magnitude of harm that would result to the United States and its citizens from such an attack, combine to justify action by the United States to defend itself;

Whereas United Nations Security Council Resolution 678 (1990) authorizes the use of all necessary means to enforce United Nations Security Council Resolution 660 (1990) and subsequent relevant resolutions and to compel Iraq to cease certain activities that threaten international peace and security, including the development of weapons of mass destruction and refusal or obstruction of United Nations weapons inspections in violation of United Nations Security Council Resolution 687 (1991), repression of its civilian population in violation of United Nations Security Council Resolution 688 (1991), and threatening its neighbors or United Nations operations in Iraq in violation of United Nations Security Council Resolution 949 (1994);

Whereas in the Authorization for Use of Military Force Against Iraq Resolution (Public Law 102–1), Congress has authorized the President "to use United States Armed Forces pursuant to United Nations Security Council Resolution 678 (1990) . . . ;

Whereas in December 1991, Congress expressed its sense that it "supports the use of all necessary means to achieve the goals of United Nations Security Council Resolution 687 as being consistent with the Authorization of Use of Military Force Against Iraq Resolution (Public Law 102–1)," that Iraq's repression of its civilian population violates United Nations Security Council Resolution 688 and "constitutes a continuing threat to the peace, security, and stability of the Persian Gulf region," and that Congress, "supports the use of all necessary means to achieve the goals of United Nations Security Council Resolution 688";

Whereas the Iraq Liberation Act of 1998 (Public Law 105–338) expressed the sense of Congress that it should be the policy of the United States to support efforts to remove from power the current Iraqi regime and promote the emergence of a democratic government to replace that regime;

Whereas on September 12, 2002, President Bush committed the United States to "work with the United Nations Security Council to meet our common challenge" posed by Iraq and to "work for the necessary resolutions," while also making clear that "the Security Council resolutions will be enforced, and the just demands of peace and security will be met, or action will be unavoidable";

Whereas the United States is determined to prosecute the war on terrorism and Iraq's ongoing support for international terrorist groups combined with its development of weapons of mass destruction in direct violation of its obligations under the 1991 cease-fire and other United Nations Security Council resolutions make clear that it is in the national security interests of the United States and in furtherance of the war on terrorism that all relevant United Nations Security Council resolutions be enforced, including through the use of force if necessary;

Whereas Congress has taken steps to pursue vigorously the war on terrorism through the provision of authorities and funding requested by the President to take the necessary actions against international terrorists and terrorist organizations, including those nations, organizations, or persons who planned, authorized, committed, or aided the terrorist attacks that occurred on September 11, 2001, or harbored such persons or organizations;

Whereas the President and Congress are determined to continue to take all appropriate actions against international terrorists and terrorist organizations, including those nations, organizations, or persons who planned, authorized, committed, or aided the terrorist attacks that occurred on September 11, 2001, or harbored such persons or organizations;

Whereas the President has authority under the Constitution to take action in order to deter and prevent acts of international terrorism against the United States, as Congress recognized in the joint resolution on Authorization for Use of Military Force (Public Law 107–40); and

Whereas it is in the national security interests of the United States to restore international peace and security to the Persian Gulf region:

Now, therefore, be it Resolved by the Senate and House of Representatives of the United States of America in Congress assembled,

SEC. 1. SHORT TITLE.

This joint resolution may be cited as the "Authorization for Use of Military Force Against Iraq Resolution of 2002".

Authorization for Use of Military Force Against Iraq Resolution of 2002.

SEC. 2. SUPPORT FOR UNITED STATES DIPLOMATIC EFFORTS.

The Congress of the United States supports the efforts by the President to—

(1) strictly enforce through the United Nations Security Council all relevant Security Council resolutions regarding Iraq and encourages him in those efforts; and

(2) obtain prompt and decisive action by the Security Council to ensure that Iraq abandons its strategy of delay, evasion and noncompliance and promptly and strictly complies with all relevant Security Council resolutions regarding Iraq.

SEC. 3. AUTHORIZATION FOR USE OF UNITED STATES ARMED FORCES.

(a) AUTHORIZATION.— The President is authorized to use the Armed Forces of the United States as he determines to be necessary and appropriate in order to—

(1) defend the national security of the United States against the continuing threat posed by Iraq; and

(2) enforce all relevant United Nations Security Council resolutions regarding Iraq.

(b) PRESIDENTIAL DETERMINATION.— In connection with the exercise of the authority granted in subsection (a) to use force the President shall, prior to such exercise or as soon thereafter as may be feasible, but no later than 48 hours after exercising such authority, make available to the Speaker of the House of Representatives and the President pro tempore of the Senate his determination that—

(1) reliance by the United States on further diplomatic or other peaceful means alone either (A) will not adequately protect the national security of the United States against the continuing threat posed by Iraq or (B) is not likely to lead to enforcement of all relevant United Nations Security Council resolutions regarding Iraq; and

(2) acting pursuant to this joint resolution is consistent with the United States and other countries continuing to take the necessary actions against international terrorist and terrorist organizations, including those nations, organizations, or persons who planned, authorized, committed or aided the terrorist attacks that occurred on September 11, 2001.

(c) WAR POWERS RESOLUTION REQUIREMENTS.

(1) *SPECIFIC STATUTORY AUTHORIZATION.—* Consistent with section 8(a)(1) of the War Powers Resolution, the Congress declares that this section is intended to constitute specific statutory authorization within the meaning of section 5(b) of the War Powers Resolution.

(2) *APPLICABILITY OF OTHER REQUIREMENTS.—* Nothing in this joint resolution supersedes any requirement of the War Powers Resolution.

Strategy for Homeland Defense and Civil Support, Department of Defense, June 2005

Foreword. Protecting the United States from direct attack is the highest priority of the Department of Defense. The military has traditionally secured the United States by projecting power overseas. While our current missions abroad continue to play a vital role for the security of our Nation, the terrorist attacks of September 11, 2001 emphasized that we are confronting fundamentally different challenges from those faced during the Cold War . . .

The Strategy for Homeland Defense and Civil Support marks the next significant milestone in reshaping the Department's approach to homeland defense. Building upon the concept of an active, layered defense outlined in the National Defense Strategy, the Strategy for Homeland Defense and Civil Support constitutes the Department's vision for transforming homeland defense and civil support capabilities. It will fundamentally change the Department's approach to homeland defense in an historic and important way . . .

Executive Summary. . . .To defeat 21st century threats, we must think and act innovatively. Our adversaries consider US territory an integral part of a global theater of combat. We must therefore have a strategy that applies to the domestic context the key principles that are driving the transformation of US power projection and joint expeditionary warfare.

Protecting the United States in the ten year timeframe covered by this Strategy requires an active, layered defense. This active, layered defense is global, seamlessly integrating US capabilities in the forward regions of the world, the global commons of space and cyberspace, in the geographic approaches to US territory, and within the United States. It is a defense in depth. To be effective, it requires superior intelligence collection, fusion, and analysis, calculated deterrence of enemies, a layered system of mutually supporting defensive measures that are neither passive nor ad hoc, and the capability to mass and focus sufficient warfighting assets to defeat any attack.

Capabilities for Homeland Defense and Civil Support. Consistent with the National Defense Strategy's call to develop and sustain key operational capabilities, the Strategy for Homeland Defense and Civil Support promotes the development of core capabilities to achieve its objectives. Prominent capability themes include:

- Intelligence, Surveillance, and Reconnaissance Capabilities.
  The Department of Defense requires current and actionable intelligence identifying potential threats to US territory. DoD must also ensure that it can identify and track suspect traffic approaching the United States. DoD must conduct reconnaissance and surveillance to examine wide areas of the maritime and air domains and, working with lead domestic partners and Canada and Mexico in the land domain, discover potential threats before they reach the United States.
- Information Sharing.
  Together with domestic and international partners, DoD will integrate and share information collected from a wide range of sources. The events of September 11, 2001 highlighted the need to share information across Federal agencies and, increasingly, with state, local, and tribal authorities, the private sector, and international partners.
- Joint Operational Capabilities for Homeland Defense.
  DoD will continue to transform US military forces to execute homeland defense missions in the forward regions, approaches, US homeland, and global commons.
- Interagency and Intergovernmental Coordination.
  The Department of Defense and our domestic and international partners will continue to cooperate closely in the execution of homeland defense and civil support missions.

John Warner National Defense Authorization Act for Fiscal Year 2007

Section 1076 of this Act modified the Insurrection Act expanding the opportunities for the President to authorize use of the military. These changes were repealed by the National Defense Authorization Act for Fiscal Year 2008, below, which caused the Insurrection Act to return to its earlier version. The current version of the statute is at the beginning of this chapter.

SEC. 1076. USE OF THE ARMED FORCES IN MAJOR PUBLIC EMERGENCIES.

(a) USE OF THE ARMED FORCES AUTHORIZED.

(1) *IN GENERAL.—* Section 333 of title 10, United States Code, is amended to read as follows:

"§ 333. Major public emergencies; interference with State and Federal law

"*(a) USE OF ARMED FORCES IN MAJOR PUBLIC EMERGENCIES.*

(1) The President may employ the armed forces, including the National Guard in Federal service, to—
  "(A) restore public order and enforce the laws of the United States when, as a result of a natural disaster, epidemic, or other serious public health emergency, terrorist attack or incident, or other condition in any State or possession of the United States, the President determines that—
    "(i) domestic violence has occurred to such an extent that the constituted authorities of the State or possession are incapable of maintaining public order; and
    "(ii) such violence results in a condition described in paragraph (2); or
  "(B) suppress, in a State, any insurrection, domestic violence, unlawful combination, or conspiracy if such insurrection, violation, combination, or conspiracy results in a condition described in paragraph (2).
"(2) A condition described in this paragraph is a condition that—
  "(A) so hinders the execution of the laws of a State or possession, as applicable, and of the United States within that State or possession, that any part or class of its people is deprived of a right, privilege, immunity, or protection named in the Constitution and secured by law, and the constituted authorities of that State or possession are unable, fail, or refuse to protect that right, privilege, or immunity, or to give that protection; or
  "(B) opposes or obstructs the execution of the laws of the United States or impedes the course of justice under those laws.
"(3) In any situation covered by paragraph (1)(B), the State shall be considered to have denied the equal protection of the laws secured by the Constitution.

National Defense Authorization Act for Fiscal Year 2008, January 28, 2008

(a) INTERFERENCE WITH STATE AND FEDERAL LAWS.

(1) *IN GENERAL.—* Section 333 of title 10, United States Code, is amended to read as follows:

"§ 333. INTERFERENCE WITH STATE AND FEDERAL LAW

"The President, by using the militia or the armed forces, or both, or by any other means, shall take such measures as he considers necessary to suppress, in a State, any insurrection, domestic violence, unlawful combination, or conspiracy, if it—

"(1) so hinders the execution of the laws of that State, and of the United States within the State, that any part or class of its people is deprived of a right, privilege, immunity, or protection named in the Constitution and secured by law, and the constituted authorities of that State are unable, fail, or refuse to protect that right, privilege, or immunity, or to give that protection; or

"(2) opposes or obstructs the execution of the laws of the United States or impedes the course of justice under those laws.

In any situation covered by clause (1), the State shall be considered to have denied the equal protection of the laws secured by the Constitution."

Northcom's CBRNE Consequence Management Response Force, October 1, 2008

U.S. Air Force News

"For the first time in its existence, U.S. Northern Command is gaining a dedicated force to respond to potential chemical, biological, radiological, nuclear and high-yield explosive (CBRNE) incidents in the homeland.

"We are now building the first of three CBRNE Consequence Management Response Forces," said USNORTHCOM Commander Gen. Gene Renuart. "On the first of October, we'll have an organized force, a trained force, an equipped force, a force that has adequate command and control and is on quick response - 48 hours - to head off to a large-scale nuclear, chemical, biological event that might require Department of Defense support."

The CBRNE Consequence Management Response Force, or CCMRF, is a team of about 4,700 joint personnel that would deploy as the Department of Defense's initial response force for a CBRNE incident. Its capabilities include search and rescue, decontamination, medical, aviation, communications and logistical support.

Although CCMRFs are a joint force comprised of Soldiers, Sailors, Airmen and Marines, the first CCMRF will fall under the operational control of USNORTHCOM's Joint Force Land Component Command, U.S. Army North, located in San Antonio. Joint Task Force Civil Support, USNORTHCOM's subordinate command in Fort Monroe, Va., would serve as the operational headquarters and work closely with state and local officials and first responders.

Army Times

". . .It is not the first time an active-duty unit has been tapped to help at home. In August 2005, for example, when Hurricane Katrina unleashed hell in Mississippi and Louisiana, several active-duty units were pulled from various posts and mobilized to those areas. But this new mission marks the first time an active unit has been given a dedicated assignment to NorthCom, a joint command established in 2002 to provide command and control for federal homeland defense efforts and coordinate defense support of civil authorities . . .

They may be called upon to help with civil unrest and crowd control or to deal with potentially horrific scenarios such as massive poisoning and chaos in response to a chemical, biological, radiological, nuclear or high-yield explosive, or CBRNE, attack. Training for homeland scenarios has already begun at Fort Stewart and includes specialty tasks such as knowing how to use the "jaws of life" to extract a person from a mangled vehicle; extra medical training for a CBRNE incident; and working with U.S. Forestry Service experts on how to go in with chainsaws and cut and clear trees to clear a road or area.

ENDNOTES

1. The Constitution of the United States of America. http://www.archives.gov/exhibits/charters/constitution_transcript.html.
2. U.S. Constitution, Amendment III, 1791. http://www.law.cornell.edu/constitution/constitution.table.html#amendments.
3. U.S. Constitution, Amendments. http://www.law.cornell.edu/constitution/constitution.table.html#amendments.
4. War Powers Resolution of 1973, Public Law 93–148, November 7, 1973, 50 USC b1541, *et. seq.*
5. Authorization for Military Action Against Iraq Resolution, January 14, 1991, P.L. 102–1. http://www.milnet.com/public-law-102-1.html.
6. Authorization for Use of Military Force, P.L. 107–40, September 18, 2001. http://thomas.loc.gov/cgi-bin/bdquery/z?d107:S.J.Res23
7. Patriot Act, October 26 2001. http://thomas.loc.gov/cgi-bin/bdquery/z?d107:hr03162:%5D.
8. U.S. Northern Command History. http://www.northcom.mil/About/history_education/history.html.
9. Global Security.org. http://www.globalsecurity.org/military/agency/dod/northcom.htm.
10. Authorization for Use of Military Force Against Iraq Resolution Of 2002. Public Law 107–243, October 16, 2002. http://frwebgate.access.gpo.gov/cgi-bin/getdoc.cgi?dbname=107_cong_public_laws&docid=f:publ243.107.pdf.

11. Strategy for Homeland Defense and Civil Support, Department of Defense, June 2005. http://www.defenselink.mil/news/Jun2005/d20050630homeland.pdf.
12. John Warner National Defense Authorization Act for Fiscal Year 2007, October 17, 2006.
13. National Defense Authorization Act for Fiscal Year 2008, PUBLIC LAW 110–181, January 28, 2008. http://www.dod.mil/dodgc/olc/docs/pl110-181.pdf.
14. Northcom's CBRNE Consequence Management Response Force, October 1, 2008. U.S. Air Force News. http://www.af.mil/news/story.asp?id=123117765.
15. "Brigade homeland tours start October 1," by Gina Cavallaro, Army Times, September 30, 2008. http://www.armytimes.com/news/2008/09/army_homeland_090708w/.
16. Black's Law dictionary, Revised Fourth Edition, West Publishing Co., 1968.
17. "Legal Aspects of Domestic Employment of the Army," by Thomas R. Lujan, Parameters, Autumn 1997. pp. 82–97. http://www.carlisle.army.mil/USAWC/parameters/97autumn/lujan.htm.

ADDITIONAL RESOURCES

Authorization on Use of Military Force

"Armies in Homeland Security: American and European Perspectives. Edited by John L. Clark, National Defense University Press, 2006. This text examines the role and responsibilities of armies in homeland security in different nations, including: United Kingdom, Germany, Hungary, Italy, Austria, Bulgaria, Ukraine, Romania, France, and the European Union. Chapter 1 is about America and includes more material than I am able to include in this text.

"War Powers Resolution: Presidential Compliance," by Richard F. Grimmett, September 23, 2009, Congressional Research Service, RL33532, http://opencrs.com/document/RL33532/

"Authorization For Use Of Military Force in Response to the 9/11 Attacks (P.L. 107-40): Legislative History," by Richard F. Grimmett, CRS, Order Code RS22357, Updated January 16, 2007, http://www.fas.org/sgp/crs/natsec/RS22357.pdf

"Border Security and Military Support: Legal Authorizations and Restrictions," by Stephen R. Viña, CRS RS22443, Updated May 23, 2006, http://www.fas.org/sgp/crs/homesec/RS22443.pdf

"Declarations of War and Authorizations for the Use of Military Force: Historical Background and Legal Implications," Aackerman and Richard F. Grimmett, CRS RL31133, January 14, 2003, http://opencrs.com/document/RL31133/2003-01-14

Posse Comitatus

"The Posse Comitatus Act and Homeland Security," John R. Brinkerhoff, February 2002 http://www.homelandsecurity.org/journal/articles/brinkerhoffpossecomitatus.htm

Overview Of The Posse Comitatus Act, Rand, 2001, http://www.rand.org/pubs/monograph_reports/MR1251/MR1251.AppD.pdf

The Myth of Posse Comitatus, Major Craig T. Trebilcock, U.S. Army Reserve, October 2000, http://www.homelandsecurity.org/journal/Articles/Trebilcock.htm

"Legal Aspects of Domestic Employment of the Army," by Thomas R. Lujan, Parameters, Autumn 1997, pp. 82-97, http://www.carlisle.army.mil/USAWC/parameters/97autumn/lujan.htm

Civil Support

DOD Civil Support During the 2007 and 2008 California Wildland Fires, Department of Defense Office of Inspector General, D-2010-015, Nov. 13, 2009, http://www.dodig.mil/Audit/reports/fy2010/10-015.pdf

"Army Support during the Hurricane Katrina Disaster" by James A. Wombwell, The Long War Series, Occasional Paper 29, Combat Studies Institute (CSI), http://cgsc.leavenworth.army.mil/carl/download/csipubs/wombwell.pdf

"The Role of the Department of Defense During A Flu Pandemic," by Lawrence Kapp and Don J. Jansen, June 4, 2009, CRS R40619, http://opencrs.com/document/RL33512

"Operationalizing Military Support to Civil Authorities, CNIC prepares Navy regional and installation managers for emergency management," By Capt. BJ Keepers and Dr. Raymond Roll, October – December 2008, http://www.chips.navy.mil/archives/08_Oct/PDF/CNIC.pdf

"Department of Defense Support to Domestic Incidents," The Office of the Assistant Secretary of Defense/Homeland Defense and America's Security Affairs, January 2008, http://www.fema.gov/pdf/emergency/nrf/DOD_SupportToDomesticIncidents.pdf

"Declarations of War and Authorizations for the Use of Military Force: Historical Background and Legal Implications, Jennifer K. Elsea and Richard F. Grimmett, March 8, 2007, CRS RL31133, http://fpc.state.gov/documents/organization/82969.pdf

"Military Support To Civil Authorities: The Role Of The Department Of Defense In Support Of Homeland Defense," A Report Prepared by the Federal Research Division, Library of Congress under an Interagency Agreement with the Commission on the National Guard and Reserves, February 2007, by Alice R. Buchalter http://www.loc.gov/rr/frd/pdf-files/CNGR_Milit-Support-Civil-Authorities.pdf

"The Use of Federal Troops for Disaster Assistance: Legal Issues," by Jennifer K. Elsea, CRS RS22266, September 16, 2005, http://www.au.af.mil/au/awc/awcgate/crs/rs22266.pdf

Triage for Civil Support (2004). Using Military Medical Assets to Respond to Terrorist Attacks," http://www.rand.org/pubs/monographs/MG217/

U.S. Northern Command (USNORTHCOM) was established Oct. 1, 2002 to provide command and control of Department of Defense (DOD) homeland defense efforts and to coordinate defense support of civil authorities. USNORTHCOM defends America's homeland — protecting our people, national power, and freedom of action. http://www.northcom.mil/About/index.html

"Military Support of Civil Authorities—A New Focus for a New Millennium," Major General Bruce M. Lawlor, Commander, Joint Task Force–Civil Support, October 2000 (Updated September 2001), http://www.homelandsecurity.org/journal/articles/Lawlor.htm

23

DETENTION AND TREATMENT OF TERRORISTS

This chapter, beginning with the United Nations Charter in 1945, the Universal Declaration of Human Rights in 1948, and the Fourth Geneva Convention of 1949, discusses the major authorities related to detention and treatment of terrorists.

SOURCES

- United Nations Charter, June 26, 1945
- The United Nations International Covenant on Civil and Political Rights, December 16, 1966[1]
- Declaration On The Protection Of All Persons From Being Subjected To Torture And Other Cruel, Inhuman Or Degrading Treatment Or Punishment, December 9, 1975[2]
- Convention Against Torture And Other Cruel, Inhuman Or Degrading Treatment Or Punishment December 10, 1984[3]
- Executive Order 12949–Foreign Intelligence Physical Searches February 9, 1995[4]
- Military Order of November 13, 2001—Detention, Treatment, and Trial of Certain Non-Citizens in the War Against Terrorism[5]
- Department of Defense, Military Commission order No. 1, Procedures for Trial by Military commission of Certain Non-United States Citizens in the War Against Terrorism, March 21, 2002[6]
- Detainee Treatment Act Of 2005[7]
- Military Commissions Act Of 2006[8]

- Executive Order 13425 of February 14, 2007, Trial of Alien Unlawful Enemy Combatants by Military, Commission[9]
- Executive Order 13440—Interpretation of the Geneva Conventions Common Article 3 as Applied to a Program of Detention and Interrogation Operated by the Central Intelligence Agency, July 24, 2007[10]
- Executive Order 13492 of January 22, 2009, Review and Disposition of Individuals Detained At the Guantánamo Bay Naval Base and Closure of Detention Facilities[11]
- Executive Order 13493 of January 22, 2009, Review of Detention Policy Options[12]
- Executive Order 13491—Ensuring Lawful Interrogations, January 27, 2009[13]
- Military Commissions Act of 2009[14]

Charter of The United Nations, June 26, 1945[15]

CHAPTER IX: INTERNATIONAL ECONOMIC AND SOCIAL COOPERATION

Article 55 With a view to the creation of conditions of stability and well-being which are necessary for peaceful and friendly relations among nations based on respect for the principle of equal rights and self-determination of peoples, the United Nations shall promote:

higher standards of living, full employment, and conditions of economic and social progress and development;

solutions of international economic, social, health, and related problems; and international cultural and educational cooperation; and

Foundations of Homeland Security: Law and Policy, First Edition. Martin J. Alperen.
© 2011 John Wiley & Sons, Inc. Published 2011 by John Wiley & Sons, Inc.

universal respect for, and observance of, human rights and fundamental freedoms for all without distinction as to race, sex, language, or religion.

Universal Declaration of Human Rights, December 10, 1948[16]

PREAMBLE Whereas recognition of the inherent dignity and of the equal and inalienable rights of all members of the human family is the foundation of freedom, justice and peace in the world,

Whereas disregard and contempt for human rights have resulted in barbarous acts which have outraged the conscience of mankind, and the advent of a world in which human beings shall enjoy freedom of speech and belief and freedom from fear and want has been proclaimed as the highest aspiration of the common people,

Whereas it is essential, if man is not to be compelled to have recourse, as a last resort, to rebellion against tyranny and oppression, that human rights should be protected by the rule of law,

Whereas it is essential to promote the development of friendly relations between nations,

Whereas the peoples of the United Nations have in the Charter reaffirmed their faith in fundamental human rights, in the dignity and worth of the human person and in the equal rights of men and women and have determined to promote social progress and better standards of life in larger freedom,

Whereas Member States have pledged themselves to achieve, in co-operation with the United Nations, the promotion of universal respect for and observance of human rights and fundamental freedoms,

Whereas a common understanding of these rights and freedoms is of the greatest importance for the full realization of this pledge,

Now, Therefore THE GENERAL ASSEMBLY proclaims THIS UNIVERSAL DECLARATION OF HUMAN RIGHTS as a common standard of achievement for all peoples and all nations, to the end that every individual and every organ of society, keeping this Declaration constantly in mind, shall strive by teaching and education to promote respect for these rights and freedoms and by progressive measures, national and international, to secure their universal and effective recognition and observance, both among the peoples of Member States themselves and among the peoples of territories under their jurisdiction.

Article 5 No one shall be subjected to torture or to cruel, inhuman or degrading treatment or punishment.

The Fourth Geneva Convention, August 12, 1949[17]

Article 3 In the case of armed conflict not of an international character occurring in the territory of one of the High Contracting Parties, each Party to the conflict shall be bound to apply, as a minimum, the following provisions:

(1) Persons taking no active part in the hostilities, including members of armed forces who have laid down their arms and those placed hors de combat by sickness, wounds, detention, or any other cause, shall in all circumstances be treated humanely, without any adverse distinction founded on race, colour, religion or faith, sex, birth or wealth, or any other similar criteria.

To this end the following acts are and shall remain prohibited at any time and in any place whatsoever with respect to the above-mentioned persons:

(a) violence to life and person, in particular murder of all kinds, mutilation, cruel treatment and torture;

(b) taking of hostages;

(c) outrages upon personal dignity, in particular humiliating and degrading treatment;

(d) the passing of sentences and the carrying out of executions without previous judgment pronounced by a regularly constituted court, affording all the judicial guarantees which are recognized as indispensable by civilized peoples.

The United Nations International Covenant on Civil and Political Rights, December 10, 1966

PREAMBLE The States Parties to the present Covenant,

Considering that, in accordance with the principles proclaimed in the Charter of the United Nations, recognition of the inherent dignity and of the equal and inalienable rights of all members of the human family is the foundation of freedom, justice and peace in the world,

Recognizing that these rights derive from the inherent dignity of the human person,

Recognizing that, in accordance with the Universal Declaration of Human Rights, the ideal of free human beings enjoying civil and political freedom and freedom from fear and want can only be achieved if conditions are created whereby everyone may enjoy his civil and political rights, as well as his economic, social and cultural rights,

Considering the obligation of States under the Charter of the United Nations to promote universal respect for, and observance of, human rights and freedoms,

Realizing that the individual, having duties to other individuals and to the community to which he belongs, is under a responsibility to strive for the promotion and observance of the rights recognized in the present Covenant,

Agree upon the following articles:

Article 7 No one shall be subjected to torture or to cruel, inhuman or degrading treatment or punishment. In particular, no one shall be subjected without his free consent to medical or scientific experimentation.

Declaration On The Protection Of All Persons From Being Subjected To Torture And Other Cruel, Inhuman Or Degrading Treatment Or Punishment, December 9, 1975

Article 1 1. For the purpose of this Declaration, torture means any act by which severe pain or suffering, whether physical or mental, is intentionally inflicted by or at the instigation of a public official on a person for such purposes as obtaining from him or a third person information or confession, punishing him for an act he has committed or is suspected of having committed, or intimidating him or other persons. It does not include pain or suffering arising only from, inherent in or incidental to, lawful sanctions to the extent consistent with the Standard Minimum Rules for the Treatment of Prisoners.

2. Torture constitutes an aggravated and deliberate form of cruel, inhuman or degrading treatment or punishment.

Article 2 Any act of torture or other cruel, inhuman or degrading treatment or punishment is an offence to human dignity and shall be condemned as a denial of the purposes of the Charter of the United Nations and as a violation of the human rights and fundamental freedoms proclaimed in the Universal Declaration of Human Rights.

Article 3 No State may permit or tolerate torture or other cruel, inhuman or degrading treatment or punishment. Exceptional circumstances such as a state of war or a threat of war, internal political instability or any other public emergency may not be invoked as a justification of torture or other cruel, inhuman or degrading treatment or punishment.

Article 4 Each State shall, in accordance with the provisions of this Declaration, take effective measures to prevent torture and other cruel, inhuman or degrading treatment or punishment from being practised within its jurisdiction.

Article 5 The training of law enforcement personnel and of other public officials who may be responsible for persons deprived of their liberty shall ensure that full account is taken of the prohibition against torture and other cruel, inhuman or degrading treatment or punishment. This prohibition shall also, where appropriate, be included in such general rules or instructions as are issued in regard to the duties and functions of anyone who may be involved in the custody or treatment of such persons.

Article 6 Each State shall keep under systematic review interrogation methods and practices as well as arrangements for the custody and treatment of persons deprived of their liberty in its territory, with a view to preventing any cases of torture or other cruel, inhuman or degrading treatment or punishment.

Article 7 Each State shall ensure that all acts of torture as defined in article 1 are offences under its criminal law. The same shall apply in regard to acts which constitute participation in, complicity in, incitement to or an attempt to commit torture.

Article 8 Any person who alleges that he has been subjected to torture or other cruel, inhuman or degrading treatment or punishment by or at the instigation of a public official shall have the right to complain to, and to have his case impartially examined by, the competent authorities of the State concerned.

Article 9 Wherever there is reasonable ground to believe that an act of torture as defined in article 1 has been committed, the competent authorities of the State concerned shall promptly proceed to an impartial investigation even if there has been no formal complaint.

Article 10 If an investigation under article 8 or article 9 establishes that an act of torture as defined in article 1 appears to have been committed, criminal proceedings shall be instituted against the alleged offender or offenders in accordance with national law. If an allegation of other forms of cruel, inhuman or degrading treatment or punishment is considered to be well founded, the alleged offender or offenders shall be subject to criminal, disciplinary or other appropriate proceedings.

Article 11 Where it is proved that an act of torture or other cruel, inhuman or grading treatment or punishment has been committed by or at the instigation of a public official, the victim shall be afforded redress and compensation in accordance with national law.

Article 12 Any statement which is established to have been made as a result of torture or other cruel, inhuman or degrading treatment or punishment may not be invoked as evidence against the person concerned or against any other person in any proceedings.

Convention Against Torture and Other Cruel, Inhuman or Degrading Treatment or Punishment, December 10, 1984[18]

The States Parties to this Convention, Considering that, in accordance with the principles proclaimed in the Charter of the United Nations, recognition of the equal and inalienable rights of all members of the human family is the foundation of freedom, justice and peace in the world, Recognizing that those rights derive from the inherent dignity of the human person... Desiring to make more effective the struggle against torture and other cruel, inhuman or degrading treatment or punishment throughout the world, Have agreed as follows:

Part I

Article 1 1. For the purposes of this Convention, the term "torture" means any act by which severe pain or suffering, whether physical or mental, is intentionally inflicted on a person for such purposes as obtaining from him or a third person information or a confession, punishing him for an act he or a third person has committed or is suspected of having committed, or intimidating or coercing him or a third person, or for any reason based on discrimination of any kind, when such pain or suffering is inflicted by or at the instigation of or with the consent or acquiescence of a public official or other person acting in an official capacity. It does not include pain or suffering arising only from, inherent in or incidental to lawful sanctions.

Article 2 1. Each State Party shall take effective legislative, administrative, judicial or other measures to prevent acts of torture in any territory under its jurisdiction.

2. No exceptional circumstances whatsoever, whether a state of war or a threat of war, internal political instability or any other public emergency, may be invoked as a justification of torture.

3. An order from a superior officer or a public authority may not be invoked as a justification of torture.

Article 3 1. No State Party shall expel, return (refouler) or extradite a person to another State where there are substantial grounds for believing that he would be in danger of being subjected to torture.

2. For the purpose of determining whether there are such grounds, the competent authorities shall take into account all relevant considerations including, where applicable, the existence in the State concerned of a consistent pattern of gross, flagrant or mass violations of human rights.

Article 4 1. Each State Party shall ensure that all acts of torture are offences under its criminal law. The same shall apply to an attempt to commit torture and to an act by any person which constitutes complicity or participation in torture.

2. Each State Party shall make these offences punishable by appropriate penalties which take into account their grave nature.

Article 5 1. Each State Party shall take such measures as may be necessary to establish its jurisdiction over the offences referred to in article 4 in the following cases:

(a) When the offences are committed in any territory under its jurisdiction or on board a ship or aircraft registered in that State;

(b) When the alleged offender is a national of that State;

(c) When the victim is a national of that State if that State considers it appropriate.

2. Each State Party shall likewise take such measures as may be necessary to establish its jurisdiction over such offences in cases where the alleged offender is present in any territory under its jurisdiction and it does not extradite him pursuant to article 8 to any of the States mentioned in paragraph 1 of this article.

Article 8 1. The offences referred to in article 4 shall be deemed to be included as extraditable offences in any extradition treaty existing between States Parties. States Parties undertake to include such offences as extraditable offences in every extradition treaty to be concluded between them.

Article 10 1. Each State Party shall ensure that education and information regarding the prohibition against torture are fully included in the training of law enforcement personnel, civil or military, medical personnel, public officials and other persons who may be involved in the custody, interrogation or treatment of any individual subjected to any form of arrest, detention or imprisonment.

2. Each State Party shall include this prohibition in the rules or instructions issued in regard to the duties and functions of any such persons.

Article 11 Each State Party shall keep under systematic review interrogation rules, instructions, methods and practices as well as arrangements for the custody and treatment of persons subjected to any form of arrest, detention or imprisonment in any territory under its jurisdiction, with a view to preventing any cases of torture.

Article 13 Each State Party shall ensure that any individual who alleges he has been subjected to torture in any territory under its jurisdiction has the right to complain to, and to have his case promptly and impartially examined by, its competent authorities. Steps shall be taken to ensure that the complainant and witnesses are protected against all ill-treatment or intimidation as a consequence of his complaint or any evidence given.

Article 14 1. Each State Party shall ensure in its legal system that the victim of an act of torture obtains redress and has an enforceable right to fair and adequate compensation, including the means for as full rehabilitation as possible. In the event of the death of the victim as a result of an act of torture, his dependants shall be entitled to compensation.

2. Nothing in this article shall affect any right of the victim or other persons to compensation which may exist under national law.

Article 15 Each State Party shall ensure that any statement which is established to have been made as a result of torture shall not be invoked as evidence in any proceedings, except against a person accused of torture as evidence that the statement was made.

Article 16 1. Each State Party shall undertake to prevent in any territory under its jurisdiction other acts of cruel, inhuman or degrading treatment or punishment which do not amount to torture as defined in article 1, when such acts are committed by or at the instigation of or with the consent or acquiescence of a public official or other person acting in an official capacity. In particular, the obligations contained in articles 10, 11, 12 and 13 shall apply with the substitution for references to torture of references to other forms of cruel, inhuman or degrading treatment or punishment.

2. The provisions of this Convention are without prejudice to the provisions of any other international instrument or national law which prohibits cruel, inhuman or degrading treatment or punishment or which relates to extradition or expulsion.

Executive Order 12949—Foreign Intelligence Physical Searches, February 9, 1995

By the authority vested in me as President by the Constitution and the laws of the United States, including sections 302 and 303 of the Foreign Intelligence Surveillance Act of 1978 ("Act") (50 U.S.C. 1801, et seq.), as amended by Public Law 103- 359, and in order to provide for the authorization of physical searches for foreign intelligence purposes as set forth in the Act, it is hereby ordered as follows:

Sec. 1.

Pursuant to section 302(a)(1) of the Act, the Attorney General is authorized to approve physical searches, without a court order, to acquire foreign intelligence information for periods of up to one year, if the Attorney General makes the certifications required by that section.

Sec. 2.

Pursuant to section 302(b) of the Act, the Attorney General is authorized to approve applications to the Foreign Intelligence Surveillance Court under section 303 of the Act to obtain orders for physical searches for the purpose of collecting foreign intelligence information.

Sec. 3.

Pursuant to section 303(a)(7) of the Act, the following officials, each of whom is employed in the area of national security or defense, is designated to make the certifications required by section 303(a)(7) of the Act in support of applications to conduct physical searches:

- (a) Secretary of State;
- (b) Secretary of Defense;
- (c) Director of Central Intelligence;
- (d) Director of the Federal Bureau of Investigation;
- (e) Deputy Secretary of State;
- (f) Deputy Secretary of Defense; and
- (g) Deputy Director of Central Intelligence.

None of the above officials, nor anyone officially acting in that capacity, may exercise the authority to make the above certifications, unless that official has been appointed by the President, by and with the advice and consent of the Senate.

Military Order of November 13, 2001—Detention, Treatment, and Trial of Certain Non-Citizens In The War Against Terrorism

By the authority vested in me as President and as Commander in Chief of the Armed Forces of the United States by the Constitution and the laws of the United States of America, including the Authorization for Use of Military Force Joint Resolution (Public Law 107–40, 115 Stat. 224) and sections 821 and 836 of title 10, United States Code, it is hereby ordered as follows:

Sec. 1. Findings.

- (e) To protect the United States and its citizens, and for the effective conduct of military operations and prevention of terrorist attacks, it is necessary for individuals subject to this order pursuant to section 2 hereof to be detained, and, when tried, to be tried for violations of the laws of war and other applicable laws by military tribunals.
- (f) Given the danger to the safety of the United States and the nature of international terrorism, and to the extent provided by and under this order, I find consistent with section 836 of title 10, United States Code, that it is not practicable to apply in military commissions under this order the principles of law and the rules of evidence generally recognized in the trial of criminal cases in the United States district courts.
- (g) Having fully considered the magnitude of the potential deaths, injuries, and property destruction that would result from potential acts of terrorism against the United States, and the probability that such acts will occur, I have determined that an extraordinary emergency exists for national defense purposes, that this emergency constitutes an urgent and compelling government interest, and that issuance of this order is necessary to meet the emergency.

Sec. 2. Definition and Policy.

- (a) The term "individual subject to this order" shall mean any individual who is not a United States citizen with respect to whom I determine from time to time in writing that: there is reason to believe that such individual, at the relevant times, (i) is or was a member of the organization known as al Qaida; (ii) has engaged in, aided or abetted, or conspired to commit, acts of international terrorism, or acts in preparation therefor, that have caused, threaten to cause, or have as their aim to cause, injury to or adverse effects on the United States, its citizens, national security, foreign policy, or economy; or (iii) has knowingly harbored one or more individuals described in subparagraphs (i) or (ii) of subsection 2(a)(1) of this order; and (2) it is in the interest of the United States that such individual be subject to this order.

(b) It is the policy of the United States that the Secretary of Defense shall take all necessary measures to ensure that any individual subject to this order is detained in accordance with section 3, and, if the individual is to be tried, that such individual is tried only in accordance with section

(c) It is further the policy of the United States that any individual subject to this order who is not already under the control of the Secretary of Defense but who is under the control of any other officer or agent of the United States or any State shall, upon delivery of a copy of such written determination to such officer or agent, forthwith be placed under the control of the Secretary of Defense.

Sec. 3. Detention Authority of the Secretary of Defense.

Any individual subject to this order shall be—

(a) detained at an appropriate location designated by the Secretary of Defense outside or within the United States;

(b) treated humanely, without any adverse distinction based on race, color, religion, gender, birth, wealth, or any similar criteria;

(c) afforded adequate food, drinking water, shelter, clothing, and medical treatment;

(d) allowed the free exercise of religion consistent with the requirements of such detention; and

(e) detained in accordance with such other conditions as the Secretary of Defense may prescribe.

Sec. 4. Authority of the Secretary of Defense Regarding Trials of Individuals Subject to this Order.

(a) Any individual subject to this order shall, when tried, be tried by military commission for any and all offenses triable by military commission that such

individual is alleged to have committed, and may be punished in accordance with the penalties provided under applicable law, including life imprisonment or death.

(b) As a military function and in light of the findings in section 1, including subsection (f) thereof, the Secretary of Defense shall issue such orders and regulations, including orders for the appointment of one or more military commissions, as may be necessary to carry out subsection (a) of this section.

(c) Orders and regulations issued under subsection (b) of this section shall include, but not be limited to, rules for the conduct of the proceedings of military commissions, including pretrial, trial, and post-trial procedures, modes of proof, issuance of process, and qualifications of attorneys, which shall at a minimum provide for—

(1) military commissions to sit at any time and any place, consistent with such guidance regarding time and place as the Secretary of Defense may provide;

(2) a full and fair trial, with the military commission sitting as the triers of both fact and law;

(3) admission of such evidence as would, in the opinion of the presiding officer of the military commission (or instead, if any other member of the commission so requests at the time the presiding officer renders that opinion, the opinion of the commission rendered at that time by a majority of the commission), have probative value to a reasonable person;

(4) in a manner consistent with the protection of information classified or classifiable under Executive Order 12958 of April 17, 1995, as amended, or any successor Executive Order, protected by statute or rule from unauthorized disclosure, or otherwise protected by law, (A) the handling of, admission into evidence of, and access to materials and information, and (B) the conduct, closure of, and access to proceedings;

(5) conduct of the prosecution by one or more attorneys designated by the Secretary of Defense and conduct of the defense by attorneys for the individual subject to this order;

(6) conviction only upon the concurrence of two-thirds of the members of the commission present at the time of the vote, a majority being present;

(7) sentencing only upon the concurrence of two-thirds of the members of the commission present at the time of the vote, a majority being present; and

(8) submission of the record of the trial, including any conviction or sentence, for review and final decision by me or by the Secretary of Defense if so designated by me for that purpose.

Sec. 7. Relationship to Other Law and Forums.

(b) With respect to any individual subject to this order—

(1) military tribunals shall have exclusive jurisdiction with respect to offenses by the individual; and

(2) the individual shall not be privileged to seek any remedy or maintain any proceeding, directly or indirectly, or to have any such remedy or proceeding sought on the individual's behalf, in (i) any court of the United States, or any State thereof, (ii) any court of any foreign nation, or (iii) any international tribunal.

(e) I reserve the authority to direct the Secretary of Defense, at any time hereafter, to transfer to a governmental authority control of any individual subject to this order. Nothing in this order shall be construed to limit the authority of any such governmental authority to prosecute any individual for whom control is transferred.

Department of Defense, Military Commission Order No. 1, Procedures for Trial by Military Commission of Certain Non-United States Citizens in the War Against Terrorism, March 21, 2002

1. PURPOSE This Order implements policy, assigns responsibilities, and prescribes procedures under references (a) and (b) for trials before military commissions of individuals subject to the President's Military Order. These procedures shall be implemented and construed so as to ensure that any such individual receives a full and fair trial before a military commission, as required by the President's Military Order. Unless otherwise directed by the Secretary of Defense, and except for supplemental procedures established pursuant to the President's Military Order or this Order, the procedures prescribed herein and no others shall govern such trials.

2. ESTABLISHMENT OF MILITARY COMMISSIONS In accordance with the President's Military Order, the Secretary of Defense or a designee ("Appointing Authority") may issue orders from time to time appointing one or more military commissions to try individuals subject to the President's Military Order and appointing any other personnel necessary to facilitate such trials.

3. JURISDICTION

A. Over Persons A military commission appointed under this Order ("Commission") shall have jurisdiction over only an individual or individuals ("the Accused") (1) subject to the President's Military Order and (2) alleged to have committed an offense in a charge that has been referred to the Commission by the Appointing Authority.

B. Over Offenses Commissions established hereunder shall have jurisdiction over violations of the laws of war and all other offenses triable by military commission.

C. Maintaining Integrity of Commission Proceedings The Commission may exercise jurisdiction over participants in its proceedings as necessary to preserve the integrity and order of the proceedings.

5. PROCEDURES ACCORDED THE ACCUSED The following procedures shall apply with respect to the Accused:

A. The Prosecution shall furnish to the Accused, sufficiently in advance of trial to prepare a defense, a copy of the charges in English and, if appropriate, in another language that the Accused understands.

B. The Accused shall be presumed innocent until proven guilty.

C. A Commission member shall vote for a finding of Guilty as to an offense if and only if that member is convinced beyond a reasonable doubt, based on the evidence admitted at trial, that the Accused is guilty of the offense.

D. At least one Detailed Defense Counsel shall be made available to the Accused sufficiently in advance of trial to prepare a defense and until any findings and sentence become final in accordance with Section 6(H)(2).

E. The Prosecution shall provide the Defense with access to evidence the Prosecution intends to introduce at trial and with access to evidence known to the Prosecution that tends to exculpate the Accused. Such access shall be consistent with Section 6(D)(5) and subject to Section 9.

F. The Accused shall not be required to testify during trial. A Commission shall draw no adverse inference from an Accused's decision not to testify. This subsection shall not preclude admission of evidence of prior statements or conduct of the Accused.

G. If the Accused so elects, the Accused may testify at trial on the Accused's own behalf and shall then be subject to cross-examination.

H. The Accused may obtain witnesses and documents for the Accused's defense, to the extent necessary and reasonably available as determined by the Presiding Officer. Such access shall be consistent with the requirements of Section 6(D)(5) and subject to Section 9. The Appointing Authority shall order that such investigative or other resources be made available to the Defense as the Appointing Authority deems necessary for a full and fair trial.

I. The Accused may have Defense Counsel present evidence at trial in the Accused's defense and cross-examine each witness presented by the Prosecution who appears before the Commission.

J. The Prosecution shall ensure that the substance of the charges, the proceedings, and any documentary evidence are provided in English and, if appropriate, in another language that the Accused understands. The Appointing Authority may appoint one or more interpreters to assist the Defense, as necessary.

K. The Accused may be present at every stage of the trial before the Commission, consistent with Section 6(B)(3), unless the Accused engages in disruptive conduct that justifies exclusion by the Presiding Officer. Detailed Defense Counsel may not be excluded from any trial proceeding or portion thereof.

L. Except by order of the Commission for good cause shown, the Prosecution shall provide the Defense with access before sentencing proceedings to evidence the Prosecution intends to present in such proceedings. Such access shall be consistent with Section 6(D)(5) and subject to Section 9.

M. The Accused may make a statement during sentencing proceedings.

N. The Accused may have Defense Counsel submit evidence to the Commission during sentencing proceedings.

O. The Accused shall be afforded a trial open to the public (except proceedings closed by the Presiding Officer), consistent with Section 6(B).

P. The Accused shall not again be tried by any Commission for a charge once a Commission's finding on that charge becomes final in accordance with Section 6(H)(2).

6. EVIDENCE

(1) Admissibility Evidence shall be admitted if, in the opinion of the Presiding Officer (or instead, if any other member of the Commission so requests at the time the Presiding Officer renders that opinion, the opinion of the Commission rendered at that time by a majority of the Commission), the evidence would have probative value to a reasonable person.

Detainee Treatment Act Of 2005

TITLE X—MATTERS RELATING TO DETAINEES

SEC. 1001. SHORT TITLE.

This title may be cited as the 'Detainee Treatment Act of 2005'.

SEC. 1002. UNIFORM STANDARDS FOR THE INTERROGATION OF PERSONS UNDER THE DETENTION OF THE DEPARTMENT OF DEFENSE.

(a) IN GENERAL.— No person in the custody or under the effective control of the Department of Defense or under detention in a Department of Defense facility shall be subject to any treatment or technique of interrogation not authorized by and listed in the United States Army Field Manual on Intelligence Interrogation.

(b) APPLICABILITY.— Subsection (a) shall not apply with respect to any person in the custody or under the effective control of the Department of Defense pursuant to a criminal law or immigration law of the United States.

(c) CONSTRUCTION.— Nothing in this section shall be construed to affect the rights under the United States Constitution of any person in the custody or under the physical jurisdiction of the United States.

SEC. 1003. PROHIBITION ON CRUEL, INHUMAN, OR DEGRADING TREATMENT OR PUNISHMENT OF PERSONS UNDER CUSTODY OR CONTROL OF THE UNITED STATES GOVERNMENT.

(a) IN GENERAL.— No individual in the custody or under the physical control of the United States Government, regardless of nationality or physical location, shall be subject to cruel, inhuman, or degrading treatment or punishment.

(b) CONSTRUCTION.— Nothing in this section shall be construed to impose any geographical limitation on the applicability of the prohibition against cruel, inhuman, or degrading treatment or punishment under this section.

(c) LIMITATION ON SUPERSEDURE.— The provisions of this section shall not be superseded, except by a provision of law enacted after the date of the enactment of this Act which specifically repeals, modifies, or supersedes the provisions of this section.

(d) CRUEL, INHUMAN, OR DEGRADING TREATMENT OR PUNISHMENT DEFINED.— In this section, the term 'cruel, inhuman, or degrading treatment or punishment' means the cruel, unusual, and inhumane treatment or punishment prohibited by the Fifth, Eighth, and Fourteenth Amendments to the Constitution of the United States, as defined in the United States Reservations, Declarations and Understandings to the United Nations Convention Against Torture and Other Forms of Cruel, Inhuman or Degrading Treatment or Punishment done at New York, December 10, 1984.

SEC. 1004. PROTECTION OF UNITED STATES GOVERNMENT PERSONNEL ENGAGED IN AUTHORIZED INTERROGATIONS.

(a) PROTECTION OF UNITED STATES GOVERNMENT PERSONNEL.— In any civil action or criminal prosecution against an officer, employee, member of the Armed Forces, or other agent of the United States Government who is a United States person, arising out of the officer, employee, member of the Armed Forces, or other agent's engaging in specific operational practices, that involve detention and interrogation of aliens who the President or his designees have determined are believed to be engaged in or associated with international terrorist activity that poses a serious, continuing threat to the United States, its interests, or its allies, and that were officially authorized and determined to be lawful at the time that they were conducted, it shall be a defense that such officer, employee, member of the Armed Forces, or other agent did not know that the practices were unlawful and a person of ordinary sense and understanding would not know the practices were unlawful. Good faith reliance on advice of counsel should be an important factor, among others, to consider in assessing whether a person of ordinary sense and understanding would have known the practices to be unlawful. Nothing in this section shall be construed to limit or extinguish any defense or protection otherwise available to any person or entity from suit, civil or criminal liability, or damages, or to provide immunity from prosecution for any criminal offense by the proper authorities.

(b) COUNSEL.— The United States Government may provide or employ counsel, and pay counsel fees, court costs, bail, and other expenses incident to the representation of an officer, employee, member of the Armed Forces, or other agent described in subsection (a), with respect to any civil action or criminal prosecution arising out of practices described in that subsection, under the same conditions, and to the same extent, to which such services and payments are authorized under section 1037 of title 10, United States Code.

SEC. 1005. PROCEDURES FOR STATUS REVIEW OF DETAINEES OUTSIDE THE UNITED STATES.

(a) *Submittal of Procedures for Status Review of Detainees at Guantánamo Bay, Cuba, and in Afghanistan and Iraq.*

(1) IN GENERAL.— Not later than 180 days after the date of the enactment of this Act, the Secretary of Defense shall submit to the Committee on Armed Services and the Committee on the Judiciary of the Senate and the Committee on Armed Services and the Committee on the Judiciary of the House of Representatives a report setting forth–

(A) the procedures of the Combatant Status Review Tribunals and the Administrative Review Boards established by direction of the Secretary of Defense that are in operation at Guantánamo Bay, Cuba, for determining the status of the detainees held at Guantánamo Bay or to provide an annual review to determine the need to continue to detain an alien who is a detainee; and

(B) the procedures in operation in Afghanistan and Iraq for a determination of the status of aliens detained in the custody or under the physical control of the Department of Defense in those countries.

(2) DESIGNATED CIVILIAN OFFICIAL.— The procedures submitted to Congress pursuant to paragraph (1)(A) shall ensure that the official of the Department of Defense who is designated by the President or Secretary of Defense to be the final review authority within the Department of Defense with respect to decisions of any such tribunal or board (referred to as the 'Designated Civilian Official') shall be a civilian officer of the Department of Defense holding an office to which appointments are required by law to be made by the President, by and with the advice and consent of the Senate.

(3) CONSIDERATION OF NEW EVIDENCE.— The procedures submitted under paragraph (1)(A) shall provide for periodic review of any new evidence that may become available relating to the enemy combatant status of a detainee.

(b) *Consideration of Statements Derived With Coercion.*

(1) ASSESSMENT.— The procedures submitted to Congress pursuant to subsection (a)(1)(A) shall ensure that a Combatant Status Review Tribunal or Administrative Review Board, or any similar or successor administrative tribunal or board, in making a determination of status or disposition of any detainee under such procedures, shall, to the extent practicable, assess–

(A) whether any statement derived from or relating to such detainee was obtained as a result of coercion; and

(B) the probative value (if any) of any such statement.

(2) APPLICABILITY.— Paragraph (1) applies with respect to any proceeding beginning on or after the date of the enactment of this Act.

(e) *Judicial Review of Detention of Enemy Combatants.*

(1) IN GENERAL.— Section 2241 of title 28, United States Code, is amended by adding at the end the following:

'(e) Except as provided in section 1005 of the Detainee Treatment Act of 2005, no court, justice, or judge shall have jurisdiction to hear or consider–

'(1) an application for a writ of habeas corpus filed by or on behalf of an alien detained by the Department of Defense at Guantánamo Bay, Cuba; or

'(2) any other action against the United States or its agents relating to any aspect of the detention by the Department of Defense of an alien at Guantánamo Bay, Cuba, who–

'(A) is currently in military custody; or

'(B) has been determined by the United States Court of Appeals for the District of Columbia Circuit in accordance with the procedures set forth in section 1005(e) of the Detainee Treatment Act of 2005 to have been properly detained as an enemy combatant.'

Military Commissions Act of 2006[19]

An Act to authorize trial by military commission for violations of the law of war, and for other purposes.

Be it enacted by the Senate and House of Representatives of the United States of America in Congress assembled,

(a) Short Title.–This Act may be cited as the ''Military Commissions Act of 2006''.

SEC. 2. CONSTRUCTION OF PRESIDENTIAL AUTHORITY TO ESTABLISH MILITARY COMMISSIONS.

The authority to establish military commissions under Chapter 47A of title 10, United States Code, as added by section 3(a), may not be construed to alter or limit the authority of the President under the Constitution of the United States and laws of the United States to establish military commissions for areas declared to be under martial law or in occupied territories should circumstances so require.

SEC. 3. MILITARY COMMISSIONS.

(a) *Military Commissions.*

(1) IN GENERAL.— Subtitle A of title 10, United States Code, is amended by inserting after chapter 47 the following new chapter:

''Sec. 948a. Definitions

''In this chapter:

''(1) *UNLAWFUL ENEMY COMBATANT.—* (A) The term 'unlawful enemy combatant' means—

''(i) a person who has engaged in hostilities or who has purposefully and materially supported hostilities against the United States or its co-belligerents who is not a lawful enemy combatant (including a person who is part of the Taliban, al Qaeda, or associated forces); or

''(ii) a person who, before, on, or after the date of the enactment of the Military Commissions Act of 2006, has been determined to be an unlawful enemy combatant by a Combatant Status Review Tribunal or another competent tribunal established under the authority of the President or the Secretary of Defense.

''(B) Co-belligerent.—In this paragraph, the term 'co-belligerent', with respect to the United States, means any State or armed force joining and directly engaged with the United States in hostilities or directly supporting hostilities against a common enemy.

''(2) *LAWFUL ENEMY COMBATANT.—* The term 'lawful enemy combatant' means a person who is—

''(A) a member of the regular forces of a State party engaged in hostilities against the United States;

''(B) a member of a militia, volunteer corps, or organized resistance movement belonging to a State party engaged in such hostilities, which are under responsible command, wear a fixed distinctive sign recognizable at a distance, carry their arms openly, and abide by the law of war; or

''(C) a member of a regular armed force who professes allegiance to a government engaged in such hostilities, but not recognized by the United States.

(3) *ALIEN.—* The term 'alien' means a person who is not a citizen of the United States.

(4) *CLASSIFIED INFORMATION.—* The term 'classified information' means the following:

''(A) Any information or material that has been determined by the United States Government pursuant to statute, Executive order, or regulation to require protection against unauthorized disclosure for reasons of national security.

''(B) Any restricted data, as that term is defined in section 11 y. of the Atomic Energy Act of 1954 (42 U.S.C. 2014(y)).

''(5) *GENEVA CONVENTIONS.–* The term 'Geneva Conventions' means the international conventions signed at Geneva on August 12, 1949.

''Sec. 948b. Military Commissions Generally

''**(a) PURPOSE.—** This chapter establishes procedures governing the use of military commissions to try alien unlawful enemy combatants engaged in hostilities against the United States for violations of the law of war and other offenses triable by military commission.

"(b) AUTHORITY FOR MILITARY COMMISSIONS UNDER THIS CHAPTER.— The President is authorized to establish military commissions under this chapter for offenses triable by military commission as provided in this chapter.

"(c) CONSTRUCTION OF PROVISIONS.— The procedures for military commissions set forth in this chapter are based upon the procedures for trial by general courts-martial under Chapter 47 of this title (the Uniform Code of Military Justice). Chapter 47 of this title does not, by its terms, apply to trial by military commission except as specifically provided in this chapter. The judicial construction and application of that chapter are not binding on military commissions established under this chapter.

"(d) INAPPLICABILITY OF CERTAIN PROVISIONS.— (1) The following provisions of this title shall not apply to trial by military commission under this chapter:

> "(A) Section 810 (article 10 of the Uniform Code of Military Justice), relating to speedy trial, including any rule of courts-martial relating to speedy trial.
>
> "(B) Sections 831(a), (b), and (d) (articles 31(a), (b), (d) of the Uniform Code of Military Justice), relating to compulsory self-incrimination.
>
> "(C) Section 832 (article 32 of the Uniform Code of Military Justice), relating to pretrial investigation.

"(2) Other provisions of chapter 47 of this title shall apply to trial by military commission under this chapter only to the extent provided by this chapter.

"(e) TREATMENT OF RULINGS AND PRECEDENTS.— The findings, holdings, interpretations, and other precedents of military commissions under this chapter may not be introduced or considered in any hearing, trial, or other proceeding of a court-martial convened under chapter 47 of this title. The findings, holdings, interpretations, and other precedents of military commissions under this chapter may not form the basis of any holding, decision, or other determination of a court-martial convened under that chapter.

"(f) STATUS OF COMMISSIONS UNDER COMMON ARTICLE 3.— A military commission established under this chapter is a regularly constituted court, affording all the necessary 'judicial guarantees which are recognized as indispensable by civilized peoples' for purposes of common Article 3 of the Geneva Conventions.

"(g) GENEVA CONVENTIONS NOT ESTABLISHING SOURCE OF RIGHTS.— No alien unlawful enemy combatant subject to trial by military commission under this chapter may invoke the Geneva Conventions as a source of rights.

"Sec. 948c. Persons Subject to Military Commissions

"Any alien unlawful enemy combatant is subject to trial by military commission under this chapter.

"Sec. 948d. Jurisdiction of Military Commissions

"(a) JURISDICTION.— A military commission under this chapter shall have jurisdiction to try any offense made punishable by this chapter or the law of war when committed by an alien unlawful enemy combatant before, on, or after September 11, 2001.

"(b) LAWFUL ENEMY COMBATANTS.— Military commissions under this chapter shall not have jurisdiction over lawful enemy combatants. Lawful enemy combatants who violate the law of war are subject to chapter 47 of this title. Courts-martial established under that chapter shall have jurisdiction to try a lawful enemy combatant for any offense made punishable under this chapter.

"(c) DETERMINATION OF UNLAWFUL ENEMY COMBATANT STATUS DISPOSITIVE.— A finding, whether before, on, or after the date of the enactment of the Military Commissions Act of 2006, by a Combatant Status Review Tribunal or another competent tribunal established under the authority of the President or the Secretary of Defense that a person is an unlawful enemy combatant is dispositive for purposes of jurisdiction for trial by military commission under this chapter.

"(d) PUNISHMENTS.— A military commission under this chapter may, under such limitations as the Secretary of Defense may prescribe, adjudge any punishment not forbidden by this chapter, including the penalty of death when authorized under this chapter or the law of war.

"SUBCHAPTER II—COMPOSITION OF MILITARY COMMISSIONS

"Sec. 948h. Who May Convene Military Commissions

"Military commissions under this chapter may be convened by the Secretary of Defense or by any officer or official of the United States designated by the Secretary for that purpose.

"Sec. 948i. Who May Serve on Military Commissions

"(a) IN GENERAL.— Any commissioned officer of the armed forces on active duty is eligible to serve on a military commission under this chapter.

"(b) DETAIL OF MEMBERS.— When convening a military commission under this chapter, the convening authority shall detail as members of the commission such members of the armed forces eligible under subsection (a), as in the opinion of the convening authority, are best qualified for the duty by reason of age, education, training, experience, length of service, and judicial temperament. No member of an armed force is eligible to serve as a member of a military commission when such member is the accuser or a witness for the prosecution or has acted as an investigator or counsel in the same case.

"Sec. 948j. Military Judge of a Military Commission

"(b) QUALIFICATIONS.— A military judge shall be a commissioned officer of the armed forces who is a member of the bar of a Federal court, or a member of the bar of the highest court of a State, and who is certified to be qualified for duty under section 826 of this title (article 26 of the Uniform Code of Military Justice) as a military judge in general courts-martial by the Judge Advocate General of the armed force of which such military judge is a member.

Executive Order 13425 of February 14, 2007, Trial of Alien Unlawful Enemy Combatants By Military Commission

By the authority vested in me as President by the Constitution and the laws of the United States of America, including the Military Commissions Act of 2006 (Public Law 109–366), the Authorization for Use of Military Force (Public Law 107–40), and section 948b(b) of title 10, United States Code, it is hereby ordered as follows:

Sec. 1. Establishment of Military Commissions.

There are hereby established military commissions to try alien unlawful enemy combatants for offenses triable by military commission as provided in chapter 47A of title 10.

Sec. 2. Definitions.

As used in this order:

(a) "unlawful enemy combatant" has the meaning provided for that term in section 948a(1) of title 10; and

(b) "alien" means a person who is not a citizen of the United States.

Sec. 3. Supersedure.

This order supersedes any provision of the President's Military Order of November 13, 2001 (66 Fed. Reg. 57,833), that relates to trial by military commission...

Executive Order 13440—Interpretation Of The Geneva Conventions Common Article 3 As Applied To A Program Of Detention And Interrogation Operated By The Central Intelligence Agency, July 24, 2007

Interpretation of the Geneva Conventions Common Article 3 as Applied to a Program of Detention and Interrogation Operated by the Central Intelligence Agency

By the authority vested in me as President and Commander in Chief of the Armed Forces by the Constitution and the laws of the United States of America, including the Authorization for Use of Military Force (Public Law 107–40), the Military Commissions Act of 2006 (Public Law 109–366), and section 301 of title 3, United States Code, it is hereby ordered as follows:

Sec. 1. General Determinations.

(a) The United States is engaged in an armed conflict with al Qaeda, the Taliban, and associated forces... On February 7, 2002, I determined for the United States that members of al Qaeda, the Taliban, and associated forces are unlawful enemy combatants who are not entitled to the protections that the Third Geneva Convention provides to prisoners of war. I hereby reaffirm that determination.

(b) The Military Commissions Act defines certain prohibitions of Common Article 3 for United States law, and it reaffirms and reinforces the authority of the President to interpret the meaning and application of the Geneva Conventions.

Sec. 2. Definitions.

As used in this order:

(a) "Common Article 3" means Article 3 of the Geneva Conventions.

(b) "Geneva Conventions" means:

(i) the Convention for the Amelioration of the Condition of the Wounded and Sick in Armed Forces in the Field, done at Geneva August 12, 1949 (6 UST 3114);

(ii) the Convention for the Amelioration of the Condition of Wounded, Sick and Shipwrecked Members of Armed Forces at Sea, done at Geneva August 12, 1949 (6 UST 3217);

(iii) the Convention Relative to the Treatment of Prisoners of War, done at Geneva August 12, 1949 (6 UST 3316); and

(iv) the Convention Relative to the Protection of Civilian Persons in Time of War, done at Geneva August 12, 1949 (6 UST 3516).

(c) "Cruel, inhuman, or degrading treatment or punishment" means the cruel, unusual, and inhumane treatment or punishment prohibited by the Fifth, Eighth, and Fourteenth Amendments to the Constitution of the United States.

Sec. 3. Compliance of a Central Intelligence Agency Detention and Interrogation Program with Common Article 3.

(a) Pursuant to the authority of the President under the Constitution and the laws of the United States, including the Military Commissions Act of 2006, this order interprets the meaning and application of the text of Common Article 3 with respect to certain detentions and interrogations, and shall be treated as authoritative for all purposes as a matter of United States law, including satisfaction of the international obligations of the United States. I hereby determine that Common Article 3 shall apply to a program of detention and interrogation operated by the Central Intelligence Agency as set forth in this section. The requirements set forth in this section shall be applied with respect to detainees in such program without adverse distinction as to their race, color, religion or faith, sex, birth, or wealth.

(b) I hereby determine that a program of detention and interrogation approved by the Director of the Central Intelligence Agency fully complies with the obligations of the United States under Common Article 3, provided that:

  (i) the conditions of confinement and interrogation practices of the program do not include:

   (A) torture, as defined in section 2340 of title 18, United States Code;

   (B) any of the acts prohibited by section 2441(d) of title 18, United States Code, including murder, torture, cruel or inhuman treatment, mutilation or maiming, intentionally causing serious bodily injury, rape, sexual assault or abuse, taking of hostages, or performing of biological experiments;

   (C) other acts of violence serious enough to be considered comparable to murder, torture, mutilation, and cruel or inhuman treatment, as defined in section 2441(d) of title 18, United States Code;

   (D) any other acts of cruel, inhuman, or degrading treatment or punishment prohibited by the Military Commissions Act (subsection 6(c) of Public Law 109–366) and the Detainee Treatment Act of 2005 (section 1003 of Public

Law 109–148 and section 1403 of Public Law 109–163);

   (E) willful and outrageous acts of personal abuse done for the purpose of humiliating or degrading the individual in a manner so serious that any reasonable person, considering the circumstances, would deem the acts to be beyond the bounds of human decency, such as sexual or sexually indecent acts undertaken for the purpose of humiliation, forcing the individual to perform sexual acts or to pose sexually, threatening the individual with sexual mutilation, or using the individual as a human shield; or

   (F) acts intended to denigrate the religion, religious practices, or religious objects of the individual;

  (ii) the conditions of confinement and interrogation practices are to be used with an alien detainee who is determined by the Director of the Central Intelligence Agency:

   (A) to be a member or part of or supporting al Qaeda, the Taliban, or associated organizations; and

   (B) likely to be in possession of information that:

    (1) could assist in detecting, mitigating, or preventing terrorist attacks, such as attacks within the United States or against its Armed Forces or other personnel, citizens, or facilities, or against allies or other countries cooperating in the war on terror with the United States, or their armed forces or other personnel, citizens, or facilities; or

    (2) could assist in locating the senior leadership of al Qaeda, the Taliban, or associated forces;

  (iii) the interrogation practices are determined by the Director of the Central Intelligence Agency, based upon professional advice, to be safe for use with each detainee with whom they are used; and

  (iv) detainees in the program receive the basic necessities of life, including adequate food and water, shelter from the elements, necessary clothing, protection from extremes of heat and cold, and essential medical care.

(c) The Director of the Central Intelligence Agency shall issue written policies to govern the program, including guidelines for Central Intelligence Agency personnel that implement paragraphs (i)(C), (E), and (F) of subsection 3(b) of this order, and including requirements to ensure:

(i) safe and professional operation of the program;

(ii) the development of an approved plan of interrogation tailored for each detainee in the program to be interrogated, consistent with subsection 3(b)(iv) of this order;

(iii) appropriate training for interrogators and all personnel operating the program;

(iv) effective monitoring of the program, including with respect to medical matters, to ensure the safety of those in the program; and

(v) compliance with applicable law and this order.

Sec. 5. General Provisions.

(a) Subject to subsection (b) of this section, this order is not intended to, and does not, create any right or benefit, substantive or procedural, enforceable at law or in equity, against the United States, its departments, agencies, or other entities, its officers or employees, or any other person.

(b) Nothing in this order shall be construed to prevent or limit reliance upon this order in a civil, criminal, or administrative proceeding, or otherwise, by the Central Intelligence Agency or by any individual acting on behalf of the Central Intelligence Agency in connection with the program addressed in this order.

Executive Order 13491—Ensuring Lawful Interrogations, January 22, 2009

By the authority vested in me by the Constitution and the laws of the United States of America, in order to improve the effectiveness of human intelligence-gathering, to promote the safe, lawful, and humane treatment of individuals in United States custody and of United States personnel who are detained in armed conflicts, to ensure compliance with the treaty obligations of the United States, including the Geneva Conventions, and to take care that the laws of the United States are faithfully executed, I hereby order as follows:

Sec. 1. Revocation.

Executive Order 13440 of July 20, 2007, is revoked. All executive directives, orders, and regulations inconsistent with this order, including but not limited to those issued to or by the Central Intelligence Agency (CIA) from September 11, 2001, to January 20, 2009, concerning detention or the interrogation of detained individuals, are revoked to the extent of their inconsistency with this order. Heads of departments and agencies shall take all necessary steps to ensure that all directives, orders, and regulations of their respective departments or agencies are consistent with this order. Upon request, the Attorney General shall provide guidance about which directives, orders, and regulations are inconsistent with this order.

Sec. 2. Definitions.

As used in this order:

(a) "Army Field Manual 2–22.3" means FM 2–22.3, Human Intelligence Collector Operations, issued by the Department of the Army on September 6, 2006.

(b) "Army Field Manual 34–52" means FM 34–52, Intelligence Interrogation, issued by the Department of the Army on May 8, 1987.

(c) "Common Article 3" means Article 3 of each of the Geneva Conventions.

(d) "Convention Against Torture" means the Convention Against Torture and Other Cruel, Inhuman or Degrading Treatment or Punishment, December 10, 1984, 1465 U.N.T.S. 85, S. Treaty Doc. No. 100–20 (1988).

(e) "Geneva Conventions" means:

(i) the Convention for the Amelioration of the Condition of the Wounded and Sick in Armed Forces in the Field, August 12, 1949 (6 UST 3114);

(ii) the Convention for the Amelioration of the Condition of Wounded, Sick and Shipwrecked Members of Armed Forces at Sea, August 12, 1949 (6 UST 3217);

(iii) the Convention Relative to the Treatment of Prisoners of War, August 12, 1949 (6 UST 3316); and

(iv) the Convention Relative to the Protection of Civilian Persons in Time of War, August 12, 1949 (6 UST 3516).

(f) "Treated humanely," "violence to life and person," "murder of all kinds," "mutilation," "cruel treatment," "torture," "outrages upon personal dignity," and "humiliating and degrading treatment" refer to, and have the same meaning as, those same terms in Common Article 3.

(g) The terms "detention facilities" and "detention facility" in section 4(a) of this order do not refer to facilities used only to hold people on a short-term, transitory basis.

Sec. 3. Standards and Practices for Interrogation of Individuals in the Custody or Control of the United States in Armed Conflicts.

(a) *Common Article 3 Standards as a Minimum Baseline.* Consistent with the requirements of the Federal torture statute, 18 U.S.C. 2340–2340A, section 1003 of the Detainee Treatment Act of 2005, 42 U.S.C. 2000dd, the Convention Against Torture, Common Article 3, and other laws regulating the treatment and interrogation of individuals detained in any armed conflict, such persons shall in all circumstances be treated humanely and shall not be subjected to violence to life and person (including murder of all kinds, mutilation, cruel treatment, and torture), nor to outrages upon personal dignity (including humiliating and degrading treatment), whenever such individuals are in the custody or under the effective control of an officer, employee, or other agent of the United States Government or detained within a facility owned, operated, or controlled by a department or agency of the United States.

(b) *Interrogation Techniques and Interrogation-Related Treatment.* Effective immediately, an individual in the custody or under the effective control of an officer, employee, or other agent of the United States Government, or detained within a facility owned, operated, or controlled by a department or agency of the United States, in any armed conflict, shall not be subjected to any interrogation technique or approach, or any treatment related to interrogation, that is not authorized by and listed in Army Field Manual 2–22.3 (Manual). Interrogation techniques, approaches, and treatments described in the Manual shall be implemented strictly in accord with the principles, processes, conditions, and limitations the Manual prescribes. Where processes required by the Manual, such as a requirement of approval by specified Department of Defense officials, are inapposite to a department or an agency other than the Department of Defense, such a department or agency shall use processes that are substantially equivalent to the processes the Manual prescribes for the Department of Defense. Nothing in this section shall preclude the Federal Bureau of Investigation, or other Federal law enforcement agencies, from continuing to use authorized, non-coercive techniques of interrogation that are designed to elicit voluntary statements and do not involve the use of force, threats, or promises.

(c) *Interpretations of Common Article 3 and the Army Field Manual.* From this day forward, unless the Attorney General with appropriate consultation provides further guidance, officers, employees, and other agents of the United States Government may, in conducting interrogations, act in reliance upon Army Field Manual 2–22.3, but may not, in conducting interrogations, rely upon any interpretation of the law governing interrogation—including interpretations of Federal criminal laws, the Convention Against Torture, Common Article 3, Army Field Manual 2–22.3, and its predecessor document, Army Field Manual 34–52—issued by the Department of Justice between September 11, 2001, and January 20, 2009.

Sec. 4. Prohibition of Certain Detention Facilities, and Red Cross Access to Detained Individuals.

(a) *CIA Detention.* The CIA shall close as expeditiously as possible any detention facilities that it currently operates and shall not operate any such detention facility in the future.

(b) *International Committee of the Red Cross Access to Detained Individuals.* All departments and agencies of the Federal Government shall provide the International Committee of the Red Cross with notification of, and timely access to, any individual detained in any armed conflict in the custody or under the effective control of an officer, employee, or other agent of the United States Government or detained within a facility owned, operated, or controlled by a department or agency of the United States Government, consistent with Department of Defense regulations and policies.

Sec. 5. Special Interagency Task Force on Interrogation and Transfer Policies.

(a) *Establishment of Special Interagency Task Force.* There shall be established a Special Task Force on Interrogation and Transfer Policies (Special Task Force) to review interrogation and transfer policies.

(e) *Mission.* The mission of the Special Task Force shall be:

(i) to study and evaluate whether the interrogation practices and techniques in Army Field Manual 2–22.3, when employed by departments or agencies outside the military, provide an appropriate means of acquiring the intelligence necessary to protect the Nation, and, if warranted, to recommend any additional or different guidance for other departments or agencies; and

(ii) to study and evaluate the practices of transferring individuals to other nations in order to ensure that such practices comply with the domestic laws, international obligations, and policies of the United States and do not result in the transfer of individuals to other nations to face torture or otherwise for the purpose, or with the effect, of undermining or circumventing the commitments or obligations of the United States to ensure the humane treatment of individuals in its custody or control.

Executive Order 13492 of January 22, 2009, Review and Disposition of Individuals Detained At the Guantánamo Bay Naval Base And Closure Of Detention Facilities

By the authority vested in me as President by the Constitution and the laws of the United States of America, in order to effect the appropriate disposition of individuals currently detained by the Department of Defense at the Guantánamo Bay Naval Base (Guantánamo) and promptly to close detention facilities at Guantánamo, consistent with the national security and foreign policy interests of the United States and the interests of justice, I hereby order as follows:

Sec. 1. Definitions.

As used in this order:

(a) "Common Article 3" means Article 3 of each of the Geneva Conventions.

(b) "Geneva Conventions" means:

    (i) the Convention for the Amelioration of the Condition of the Wounded and Sick in Armed Forces in the Field, August 12, 1949 (6 UST 3114);

    (ii) the Convention for the Amelioration of the Condition of Wounded, Sick and Shipwrecked Members of Armed Forces at Sea, August 12, 1949 (6 UST 3217);

    (iii) the Convention Relative to the Treatment of Prisoners of War, August 12, 1949 (6 UST 3316); and

    (iv) the Convention Relative to the Protection of Civilian Persons in Time of War, August 12, 1949 (6 UST 3516).

(c) "Individuals currently detained at Guantánamo" and "individuals covered by this order" mean individuals currently detained by the Department of Defense in facilities at the Guantánamo Bay Naval Base whom the Department of Defense has ever determined to be, or treated as, enemy combatants.

Sec. 2. Findings.

(a) Over the past 7 years, approximately 800 individuals whom the Department of Defense has ever determined to be, or treated as, enemy combatants have been detained at Guantánamo. The Federal Government has moved more than 500 such detainees from Guantánamo, either by returning them to their home country or by releasing or transferring them to a third country. The Department of Defense has determined that a number of the individuals currently detained at Guantánamo are eligible for such transfer or release.

(b) Some individuals currently detained at Guantánamo have been there for more than 6 years, and most have been detained for at least 4 years. In view of the significant concerns raised by these detentions, both within the United States and internationally, prompt and appropriate disposition of the individuals currently detained at Guantánamo and closure of the facilities in which they are detained would further the national security and foreign policy interests of the United States and the interests of justice. Merely closing the facilities without promptly determining the appropriate disposition of the individuals detained would not adequately serve those interests. To the extent practicable, the prompt and appropriate disposition of the individuals detained at Guantánamo should precede the closure of the detention facilities at Guantánamo.

(c) The individuals currently detained at Guantánamo have the constitutional privilege of the writ of habeas corpus. Most of those individuals have filed petitions for a writ of habeas corpus in Federal court challenging the lawfulness of their detention.

(d) It is in the interests of the United States that the executive branch undertake a prompt and thorough review of the factual and legal bases for the continued detention of all individuals currently held at Guantánamo, and of whether their continued detention is in the national security and foreign policy interests of the United States and in the interests of justice. The unusual circumstances associated with detentions at Guantánamo require a comprehensive interagency review.

(e) New diplomatic efforts may result in an appropriate disposition of a substantial number of individuals currently detained at Guantánamo.

(f) Some individuals currently detained at Guantánamo may have committed offenses for which they should be prosecuted. It is in the interests of the United States to review whether and how any such individuals can and should be prosecuted.

(g) It is in the interests of the United States that the executive branch conduct a prompt and thorough review of the circumstances of the individuals currently detained at Guantánamo who have been charged with offenses before military commissions pursuant to the Military Commissions Act of 2006, Public Law 109–366, as well as of the military commission process more generally.

Sec. 3. Closure of Detention Facilities at Guantánamo.

The detention facilities at Guantánamo for individuals covered by this order shall be closed as soon as practicable, and no later than 1 year from the date of this order. If any individuals covered by this order remain in detention at Guantánamo at the time of closure of those detention facilities, they shall be returned to their home country, released, transferred to a third country, or transferred to another United States detention facility in a manner consistent with law and the national security and foreign policy interests of the United States.

Sec. 4. Immediate Review of All Guantánamo Detentions.

(a) *Scope and Timing of Review.* A review of the status of each individual currently detained at Guantánamo (Review) shall commence immediately.

Executive Order 13493 of January 22, 2009, Review of Detention Policy Options

By the authority vested in me as President by the Constitution and the laws of the United States of America, in order to develop policies for the detention, trial, transfer, release, or other disposition of individuals captured or apprehended in connection with armed conflicts and counterterrorism operations that are consistent with the national security and foreign policy interests of the United States and the interests of justice, I hereby order as follows:

Sec. 1. Special Interagency Task Force on Detainee Disposition.

(a) *Establishment of Special Interagency Task Force.* There shall be established a Special Task Force on Detainee Disposition (Special Task Force) to identify lawful options for the disposition of individuals captured or apprehended in connection with armed conflicts and counterterrorism operations.

(e) *Mission.* The mission of the Special Task Force shall be to conduct a comprehensive review of the lawful options available to the Federal Government with respect to the apprehension, detention, trial, transfer, release, or other disposition of individuals captured or apprehended in connection with armed conflicts and counterterrorism operations, and to identify such options as are consistent with the national security and foreign policy interests of the United States and the interests of justice.

Military Commissions Act of 2009[20]

SEC. 1801. SHORT TITLE. This title may be cited as the "Military Commissions Act of 2009".

SEC. 1802. MILITARY COMMISSIONS. Chapter 47A of title 10, United States Code, is amended to read as follows:

"§ 948a. Definitions

"In this chapter:

"(1) ALIEN.— The term 'alien' means an individual who is not a citizen of the United States.

"(3) COALITION PARTNER.— The term 'coalition partner', with respect to hostilities engaged in by the United States, means any State or armed force directly engaged along with the United States in such hostilities or providing direct operational support to the United States in connection with such hostilities.

"(6) PRIVILEGED BELLIGERENT.— The term 'privileged belligerent' means an individual belonging to one of the eight categories enumerated in Article 4 of the Geneva Convention Relative to the Treatment of Prisoners of War.

"(7) UNPRIVILEGED ENEMY BELLIGERENT.— The term 'unprivileged enemy belligerent' means an individual (other than a privileged belligerent) who—

"(A) has engaged in hostilities against the United States or its coalition partners;

"(B) has purposefully and materially supported hostilities against the United States or its coalition partners; or

"(C) was a part of al Qaeda at the time of the alleged offense under this chapter.

"(9) HOSTILITIES.— The term 'hostilities' means any conflict subject to the laws of war.

"§ 948b. Military Commissions Generally

"(a) PURPOSE.— This chapter establishes procedures governing the use of military commissions to try alien unprivileged enemy belligerents for violations of the law of war and other offenses triable by military commission.

"(b) AUTHORITY FOR MILITARY COMMISSIONS UNDER THIS CHAPTER.— The President is authorized to establish military commissions under this chapter for offenses triable by military commission as provided in this chapter.

"(c) CONSTRUCTION OF PROVISIONS.— The procedures for military commissions set forth in this chapter are based upon the procedures for trial by general courts-martial under chapter 47 of this title (the Uniform Code of Military Justice). Chapter 47 of this title does not, by its terms, apply to trial by military commission except as specifically provided therein or in this chapter, and many of the provisions of chapter 47 of this title are by their terms inapplicable to military commissions. The judicial construction and application of chapter 47 of this title, while instructive, is therefore not of its own force binding on military commissions established under this chapter.

"(d) INAPPLICABILITY OF CERTAIN PROVISIONS.— (1) The following provisions of this title shall not apply to trial by military commission under this chapter:

"(A) Section 810 (article 10 of the Uniform Code of Military Justice), relating to speedy trial, including any rule of courtsmartial relating to speedy trial.

"(B) Sections 831(a), (b), and (d) (articles 31(a), (b), and (d) of the Uniform Code of Military Justice), relating to compulsory self-incrimination.

"(C) Section 832 (article 32 of the Uniform Code of Military Justice), relating to pretrial investigation.

"(2) Other provisions of chapter 47 of this title shall apply to trial by military commission under this chapter only to the extent provided by the terms of such provisions or by this chapter.

"(e) GENEVA CONVENTIONS NOT ESTABLISHING PRIVATE RIGHT OF ACTION.—

No alien unprivileged enemy belligerent subject to trial by military commission under this chapter may invoke the Geneva Conventions as a basis for a private right of action.

"§ 948c. Persons Subject to Military Commissions

"Any alien unprivileged enemy belligerent is subject to trial by military commission as set forth in this chapter.

"§ 948d. Jurisdiction of Military Commissions

"A military commission under this chapter shall have jurisdiction to try persons subject to this chapter for any offense made punishable by this chapter, sections 904 and 906 of this title (articles 104 and 106 of the Uniform Code of Military Justice), or the law of war, whether such offense was committed before, on, or after September 11, 2001, and may, under such limitations as the President may prescribe, adjudge any punishment not forbidden by this chapter, including the penalty of death when specifically authorized under this chapter. A military commission is a competent tribunal to make a finding sufficient for jurisdiction.

"§ 948j. Military judge of a military commission

"(a) DETAIL OF MILITARY JUDGE.—

A military judge shall be detailed to each military commission under this chapter. The Secretary of Defense shall prescribe regulations providing for the manner in which military judges are so detailed to military commissions. The military judge shall preside over each military commission to which such military judge has been detailed.

ENDNOTES

1. The United Nations International Covenant On Civil And Political Rights. http://www.hrweb.org/legal/cpr.html.
2. Declaration On The Protection Of All Persons From Being Subjected To Torture And Other Cruel, Inhuman Or Degrading Treatment Or Punishment, December 9, 1975. http://www.un-documents.net/dpptcidt.htm.
3. Convention Against Torture And Other Cruel, Inhuman or Degrading Treatment or Punishment, December 10, 1984. http://untreaty.un.org/english/treatyevent2001/pdf/07e.pdf.
4. Executive Order 12949–Foreign Intelligence Physical Searches, February 9, 1995, 60 FR 8169; February 13, 1995. http://www.fas.org/irp/offdocs/eo/eo-12949.htm.
5. Military Order of November 13, 2001—Detention, Treatment, and Trial of Certain Non-Citizens in the War Against Terrorism. http://frwebgate.access.gpo.gov/cgi-bin/getdoc.cgi?dbname=2001_register&docid=01-28904-filed.pdf.
6. Department of Defense, Military Commission order No. 1, Procedures for Trial by Military commission of Certain Non-United States Citizens in the War Against Terrorism, March 21, 2002. http://www.defenselink.mil/news/Mar2002/d20020321ord.pdf.
7. Detainee Treatment Act of 2005, [as included in the Department of Defense Appropriations Act, 2006, December 30, 2005. http://thomas.loc.gov/cgi-bin/query] http://jurist.law.pitt.edu/gazette/2005/12/detainee-treatment-act-of-2005-white.php.
8. Military Commissions Act Of 2006, Public Law 109–366. http://frwebgate.access.gpo.gov/cgi-bin/getdoc.cgi?dbname=109_cong_public_laws&docid=f:publ366.109.
9. Executive Order 13425 of February 14, 2007, Trial of Alien Unlawful Enemy Combatants by Military, Commission, Federal Register Vol. 72, No. 33. http://edocket.access.gpo.gov/2007/pdf/07-780.pdf.
10. Executive Order 13440—Interpretation of the Geneva Conventions Common Article 3 as Applied to a Program of Detention and Interrogation Operated by the Central Intelligence Agency, July 24, 2007, Federal Register Vol. 72, No. 14. http://edocket.access.gpo.gov/2007/pdf/07-3656.pdf.
11. Executive Order 13492 of January 22, 2009, Review and Disposition of Individuals Detained At the Guantanamo Bay Naval Base and Closure of Detention Facilities. http://edocket.access.gpo.gov/2009/pdf/E9-1893.pdf.
12. Executive Order 13493 of January 22, 2009, Review of Detention Policy Options. http://edocket.access.gpo.gov/2009/pdf/E9-1895.pdf.
13. Executive Order 13491—Ensuring Lawful Interrogations, January 27, 2009. http://edocket.access.gpo.gov/2009/pdf/E9-1885.pdf.
14. Military Commissions Act of 2009, Public Law 111–84. http://frwebgate.access.gpo.gov/cgi-bin/getdoc.cgi?dbname=111_cong_bills&docid=f:h2647enr.txt.pdf.
15. Charter of the United Nations. http://www2.ohchr.org/english/law/.

16. Universal Declaration of Human Rights, December 10, 1948. http://www.un.org/en/documents/udhr/index.shtml#ap.

17. The Fourth Geneva Convention, (August 12, 1949). http://www.jewishvirtuallibrary.org/jsource/History/Human_Rights/geneva1.html.

18. Convention Against Torture And Other Cruel, Inhuman or Degrading Treatment or Punishment. http://untreaty.un.org/english/treatyevent2001/pdf/07e.pdf.

19. Military Commissions Act Of 2006, [Page 120 STAT. 2600], Public Law 109–366. http://frwebgate.access.gpo.gov/cgi-bin/getdoc.cgi?dbname=109_cong_public_laws&docid=f:publ366.109.

20. Military Commissions Act of 2009, Public Law 111–84. October 28, 2009. http://frwebgate.access.gpo.gov/cgi-bin/getdoc.cgi?dbname=111_cong_bills&docid=f:h2647enr.txt.pdf.

ADDITIONAL RESOURCES

"Not a Suicide Pact, The Constitution in a Time of National Emergency," by Richard A. Posner, Oxford University Press, 2006.

"Closing the Guantanamo Detention Center: Legal Issues," by Michael John Garcia, Elizabeth B. Bazan, R. Chuck Mason, Edward C. Liu, and Anna C. Henning, Congressional Research Service, R40139, November 2009, http://opencrs.com/document/R40139/

"Comparison of Rights in Military Commission Trials and Trials in Federal Criminal Court," by Jennifer K. Elsea, Congressional Research Service, November 19, 2009, R40932, http://opencrs.com/document/R40932/

"Guantanamo Detention Center: Legislative Activity in the 111th Congress," by Anna C. Henning, Congressional Research Service, R40754, November 6, 2009, http://opencrs.com/document/R40754/

"A Review of the FBI's Involvement in and Observations of Detainee Interrogations in Guantanamo Bay, Afghanistan, and Iraq," October 2009 (Revised), U.S. Department of Justice, Office of Inspector General, http://www.justice.gov/oig/special/s0910.pdf

"USA must grant Bagram detainees access to US courts," Amnesty International, September 16, 2009, http://www.amnesty.org/en/news-and-updates/report/usa-must-grant-bagram-detainees-access-us-courts-20090916

"Enemy Combatant Detainees: *Habeas Corpus* Challenges in Federal Court," by Jennifer K. Elsea, Kenneth R. Thomas, Michael John Garcia, September 15, 2009, Congressional Research Service, RL33180, http://opencrs.com/document/RL33180/

"The Military Commissions Act of 2006: Background and Proposed Amendments," Jennifer K. Elsea, CRS September 8, 2009, R40752, http://opencrs.com/document/R40752/

"Renditions: Constraints Imposed by Laws on Torture," Michael John Garcia, September 8, 2009, Congressional Research Service, RL32890, http://opencrs.com/document/RL32890/

Unclassified Report on the President's Surveillance Program United States. Dept. of Justice. Office of the Inspector General; United States. Central Intelligence Agency. Office of Inspector General; United States. Office of the Director of National Intelligence. Office of the Inspector General; United States. Dept. of Defense. Office of the Inspector General; United States. National Security Agency. Office of Inspector General. 10 July 2009, http://judiciary.house.gov/hearings/pdf/IGTSPReport090710.pdf

Detainee Abuse Reviewed, Brookings Institute. This site lists several Brookings articles about detaining terrorists and Guantanamo Bay. http://www.brookings.edu/multimedia/video/2009/0828_detainees_wittes.aspx

Military Law and Legal Links, Air War College. Website with extensive resources and links related to military law. http://www.au.af.mil/au/awc/awcgate/awc-law.htm

Obama Administration To Revive Fatally Flawed Military Commissions, Decision Strikes Blow To Due Process And Rule Of Law, ACLU, 5/15/2009, http://www.aclu.org/safefree/detention/39601prs20090515.html

World Today, Volume 65, Number 8/9, August 2009, three articles about Geneva Conventions. http://www.chathamhouse.org.uk/publications/twt/current/Geneva Conventions Sixty Years On: Changing War, Changing Law, Adam Roberts The Geneva Conventions: Safeguarding Civilians, Barbara Stocking Geneva Conventions and the Media: Bearing Witness, Nik Gowing

"Analysis of /Selected Legislative Proposals, Addressing Guantanamo Detainees," by Anna C. Henning, May 11, 2009, CRS R40419, http://opencrs.com/document/R40419

Enemy Combatant Detainees: Habeas Corpus Challenges in Federal Court April 07, 2009, CRS RL33180, http://opencrs.com/document/RL33180/2009-04-07

The Military Commissions Act of 2006: Analysis of Procedural Rules and Comparison with Previous DOD Rules and the Uniform Code of Military Justice, Congressional Research Service, Updated September 27, 2007, Jennifer K. Elsea, RL33688, http://fas.org/sgp/crs/natsec/RL33688.pdf

Justice delayed and justice denied? Trials under the Military Commissions Act, Amnesty International, Index Number: AMR 51/044/2007, Date Published: 22 March 2007, http://www.amnesty.org/en/library/info/AMR51/044/2007 Also see Amnesty International http://www.amnestyusa.org/war-on-terror/fair-trials/page.do?id=1041195

DoD Releases Military Commissions Manual, by Sgt. Sara Wood, USA American Forces Press Service, Jan. 18, 2007, http://www.defenselink.mil/news/newsarticle.aspx?id=2745

Treatment of "Battlefield Detainees" in the War on Terrorism, Updated November 14, 2006, Jennifer K. Elsea, CRS RL31367, http://fpc.state.gov/documents/organization/76896.pdf

Stanford Report, Military Commissions Act a 'poisoned chalice,' scholar warns during symposium, by Lisa Trei, October 25, 2006, http://news.stanford.edu/news/2006/october25/human-102506.html

The death of habeas corpus, Keith Olbermann: 'The president has now succeeded where no one has before,' MSNBC, Commentary, Countdown, Oct. 11, 2006, http://www.msnbc.msn.com/id/15220450/

The War Crimes Act: Current Issues, Updated October 2, 2006, Michael John Garcia, CRS RL33662, http://www.au.af.mil/au/awc/awcgate/crs/rl33662.pdf

The Department of Defense Rules for Military Commissions: Analysis of Procedural Rules and Comparison with Proposed Legislation and the Uniform Code of Military Justice, Congressional Research Service, Updated September 25, 2006, Jennifer K. Elsea, RL31600, http://ftp.fas.org/sgp/crs/natsec/RL31600.pdf

The Department of Defense Rules for Military, Commissions: Analysis of Procedural Rules and Comparison with Proposed Legislation and the Uniform Code of Military Justice, Updated August 4, 2005, Jennifer Elsea, CRS RL31600, http://www.fas.org/irp/crs/RL31600.pdf

24

RESILIENCY AND A CULTURE OF PREPAREDNESS

"Greater civilian participation is necessary both to make military operations successful and to relieve stress on the men and women of the armed forces. Having permanent civilian capabilities available and using them early could also make it less likely that military forces will need to be deployed in the first place."

–National Defense Strategy, June 2008[1]

This chapter discusses efforts to foster a culture of preparedness and resiliency.

SOURCES

- National Strategy for the Physical Protection of Critical Infrastructures and Key Assets, February 2002[2]
- HSPD 8 (22). National Preparedness, December 17, 2003[3]
- HSPD 21 (20). Public Health and Medical Preparedness, October 18, 2007[4]
- 2008 National Defense Strategy[5]
- Top Ten Challenges Facing the Next Secretary of Homeland Security, Homeland Security Advisory Council, September 11, 2008[6]
- Homeland Security 3.0, Building a National Enterprise to Keep America Safe, Free, and Prosperous, September 18, 2008[7]

National Strategy for the Physical Protection of Critical Infrastructures and Key Assets, February 2002

National Resilience: Sustaining Protection for the Long Term. . . .Resilience is characteristic of most U.S. communities, and it is reflected in the ways they cope with natural disasters. Over time, residents of communities in areas that are persistently subjected to natural disasters become accustomed to what to expect when one occurs. Institutions and residents in such areas grow to understand the nature of catastrophic events, as well as their roles and responsibilities in managing their aftereffects. They are also familiar with and rely on trusted community systems and resources that are in place to support protection, response, and recovery efforts. As a result, they have confidence in their communities' abilities to contend with the aftermath of disasters and learn from each event.

Institutions and residents nationwide must likewise come to understand the nature of terrorism, its consequences, and the role they play in combating it. Ideally, they will become familiar with and have confidence in the protection, response, and recovery mechanisms that exist within their communities. Together with local officials, private organizations and residents must work to improve these systems and resources to meet the challenge of safeguarding our country from terrorists.

Our challenge is to identify, build upon, and apply the lessons learned from the September 11 attacks to anticipate and protect against future terrorist attacks on our critical infrastructures and key assets. Our ability to do so will determine how successfully we adapt to the current dynamic threat environment and whether we can emerge as a stronger, more vibrant nation with our values and way of life intact.

HSPD 8. National Preparedness, December 17, 2003

(22). Citizen Participation. The Secretary shall work with other appropriate Federal departments and agencies as well as State and local governments and the private sector to

Foundations of Homeland Security: Law and Policy, First Edition. Martin J. Alperen.
© 2011 John Wiley & Sons, Inc. Published 2011 by John Wiley & Sons, Inc.

encourage active citizen participation and involvement in preparedness efforts. The Secretary shall periodically review and identify the best community practices for integrating private citizen capabilities into local preparedness efforts.

HSPD 21. Public Health And Medical Preparedness, October 18, 2007

(20). Community Resilience: The above components address the supply side of the preparedness function, ultimately providing enhanced services to our citizens. The demand side is of equal importance. Where local civic leaders, citizens, and families are educated regarding threats and are empowered to mitigate their own risk, where they are practiced in responding to events, where they have social networks to fall back upon, and where they have familiarity with local public health and medical systems, there will be community resilience that will significantly attenuate the requirement for additional assistance. The Federal Government must formulate a comprehensive plan for promoting community public health and medical preparedness to assist State and local authorities in building resilient communities in the face of potential catastrophic health events.

2008 National Defense Strategy

"...We as a nation must strengthen not only our military capabilities, but also reinvigorate other important elements of national power and develop the capability to integrate, tailor, and apply these tools as needed. We must tap the full strength of America and its people...

The Department of Defense has taken on many of these burdens. Our forces have stepped up to the task of long-term reconstruction, development and governance. The U.S. Armed Forces will need to institutionalize and retain these capabilities, but this is no replacement for civilian involvement and expertise. The United States must improve its ability to deploy civilian expertise rapidly, and continue to increase effectiveness by joining with organizations and people outside of government – untapped resources with enormous potential. We can make better use of the expertise of our universities and of industry to assist in reconstruction and long-term improvements to economic vitality and good governance. Greater civilian participation is necessary both to make military operations successful and to relieve stress on the men and women of the armed forces. Having permanent civilian capabilities available and using them early could also make it less likely that military forces will need to be deployed in the first place."

Top Ten Challenges Facing The Next Secretary Of Homeland Security, Homeland Security Advisory Council, September 11, 2008

"... iv. *Strategic Initiatives.* In addition to the previous objectives, there are a number of strategic national challenges that the next Secretary will need to address. These include shifting our preparedness and protection efforts towards a concept of national resiliency, finding the right balance between security and openness at our borders, and building the framework that will support a risk management approach to the homeland.

Key Challenge 7: Lead The Building of a Resilient America. Critical infrastructure is the enabler of our national economic and social activity and therefore, a central focus of our homeland security efforts. While the Department's role in promoting infrastructure protection is important, recent infrastructure failures and their cascading consequences have demonstrated that a focus based solely on protection is not enough. As a nation, we cannot protect everything, against all things, at all times, and at all costs. Fortress America thinking is an unattainable goal and the wrong national strategy ... The ability to absorb the blows and quickly snap back from the consequences of any event, natural or manmade, will be the measure of long-term security success. The Nation-wide application of a "resilience metric" (i.e., time to reconstitution of every day services and routines of life) builds on traditional, sector-focused protection efforts and provides the means to objectively assess, triage, and significantly mitigate and effectively manage the initial and cascading consequences of infrastructure service disruption, regardless of cause. An all-hazards approach to building resiliency should become an overarching theme throughout our homeland security enterprises.

Public-private partnerships. Resilience is a unifying goal that must be addressed by the entire Federal Government and Nation. Thus, the new Secretary must ensure that DHS policies and programs empower, enable and leverage the experience, vision and innovation that reside in private sector, community, state and regional-based resilience efforts. Ensure continuous improvement in national resilience by actively engaging and acting upon private-sector and academic-sector thought ... As an extension of the above, the government must also support the development of a nationwide system of community-based, cross-sector, resilience-focused partnerships to empower communities to collaborate in their collective best interests."

Homeland Security 3.0, Building A National Enterprise To Keep America Safe, Free, And Prosperous, September 18, 2008[8]

FINDING #1: Energizing and engaging individuals in efforts to improve the safety of their families and communities must be the centerpiece of a national homeland security enterprise. Voluntary community actions have been a longstanding American way of solving thorny problems. Embodied in the U.S. Constitution, the principles of limited government and federalism give citizens and local communities the greatest role in shaping their lives. Government simply cannot be at all places at all times to protect against all contingencies. This principle is evident in the 10th Amendment, which states, "The powers not delegated to the United States by the Constitution, nor prohibited by it to the States, are reserved to the States respectively, or to the people."

In matters relating to their communities, local jurisdictions have the preponderance of authority and autonomy. Moreover, they will be the first on the scene and the first to act in the aftermath of a disaster. The best communities accept these responsibilities and take an all-hazards approach to emergency and public safety planning and preparedness by optimizing community responses to meet the range of natural and manmade dangers (e.g., storms, floods, terrorist incidents, and other malicious acts)...

FINDING #3: Despite a presidential directive (HSPD–7)[9] that emphasized the importance of grassroots efforts, many factors have worked against establishing a national culture of preparedness. The first factor is the "not me" syndrome. In the aftermath of Hurricane Katrina and just before hurricane season started in 2006, the American Red Cross polled Americans in hurricane-prone areas on their preparedness activities. Given the sheer devastation and extensive reporting on the impact of Hurricane Katrina, most Americans saw hours of videos and pictures that should have driven home the importance of being prepared. Yet the poll results indicated that the vast majority of households had failed to take even the most basic steps, such as establishing a meeting place, making an evacuation plan, or selecting an emergency contact. According to a Harris poll one year later, the numbers remained largely unchanged. Americans are largely ambivalent to preparedness because they do not believe that they will ever be victims. This is equally true with preparedness for terrorist incidents. The reality is that most Americans live in areas where the risk of and potential danger from a catastrophic incident such as a terrorist attack or natural disaster (except for cybersecurity and pandemic flu) is low.

The second factor is the government's impaired credibility. A pattern over several years of raising and lowering alert levels and of misunderstanding the major threats of the day has led to a public wary and doubtful of government warnings. In regard to terrorism, when the government continues to warn the public that "it's not a matter of if, but when we will be attacked," the question for some becomes "Why should we prepare if the government is just going to get it wrong again?"

The third factor is failed government leadership. Not until a private initiative brought the Ready.gov program in its entirety to federal officials did the government even try to engage individuals and communities in preparedness. Right or wrong, the only elements of the readiness program that

people still remember are to buy duct tape and go shopping. Regrettably, when the public was most open to government guidance, botched communications and/or flawed reporting made a mockery of the value of preparedness and the serious steps that individuals can take to help themselves and their communities.

ENDNOTES

1. National Defense Strategy, June 2008. http://www.defenselink.mil/news/2008%20national%20defense%20strategy.pdf.
2. National Strategy for the Physical Protection of Critical Infrastructures and Key Assets, February, 2002. http://www.dhs.gov/xlibrary/assets/Physical_Strategy.pdf.
3. HSPD 8, December 17, 2003. http://www.dhs.gov/xabout/laws/gc_1215444247124.shtm.
4. HSPD 21, http://www.dhs.gov/xabout/laws/gc_1219263961449.shtm.
5. 2008 National Defense Strategy, June 2008, p. 17. http://www.defenselink.mil/news/2008%20national%20defense%20strategy.pdf.
6. Top Ten Challenges...Homeland Security Advisory Council, September 11, 2008. http://www.dhs.gov/xlibrary/assets/hsac_dhs_top_10_challenges_report.pdf.
7. David Heyman and James Jay Carafano, Ph.D., "Homeland Security 3.0, Building a National Enterprise to Keep America Safe, Free, and Prosperous," The Heritage Foundation Special Report, Center for Strategic and International Studies, SR-23, September 18, 2008, p. 5. http://www.heritage.org/Research/HomelandDefense/upload/sr_23.pdf.
8. David Heyman and James Jay Carafano, Ph.D., "Homeland Security 3.0, Building a National Enterprise to Keep America Safe, Free, and Prosperous," The Heritage Foundation Special Report, Center for Strategic and International Studies, SR-23, September 18, 2008, p.5. http://www.heritage.org/Research/HomelandDefense/upload/sr_23.pdf. (accessed May 11, 2009).
9. This author disagrees with the characterization of HSPD7 but agrees with the remainder of Finding #3.

ADDITIONAL RESOURCES

Defense Horizon, no. 69 - To Build Resilience: Leader Influence on Mental Hardiness, by Paul T. Bartone, Charles L. Barry, and Robert E. Armstrong, Center for Technology and National Security Policy, November 2009, http://www.ndu.edu/inss/press/dh/DH69.pdf

"Exploring the Relationship between Homeland Security Information Sharing & Local Emergency Preparedness." Hamilton Bean, *Homeland Security Affairs* V, no. 2 (May 2009), http://www.hsaj.org/?article=5.2.5

25

EUROPEAN HOMELAND SECURITY: A WORK IN PROGRESS

JOHN L. CLARKE

George C. Marshall European Center for Security Studies

INTRODUCTION: SECURING THE EUROPEAN HOMELAND – A CAUTIONARY TALE

Though it appears that it has taken the attacks in London and Madrid, as well as many attempted attacks, to bring it home, there can no longer be any gainsaying that Europe is under attack. Given the open nature of European society, the target of the attacks is not only national governments, but also the fabric of European, and, by extension, Western culture. Europe's great experiment in creating an ever-closer union is itself a target, for if terrorists succeed, they may convince large segments of European society that security is indeed divisible; that safety can be purchased through accommodation to terror; and that guns, guards and gates are the only tools available to societies to defend themselves. This is the unfortunate conclusion one must draw to if Europe is not able to summon the courage and resources to respond as a union to these challenges. This study examines how Europe, and specifically the European Union, has responded over the past decade to these challenges and how the EU is measuring up to the new range of threats presented by terrorists and catastrophic attacks.

It is a cautionary tale, for while Europe's political leaders clearly recognize the threats and the dangers they pose, the record of Europe's accomplishment has not proceeded as rapidly as the threat has grown. It would be most regrettable if it took an attack of catastrophic proportions to bring Europeans to the understanding that actions, not words, are the currency understood by terrorists and that the security

of one state, or city, is inextricably bound up with that of its neighbors.

While the September 11, 2001 attacks may have changed the strategic landscape for the United States with regard to the threat posed by terrorism, Europeans have long claimed to have a much greater store of experience, and therefore wisdom, with regard to these threats. After all, European countries have been confronted with a broad range of threats over the past few decades, from IRA bombings in London to ETA bombings in Madrid, as well as Corsican, Breton, South Tyrolean, Red Brigades, Red Army Faction terrorists…the list goes on.

But the Paris, Moscow, Madrid and London mass transit bombings, as well as numerous attempted attacks, ought to have changed the perception that Europeans intrinsically know how to manage these threats in a superior and more effective manner when compared to the United States. While separatist and extremist groups posed a serious threat – and, indeed, some still do – the threat posed by religiously motivated extremist groups is fundamentally and qualitatively different.

Nearly a decade after the events of 11th September 2001, and now five years after the London bombing of July 2005, much progress has been made on both sides of the Atlantic—but much remains to be done.

While many express the view that the campaigns in Iraq and Afghanistan have exacerbated the global terrorist threat, it seems reasonable to conclude that, given the trends in the Muslim world, the threat would have continued to grow in any event.

On the positive side of the ledger, the number of successful attacks in both Europe and America has been less than many would have imagined after the attacks of

Foundations of Homeland Security: Law and Policy, First Edition. Martin J. Alperen.
© 2011 John Wiley & Sons, Inc. Published 2011 by John Wiley & Sons, Inc.

September 2001—and far less sophisticated as well. The failure of the recent attempted car bombing attacks in London and Glasgow as well as the airline bombing attempt over Detroit points to the still-extant lack of sophistication on the part of would-be bombers.

Of great importance, the much-feared attack with weapons of mass destruction (WMD) has not happened–yet. However, the use of chlorine gas attacks in Iraq points to the increasingly probability that industrial gases maybe used in future attacks in Europe or the US.

In addition, an unknown number—at least to the public—of attacks have been prevented, through the undeniable disruption of terrorist networks and through increased security measures. Of perhaps even greater importance, high-quality intelligence work has resulted in the prevention and, indeed, preemption, of a number of potential attacks.

Of course, these successes have come at some price to the individual liberties treasured on both sides of the Atlantic. But it should be noted that the public has, thus far, been very accepting of the additional burdens placed on their societies. It seems fair to say that the balance between liberty and security has become more stable in recent years. But the fact remains that the greatest threat to these freedoms is the next terrorist attack. If that attack involves large numbers of casualties, or the use of WMD, then the public will demand, and governments will supply, security measures which may have a significant impact on liberty.

That said, much remains to be done, and the approaches countering terrorism on both sides of the Atlantic remain significantly different. Indeed, these approaches have settled into caricatures that, regrettably, inform much public opinion in Europe and America.

Europe is viewed in Washington as essentially soft on terrorism and, even more damaging, as a potential source of threat to the US. Americans are cognizant that many threats may emanate from Europe in the form of visitors who do not require visas or even illegal immigrants. The Ft. Dix, New Jersey plan involved Albanian immigrants who had come in the aftermath of the wars in former Yugoslavia.

On the other hand, the US is viewed as far too muscular in its approach to terror. It stands accused by much elite opinion in Europe as placing far too much emphasis on the role of military force in preventing and preempting terrorism. European newspapers are replete with cartoons depicting Uncle Sam as Rambo. It is particularly telling that substantial minorities in most Europeans countries—usually around a third of those asked—cite the United States as the greatest threat to security.

Of course, these are caricatures—but, as with many caricatures, they have some elements of truth. Europe does prefer to treat terrorism essentially as a law enforcement problem only—perhaps because Europe lacks the kinds and number of military forces that it could use, assuming it had the political will to do so.

Moreover, Europe, still composed of independent countries, lacks the federal structure of the United States. The difficulties with establishing a common approach to combating terrorism are well known in a region where it remains a national responsibility and it is still easier for a terrorist to move between countries than it is for a police officer to do so in the pursuit of his duties.

Europe has produced an impressive number of actions plans and other measures related to counterterrorism, but the fact remains that it is up to the members to develop the national legislation necessary to implement them.

In the United States, the challenges are different, but no less serious. Whereas Europe has had long experience with domestic terrorists, the US has little; whereas Europe spent the whole Cold War providing homeland defense, the US did not; and whereas most European countries have a ministry of the interior, a domestic intelligence service and a national police force, America lacks all three.

America's response to the attacks nine years ago was to make the biggest change in government since World War II: the creation of the Department of Homeland Security. But the DHS is only vaguely similar to most ministries of the interior or internal security in Europe. It lacks both intelligence and law enforcement capabilities that are commonly found in these ministries. And the DHS was (and remains) overwhelmingly focused on combating terrorism, though this focus has changed somewhat in the aftermath of Hurricane Katrina, to what the Americans call an "all hazards" approach.

There are important differences in strategy as well. America, having suffered 3000 dead in one attack and having been threatened by opponents with the intent and capability to employ WMD, is overwhelmingly concerned with *catastrophic* terrorism. In response, the US has evolved a *capabilities-based* strategy; that is, the Americans will consider what the enemy is capable of doing and take actions to prevent those attacks from occurring.

Risk assessment, key to any counter terror strategy, will be based on the *criticality* and *vulnerability* of potential targets. Key assets, such as aviation and nuclear power, will be hardened to prevent an attack from occurring, and the vulnerability of all assets will be reduced to a minimum consistent with acceptable risk. This also involves a recognition that, particularly after the intelligence failures of the past half decade, surprise will always be with us and intelligence will never be perfect.

Moreover, given the potential for catastrophic terrorism, every effort must be made to prevent and preempt terrorist attacks *before* they occur—even if this means the employment of armed force, where appropriate and possible. From the US perspective, these kinds of terrorist groups are not amenable to traditional concepts of deterrence and dissuasion; they have no demands that can be negotiated, only complied with (withdraw from the Mid-East, abandon Israel, etc).

This approach contrasts sharply with that of the EU and many of its member states. Not believing themselves threatened in the same way as the US (which, it must be said, many in Europe feel it has brought upon itself) and not possessing the same range of capabilities, the Europeans understandably have adopted a different approach.

Lacking a "United States of Europe," each state has had to fend for itself. The result has been a hodge-podge of approaches, with some European states, such as France and the UK, far more robust than others. Other states in Europe are only now beginning to grapple with the domestic threat.

While Europe has far greater experience with terrorism, going back to the 1970's (ETA, IRA, RAF, etc) those group were not focused on catastrophic levels of damage and had at least some kind of negotiable demands (independence for the Basque region, a united Ireland). This kind of terrorism was "manageable" and of a different magnitude when compared to today's threats.

Unlike the US capabilities-based approach, many European countries have adopted a *threat-based* approach, counting on intelligence to give them advance warning of a potential threat and enabling them to take action to prevent it. This strategy puts a premium on good quality, *actionable* intelligence—not an easy task, given the nature of the terrorist enemy.

European risk assessments are based on *probability*, rather than criticality and vulnerability. This approach accepts that there will be attacks and that the main focus of the government's effort must be on recovering from the attacks, or *resilience*, the term used by the UK.

While these strategic differences exist, one should not make too much of them. Both the US and Europe employ all the instruments of power in their fight against terrorism. The Europeans are well represented in military operations in Afghanistan, and the US has a vigorous law enforcement effort which has yielded significant successes—witness the arrest of six suspects who may have planned to attack Ft. Dix.

Indeed, on many issues, there is a great similarity on how to respond to those attacks that do occur. While the US may put a bit more emphasis on trying to prevent attacks, the lessons learned after September 11th and Hurricane Katrina are now clear, and great effort has been made to ensure that the US can recover as quickly as possible. The UK concept of resiliency has fast become the standard for many countries, though few can match the British approach—UK authorities are clear that the next attack is a question of *when*, not *if*.

There remain, of course, a number of issues to be resolved. For example, there is still the problem of air passenger data, in which the US wants more comprehensive information on passengers flying to the US than the Europeans are willing to provide at present. But the level of cooperation between the two continents is significant, if unpublicized.

Security officials on both sides of the Atlantic understand that, in the world we live in today, security cannot be allowed to become divisible. That is, when terrorists can strike the weakest link in an alliance, the danger is that others will seek a separate peace. In a world of terrorists trying to acquire WMD, this is a recipe for catastrophe. And terrorists are working hard to convince people that a strong transatlantic security bond is no longer an asset, but has become a liability.

The lack of a common perception of the threat across the Atlantic represents the biggest problem in transatlantic homeland security. Alliances are predicated on a shared sense of risk. That does not now exist. Will the terrorists succeed where the Soviet Union failed, in convincing Europeans and Americans to abandon their solidarity and seek that separate peace? Therein lies the great danger for us all.

But the Paris, Moscow, Madrid and, now, London mass transit bombings ought to have changed the perception that Europeans intrinsically know how to manage these threats in a superior and more effective manner when compared to the United States. While separatist and extremist groups posed a serious threat – and indeed, some still do – the threat posed by religiously motivated extremist groups is fundamentally and qualitatively different.

The advent of mass casualty suicide attacks and the ever-present threat of an attack with weapons of mass destruction have, or should have, changed the calculus. The European threat-based approach of managing threats as they arise and relying on law enforcement procedures in dealing with them has now been called into question. The extent to which this approach relies on timely and high quality intelligence has been highlighted by the failure of the intelligence services to detect and prevent recent attacks. While Europe is, understandably, far from adopting the capabilities-based approach of the US, its threat based approach, as outlined in this study, is clearly in need of a major shift in direction and focus.

This is of particular importance in a Europe of 27 members, with its transparent borders and ease of movement. For the fact is that the struggle against terrorism in Europe remains very much a national effort, despite the rhetoric of the common EU approach, with its action plans and initiatives, to the contrary. Nearly all of the important steps taken to quell terrorism are found at the level of the member states, particularly in the judicial and law enforcement areas. As this study will demonstrate, Europe, and the EU in particular, does not lack for plans and programs in the area of fighting terrorism. But it does lack the ability to carry out many of these programs, as the EU lacks the power of a national government to implement these programs. Cross border cooperation, while hugely important and growing, remains largely informal.[1] It is a sad testament that it remains easier for a terrorist to cross borders in Europe than it is for a policeman in pursuit of his duties.

The problems begin with terminology. There is little agreement on where public security ends and counterterrorism begins. Indeed, the terms themselves create confusion. Commentators and academics routinely employ the terms "antiterrorism" and "counterterrorism" and, even, "fighting terrorism" and "combating terrorism" nearly interchangeably. From an operational perspective, this creates the potential for serious misunderstanding, as these terms have quite different operational contexts. Antiterrorism should be understood to mean primarily defensive measures, such as security patrols and observation technology, as well as the hardening of potential targets. Counterterrorism, on the other hand, is best understood as meaning active measures to interdict and preempt potential terrorist attacks. Counterterrorism measures may employ not only law enforcement activities but also offensive military operations where appropriate. As to fighting and combating terrorism, they are largely devoid of any operational context and serve principally as literary devices whose resonance is found largely among the media.

These distinctions are of great importance when discussing homeland security as this concept embraces a broad and comprehensive array of anti- and counter terrorist measures. Yet the term homeland security affords us the most comprehensive concept for addressing these issues, even if this term carries its own difficult baggage.

Europe, the US and Homeland Security: Mutual Misunderstanding

"Homeland security" is of distinct US coinage. As such, the term tends to sit uneasily with Europeans, partly because it comes from across the Atlantic, partly because it was conceived by a US administration whose rhetoric tends to antagonize many European polities and partly because it contains vague but worrisome implications for personal privacy. But the principal difficulty is that the logic of a comprehensive homeland security approach would require Europe's political leaders to make some unpalatable decisions.

To secure one's domestic territory in a global sense against terrorist attack, as both US and EU leaderships now aim to do, requires a mobilization of all available means to prevent those attacks or, at a minimum, an elaboration of policy that takes into account all those means. This would embrace, of course, the possible uses of intelligence assets and military resources to prevent or deal with the consequences of a terrorist attack which would require that policymakers review all of their options, to include military ones, if they are to produce effective policy in this area.

Moreover, homeland security, as currently construed in the US, remains outside the purview of the organs of the European Union. It is not, in the EU view, a defined policy area, particularly as it spans a number of policy domains in the EU, such as Justice and Home Affairs, as well as defense and security policy.[2] This renders any formal review problematical, as it would invariably involve a review and harmonization of 27 national homeland security policies.

Such a review has thus far proven extraordinarily difficult in a union of 27 national governments, and particularly among those with long histories of independent foreign and military action. True reform would, inevitably, involve transferring real power and authority, such as investigational and prosecutorial powers, from the national governments to Brussels. Any hint in Brussels of EU responsibility or authority for internal security within the member states remains official anathema in many capitals. The bombings in Madrid and London have aroused much rhetoric that this must change, but little seems to have been really accomplished as yet.

Instead of directly confronting these threats with the necessary institutional adaptations, many EU policymakers use a less confrontational language. They don't refer to homeland security. Europeans prefer terms such as "domestic security," "public security" or, even, "internal security," despite the historical implications of these terms. They refer to "security for the citizen" or "an area of justice, freedom and security" for the EU. These terms are seen to offer both political and pragmatic advantages compared to an ostensibly more hard-edged, comprehensive, US concept of homeland security.

The political advantage is: the Europeans conceive the fight between good and evil in the world, and their political vision and approach to it, in ways that substantially diverge from those of the United States.[3] Due to its own more recent and brutal history, the Old World has drawn certain lessons. According to this logic, Europe is beyond an automatic reliance on brute force; it shies away from direct confrontation in favor of dialogue and positive incentives-based persuasion; it favors the collegial; it seeks the mantle of legitimacy conferred by multilateral versus bilateral solutions; it hands out generous amounts of foreign aid unencumbered by restrictions; and it is always careful in its rhetoric to stress the need for sustainable growth and a fair division of wealth among nations as the keys to international stability and respect for human rights.[4]

This world-view rather neatly stands the EU in sharp contrast to a United States that, rightly or wrongly, is increasingly viewed from abroad as a military bully in a china shop that smashes whatever it wants, whenever it wants in the name of national security. This line of thinking allows the EU to float on the idea that the security of its homeland is not quite as susceptible to attack as that of the United States.

Despite Europe's 30-year battles with domestic terrorism (Spain, Italy, France, Northern Ireland, etc.) and despite the horrific events of the March 2004 bombings in Madrid and those in London in July 2005, as well as the incidents in Germany and the UK in the summer of 2007, there is no denying a certain tendency among a large segment of Europe's polity that, if it can keep the terminology of its rhetoric fine-tuned just so, if it can combine this with the right kinds of humanitarian and development aid, if it can manufacture enough dialogue with potential enemies, if it can placate largely unassimilated domestic minorities, and keep its political distance from the US, then it will defuse or at least minimize the terrorist threat to Europe.[5]

The great danger with this approach is that it provides the opportunity for terrorists to, as noted, succeed where the Soviet Union failed: in persuading many in Europe that the security of the western Alliance is divisible, that Europe can achieve a separate accommodation with the common enemy, and that a close security relationship with the United States has become a liability instead of an asset. As the events in Spain have shown, governments can be persuaded to alter their policies along these lines. The significantly divergent threat assessments of the US and its European (and Canadian) allies is evidence that this approach offers much promise for terrorists bent on causing irreparable damage to the western alliance.

The EU's preference for "security of the citizen" over "homeland security" is not of particularly great utility as a basis for establishing a policy for counter- and anti-terrorism.

But it is Europe's own concept, designed to accommodate an agenda that reflects the homeland security policy goals which 27 national capitals have been able to agree upon, if somewhat reluctantly, and which can only be achieved at the level of the EU. Together, these two terminological devices go some way toward explaining why the EU has ragged fissures in its homeland security policy. Europe's careful choice of words and slogans yields two concrete observations about its homeland security obligations and why these fissures exist. One is the obvious fact that the European continent is surrounded on three sides – southern, southeastern and eastern – by instability, poverty, dubious political regimes and cultural-religious societies that have too little in common with Europe's long and arduous march to secular democracy. Europe also possesses sizeable minorities that remain largely unassimilated into the national societies in which they live. The EU is an institution riddled with policy gaps, split responsibilities, power struggles between national and EU authorities, divisions of policy labor, legal restrictions of nightmarish complexity precluding rapid implementation of homeland security decisions and, lastly, contradictions in doctrine that have a direct bearing on the development and implementation of homeland security across the EU.

As a result of these two factors – fear of provoking potential enemies and the EU/national institutional atomization – there is no open and healthy discussion in Europe by its politicians, bureaucrats, diplomats and its military hierarchies about how to carry out the EU's commitment to create a "security of the citizen."[6] These actors tend to avoid the subject, making oblique references to scenarios that imply a vague future need for more coordination between national security institutions, they explore and perhaps even agree on one bilateral security arrangement or another, they work up a paper exercise or two, or issue impressive-sounding initiatives. But what Europe lacks is serious preparation for the new kinds of terror threats, replete with active cross border planning and including realistic exercises involving security and military forces.

To be fair, a terrorist-engineered event whose impact spread across multiple frontiers in Europe, particularly involving the use of weapons of mass destruction would unavoidably create chaos, regardless of the level of planning and preparation. But a response mechanism that cannot automatically rely on pan-European security and military forces and logistics and which is not predicated on clear predefined security forces command chains that account for all of Europe's internal frontier regions will lead to "anarchy." Europe is not prepared in this regard.

This is not to say that Europe is doomed to ineffectiveness. It is not. There are cause-and effect lags on both sides of the Atlantic. Indeed, in certain policy areas the EU is moving faster than the United States, which cannot guarantee the inviolability of its own borders and which faces enormous logistical and administrative challenges in fusing its 22 national agencies and 180,000 government workers into an effective Department of Homeland Defense.[7] The EU's law enforcement agencies have a long, if informal, tradition of working together, a cross-border practice that is now spreading to other national agencies and ministries of the 27 member states. For example, cooperation in setting up common databases among its judicial and border control authorities in the fight against terrorism is making good progress. The EU is also consolidating its coordination of civil-emergency response networks and identifying national inventories of medical supplies, transport equipment and other stocks that can be shifted from one member state to another for disaster relief.[8]

But national sovereignty remains the greatest barrier to increased cooperation. National sovereignty is an old issue in Europe but it is a tenacious one. Nonetheless, it is under slow but steady attack via the EU's inexorable, if sometimes imperceptible, march into policy domains that have been the exclusive remit of individual countries. The evident failure of the EU constitution may retard this process, but it will not end it. Europe's national bureaucracies and its politicians know this. Some sense it instinctively and accept the inevitable; others demand a clawing back of EU authority. Many member states are doing their best to prevent this and, in the short term, they may succeed in winning tactical skirmishes. The recent bombings in London have conclusively demonstrated that great dangers exist in Europe, including the danger of suicide bombers. It remains, however, to be seen how the continent responds. Many are calling this Europe's wake-up call; but they did that after the 2004 Madrid bombing as well, to little avail. Given this unfortunate situation, it is worth recalling how Europe has approached the issue of homeland security in historical context.

The Evolution of EU Homeland Security

As in the United States, the fall of the Berlin Wall and the Cold War's end meant Europe could focus on the less contentious problems of domestic security such as organized crime, illegal immigration, drug-running networks and money laundering activities. While the instability and tensions produced by the Balkan wars of the mid-1990s certainly contributed to – and continue to exacerbate – these headaches, the region's security defaulted to NATO militaries to sort out, leaving the EU to spend the large part of the 1990s refining legislation to tackle its more prosaic domestic challenges and trying to push national law enforcement agencies to work more closely together. Driven in equal measure by a need to crack down on financial crime and a desire by its member states to squeeze undeclared tax revenues, for instance, the EU passed a series of directives to clamp down on bank secrecy and money laundering.[9] It also spent considerable energy encouraging more cooperation among national judicial authorities, though the effect of that campaign remained rather limited until the end of the decade.

Perhaps more significant from the point of view of shared domestic security was the decision in 1992 to create Europol, the pan-European policy agency in The Hague.[10] This was a step in the right direction, though a limited one since Europol was not given the authority to request information from national law enforcement agencies; its role was merely to facilitate/coordinate requests coming from national authorities. But it prefigured more significant cross-border law enforcement developments to come. In the same fashion, the Schengen countries, named after the Luxembourg town where their agreement was signed in 1985, began allowing citizens to circulate freely within their collective territory. To enable this, a common database of visa files, known as the Schengen Information System (SIS), was developed. This would lay the groundwork for later EU decisions to exploit this database and link it to new ones for homeland security applications.

Despite the above formal moves, cross-border judicial and law enforcement cooperation in Europe throughout the 1990s tended to remain voluntary, ad hoc and based on nonbinding political agreements. Information was provided and coordinated among national authorities according to a case at hand, though often not very quickly. Intelligence agencies, both military and civilian, continued to go their own way and did not enter the policy picture.

Three events changed this. One was the agreement by EU leaders in Tampere, Finland in October 1999 on a new agenda of home affairs objectives. Part of the reason behind this was a recognition that cross-border cooperation in home affairs and judicial matters was not working very well, or at least not fast enough to keep up with the EU's unfolding single market and the criminal elements taking advantage of its increasingly borderless internal structure. The other reason was the EU's looming enlargement in 2004 to take in a large chunk of Central Europe. Worries in EU capitals about the newcomers' porous borders and corruption were a major spur behind their decision to tighten cooperation.

The five-year Tampere agenda laid down a wide range of objectives, both political and legislative, in order to tighten cooperation among the EU nations' judicial and law enforcement authorities, while guaranteeing civil liberties. These covered measures to create a common policy on asylum and immigration; integrated management of the EU external frontiers, including the formation in 2005 of an EU border management agency; harmonization of law enforcement instruments; and better use of Europol and other international fora to fight cross-border crime and regional terrorism within the union such as Spain's Basque separatist rebels.

Initial progress on Tampere was slow, however, until the second event came along – the September 2001 terrorist attacks – which catalyzed Europe's home affairs agenda, causing Tampere to accelerate dramatically. EU leaders quickly adopted an action plan for fighting terrorism since it was evident the EU would not be able to cooperate effectively or quickly enough with the United States or other international actors in matters of surveillance, intelligence, law enforcement and other security imperatives unless it first vastly strengthened internal coordination among its member states.[11] A second and perhaps more embarrassing spur was the fact that US intelligence agencies traced many of the logistical links supporting the 9/11 attacks to terrorist operatives based in EU countries.

One consequence of this re-energized Tampere program was that European Commission emerged determined to deflect US designs to impose some of its homeland security imperatives on Europe, particularly via Washington's use of bilateral divide-and-conquer techniques. A good illustration of this was the US administration's moves in 2002-2003 to strike accords with individual EU nations to bind them to its maritime Container Security Initiative – moves blocked by the Commission and replaced with an overarching EU-US agreement.[12] This, however, was more a tactical measure by EU authorities rather than one of substantive opposition: both sides of the Atlantic largely agree on the ways their bureaucracies must work together to counter terrorism. Indeed, the EU later issued its Port Security Directive, designed to enhance the security of 780 ports in the EU.[13]

Other measures included the setting up of the EU's Monitoring and Information Center (MIC) as a pan-EU rapid alert system enabling one member state to centrally alert all others of natural and man-made disasters. This was followed in May 2002 by two complementary rapid alert systems, BICHAT and ECURIE, for biological and radiological events, respectively.

In addition, the EU agreed to establish a common border management agency, which commenced operations in 2005. This organization, known as the European Agency for

External Borders, is headquartered in Warsaw and designed to encourage the cooperation of national border security agencies. Another key measure now in force involves the establishment of the Europe-wide arrest warrant, which came into force on March 1 2004.

This has been the subject of much interest with the case of Mamoun Darkazanli, a Syrian-German national and suspected al-Qaeda member who was wanted by Spanish authorities. On July 18, 2005, the German Constitutional Court struck down a German law designed to implement the European arrest warrant, thus rendering the extradition case moot. This case has seriously complicated the development of European judicial cooperation on terrorist matters.

The third galvanizing event and the one with the most ramifications for Europe's homeland security agenda was the March 11, 2004 bombings in Madrid, which killed 191 and wounded another 1,800. As fate would have it, the bombings occurred in the same year the EU was due to review and update its Tampere agenda. The result was to accelerate that review and to produce yet another strengthened five-year set of home affairs objectives. Approved by national leaders in November 2004 when the Dutch government held the EU's rotating six-month presidency, it is known as The Hague Program. It essentially builds on and expands Tampere's objectives for the period 2005-2010.

The program's overriding focus is on establishing a common immigration and asylum policy for the member states. The Hague Program calls for the EU to: make police information available between all EU countries (threats to the security of another EU state must be communicated immediately); address the factors that contribute to fundamentalism and to the involvement of individuals in terrorist activities; make greater use of Europol, the EU's police office, and Eurojust, EU's judicial cooperation body; and ensure greater civil and criminal justice cooperation across borders and the full application of the principle of mutual recognition. It was designed to ensure that the upgraded Schengen Information System (SISII) functions as designed, as well as trying to improve the sharing of other intelligence related to security.[14]

An updated Action Plan was also approved by the Commission in December 2004. It focused on seven principal areas, including working to counter terrorist financing; enhancing the role of Eurojust and Europol in the fight against terrorism; establishing a central database of visa applications; setting up emergency response unit (ARGOS); and establishing measures to protect energy, health, transport and communications infrastructures.[15]

Perhaps the initiative that has gained the most attention was the appointment of Dutchman Gijs de Vries to the new post of "counterterrorism coordinator" and the tasking of Javier Solana, the EU's top official for security and defense policy, to widen cooperation among national intelligence services across the EU. In the interim, much criticism has been heaped on this decision, with many noting that the coordi-

nators office has no power and no funding authority, thus significantly weakening the position. His replacement, Gilles de Kerchove, has not been more successful in raising the profile of this position.

In addition, a special meeting of the interior ministers of the member countries was called in July 2005 by the UK presidency, in the immediate aftermath of the London underground bombings. While none of the measures called for in the declaration are new, deadlines have been brought forward for a number of them. It should be noted that more than half of the items in the action plan have resulted in decisions at the EU level; the difficulties lay largely in implementation. In December 2008 a decision was finally reached on the European Evidence warrant after years of haggling.[16]

This sense of urgency is most welcome; but, again, the EU track record is not encouraging, particularly given the lack of momentum brought about by the constitutional crisis. In the years since then, the number of EU initiatives has dwindled to a handful, despite the attacks at UK airports and other incidents. Those that are in effect seem to be observed only perfunctorily. As in the past, the responsibility for managing homeland security tasks remains national in nature. While cooperation between national intelligence and counterterrorism services is good, it is no substitute for concerted action on the EU level.

As things stand today (January 2010), the EU is regrettably not much closer to achieving the lofty goals of its many action plans, nor is it necessarily better positioned to deal with any attacks that may come. Europe has, instead, been most fortunate. A number of terrorist attacks have been prevented, such as the Sauerland bomb plot of September 2007, and those that have been conducted have not been very successful, such as the Glasgow airport attack of July 2007.

Homeland Security Challenges for Europe: Key Concerns and Recommendations

Intelligence and Warning Collecting and sharing intelligence remains a major obstacle to European homeland security efforts. A proposal by Austria and Belgium to develop a Europe-wide intelligence agency has not progressed, as it has encountered resistance on the part of other members.

This has been compounded by certain difficulties of intelligence sharing on the national level; Germany, for example, has consistently encountered problems in sharing intelligence among the sixteen provincial-level (Länder) interior ministries (who are responsible for most police functions in Germany) as well as with the federal-level interior ministry.

However, progress has been achieved in the ongoing attempts to reconcile differences in the various crime, immigration and terrorist warning data banks, particularly the SIS II and the Eurodac data banks. In addition, there have been reports of low-visibility counterterrorism centers, such as the so-called "Alliance Base," said to be located in Paris, in which intelligence agents and special operations force personnel are able to combine resources and plan operations. These facilities permit intelligence officers to see law enforcement documents from their own countries, which in many cases would be prohibited by national law.[17]

In addition, the establishment of a round-the-clock situation center at the EU has been instrumental in increasing the warning capabilities of the member states, as they are now able to share warning data. Warning remains a problem area, as evidenced by the lack of warning in advance of the London attacks. Indeed, British authorities actually downgraded their warning level in the weeks preceding the attacks.[18]

What is clear is that the level of intelligence "sharing" (a term disliked by intelligence professionals) must increase, even if politics require that it remain largely informal. In particular, a lessons-learned function, focused on intelligence failure, ought to be instituted. Moreover, the wall between security intelligence and law enforcement, while key to the protection of civil liberties, must be reviewed and procedures instituted to allow for some level of permeability, consistent with maintaining an acceptable balance between security and liberty. In addition, changes to national laws should be considered to enable legal investigations to use intelligence generated by security services in terrorism-related cases.[19] Given the potential threat of catastrophic terrorism, the current opaque nature of these walls is no longer acceptable, and some of this information must be shared not only by national officials but also with international partners. It is simply unacceptable that cross-border cooperation is easier for those bent on destruction than it is for those charged with securing the homeland.[20]

Critical Infrastructure Protection

Critical infrastructure, which encompasses systems such as energy, water, public health, telecommunications, finance and banking, agriculture, and other systems such as chemical plants, represent potential targets for terrorist attacks. As much of the infrastructure in Europe, as in the US, is in private hands, responsibility for protecting these systems must necessarily be a joint public-private undertaking. Moreover, much of the infrastructure in Europe is interconnected. For example, an energy system failure in one country could have a devastating effect in other countries.

Key to protecting these systems is an accurate assessment of the criticality and vulnerability of the systems. Databases to support these assessments must be developed. The EU is lagging behind the US in this area, as much of the key infrastructure has yet to be catalogued. Even the basic concept of what constitutes critical infrastructure can vary from country to country. The European Commission authorized Euro 140 million for the period 2005-2010 to identify and prioritize vulnerabilities to critical infrastructure.[21] This is an important start to this effort, but much more effort and money will be required to ensure the security of critical infrastructure

across Europe. It is equally important to develop common assessment criteria, so that intelligent risk management decisions can be made on which systems are most in need of protection on a Europe-wide basis.

Transportation Security

In the aftermath of the mass transit bombings in Madrid and London, much attention has been focused on the security of transportation systems. To an even greater extent than in the US, Europeans depend heavily on mass transit. That these systems are highly vulnerable is well known; recent events have shown that it is nearly impossible to provide total security for these systems while at the same time ensuring the convenience, efficiency and accessibility that makes these systems so useful. Moreover, a significant portion of European transportation originates in one country and terminates in another, or passes through several states, making a coordinated response essential.

While much attention has been focused on underground rail systems, other parts of the transportation network remain vulnerable, notably bridges and tunnels, rail transportation of hazardous materials as well as aviation security. While much has been done to enhance aviation security, it remains vulnerable due to the large number of unsecured general aviation facilities. Nevertheless, transportation security remains a bright spot on the European homeland security scene. European standards have been consistently higher than those of the US, although port security remains an area in which improvement is needed. One area that would yield immediate benefit is an enhanced passenger awareness program, built on the lessons learned from Madrid and London.

Catastrophic Terrorism

Europeans seem not to take the threat posed by terrorist employment of weapons of mass destruction (here defined as the use of chemical, biological, radiological or nuclear weapons, or CBRN weapons) as seriously, or likely, as do Americans. Much of the US homeland security effort is focused on the prevention of and recovery from these kinds of attacks while the European focus seems to be more on the kinds of high explosive attacks seen in Madrid and London – despite the fact that police in several countries have uncovered plans for such attacks.[22] This is not to say that national governments have not considered these possibilities and taken some measures to assure a response capability; but there has been little consideration and action at the level of the EU. There have been a number of studies conducted in recent months on the state of Europe's preparedness, particularly with regard to bioterrorism.[23] Another area of great concern has been the dangers posed by radiological dispersion devices (RDD), or "dirty bombs." There is significant concern in a number of European countries that terrorists may resort to the use of these devices, as their fabrication poses little problem.[24]

Some important steps have been taken at the European level, notably the formation of a CBRN defense battalion at

NATO, but much of the effort in the area of defense and response to catastrophic terrorism remains at the national level.[25] Given that the employment of any of these weapons would have immediate international impact, it would seem that this is an area in which considerable progress should be made.

Emergency Preparation and Response As noted above, attacks with weapons of mass destruction are likely to have significant impact not only within the target country, but also in neighboring states. As such, close cooperation between emergency response forces, particularly in the area of public health, is essential. Biological vectors, such as anthrax, or chemical contaminants can be transmitted rapidly from one city to another in Europe, and first responders must be prepared to deal with them.

While Europe has well trained and numerous emergency response organizations on the national and local level, a catastrophic event is likely to challenge even the best prepared. Thus, some level of cooperation within Europe is necessary, if only to avoid unnecessary duplication. Some lessons can be learned from efforts to rationalize military forces within Europe and apply them to emergency response forces. At a minimum, standards for emergency response equipment and training standards for personnel represent areas in which the EU could make significant progress. There are a number of voluntary organizations in Europe, such as firefighters, law enforcement and toxicologist associations, but clearly much more can be done at the EU level to provide for common standards.

The Role of Military Forces in European Homeland Security One area that ought to figure prominently in Europe's response to terrorism is the role that military forces ought to play in securing the common homeland. This area has received a great deal of recent attention in the US, with the establishment of a military command responsible for North America. Of interest, this is an area in which Europeans have significantly more experience than the Americans. European military forces have routinely been deployed to secure key installations and other critical infrastructure against attacks by nationalist terror groups such as the IRA and the Red Brigades. Moreover, military forces have participated in counterinsurgency and policing operations in many countries, such as Italy, Spain and the UK.

Many European countries possess specialized paramilitary forces such as the Gendarmerie, Carabinieri and Guardia Civil, which, while not necessarily designed for the purpose, have proven to be of great utility in anti- and counterterrorism operations. These forces are able to bridge the gap between military and law enforcement operations, particularly with regard to the use of force. Curiously, the evolving European common defense and security policy makes no mention of the defense and security of the homeland. At the EU level,

there is very little discussion of the employment of defense and military capabilities in any of these documents, except for incidental references to civil/military coordination for certain kinds of civil disasters.

Moreover, many of the member states, such as Germany, have a broad range of restrictions on the employment of military forces in domestic contingencies. Thus, the employment of military forces in a domestic environment remains very much in the hands of the member states. An example of this approach is found in the member states' adoption in late 2002 of a program to improve cooperation across the EU to guard against and limit the effects of chemical, biological, radiological and nuclear (CBRN) threats – risks that Europe's armies have long trained to deal with because of the Cold War. There is only a single reference to national military capabilities in the policy objectives listed in the document's operational annex.[26] One would imagine that this would be an area ripe for the establishment of common policy, as the defense of every member is inextricably bound up with that of its neighbors.

Conclusion It is, perhaps, an ultimate irony: terrorists in Europe think more European than many of Europe's homeland security-related agencies.[27] They enjoy the freedoms granted them by governments and turn those liberties against those same governments. They plan attacks in one country and execute them in the next. National governments, traditionally the standard-bearers of the fight against terrorists in Europe, are finding that there are limits to what they can accomplish in an expanded EU. The stark fact of international terrorism since September 2001, and particularly its deadly impact in Europe in March 2004 and July 2005, has forced national and EU policymakers to start addressing, if gingerly, new strategic issues and to re-think older ones – issues that have military implications for homeland security, even if those implications remain unvoiced or played down in official public discourse for the time being.

ENDNOTES*

1. Keohane, Daniel, "The EU and Counter-terrorism", Centre for European Reform, London, 2005, p. 2.
2. Keohane, ibid., p. 3.
3. See Kagan, Robert, "Power and Weakness", Policy Review, June 2002.
4. Tigner, Brooks, "The High Hanging Fruit of EU Homeland Security", unpublished, p. 2.

*Author's note: some of the material in this chapter was first published by the Bertelsmann Foundation in *Securing the European Homeland: The EU, Terrorism and Homeland Security*; Gutersloh, Germany, 2005 and is reprinted here with the permission of the publisher.

5. Tigner, ibid., p. 4. See also Clarke, John L., "Is Transatlantic Security Divisible? Securing the Transatlantic Homeland", EuroFuture, Summer 2004, p. 54.

6. Tigner, p. 3.

7. For an elaboration of the US approach, see Clarke, John L., "The United States, Europe and Homeland Security: Seeing Soft Security Concerns through a Counterterrorist Lens", in Aldis, Anne and Graeme P. Herd, Soft Security Threats and European Security, New York 2005, pp. 117–138.

8. Tigner, p. 4.

9. See Directive 91/308/EEC of the Council of June 10, 1991 on prevention of the use of the financial system for the purpose of money laundering, EU Official Journal L 166, June 28, 1991, p. 0077–0083; and the subsequent amending Directive 2001/97/EC of December 4, 2001, Official Journal L 344, December 28, 2001, p. 0076–0082.

10. For the history, structure and functioning of Europol. See http://www.europol.eu.int.

11. See www.euractiv.com/Artilce?tcmuri:29-136674-16&type=LinksDossier.

12. See European Commission press release of November 11, 2003 (IP/03/1565) announcing the agreement in principle, which led to formal signatures three months later.

13. See www.euractiv.com/Article?tcmuri=tcm:29-134414-16&type=News.

14. See www.eurative.com/Article?tcmuri=tcm:29-130657-16& type=LinksDossier.

15. See http://register.consilium.eu.int/pdf/en/04/st14/st14330-re01.en04.pdf.

16. See www.eurativ.com.Article?tcmuri=tcm:29-142468-16&type=news.

17. Priest, Dana, "Help from France Key in Covert Operations", Washington Post, July 3, 2005, p. 1. (accessed at UK Rephttp://www.washingtonpost.com/wp-wyn/content/article/2005/07/02/AR2005070201361.htmlort).

18. Sciolino, Elaine, "Linked Risk and Iraq" N.Y. Times, July 18, 2005. (accessed at http://www.iht.com/articles/2005/07/19/news/alert.php).

19. See Falkenrath, Richard, "Europe's Dangerous Complacency", Financial Times, July 7, 2004. (accessed at http://www.brookings.edu/views/op-ed/fellows/falkenrath20040707.htm).

20. For a discussion of the challenges of intelligence cooperation in Europe, see "The Fight Within", The Economist, July 23–29, 2005, pp. 27–28.

21. See New Defense Agenda, "Strategic Priorities for Protecting Europe's Infrastructure Against Terrorism". (accessed at http://www.forumEurope.com/publication/NDA_SOD_27June2005.pdf).

22. See, inter alia, "Spain: Al Qaeda Planned Chemical Attack" Washington Times, May 3, 2005. (accessed at http://washingtontimes.com/upi-breaking/20050503-073413-4680r.htm); "UK Chemical Attack Foiled" CNN.com, April 4, 2004. (accessed at http://edition.cnn.com/2004/WORLD/europe/04/06/britain.attack.plot/).

23. See "Countering Bioterrorism: How can Europe and the United States Work Together?", The New Defense Agenda, April 2005 (accessed at http://www.forum-europe.com/publication/EUUS_CounteringBioterrorism_April27.pdf).

24. Italian authorities are reported to be concerned about the use of RDDs. See http://www.agi.it/english/news.pl?doc=200507161801-1127-RT1-CRO-0-NF11&page=0&id=agionline-eng.oggitalia.

25. For more information on this battalion. See http://www.nato.int/docu/pr/2003/p031126e.htm.

26. See Council document 14627/02 of November 21, 2002. Stating that the EU's security and defense instruments are designed only for external use and not for application inside the Union, the footnote's last sentence pretty well sums up the situation: "The use of national military capabilities and specialized units for support of the protection of civilian populations may only be provided, case by case, on a bilateral basis or through the Community mechanism."

27. Munchau, Wolfgang, "Europe Must Tackle Terrorism", Financial Times, July 10, 2005. (accessed at http:// news.ft.com/cms/s/930466c8-f16c-11d9-9c3e-00000e2711c8.html).

ADDITIONAL RESOURCES

"Armies in Homeland Security: American and European Perspectives," John L. Clarke, Ed., National Defense University Press, 2006.

"Finding Security in an Age of Uncertainty: German and American Counterterrorism Policies," by Frank Gadinger and Dorle Hellmuth, 2009, American Institute for Contemporary German Studies, http://www.aicgs.org/documents/pubs/polrep41.pdf

"Transatlantic Counterterrorism Policy: Cultural, Economic, and Financial Aspects," by Kirsten Verclas, American Institute for Contemporary German Studies, December 2009, http://www.aicgs.org/documents/pubs/issuebrief34.pdf

"Cameron's Europe: Can the Conservatives Achieve Their EU Objectives?" By Charles Grant, Centre for European Reform, http://www.cer.org.uk/pdf/essay_936_dec09.pdf

"Obama's "Eisenhower Moment:" American Strategic Choices and the Transatlantic Defense Relationship," by Edwina S. Campbell, "France's New NATO Policy: Leveraging a Realignment of the Alliance?" by Gisela Muller-Brandeck-Bocquet "Asymmetric Interdependence: Do America and Europe Need Each Other?" by Beate Neuss, Air University, Strategic Studies Quarterly, Winter 2009, v. 3, no. 4 http://www.au.af.mil/au/ssq/2009/Winter/Winter09.pdf

"Shoulder to Shoulder: Forging a strategic US-EU partnership," Lead authors Daniel S. Hamilton and Frances G. Burwell, Atlantic Council December 2009, http://www.acus.org/files/ publication_pdfs/65/US-EUPartnership.pdf

"A Shift in Terrorist Strategy Threatens Italian National Security," *Terrorism Monitor*, v. 7, no. 35, November 20 2009 http://www.jamestown.org/uploads/media/TM_007_a3f2f1.pdf

"A New Security Architecture for Europe? Russian Proposal and Western Reactions," Egmont Institute, Royal Institute for International Relations, by Patrick Nopens, Nov. 2009, http://www.irri-kiib.be/papers/09/other/Nopens%20on%20 Medvedev%20Proposals%203.pdf

"A Shift in Terrorist Strategy Threatens Italian National Security," by Dario Cristiani, *Terrorism Monitor*, v. 7, no. 35, November 20 2009 http://www.jamestown.org/ uploads/media/TM_007_a3f2f1.pdf

"Security without the United States? Europe's Perception of NATO," by Gen Klaus Naumann, Bundeswehr, Retired, *Strategic Studies Quarterly*, Fall 2009, v. 3, no. 3 http://www. au.af.mil/au/ssq/2009/Fall/Fall09.pdf

"Shared Challenges–Joint Solutions? The United States and Europe Face New Global Security Risks–High Times for Grand Strategy," by Ralph Rotte & Christoph Schwarz, *Strategic Studies Quarterly*, Fall 2009, v. 3, no. 3 http://www.au.af.mil/ au/ssq/2009/Fall/Fall09.pdf

"Missile Defence - A View from Europe," by Dr. Michael Rance,

"US /Netherlands Cooperative Ballistic Missile Defense Initiative," by Roger L. Priem, "Net-Centricity Operational: Sweden's Security Management System," by Michael Mohr, *Common Defense Quarterly*, Fall 2009 http://ipaperus.ipaperus.com/ commondefensequarterly/CommonDefenseQuarterlyFallIssue 2009/

"European Union Policy on CBRN security: A Primer;" by Alok Rashmi Mukhopadhyay, CBW Magazine: Journal on Chemical and Biological Weapons," Institute for Defence Studies and Analyses, v. 2, no. 4, July-September 2009, http://www.idsa.in/cbwmagazine/EuropeanUnionPolicyon CBRNsecurity_armukhopadhyay_0909

"The national security strategy of the United Kingdom: update 2009 security for the next generation," Presented to Parliament by the Prime Minister, by Command of Her Majesty, Cm 7590, 25 June 2009, http://www.official-documents. gov.uk/document/cm75/7590/7590.pdf

"U.S.-EU Cooperation Against Terrorism," by Kristin Archick, Congressional Research Service RS22030, January 28, 2008, http://wikileaks.org/leak/crs/RS22030.pdf

"European Approaches to Homeland Security and Counterterrorism," by Kristin Archick, Coordinator; Carl Ek, Paul Gallis, Francis T. Miko, and Steven Woehrel Congressional Research Service, July 24, 2006, RL33573, http://opencrs.com/ document/RL33573/

"Europe and Counterterrorism: Strengthening Police and Judicial Cooperation," by Kristin Archick, Congressional Research Service RL31509, Updated October 15, 2004, http://wikileaks.org/ leak/crs/RL31509.pdf

"European Counterterrorist Efforts: Political Will and Diverse Responses in the First Year After September 11" October 17, 2002, by Paul Gallis, Congressional Research Service, RL31612, http://opencrs.com/document/RL31612/

European Law Enforcement Agency, http://www.europol.europa. eu/ European Commission, statistics. http://epp.eurostat.ec. europa.eu/portal/page/portal/eurostat/home/

Homeland Security Europe, www.homelandsecurityeu.com

Seceur, The Business of EU Security Policy, http://www. seceur.info/

International Rescue and Emergency Care Association, http://www.ireca.org/

European Biosafety Association, http://www.ebsaweb.eu/

The European Association for Bioindustries, http://www. europabio.org/index.htm

Metropolitan Police, London, anti-terrorist hotline, http://www. met.police.uk/so/at_hotline.htm

26

CHINA AND JAPAN: APPROACHES TO DOMESTIC AND TRANSNATIONAL TERRORISM

MANUEL MANRIQUEZ

To many Americans, the September 11, 2001 terrorist attacks on the World Trade Center towers and the Pentagon were a shock unlike any they had experienced before. Even people who lived hundreds or thousands of miles away felt fear, anger, and sorrow over the tremendous loss of life and the breach of national security that revealed America's vulnerability to transnational terrorist attacks. In 1995, Japan experienced a similarly striking (yet not as destructive) attack perpetrated by members of a domestic terrorist group known as Aum Shinrikyo. Preaching an apocalyptic vision of the world's demise, the group's leader, Shoko Asahara, planned and initiated a coordinated attack on a number of Tokyo subway trains using sarin gas; members of the Aum cult released the deadly nerve agent inside train cars, killing 12 people and injuring thousands (U.S. Department of State 2008). In the aftermath of that incident, Japanese leaders faced a pressing need to make policy decisions designed to prevent such attacks in the future, much like the George W. Bush administration did after 9/11.

Indeed, the threat of further terrorist attacks necessitates an effective response by the target nation's policymakers and national security institutions. Like many western states, the two major powers of East Asia highlighted in this chapter face distinct issues related to combating terrorism, in both transnational and domestic contexts. These countries seek to address terrorist threats through anti-terrorism law and policy as well as counter-terrorism law enforcement and military operations. The specific terrorist activities that shape each country's anti-terrorism/counter-terrorism policies have their own particular characteristics. Thus, leaders from each country must strike a balance between the internal issues that require official responses as well as the global issues that, in their capacity as members of the international community, present these nations with challenging choices concerning how to engage in cooperative multinational efforts to combat terrorism.

The People's Republic of China (PRC or China) and Japan are interesting cases to examine concerning official responses to terrorism because they each must balance competing national interests. The inherent tensions between these interests present challenges that are unique to each country as political obligations/opportunities and security imperatives pull policymakers from the respective countries in different directions. For China, the most notable "terrorist" threats originate from ethnic Uyghur separatists of Northwestern China's semi-autonomous Xinjiang province. These separatists have carried out countless attacks—in Xinjiang and other parts of China—ranging from street fights to bombings of civilian targets (Yuan 2003, 131). While China is eager to neutralize the threat such elements pose in the name of fighting terrorism, PRC leaders do not wish to further legitimize U.S. military intervention in the Middle East and Central/South Asia by playing up the Uyghur "terrorist threat" to too great an extent. Japan on the other hand, still requires the protection of U.S. military forces and other benefits that the U.S.-Japan alliance provides. Therefore, Japanese leaders seek to support the U.S. with respect to its anti-terrorism/counter-terrorism efforts—however, constitutional constraints on Japan's defense institutions and overseas military activities render it a reluctant partner in overseas counter-terrorism operations despite U.S. pressure to adopt a more collaborative role in such endeavors.

In examining the above issues, this chapter presents in-depth analysis of China's and Japan's policy approaches to domestic and transnational terrorist threats and examines

Foundations of Homeland Security: Law and Policy, First Edition. Martin J. Alperen.
© 2011 John Wiley & Sons, Inc. Published 2011 by John Wiley & Sons, Inc.

the nature of those threats, including the attendant complicating factors tied to each nation's interests. Consistent with the content of the book, this chapter offers an analysis of Chinese and Japanese "homeland security" issues as the term is commonly conceived of in the United States: in relation to anti-terrorism and counter-terrorism efforts. Although the term "homeland security" does not enjoy common usage in East Asia, the book's emphasis on relevant American law and policy renders usage of the term useful in that the analysis featured here parallels that of the book.

It is essential to note that there are ongoing debates among terrorism specialists, security analysts, and scholars as to which acts, including those mentioned above, truly constitute "terrorism." While there is not a uniform definition of the term, the purpose of this chapter is not to take a firm position in the debate, but to analyze the relevant approaches each government has taken and is currently taking toward what they perceive as or argue equates to terrorism. To the extent that China in particular may benefit from designating certain activities as terrorism, this chapter will look briefly at the strategies behind such designations.

The People's Republic of China

Strategic Overview The People's Republic of China is the world's most populous country and one of its most ethnically diverse. It is also the fourth largest country in the world (after Russia, Canada, and the United States); and it shares land borders with fourteen countries—far more than either Canada or the U.S. and equally as many as Russia (Central Intelligence Agency 2009). Among these countries, Afghanistan, Burma (Myanmar), North Korea, and Pakistan are highly unstable with respect to governance and/or security. In addition to Afghanistan and Pakistan, many others continue to experience local insurgencies and civil armed conflict, including China's regional rival India, which has struggled with separatist militant groups in Kashmir (a disputed region of Northwest India that borders China) since 1989. The pro-Pakistan Islamic militant group Hizb-ul Mujahideen is the most prominent "Jihadist" organization in Kashmir and it is at the center of the regional struggle, which poses a major threat to stability in that part of the world (Leather 2002, 10-12). Coupled with the threat of "Jihadist" ideals spreading across Asia, the ongoing political unrest among Asian Muslims in general poses a significant security concern for the Chinese Communist Party (CCP) which has a monopoly on national security policymaking in China.

The PRC includes five semi-autonomous regions, including Xinjiang and Tibet—both of which are problem areas for the Chinese government due to ongoing separatist activities in those provinces. As far as terrorism is concerned, Xinjiang is China's top security concern. However,

to understand China's approach toward meeting the security threat that Xinjiang-based separatism and terrorism pose, it is essential to place the matter in a broader context that focuses on overall Chinese security and territorial concerns.

Unlike Japan and South Korea, China is in the unique position of seeking great power status and perhaps challenging U.S. hegemony and dominance in the Asia-Pacific region and possibly beyond. This means that CCP leaders are acutely aware of world opinion concerning China's legitimacy as a great power. The effect of this insecurity is a preoccupation with territorial integrity and regional stability. Therefore, PRC policymakers' primary regional concerns are the status of Taiwan's sovereignty, territorial disputes with Japan and others, and security instability in South Asia (Pakistan and India) and the Korean Peninsula (Li 2009, 85). Chinese leaders are also increasingly concerned about encirclement by the United States as American military forces are currently stationed in nearby countries: Japan, South Korea, the Philippines, Afghanistan, and Kyrgyzstan (Leheny 2005, 252). However, Uzbekistan—a member of the Shanghai Cooperation Organization (SCO)—did manage to evict U.S. forces from an air base known as K2, perhaps at the behest of China which is a leading member of the SCO (Wright, Tyson 2005). Taking into consideration the fact that U.S. Naval vessels also patrol areas of the South China Sea near Taiwan and China's Hainan Island, examination of a map of China and the surrounding areas does reveal a pattern of U.S. encirclement of China. Whether or not this indicates an intentional effort on behalf of American military and political strategists to contain China is beside the point, nor will this analyst argue for either position; it is simply important to note that Chinese perceptions of encirclement by the U.S. may have a basis in reality due to the geographic positioning of U.S. military forces.

Chinese leaders have long espoused a "One China" policy. The precise definition of the term is complicated, but essentially the policy asserts that Taiwan is a rogue province of the PRC and will one day be reincorporated and placed under mainland governance. This standard also governs the status of Tibet and Xinjiang. Ultimately, Chinese leaders will never willingly give up control of any of the nation's semi-autonomous regions nor does it react favorably to official Taiwanese assertions of its independence. However, China must tread carefully in its approach to Taiwan so as not to come into military conflict with the United States—Taiwan's main ally in the region and its top military weapons supplier. When it can, China uses swift military and police action to quell dissent and imprison, torture, and/or execute radical militants, political dissidents and activists. Prime examples of China's brutality against peaceful demonstrators include the well-known incidents of the 1989 massacre of protestors in Tiananmen Square and allegations of harsh treatment, including execution and torture, of Falun Gong (a Bhuddism-oriented religious group) members who refused to renounce their beliefs (Lum 2006, summary). With that in mind, we can weigh the implications of violent Uyghur separatism in Xinjiang.

Xinjiang: Home to China's "Three Evil Forces" China's national security issues are all connected and most concern the CCP's need to stay in power and maintain political legitimacy. In a country where the freedom to criticize the government is suppressed and where the absence of a free press is designed to keep the population loyal to the CCP, any perception of the PRC's vulnerability or weakness under Communist rule is a threat to the state. Therefore, the CCP maintains a tight grip on the flow of information about insurgency and "terrorism" in the Xinjiang Uyghur Autonomous Region (XUAR). This makes assessing the nature of violent attacks in Xinjiang and elsewhere quite difficult. According to Chinese officials, the "three evils" expressed as "terrorism, separatism (or splittism), and extremism" are linked and such phenomena can be traced to various violent non-Han (Han are the majority ethnic group in China, comprising about 92% of the population) minority groups—typically Muslim Uyghurs from Xinjiang (Roy 2006, 1). Although there is some question about the validity of the claim, Chinese leaders have long asserted that some of these groups constitute a transnational terrorist threat. For its part, the United States has weighed in on the matter, designating only one group, the East Turkistan Islamic Movement (ETIM), as a terrorist organization (Li 2009, 103). The U.S. State Department also claims that this same Xinjiang-based group has connections to al Qaeda (Wayne 2008, 44).

Undoubtedly, there have been numerous suicide bombings and other attacks against civilian targets that may in some cases be accurately described as terrorist attacks. Yet, there is wide disagreement among scholars as to the exact nature of so-called "terrorist attacks" in China. Although it is probable that some attacks are motivated by Islamist ideals, the debate continues over whether global "Jihad" is a powerful motivating factor among Muslims in China. One key point to consider is that Tamil rebels in Sri Lanka have a decades-long history of carrying out suicide bombings and they are neither Muslim nor particularly motivated by religious ideals (Welshans 2007, 2-4). Nevertheless, Chinese officials continue to claim that many attacks perpetrated by radical groups from the XUAR are religiously motivated and that Islamist forces have had a growing impact on insurgency and "terrorism" in Xinjiang—especially after 9/11 (Wayne 2008, 23). However perspectives differ on the precise influence of Muslim fundamentalism, it can be inferred from these debates that suppression of religious freedoms and the encroachment of Han Chinese into predominantly Muslim areas throughout China—and in the XUAR in particular—have fomented insurgency and terrorist-style attacks in China by groups and individuals that are primarily motivated by a common disdain

toward China's central government and the police and military forces it uses to keep order.

The list of bombings, riots, shootings, assassinations, cases of arson and other violent attacks executed by radical Xinjiang-based separatist groups is quite lengthy. Such attacks began to occur with stunning frequency in the early 1990s and continued throughout the decade—they include a riot in southwestern Xinjiang on April 5, 1990 wherein 30 people were killed; the first bombing of a bus in Urumqi (capital of the XUAR) on February 5, 1992; a riot in Yili Kazak Autonomous Prefecture that killed ten and injured 200; three bus bombings in Urumqi on February 25, 1997 that killed nine and wounded 74; the bombing of a bus in Beijing on March 7, 1997 that killed two and injured 30; and other bombings, shootings, and cases of arson occurring in Xinjiang in 1999 (Yuan 2003, 131). This is just a sampling of the most well-known attacks in China during the 1990s, and while it is difficult to confirm the veracity of some of these claims, officials from China's Information Office of State Council claim that terrorists are responsible for more than 200 violent incidents which caused 160 deaths and 440 injuries between 1990 and 2001(Wayne 2008, 42).

The various groups implicated in these attacks are primarily associated with the Uyghur movement to gain independence from China. These groups then are clearly motivated by nationalism for what they call "East Turkistan"; "Xinjiang" being a Chinese term for the region. The Uyghur people belong to the Turkic ethno-linguistic group and therefore identify with other peoples from that group which includes Kazakhs, Kyrgyz, Turkish, and Uzbeks among others. The most prominent radical groups, and those most frequently linked to terrorism by Chinese officials are the aforementioned ETIM, the East Turkistan Liberation Organization (with ties to a group based in Uzbekistan that is allied with al Qaeda), the United Revolutionary Front of East Turkistan (which has ties with several terrorist groups in Kazakhstan), and the Uyghur Liberation Organization (which has attempted to enter mainstream politics outside of China but has failed to completely renounce the use of violence to achieve its political goals); there are of course other notable groups, but the notion that they are active terrorist organizations or that they have established links with notable transnational terrorist groups remains dubious (Ibid, 44–47).

In almost any case of "terrorist" activity in China, it is difficult to attribute responsibility for particular attacks. China's claims as to what group is to blame for a given attack must be regarded with a measure of skepticism given the lack of independent verification. Nevertheless, one can safely assume that attacks are not fabricated as it is not in the CCP's interest to highlight social instability or political unrest. At the same time, in the words of Asia specialist David Leheny, Chinese leaders have "long sought a free hand to crack down on Uyghurs pushing for independence or autonomy" (2005, 252).

Therefore, the "War on Terror" espoused by former U.S. President George W. Bush, may have lent credence to China's own anti-terrorism campaign in Xinjiang. In this way, 9/11 was a game changer for China almost as much as it was for the United States.

Linking Radical Uyghur Groups to "Terrorism" and al Qaeda Xinjiang is not the only origin of alleged terrorist activities in China, nor are Xinjiang's Uyghurs the only ethnic minority group to feature alleged terrorists among their numbers. Still, Xinjiang is the focal point for the PRC's counter-terrorism operations and the targeted groups are primarily based in that region. A report released by Chinese authorities in 2002 states that Xinjiang's "East Turkistan" groups have links to al Qaeda and are responsible for numerous terrorist attacks in the 1990s (Information Office of the State Council, China 2003). Furthermore, Chinese leaders claim that approximately 1,000 Uyghurs travelled to Afghanistan to train under al Qaeda supervision and that over 100 of them returned to China to wage a "Jihad" against Chinese rule in Xinjiang; they further assert that 300 were killed or captured fighting American military units in Afghanistan and 600 escaped into Pakistan's northern tribal region (Van Wie Davis 2008).

Yet, the purported link between Uyghur separatist groups in Xinjiang and al Qaeda appears tenuous as there is strong evidence to suggest that the overthrow of Chinese rule in Xinjiang is not at the forefront of al Qaeda's agenda. In 2004, the ETIM's deputy leader claimed that Osama bin Laden did not directly support the separatist Uyghur "non-Arab cause of overthrowing China's rule," although he did allow certain Uyghurs to be trained at his camps in Afghanistan (Kan 2009, 7). The absence of the issue in a long list of grievances expressed by al Qaeda's second in command, Ayman al-Zawahiri, on September 10, 2008, further illustrates the lack of concern over the radical Uyghurs' separatist agenda by the world's most menacing transnational terrorist network (Ibid). Furthermore, in direct contrast to PRC assertions that Chinese authorities are fighting "terrorists" in Xinjiang, an official PRC journal published in 1998 stated that China has neither domestic nor transnational terrorist groups (Kan 2009, 8).

The PRC's case against the group most frequently associated with terrorism in China during the 1990s, the ETIM, remains unsubstantiated due to the absence of any group called ETIM having taken responsibility for violent attacks at any time during that decade (Ibid, 6). Moreover, the leader of the ETIM, Hasan Mahsum, stated in 2002 that the organization had no links to al Qaeda. This is the same individual who was placed at the top of China's list of most wanted terrorists in December 2003 despite the fact that he had already been killed while fighting Pakistani military in South Waziristan (Ibid, 7). This calls into question the quality of China's assertions about active terrorists in the PRC. China's claims are

further weakened by the fact that PRC officials have painted Falun Gong, the aforementioned nonviolent religious group, and some Tibetan groups with the same brush—linking them to terrorism (Ibid, 6). This is indicative of PRC leaders' desire to label most separatist elements in China as "terrorists."

Regardless of the inconsistency of China's claims, it is plausible that radical Uyghur groups in Xinjiang have had some level of involvement with either the Taliban or al Qaeda, as the evidence that Uyghurs were captured by U.S. forces in Afghanistan is incontrovertible. Of the 22 Uyghurs imprisoned at the U.S. detention center in Guantanamo Bay, Cuba, ten were allegedly training in Afghanistan to fight for independence from the PRC and seven were members of al Qaeda. Such evidence lends credence to the notion that certain Uyghur elements and al Qaeda share similar interests in that armed resistance and the use of terrorist tactics are acceptable means of achieving their respective political ends. Thus, it stands to reason that there may be some ideational links between radical Uyghur groups and al Qaeda even if there are no substantial organizational links.

China's Policy Approach to Domestic Terrorism The CCP government maintains its legitimacy, both at home and abroad, by providing its people with security and expanding economic prosperity. It is essential in this endeavor for China's leaders to project the sense that the country's internal political problems are under control. Observers often point out that if China fails to maintain its internal and peripheral security, its prospects of achieving "great power status" in the world will be significantly diminished (Li 2009, 185). It follows that it is in the CCP's best interests to limit the amount and quality of information about Xinjiang-based radical groups and the attacks they are allegedly responsible for. At the same time, in order for Chinese authorities to avoid a greater degree of international scrutiny of the policies and tactics that they carry out to deal with such matters, it is also in their best interests to make a plausible case that the groups in question are indeed terrorists. This tension between the Chinese leadership's competing interests is played out in the country's policies and practices in dealing with threats to internal security stability.

The Chinese lawmaking process is not transparent and anti-terrorism laws are not part of the public record as they are in liberal democracies. Therefore, the most effective way to analyze domestic Chinese anti-terrorism and counter-terrorism policies is to emphasize an examination of policy in action rather than in theory. This is the approach taken here. Overall, PRC domestic anti-terrorism/counter-terrorism policies consist of restricting the flow of free information about terrorist attacks and the military/law enforcement responses to them; the use of rapid and deadly force to crack down on radical groups in China and to preempt terrorist attacks; the probable, yet difficult to verify, use of clandestine intelligence agents in the targeted areas; and a bottom-up method of counter-insurgency that includes the incorporation of problem regions into the state apparatus and the wider Chinese society. This last method effectively renders so-called "autonomous regions" much less independent than the term coveys (Wayne 2008, 24–25).

In shaping the information available to the public about Uyghur and other separatist groups in China, the government uses its state-run media to deliver official accounts of "terrorist" incidents and responses to those incidents. In tandem with the Chinese authorities' efforts to severely restrict foreign journalists' access to sensitive areas (e.g. Xinjiang) and limiting the availability of information about particular incidents and official actions, the Chinese government's manipulation of relevant news and reporting on the issues is a powerful tool to help Beijing avoid international and domestic scrutiny of its counter-terrorism tactics. Moreover, there have been various reports of Chinese security agents detaining foreign journalists. Some of the most recent accounts of such occurrences concern cases wherein the paramilitary People's Armed Police (PAP) detained and in one instance beat Japanese reporters who were covering the aftermath of bombings in Xinjiang around the time of the 2008 Olympic Games in Beijing (Kan 2009, 19). Reports of other incidents involving forceful detentions, abuse, and the deleting of foreign journalists' photographs around that time (August 2008) reveal a pattern of Chinese security personnel mistreating journalists and reporters (Ibid, 20). While attempts to silence the media—particularly members of the foreign press who attempt to cover issues that the Chinese government does not want to be highlighted—is part of the larger PRC effort to limit the flow of information inside China and abroad, it is clearly also an element in the fight against domestic radical groups as lending those groups a voice encourages the public to consider whether or not they have legitimate cause for their dissent and insurrection.

Chinese officials have long relied on the use of force to dismantle radical groups and to preempt attacks from these groups as well as to quell civil unrest. China uses both military and police forces for these purposes and the PAP has a central role in cracking down on suspected terrorists and other extremists throughout the country (Lam 2010, 3). In Xinjiang, the local police, China's Public Security Bureau (akin to the FBI), and elements of the People's Liberation Army (PLA) have also been active in the fight against China's "three evil forces" of "terrorism, separatism, and extremism." In 1996 Chinese authorities began to implement a new policy agenda designed to target "major criminals" and "terrorists"; the ongoing "Strike Hard" campaign, includes widespread detentions and summary executions (Kan 2009, 8; Wayne 2008, 10). Executions in particular, are meant to have a deterrent effect on those intending to violently oppose Beijing's rule. One of the most well-known instances of this is the April 9, 2009 executions of two Uyghur men for an alleged terrorist bombing on August 4, 2008—just before the

Olympic Games began in Beijing—that reportedly killed 16 PAP security agents; the executions were announced to about 4,000 local officials and residents gathered at a stadium in Kashgar, an administrative center in the XUAR (Kan 2009, 19-20; Voice of America 2009).

Due to the high degree of international attention around the time of the Beijing Olympics in August 2008, Chinese authorities concentrated an exceptional amount of law enforcement and military activity on preventing radical groups from attacking sensitive targets in Beijing as well as in Xinjiang. In the first half of 2008, leading up to the Olympics, Chinese authorities reportedly rounded up 82 suspected terrorists in Urumqi and 12 terrorist groups in Kashgar (U.S. Department of State 2009, 38). China's mass police actions during this time draw attention to the most detectable component of the CCP's preemptive counter-terrorism policy.

Indeed, in the XUAR, the police and military are ubiquitous. There may truly be a need for extremely tight security in Xinjiang—however, it is probable that the vast security presence in the region serves as a means to deter both violent and non-violent public opposition to PRC rule and not just to protect sensitive locations and assets. In addition to a heavy police presence, the PAP and PLA number about 150,000 to 200,000 at a given time in Xinjiang; but perhaps more astonishing is the size of the paramilitary Xinjiang Construction and Production Corps (XCPC) which totals about 2.5 million, just less than 1 million of whom are workers (Wayne 2008, 74, 78). While many XCPC personnel are involved in construction and farming projects, the institution traces its roots to the PLA occupation of Xinjiang before it became an official province. Consistent with its origins, the XCPC is responsible for border security and for establishing a large security presence overall (Ibid, 78).

Some of the less visible components of counter-terrorism policy may actually be more effective because they do not engender violent retribution in the form of vengeance-driven attacks for perceived acts of oppression (Wayne 2008, 8). Whereas mass arrests, widely publicized executions, and other direct police and military actions are likely to intensify hostility and resentment toward Chinese authorities, clandestine counter-terrorism activities have the potential to yield results without the inevitable backlash. Moreover, clandestine counter-terrorism activities are difficult to detect—so spies and informants can operate for long periods of time without being discovered. Undoubtedly, spies and informants as well as many local police officers are Uyghurs or other ethnic minorities from the region. Martin I. Wayne, a specialist on China's counter-terrorism and counter-insurgency policies in Xinjiang states that after 9/11 "Spies and informants reportedly penetrated an increasing number of institutions in society, including greater surveillance of religious gatherings" (Wayne 2007, 42).

Perhaps the most notable anti-terrorism/anti-insurgency technique that Chinese policymakers use is the subversion of minority culture and the integration of Xinjiang into wider Chinese society—which effectively impacts the political will of Xinjiang's ethnic minorities. Indeed this is part of a wider policy of integrating outlying regions into the Han-centric Chinese polity and society and it has been going on since the early days of the PRC—although the precise shape of the policy has altered over the years. The CCP's methods of achieving integration and manipulating the political will of the non-Han population include government-sponsored migration of Hans into Xinjiang and the strict regulation of education and religious practice.

Continuous Han migration is an approach that has slowly tipped the balance of Xinjiang's population in favor of a slight Han majority or at least a plurality. Estimates vary, but essentially Hans now make up about 50% of Xinjiang's total population (this includes the vast number of Han security personnel), whereas in the early 1950s they made up about 5% of the population (Wayne 2008, 74; Kan 2009, 5). According to official Chinese sources, Xinjiang is home to 13 major ethnic groups, including the Han and the Uyghur people among 11 other largely Turkic/Muslim groups; with Uyghurs comprising perhaps less than 45% of the XUAR's population (Bhattacharji 2009). The steady influx of Han's into Xinjiang and the perceived marginalization of other ethnic groups both politically and economically is one of the most contentious issues in the region. Although Chinese officials deny that advancing demographic change is the primary motivation behind continued Han migration to Xinjiang, the trend has "fueled Uyghur discontent as Han and Uyghurs compete over limited jobs and natural resources" (Ibid). The same can be said for official positions in the local CCP leadership. Finally, where anti-terrorism and anti-insurgency policy is concerned, the "Hanization" of Xinjiang may also be central to the CCP's efforts to diminish the influence of separatist groups and other dissenters.

Another of the PRC's most prevalent means of controlling dissent and manipulating the political will of Xinjiang's Muslims is the strict regulation of religious practice. The CCP has sought to restrict the free practice of religion in Xinjiang since taking control of the province shortly after routing the nationalist Kuomintang in 1949—with a period of relaxation of restrictions under Deng Xiaoping in 1979 (Welshans 2007, 28). The CCP began tightening restrictions on religious practices again in the early 1990s as part of a crackdown on Xinjiang's Muslims in response to public demonstrations in the late 1980s and a violent mass uprising in 1990 (Bovingdon 2004, viii). These restrictions continue today; currently, PRC policy restricts individuals under the age of 18 from engaging in formal religious training (Wayne 2008, 25). Moreover, in Xinjiang, where religious restrictions are the most severe, the repression of Islam has included "the closure of mosques" and "the supervision and dismissal of clerics" (Bovingdon 2004, viii). This is no small matter for Muslims in Xinjiang because Islam is a fundamental part of their daily lives as well as their spiritual and cultural expression. Yet Chinese leaders view the practice of religion as a potential threat to the integrity of the atheist state and CCP authority. Likewise, they fear that the free practice of Islam encourages radicalism among Uyghurs and other Muslims in China. According to an Amnesty International report on China's repression of Uyghurs in Xinjiang, the PRC government accuses people attempting to practice religion peacefully of "separatism" and it persecutes religious leaders and Muslim opposition figures linking them to "terrorism" (2002, 7).

Where education is concerned, PRC policy is equally restrictive. Overall, education policy in China is essentially designed to mold youth into good, obedient citizens rather than to encourage students to think independently and creatively (Wayne 2008, 24). In Xinjiang specifically, education policy is geared toward incorporating youths of Uyghur and other non-Han ethnicities into Chinese society (Ibid). Language instruction is a particularly salient example of this method of incorporation. In the XUAR's schools, students are mainly taught Mandarin while the traditional languages, including the Uyghur language, are sidelined (Lam 2009). Meanwhile, under the "bilingual education" policy, schools that taught only in ethnic minority languages were abolished altogether (Uyghur Human Rights Project 2008). Clearly this is not a policy solely designed as an anti-terrorism measure, but this manner of subverting minority culture is an important component of the CCP's overall effort to render the society of Xinjiang hostile to the growth and spread of radicalism and separatism. However, like many of the social policies examined above, it likely helps to provoke resentment of the CCP and the XUAR government among minority groups.

Although violence in Xinjiang decreased significantly throughout most of the first decade of the 21st century—perhaps due to China's use of the multi-faceted police, military, and social anti-terrorism/counter-terrorism approach outlined above—social unrest in Xinjiang manifested in the form of violent riots and attacks against Han residents of the province in the summer of 2009. Through this anti-Han violence, a small fraction of Xinjiang's Uyghur population illustrated their deep bitterness over Han encroachment and the central government's harsh repression of Uyghur dissent that is at the heart of broader minority discontent. Despite the appearance of short-term success that the relative calm of 2001 to 2008 seems to have demonstrated, CCP policymakers will likely find it difficult to address the long-term separatist or "terrorist" threats as long as Uyghurs and other minorities in Xinjiang perceive the PRC policy in Xinjiang as unjust and oppressive.

China and America's "War on Terror" PRC domestic anti-terrorism and counter-terrorism policies became more aggressive after September 11, 2001. Indeed, China's assertions about the threat of transnational terrorism within its own borders may have some basis in reality due to the possible links that East Turkistan groups have with foreign extremist groups. However, many outside observers note that separatists in Xinjiang are largely motivated by nationalist ideals, not the Islamist ideology which opposes the presence of Western influence in Muslim countries; after all, China is not the West, nor does the Chinese military have a visible presence in the Middle East or North Africa. Not surprisingly, the perspectives of China's elites on America's campaign against transnational terrorist elements are consistent with the differences between China's and America's primary terrorism concerns. Whereas the United States is focused on combating terrorism abroad through military means, China is more focused on combating internal "terrorist" threats.

Concerning the 9/11 attacks in particular, Chinese analysts are in agreement that they constitute terrorism "of an extreme and evil nature" and that they are essentially bad for the world as well as the United States (Li 2009, 80). However, these analysts are generally in agreement with the Chinese public—to the extent that public opinion in the PRC can be assessed—in that they believe responsibility for 9/11 largely resides with the U.S. due to its hegemonic international political and economic policies; moreover, China specialist Rex Li points out, "there is a consensus among Chinese security analysts that America is the major source of global instability" due to U.S. designs on maintaining a "unipolar global system" (Ibid, 82). The argument here is that America's often unilateral approach to global affairs creates enemies in countries where U.S. foreign policy is to blame for poverty as well as regional insecurity and social instability.

Nevertheless, Chinese leaders responded to 9/11 with words of support for the United States. Then PRC President Jiang Zemin and Foreign Minister Tang Jiaxun both contacted Bush Administration officials to express their concern over the attacks, with the latter placing a call to Secretary of State Colin Powell stating that "the Chinese people stand with the American people" (Hassig 2002, 3). Such amicable responses from China's leadership came as no surprise to many China observers. As a number of analysts note—with varying degrees of criticism and certainty—the CCP likely pledged its support for U.S. anti-terrorism efforts to justify a crackdown on separatist groups the regime labeled as "terrorists" (Leheny 2005, 251; Hassig 2002, 2; Chung 2002; Kan 2009, 4). Taking inconsistencies in official Chinese statements into account, the notion that the PRC used 9/11 as a pretext to wage its own "War on Terror" certainly holds water.

PRC leaders had other reasons to support Washington's international post-9/11 security agenda despite their misgivings about the pending U.S. military invasion of Afghanistan. A report published by the Institute for Defense Analysis (a federally funded non-profit corporation) points out that Beijing sought to mend fences with Washington after the PRC detained the 24 U.S. military personnel that made up the crew of an EP-3 reconnaissance aircraft which was forced to make an emergency landing at a Chinese Naval base after accidentally colliding with a Chinese fighter jet in mid-air (Hassig 2002, 3). The collision and subsequent detention of the American EP-3 crew caused a flaring of tensions between the PRC and the U.S. that Beijing wished to move beyond. This matter, in addition to the PRC's desire to crack down on Uyghur separatists without facing condemnation of its actions from the United States, motivated Chinese policymakers to provide limited support for the U.S. response to 9/11.

The first significant sign that China was willing to approve the U.S. response to 9/11 came one day after the attacks when the PRC, in its capacity as a permanent member of the United Nations Security Council (UNSC), voted with all other UNSC members to pass Resolution 1368 (Gill, Huang 2009, 11). Each permanent member of the UNSC wields veto power over any resolution considered by that body (permanent members are China, France, Russia, the United Kingdom, and the United States). Resolution 1368, which authorized the U.S.-led invasion of Afghanistan, would not have passed without China's support. The affirmative PRC vote on UNSC Resolution 1368 meant that Beijing openly recognized The United States' right to respond militarily to the 9/11 attacks even though it meant that U.S. military forces entering Afghanistan would be stationed on China's Western flank as well as directly to the East (in South Korea and Japan). Such an endorsement is especially unusual for China given the PRC's aversion to approving military invasions of a sovereign country. Thus, the strategic calculation in Beijing must have been that it was worth risking encirclement of China by U.S. military forces and possibly a long-term presence of U.S. troops in Central Asia because it allowed the PRC more latitude in dealing with Xinjiang's separatists and the ongoing situation with Taiwan while also improving Sino-U.S. relations on the heels of the EP-3 incident (Hassig 2002, 11).

The PRC further solidified its position in support of the U.S. when it voted to pass UNSC Resolution 1373, which was essentially a reaffirmation of Resolution 1368 but went further by expressing the need to suppress terrorist financing. However, Jiang Zemin belied CCP anxieties over U.S. military presence in Afghanistan when he told British Prime Minister Tony Blair in a phone conversation on September 18, 2001 that the "War on Terrorism" required "conclusive evidence," compliance with the U.N. Charter, and a "role for the Security Council" (Kan 2009, 1). To be sure, Chinese policymakers found themselves in a quandary over the October 2001 U.S.-led invasion of Afghanistan.

During the lead up to the invasion, PRC officials maintained close contact with China's regional ally, Pakistan. Then Pakistani President Pervez Musharraf visited China shortly after the 9/11 attacks and again in December 2001. During those trips China pledged over a million dollars in initial aid to Pakistan while also facilitating contact between U.S. and Pakistani officials (Reilly 2002, 3). In this way, China helped ease U.S.-Pakistan relations, which served Washington's interests as well as Pakistan's and China's. China also took early action in pledging aid for eventual Afghan reconstruction efforts at an international conference in Tokyo, Japan that took place in late January 2002 (Hassig 2002, 7). Around the same time, China's Foreign Ministry promised to make an effort to prevent Osama bin Laden or any other al Qaeda elements from entering China (Ibid). These efforts came in lieu of military assistance, which China completely withheld.

After the U.S.-led invasion of Afghanistan, China vacillated in its cooperation with the United States. At a UN meeting in September 2002, PRC Foreign Minister Tang Jiaxun expressed China's doubts about U.S. actions in Afghanistan when he said, "efforts should be made to prevent the arbitrary expansion" of America's "War on Terror" (Li 2009, 83). Such language may have surprised U.S. leaders, as one month earlier Washington succumbed to Chinese pressure and designated China's Xinjiang enemy number one, the separatist Uyghur group ETIM, as a terrorist organization. Yet, there was much give and take between China and the U.S. after the Afghan invasion. In 2001 and 2002, the two countries established a number of cooperative initiatives. In October 2001, Beijing and Washington established a consultative mechanism to coordinate anti-terrorism efforts; and one year later, the PRC agreed to host a Federal Bureau of Investigation (FBI) office in Beijing to enhance counter-terrorism efforts (U.S. Department of State 2009, 39). Shortly thereafter, the FBI announced that it would provide security assistance to the PRC authorities for the 2008 Beijing Olympic Games, ostensibly to prevent potential terrorist attacks (Li 2009, 95).

This spirit of cooperation did not manifest in early 2003, when China sided with France and Germany to oppose the U.S. invasion of Iraq and push for more deliberation and inspections of Iraq's suspected weapons of mass destruction (WMD)-related sites. In principal, PRC policymakers reject preemptive war and they generally feel that "the Bush Administration's approach to counter-terrorism [was] overly aggressive, diplomatically impatient, and [paid] too little attention to the political and economic discontent in the Third World that gives rise to terror activities" (Roy 2006, 1). Thus, China's support for America's "War on Terror" had clear boundaries and even tacit approval of another invasion of an Asian nation was out of the question.

Whereas the United States' Iraq invasion was a sore point between Beijing and Washington, it apparently did not hamper Sino-U.S. cooperation in other areas, most notably around efforts to combat financing for terrorist groups and to a lesser degree fighting the spread of WMD and related materials and components. A report published by the U.S. Department of State specifies, "terrorist financing is a criminal offense in China" (2009, 38). The report goes on to list China's efforts to combat such activities; they include membership in international institutions such as the Financial Action Task Force and the Eurasian Group, which are designed to fight international money laundering as well as terrorist financing (Ibid). Moreover, in May 2009, China joined the Egmont Group, which coordinates financial intelligence units (specialized government agencies that also work against money laundering and terrorist financing) across 116 nations (The Egmont Group 2009).

Where combating the proliferation of WMD and related materials and components is concerned, China cooperates with the United States and its allies on some matters and is obstructive or simply non-cooperative on others. In the face of criticism over its role as a weapons proliferator with ties to regimes that allegedly support terrorist activities, such as Iran and North Korea, PRC officials are quick to point out that they are cooperative in the context of multilateral negotiations with the DPRK on the denuclearization of the Korean Peninsula and in supporting UNSC moves to sanction Iran over its alleged nuclear program (Kan 2009, 22).

On the first point, PRC leaders are right to stress the importance of their role in negotiations with North Korea. It is probable that without the steady influence of China—North Korea's long-time ally—the multilateral diplomatic talks on denuclearization, known as the "six-party talks," would not be possible. The PRC places pressure on the Kim regime to engage in the talks, and although they frequently stall, it is the only diplomatic process wherein progress towards North Korean denuclearization is discussed between the United States and the DPRK. Despite China's crucial role in the six-party talks, Beijing has a history of supporting North Korea's ballistic and cruise missile development programs. From the early 1970s until 2001, China is suspected of transferring cruise missiles and ballistic missile components and related technological knowledge to the DPRK (Nuclear Threat Initiative 2003). Since that time however, it appears that Beijing has been more cooperative with international efforts to limit transfers of potential nuclear-weapon delivery systems to North Korea. U.S. concerns about the DPRK transferring WMD technology and knowledge to terrorist groups may be one motivating factor behind the PRC's backing on this issue, but the most influential factor is most likely the PRC's desire to limit the North Korean nuclear threat. This is largely due to the fact that it is in China's interest to prevent South Korea and Japan from considering plans to develop nuclear weapons of their own to strengthen nuclear deterrent capabilities if North Korea successfully develops ballistic missiles armed with nuclear warheads.

Whereas Beijing has been increasingly cooperative on matters concerning North Korea, the U.S.-led international ship inspection regime known as the Proliferation Security Initiative (PSI) is essentially in conflict with the PRC's foreign policy strategy. PSI is not an explicit anti-terrorism mechanism, but its central aim, which is to coordinate international efforts to interdict ships carrying WMD and missile-related equipment and/or material, is consistent with efforts to prevent the transfer of such items to terrorist groups. Nevertheless, Chinese leaders have chosen not to participate in PSI exercises over concerns that such activities, which take place in Asia-Pacific waters, are of questionable legality and because they pose a threat to North Korean shipping and thus regional stability (Lieggi 2008). On the other hand, China has cooperated with other key international efforts to prevent the illegal transfer of nuclear-weapons related technology and material. Most notably, the PRC is a partner in the multinational Global Initiative to Combat Nuclear Terrorism (GICNT). The 76 nation-strong GICNT group "offers a comprehensive approach to strengthening all defensive layers necessary to prevent, protect against, and respond comprehensively to the nuclear terrorist threat" (U.S. Department of State 2009, 192). Additionally, China collaborates with the U.S. Customs and Border Protection agency under the Department of Homeland Security on its Container Security Initiative (CSI) and with the U.S. Energy Department's National Nuclear Security Administration on the Megaports Initiative. The CSI, with active high-tech container screening and inspections at various high-volume foreign ports, is intended to prevent the delivery of weapons for use by terrorists in the United States, whereas the Megaports Initiative is designed to detect nuclear/radioactive materials that have the potential to be used in the making of "dirty bombs" or other weapons (U.S. Department of Homeland Security; U.S. Department of State 2009, 37).

By examining China's level of participation in global anti-terrorism efforts and its cooperation with many major U.S. anti-terrorism initiatives, China's approach to transnational terrorism becomes clear: PRC policymakers are willing to support actions that limit the ability of terrorist groups to secure financing and WMD, but not at the expense of East Asian regional stability. Nor are they willing to pledge direct military support for U.S. and NATO counter-terrorism actions in the Middle East and Central Asia, but they are amenable to providing financial support to help stabilize the security situation in Pakistan and Afghanistan. Overall, China's leaders do not want U.S. forces stationed close to their borders as they have sought to limit U.S. influence in the areas surrounding China. The PRC's support for the Kim regime in North Korea—which, if it falls, will surely pose the risk of U.S. and South Korean troops coming close to China's border with the DPRK—and China's efforts to push the U.S. military out of the Central Asian Republics through the SCO illustrates this point. The strategic calculus among CCP leaders must certainly be that it is in China's interest to support multinational efforts to combat terrorism and to some extent help the U.S. and its allies in this endeavor as well. However, the tension between China's support for American anti-terrorism activities and its anxiety over encirclement by U.S. military forces reveals that it is not in China's interest to al-

low the U.S. a free hand to operate without constraints in the PRC's neighborhood.

China's Regional Counter-terrorism Efforts The SCO sprang from the "Shanghai Five" group (included all SCO members except for Uzbekistan), which arose from the need to fill the power vacuum left by the collapse of the Soviet Union and the resultant independence of the Central Asian republics. Formally, the SCO was founded in June 2001, although the "Shanghai Five" group began meeting in 1996. The SCO coordinates policy on a wide scope of issues, regional security and economic development chief among them. In 2000, before the group officially became the SCO, the PRC shifted the group's counter-terrorism focus to deal with the aforementioned "three evils" (Kan 2009, 23). Whereas China at times rejected U.S. invitations to participate in counter-terrorism exercises, most notably PSI maritime activities, the PRC has been at the forefront of counter-terrorism military exercises with its SCO partners and other key regional players.

After the 9/11 attacks, China's leadership role in the SCO expanded as counter-terrorism initiatives gained prominence. In 2002, China and its SCO partners executed the first in a series of counter-terrorism exercises which took place in Kazakhstan and in Xinjiang (Yuan 2003, 134). Further counter-terrorism exercises were executed in 2003—and in 2004, the PLA carried out joint counter-terrorism exercises with Pakistan and then with India, one of China's most powerful regional rivals (Gill, Huang 2009, 18). In 2006, China held joint counter-terrorism exercises with Tajikistan and again with the Thai military in 2007—and in 2005, 2007, and 2009, the PLA and the Russian military carried out counter-terrorism exercises on Russian and Chinese territory (Ibid, 18-19).

The emphasis of counter-terrorism in these bilateral and multilateral military exercises illustrates the degree to which China and its regional partners take the threat of terrorism—or at least asymmetrical warfare—seriously. For China and each of these nations, domestic insurgencies and the possibility of cross-border cooperation between separatist or terrorist groups are a reality. Indeed, China has a stake in helping to maintain regional stability by cooperating with its neighbors on security initiatives and counter-terrorism exercises. However, China's Xinjiang issue is, for now, primarily a matter for the PRC to handle.

Japan

Strategic Overview Japan has long enjoyed its status as the second largest economy in the world in terms of Real Gross Domestic Product (GDP)—although as this book goes to press, new estimates suggest that China's economy has already overtaken Japan's or will do so in 2010 (Conway 2009; McIntyre 2009). As an island nation with a dearth of natural resources, Japan has historically relied on imports for most essential natural resources and has thrived on an export-oriented economy. Japan achieved its status as a global economic powerhouse through U.S. patronage and preferential trade policy as well as the country's own well-designed economic growth model and technological innovation. Japanese policymakers have also enjoyed rare advantages in economic planning thanks to the small percentage of the nation's annual budget dedicated to military expenditures: in 1967, the Japanese government limited defense spending to less than 1% of annual GDP (Samuels 2007, 41). It has remained near this mark due in large part to the security benefits of the U.S.-Japan alliance, including the provision of the U.S. nuclear umbrella and other direct security measures as well as collaboration between Japan's and America's Defense establishments and intelligence sharing.

Despite the overall success of the alliance, formally in place since 1952, Japanese relations with its neighbors and the United States are vulnerable due to the prevalence of a number of sensitive issues. In the context of East Asian regional relations, China, North Korea, and to a lesser extent South Korea, remain concerned about the potential resurgence of Japanese militarism. The WWII-era atrocities perpetrated by the Imperial Japanese military and the alleged lack of remorse or repentance over these matters among key Japanese elites has prevented many of Japan's neighbors from expressing full forgiveness for Japan's past crimes. Therefore, Japan faces pressure from its most powerful neighbors to limit the capacity and scope of its military activities. Where Japan and the U.S. are concerned, the alliance was seemingly flawless until Japan failed to meet U.S. and international expectations in its response to the 1990-91 Gulf War, for which it provided $13 billion in aid rather than sending support personnel or man-power of any kind. To its great shame, Japan was accused of using "checkbook diplomacy" in lieu of pledging more substantial international support to its allies (Green 2001, 202). Further weaknesses in the alliance have surfaced since that time, although Japanese policymakers have attempted to address these issues with some degree of success.

Japan's role with respect to national defense and international security is limited by the nation's post-WWII constitution, which strictly prohibits the "threat or use of force as means of settling international disputes" (Constitution of Japan 1946). Subsequent interpretations of constitutional restrictions expressed in Article 9 of what is known as Japan's "Peace Constitution," have gradually loosened restrictions on the nation's defense and security capabilities. However, Japan's right to "collective self-defense"—a term referring to the country's ability to aid its alliance partner, the United States, in executing regional security/military operations for the benefit of both parties—remains a contentious issue. Whereas American leaders have frequently applied pressure on the Japanese government to engage in a broader range of military support missions, opposition to such activities among

the public and some Japanese parliamentarians as well as the difficulty of amending the constitution or altering the current interpretation of its strictures, has prevented Japan from satisfying Washington's predilections.

Thus, Japanese leaders face challenging conditions in the international system. While they are inclined to answer U.S. calls to act in matters concerning terrorism, the extent of their actions is severely hampered by the aforementioned domestic and regional conditions. Moreover, Japan, unlike China, does not face the destabilizing threat of internal separatism. Still, Japan's experiences with Aum Shinrikyo and the North Korean missile/nuclear threat have gradually moved public opinion toward greater support of lifting some restrictions on the nation's defense and security capabilities—just as they have facilitated debates in the Diet (Japanese Parliament) over the use of force abroad and "collective self-defense." With the advent of Japan's new centrist government in September 2009, which replaced the conservative Liberal Democratic Party (LDP), some moves toward greater latitude in Japanese military operations—including anti-terrorism efforts—have been reversed or halted.

Japan's Experience with North Korean "Terrorism" A high degree of enmity currently exists between North Korea and Japan. This is largely due to a several key factors. They are as follows: atrocities carried out against the Korean people by Japan's occupation force during the colonization of the Korean Peninsula (1910-1945); Japan's alignment with the United States against North Korea during and after the Korean War of 1950-1953; anti-Japanese sentiments and rhetoric espoused by the Stalinist Kim regime of North Korea; the abduction of Japanese citizens by North Korean operatives in the 1970s and 80s; provocative North Korean missile and nuclear tests; and, Japan's enhancement of its military capabilities—which is viewed as threatening by the DPRK.

The degree to which political tensions exist between Japan and North Korea have been exacerbated by the issues listed above, not least of which is the DPRK's acerbic rhetoric denouncing Japan's efforts to re-invade the Korean Peninsula. The suggestion that this could even be a remote possibility given the current political and security environments in East Asia is highly disingenuous. However, official North Korean rhetoric aims to stir up domestic ire toward the Kim regime's adversaries, not to present a valid assessment of threats to the DPRK.

Due in large part to the isolation of North Korea, which is often called the "Hermit Kingdom," as well as the disproportionality of DPRK military forces versus those of the United States, South Korea, and Japan, the Kim regime has historically resorted to using various forms of asymmetrical warfare against its three adversaries. Some of these methods equate to acts of terrorism; most have been aimed at South Korean citizens and the Republic of Korea's government, which

North Korean leaders have long accused of being a "puppet" of the American "Imperialists." Examples include airplane hijackings, attempted or successful assassinations of high-ranking ROK leaders and South Korean citizens, numerous abductions of South Korean nationals, and the infamous mid-air bombing of a Korean Airlines passenger plane by North Korean agents in November 1987 (Fischer 2007, 3-10).

Where Japan is concerned, North Korea has been accused of carrying out terrorist acts in the form of abductions of Japanese nationals by North Korean operatives. Evidence of these abductions began to appear in the early 1980s with the arrest of a North Korean agent who attempted to pass as a Japanese citizen by using an alias and corresponding citizenship papers that belonged to a missing person (Samuels 2007, 149). More evidence surfaced when, in January 1988, a North Korean agent, captured in connection to the Korean Airlines bombing attack in 1987, confessed to having been trained to pass as Japanese by a Japanese woman who was believed to have been kidnapped by North Korean operatives (Fischer 2007, 10). Japanese authorities assert that overall, at least 17 Japanese citizens were abducted by North Korean agents throughout the 1970s and 80s (Government of Japan). Despite the mounting evidence and the North Korean airline bomber's confession, DPRK officials continuously denied abduction allegations until September 2002, when, during a rare visit by a sitting Japanese prime minister to North Korea, Kim Jong-Il admitted to Junichiro Koizumi that 13 abductions had taken place (Samuels 2007, 149). Subsequently, North Korea released five of the abductees, claiming that the remaining abductees were deceased. North Korean authorities also provided evidence of the remaining abductees' deaths, but Japanese officials believed the evidence fraudulent and have continued to press North Korea to come clean over the whereabouts of the remaining abductees (Chanlett-Avery 2008, 3).

Due in part to anger over the abductions among the Japanese public, Japanese officials, with the support of the Bush administration, pressured North Korea to resolve the abductions issue in the context of the six-party talks aimed at achieving North Korean denuclearization. Although the talks—which include China, Japan, North Korea, Russia, South Korea, and the United States—were initially conceived to negotiate an end to North Korea's nuclear weapons programs in return for economic and diplomatic concessions provided to the DPRK by the other participants, they have also featured discussion of other grievances against North Korea. Due to the fact that Japan and North Korea do not enjoy normal diplomatic relations, the six-party talks have been the only venue through which negotiations over the abductions issue can occur.

It is the Japanese government's unyielding policy to continue to seek a resolution of the abductions issue through the six-party process. However, this has presented Japanese officials with difficulties that may not soon be overcome.

First, in 2007 the Bush administration began to drift away from its insistence on resolving the abductions issue as part of an overall denuclearization deal in the six-party talks, insisting that a lack of resolution on the issue would not prevent a denuclearization deal (Chanlett-Avery 2008, 2). Washington's vacillation on the issue raised concerns among Japanese leaders that the Bush administration might abandon the matter altogether in favor of a quicker and easier denuclearization process. The second problem is that the Japanese position was undermined when, in October 2008, Washington removed North Korea from its list of "state sponsors of terrorism" as part of a deal that traded the DPRK terror list removal and the lifting of U.S. sanctions on North Korea for the dismantlement of the DPRK's plutonium enrichment facility at Yongbyon and a complete and verifiable declaration of its nuclear activities (Niksch 2009, 1). The deal, originally conceived in early 2007, did not stipulate a resolution of the abductions issue. The third problem is the fragility of talks and the tendency for the six-party process to break-down, forcing the parties to expend great diplomatic energy and time toward restarting the talks. As of the publication of this text, the six-party process has been stalled since December 2008 without a near-term date for resumption of the talks as yet agreed upon.

Although North Korea has not been implicated in any terrorism-related activities since the 1987 Korean Airlines bombing, the country's penchant for continued missile and nuclear testing against international will does not bode well for Japan's chances at resolving the abductions issue with North Korea in the near future. As high-level negotiations between Washington and Pyongyang over resumption of the six-party talks continue, it remains unclear whether the Obama administration will prioritize the issue if talks resume, despite frequent mention of the issue from Obama and members of his administration—including a recent statement by Secretary of State Hillary Clinton wherein she said that America will "never forget the families of the abducted, whom I met in Japan last February. I heard their stories, I looked at their pictures, and I carry that in my heart" (The Korea Herald 2010).

In addition to the abductions, which constitute the only clear acts of terrorism aimed directly at Japan by the DPRK, North Korea also poses a nuclear-proliferation risk. This risk is often cited in discussions about nuclear terrorism because it is feared that if the DPRK government collapses or if the Kim regime becomes more financially desperate, it is possible that its nuclear assets may fall into the hands of transnational terrorists or that the regime will transfer such assets to a terrorist group (Cha 2004, 144). This would be a problem for the United States and all of its allies, as any one nation that is perceived as a U.S. collaborator would be a potential target. Yet, at this time, such a scenario is unlikely due to the Kim regime's desire to gain concessions from the U.S. and its allies, including the lifting of sanctions on North Korea, a negotiated peace treaty formally ending the Korean War, and the normalization of U.S.-DPRK relations.

Finally, one more sore point between the DPRK and Japan continues to hurt the possibilities for a long overdue rapprochement between the two nations: North Korean leaders continue to harbor members of the Red Faction Army or "Yodo-go group"—a Japanese domestic radical leftist organization that orchestrated the hijacking of Japan Airlines flight 351 in 1970 (Prime Minister of Japan and His Cabinet). While this issue is not at the forefront of discussions over possibilities for peace between North Korea and Japan, it is one more example of a North Korean link to terrorism that renders an amicable dialogue between the two countries less likely.

Japan's 1995 "Shocks" and Official Responses

The Japanese public and the government suffered two shocks in the first quarter of 1995. The first occurred early in the morning on January 17, 1995, when a magnitude 7.2 earthquake hit the Kansai region of southern Japan with devastating results; Kobe City in Hyogo Prefecture was the hardest hit urban area. This seismic event, which the Japanese government called "The Great Hanshin Earthquake Disaster" (henceforth referred to as the Kobe earthquake), caused the deaths of over 5,000 people and about 30,000 injuries as well as severe damage from fire and structural collapses totaling approximately ¥9.63 trillion or $96.3 billion (Bardet 1995). In the aftermath of the earthquake, Japanese authorities failed to provide relief quickly and effectively. The primary reasons behind this failure are as follows: a lack of disaster preparedness on the part of Kobe City authorities; poor reporting and response mechanisms between local authorities and the central government in Tokyo; obstructive bureaucratic restrictions on foreign aid; the reluctance of Japanese officials to accept assistance from foreign countries; prejudicial treatment of foreign residents affected by the earthquake; and, inaccurate reporting by Japan's mass media that misrepresented the aftermath as calm and orderly despite the fact that eye-witnesses reported observing widespread chaos on the ground (Fukushima 1995).

The second shock of 1995 occurred on March 20, when members of the extremist-religious cult, Aum Shinrikyo, carried out the sarin gas attacks on the Tokyo subway system mentioned in the introduction of this chapter. Although the attacks did kill 12 people and likely injured thousands (estimates are inconsistent), they were initially conceived of as a complex plan to kill millions of Japanese and bring about Armageddon. The March 1995 attacks were only executed as a diversionary tactic meant to confuse officials who were supposedly planning a series of raids on Aum complexes—this according to rumors that Aum was tipped off about the impending police actions (Lifton 1999, 40). Despite the fact that members of the Aum cult had already carried out a sarin gas attack in the small Japanese mountain town of Matsumoto in June 1994, killing seven people and injuring three judges who were set to preside over a court case involving the fraudulent land deals of Aum members, police investigators failed to make a connection between that incident and Aum Shinrikyo (Ibid, 39-40). If police had made the connection, the March 1995 Tokyo subway attacks might have been prevented. In this case, both local police and government officials performed poorly in advance of the attacks and in response to them.

Thus, in contrast to the Kobe earthquake, Japanese authorities likely had the opportunity to prevent the second Aum cult sarin gas attack. Robyn Pangi, a specialist on disaster preparedness and state/local responses to terrorism, points out that where police investigators failed or were unwilling to make a connection between the first use of sarin gas and organized terrorism—instead choosing to designate the creation and release of sarin gas as an accident—the media "emphasized the improbability of making sarin by accident and raised the possibility of a link between Aum Shinrikyo and the Matsumoto attack" (Pangi 2002, 7). Pangi identifies further police inefficacy in that they refused to execute an aggressive investigation of Aum even after tests on soil from outside an Aum complex revealed traces of the rare nerve agent (Ibid). Given such evidence of official negligence, it is all but certain that the local police were ill-prepared to properly respond to any type of terrorist attack on Japanese soil.

The overall unpreparedness of both local and national officials is also apparent in the response to the 1995 Tokyo subway attacks. When these attacks occurred, only two months after the Kobe earthquake, many of the same issues that plagued Japanese authorities in the post-earthquake rescue and recovery efforts were still present. However, the nature of chemical attacks, and indeed any WMD attack, is quite different than that of a natural disaster. Responses to such attacks require a different set of procedures and response mechanisms, including specially trained mass-casualty medical personnel, decontamination teams, preparations and provisions for evacuations and quarantining, public emergency notification and warning systems, post-incident environmental analysis, and provisions for psychological assessments and counseling (Pangi 2002, 9). Unfortunately for the victims of the Tokyo subway attacks, Japanese anti-terrorism policy and terrorist attack response mechanisms were ill suited for the largest ever chemical attack against a civilian population by a terrorist organization.

If Japan's lax homeland security policies were responsible for the poor quality of response and recovery efforts after the Kobe earthquake and Aum Shinrikyo's Tokyo subway attacks, the government's loose regulatory approach toward religious groups helped create the conditions that made it possible for the latter incident to occur. In stark contrast to the severe lack of religious freedom in China, religious groups and individuals in Japan have enjoyed the freedom to practice their beliefs and traditions since the fall of Imperial Japan as the country's 1946 constitution provides that "Freedom of religion is guaranteed to all" (Constitution of Japan 1946). According to a United States' Bureau of Democracy, Human Rights, and Labor report, this is true in practice and "there is a generally amicable relationship among religious groups in society" which contributes to religious freedom (U.S. Department of State 2006). However, under Japan's 1951 Religious Corporation Law and the 1946 constitution, protections for religious groups—including tax exempt status and restrictions on government intrusion into the affairs of officially recognized religious organizations—rendered any investigations into their activities highly unlikely as authorities typically avoided taking any measures that could be perceived as religious persecution. In addition to these protections, official intelligence gathering was also severely constrained; limitations included a ban on preventive surveillance activities and inter-prefectural police rivalries which hindered effective information sharing practices (Pangi 2002, 4). As a result of the structural weaknesses of police activities and the lack of motivation to investigate Aum's activities, the cult was able to stockpile large amounts of harmful chemical and biological materials and vast sums of cash; it also procured a Russian helicopter intended for use in the 1995 sarin gas attack originally planned for October of that year (Ibid, 4; Lifton 1999, 40).

The severity of the 1995 shocks and Japanese policymakers' failure to prevent and prepare for a WMD terrorist attack led Tokyo and the Diet to enact new domestic legal and policy measures. These measures include amendment of the 1951 Religious Corporation Law to allow police greater latitude in dealing with groups suspected of involvement in illegal activities, a loosening of restrictions on police surveillance and wire-tapping, and a restructuring of the national and local disaster and WMD attack response mechanisms. Moreover, in prosecuting the Aum cult in connection to the Tokyo subway attacks, Japan's Supreme Court invoked Article 81 of the existing Religious Corporation Law to dissolve the group in a 1996 case known as *Aum Shinrikyo v. Doi* (Beckman 2007, 141).

The abovementioned 1996 amendments of the Religious Corporation Law grant law enforcement agencies and the government wider authority over regulation and oversight of Japan's officially recognized religious groups while also placing more stringent requirements on such groups to report financial assets and earnings (Department of State 2006). Additionally, the amendments provide recourse to any person(s) to, upon injury or relevant offense, call upon authorities to review a group's official certification as a religious corporation (Beckman 2007, 142). The amendments also require any religious organization to provide a list of active leaders and/or executive members to relevant authorities as part of the normal registration process. Finally, a key amendment allows police and government authorities to do something that

would have been tantamount to religious persecution under previous law:

> Members of the religious group can be questioned by the government as to the group's corporate status when the authorities have reason to suspect that cause exists "(1) to suspend profit-making activities [of the group]; (2) to rescind the certification of incorporation; or (3) to dissolve the corporation pursuant to section 81 (1)(i)–(iv)" (Ibid).

Other laws were amended or created to broaden the scope of police capabilities in dealing with organized crime and terrorist groups. Shortly after the 1995 sarin gas attacks, the Diet passed new legislation entitled the Law Related to the Prevention of Bodily Harm Caused by Sarin and Other Substances. This narrowly defined legislative measure clearly applied to the Aum cult's sarin gas attacks as it expressed the prohibition of the manufacturing, possession, and use of the specific chemical agent utilized in the 1994 and 1995 Aum attacks in Matsumoto and Tokyo (Howitt, Pangi 2003, 403). Subsequently, the Diet amended Japan's Police Law to allow police to cross prefectural boundaries in pursuit and in investigations of organized crime groups (synonymous with terrorist organizations). And in 1999, the Diet passed the Group Regulation Act, which included the legalization of police surveillance in certain cases and was designed to "regulate groups that have committed indiscriminate mass murder"—an obvious reference to Aum Shinrikyo (Pangi 2002, 34).

As for changes to Japan's disaster and WMD attack prevention and preparation practices, policymakers enacted various new measures and directives. These include information sharing between Japan's Self-Defense Forces (SDF) and the Police; specialized training for first responders; emergency planning for WMD attacks; large and small-scale disaster drills; the formalization of a broad national response plan; improvements to communication systems to better coordinate between responsible agencies; the provision of protective gear, decontamination kits, and harmful chemical/biological agent detection devices to various police departments; the founding of the Tokyo National Disaster Center in July 1995; the development of plans for hospitals to handle mass casualties; and the training of mental health professionals to assist victims of an attack or disaster in coping with psychological issues that may arise (Pangi 2002, 9–38).

These broad measures have yet to be fully tested as no WMD attack has occurred on Japanese soil since Aum Shinrikyo's attacks on the Tokyo subways in 1995. Nevertheless, the September 11, 2001 Twin Tower and Pentagon aircraft bombings served as a wakeup call for Japanese officials and the Japanese people to the reality of transnational terrorism and the potential for large-scale attacks from outside a nation's borders. The fact that 24 Japanese nationals were killed on 9/11 made the emotional responses of many people in

Japan more acute and may have bolstered public support for Japan's post-9/11 response in favor of helping the Bush administration in its "War on Terror" (Weston 2008, 43). Despite Tokyo's inevitable backing of the U.S. invasion of Afghanistan after 9/11, Japan's defense capabilities were still hampered by the nation's long history of "pacifism".

Japan and America's "War on Terror" Given that Japan is one of the United States' closest allies, and certainly its most significant collaborator on security matters in East Asia, it was inevitable that Japanese leaders would pledge their support for Washington's response to the 9/11 attacks. Immediately after the attacks, then Japanese Prime Minister Junichiro Koizumi summed up Japan's official position when he said, "We can never forgive such a dastardly and outrageous act. On behalf of the people of Japan, I express my condolence to the American people from the bottom of my heart. This sort of terrorism will never be forgiven and we feel strong anger" (Hassig 2002, 3). Indeed, opinion polls taken after 9/11 indicate that a plurality of the Japanese people did support the invasion of Afghanistan. In a *Yomiuri Shimbun* (Japan's most widely circulated daily newspaper) poll taken in late September 2001, 44.1 percent of respondents supported U.S. war preparations while 26.7 percent were opposed and the remaining 30.2 percent were unsure or unable to answer (Midford 2008, 15). For a country with a profoundly traumatic experience of war, including the Atomic bombings of Hiroshima and Nagasaki, support for war plans is extremely rare. To reinforce this point, cross-national polling data from the Pew Foundation indicates that the Japanese public supported the "War on Terror" well into 2002, with 61 percent in favor and 32 percent opposed (Ibid, 20).

As the United States and Britain went to war in Afghanistan, Prime Minister Koizumi—who enjoyed significant popularity throughout his tenure—made good on a promise he made on September 19, 2001 to actively support the American military response to 9/11 (Shinoda 2007, 86). Against the flow of Japanese tradition since the fall of Imperial Japan at the end of WWII, Koizumi ushered legislation through the Diet that authorized the deployment of Japan's SDF abroad in support of an active war effort (Ibid). The Anti-Terrorism Special Measures Law, promulgated in October 2001, set the stage for the dispatch of support and refueling vessels to the Indian Ocean. While such a move would not be considered a milestone for other developed nations, for Japan it signaled a sea change in security and defense policy. Prime Minister Koizumi acted even more quickly in devising his administration's strategic approach to the issues presented by 9/11—within one hour of the attacks he initiated an inter-ministerial task force under his leadership; and by the morning of September 12, he had issued initiatives to protect U.S. military forces in Japan and to

send SDF personnel abroad if deemed necessary (Samuels 2007, 95).

Regardless of the swift action that the Koizumi administration took "on behalf of the people of Japan," Morimoto Satoshi, a foreign policy/security adviser to the Japanese government, belied Japanese anxieties that bear a striking resemblance to China's concerns. In no uncertain terms, Satoshi pointed to concerns that the United States was increasingly "hegemonic in its interaction with other countries. . ." (Pyle 2007, 352). Still, the hawkish Koizumi continued to support the U.S. "War on Terror" until he stepped down from the premiership in September 2006. However, Koizumi's policies broke with trends in public opinion on the invasion of Iraq. The Bush administration spent months making the case that Iraq was connected to the global terrorist threat before the U.S. invasion of that country in March 2003. As Koizumi pledged his support for that effort as well, framing his stance in the context of the North Korean nuclear/missile threat—which concerned both the U.S. and Japan—public opinion polls in Japan indicated undeniable opposition to the invasion of Iraq (Shinoda 2007, 109). An Opinion poll run by *Asahi Shimbun* (Japan's second most widely circulated daily newspaper) on March 20-21, 2003 resulted in 59 percent opposed to the Iraq invasion and 31 percent in favor; the same paper ran polls later in March and again in April that indicated a stable trend of majority opposition to the Iraq War (Midford 2008, 16). The LDP, which ruled Japan from 1955 until 2009 with only one 11-month break in the early 1990s, has always been more conservative and hawkish in foreign affairs than the majority of the public. However, Prime Minister Koizumi espoused policies in relation to the "War on Terror" that were more hawkish than many of his LDP colleagues' positions. Despite continued support among many LDP leaders, the Iraq War remains to this day an unpopular war in Japan.

It almost goes without saying that Japan has supported all of Washington's anti-terrorism polices since 9/11. For example, the Japanese government has unflinchingly backed the U.S. in its endeavors to pass UN anti-terrorism resolutions. Tokyo has also backed American anti-terrorism/counterterrorism measures through financial assistance and the provision of transport, medicine, and other supplies (Hassig 2002, 5). Moreover, Japan has maintained a close partnership with the U.S. on the aforementioned Proliferation Security Initiative. None of this is unusual given Japan's reliance on the United States for regional security, weapons systems transfers, and various other forms of assistance. What is unusual is that, under the LDP, Japan took the unprecedented step of providing SDF ground troops for non-combat support missions in Iraq which began in January 2004 and ended in 2006 without a single SDF casualty or any shots fired by Japanese troops (Samuels 2007, 98). The 2003 Law Concerning Special Measures on Humanitarian and Reconstruction Assistance, which authorized this move, was another Koizumi initiative (Tsuchiyama 2007, 47-48). Considering the constitutional restrictions on Japan's military capabilities and the restrictive interpretation of Article 9 that prohibited "collective self-defense," the dispatch of SDF personnel to Iraq was a remarkable move toward weakening those restrictions and breaking a long-time taboo in Japan against the involvement of the Japanese military in any overseas capacity save non-violent UN sanctioned Peace Keeping Operations.

Under the leadership of Prime Minister Koizumi and his successors, the LDP pushed toward a wider defense role in support of the U.S.—which unnerved Chinese leaders as well as the Kim regime in North Korea. However, that momentum stopped with the victory of the Democratic Party of Japan (DPJ) in the Lower House (the more powerful of the two parliamentary bodies) elections of August 30, 2009. DPJ leaders, party heavyweight Ichiro Ozawa chief among them, had already made it clear that they opposed the Maritime Self-Defense Force (MSDF) refueling mission in the Indian Ocean on the grounds that the law authorizing it failed to specify that any deployment of SDF assets and personnel overseas must first be approved by the Diet (Easley, Kotani, and Mori 2010, 51). Finally, on January 15, 2010, almost four months to the day after Prime Minister Yukio Hatoyama assumed office, Japan's Minister of Defense, Toshimi Kitazawa, ordered the MSDF support vessels to return to Japan (Asahi Shimbun 2010). With that order, Japan ended its unyielding support of U.S. counter-terrorism operations in Central Asia.

Conclusion Despite a resurgence of violence in Xinjiang leading up to the 2008 Olympic Games in Beijing and in the summer of 2009, it remains difficult for China to make the case that Xinjiang separatist groups constitute a regional or transnational terrorist threat. That is precisely because such groups are clear in their pursuit of independence from China and the realization of an "East Turkistan" republic. Furthermore, the reported killing of approximately 200 Han Chinese by disgruntled Uyghurs in Xinjiang in July 2009 resembled acute civil unrest far more than terrorism. And although the Chinese government claimed that the riots and killings in Xinjiang were instigated by exiled Uyghur separatists, the use of syringes by many Uyghur attackers is quite different than bombings and other previous separatist tactics (BBC News 2009).

While China's cooperation with regional partners regarding counter-terrorism arguably has a valid purpose for combating regional threats, the local nature of the threat in Xinjiang dictates that PRC policy will remain focused on maintaining internal stability. For China, keeping its own house in order is priority number one. When it is sensible and convenient to cooperate with regional partners, China will do so; but where separatists in Xinjiang are concerned, the only hand cracking down on alleged "terrorists" will belong to the PRC.

Thus, it stands to reason that while Chinese leaders will likely keep a safe distance from most U.S. counter-terrorism efforts and apply pressure whenever and wherever possible to prevent U.S. forces from encircling the PRC, they will also refrain from posing a direct challenge to Washington's anti-terrorism and counter-terrorism initiatives in the Middle East and South/Central Asia. As long as combating Uyghur separatism in Xinjiang remains an important goal for China, it behooves Chinese policymakers to maintain a tolerant stance in regard to U.S. military actions against terrorism so as not to incur greater scrutiny of Chinese security policy in Xinjiang.

Moreover, it is increasingly beneficial for Chinese leaders to cast the regime as a cooperative member of the international community, especially concerning terrorism—a threat that all nations fundamentally oppose. Case in point: despite rising tensions between Washington and Beijing in early 2010 over the Obama administration's arms sales to Taiwan and President Obama's meeting with the Tibetan spiritual leader, the Dalai Lama, Chinese President Hu Jintao attended the U.S. sponsored Nuclear Security Summit in April 2010. President Hu's presence at the summit—arranged by President Obama to enhance international cooperation aimed at securing nuclear material/weapons and keep them out of the hands of terrorist groups, was the clearest sign moving forward that China is on board with broad international initiatives to combat the transnational terrorist threat.

For Japan, its experience with Aum Shinrikyo is still a fresh reminder that domestic terrorism is an issue for which sensible and relevant policies must be maintained. Although the Aum cult was disbanded and many of its leaders prosecuted (some currently face the death penalty), the organization resurfaced under the name Aleph. Japan's revised domestic laws and policies will allow authorities to keep a close eye on that organization's activities. Yet, Japanese leaders must approach the domestic terrorism issue with flexible policymaking and aggressive law enforcement, neither of which are approaches that Japan is historically adept at. While North Korea does not currently pose a conventional terrorist threat, the abduction issue remains unresolved and the only venue through which it can be addressed (six-party talks) is typically slow to yield results. Nevertheless, Japan should seek the Obama administration's backing on the issue within the six-party framework. It is Japan's best hope for a resolution of that issue.

Overall, the most salient challenges for Japan in terms of combating terrorism are the structural and normative obstacles preventing full cooperation with the United States. Now that the DPJ-led government has made it clear that there are limits to its support of U.S. efforts to combat terrorism, the Obama administration will be inclined to put pressure on Tokyo to pledge other forms of support. If Tokyo is unable or unwilling to grant alternative forms of cooperation or support, the U.S. may distance itself from Japan, rendering Japan more vulnerable to regional security instability vis-à-vis China and North Korea, but perhaps less of a target for transnational terrorists with an eye toward harming U.S. allies.

ADDITIONAL RESOURCES

Chung CP. 2004. The Shanghai Co-operation Organization: China's Changing Influence in Central Asia. The China Quarterly. **180**(1): 989–1009.

Emmers R. 2009. Comprehensive Security and Resilience in Southeast Asia: ASEAN's Approach to Terrorism. Pacific Review. **22**(2): 159–177.

Hassig KO. 2003. Community Response to Terrorism: The South Korean Model. Ft. Belvoir (VA): Defense Technical Information Center. Available at http://handle.dtic.mil/100.2/ADA419007.

Hastings JV. 2005. Perceiving a Single Chinese State: Escalation and Violence in Uighur Protests. Problems of Post-Communism. **52**(1): 28–38.

Jones DM, Smith M. 2005. Terrorism: China and the Asia Pacific – Dragon Stirs. The World Today. **61**(8): 35.

Katzenstein PJ. 2008. Rethinking Japanese Security: Internal and External Dimensions. Security and Governance Series. London (UK): Routledge.

Lutz JM, Lutz BJ. 2008. Global Terrorism. London (UK): Routledge.

McCleskey E, McCord D, Leetz J, Markey J. 2007. Underlying Reasons for Success and Failure of Terrorist Attacks: Selected Case Studies. Ft. Belvoir (VA): Defense Technical Information Center.

Niksch LA. 2002. North Korea and Terrorism: the Yokota Megumi Factor. Korean Journal of Defense Analysis. **14**: 7–24.

Reader I. 2000. Religious Violence in Contemporary Japan: the Case of Aum Shinrikyo. Honolulu (HI): University of Hawai'i Press.

Shen S. 2006. Chinese Response to Anti-terrorism. New York (NY): Nova Science Publishers.

Suh JJ, Katzenstein PJ, Carlson A. 2004. Rethinking Security in East Asia: Identity, Power, and Efficiency. Studies in Asian Security. Stanford (CA): Stanford University Press.

Tan A. 2005. Singapore: Recent Developments in Terrorism and Japan's Role. Asia Pacific Review. **12**(2): 71–91.

BIBLIOGRAPHY

Amnesty International. 2002. People's Republic of China: China's Anti-terrorism Legislation and Repression in the Xinjiang Uighur Autonomous Region. Available at http://www.amnesty.org/en/library/asset/ASA17/010/2002/en/f8e02362-d873-11dd-9df8-936c90684588/asa170102002en.pdf. (accessed December 17, 2009).

Asahi Shimbun. 2010. Japan Ends MSDF Refueling Mission. Politics section, Online edition, January 16. Available at http://

www.asahi.com/english/Herald-asahi/TKY201001160143.html. (accessed January 16, 2010).

Bardet JP. 1995. The Great Hanshin Earthquake Disaster: Preliminary Investigation Report; February 10, 1995. Los Angeles (CA): Dept. of Civil Engineering, University of Southern California.

BBC News. 2009. Chinese Break Up "Needle" Riots. Asia-Pacific section, September 4. Available at http://news.bbc.co.uk/2/hi/asia-pacific/8237259.stm. (accessed January 18, 2010).

Beckman J. 2007. Comparative Legal Approaches to Homeland Security and Anti-terrorism. Homeland Security Series. Aldershot (UK): Ashgate Publishing.

Bhattacharji P. 2009. Uighurs and China's Xinjiang Region. Council on Foreign Relations. Available at http://www.cfr.org/publication/16870./ (accessed December 19, 2009).

Bovingdon G. 2004. Autonomy in Xinjiang: Han Nationalist imperatives and Uyghur discontent. Washington (DC): East-West Center.

Cha VD. 2004. Korea: a Peninsula in Crisis and Flux. In Confronting Terrorism in the Pursuit of Power by Tellis AJ, Wills M (editors). Strategic Asia, 2004–05. Seattle (WA): National Bureau of Asian Research. p. 139–162.

Central Intelligence Agency. 2009. The World Factbook: China. Available at https://www.cia.gov/library/publications/the-world-factbook/geos/ch.html. (accessed December 24, 2009).

Chanlett-Avery E. 2008. North Korea's Abduction of Japanese Citizens and the Six-Party Talks. CRS Report for Congress, RS2284. Washington (DC): Congressional Research Service, Library of Congress.

Chung CP. 2002. China's "War on Terror": September 11 and Uighur Separatism. Council on Foreign Relations. Available at http://www.cfr.org/publication/4765/chinas_war_on_terror.html. (accessed January 5, 2010).

Constitution of Japan. 1946. Available at http://www.constitution.org/cons/japan.txt. (accessed January 03, 2010).

Conway E. 2009. Chinese Economy Overtakes Japan. *UK Telegraph*, December 26, Economics section, Online edition. Available at http://www.telegraph.co.uk/finance/economics/6890189/Chinese-economy-overtakes-Japan.html. (accessed December 29, 2009).

Easley LE, Kotani T, Mori A. 2010. Electing a New Japanese Security Policy? Examining Foreign Policy Visions within the Democratic Party of Japan. In: Asia Policy, number 9 (January 2010). Seattle (WA): National Bureau of Asian Research. p. 45–66.

The Egmont Group. 2009. International Bulletin. Available at www.egmontgroup.org/library/download/50. (accessed January 12, 2010).

Fischer H. 2007. North Korean Provocative Actions, 1950–2007. CRS Report for Congress, RL30004. Washington (DC): Congressional Research Service, Library of Congress.

Fukushima GS. 1995. The Great Hanshin Earthquake. Japan Policy Research Institute. Occasional Paper No. 2. Available at http://www.jpri.org/publications/occasionalpapers/op2.html. (accessed January 3, 2010).

Gill B, Huang CH. 2009. China's Expanding Role in Peacekeeping: Prospects and Policy Implications. Stockholm International Peace Research Institute, Policy Paper (25).

Government of Japan. 2009. Abductions of Japanese Citizens by North Korea. Headquarters for the Abduction Issue. Available at http://www.rachi.go.jp/en/ratimondai/syousai.html. (accessed January 5, 2010).

Green MJ. 2001. Japan's Reluctant Realism: Foreign Policy Challenges in an Era of Uncertain Power. New York (NY): Palgrave.

Hassig KO. 2002. The United States and East Asia after 9/11. IDA document, D-2774. Alexandria (VA): Institute for Defense Analyses.

Howitt AM, Pangi RL. 2003. Countering terrorism dimensions of preparedness. Cambridge, (MA): MIT Press.

Information Office of the State Council, China. 2003. "East Turkistan" Terrorist Forces Cannot Get Away with Impunity. Available at http://au.china-embassy.org/eng/xw/t45631.htm. (accessed December 28, 2009).

Kan SA. 2009. U.S.-China Counterterrorism Cooperation: Issues for U.S. Policy. CRS Report for Congress, RL33001. Washington (DC): Congressional Research Service, Library of Congress.

The Korea Herald. 2010. N.K. Nukes Among Obama's Foreign Policy Victories. National Section, Online Edition, January 13. Available at http://www.koreaherald.co.kr/NEWKHSITE/data/html_dir/2010/01/13/201001130061.asp. (accessed January 15, 2010).

Lam W. 2009. The Xinjiang Crisis: A Test for Beijing's Carrot-and-Stick Strategy. The Jamestown Foundation. *China Brief: a Journal of Analysis and Information*; IX: 15 (July 2003). Available at http://www.jamestown.org/programs/chinabrief/single/?tx_ttnews[tt_news]=35307&tx_ttnews[backPid]=459&no_cache=1. (accessed January 13, 2010).

Lam W. 2010. Major Reshuffles in China's Military and Security Leadership. The Jamestown Foundation. *China Brief: a Journal of Analysis and Information*; 10(1). Available at http://www.jamestown.org/uploads/media/cb_010_05.pdf. (accessed January 11, 2010).

Leather K. 2002. Kashmiri Separatists: Origins, Competing Ideologies, and Prospects for Resolution of the Conflict. CRS Report for Congress, RL31587. Washington (DC): Congressional Research Service, Library of Congress.

Leheny D. 2005. The War on Terrorism in Asia and the Possibility of Secret Regionalism. In Remapping East Asia: the Construction of a Region. Ithaca (NY): Cornell University Press. p. 236–255.

Li R. 2009. A Rising China and Security in East Asia: Identity Construction and Security Discourse. London (UK): Routledge.

Lieggi L. 2008. Proliferation Security Initiative Exercise Hosted by Japan Shows Growing Interest in Asia But No Sea Change in Key Outsider States. WMD Insights. Available at http://www.wmdinsights.com/I21/I21_EA1_ProliferationSecurity.htm. (accessed January 12, 2010).

Lifton RJ. 1999. Destroying the World to Save it: Aum Shinrikyo, Apocalyptic Violence, and the New Global Terrorism. New York (NY): Henry Holt and Co.

Lum T. 2006. China and Falun Gong. CRS Report to Congress, RL33437. Washington (DC): Congressional Research Service, Library of Congress.

McIntyre DA. 2009. China Is Now The World's Second Largest Economy. 24/7 WallSt, Dec 27. Available at http://247wallst.com/2009/12/27/china-is-almost-certainly-worlds-second-largest-economy/. (accessed January 05, 2010).

Midford P. 2008. Japanese Mass Opinion Toward the War on Terrorism. In Japanese Public Opinion and the War on Terrorism by Eldridge RD, Midford P (editors). New York (NY): Palgrave Macmillan. p 11–42.

Niksch LA. 2009. North Korea: Terrorism List Removal. CRS Report for Congress, RL30613. Washington (DC): Congressional Research Service, Library of Congress.

Nuclear Threat Initiative. 2003. North Korea Profile: Missile; Import/Export. Available at http://nti.org/e_research/profiles/NK/Missile/66.html. (accessed January 4, 2010).

Prime Minister of Japan and His Cabinet. The Abduction of Japanese Citizens by North Korea. Available at http://www.kantei.go.jp/foreign/abduction/unresolved.html. (accessed December 26, 2009).

Pyle KB. 2007. Japan Rising: the Resurgence of Japanese Power and Purpose. A Century Foundation Book. New York (NY): Public Affairs.

Reilly J. 2002. The U.S. "War on Terror" and East Asia. Foreign Policy in Focus: Policy Report.

Roy D. 2006. Lukewarm Partner: Chinese Support for U.S. Counter-Terrorism in Southeast Asia. Ft. Belvoir (VA): Defense Technical Information Center. Available at http://handle.dtic.mil/100.2/ADA445080. (accessed December 16, 2009).

Samuels RJ. 2007. Securing Japan: Tokyo's Grand Strategy and the Future of East Asia. Ithaca (NY): Cornell University Press.

Shinoda T. 2007. Koizumi Diplomacy: Japan's Kantei Approach to Foreign and Defense Affairs. Seattle (WA): University of Washington Press.

Tsuchiyama J. 2007. War Renunciation, Article 9, and Security Policy. In Japan in International Politics: the Foreign Policies of an Adaptive State by Berger TU, Mochizuki M, Tsuchiyama J (editors). Boulder (CO): Lynne Rienner Publishers. p. 47–74.

U.S. Department of Homeland Security. CSI: Container Security Initiative. Available at http://www.cbp.gov/xp/cgov/trade/cargo_security/csi./ (accessed December 30, 2009).

U.S. Department of State. 2006. International Religious Freedom Report: Japan. Available at http://www.state.gov/g/drl/rls/irf/2006/71342.htm. (accessed January 3, 2010).

U.S. Department of State. 2008. Country Reports on Terrorism 2007. Washington DC Office of the Coordinator for Counterterrorism. Ft. Belvoir (VA): Defense Technical Information Center.

U.S. Department of State. 2009. Country Reports on Terrorism 2008. Washington DC Office of the Coordinator for Counterterrorism. Ft. Belvoir (VA): Defense Technical Information Center.

Uyghur Human Rights Project. 2008. State Department Report Highlights Human Rights Abuses Against Uyghurs. Available at http://www.uhrp.org/articles/817/1/State-Department-report-highlights-human-rights-abuses-against-Uyghurs-/index.html. (accessed December 17, 2009).

Van Wie Davis E. 2008. Uyghur Muslim Ethnic Separatism in Xinjiang, China. Asian Affairs: an American Review. Available at http://www.apcss.org/Publications/APCSS–%20Uyghur%20Muslim%20Separatism%20in%20Xinjiang.doc. (accessed December 28, 2009).

Voice of America. 2009. China Executes 2 for Attack in Xinjiang. Available at http://www1.voanews.com/english/news/a-13-2009-04-09-voa51-68732282.html. (accessed January 3, 2010).

Wayne MI. 2007. Five Lessons from China's War on Terror. Joint Force Quarterly. **47**: 42–47.

Wayne MI. 2008. China's War on Terrorism: Counter-insurgency, Politics, and Internal Security. London (UK): Routledge.

Welshans, KC. 2007. Nationalism and Islamic Identity in Xinjiang [Thesis]. Monterey (CA): Naval Postgraduate School. Available at http://handle.dtic.mil/100.2/ADA475738. (accessed December 20, 2009).

Weston SA. 2008. Framing the Japanese Homeland Security Debate: Mass media and Public Opinion. In Japanese Public Opinion and the War on Terrorism by Eldridge RD, Midford P (editors). New York (NY): Palgrave Macmillan. p. 43–89.

Wright R, Tyson AS. 2005. U.S. Evicted From Air Base in Uzbekistan. *Washington Post*, July 30, World/Asia Pacific section, Online edition. Available at http://www.washingtonpost.com/wp-dyn/content/article/2005/07/29/AR2005072902038.html. (accessed December 28, 2009).

Yuan JD. 2003. China and the Shanghai Cooperation Organization: Anti-Terrorism and Beijing's Central Asia Policy. Politologiske Studier *6*. **2**: 128–139.

27

TEACHING IDEAS

The 'Additional Resources' and footnotes can be used to supplement the text as time, resources, and depth of study dictate.

Chapter 1. Introduction. Are global warming, population growth, national dependence on foreign oil, deprivation of human rights and equality, matters of homeland/national security?

Is there a new, hopeful, political climate?[1] Can this influence anything?

Should we act now to avoid conflict twenty years from now?

Can what the United States does or does not do now influence the social environment worldwide and resonate in its homeland security/national security implications for decades to come?

This Chapter lists different definitions of terrorism. Does anything change depending upon which definition is used?

Chapter 2. Strategic Environment. This chapter presents mostly U.S. Government opinion from official documents. Do these reflect an objective reality? What other sources should influence our decision-making?

Chapter 3. Homeland Security Council. There is a National Security Council and a Homeland Security Council. Is there an advantage to two councils?

Should we change the Homeland Security Council and our entire national security/ homeland security structure and process?

Foundations of Homeland Security: Law and Policy, First Edition. Martin J. Alperen.
© 2011 John Wiley & Sons, Inc. Published 2011 by John Wiley & Sons, Inc.

Chapter 4. Intelligence. Criticisms about our intelligence system include the problems of strict agency stovepiped missions, competitive agency cultures, and the inability for interagency coordination and collaboration. Our national security structure was formulated sixty years ago for a world and threats that mostly no longer exist. How can we organize our government to better reflect changes in the world?

How can necessary global police cooperation happen without unprecedented information sharing?

Chapter 5. The Department of Homeland Security (DHS).

Chapter 6. The Federal Emergency Management Agency (FEMA). DHS incorporated FEMA. Was it helpful? Should FEMA be independent of DHS?

What would happen if they were separate agencies? Is the structure of DHS favorable to its mission? Is the DHS Mission broad enough/too broad? How about FEMAs?

Compare the DHS and FEMA mission statements from Chapter 1. Is there a substantive difference?

Was the Select Bipartisan Report discussed here accurate? Was it complete?

Does PKEMRA address the issues raised in the Report?

What sections of PKEMRA address specific issues raised in the Select Bipartisan Report?

Despite PKEMRA there are still many unanswered questions. Some are mundane such should we build homes in flood zones. Others are more serious and not yet answered. What do we do, for example, in the event a person contaminated, perhaps with a deadly and contagious pathogen, when they panic and refuse to stay away from others, or try to enter an emergency room or shelter without decontamination and risk the entire facility and others' lives?

Chapter 7. National Security Strategy of the United States of America.

Chapter 8. National Strategy for Combating Terrorism.

Chapter 9. National Strategy for Homeland Security. Evaluate the strategies. Would you know what to do after reading this strategy? Does it provide guidance? Was anything ever done with its recommendations? Evaluate what was done and the effect of the strategy on our nation's security.

Chapter 10. Border Security. The last entry in this chapter is the National Southwest Border Counternarcotics Strategy from June 2009. Are there similarities between narcotics trafficking and terrorism?

Could terrorists use the same transportation routes and methods?

Chapter 11. Critical Infrastructure. Does infrastructure affect resiliency?

Can we assume failing infrastructure means catastrophes are more likely?

Does failing infrastructure mean it would be that much easier for a terrorist to do damage?

If terrorists can do more damage against weak infrastructure, does this mean terrorists are more likely to try an attack against a weak infrastructure than against a strong or resilient one?

Should rebuilding failing infrastructure become a national priority?

Chapter 12. Cyber Security. Have we set up mechanisms to protect our cyber systems? Are they effective? Is cyber security a realistic possibility?

Chapter 13. Agriculture and Food. How well have we addressed the "farm to table" system? What are the weak links.

Chapter 14. Transportation. The aviation International Outreach Plan includes the language, "Consistent with NSPD-47/HSPD-16, this plan establishes the following objectives: a *coordinated policy* for United States Government aviation security activities..." Taking US policy as a whole, do we have a coordinated policy?

What is the most effective way to obtain international cooperation?

Chapter 15. Weapons of Mass Destruction (WMD). Congress passed the Implementing Recommendations of the 9/11 Commission Act of 2007 establishing the position of WMD Coordinator to advise the President. Is a WMD Coordinator the answer to this problem?

World At Risk: The Report of the Commission on the Prevention of WMD Proliferation and Terrorism,[2] lists 13

recommendations. Are these 13 recommendations covered by current DHS policies or are they new ideas?

Chapter 16. Biodefense and WMD Countermeasures. In view of the easy proliferation of biohazards, can we possibly do an adequate job with biodefense and WMD Countermeasures? How do we keep abreast of the most recent threats?

Chapter 17. National Continuity Policy. Design a COOP Plan using all the resources listed at end of the COOP Chapter.

Create a plan to protect this school.

Chapter 18. Identification Issues. Evaluate the Real ID Act. Do we need a non-alterable and reliable form of id? What about privacy concerns?

Chapter 19. Emergency Preparedness and Response. Are we more prepared today than in 2001? In what ways is this preparedness helpful?

Is the Homeland Security Advisory System helpful? What about deciding to withhold notice of change of a threat Condition? Why would that be done?

Chapter 20. National Incident Management System (NIMS). Is it logical to have NIMS? Could we be prepared without it?

Chapter 21. National Response Framework (NRF). Does the NRF tie it all together?

Chapter 22. Authority to Use Military Force. After reading this chapter, is it clear under which circumstances you might see federal troops providing local law enforcement?

Chapter 23. Detention and Treatment of Terrorists. Provide a chronological synopsis of developments from the Military Order of November 13, 2001, to date, regarding some aspect of the detention and treatment of terrorists. How has the ability to detain changed? What are the limits on interrogation? Trace the development of the trial mechanism we will use to try detainees. Evaluate the guidelines for interrogation.

Chapter 24. Resiliency and a Culture of Preparedness. What is resiliency and why is it important?

Is a resilient community less likely to be a terrorist target? One line of reasoning believes that if a community (or a piece of infrastructure) can be so resilient that it will recover quickly from whatever happens, then dramatic video of destruction will be minimized and such a terrorist mission would not be a great success. Would terrorists choose a less resilient target?

Chapter 25. European Homeland Security: a Work in Progress. What can the U.S. learn from Europe. What can they learn from us?

Chapter 26. Asian Homeland Security. Does violence perpetrated by Uyghur separatists in Xinjiang equate to terrorism?

Are Chinese policymakers justified in limiting religious freedom in Xinjiang as part of Beijing's overall "anti-terrorism" strategy?

Should Uyghur separatists who are arrested in connection with bombings or other violent attacks be granted the right to stand trial or are summary executions a more effective approach?

Do the terrorist attacks perpetrated by Aum Shinrikyo signal a need for greater official scrutiny of religious organizations? What should be the criteria for organizations that pose the greatest potential security threat?

How can Japan cooperate with the United States regarding counter-terrorism (beyond pledging financial assistance) without deploying troops near combat zones?

ENDNOTES

1. "With the election of President Barack Obama, the United States and the world are expecting a new approach to countering terrorism … The administration should capitalize on a unique opportunity to emphasize Barack Obama's widely admired personal story and interest in engaging the world to weaken key elements of the al-Qa'ida "narrative." The weakening of this narrative could, in turn, reduce the terrorist group's recruitment capabilities and capacity to garner sympathy from the Muslim world." Tom Sanderson. President Obama's Overseas Terrorism Challenge. Combating Terrorism Center At West Point, CTC Sentinel. Vol. 2, Issue 4. April 2009, p. 8. http://www.ctc.usma.edu/sentinel/CTCSentinel-Vol2Iss4.pdf.
2. World At Risk: The Report of the Commission on the Prevention of WMD Proliferation and Terrorism. http://www.preventwmd.gov/report/.

INDEX

Foundations of Homeland Security: Law and Policy, First Edition. Martin J. Alperen.
© 2011 John Wiley & Sons, Inc. Published 2011 by John Wiley & Sons, Inc.